Lecture Notes in Computer Science 4939

Commenced Publication in 1973
Founding and Former Series Editors:
Gerhard Goos, Juris Hartmanis, and Jan van Leeuwen

Ronald Cramer (Ed.)

Public Key Cryptography – PKC 2008

11th International Workshop
on Practice and Theory in Public Key Cryptography
Barcelona, Spain, March 9-12, 2008
Proceedings

 Springer

Volume Editor

Ronald Cramer
CWI Amsterdam and
Leiden University
The Netherlands
E-mail: ronald.cramer@cwi.nl

Library of Congress Control Number: 2008921494

CR Subject Classification (1998): E.3, F.2.1-2, C.2.0, K.4.4, K.6.5

LNCS Sublibrary: SL 4 – Security and Cryptology

ISSN	0302-9743
ISBN-10	3-540-78439-X Springer Berlin Heidelberg New York
ISBN-13	978-3-540-78439-5 Springer Berlin Heidelberg New York

Springer is a part of Springer Science+Business Media

springer.com

© International Association for Cryptologic Research 2008
Printed in Germany

Typesetting: Camera-ready by author, data conversion by Scientific Publishing Services, Chennai, India
Printed on acid-free paper   SPIN: 12234431   06/3180   5 4 3 2 1 0

Preface

These are the Proceedings of the 11th International Workshop on Practice and Theory in Public Key Cryptography – PKC 2008. The workshop was held in Barcelona, Spain, March 9–12, 2008.

It was sponsored by the International Association for Cryptologic Research (IACR; see www.iacr.org), this year in cooperation with MAK, the Research Group on Mathematics Applied to Cryptography at UPC, the Polytechnical University of Catalonia. The General Chair, Carles Padró, was responsible for chairing the Local Organization Committee, for handling publicity and for attracting funding from sponsors.

The PKC 2008 Program Committee (PC) consisted of 30 internationally renowned experts. Their names and affiliations are listed further on in these proceedings. By the September 7, 2007 submission deadline the PC had received 71 submissions via the IACR Electronic Submission Server. The subsequent selection process was divided into two phases, as usual. In the review phase each submission was carefully scrutinized by at least three independent reviewers, and the review reports, often extensive, were committed to the IACR Web Review System. These were taken as the starting point for the PC-wide Web-based discussion phase. During this phase, additional reports were provided as needed, and the PC eventually had some 258 reports at its disposal. In addition, the discussions generated more than 650 messages, all posted in the system. During the entire PC phase, which started on April 12, 2006 with the invitation by the PKC Steering Committee, and which continued until March 2008, more than 500 e-mail messages were communicated. Moreover, the PC received much appreciated assistance by a large body of external reviewers. Their names are also listed in these proceedings.

The selection process for PKC 2008 was finalized by the end of November 2007. After notification of acceptance, the authors were provided with the review comments and were granted three weeks to prepare the final versions, which were due by December 14, 2007. These final versions were not subjected to further scrutiny by the PC and their authors bear full responsibility. The Program Committee worked hard to select a balanced, solid and interesting scientific program, and I thank them very much for their efforts.

After consultation with the PC, I decided to grant the PKC 2008 "Best Paper Award" to Vadim Lyubashevsky (University of California at San Diego), for his paper "Lattice-Based Identification Schemes Secure Under Active Attacks". Besides the above-mentioned 21 regular presentations, the PKC 2008 scientific program featured three invited speakers: David Naccache (ENS, Paris) on "Cryptographic Test Correction", Jean-Jacques Quisquater (Université Catholique de Louvain) on "How to Secretly Extract Hidden Secret Keys: A State of the Attacks", and Victor Shoup (New York University) on "The Role of Discrete

Logarithms in Designing Secure Crypto-Systems". David Naccache also contributed (unrefereed) notes for his lecture, which are also included in this volume.

CWI[1] in Amsterdam and the Mathematical Institute at Leiden University, my employers, are gratefully acknowledged for their support. Also many thanks to Springer for their collaboration. Thanks to Shai Halevi for his IACR Web-handling system.

Eike Kiltz from the CWI group, besides serving as a member of the PC, provided lots of general assistance to the Chair, particularly when setting up and running the Web system and when preparing this volume. I thank Carles Padró, PKC 2008 General Chair, for our smooth and very pleasant collaboration. Finally, we thank our sponsors the Spanish Ministry of Education and Science, and UPC.

January 2008   Ronald Cramer

---

[1] CWI is the National Research Institute for Mathematics and Computer Science in the Netherlands

PKC 2008

The 11th International Workshop on Practice and Theory in Public Key Cryptography

Universitat Politècnica de Catalunya, Barcelona, Spain
March 9–12, 2008

Sponsored by the *International Association for Cryptologic Research (IACR)*

Organized in cooperation with the
Research Group on Mathematics Applied to Cryptography at UPC

General Chair

Carles Padró, UPC, Spain

Program Chair

Ronald Cramer, CWI Amsterdam and Leiden University, The Netherlands

Local Organizing Committee

Javier López, Ignacio Gracia, Jaume Martí, Sebastià Martín, Carles Padró and
Jorge L. Villar

PKC Steering Committee

Ronald Cramer	CWI and Leiden University, The Netherlands
Yvo Desmedt	UCL, UK
Hideki Imai	University of Tokyo, Japan
David Naccache	ENS, France
Tatsuaki Okamoto	NTT, Japan
Jacques Stern	ENS, France
Moti Yung	Columbia University and Google, USA
Yuliang Zheng	University of North Carolina, USA

Program Committee

Michel Abdalla	ENS, France
Masayuki Abe	NTT, Japan
Alexandra Boldyreva	Georgia Tech, USA
Jung Hee Cheon	Seoul National University, South Korea
Ronald Cramer	CWI and Leiden University, The Netherlands
Matthias Fitzi	ETH, Switzerland
Matthew Franklin	UC Davis, USA
Steven Galbraith	Royal Holloway, UK
Juan A. Garay	Bell Labs, USA
Rosario Gennaro	IBM Research, USA
Craig Gentry	Stanford University, USA
Kristian Gjøsteen	NTNU, Norway
Maria I. González Vasco	University Rey Juan Carlos, Spain
Jens Groth	UCL, UK
Yuval Ishai	Technion, Israel and UCLA, USA
Eike Kiltz	CWI, The Netherlands
Kaoru Kurosawa	Ibaraki University, Japan
Wenbo Mao	HP Labs, China
Alexander May	University of Bochum, Germany
Jesper Buus Nielsen	Aarhus University, Denmark
Berry Schoenmakers	TU Eindhoven, The Netherlands
abhi shelat	University of Virginia, USA
Victor Shoup	New York University, USA
Martijn Stam	EPFL, Switzerland
Rainer Steinwandt	Florida Atlantic University, USA
Tsuyoshi Takagi	Future University of Hakodate, Japan
Edlyn Teske	University Waterloo, Canada
Ramarathnam Venkatesan	Microsoft, USA & India
Jorge Villar Santos	UPC, Spain
Moti Yung	Columbia University and Google, USA

External Reviewers

Toru Akishita	Pierre-Alain Fouque	Sang Geun Hahn
Jean-Luc Beuchat	Jun Furukawa	Daewan Han
Raghav Bhaskar	Phong Nguyen	Goichiro Hanaoka
Johannes Blömer	Nicolas Gama	Darrel Hankerson
David Cash	Willi Geiselmann	Anwar Hasan
Nishanth Chandran	Kenneth Giuliani	Swee-Huay Heng
Carlos Cid	Jason Gower	Nick Howgrave-Graham
Iwan Duursma	Nishanth Chandran	David Jao
Serge Fehr	Vipul Goyal	Marc Joye
Marc Fischlin	Matt Green	Waldyr Benits Jr.

Table of Contents

Session IV: Identification, Broadcast and Key Agreement

Session V: Implementation of Fast Arithmetic

Session VI: Digital Signatures (II)

Session VII: Algebraic and Number Theoretical Cryptanalysis (II)

Session VIII: Public Key Encryption

Total Break of the ℓ-IC Signature Scheme

Pierre-Alain Fouque[1], Gilles Macario-Rat[2],
Ludovic Perret[3], and Jacques Stern[1]

[1] ENS/CNRS/INRIA
Pierre-Alain.Fouque@ens.fr, Jacques.Stern@ens.fr
[2] Orange Labs
gilles.macariorat@orange-ftgroup.com
[3] UMPC/LIP6/SPIRAL & INRIA/SALSA
ludovic.perret@lip6.fr

Abstract. In this paper, we describe efficient forgery and full-key recovery attacks on the ℓ-IC$^-$ signature scheme recently proposed at PKC
2007. This cryptosystem is a multivariate scheme based on a new internal
quadratic primitive which avoids some drawbacks of previous multivariate schemes: the scheme is extremely fast since it requires one exponentiation in a finite field of medium size and the public key is shorter than
in many multivariate signature schemes. Our attacks rely on the recent
cryptanalytic tool developed by Dubois *et al.* against the SFLASH signature scheme. However, the final stage of the attacks requires the use
of Gröbner basis techniques to conclude to actually forge a signature
(resp. to recover the secret key). For the forgery attack, this is due to
the fact that Patarin's attack is much more difficult to mount against
ℓ-IC. The key recovery attack is also very efficient since it is faster to
recover equivalent secret keys than to forge.

1 Introduction

Multivariate cryptography proposes efficient cryptographic schemes well-suited
for low computational devices. Since the underlying problem is not known to be
easy in the quantum model, these schemes have been considered by standard-
ization bodies as alternatives to RSA or DLog based schemes. For instance, in
2003, one promising signature scheme, called SFLASH, has been selected by the
NESSIE project. SFLASH is based on the C^* cryptosystem [20] proposed by
Matsumoto and Imai in 1988 and broken by Patarin in 1995 [21]. Following an
idea of Shamir [25], Patarin, Goubin and Courtois proposed SFLASH [24] by
removing some equations of the system. The scheme is also called C^{*-} and the
generic transformation of removing equations is called the "Minus" transformation which can be applied to many multivariate schemes.

The security of multivariate public-key cryptosystems is related to the problem of solving systems of quadratic or higher degree equations in many variables.
This problem is known to be NP-hard and it seems to be also difficult on average. The today most efficient algorithms to solve this generic problem are Gröbner

R. Cramer (Ed.): PKC 2008, LNCS 4939, pp. 1–17, 2008.

basis algorithms whose complexity is exponential[1] in time and space. But this general tool can perform much better in the cryptographic context since the security does not rely on hard instances. As usual in multivariate cryptography, esay instances of this NP-hard problem are hidden using linear mappings and in some cases, Gröbner basis algorithms are able to recover the hidden structure [15]. Fortunately, some countermeasures are known to avoid this kind of attack such as the Minus transformation. But are they sufficient to avoid all attack?

Recently, some breakthrough results [11,10] have been achieved in the cryptanalysis of multivariate schemes and have led to the efficient break of SFLASH in practice. In this work, some cryptanalytic tools have been developed which are very generic and efficient since only linear and bilinear algebra are used. They can be seen as differential cryptanalysis applied on multivariate scheme but the treatment of the differential of the public key is the main important point. The idea is to compute the differential of the public key and then to study the differential function as a bilinear function when the internal mapping is a quadratic function. The differential mapping at some point, or fix difference, is a linear map, but if we let the point vary, we get a bilinear map. Then, in [11], the authors are able to characterize the self-adjoint operators of these bilinear functions, also called skew-symmetric linear map with respect to the bilinear function, and they show that they can be used to recover missing coordinates. For SFLASH, they show that they correspond to the conjugate by one linear and secret map of the multiplications in the extension. Finally, once all the missing equations have been recovered, Patarin's attack can be used to forge a signature for any message.

Main Results. The ℓ-IC signature scheme has been proposed by Ding, Wolf and Yang at PKC 2007. They propose a new quadratic function based on the Cremona mapping over $\mathbb{E}$, an extension of a finite field. The advantages are that this function is more efficient to invert than SFLASH since it requires only one inversion in the finite field of q^k elements, and it provides shorter public key. The number of quadratic polynomials of the public key $\boldsymbol{P}$ is $|q|n$ where n is the product of the extension degree k and ℓ the number of coordinates of the Cremona map and $|q|$ is the bitlength of the small field $\mathbb{K}$. It can be seen that the parameter k must be large enough to avoid some attack, and ℓ must be small if we want to have short public key. In general, ℓ will be equal to 3 or 5, in the parameters proposed by the authors.

In this paper, we show that the recent tools developed for SFLASH are generic and can be used to other multivariate schemes. We will use these tools to recover the missing coordinates of the ℓ-IC$^-$ scheme. Once the whole set of equations of the public key is recovered, Gröbner basis techniques can be used either to forge a signature for any message or to recover the secret key. The key recovery uses the fact that we are able to characterize and recover equivalent secret keys. More precisely, we recover two linear mappings S_0 and T_0 such that if we compose the public key $\boldsymbol{P}$ with them, $T_0^{-1} \circ \boldsymbol{P} \circ S_0^{-1}$, the new system of polynomials

---

[1] For systems with a finite number of solutions.

are equivalent to $T' \circ \boldsymbol{F} \circ S'$, where $\boldsymbol{F}$ is the central mapping and S' and T' are two linear mappings defined over the extension $\mathbb{E}$ and not over $\mathbb{K}$. Finally, the description of a ℓ-IC public key in $\mathbb{E}$ is easy to invert using Gröbner basis technique, since the number of unknown is small provided ℓ is small.

Organization of the Paper. In Section 2, we recall some classical definitions and properties of Gröbner basis. Then, in Section 3, we describe the ℓ-IC$^-$ signature scheme. We also describe the scheme $\ell = 3$, which is the version proposed in [9]. In Section 4, we describe a special property of the differential of this new quadratic scheme. This property, together with Gröbner basis techniques, will permit us to mount an efficient forgery (Section 5) and full key recovery attacks (Section 6).

2 Gröbner Basics

We present here Gröbner basis and some of their properties. We will touch here only a restricted aspect of this theory. For a more thorough introduction to this topic, we refer the interested reader to [1,8].

2.1 Definition – Property

We will denote by $\mathbb{K}$ a finite field of $q = p^r$ elements (p a prime, and $r \geq 1$). We shall call *ideal generated* by $p_1, \ldots, p_s \in \mathbb{K}[x_1, \ldots, x_n]$, denoted by $\langle p_1, \ldots, p_s \rangle$, the set:

$$\mathcal{I} = \langle p_1, \ldots, p_s \rangle = \left\{ \sum_{k=1}^{s} p_k u_k : u_1, \ldots, u_k \in \mathbb{K}[x_1, \ldots, x_n] \right\} \subseteq \mathbb{K}[x_1, \ldots, x_n].$$

We will denote by $V_{\mathbb{K}}(\mathcal{I}) = \left\{ \mathbf{z} \in \mathbb{F}_q^n : p_i(\mathbf{z}) = 0 \, \forall i, 1 \leq i \leq s \right\}$ the *variety associated* to $\mathcal{I}$. Gröbner bases offer an explicit method for describing varieties. Informally, a Gröbner basis of an ideal $\mathcal{I}$ is a computable generating set of $\mathcal{I}$ with "good" algorithmic properties. These bases are defined with respect to *monomial orderings*. For instance, the *lexicographical* (Lex) and *degree reverse lexicographical* (DRL) orderings – which are widely used in practice – are defined as follows:

Definition 1. *Let $\alpha = (\alpha_1, \ldots, \alpha_n)$ and $\beta = (\beta_1, \ldots, \beta_n) \in \mathbb{N}^n$. Then:*
- $x_1^{\alpha_1} \cdots x_n^{\alpha_n} \succ_{\text{Lex}} x_1^{\beta_1} \cdots x_1^{\beta_n}$ *if the left-most nonzero entry of $\alpha - \beta$ is positive.*
- $x_1^{\alpha_1} \cdots x_n^{\alpha_n} \succ_{\text{DRL}} x_1^{\beta_1} \cdots x_n^{\beta_n}$ *if $\sum_{i=1}^{n} \alpha_i > \sum_{i=1}^{n} \beta_i$, or $\sum_{i=1}^{n} \alpha_i = \sum_{i=1}^{n} \beta_i$ and the right-most nonzero entry of $\alpha - \beta$ is negative.*

Once a (total) monomial ordering is fixed, we can introduce the following definitions:

Definition 2. *We shall call* total degree *of a monomial $x_1^{\alpha_1} \cdots x_n^{\alpha_n}$ the sum $\sum_{i=1}^{n} \alpha_i$. The* leading monomial *of $p \in \mathbb{K}[x_1, \ldots, x_n]$ is the largest monomial (w.r.t. some monomial ordering $\prec$) among the monomials of p. This leading monomial will be denoted by $\text{LM}(p, \prec)$. The* degree *of p, denoted $\deg(p)$, is the total degree of $\text{LM}(p, \prec)$.*

We are now in a position to define more precisely the notion of Gröbner basis.

Definition 3. *A set of polynomials* $G \subset \mathbb{K}[x_1, \ldots, x_n]$ *is a* Gröbner basis – *w.r.t. a monomial ordering* $\prec$ – *of an ideal* $\mathcal{I}$ *in* $\mathbb{K}[x_1, \ldots, x_n]$ *if, for all* $p \in \mathcal{I}$, *there exists* $g \in G$ *such that* $\mathrm{LM}(g, \prec)$ *divides* $\mathrm{LM}(p, \prec)$.

Gröbner bases computed for a lexicographical ordering (Lex-Gröbner bases) permit to easily describe varieties. A Lex-Gröbner basis of a *zero-dimensional system* (i.e. with a finite number of zeroes over the algebraic closure) is always as follows

$$\{f_1(x_1) = 0, f_2(x_1, x_2) = 0, \ldots, f_{k_2}(x_1, x_2) = 0, \ldots, f_{k_n}(x_1, \ldots, x_n)\}$$

To compute the variety, we simply have to successively eliminate variables by computing zeroes of univariate polynomials and back-substituting the results.

From a practical point of view, computing (directly) a Lex-Gröbner basis is much slower that computing a Gröbner basis w.r.t. another monomial ordering. On the other hand, it is well known that computing degree reverse lexicographical Gröbner bases (DRL-Gröbner bases) is much faster in practice. The FLGM algorithm [14] permits – in the zero-dimensional case – to efficiently solve this issue. This algorithm use the knowledge of a Gröbner basis computed for a given order to construct a Gröbner for another order. The complexity of this algorithm is polynomial in the number of solutions of the ideal considered.

DRL-Gröbner bases have another interesting property. Namely, these bases permit to recover low-degree relations between the inputs/outputs of a vectorial function $\mathbf{f} = (f_1, \ldots, f_m) : \mathbb{K}^n \to \mathbb{K}^m$.

Proposition 1. *Let* $\mathbf{f} = (f_1, \ldots, f_m)$ *be polynomials of* $\mathbb{K}[x_1, \ldots, x_n]$. *We shall call* ideal of relations *of* $\mathbf{f}$ *the set:*

$$\mathcal{I}_{\mathcal{R}}(\mathbf{f}) = \langle z_1 - f_1(x_1, \ldots, x_n), \ldots, z_m - f_m(x_1, \ldots, x_n) \rangle \in \mathbb{K}[x_1, \ldots, x_n, z_1, \ldots, z_m].$$

If $\mathcal{I}_{\mathcal{R}}(\mathbf{f})$ *is radical, then a DRL-Gröbner basis* G *(with* $x_1 > \cdots > x_n > z_1 > \cdots > z_m$) *of* $\mathcal{I}_{\mathcal{R}}(\mathbf{f})$ *describes all the (independent) algebraic relations between the inputs/outputs of* $\mathbf{f}$. *In particular,* G *contains a linear basis of the polynomials* $Q \in \mathcal{I}_{\mathcal{R}}(\mathbf{f})$ *s. t.:*

$$\deg(Q) = \min_{P \in \mathcal{I}_{\mathcal{R}}(\mathbf{f})}\big(\deg(P)\big).$$

Note that in the cryptographic context, the ideals (of relations) are usually radicals. We can indeed always include the field equations. So, this condition is not really restrictive.

2.2 Computing Gröbner Bases

The historical method for computing Gröbner bases is Buchberger's algorithm [6,5]. Recently, more efficient algorithms have been proposed, namely the F_4 and F_5 algorithms [12,13]. These algorithms are based on the intensive use of linear algebra techniques. Precisely, F_4 can be viewed as the "gentle" meeting of Buchberger's algorithm and Macaulay ideas [19]. In short, the arbitrary choices – which limit the practical efficiency of Buchberger's algorithm – are replaced in F_4 by computational strategies related to classical linear algebra problems (mainly the computation of a row echelon form).

In [13], a new criterion (the so-called F_5 criterion) for detecting useless computations has been proposed. It is worth pointing out that Buchberger's algorithm spends 90% of its time to perform these useless computations. Under some regularity conditions, it has been proved that all useless computations can be avoided. A new algorithm, called F_5, has then been developed using this criterion and linear algebra methods. Briefly, F_5 constructs incrementally the following matrices in degree d:

$$A_d = \begin{matrix} & m_1 \succ m_2 \succ m_3 \ldots \\ t_1 f_1 \\ t_2 f_2 \\ t_3 f_3 \\ \ldots \end{matrix} \begin{bmatrix} \ldots & \ldots & \ldots & \ldots \\ \ldots & \ldots & \ldots & \ldots \\ \ldots & \ldots & \ldots & \ldots \\ \ldots & \ldots & \ldots & \ldots \end{bmatrix}$$

where the indices of the columns are monomials sorted for the admissible ordering $\prec$ and the rows are product of some polynomials f_i by some monomials t_j such that $\deg(t_j f_i) \leq d$. For a *regular system* [13] (resp. *semi-regular system* [3,4]) the matrices A_d are of full rank. In a second step, row echelon forms of theses matrices are computed, i.e.

$$A'_d = \begin{matrix} & m_1 \ m_2 \ m_3 \ \ldots \\ t_1 f_1 \\ t_2 f_2 \\ t_3 f_3 \\ \ldots \end{matrix} \begin{bmatrix} 1 & 0 & 0 & \ldots \\ 0 & 1 & 0 & \ldots \\ 0 & 0 & 1 & \ldots \\ 0 & 0 & 0 & \ldots \end{bmatrix}$$

For a sufficiently large d, A'_d contains a Gröbner basis of the considered ideal. An important parameter to evaluate the complexity of F_5 is the maximal degree d_{reg} occurring in the computation and the size $N_{d_{\mathrm{reg}}}$ of the matrix $A_{d_{\mathrm{reg}}}$. The overall cost is dominated by $N_{d_{\mathrm{reg}}}^{\omega}$, with $2 \leq \omega < 3$ denoting the linear algebra constant. Very roughly, $N_{d_{\mathrm{reg}}}$ can be approximated by $\mathcal{O}(n^{d_{\mathrm{reg}}})$ yielding to a global complexity of:

$$\mathcal{O}(n^{\omega \cdot d_{\mathrm{reg}}});$$

more details on this complexity analysis, and further complexity results, can be found in [3,4].

To date, F_5 is the most efficient method for computing Gröbner bases, and hence zero-dimensional varieties. From a practical point of view, the gap with other algorithms computing Gröbner bases is consequent. Notably, it has been proved [2] from both a theoretical and practical point of view that XL [7] – which is an algorithm proposed by the cryptographic community for solving overdefined system of equations – is a redundant version of F_4 and less efficient than F_5.

3   The ℓ-IC$^-$ Signature Scheme

In this part, we describe the ℓ-IC$^-$ multivariate signature scheme proposed at PKC'07 by Ding, Wolf and Yang [9]. Note that our description differs from the original description given by the authors of [9]; allowing us to present our attacks in a concise way.

The design principle of ℓ-IC schemes is classical in multivariate cryptography. Namely, we start from a well chosen algebraic system $\mathbf{F}$ which is "easy" to solve, and then hide this central system using linear and invertible transformations S and T following the idea of McEliece's cryptosystem:

$$\mathbf{P} = T \circ \mathbf{F} \circ S. \tag{1}$$

For ℓ-IC, the central function $\mathbf{F}$ in $\mathbb{E}[X_1, X_2, \ldots, X_\ell]^\ell$ is obtained by considering the so-called *Cremona mapping* which is defined – over an extension $\mathbb{E}$ of degree k of $\mathbb{K}$ – as follows:

$$\mathbf{F}(X_1, X_2, \ldots, X_\ell) = (X_1^{q^{\lambda_1}} X_2, X_2^{q^{\lambda_2}} X_3, \ldots, X_\ell^{q^{\lambda_\ell}} X_1). \tag{2}$$

This function can be invertible for well chosen parameters and it is efficient to invert since only one inversion in $\mathbb{E}$ is required: once X_1 is recover, only division are needed.

The public key consists in $\mathbf{P}$ and to sign a message $\boldsymbol{m}$ of n bits, we inverse it using T, compute an inverse of $\mathbf{F}$, and finally inverse S to find a preimage $\boldsymbol{s}$ of $\boldsymbol{m}$ for the function $\mathbf{P}$. To verify a signature $\boldsymbol{s}$, it is sufficient to evaluate the public key $\mathbf{P}$ and check that it is equal to the message $\boldsymbol{m}$.

We introduce now some notations in order to provide a compact representation of $\mathbf{F}$. We will denote by $x \otimes y$ the component-wise multiplication of $x = (x_1, x_2, \ldots, x_\ell)$ and $y = (y_1, y_2, \ldots, y_\ell)$, i.e.:

$$x \otimes y = (x_1 y_1, x_2 y_2, \ldots, x_\ell y_\ell).$$

Moreover, $\mathcal{R}$ will denote the left rotation operator, namely:

$$\mathcal{R}(x) = (x_2, x_3, \ldots, x_\ell, x_1).$$

Finally, if $\Lambda = (\lambda_1, \ldots, \lambda_\ell) \in \mathbb{N}^\ell$, then $\mathcal{E}_\Lambda$ will denote:

$$\mathcal{E}_\Lambda(x) = (x_1^{q^{\lambda_1}}, \ldots, x_\ell^{q^{\lambda_\ell}}).$$

With these notations, the central map $\mathbf{F}$ can be expressed as:

$$\mathbf{F}(x) = \mathcal{E}_\Lambda(x) \otimes \mathcal{R}(x).$$

In order to combine $\mathbf{F}$ with the two secret transformations S and T, we have to consider some canonical bijection Φ of $\mathbb{K}^{k\ell}$ onto $\mathbb{E}^\ell$. So, $\mathbf{F}$ operates on $\mathbb{E}^\ell$ and

$\Phi^{-1} \circ \mathbf{F} \circ \Phi$ operates on $\mathbb{K}^{k\ell}$. In the sequel, we may avoid the writing of Φ when the context is obvious. Hence, we can express $\mathbf{F}$ and therefore the public key $\mathbf{P}$ as a system of $n = \ell \cdot k$ polynomials of n variables over $\mathbb{K}$. Since S, T, $\mathcal{R}$, and $\mathcal{E}_\Lambda$ are $\mathbb{K}$–linear, the polynomials of $\mathbf{P}$ are quadratic over the n variables of $\mathbb{K}$. In expression (1), note that S can be seen as a change of input variables of $\mathbf{F}$, and T as a change of output variables of $\mathbf{F}$.

We now would like to consider the simplest expressions for $\mathbf{F}$. The authors of [9] remarked that it is useless to consider expression like $\mathbf{F}(x) = \mathcal{E}_{\Lambda_1}(x) \otimes \mathcal{R}(\mathcal{E}_{\Lambda_2}(x))$. The exponentiation $\mathcal{E}_{\Lambda_2}$ would be absorbed by the morphism S. In the same spirit, if we consider

$$\Lambda' = (\lambda_2 + \ldots + \lambda_\ell, \lambda_3 + \ldots + \lambda_\ell, \ldots, \lambda_\ell, 0),$$

$$\Lambda'' = (\lambda_1 + \ldots + \lambda_\ell, 0, \ldots, 0),$$

$$\Lambda''' = (0, \lambda_2 + \ldots + \lambda_\ell, \lambda_3 + \ldots + \lambda_\ell, \ldots, \lambda_\ell)$$

then we have the following equality:

$$\mathcal{E}_{\Lambda'}\big(\mathcal{E}_\Lambda(x) \otimes \mathcal{R}(x)\big) = \mathcal{E}_{\Lambda''}(\mathcal{E}_{\Lambda'''}(x)) \otimes \mathcal{R}(\mathcal{E}_{\Lambda'''}(x)).$$

The exponentiation $\mathcal{E}_{\Lambda'}$ would be absorbed by the external transformation T. For Λ, we can then limit the choice to vectors such as $(\lambda, 0, \ldots, 0)$. Thus, a simple expression for $\mathbf{F}$ is given as follows:

$$\mathbf{F}(X_1, X_2, \ldots, X_\ell) = (X_1^{q^\lambda} X_2, X_2 X_3, \ldots, X_\ell X_1),$$

for some integer λ.

Ding, Wolf and Yang gave explicit formulae [9] for inverting $\mathbf{F}$ when possible, since invertibility of $\mathbf{F}$ is required in the signature scheme:

- If ℓ is even, we must have $\gcd(q^\lambda - 1, q^k - 1) = 1$. Since $q - 1$ divides $q^\lambda - 1$ and $q^k - 1$, we must have $q = 2$.
- If ℓ is odd, we must have $\gcd(q^\lambda + 1, q^k - 1) = 1$. So in this second case, the choices are $\lambda = 0$ when q is even and otherwise $\lambda > 0$ and $k/\gcd(k, \lambda)$ odd (according to [11]).

Then, for a practical signature scheme, the authors of [9] have considered the effects of some known attacks and some modified versions of the main scheme ℓ-IC supposed to defeat those attacks. Particularly for ℓ even, ℓ-IC scheme is vulnerable to the UOV attack [18,17]. So even values of ℓ should be avoided. Then, the authors suggested a modified version, the "Minus" scheme, named ℓIC^-. The point is to remove r polynomials among the description of $\mathbf{P}$. To sign a message m of $(n-r)$ bits, first add r random bits to the message, proceed as in the ℓ-ICscheme, and then discard those r random bits. It increases the complexity of Patarin and Faugère-Joux attacks by a factor q^r. As a counterpart, the scheme can only be used for signature since exhaustive search is also impossible for legitimate user.

In the sequel, we will denote by $\mathbf{P_\Pi} \in \mathbb{E}[X_1, X_2, \ldots, X_\ell]^\ell$ the corresponding truncated public key (*i.e.* the composition of $\mathbf{P}$ with a suitable projection $\mathbf{\Pi}$). Finally, the authors propose the following sets of parameters:

$\#\mathbb{K}$	ℓ	k	n	$n - r$	Security estimation
2^8	3	10	30	20	2^{80}
2^8	3	12	36	24	2^{96}
2^8	3	16	48	32	2^{128}

4   Differential and Multiplication of ℓ-IC

In this part, we present some tools adapted for the cryptanalysis of multivariate systems. We introduce the definition of the differential and we show a special property of the differential of the central map $\mathbf{F}$ of ℓ-IC. In the next section, we show that this property translated onto the public key enables to retrieve special linear applications, which breaks the "Minus" scheme of ℓIC^-.

4.1   Differential of the Public Key

For a generic application $\mathbf{F}$ in one variable, its differential $\mathbf{DF}$ is a symmetric function in two variables defined as:

$$\mathbf{DF(X, A)} = \mathbf{F(X + A)} - \mathbf{F(X)} - \mathbf{F(A)} + \mathbf{F(0)}.$$

In the case of the central map $\mathbf{F}$ of ℓ-IC, we get explicitly:

$$\mathbf{DF(X, A)} = \mathcal{E}_\Lambda(\mathbf{X}) \otimes \mathcal{R}(\mathbf{A}) + \mathcal{E}_\Lambda(\mathbf{A}) \otimes \mathcal{R}(\mathbf{X}).$$

Note that when $\mathbf{F}$ is quadratic function, $\mathbf{DF}$ is symmetric bilinear function.

The differential $\mathbf{DP}$ of the public key $\mathbf{P}$ is also a bilinear symmetric function and is linked to the differential of the central map $\mathbf{F}$ by the following relation:

$$\mathbf{DP(X, A)} = T(\mathbf{DF}(S(\mathbf{X}), S(\mathbf{A}))).$$

Furthermore, the differential $\mathbf{DP}$ can be explicitly computed from the expression of the public key $\mathbf{P}$ since the differential operator operates linearly on functions and it can be easily computed on monomials.

4.2   Characteristic Properties of the Multiplications

Since $\mathcal{R}$ and $\mathcal{E}_\Lambda$ are multiplicative,*i.e.* for all $(\mathbf{X, A})$, $\mathcal{R}(\mathbf{X} \otimes \mathbf{A}) = \mathcal{R}(\mathbf{X}) \otimes \mathcal{R}(\mathbf{A})$ and $\mathcal{E}_\Lambda(\mathbf{X} \otimes \mathbf{A}) = \mathcal{E}_\Lambda(\mathbf{X}) \otimes \mathcal{E}_\Lambda(\mathbf{A})$, we have the multiplicative property of the differential $\mathbf{DF}$, for all ξ, $\mathbf{X}$, $\mathbf{A}$ in $\mathbb{E}^\ell$:

$$\mathbf{DF}(\xi \otimes \mathbf{X, A}) + \mathbf{DF}(\mathbf{X}, \xi \otimes \mathbf{A}) = (\mathcal{E}_\Lambda(\xi) + \mathcal{R}(\xi)) \otimes \mathbf{DF(X, A)}. \qquad (3)$$

For simplicity, we now introduce the following notations: $M_\xi(\mathbf{X}) = \xi \otimes \mathbf{X}$ the multiplication by ξ in $\mathbb{E}^\ell$ and $N_\xi = S^{-1} \circ M_\xi \circ S$ and $L(\xi) = \mathcal{E}_\Lambda(\xi) + \mathcal{R}(\xi)$.

The key idea is the following statement.

Lemma 1. *The $\mathbb{K}$-linear applications M that satisfy for all $\mathbf{X}$, $\mathbf{A}$ in $\mathbb{E}^\ell$:*

$$\mathbf{DF}(M(\mathbf{X}), \mathbf{A}) + \mathbf{DF}(\mathbf{X}, M(\mathbf{A})) = 0 \tag{4}$$

are precisely the multiplications M_ξ with ξ satisfying $L(\xi) = 0$.

Proof. Due to the property (3), we first look for the linear applications M and M' that satisfy for all $\mathbf{X}$, $\mathbf{A}$ in $\mathbb{E}^\ell$:

$$\mathbf{DF}(M(\mathbf{X}), \mathbf{A}) + \mathbf{DF}(\mathbf{X}, M(\mathbf{A})) = M'(\mathbf{DF}(\mathbf{X}, \mathbf{A})). \tag{5}$$

We now express M and M' in a well chosen basis, and then we show that the coordinates of M are those of the multiplications. Indeed, any $\mathbb{K}$-linear application over $\mathbb{E}$ can be uniquely expressed as $\sum_{v=0}^{k-1} \alpha_v x^{q^v}$ with $(\alpha_0, \ldots, \alpha_{k-1})$ in $\mathbb{E}^k$. Hence, the w-th coordinate of $M(X)$ and $M'(X)$ can be expressed respectively as:

$$\sum_{u=0}^{\ell-1} \sum_{v=0}^{k-1} \alpha_{u,v,w} X_w^{q^v} \quad \text{and} \quad \sum_{u=0}^{\ell-1} \sum_{v=0}^{k-1} \beta_{u,v,w} X_w^{q^v},$$

for some $\alpha_{u,v,w}$ and $\beta_{u,v,w}$ in $\mathbb{E}$. The function $\mathbf{F}$ is defined as in (2), so the w-th coordinate of $\mathbf{DF}(\mathbf{X}, \mathbf{A})$ is

$$X_w^{q^{\lambda_w}} A_{w+1} + A_w^{q^{\lambda_w}} X_{w+1}.$$

Then by considering the w-th coordinate of equation (5) we get:

$$\sum_{u=0}^{\ell-1} \sum_{v=0}^{k-1} \alpha_{u,v,w}^{q^{\lambda_w}} \left(X_u^{q^{v+\lambda_w}} A_{w+1} + A_w^{q^{v+\lambda_w}} X_{w+1} \right) + \alpha_{u,v,w+1} \left(X_u^{q^v} A_w^{\lambda_w} + A_w^{q^v} X_w^{\lambda_w} \right)$$

$$= \sum_{u=0}^{\ell-1} \sum_{v=0}^{k-1} \beta_{u,v,w} \left(X_u^{q^{\lambda_u}} A_{u+1} + A_u^{q^\lambda} X_{u+1} \right)^{q^v} \tag{6}$$

The functions $X_a^{q^b} A_c^{q^d}$ are linearly independent. So, we can derive as many relations as the number of these functions, for each coordinate equation (6). Since one given coefficient $\alpha_{a,b,c}$ occurs at most four times in all these relations, we can see that many of them are null, since corresponding relations are trivial. Coefficients $\alpha_{u,v,w}$ appearing in non trivial relations have the following indexes: $(w, 0, w)$, $(w+1, -\lambda_w, w)$, $(w+2, -\lambda_w-\lambda_{w+1}, w)$, $(w+1, 0, w+1)$, $(w, \lambda_w, w+1)$, $(w-1, \lambda_w + \lambda_{w-1}, w+1)$. At this point, we must recall that "$w+1$" is in fact the successor of w in $(0, \ldots, \ell-1)$ or that w are taken modℓ. Hence we may consider that "$\ell+1 = 1$" and "$1 - 1 = \ell$". This is why we now have to consider two cases: $(\ell = 3, q$ even$)$, and $(\ell = 3, q$ odd$)$ or $\ell \geq 5$.

- In the first case $(\ell = 3, q$ even$)$, there are two kinds of "side effect", since "$w-1 = w+2$" for indexes, and "$X+X = 0$" in $\mathbb{E}$. In this case, we have $\Lambda = (0, 0, 0)$, and $F(X) = X \otimes \mathcal{R}(X)$. The solutions of equation (5) are in fact the $\mathbb{E}$-linear applications over $\mathbb{E}^\ell$. One can check easily that in this case, solutions

M of equation (5) can be expressed as $\alpha \otimes X + \beta \otimes \mathcal{R}(X) + \gamma \otimes \mathcal{R}(\mathcal{R}(X))$, for some α, β, and γ in $\mathbb{E}$. Nevertheless, since in equation (4), is in fact equation (5) where $M' = 0$, the only non trivial relations are: $\alpha_{1,0,1} = \alpha_{2,0,2} = \alpha_{3,0,3}$. Hence we have $M(X) = (\alpha_{1,0,1}X_1, \alpha_{2,0,2}X_2, \alpha_{3,0,3}X_3) = (\alpha_{1,0,1}, \alpha_{2,0,2}, \alpha_{3,0,3}) \otimes X$.

– In the second case, the only non trivial relations that remain are: $\alpha_{w,0,w}^{q^{\lambda_w}} + \alpha_{w+1,0,w+1} = \beta_{w,0,w}$. Hence the result: $M(X) = \alpha \otimes X$, $M'(X) = (\mathcal{E}_\Lambda(\alpha) + \mathcal{R}(\alpha)) \otimes X$. When $M' = 0$, we must have $\mathcal{E}_\Lambda(\alpha) + \mathcal{R}(\alpha) = 0$.   □

By translating this result in the public key with the following property:

$$\mathbf{DP}(N_\xi(\mathbf{X}), \mathbf{A}) + \mathbf{DP}(\mathbf{X}, N_\xi(\mathbf{A})) = T(M_{L(\xi)}(\mathbf{DF}(S(\mathbf{X}), S(\mathbf{A})))) \qquad (7)$$

we get the next result:

Lemma 2. *The linear applications M that satisfy for all $\mathbf{X}$, $\mathbf{A}$ in $\mathbb{E}^\ell$:*

$$\mathbf{DP}(M(\mathbf{X}), \mathbf{A}) + \mathbf{DP}(\mathbf{X}, M(\mathbf{A})) = 0 \qquad (8)$$

are the "multiplications" N_ξ, i.e. the conjugates by S of the multiplications M_ξ with ξ satisfying $L(\xi) = 0$.

We emphasize here that finding the applications of the lemma 2 can be practically achieved, since it can be reduced to the resolution of a linear system.

To conclude this section, we give here the solutions of $L(\xi) = 0$. We need to show that $\xi = 0$ is not the only solution, and more precisely that there exist solutions whose coordinates are in $\mathbb{E}$ but not in $\mathbb{K}$. This result will be useful later.

Lemma 3. *There are non trivial solutions of equation $L(\xi) = 0$ that are not in $\mathbb{K}^\ell$.*

– *When q is even, then $\lambda = 0$. The solutions satisfy $\xi_1 = \xi_2 = \ldots = \xi_\ell$. So $\xi = (\alpha, \ldots, \alpha)$ with α in $\mathbb{E}$.*

– *When q is odd, the solutions satisfy $\xi_1^{q^\lambda} + \xi_2 = \xi_2 + \xi_3 = \ldots = \xi_\ell + \xi_1 = 0$. So $\xi = (\alpha, \alpha, -\alpha, \ldots, \alpha, -\alpha)$ with α in $\mathbb{E}$ satisfying $\alpha^{q^\lambda} + \alpha = 0$. Since $\gcd(q^\lambda - 1, q^k - 1) \geq q - 1 > 1$, equation $\alpha^{q^\lambda} + \alpha = 0$ admits solutions in $\mathbb{E} \setminus \mathbb{K}$.*

5   Practical Cryptanalysis of ℓ-IC$^-$ for Small ℓ

From now, we focus our attention to the practical cryptanalysis of the 3-IC$^-$ signature scheme. This is the signature scheme proposed in [9]. However, we would like to emphasize that the next attack can be easily extended to any ℓ-IC$^-$ signature scheme.

5.1   Roadmap of the Attack

The goal of the attack is to recover – from the truncated public key $\mathbf{P}_{\Pi}$ – the equations that were removed. Namely, to recover the whole set of polynomials $\mathbf{P}$. Once these equations are recovered, the scheme is completely broken since a signature can be efficiently forged using Gröbner bases. The principle of the attack is very similar to the one described against SFLASH in [10]. First, we recover an invariant matrix N_{ξ} for the mapping $\mathbf{DP}$. This is done by solving a linear system generated from the (public) components of $\mathbf{DP}_{\Pi}$ (see Section 4). This matrix will then permit to reconstruct the whole public key $\mathbf{P}$ as we describe in the sequel.

5.2   Description of the Attack

What we have to do is first finding one suitable linear application M satisfying:

$$\mathbf{DP}_{\Pi}\big(M(\mathbf{X}), \mathbf{A}\big) + \mathbf{DP}_{\Pi}\big(\mathbf{X}, M(\mathbf{A})\big) = 0.$$

If r the number of missing coordinates is not too high, all solutions are indeed "multiplications" N_{ξ} according to section 4.

We recall that $N_{\xi} = S^{-1} M_{\xi} S$, M_{ξ} being the matrix of multiplication by ξ in $\mathbb{E}^{\ell}$. Since we have the following relation:

$$
\begin{aligned}
\mathbf{P}_{\Pi} \circ N_{\xi} &= \Pi \circ T \circ \mathbf{F} \circ S \circ N_{\xi} \\
&= \Pi \circ T \circ \mathbf{F} \circ S \circ S^{-1} \circ M_{\xi} \circ S \\
&= \Pi \circ T \circ \mathbf{F} \circ M_{\xi} \circ S \\
&= \Pi \circ T \circ M_{F(\xi)} \circ \mathbf{F} \circ S \\
&= \Pi \circ T \circ M_{F(\xi)} \circ T^{-1} \circ T \circ \mathbf{F} \circ S \\
&= \Pi \circ T \circ M_{F(\xi)} \circ T^{-1} \circ \mathbf{P},
\end{aligned}
$$

by composing the public key $\mathbf{P}_{\Pi}$ by N_{ξ}, we get another set of $(n - r)$ equations. We select randomly r equations among this set. It is very likely that this new set will be independent from the $(n - r)$ of P_{Π}. This is indeed the case if ξ does not have all its coordinates in $\mathbb{K}$ or more precisely if M_{ξ} is not diagonal. So, we have in some sense recovered the equations removed. We quoted below some experimental results that we obtained for ℓ-IC$^-$. We have done these experiments using the computer algebra Magma[2]. In this table, T_{rec} is the time to reconstruct the missing equations with our approach.

$\#\mathbb{K}$	ℓ	k	n	r	T_{rec}
2^8	3	10	30	20	12 s.
2^8	3	12	36	24	31 s.
2^8	3	16	48	32	2 min.
2^8	5	10	50	4	3 min
2^8	5	12	60	4	8 min.
2^8	5	16	80	4	36 min.

---

[2] http://magma.maths.usyd.edu.au/magma/

Equations Linking Input and Output. It remains anyway to actually forge a signature using this additional knowledge. To this end, we can first try to mimic Patarin's attack on C*. It can be noted that Patarin's bilinear equations also exist for ℓ-IC. For instance, when $\ell = 3$, we can see that:

$$\begin{cases} Y_1 = X_1 X_2 \\ Y_2 = X_2 X_3 \\ Y_3 = X_3 X_1 \end{cases} \quad \text{implies} \quad \begin{cases} X_3 Y_1 = X_1 Y_2 \\ X_2 Y_3 = X_3 Y_1 \\ X_1 Y_2 = X_2 Y_3 \end{cases}.$$

These are bilinear equations between the input $\mathbf{X} = (X_1, X_2, X_3)$ and output $\mathbf{Y} = (Y_1, Y_2, Y_3)$ of the function $\mathbf{F}$. However, the last bilinear equation is not independent from the two previous ones. We have then only $2k$ independent equations in $\mathbb{K}$. In order to have enough independent equations, we can try to add:

$$Y_1 Y_2 = X_1 X_2^2 X_3 = X_2^2 Y_3.$$

This last equation permits to obtain k additional independent equations. It is not bilinear in the left hand side. But, this is not really an issue, since the right hand side is bilinear when char($\mathbb{E}$)= 2.

We mention that these equations can be recovered automatically using Gröbner bases. To do so, we consider the ideal of relations:

$$\mathcal{I}_\mathcal{R}(\mathbf{F}) = \langle Y_1 - X_1 X_2, Y_2 - X_2 X_3, Y_3 - X_1 X_3 \rangle \in \mathbb{K}[X_1, X_2, X_3, Y_1, Y_2, Y_3].$$

This ideal is radical. Thus, a DRL-Gröbner basis G (with $X_1 > \cdots > X_3 > Y_1 > \cdots > Y_3$) of $\mathcal{I}_\mathcal{R}(\mathbf{F})$ contains a generator set of all the algebraic (independent) relations between the inputs/outputs of $\mathbf{F}$ (see Property 1). In this particular case, we obtain instantaneously (using the computer algebra system Magma) the following basis:

$$[X_1 X_2 + Y_1, X_1 X_3 + Y_3, X_2 X_3 + Y_2, X_3 Y_1 + X_2 Y_3, X_1 Y_2 + X_2 Y_3, X_2^2 Y_3 + Y_1 Y_2].$$

Anyway, this approach does not permit to efficiently forge a signature. Unfortunately, if we try to reconstruct the corresponding equations from the (whole) public key $\mathbf{P}$, we need 2^{48} operations for the first set of parameters.

Signature Forgery. To conclude the attack, we will use another classical property of Gröbner basis. Once all the polynomials of $\mathbf{P}$ recovered, it is not difficult to forge a signature of a message $\boldsymbol{m} \in \mathbb{K}^n$ by computing a solution of the nonlinear system:

$$\mathbf{P}(\mathbf{X}) - \boldsymbol{m}, \tag{9}$$

which can be done in practice for real sizes of the parameters. This behavior was already suspected by the authors of the scheme [9]. However, for the sake of completeness, we quoted below some experimental results that we obtained for ℓ-IC. We have done these experiments using Magma (v2.13-12) which includes a very efficient implementation of the Gröbner basis algorithm F$_4$.

$\#\mathbb{K}$	ℓ	k	n	d_{reg}	T
2^8	3	10	30	4	0.7 s.
2^8	3	12	36	4	2 s.
2^8	3	16	48	4	11 s.
2^8	5	10	50	4	12 s.
2^8	5	12	60	4	39 s.
2^8	5	16	80	4	209 s.

In this table, T denotes the amount of time needed to compute a solution of the system (9), for randomly chosen (non-zero) messages $\boldsymbol{m} \in \mathbb{K}^n$ (i.e. to forge a valid signature for $\boldsymbol{m}$). We mention that T is the time of computing Gröbner basis plus the time to compute the solution from this Gröbner basis. We have also reported the maximum degree d_{reg} reached during Gröbner bases computations. It appears that this degree is bounded from above by a constant (4), leading then to an experimental complexity for systems arising in ℓ-IC (ℓ odd) of:

$$\mathcal{O}(n^{4 \cdot \omega}), \text{ with } 2 \leq \omega < 3 \text{ denoting the linear algebra constant.}$$

This implies that whole attack presented in this part is polynomial (in the number n of variables).

6   A Key-Recovery Attack for ℓ-IC$^-$ for Small ℓ

In this part, we show that we can go one step further in the cryptanalysis of the ℓ-IC$^-$ scheme. Namely, we can recover the secret key (T, S), or at least one equivalent description, when ℓ is small. As previously, this attack will combine differential and Gröbner bases techniques. We will only consider the case q even, but once again this attack can easily be extended to other cases. Finally, the attack does not need to have the definition of the irreducible polynomial which defines the medium field $\mathbb{E}$ since this isomorphism can be absorbed in the equivalent key.

6.1   Equivalent Secret Keys

For an attacker, a total break of ℓ-IC is equivalent to finding a description of $\mathbf{P}$ such as $\mathbf{P} = T \circ \mathbf{F} \circ S$. In fact, this description is not unique. Indeed, it can be seen that there exist many equivalent keys [27]. For instance, since $M_{\mathbf{F}(\xi)} \circ \mathbf{F} = \mathbf{F} \circ M_\xi$, then $(T \circ M_{\mathbf{F}(\xi)}^{-1}, M_\xi \circ S)$ is another valid description. We notice here that M_ξ is not only $\mathbb{K}$-linear, but also $\mathbb{E}$-linear. So, more generally, we have to face the problem of finding an equivalent description (T', S') where $T^{-1} \circ T'$ and $S' \circ S^{-1}$ are $\mathbb{E}$-linear.

In the sequel, we will use the fact that a matrix of a $\mathbb{K}$-linear application which is also $\mathbb{E}$-linear can be viewed as a $k\ell \times k\ell$-matrix over $\mathbb{K}$ but also as a $\ell \times \ell$-block matrix whose blocks are multiplications by elements of $\mathbb{E}$.

6.2   Roadmap of the Attack

To recover one such equivalent secret key, we consider that S and T can be decomposed into one $\mathbb{K}$-linear part and one $\mathbb{E}$-linear part, according to the previous subsection. In the first part of the attack, we will find the part of S and of T in $\mathbb{K}$ and then the parts in $\mathbb{E}$. To recover the part of S in $\mathbb{K}$, called S_0, we will use the invariants N_ξ that we recover using the differential of the public key. Then, once S_0 is recovered, we will find the part of T in $\mathbb{K}$, called T_0, using the differential $\mathbf{DP}$. In fact, $\mathbf{DP}$ depends linearly on S and T and if we compose $\mathbf{DP}$ by S_0^{-1}, then we are able to cancel the part of S in $\mathbf{DP}$. Using some clever ideas we are able to reconstruct some T_0. Finally, we find the part of S and T in $\mathbb{E}$ using Gröbner basis algorithms on the public equation composed on the right by S_0^{-1} and on the left by T_0^{-1}. The problem can then be described in $\mathbb{E}$ instead of $\mathbb{K}$. In such a case, we have reduced the number of variables to $2 \times \ell^2$. Due to the special form of the equations, the two sets of variables are separated, Gröbner basis algorithms are very efficient.

6.3   Description of the Attack

Resolution of S_0. We suppose that we have already recovered the multiplication matrix N_ξ (we have then all the polynomials of $\mathbf{P}$). We recall that:

$$SN_\xi = M_\xi S,$$

M_ξ being a block-diagonal matrix and since $\xi = (\alpha, \alpha, \alpha)$, each block of the diagonal corresponds to the same multiplication matrix by α element of $\mathbb{E}$. Our goal is to recover S from this equality.

To this end, we try to find M_ξ. Observe that α is an element of the multiplicative group $\mathbb{E}^*$ of $\mathbb{E}$. We know that $\mathbb{E}^*$ is of order $q^k - 1$. Due to the choice of the parameters, we can isolate a small subgroup of $\mathbb{E}^*$, not totally included in $\mathbb{K}^*$. Note that elements of $\mathbb{K}$ must be avoided, otherwise M_ξ would be totally diagonal, leading then to linearly dependent equations.

In our example, $q = 256$ and $k = 10, 12, 16$. Since k is even, a good candidate for the order is $o = q + 1$, but any smaller value prime with $q - 1$ will be possible. Consequently, by raising N_ξ to the power $a = (q^k - 1)/o$ we get:

$$N_\xi^a = S^{-1} M_\xi^a S = S^{-1} M_\xi^a S,$$

and ξ^a is of order o. Finally, we can test all elements ρ of order o. For each of them, we try to solve:

$$XN_\xi^a = M_\rho X.$$

Let's suppose that X_1 and X_2 are two particular invertible solutions of this equation. Then $Y = X_1 X_2^{-1}$ must satisfy the equation:

$$YM_\rho = M_\rho Y.$$

So, at this step, the solutions for S form the right coset of any particular solution and the subgroup of ℓ-by-ℓ block-matrices of elements of $\mathbb{K}$, which precisely commute with M_ρ. These are exactly the $\mathbb{E}$-linear applications. So, we can pick at random some invertible solution S_0.

Resolution of T_0. Next step is to obtain a similar description for T. We would like to gain some information on T from the differential of the public key using linear algebra. We recall that:

$$\mathbf{DP}(\mathbf{X}, \mathbf{A}) = T(\mathbf{DF}(S(\mathbf{X}), S(\mathbf{A}))).$$

From now, it will be easier to fix the first variable and to see $\mathbf{DP_X}(\mathbf{A})$ as a linear mapping or equivalently as a matrix. So let's consider v_1 a fixed random vector. Then, consider the expression:

$$\mathbf{DP}_{v_1} \circ S_0^{-1} = T \circ \mathbf{DF}_{S(v_1)} \circ S \circ S_0^{-1}.$$

It is important to note that $\mathbf{DF}_{S(v_1)} \circ S \circ S_0^{-1}$ is actually $\mathbb{E}$-linear, not only $\mathbb{K}$-linear. The matrix $\mathbf{DP}_{v_1} \circ S_0^{-1}$ is therefore the product of T and an unknown ℓ-by-ℓ block-matrix of elements of $\mathbb{E}$. Unfortunately, this matrix is not invertible due to the underlying structure of $\mathbf{DF}$. However, this issue can be easily resolved by picking at random a second vector v_2 and some matrix R with ℓ-by-ℓ block-multiplications (i.e. R is $\mathbb{E}$-linear) and computing the matrix $\mathbf{DP}_{v_1} \circ S_0^{-1} + \mathbf{DP}_{v_2} \circ S_0^{-1} \circ R$. All possible results can be seen as a left coset which contains the real value of T. So, it suffices to pick any value T_0, provided it is invertible.

Resolution of T' and S'. In the last step, we compose the public equations on the right by S_0^{-1} and on the left by T_0^{-1}, the result is public equations expressed in $\mathbb{E}$ instead of $\mathbb{K}$. As explained in [16], we can recover the components of T' and S' by solving an algebraic system of equations. In our case, we have reduced the number of variables to $2 \times \ell^2$. This is due to the fact we are working over $\mathbb{E}$ instead of $\mathbb{K}$. Here, the number of unknowns is very small (2×3^2, for the parameters considerd). The last unknown parameters can easily be retrieved (within a second) using Gröbner bases techniques, as illustrated in the table below:

$\#\mathbb{K}$	ℓ	k	n	T
2^8	3	10	30	0.1 s.
2^8	3	12	36	0.1 s.
2^8	3	16	48	0.1 s.
2^8	5	10	50	0.3 s.
2^8	5	12	60	0.3 s.
2^8	5	16	80	0.3 s.

7   Conclusion

We have presented a forgery attack and a key recovery attack on the parameters of the ℓ-IC$^-$ signature scheme proposed in the original paper. We also briefy mention that this attack can be extended to all other choices of parameters. The main worry when proposing a multivariate scheme is that the Minus Transformation can be used with attention now, due to the differential attack. Finally, for this scheme and contrary to the SFLASH signature scheme, we show that it is possible to recover the secret keys S and T.

Acknowledgements

The first and last authors are very grateful to Adi Shamir for interesting discussions on this subject.

The work described in this paper has been supported by the ANR MAC project and by the European Commission through the IST Program under contract IST-2002-507932 ECRYPT.

References

1. Adams, W.W., Loustaunau, P.: An Introduction to Gröbner Bases. In: Graduate Studies in Mathematics, vol. 3, AMS (1994)
2. Ars, G., Faugère, J.-C., Imai, H., Kawazoe, M., Sugita, M.: Comparison Between XL and Gröbner Basis Algorithms. In: Lee, P.J. (ed.) ASIACRYPT 2004. LNCS, vol. 3329, pp. 338–353. Springer, Heidelberg (2004)
3. Bardet, M.: Étude des Systèmes Algébriques Surdéterminés. Applications aux Codes Correcteurs et à la Cryptographie. PhD thesis, Université de Paris VI, Thèse de Doctorat (2004)
4. Bardet, M., Faugère, J.-C., Salvy, B., Yang, B.-Y.: Asymptotic Behaviour of the Degree of Regularity of Semi-Regular Polynomial Systems. In: MEGA 2005, Eighth International Symposium on Effective Methods in Algebraic Geometry (2005)
5. Buchberger, B.: Gröbner Bases: an Algorithmic Method in Polynomial Ideal Theory.. In: Bose, R.e. (ed.) Recent trends in multidimensional systems theory (1985)
6. Buchberger, B., Collins, G.-E., Loos, R.: Computer Algebra Symbolic and Algebraic Computation., 2nd edn. Springer, Heidelberg (1992)
7. Courtois, N., Klimov, A., Patarin, J., Shamir, A.: Efficient Algorithms for Solving Overdefined Systems of Multivariate Polynomial Equations. In: Preneel, B. (ed.) EUROCRYPT 2000. LNCS, vol. 1807, pp. 392–407. Springer, Heidelberg (2000)
8. Cox, D.A., Little, J.B., O'Shea, D.: Ideals, Varieties, and Algorithms: an Introduction to Computational Algebraix Geometry and Commutative Algebra. Undergraduate Texts in Mathematics. Springer, Heidelberg (1992)
9. Ding, J., Wolf, C., Yang, B.-Y.: ℓ-Invertible Cycles for Multivariate Quadratic Public Key Cryptography. In: Okamoto, T., Wang, X. (eds.) PKC 2007. LNCS, vol. 4450, pp. 266–281. Springer, Heidelberg (2007)
10. Dubois, V., Fouque, P.-A., Shamir, A., Stern, J.: Practical Cryptanalysis of SFLASH. In: Menezes, A. (ed.) CRYPTO 2007. LNCS, vol. 4622, Springer, Heidelberg (2007)
11. Dubois, V., Fouque, P.-A., Stern, J.: Cryptanalysis of SFLASH with Slightly Modified Parameters. In: Naor, M. (ed.) EUROCRYPT 2007. LNCS, vol. 4515, pp. 264–275. Springer, Heidelberg (2007)
12. Faugère, J.-C.: A New Efficient Algorithm for Computing Gröbner Basis: F_4. Journal of Pure and Applied Algebra 139, 61–68 (1999)
13. Faugère, J.-C.: A New Efficient Algorithm for Computing Gröbner Basis without Reduction to Zero: F_5. In: ISSAC, pp. 75–81. ACM Press, New York (2002)
14. Faugère, J.-C., Gianni, P., Lazard, D., Mora, T.: Efficient Computation of Zero-Dimensional Gröbner Bases by Change of Ordering. Journal of Symbolic Computation 16(4), 329–344 (1993)
15. Faugère, J.-C., Joux, A.: Algebraic Cryptanalysis of Hidden Field Equation (HFE) Cryptosystems using Gröbner Bases. In: Boneh, D. (ed.) CRYPTO 2003. LNCS, vol. 2729, pp. 44–60. Springer, Heidelberg (2003)

16. Faugère, J.-C., Perret, L.: Polynomial Equivalence Problems: Algorithmic and The-
    oretical Aspects. In: Vaudenay, S. (ed.) EUROCRYPT 2006. LNCS, vol. 4004, pp.
    30–47. Springer, Heidelberg (2006)
17. Kipnis, A., Patarin, J., Goubin, L.: Unbalanced Oil and Vinegar Signature Schemes.
    In: Stern, J. (ed.) EUROCRYPT 1999. LNCS, vol. 1592, pp. 206–222. Springer,
    Heidelberg (1999)
18. Kipnis, A., Shamir, A.: Cryptanalysis of the Oil & Vinegar Signature Scheme.
    In: Krawczyk, H. (ed.) CRYPTO 1998. LNCS, vol. 1462, pp. 257–266. Springer,
    Heidelberg (1998)
19. Macaulay, F.S.: The Algebraic Theory of Modular Systems. Cambridge University
    Press, Cambridge (1916)
20. Matsumoto, T., Imai, H.: Public Quadratic Polynominal-Tuples for Efficient
    Signature-Verification and Message-Encryption. In: Günther, C.G. (ed.) EURO-
    CRYPT 1988. LNCS, vol. 330, pp. 419–453. Springer, Heidelberg (1988)
21. Patarin, J.: Cryptanalysis of the Matsumoto and Imai Public Key Scheme of Euro-
    crypt 1988. In: Coppersmith, D. (ed.) CRYPTO 1995. LNCS, vol. 963, pp. 248–261.
    Springer, Heidelberg (1995)
22. Patarin, J.: Asymmetric Cryptography with a Hidden Monomial. In: Koblitz, N.
    (ed.) CRYPTO 1996. LNCS, vol. 1109, pp. 45–60. Springer, Heidelberg (1996)
23. Patarin, J.: Hidden Fields Equations (HFE) and Isomorphisms of Polynomials
    (IP): Two New Families of Asymmetric Algorithms. In: Maurer, U.M. (ed.) EU-
    ROCRYPT 1996. LNCS, vol. 1070, pp. 33–48. Springer, Heidelberg (1996)
24. Patarin, J., Courtois, N., Goubin, L.: FLASH, a Fast Multivariate Signature Al-
    gorithm. In: Naccache, D. (ed.) CT-RSA 2001. LNCS, vol. 2020, pp. 298–307.
    Springer, Heidelberg (2001)
25. Shamir, A.: Efficient Signature Schemes Based on Birational Permutations. In:
    Stinson, D.R. (ed.) CRYPTO 1993. LNCS, vol. 773, pp. 1–12. Springer, Heidelberg
    (1994)
26. Shor, P.W.: Polynomial-Time Algorithms for Prime Factorization and Discrete
    Logarithms on a Quantum Computer. SIAM J. Computing 26, 1484–1509 (1997)
27. Wolf, C., Preneel, B.: Equivalent Keys in HFE, C*, and Variations. In: Dawson,
    E., Vaudenay, S. (eds.) Mycrypt 2005. LNCS, vol. 3715, pp. 33–49. Springer, Hei-
    delberg (2005)
28. Wolf, C., Preneel, B.: Taxonomy of Public Key Schemes based on the problem
    of Multivariate Quadratic equations. Cryptology ePrint Archive, Report 2005/077
    (2005), http://eprint.iacr.org/

Recovering NTRU Secret Key from Inversion Oracles

Petros Mol[1] and Moti Yung[2]

[1] University of California, San Diego
pmol@cs.ucsd.edu
[2] Google Inc., Columbia University
moti@cs.columbia.edu

Abstract. We consider the NTRU encryption scheme as lately suggested for use, and study the connection between inverting the NTRU primitive (i.e., the one-way function over the message and the blinding information which underlies the NTRU scheme) and recovering the NTRU secret key (universal breaking). We model the inverting algorithms as black-box oracles and do not take any advantage of the internal ways by which the inversion works (namely, it does not have to be done by following the standard decryption algorithm). This allows for secret key recovery directly from the output on several inversion queries even in the absence of decryption failures. Our oracles might be queried on both valid and invalid challenges e, however they are *not required* to reply (correctly) when their input is invalid. We show that key recovery can be reduced to inverting the NTRU function. The efficiency of the reduction highly depends on the specific values of the parameters. As a side-result, we connect the collisions of the NTRU function with decryption failures which helps us gain a deeper insight into the NTRU primitive.

Keywords: NTRUEncrypt, Inversion Oracles, Universal Breaking, Public-Key Cryptanalysis.

1 Introduction

For every cryptosystem the connection between recovering the secret key (i.e., universally breaking the system) and inverting the underlying (one-way) encryption function is a question of fundamental importance. The classical example is the basic Rabin cryptosystem [21] where the ability to invert instances (i.e., finding modular square roots) was shown to be equivalent to the recovery of the key, i.e., factoring; (recently, [20] extended this to all factoring based cryptosystem with a single composite). For general RSA, the question whether one can factor the modulus N querying (polynomially many times) an oracle that inverts the function $f(x) = x^e \pmod{N}$, remains a challenging open problem for almost 30 years (some work in the opposite direction can be found in [3]). Relating secret key recovery to ciphertext inversion may be used to strengthen security claim (in case key recovery is believed to be hard), and at the same time it opens the door

R. Cramer (Ed.): PKC 2008, LNCS 4939, pp. 18–36, 2008.

to chosen ciphertext attacks as was originally pointed out by Rivest regarding Rabin's scheme.

We study this connection for the NTRU Encryption scheme (NTRUEncrypt) [1] with respect to parameter sets where the secret key f has the shape $f = 1 + p * F$ for a binary polynomial F.

We note that given the state of the art, not much is known about the structure of the NTRU encryption function and the one-way properties of the basic NTRU operation, and unlike traditional public-key schemes NTRU lacks random self-reducibility which is a property often used in understanding the structure. Our investigation, in turn, is aimed at better understanding the one-way trapdoor function that underlies NTRU.

Our conceptual goal has been a "black box" reduction, i.e., treating the inversion oracle (device) as unknown (which is a stronger reduction than ones that assume specific knowledge of how the inverting algorithm works). With this goal in mind, we found that the problem of finding the secret key pair (i.e. universally breaking the scheme) can be reformulated in a way that resembles the problem of inverting a certain instance of NTRU. More specifically, rewriting the key generation equation leaks a polynomial which, for specific parameter values, can be efficiently transformed into a valid instance and thus be recovered using a black box (hypothetical) inverting algorithm.

Related Work: To the best of our knowledge, our work is the first one that studies the problem of NTRU universal breaking outside the CCA framework. All previous key recovery attacks assume access to the decryption oracle, which on input a (valid or invalid) ciphertext applies *the standard NTRU decryption process*, and use its output to retrieve information about the secret key f. All the known CCAs are not guaranteed to work unless the decryption process functions in a very specific way. These attacks retrieve f indirectly and almost all of them work only in the presence of decryption failures.

Jaulmes and Joux [15] were the first to present CCAs against NTRU. Even though their attacks need just a small number of queries to recover f, they do not seem to work for all instantiations of NTRU and require the whole output of the decryption oracle for the recovery of f. In addition, they use *invalid* ciphertexts of a very special shape and can thus be easily thwarted by a decryption machine (which simply refuses to give an output when the input is an invalid ciphertext).

In [14] the authors present 3 new chosen-ciphertext attacks against optimized NTRU (where $f = 1 + p * F$). The attacks require a very small number of queries to the decryption oracle while all the queries are on ciphertexts chosen offline and independently of the previous outputs. The main drawback of the attacks is that the oracle is queried again on *invalid ciphertexts*. In addition, the attacker needs to see the whole output of the oracle in order to fully recover the secret key f. The *reaction attacks* presented in [10] work for f of any shape and do not need to view the output of the decryption in order to recover f. The knowledge of whether the ciphertext decrypts correctly under the assumed decryption process suffices for this type of attack. The number of queries to the decryption oracle is, naturally, significantly larger than in [14].

In [12], the authors present attacks exclusively based on *valid* ciphertexts. The attacker creates the ciphertexts by encrypting valid messages and checks whether the receiver is able to decrypt them correctly (the output of the decryption is not required). These attacks work for any padding scheme and instantiation of NTRU as long as there are decryption failures. Here again the number of queries gets considerably large. In addition, these attacks seem to not have been fully implemented.

Recently, Gama and Nguyen [5] presented new CCAs on NTRU which use only valid ciphertexts chosen at random. Their attacks require the collection of a small number of decryption failures in order to recover f (but still a large number of tries in order to collect these failures). However, they require the full output of the oracle (and not just a YES/NO answer) and work only in the presence of decryption failures.

Table 1 summarizes the most representative CCAs against NTRUEncrypt. It worths noting that almost all of them (with the exception of [15] and [14]) do not work for the latest NTRU instantiations where no decryption failures occur.

Table 1. Known Chosen-Ciphertext Attacks against NTRU

Attack	# Queries	Dec.Failures	ciphertexts	type of reply	Applicability	shape of F	Ref.
Jaulmes, Joux	small	-	invalid	full output	unpadded version	NTRU-1998	[15]
Hong et al.	very small	-	invalid	full output	unpadded version	$1 + p * F$	[14]
Hoffstein,Silverman	large	required	invalid	YES/NO	unpadded version	any shape	[10]
How.-Graham et al.	large	required	valid	YES/NO	padded version	any shape	[12]
Gama, Nguyen	small	required	valid	full output	padded version	any shape	[5]

Our Results: All the aforementioned attacks work in the CCA framework and in particular assume access to *the decryption* oracle, while we assume access to *an inversion* oracle. Although the two approaches are not directly comparable, we present two main points that differentiate our analysis from the previous works.

(i) *We do not consider padding schemes:* After [15], several padding schemes have been proposed in order to enhance the security of NTRUEncrypt (semantic and CCA security) in the random oracle model [2] (see for example [9], [16] and several flaws pinpointed in [19] and [12]). However, here we are concerned only in the connection between breaking the primitive (that is the NTRU "one-way" function) and universal breaking. We work on the space of polynomials rather than in the space of binary strings. Thus we are not concerned about how the strings and the polynomials are connected. It is important to note that even the "valid" spaces might differ. Valid challenges e as defined below might not correspond to valid ciphertexts. Namely, there might be $e = h * r + m \, (mod \, q)$ for $(r, m) \in (\mathcal{B}(d_r), \mathcal{B})$ (valid challenge) which corresponds to an invalid ciphertext because r and m may not be connected via the hash functions used by the padding scheme. Therefore, our results do not work in the presence of a padding scheme and thus they are unlikely to lead to a practical attack. Still, the study of the unpadded version remains theoretically interesting and does say something about the NTRU primitive itself.

(ii) *The internal functionality of the oracle is not exploited:* All the aforementioned attacks assume that the oracle uses the standard decryption process (multiplication of the ciphertext e with f and then reduction modulo p). They all derive information about f *indirectly* from the effect this multiplication has on the input of the oracle. On the contrary, here we view the inversion oracle as a black box and make no assumption on the internal computations of the oracle. This allows for key recovery even in the absence of decryption failures (NTRU-2005). Given our "lack of knowledge" about the internals of the inversion box, it is natural that we might require a relatively large number of oracle queries. Indeed, the efficiency of the reduction highly depends on the Hamming weights d_F, d_r of polynomials F and r respectively. In particular, the number of queries required to recover the secret key is exponential to $|d_F - d_r|$.

Organization: In section 2 we give some notation and a brief description of NTRUEncrypt. Section 3 defines formally the underlying NTRU primitive and studies the connection between the number of collision pairs and decryption failures. In section 4 we define the inversion oracle and its decision counterpart. Subsequently, in section 5, we give the main results and analyze the number of queries and the success probability for finding the secret key pair with respect to each oracle. Finally in section 6 we present the conclusions and suggests directions for future research.

2   NTRU Preliminaries

2.1   Definitions and Notation

We will use $\mathcal{B}$ to denote the set of all polynomials with binary coefficients. Accordingly, we use $\mathcal{B}(d)$ to indicate the set of all polynomials with exactly d 1's and all the other coefficients set to 0 (d is the hamming weight of the binary polynomial). $\mathcal{T}$ will denote the set of ternary polynomials and $\mathcal{T}(d_1, d_2)$ the set of polynomials with exactly d_1 1s and d_2 −1s. We also use the equivalence in representation between polynomials and vectors. That is, each polynomial $p(x) = \sum_{i=0}^{k} p_i x^i$ of degree k corresponds to a vector $\vec{p} = [p_0, p_1, ..., p_k]$ and vice versa. We define the *width* of a polynomial p as

$$width(p) = max(p_0, ..., p_k) - min(p_0, ..., p_k).$$

NTRU was proposed in 1996 by Hoffstein, Pipher and Silverman [8]. All the operations take place in the ring of truncated polynomials $\mathcal{P} = \mathbb{Z}_q[X]/(X^N - 1)$. That is all the polynomials involved are of degree at most $N - 1$ with coefficients lying in an interval of width q. In this ring, addition of two polynomials (denoted "+") is defined as pairwise addition of the coefficients of the same degree and multiplication (denoted "*") is defined as convolution multiplication. That is

$$f(x) * g(x) = h(x) \text{ where } h_k = \sum_{i+j \equiv k \,(mod\, N)} f_i \cdot g_j \,(mod\, q).$$

The operator "*" is both commutative and associative. We define the *pseudo-inverse* of a polynomial p as the polynomial $P \in \mathcal{P}$ such that

$$P * p * s \equiv s \,(mod\, q)$$

for any polynomial $s \in \mathcal{P}$ such that $s(1) \equiv 0 \,(mod\, q)$.

2.2   Overview of NTRUEncrypt

Below we describe in brief the NTRU Encryption Scheme. Further details can be found in [8].

Parameter Set. For key generation, encryption and decryption process the following parameters are used:

$-N$: Determines the maximum degree of the polynomials used. N is taken to be a prime in order to prevent attacks described by Gentry [6] and sufficiently large to prevent lattice attacks such as those described in [4] and [18]. The associated NTRU lattice seems to have dimension $2N$.

$-q$: Large modulus. It is a positive integer. Its value depends on the specific instantiation.

$-p$: Small modulus. A small integer or a polynomial with small coefficients.

N, q and p depend on the desired security level. However $(p, q) = 1$ should always hold, that is p, q should generate the unit ideal.

$-\mathcal{L}_f, \mathcal{L}_g$: Private Key spaces. Sets of polynomials from which the private keys are selected.

$-\mathcal{L}_m$: Plaintext Space. Set of polynomials that represent encoded messages.

$-\mathcal{L}_r$: Blinding value space. Set of polynomials from which the temporary blinding value used during encryption is selected.

$-\psi$: A bijection between $\mathcal{L}_m \,(mod\, p)$ and $\mathcal{L}_m$.

$-center$: Centering method. An algorithm that "ensures" that the reduction modulo q is performed correctly during decryption.

Key Generation

Input: A prime N, the moduli p, q and a description of the sets $\mathcal{L}_f, \mathcal{L}_g$.
Output: The key pair $(pk, sk) = (h, (f, f_p))$.
1. Choose uniformly at random polynomials $f \in \mathcal{L}_f$ and $g \in \mathcal{L}_g$.
2. Compute $f_q \equiv f^{-1} \,(mod\, q)$ and $f_p \equiv f^{-1} \,(mod\, p)$. If f_q or f_p does not exist, go to previous step.
3. Compute $h \equiv f_q * p * g \,(mod\, q)$.
4. Return $(pk, sk) = (h, (f, f_p))$. h is the public key. The pair $(\boldsymbol{f, f_p})$ is the private key.

Encryption

Input: A message $m \in \mathcal{L}_m$ and the public key h.
Output: A ciphertext e that corresponds to m.
1. Select uniformly at random a polynomial $r \in \mathcal{L}_r$ (blinding value).
2. return $e = (h * r + m) \, (mod \, q)$.

Decryption

Input: A ciphertext e and the private key pair (f, f_p).
Output: The message $m \in \mathcal{L}_m$ that corresponds to the ciphertext e.
1. Compute $a \equiv e * f \, (mod \, q)$. $(a \equiv r * h * f + f * m \equiv p * r * g + f * m \, (mod \, q))$.
2. Using a and an appropriate centering algorithm find a polynomial A such that
   $A = p * r * g + f * m$ in $\mathbb{Z}$ and not only $mod \, q$.
3. Compute $m \, (mod \, p) = f_p * A \, (mod \, p)$.
4. Return $\psi(m \, mod \, p) \in \mathcal{L}_m$ which corresponds to the plaintext polynomial.

Remark 2.1. In most of the instantiations of the parameter set ([1], [13]), g is also taken to be invertible $mod \, q$. In that case h is invertible too. In any case, h is pseudo-invertible $mod \, q$ with H being its pseudo-inverse.

Remark 2.2. As we mentioned in the introduction, in our analysis we do not consider padding schemes. Therefore, in the encryption and decryption process, we omit the parts that describe how padding is performed. For the padded version of encryption and decryption algorithms the reader is referred to [16], [1] and [13].

2.3   Instantiations of NTRU

Since its first publication, several variants of NTRUEncrypt have appeared in the literature. This has made the analysis of NTRU a tricky task since different choices of parameter sets might significantly affect the security of the underlying NTRU primitive. Indeed, it is not yet known whether the proposed sets lead to equivalent (in terms of security) primitives. A study of the connection of the various instantiations and an analysis of their vulnerabilities with respect to certain types of attack, consists a very challenging direction for future research.

In table 2 we summarize the main instantiations of NTRU[1] (for further details the reader is referred to [5, Section 2]). Sometimes, for efficiency reasons, a combination of the above sets might be used. For example in NTRU-2001 q might be a prime or in NTRU-2005 $\mathcal{L}_r$ and F might belong in $\mathcal{X}(d)$ which denotes the set of (binary) polynomials of the from $b_1 + b_2 * b_3$ where b_i are very sparse binary polynomials with d 1s.

---

[1] Recently, in order to secure against attacks presented in [11], the NTRU parameters have been revised in [7]. The major difference is that polynomials F, g, r, m belong to the space of trinary polynomials (that is their coefficients lie in the set $\{-1, 0, 1\}$). Still, in most of the new parameter sets, f has the shape $f = 1 + p * F$ with $p = 3$. We haven't looked at reductions in these new sets, but we anticipate that similar reduction arguments apply (though the number of queries required for the reduction might grow larger since the search space grows).

Table 2. The Main NTRU Parameter Sets

Variant	q	p	$\mathcal{L}_f$	$\mathcal{L}_g$	$\mathcal{L}_m$	$\mathcal{L}_r$	F	Dec. Failures	Ref.
NTRU-1998	$2^k \in [\frac{N}{2}, N]$	3	$\mathcal{T}(d_f, d_f - 1)$	$\mathcal{T}(d_g, d_g)$	$\mathcal{T}$	$\mathcal{T}(d_r, d_r)$	-	YES	[8]
NTRU-2001	$2^k \in [\frac{N}{2}, N]$	$2 + x$	$1 + p * F$	$\mathcal{B}(d_g)$	$\mathcal{B}$	$\mathcal{B}(d_r)$	$\mathcal{B}(d_F)$	YES	[16]
NTRU-2005	prime	2	$1 + p * F$	$\mathcal{B}(d_g)$	$\mathcal{B}$	$\mathcal{B}(d_r)$	$\mathcal{B}(d_F)$	NO	[13]

3   The NTRU "One-Way" Function

In this work we consider instantiations where $f = 1 + p * F$. In these instantiations, the NTRU function is defined as follows:

Definition 3.1 (The NTRU Function)

$$\mathcal{E} : \mathcal{B}(d_r) \times \mathcal{B} \to \mathbb{Z}_q^N$$
$$(r, m) \to h * r + m \ (mod \ q)$$

The NTRU function, like the underlying functions of many other practical cryptosystems, does not have a formal proof of security in that there exists no known reduction that proves that its inversion is at least as hard as a well studied hard problem. Its security appears to be related to the hardness of some lattice problems, namely the shortest and closest vector problems (SVP, CVP). In particular, finding the secret key pair (f, g) can be reduced to finding the shortest vector in a lattice constructed by the public information (L_{CS} lattice defined in [4]) whereas inverting NTRU instances can be reduced to finding the closest lattice vector to a point. However, it is possible that both NTRU problems are easier than their lattice counterparts and thus the analogy between Finding NTRU Key/Inverting challenges and SVP/CVP might be too loose.

The underlying NTRU problem can be summarized in the following definition (first formally presented by Nguyen and Pointcheval in [19])

Definition 3.2 (The NTRU Inversion Problem). *For a given security parameter k, which specifies N, p, q as well as a random public key h and $e \equiv h * r + m \ (mod \ q)$ where $m \in \mathcal{B}$ and $r \in \mathcal{B}(d_r)$, find m. Let $\mathbf{Succ}_{NTRU}^{ow}(\mathcal{A})$ denote the success probability of any adversary $\mathcal{A}$.*

$$\mathbf{Succ}_{NTRU}^{ow}(\mathcal{A}) = Pr\left[\mathcal{A}(e, h) = m \big| (h, sk) \leftarrow \mathcal{K}(1^k), m \in \mathcal{B}, r \in_R \mathcal{B}(d_r), e \equiv h * r + m \ (mod \ q)\right]$$

The probability is taken over all the random choices made by the key generation and the encryption algorithm (h and r) as well as over all possible $m \in \mathcal{B}$. Hence, the security of NTRUEncrypt is based on the following assumption

Definition 3.3 (The NTRU Assumption). *The NTRU Inversion Problem is asymptotically hard to solve. That is, for any polynomially bounded adversary $\mathcal{A}$, $\mathbf{Succ}_{NTRU}^{ow}(\mathcal{A})$ is negligible.*

Since we are interested in efficient reductions , apart from the number of queries, we also need to bound the output of the oracles upon being asked on a specific challenge.

Definition 3.4 (Collision-Pair). *A pair* $((r_1, m_1), (r_2, m_2))$ *with* $(r_i, m_i) \in (\mathcal{B}(d_r), \mathcal{B})$, *is a NTRU collision-pair if*

$$(r_1, m_1) \neq (r_2, m_2) \quad and \quad \mathcal{E}(r_1, m_1) = \mathcal{E}(r_2, m_2).$$

Definition 3.5. *The NTRU valid challenge space is denoted by* $E_{q,h}^{d_r}$ *and contains the image of all pairs* $(r, m) \in (\mathcal{B}(d_r), \mathcal{B})$ *under NTRU function* $\mathcal{E}$. *Namely,*

$$E_{q,h}^{d_r} = \{e \in \mathbb{Z}_q^N | \exists r \in \mathcal{B}(d_r), m \in \mathcal{B} : e \equiv h * r + m \, (mod \, q)\}.$$

Definition 3.6. *Let* $e \in \mathbb{Z}_q^N$ *be a (valid or invalid) challenge. The set* $preimg(e)$ *is the set of all pairs* $(r, m) \in (\mathcal{L}_r, \mathcal{L}_m)$ *that give* e *under the NTRU function. That is*

$$preimg(e) = \{x_i = (r_i, m_i) | r_i \in \mathcal{L}_r, m_i \in \mathcal{L}_m, \, h * r_i + m_i \equiv e \, (mod \, q)\}$$

Obviously $|preimg(e)| = 0$ if $e \notin E_{q,h}^{d_r}$ and $|preimg(e)| \geq 1$ otherwise. The following proposition connects the number of collisions to the decryption failure probability.

Proposition 3.1. *On input* $e \in E_{q,h}^{d_r}$, *the standard NTRU decryption algorithm will fail to decrypt correctly with probability at least* $1 - \frac{1}{|preimg(e)|}$.

Proof. We give an intuitive proof. A less intuitive (but more formal) proof can be found in Appendix A. On input e, the standard NTRU process returns a unique message m. But there are exactly $|preimg(e)|$ distinct m's that corresponds to that e (see appendix A why these m's are distinct). Assuming (naturally) that e has emerged from the encryption of an $(r_i, m_i) \in preimg(e)$ with probability $\frac{1}{|preimg(e)|}$ (uniformly), then the inversion algorithm recovers the correct pair with probability at most $\frac{1}{|preimg(e)|}$. We say "at most" because the decryption algorithm might fail to recover any of the $(r_i, m_i) \in preimg(e)$ (due to gap or wrap failures). $\square$

The implications are straightforward. If $e \in E_{q,h}^{d_r}$ decrypts correctly, then e has a unique preimg. For example, for NTRU-2005, where decryption failures have been eliminated, this means that each valid e has a unique preimg $(r, m) \in (\mathcal{B}(r), \mathcal{B})$. Notice that the uniqueness holds not only for m (something naturally implied by perfect decryption) but for r as well. In addition, even for NTRU-2001, where decryption failures are present, the fraction of valid e that have a unique $(r, m) \in (\mathcal{B}(r), \mathcal{B})$ preimg is at least as large as the fraction of e that decrypt correctly which is (exponentially) close to one. But even for the small fraction of e that may have more than one preimages, we can argue that the number of preimages cannot grow exponentially large, otherwise the NTRU instance can be efficiently broken. Indeed, if there is a challenge e which corresponds to an exponential number of preimages, one can mount a birthday-type attack to efficiently obtain two pairs $(r_1, m_1), (r_2, m_2)$ both of which encrypt to e. We then have

$$r_1 * h + m_1 \equiv r_2 * h + m_2 \, (mod \, q) \Rightarrow (r_1 - r_2) * h \equiv m_2 - m_1 \, (mod \, q)$$

But $r_1 - r_2$ and $m_1 - m_2$ have very small norms and can be therefore used instead of f and g to invert most of the instances (of course, now the centering algorithm will perform reduction $mod\ q$ in an interval centered at zero since $r_1 - r_2$ and $m_1 - m_2$ have coefficients in $\{-1, 0, 1\}$). We summarize the above arguments in the following sentence which we only state as an assumption for scientific accuracy.

The Preimage Assumption: For each $e \in E_{q,h}^{d_r}$ the number of pairs $(r_i, m_i) \in (\mathcal{B}(d_r), \mathcal{B})$ such that $e \equiv h * r_i + m_i \ (mod\ q)$ is polynomially bounded.

4   Modeling an Inverting Algorithm with Inversion Oracles

We will use the word "challenge" for e (instead of "ciphertext") in order to avoid any confusion with Chosen-Ciphertext Attacks. An ideal inversion algorithm would invert any valid challenge e in polynomial time given only the public information. In the rest of this section we introduce our main inversion oracle and its decision version.

Definition 4.1 (orc1). *On input $e \in \mathbb{Z}_q^N$ orc1 outputs the pair(s) $(r, m) \in (\mathcal{B}(d_r), \mathcal{B})$ such that $e \equiv h * r + m \ (mod\ q)$ if $e \in E_{q,h}^{d_r}$. If $e \notin E_{q,h}^{d_r}$, orc1 gives an undefined reply denoted by "?".*

We also consider the decision version of *orc1*.

Definition 4.2 ($orc1^{DEC}$). *On input $e \in \mathbb{Z}_q^N$, $orc1^{DEC}$ outputs "YES" if $e \in E_{q,h}^{d_r}$ and "?" otherwise.*

Remark 4.1. Both *orc1* and $orc1^{DEC}$, as defined above, can be used to fully distinguish valid and invalid challenges. More interestingly, *orc1* (and $orc1^{DEC}$ with a further search similar to the one described in the proof of theorem 5.3), might recover the correct message polynomials even in cases where the standard decryption might have failed (recall that the NTRUEncrypt standard decryption process in the initial instantiations has non-zero failure probability). However, the goal here is to study how easy the key recovery problem becomes in the presence of inverting algorithms, rather than argue about properties of the algorithms themselves.

5   Universal Breaking from Inversion Oracles

We denote the problem of finding the NTRU secret key pair as $\mathcal{UB}_{NTRU}$ (Universal Breaking).

Definition 5.1. *We say that $\mathcal{UB}_{NTRU}$ is (p, orc, Q)-solvable if there exists an algorithm, polynomial in the number Q of queries, which fully recovers f with probability at least p by querying oracle orc at most Q times.*

5.1 Universal Breaking Using *orc*1

Transforming the Secret Key Equation to a Valid Inversion Instance.
From the key generation process we have

$$h \equiv f_q * p * g \,(mod\, q) \Rightarrow f * h \equiv p * g \,(mod\, q) \Rightarrow h * (1 + p * F) \equiv p * g \,(mod\, q)$$
$$\Rightarrow p_q * h + p_q * h * p * F \equiv g \,(mod\, q) \Rightarrow p_q * h + h * F \equiv g \,(mod\, q).$$

from which we can either get

$$h * F - g \equiv -p_q * h (mod\, q) \Rightarrow h * F + u - g \equiv u - p_q * h (mod\, q)$$

where $u(X) = X^{N-1} + X^{N-2} + ... + 1$ or alternatively

$$p_q * h \equiv -h * F + g \,(mod\, q) \Rightarrow p_q * h + h * u \equiv h * u - h * F + g \,(mod\, q).$$

If we now define $\bar{g} = u - g$, $\bar{F} = u - F$ these two give

$$u - p_q * h \equiv h * F + \bar{g}(mod\, q)$$
$$p_q * h + h * u \equiv h * \bar{F} + g \,(mod\, q) \tag{1}$$

where $h * u = (\sum h_i, \sum h_i, ..., \sum h_i)^T$. Summarizing, let $d = min\{|d_F - d_r|, |N - d_F - d_r|\}$.
Then the problem of key recovery takes the following form

$$t \equiv h * v + w \,(mod\, q) \qquad \text{(Secret Key Equation)}$$

where

- (I) $d = |d_F - d_r|$. Then $t \equiv u - p_q * h \,(mod\, q), v = F$ and $w = u - g$.
- (II) $d = |N - d_F - d_r|$. Then $t \equiv p_q * h + h * u \,(mod\, q), v = u - F$ and $w = g$.

with $u(X) = X^{N-1} + X^{N-2} + ... + 1$ (or $\vec{u} = (1, 1, ..., 1)^T$). It is important to note that in both cases w, v are binary. By definition, *orc*1 guarantees to output the correct pair(s) only when $e \in E_{q,h}^{d_r}$, that is when the blinding polynomial r used for encryption has exactly d_r 1's. Thus, in any case, in order to construct a polynomial that is "useful" for *orc*1, we need to transform (using an efficient and invertible transformation) the known polynomial t into a polynomial that belongs to the challenge space recognized by *orc*1. The steps of this transformation depend, as we show below, on the difference $d = |d_v - d_r|$ between the hamming weights of the polynomials v and r. We highlight below the aforementioned transformation.

(I) Let us consider the first case where $d = |d_F - d_r|$.
We get the following two subcases:

(a) $d_F \geq d_r$: Then $d_F - d_r = d$. We then have

$$t \equiv h * v + w \,(mod\, q), \quad \text{where } t \equiv u - p_q * h \,(mod\, q), v = F \text{ and } w = u - g.$$

- Suppose that $d = 0$ (Binary polynomials F and r have exactly the same hamming weight). Then we query $orc1$ on $t \in E_{q,h}^{d_r}$ and by the definition of the oracle, we expect to get $F, \bar{g}$ (and thus f, g).
- Suppose that $d = 1$ and let i be an index such that $F_i = 1$. Then $h * F + \bar{g}$, can be rewritten in the following form

$$h * F + \bar{g} = h * (F + X^i - X^i) + \bar{g},$$

Thus

$$t \equiv h * (F - X^i) + h * X^i + \bar{g} \, (mod \, q) \Rightarrow t - h * X^i \equiv h * (F - X^i) + \bar{g} \, (mod \, q).$$

But $F - X^i \in \mathcal{B}(d_r)$. Querying $orc1$ on $t - h * X^i$, we can recover $F - X^i$ and consequently F (if we know i).

- Generalizing to arbitrary $d = d_F - d_r$. Suppose that we know indices $i_1, i_2, ..., i_d$ such that $F_{i_1} = F_{i_2} = ... = F_{i_d} = 1$. Then

$$t - h * (X^{i_1} + X^{i_2} + ... + X^{i_d}) \equiv h * (F - X^{i_1} - X^{i_2} - ... - X^{i_d}) + \bar{g} \, (mod \, q).$$

where again $t - h * (X^{i_1} + X^{i_2} + ... + X^{i_d}) \in E_{q,h}^{d_r}$. If we query $orc1$ on $t - h * (X^{i_1} + X^{i_2} + ... + X^{i_d})$ we can recover $F - X^{i_1} - X^{i_2} - ... - X^{i_d}$ and consequently F.

It only remains to determine the cost of finding d indices $i_1, i_2, ..., i_d \in \{0, 1, ..., N - 1\}$ such that $F_{i_1} = F_{i_2} = ... = F_{i_d} = 1$.

(b) $d_F < d_r$: Then $d = d_r - d_F$.
- Suppose that for the indices $i_1, i_2, ..., i_d$ we know that $F_{i_1} = F_{i_2} = ... = F_{i_d} = 0$. Then

$$t + h * (X^{i_1} + X^{i_2} + ... + X^{i_d}) \equiv h * (F + X^{i_1} + X^{i_2} + ... + X^{i_d}) + \bar{g} \, (mod \, q).$$

If we query $orc1$ on $t + h * (X^{i_1} + X^{i_2} + ... + X^{i_d})$ we can recover $F + X^{i_1} + X^{i_2} + ... + X^{i_d}$ and consequently F.

(II) The case where $d = |N - d_F - d_r|$ is similar to case (I). Next we study the cost of finding the correct indices $i_1, i_2, ..., i_d$ that allow the reconstruction of F.

Computing the Cost of Finding the Correct Indices. We consider case (Ia). The analysis of the cases (Ib),(IIa) and (IIb) is completely similar.

The input is a polynomial c with N coefficients, M of which equal 1 (of course $M \leq N$). We need to guess d indices ($d \leq M$) $i_1, ..., i_d$ such that $c_{i_1} = ... = c_{i_d} = 1$ with the least possible number of tries. The only feedback we get is a "YES" whenever $c_{i_1} = ... = c_{i_d} = 1$ holds (and then we are done) and "NO" in all other cases. Let $\mu(N, M, d)$ denote the minimum number of guesses required in the worst case, if we follow an optimal strategy and $\bar{\mu}(N, M, d)$ the expected number of guesses.

Theorem 5.1. (i) $\mu(N, M, d) \leq \binom{N-M+d}{d}$.

(ii) $\bar{\mu}(N, M, d) \leq \frac{\binom{N}{d}}{\binom{M}{d}}$.

Proof. (i) We restrict our guesses to the first $N - M + d$ positions of the polynomial. Suppose that the first $N - M + d$ positions contain at most $d - 1$ 1's. Then the total number of 1's in the whole vector would be at most $d - 1 + (M - d) = M - 1$ which yields a contradiction. Thus, in the worst case, we have to try at most $\binom{N-M+d}{d}$ possible (non ordered) d-tuples.

(ii) At each step we pick a set of d indices at random from all the sets of cardinality d that have not been picked in previous guesses. Obviously this yields a smaller expected number of steps than if we just picked from all possible sets (examined or not). The number of guesses in the latter scenario follows the geometrical distribution with $p = \frac{\binom{M}{d}}{\binom{N}{d}}$. Thus the expected number of the former strategy is at most $\frac{\binom{N}{d}}{\binom{M}{d}}$. □

We note that the above bounds are rather gross estimates of the values μ and $\bar{\mu}$. The problem of minimizing the number of guesses is mainly a learning problem of independent interest.

Corollary 5.1. $\mathcal{UB}_{NTRU}$ is $(1, orc1, \mu(N, d_F, d_F - d_r))$-solvable under the Preimage Assumption.

Proof. Getting back to case (Ia) of our problem, we are searching for $d = d_F - d_r$ 1s in a vector with $M = d_F$ 1s in order to transform $t \equiv u - p_q * h \pmod{q}$ which belongs to $E_{q,h}^{d_F}$ to a $t' \in E_{q,h}^{d_r}$ and then query $orc1$ on t'. After at most $\mu(N, d_F, d_F - d_r)$ guesses the decryption oracle outputs a pair $(r, m) \in (\mathcal{B}(d_r), \mathcal{B})$. Because of the Preimage Assumption, the pairs returned upon querying the oracle on a valid challenge e are polynomially bounded. This means that the dominant factor is the number of queries addressed to $orc1$ till the correct set of indices is guessed. Then, hopefully, the r returned equals $F - X^{i_1} - X^{i_2} - ... - X^{i_d}$ and so F can be reconstructed correctly. There might be an exception to that. There might be a d-tuple of indices $(i'_1, ..., i'_d)$ such that $t - h * (X^{i'_1} + ... + X^{i'_d}) \in E_{q,h}^{d_r}$ but $F_{i'_j} = 0$ for some $j \in 1, ..., d$. Fortunately, we can detect these exceptions by reconstructing F'. Then either $F' \notin \mathcal{B}(d_F)$ or $g' \notin \mathcal{B}$, where $g' \equiv p_q * (1 + p * F') * h \pmod{q}$. The preceding analysis, however, guarantees that with at most $\mu(N, d_F, d_F - d_r)$ queries to $orc1$, we will have ended up with the correct r from which F can be reconstructed in a straightforward way. Thus, the success probability after $\mu(B, d_F, d_F - d_r)$ queries is 1. □

The same result applies to cases (Ib), (IIa) and (IIb) where d is defined properly. Hence, an upper bound for the number of the oracle queries is

$$\frac{(N - d_r)!}{d!(N - d_r - d)!} = \frac{(N - d_r)!}{d!(N - d_F)!}$$

But $\frac{(N-d_r)!}{d!(N-d_r-d)!} \leq \frac{(N-d_r)^d}{d!}$. This means that if d is a (relatively small) constant, we can solve $\mathcal{UB}_{NTRU}$ in a polynomial number of queries to $orc1$.

On the contrary, the cost of the reduction grows exponentially on d. That means that, in instantiations where $d = \omega(\log^{1+\epsilon} N)$ for some positive ϵ, the reduction is no longer polynomial.

Probabilistic Analysis. The following theorem bounds the number of queries to $orc1$ when the success probability of solving $\mathcal{UB}_{NTRU}$ is lower-bounded by ϵ.

Theorem 5.2. $\mathcal{UB}_{NTRU}$ *is* $\left(\epsilon, orc1, \binom{N}{d_F-d_r} \cdot \left(1 - (1-\epsilon)^{\overline{\left(\frac{1}{d_F-d_r}\right)}}\right)\right)$ *-solvable.*

Proof. Consider again the game of guessing d coefficients. We have in total $T = \binom{N}{d_F-d_r}$ possible (non-ordered) d-tuples $(d = d_F - d_r)$, $S = \binom{d_F}{d_F-d_r}$ of which are "winning". The probability that after Q guesses we have no winning guess is

$$Pr(fail, Q) = \left(1 - \frac{S}{T}\right) \cdot \left(1 - \frac{S}{T-1}\right) \cdots \left(1 - \frac{S}{T-Q+1}\right)$$

$$= \prod_{i=0}^{Q-1} \left(1 - \frac{S}{T-i}\right) \leq \prod_{i=0}^{Q-1} e^{-\frac{S}{T-i}},$$

where we have used that for $x \geq 0$, $1 - x \leq e^{-x}$ .Thus

$$Pr(fail, Q) \leq e^{-S \cdot \sum_{i=0}^{Q-1} \frac{1}{T-i}} = e^{-S \cdot (H_T - H_{T-Q})},$$

where $H_k = \sum_{i=1}^{k} \frac{1}{k}$ is the k-th Harmonic number. Let ϵ be the success probability, that is the probability that we guess a correct d-tuple in the first Q queries to $orc1$. Then using the approximation $H_k = \ln k$ for the harmonic number , we get

$$1 - \epsilon = Pr(fail, Q) \leq e^{-S \cdot (H_T - H_{T-Q})} \approx e^{-S \cdot (\ln T - \ln(T-Q))} = T^{-S}(T - Q)^S.$$

Thus

$$1 - \epsilon \leq \left(1 - \frac{Q}{T}\right)^S \Rightarrow Q \leq T \cdot (1 - (1-\epsilon)^{\frac{1}{S}}),$$

which completes the proof. $\square$

5.2   Replacing *orc1* with Its Decision Version

Let us now consider the decision version of $orc1$, $orc1^{DEC}$. The main result is summarized in Theorem 5.3. First we introduce Assumption 1 that simplifies the proof of the main result and makes the combinatorial arguments more clear. We then introduce a weaker assumption (Assumption 2) and sketch how one could recover the secret key under the latter.

Assumption 1: Let $\mathcal{T}$ denote the set of all polynomials with coefficients in $\{-1, 0, 1\}$. In addition let $(r_1, m_1), (r_2, m_2) \in (\mathcal{T}, \mathcal{B})$ with $r_1(1) = r_2(1)$ and $\mathcal{E}_{q,h}(r, m) = h * r + m \,(mod\, q)$. Then

$$\mathcal{E}_{q,h}(r_1, m_1) = \mathcal{E}_{q,h}(r_2, m_2) \Leftrightarrow (r_1, m_1) = (r_2, m_2).$$

Theorem 5.3. $\mathcal{UB}_{NTRU}$ is $(1, orc1^{DEC}, \binom{N-d_r}{d_F-d_r} + N + d_r - d_F - 1)$-solvable under Assumption 1.

Proof. We consider again the game of guessing d 1-coefficients where now we choose the indices $(i_1, i_2, ..., i_d)$ according to the lexicographical ordering. We first exclude the $M - d$ rightmost coefficients (coefficients that correspond to positions $N - M + d, ..., N - 1$) from our search. We begin with $(0, 1, ..., d - 1)$ and feed $orc1^{DEC}$ with $t - h * (1 + X + ... + X^{d-1})$. At each step (and as long as we get "NO" answers by $orc1^{DEC}$) we move the rightmost index 1 position to the right until it reaches the boundary position (position $N - M + d - 1$) or another index. When that happens, we move the rightmost index that can be moved 1 position to the right and initialize all its right indices right next to it (on the right). In order to make the algorithm clear, we give an example.

Let $N = 7, M = 5, d = 3$. The boundary value is $N - M + d - 1 = 4$. Then the sequence of indices we examine is the following.

$(0,1,2), (0,1,3), (0,1,4), (0,2,3), (0,2,4),(0,3,4), (1,2,3), (1,2,4), (1,3,4), (2,3,4)$.

Notice that the number of combinations we examine is at most $\binom{N-M+d}{d}$, that is the algorithm checks all the possible (non ordered) d-combinations of the first $N - M + d$ coefficients. According to theorem 5.1 at least one of those d-tuples will result to a "YES" answer from $orc1^{DEC}$. Suppose that $orc1^{DEC}$ responds "YES" after Q queries (of course $Q \leq \binom{N-M+d}{d}$) and let $(i_1^*, ..., i_d^*)$ be the configuration of indices for which the answer is "YES". Then we know that $t - h * (X^{i_1^*} + ... + X^{i_d^*}) \in E_{q,h}^{d_r}$. But

$$t - h * (X^{i_1^*} + ... + X^{i_d^*}) \equiv h * (F - X^{i_1^*} - ... - X^{i_d^*}) + \bar{g} \, (mod \, q).$$

We claim that $F_{i_1^*} = ... = F_{i_d^*} = 1$. Indeed, suppose that $F_{i_j^*} = 0$ for some j. Then $F - X^{i_1^*} - ... - X^{i_d^*}$ is no longer binary (it has at least one -1 coefficient) but still $\mathcal{E}(F - X^{i_1^*} - ... - X^{i_d^*}, \bar{g}) \equiv \mathcal{E}(r, m)$ for a pair $(r, m) \in (\mathcal{B}(d_r), \mathcal{B})$ (recall that $t - h * (X^{i_1^*} + ... + X^{i_d^*}) \in E_{q,h}^{d_r}$). This yields a contradiction according to our assumption. Thus with at most $\binom{N-M+d}{d}$ we find d indices that correspond to 1 coefficients in F.

It only remains to recover the rest of the coefficients of F. To do this we make a simple observation. For each configuration of indices, there exists one configuration previously examined that differs in exactly one index[2]. Indeed, if we move the leftmost index that has been moved one position to the left we get a configuration of indices that has already been examined. Since the previous configuration has yielded a "NO" answer the different index corresponds to a 0 coefficient in F. So, after at most $\binom{N-M+d}{d}$ queries we know d coefficients of F

---

[2] There is an exception to that. When $(i_1^*, ..., i_d^*) = (0, 1, ..., d-1)$, there is no previous configuration at all. If this is the case, we can determine the rest coefficients by simply querying $orc1^{DEC}$ on $t - h * (X^{i_1^*} + ... + X^{i_{d-1}^*} + X^i)$ for each unknown coefficient F_i. Then because of the assumption, $F_i = 1$ if and only if $t - h * (X^{i_1^*} + ... + X^{i_{d-1}^*} + X^i) \in E_{q,h}^{d_r}$.

that are equal to 1 and one 0 coefficient. Let $F_k = 0$ the known 0 coefficient. We also know that

$$t - h * (X^{i_1^*} + ... + X^{i_d^*}) \equiv h * (F - X^{i_1^*} - ... - X^{i_d^*}) + \bar{g} \, (mod \, q).$$

Thus for all other unknown coefficients

$$F_i = 1 \text{ if and only if } F - X^{i_1^*} - ... - X^{i_d^*} + X^k - X^i \in \mathcal{B}(d_r)$$

or, because of the assumption, if and only if

$$t - h * (X^{i_1^*} + ... + X^{i_d^*} - X^k + X^i) \in E_{q,h}^{d_r}.$$

So we only have to query $orc1^{DEC}$ $N - d - 1$ more times to fully recover F. Now, setting $M = d_F, d = d_F - d_r$, we get that we need at most $\binom{N-d_r}{d_F-d_r} + N + d_r - d_F - 1$ queries in total to recover F, which completes the proof.   □

Interestingly, a similar result holds if we relax Assumption 1 to Assumption 2.

Assumption 2: Let $\mathcal{T}$ as in Assumption 1. The number of pairs $(r_i, m_i) \in (\mathcal{T}, \mathcal{B})$ with constant value $r_i(1)$ that encrypt to the same $e \in \mathbb{Z}_q^N$ under $\mathcal{E}_{q,h}$ is polynomially bounded.

Theorem 5.4. $\mathcal{UB}_{NTRU}$ is $(1, orc1^{DEC}, \mathcal{O}(N) \cdot \binom{N-d_r}{d_F-d_r})$-solvable under Assumption 2.

Proof (Sketch). In the presence of (polynomially many) collisions, we just need to do an extra checking every time $orc1^{DEC}$ responds "YES" in order to see if the d-tuple of indices selected is the one that leads to the correct reconstruction of F (see details of the proof for theorem 5.3). For each checking a computational overhead of $\mathcal{O}(N)$ queries is added (the checking works in a way similar to the checking in the proof of theorem 5.3). In that case the total number of queries to $orc1^{DEC}$ is multiplied by a factor of at most $\mathcal{O}(N)$.   □

Remark 5.1. The above analysis implies that if $d_F - d_r$ is small with respect to N, we can universally break NTRUEncrypt if we have a polynomial time distinguisher between valid and invalid challenges.

Decryption Oracles and Real NTRU Parameters. The applicability of our reductions is enhanced by the set of parameters that have been proposed from time to time. Indeed both in [13] and in [1] it is suggested that during the key generation process, d_F is set equal to d_r. In addition, in the web challenges published by NTRU Cryptosystems (www.ntru.com/cryptolab/challenges.htm),the parameter sets proposed are as shown in the table below

Security	N	q	d_F	d_g	d_r
Medium	251	128	72	71	72
High	347	128	64	173	64
Highest	503	256	420	251	170

For the Medium and High level of security $d_r = d_F$, which, suggests that for theses values of parameters the problems of inverting a challenge e and finding the secret key pair, are structurally the same. For the highest level of security, however, $d = 420 + 170 - 503 = 87$ which does not allow for efficient reductions.

6 Conclusions

We have shown how inversion black-box oracles that output message polynomials corresponding to valid challenges e or that serve as decision oracles lead to a secret key recovery in the current NTRU system where $f = 1 + p * F$. The cost of recovering the secret key depends on the difference between the Hamming weights of the polynomials F and r in an exponential fashion. The reductions presented do not work in the presence of a padding scheme and thus seem unlikely to lead to any practical attacks. Still, this fundamental connection teaches us about the very structure of the cryptosystem in general. The implication is quite straightforward and should be carefully interpreted: Finding an algorithm that inverts NTRU instances in recent NTRU instantiations (and for certain parameter values), opens the door to secret key recovery within a small number of queries to that algorithm. It is important to note that there is nothing particular that makes the secret key recovery harder than inverting random instances (see equation Secret Key Equation). Indeed, the target challenge t is no less "random" than any other inversion instance, since F, g are random polynomials.

As a related future direction, we believe that coming up with more efficient reductions which further exploit the structure of the NTRU function is an interesting field for investigation. Finally, another challenging direction would be to extend the range of behavior of the black-box oracles to non-ideal ones (that fail with some probability to return the correct preimage even when being queried on valid challenges).

References

1. EESS: Consortium for Efficient Embedded Security. Efficient Embedded Security Standards #1: Implementation Aspects of NTRU and NSS, draft version 3.0 edition (July 2001)
2. Bellare, M., Rogaway, P.: Random Oracles are Practical: A Paradigm for Designing Efficient Protocols. In: ACM Conference on Computer and Communications Security, pp. 62–73 (1993)
3. Boneh, D., Venkatesan, R.: Breaking RSA May Not Be Equivalent to Factoring. In: Nyberg, K. (ed.) EUROCRYPT 1998. LNCS, vol. 1403, pp. 59–71. Springer, Heidelberg (1998)
4. Coppersmith, D., Shamir, A.: Lattice Attacks on NTRU. In: Fumy, W. (ed.) EUROCRYPT 1997. LNCS, vol. 1233, pp. 52–61. Springer, Heidelberg (1997)

5. Gama, N., Nguyen, P.Q.: New Chosen-Ciphertext Attacks on NTRU. In: Okamoto, T., Wang, X. (eds.) PKC 2007. LNCS, vol. 4450, pp. 89–106. Springer, Heidelberg (2007)
6. Gentry, C.: Key Recovery and Message Attacks on NTRU-Composite. In: Pfitzmann, B. (ed.) EUROCRYPT 2001. LNCS, vol. 2045, pp. 182–194. Springer, Heidelberg (2001)
7. Hoffstein, J., Howgrave-Graham, N., Pipher, J., Silverman, J.H., Whyte, W.: Hybrid Lattice Reduction and Meet in the Middle Resistant Parameter Selection for NTRUEncrypt, http://grouper.ieee.org/groups/1363/lattPK/submissions/ChoosingNewParameters.pdf
8. Hoffstein, J., Pipher, J., Silverman, J.H.: NTRU: A Ring-Based Public Key Cryptosystem. In: Buhler, J.P. (ed.) ANTS 1998. LNCS, vol. 1423, pp. 267–288. Springer, Heidelberg (1998)
9. Hoffstein, J., Silverman, J.H.: Protecting NTRU Against Chosen Ciphertext and Reaction Attacks. Technical report, NTRU Cryptosystems (2000), http://citeseer.ist.psu.edu/hoffstein00protecting.html
10. Hoffstein, J., Silverman, J.H.: Reaction Attacks Against the NTRU Public Key Cryptosystem. Technical Report, NTRU Cryptosystems, Report #015, version 2 (June 2000), http://citeseer.ist.psu.edu/hoffstein00reaction.html
11. Howgrave-Graham, N.: A Hybrid Lattice-Reduction and Meet-in-the-Middle Attack Against NTRU. In: Menezes, A. (ed.) CRYPTO 2007. LNCS, vol. 4622, pp. 150–169. Springer, Heidelberg (2007)
12. Howgrave-Graham, N., Nguyen, P.Q., Pointcheval, D., Proos, J., Silverman, J.H., Singer, A., Whyte, W.: The Impact of Decryption Failures on the Security of NTRU Encryption. In: Boneh, D. (ed.) CRYPTO 2003. LNCS, vol. 2729, pp. 226–246. Springer, Heidelberg (2003)
13. Howgrave-Graham, N., Silverman, J.H., Whyte, W.: Choosing Parameter Sets for NTRUEncrypt with NAEP and SVES-3. Technical Report, NTRU CRYPTOSYSTEMS (2005)
14. Hong, J., Han, J., Kwon, D., Han, D.: Chosen-Ciphertext Attacks on Optimized NTRU. Cryptology ePrint Archive: Report 2002/188 (2002)
15. Jaulmes, É., Joux, A.: A Chosen-Ciphertext Attack against NTRU. In: Bellare, M. (ed.) CRYPTO 2000. LNCS, vol. 1880, pp. 20–35. Springer, Heidelberg (2000)
16. Hoffstein, J., Silverman, J.: Optimizations for NTRU. Technical report, NTRU Cryptosystems (June 2000), http://citeseer.ist.psu.edu/693057.html
17. Näslund, M., Shparlinski, I., Whyte, W.: On the Bit Security of NTRUEncrypt. In: Desmedt, Y.G. (ed.) PKC 2003. LNCS, vol. 2567, pp. 62–70. Springer, Heidelberg (2002)
18. May, A.: Cryptanalysis of NTRU-107 (1999), http://www.informatik.tu-darmstadt.de/KP/publications/01/CryptanalysisOfNTRU.ps
19. Nguyen, P.Q., Pointcheval, D.: Analysis and Improvements of NTRU Encryption Paddings.. In: Yung, M. (ed.) CRYPTO 2002. LNCS, vol. 2442, pp. 210–225. Springer, Heidelberg (2002)
20. Paillier, P., Villar, J.L.: Trading One-Wayness Against Chosen-Ciphertext Security in Factoring-Based Encryption.. In: Lai, X., Chen, K. (eds.) ASIACRYPT 2006. LNCS, vol. 4284, pp. 252–266. Springer, Heidelberg (2006)
21. Rabin, M.O.: Digital Signatures and Public-Key Functions as Intractable as Factorization. Technical report, Cambridge (1979)

A   Proof of Theorem 3.1

Proof. For each pair $(r_i, m_i) \in preimg(e)$, we define $a_i = p * g * r_i + f * m_i$ where, as usual, f, g are the secret and auxiliary key respectively. Equation $e \equiv h * r_i + m_i \,(mod\ q)$ gives $f * e \equiv a_i \,(mod\ q)$. We need the following two lemmas.

Lemma A.1. *If $(r_i, m_i), (r_j, m_j)$ are two distinct pairs that belong to $preimg(e)$, then $(r_i \neq r_j) \wedge (m_i \neq m_j)$.*

Proof. Suppose on the contrary, that there exist $(r_i, m_i), (r_j, m_j)$ with $(r_i, m_i) \neq (r_j, m_j)$ such that $(r_i = r_j) \vee (m_i = m_j)$. Then we have the following two cases

(a) $r_i = r_j$: Then

$$h * r_i + m_i \equiv h * r_j + m_j \,(mod\ q) \stackrel{r_i = r_j}{\Rightarrow} m_i \equiv m_j \,(mod\ q).$$

But both $m_i, m_j \in \mathcal{L}_m$ and thus have small coefficients (with respect to q). Therefore $m_i = m_j$ holds over the integers which yields a contradiction.

(b) $m_1 = m_2$: Then we have

$$h * r_1 \equiv h * r_2 \,(mod\ q) \Rightarrow h * (r_1 - r_2) \equiv 0 \,(mod\ q)$$

But h has a pseudo-inverse, that is there exists a polynomial $H \in \mathcal{P}$ such that $H * h * s \equiv s \,(mod\ q)$ for any polynomial s with $s(1) \equiv 0 \,(mod\ q)$. Now notice that $(r_1 - r_2)(1) = r_1(1) - r_2(1) = d_r - d_r = 0$ (in all instantiations of NTRU the value $r(1)$ is a public constant). This gives that $H * h * (r_1 - r_2) \equiv r_1 - r_2 \,(mod\ q)$, which combined with the above equation gives $r_1 - r_2 \equiv 0 \,(mod\ q)$. This implies that $r_1 = r_2$ since both r_1 and r_2 have very small coefficients. □

Lemma A.2. *$a_i \neq a_j$ over $\mathbb{Z} \,\forall i \neq j$. That is a_is are pairwise distinct.*

Proof. Suppose that there exist distinct indices i, j such that $a_i = a_j$. First observe that $(r_i \neq r_j) \wedge (m_i \neq m_j)$, otherwise we would have

$$p * g * r_i + f * m_i = p * g * r_j + f * m_j \stackrel{\times f_q}{\Rightarrow} h * r_i + m_i \equiv h * r_j + f * m_j \,(mod\ q)$$

which clearly contradicts lemma A.1. If we multiply both sides with f_p (recall that $f_p * f = 1 + p * k$ for a polynomial k) we get

$$p * f_p * g * r_i + (1 + p * k) * m_i = p * f_p * g * r_j + (1 + p * k) * m_j \quad \text{over the integers}$$

which gives $m_i \equiv m_j \,(mod\ p)$. But p and the modulo p reduction process are selected in such a way that $m \,(mod\ p)$ for a polynomial $m \in \mathcal{L}_m$ uniquely determines m. Otherwise the decryption would be ambiguous. This means that $m_i = m_j$ over the integers which gives a contradiction. □

Back to the proof of 3.1, we have that for each pair of distinct indices i, j $a_i \neq a_j$ but $a_i \equiv a_j \, (mod \, q)$ for all pairs that collide to the same e, since $a_i \equiv a_j \equiv f * e \, (mod \, q)$. This means that there exists *at most* one index i such that all the coefficients of a_i lie in the interval dictated by the centering algorithm (let's say $[A, A+q-1]$). Indeed, if again $a_i, a_j, i \neq j$ had all their coefficients in $[A, A+q-1]$ (of range q) the equation $a_i \equiv a_j \, (mod \, q)$ would imply $a_i = a_j$ over the integers (contradiction).

Thus, the centering algorithm (and the inversion part of the decryption algorithm in general) works properly for at most one pair $(r_i, m_i) \in preimg(e)$. All the decryption algorithm sees is the challenge e and has no information on the preimage pair (r, m). Assuming (naturally) that e has emerged from the encryption of each $(r_i, m_i) \in preimg(e)$ with probability $\frac{1}{|preimg(e)|}$ (uniformly), with probability at most $\frac{1}{|preimg(e)|}$ the inversion algorithm recovers the correct pair. Thus we conclude that

$$Pr[Decryption \; succeeds | input \; is \; e] \leq \frac{1}{|preimg(e)|}.$$

□

Solving Systems of Modular Equations in One Variable: How Many RSA-Encrypted Messages Does Eve Need to Know?[*]

Alexander May and Maike Ritzenhofen

Faculty of Mathematics
Ruhr-Universität Bochum, 44780 Bochum, Germany
alex.may@ruhr-uni-bochum.de,
maike.ritzenhofen@ruhr-uni-bochum.de

Abstract. We address the problem of polynomial time solving univariate modular equations with mutually co-prime moduli. For a given system of equations we determine up to which size the common roots can be calculated efficiently. We further determine the minimum number of equations which suffice for a recovery of all common roots. The result that we obtain is superior to Håstad's original RSA broadcast attack, even if Håstad's method is combined with the best known lattice technique due to Coppersmith. Namely, our reduction uses a slightly different transformation from polynomial systems to a single polynomial. Thus, our improvement is achieved by optimal polynomial modelling rather than improved lattice techniques. Moreover, we show by a counting argument that our results cannot be improved in general. A typical application for our algorithm is an improved attack on RSA with a smaller number of polynomially related messages.

Keywords: Chinese Remaindering, Coppersmith's method, Håstad's attack, systems of univariate modular polynomials.

1 Introduction

The RSA cryptosystem [14] is the public key cryptosystem which is most widely used in practice. Therefore, it has attracted the interest of many cryptanalysts since its invention in 1977 (compare e. g. [2]). In the following, let us denote by $N = pq$ the RSA modulus with prime factors p and q, and let $\mathbb{Z}_N$ denote the ring of integers modulo N. Let e be the public exponent, and let $d = e^{-1}$ (mod $\varphi(N)$) be the private key.

Attacks on RSA intend either to factorize the modulus and thereby recover the private key, or to compute e-th roots modulo N, i. e. to decrypt ciphertexts. The equivalence or inequivalence of these two problems is still open. However, partial results are known in restricted models [3,4,10].

---

[*] This research was supported by the German Research Foundation (DFG) as part of the project MA 2536/3-1.

R. Cramer (Ed.): PKC 2008, LNCS 4939, pp. 37–46, 2008.

In this paper we deal with the problem of extracting e-th roots. This is the well-known RSA problem: Given an RSA modulus N, a public exponent e and a ciphertext $c \equiv m^e \pmod{N}$, find the corresponding plaintext m.

If $m^e < N$, the equation does not only hold in $\mathbb{Z}_N$ but over the integers, and we can calculate m easily. This implies that encrypting small messages with small public exponents is insecure.

Let us look at the inhomogeneous case. Namely, suppose the most significant bits are known so that the unknown part remains small enough. Then we get the equation $(\tilde{m} + x)^e \equiv c \pmod{N}$, with $\tilde{m}$ denoting the known, x the unknown part of the message. D. Coppersmith [6] showed that this inhomogeneous case can be solved efficiently under the same condition $x^e < N$.

Precisely, he showed that given a composite integer N and a univariate polynomial $f(x) \in \mathbb{Z}_N[x]$ of degree δ one can determine all zeros smaller than $N^{\frac{1}{\delta}}$ efficiently. Hence, $(\tilde{m} + x)^e \equiv c \pmod{N}$ can be solved if $|x| < N^{\frac{1}{e}}$.

Now we may ask what happens if we get further information in form of additional polynomials? Can we then determine larger zeros as well?

There are two variants of systems of polynomial modular equations. Either there exist equations with the same modulus or all moduli are different. The first case was considered in Coppersmith, Franklin, Patarin and Reiter [7]. They showed that it is usually sufficient to have two equations $f_1(x) \equiv 0 \pmod{N}$ and $f_2(x) \equiv 0 \pmod{N}$ in order to recover the common roots. Let a be the common solution of the two equations. Then, $f_1(x)$ and $f_2(x)$ share a factor $(x - a)$. Computing the greatest common divisor $\gcd(f_1(x), f_2(x)) \pmod{N}$ reveals this factor if it is the only common factor. In the rare cases where the greatest common divisor is not linear, the method fails and further polynomials are needed. The running time of this method is $O(\delta \log^2 \delta)$ where δ is the degree of the given polynomials.

It is worth pointing out that a scenario with two RSA encryptions under co-prime public exponents (e_1, e_2) and a common modulus N is a special case of this setting. Namely, an attacker has to find the common root m of $f_1(x) = x^{e_1} - m^{e_1}$ $(\text{mod } N)$ and $f_2(x) = x^{e_2} - m^{e_2} \pmod{N}$. G. Simmons [16] has presented a neat attack for this special setting with running time polynomial in the bitlength of (e_1, e_2). Namely, one computes integers u_1, u_2 such that $u_1 e_1 + u_2 e_2 = 1$ with the help of the Extended Euclidean Algorithm. This gives us $m = (m^{e_1})^{u_1} (m^{e_2})^{u_2}$ $(\text{mod } N)$.

In this work, we focus on equations with different moduli $N_1, N_2, \ldots, N_k \in \mathbb{N}$. Without loss of generality, we assume that all moduli are composite as modular equations over finite fields can be solved efficiently (compare e. g. [1], Chapter 7.4). We further assume that the N_i, $i = 1, \ldots, k$, are relatively prime. In case of our main application, RSA-moduli, we can otherwise compute prime factors of the N_i by computing the greatest common divisor.

Before we define our polynomial roots problem in general, let us give a motivating cryptographic application. This application was introduced by J. Håstad in [8,9] and can be considered as an analogue of Simmon's attack in the setting of different RSA moduli. A user wishes to send the same message m to several participants having different moduli and using plain RSA encryption without padding techniques. Suppose these users share the same public exponent $e = 3$. Then, an attacker obtains three equations $m^3 \equiv c_i \pmod{N_i}$ for $i = 1, 2, 3$. He can make use of the fact that the N_i are relatively prime and combine the equations by the Chinese Remainder Theorem. Thus, he gets $m^3 \pmod{N_1 N_2 N_3}$ and is able to determine m in $\mathbb{Z}$ as $m^3 < N_1 N_2 N_3$. Therefore, the attacker solves the system of polynomial equations $f_i(x) \equiv x^3 - c_i \equiv 0 \pmod{N_i}$, $i = 1, 2, 3$, with the common root m.

Now let us generalize to arbitrary polynomial equations. We define the problem of solving *systems of modular univariate polynomial equations (SMUPE-problem)*.

Definition 1 (SMUPE-problem). *Let $k \in \mathbb{N}$, $\delta_1, \ldots, \delta_k \in \mathbb{N}$, and let $N_1, \ldots, N_k \in \mathbb{N}$ be mutually co-prime composite numbers of unknown factorization. Suppose $N_1 < N_2 < \ldots < N_k$. Let $f_1(x), \ldots, f_k(x)$ be polynomials of degree $\delta_1, \ldots, \delta_k$ in $\mathbb{Z}_{N_1}[x], \ldots, \mathbb{Z}_{N_k}[x]$, respectively. Let*

$$
\begin{aligned}
f_1(x) &\equiv 0 \pmod{N_1} \\
f_2(x) &\equiv 0 \pmod{N_2} \\
&\vdots \\
f_k(x) &\equiv 0 \pmod{N_k}
\end{aligned}
\tag{1}
$$

be a system of univariate polynomial equations.

Let $X \leq N_1$, $X \in \mathbb{R}$. Find all common roots x_0 of (1) with size $|x_0| < X$.

Our goal is to compute an upper bound X for which the SMUPE-problem is solvable in time polynomial in $\prod_{i=1}^{k} \delta_i$ and in the bitlength of $\prod_{i=1}^{k} N_i$. This upper bound will give us a condition on the number of equations k in terms of δ_i and N_i. This will enable us to compute the minimal k such that the SMUPE-problem can be computed up to the bound $X = N_1$, i.e. system (1) can be solved efficiently.

J. Håstad [9] gave the following algorithm for solving the SMUPE-problem. Let $\delta \in \mathbb{N}$ be the maximum degree of all polynomials occuring in the system, i.e. $\delta := \max_{i=1,\ldots,k}\{\delta_i\}$. One first multiplies the given polynomials with $x^{\delta - \delta_i}$ to adjust their degrees. Then one combines the resulting polynomials using the Chinese Reminder Theorem to a univariate polynomial $f(x)$ with the same roots modulo $\prod_{i=1}^{k} N_i$. Applying lattice reduction methods, J. Håstad derived $k > \frac{\delta(\delta+1)}{2}$ as a lower bound on the number of polynomials for efficiently finding all roots x_0 with $|x_0| < N_1$. This bound can be easily improved to $k \geq \delta$ by directly applying Coppersmith's lattice techniques [6] to $f(x)$ (see e.g. [2]).

Our contribution: We give a different construction to combine all k polynomial equations into a single equation $f(x) \equiv 0 \pmod{\prod_{i=1}^{k} N_i}$. Instead of multiplying the polynomials by powers of x like in Håstad's approach, we take powers of the polynomials $f_i(x)$ themselves. This results in the condition $\sum_{i=1}^{k} \frac{1}{\delta_i} \geq 1$ for solving the SMUPE-problem for all x_0 with $|x_0| < N_1$. In case all polynomials share the same degree δ this corresponds to Håstad's condition $k \geq \delta$. For polynomials of different degrees, however, our new condition is superior. Especially, a few polynomials of low degree suffice.

The paper is organized as follows. In Section 2, we review Coppersmith's result from [6] and the Chinese Remainder Theorem for polynomials. In Section 3, we prove the new sufficient condition on the number of polynomials that is needed to recover all common roots efficiently. The improved RSA broadcast attack is given as an application in Section 4. In Section 5, we show that our condition cannot be improved in general by giving an example for which the condition is optimal.

2   Preliminaries

The problem of solving modular univariate polynomial equations is believed to be difficult in general. Under some restrictions on the roots however, this is not the case. In [6], D. Coppersmith showed how to provably determine zeros of modular univariate equations with sufficiently small size.

Theorem 1 (Coppersmith [6]). *Let $f(x)$ be a monic polynomial of degree $\delta \in \mathbb{N}$ in one variable modulo an integer N of unknown factorization. Let X be a bound on the desired solution x_0. If $X \leq N^{\frac{1}{\delta}}$ then we can find all integers x_0 such that $f(x_0) \equiv 0 \pmod{N}$ and $|x_0| \leq X$ in time $O(\delta^5(\delta + \log N) \log N)$.*

The running time can be achieved by using an algorithm of Nguyen, Stehlé [13] for the LLL lattice basis reduction step (see [11,12]).

The SMUPE-problem can be reduced to the problem of solving a single univariate polynomial equation by combining the equations into a single one with the same solutions. Then we can apply Theorem 1. A possible way to combine equations is by Chinese Remaindering which is described e.g. in [9,15].

Theorem 2 (Chinese Remainder Theorem). *Let $k \in \mathbb{Z}$. Let $\delta \in \mathbb{N}$, $\delta > 1$. For $i = 1, \ldots, k$ let $N_i \in \mathbb{N}$ be pairwise relatively prime numbers, and let $f_i(x) \in \mathbb{Z}[x]$ be polynomials of degree δ.*
Then there exists a unique polynomial $f(x)$ modulo $M := \prod_{i=1}^{k} N_i$ such that

$$f(x) \equiv f_i(x) \pmod{N_i} \tag{2}$$

The polynomial $f(x)$ can be determined in time $O(\delta \log^2 M)$.

Proof. Let $M := \prod_{i=1}^{k} N_i$, $M_i := \frac{M}{N_i}$ and M_i' be the inverse of M_i modulo N_i for $i = 1, \ldots, k$. The existence of such an inverse is guaranteed by $\gcd(M_i, N_i) = 1$. Then

$$f(x) = \sum_{i=1}^{k} M_i M_i' f_i(x)$$

is the desired solution. If we look at $f(x)$ modulo N_j for $j \in \{1, \ldots, k\}$, all summands with index $i \neq j$ cancel out (as N_j divides M_i) and $M_j M'_j f_j(x) \equiv f_j(x) \pmod{N_j}$.

Now suppose that $g(x)$ is another solution fulfilling the required conditions. Then, $f(x) - g(x) \equiv 0 \pmod{N_i}$ for all $i = 1, \ldots, k$, and therefore also $f(x) \equiv g(x) \pmod{M}$.

Multiplication modulo M and calculating the inverses by the Extended Euclidean Algorithm can be performed in time $O(\log^2 M)$. Determining all coefficients of f then gives us $O(\delta \log^2 M)$ for the complete algorithm. $\qquad\square$

3   An Improved Algorithm for Solving SMUPE

For notational convenience let us briefly recall the SMUPE-problem. Given $k \in \mathbb{N}$, $N_1, \ldots, N_k \in \mathbb{N}$, mutually co-prime composite numbers of unknown factorization, such that $N_1 < \ldots < N_k$, and a system of polynomial equations

$$
\begin{aligned}
f_1(x) &\equiv 0 \pmod{N_1} \\
f_2(x) &\equiv 0 \pmod{N_2} \\
&\vdots \\
f_k(x) &\equiv 0 \pmod{N_k},
\end{aligned}
\tag{1}
$$

where $f_1(x), \ldots, f_k(x)$ are of degree $\delta_1, \ldots, \delta_k \in \mathbb{N}$ in $\mathbb{Z}_{N_1}[x], \ldots, \mathbb{Z}_{N_k}[x]$, respectively.

Let $X \leq N_1$, $X \in \mathbb{R}$. Recover all solutions x_0 of (1) with $|x_0| < X$.

Considering for example Coppersmith's method (Theorem 1) for the first equation in (1), only small roots x_0 with $|x_0| < N_1^{\frac{1}{\delta_1}}$ can be found in polynomial time. By considering further equations this bound can be improved until all solutions can be found eventually.

By Håstad's algorithm in combination with Theorem 1 the condition $k \geq \delta$ with $\delta := \max_{i=1,\ldots,k}\{\delta_i\}$ is sufficient to solve a system of equations efficiently. However, this condition is clearly not optimal as the following trivial example shows. Let $N_1 < \ldots < N_4$ and take the following equations.

$$
\begin{aligned}
x^3 &\equiv c_1 \pmod{N_1} \\
x^3 &\equiv c_2 \pmod{N_2} \\
x^3 &\equiv c_3 \pmod{N_3} \\
x^5 &\equiv c_4 \pmod{N_4}
\end{aligned}
$$

Then $k = 4 < 5 = \delta$, i.e. the condition is not fulfilled. However, if we just take the first three equations, we are able to compute all common solutions smaller than N_1. This gives us the intuition that the proportion of higher and lower degrees of the polynomials ought to be taken into account. Let us now change the given example a little bit into a non-trivial one, so that no subsystem of the equations fulfills the sufficient condition.

$$x^3 \equiv c_1 \pmod{N_1}$$
$$x^3 \equiv c_2 \pmod{N_2}$$
$$x^5 \equiv c_3 \pmod{N_3}$$
$$x^5 \equiv c_4 \pmod{N_4}$$

The parameters k and δ and the N_i remain the same. Can we still determine all solutions? We notice that we can transform the first equation by squaring into

$$x^6 \equiv 2c_1 x^3 - c_1^2 \pmod{N_1^2}.$$

Applying Theorem 1 to this equation, we can find all solutions x for which $|x| < (N_1^2)^{\frac{1}{6}} = N_1^{\frac{1}{3}}$ holds. This is the same bound which we get for the roots of the original equation $x^3 \equiv c_1 \pmod{N_1}$. We proceed with the second equation in the same way, then multiply the two other equations by x and finally combine all the equations by Theorem 2 (Chinese Remainder Theorem). This gives us

$$x^6 \equiv a_1(2c_1 x^3 - c_1^2) + a_2(2c_2 x^3 - c_2^2) + a_3 x c_3 + a_4 x c_4 \pmod{N_1^2 N_2^2 N_3 N_4},$$

where the a_i are the coefficients from the Chinese Remainder Theorem, i.e. $a_i \equiv 1 \pmod{N_i}$, $a_i \equiv 0 \pmod{N_j}$, $j \neq i$. The above equation can be solved in $\mathbb{Z}$ for x with $|x| < (N_1^2 N_2^2 N_3 N_4)^{\frac{1}{6}}$. This condition is fulfilled for any x with $|x| < N_1 = (N_1^6)^{\frac{1}{6}} \leq (N_1^2 N_2^2 N_3 N_4)^{\frac{1}{6}}$. Therefore, we can determine all solutions of the above system of equations, although the condition $k \geq \delta$ is not fulfilled.

In order to generalize our approach we make the following crucial observation. Let $f(x)$ be a polynomial of degree δ. Let $f(x) \equiv 0 \pmod{N}$ for $N \in \mathbb{N}$, and let $m \in \mathbb{N}$. Then $g(x) := f^m(x) \equiv 0 \pmod{N^m}$. The solutions x with $|x| < N$ of the two equations remain unchanged. Moreover, with Coppersmith's Theorem 1 we can determine those solutions for which the condition $|x| < N^{\frac{1}{\delta}} \Leftrightarrow |x| < (N^m)^{\frac{1}{m\delta}}$ holds. Thus, Coppersmith's bound is invariant under taking powers of the polynomial $f(x)$.

As opposed to our approach, in Håstad's algorithm one does not take powers of the polynomials but multiplications of polynomials with powers of x. This increases the degree of the polynomial but leaves the modulus unchanged. Let $f(x)$ be a polynomial of degree δ with $f(x) \equiv 0 \pmod{N}$ for $N \in \mathbb{N}$. Then with $\gamma > \delta$ the equation $g(x) := x^{\gamma-\delta} f(x) \equiv 0 \pmod{N}$ contains all the solutions x of $f(x)$ with $|x| < N$. However, applying Coppersmith's method to determine roots of $g(x)$ we only get roots x with $|x| < N^{\frac{1}{\gamma}} < N^{\frac{1}{\delta}}$. So obviously, Coppersmith's bound is not invariant under multiplication with powers of x. This explains why we obtain a superior bound on the size of the roots.

In the following analysis we will restrict ourselves to monic polynomials. If one of the given polynomials $f_i(x)$ is not monic, either the coefficient of the leading monomial is invertible, or we can find a factor of the modulus. In the first case, we make the polynomial monic by multiplication with the inverse of the leading coefficient. In the latter case, we obtain for RSA moduli the complete factorization, which in turn allows for efficiently solving this polynomial equation modulo the prime factors.

Theorem 3. *Let* $(f_i, \delta_i, N_i), i = 1, \ldots, k$, *be an instance of the SMUPE-problem with monic* f_i. *Define* $M := \prod_{i=1}^{k} N_i^{\frac{\delta}{\delta_i}}$ *with* $\delta := lcm\{\delta_i, i = 1, \ldots, k\}$. *Then the SMUPE-problem can be solved for all* x_0 *with*

$$|x_0| < M^{\frac{1}{\delta}}$$

in time $O(\delta^6 \log^2 M)$.

Proof. Let x_0 be a solution of the system of polynomial equations (1). Then x_0 is a solution of

$$f_i^{\frac{\delta}{\delta_i}}(x) \equiv 0 \pmod{N_i^{\frac{\delta}{\delta_i}}} \text{ for all } i = 1, \ldots, k.$$

All these equations have common degree δ and are monic.

Combining them by Chinese Remaindering yields a polynomial $f(x)$ of degree δ such that x_0 is a solution of $f(x) \equiv 0 \pmod{M}$ with $M := \prod_{i=1}^{k} N_i^{\frac{\delta}{\delta_i}}$. Moreover, this polynomial is still monic.

For the coefficient a_δ of the monomial x^δ in $f(x)$ it holds that $a_\delta \equiv 1 \pmod{N_i^{\frac{\delta}{\delta_i}}}$ for all $i = 1, \ldots, k$ and therefore $a_\delta \equiv 1 \pmod{M}$.

The above step can be performed in time $O(\delta \log^2 M)$ by Theorem 2. With Theorem 1 all solutions x_0 of the above equation which fulfill $|x_0| \le M^{\frac{1}{\delta}} = (\prod_{i=1}^{k} N_i^{\frac{\delta}{\delta_i}})^{\frac{1}{\delta}}$ can be found in time $O(\delta^5(\delta + \log M) \log M)$. The result can therefore be obtained in time $O(\delta^6 \log^2 M)$. □

Remark 1. The same result is obtained by applying Coppersmith's method [6] directly to the polynomials $f_1(x), \ldots, f_k(x)$ instead of $f(x)$.

Theorem 3 immediately gives us a sufficient condition on k and the δ_i for solving the SMUPE-problem for all $x_0 \in \mathbb{Z}_{N_1}$.

Corollary 1. *The SMUPE-problem can be solved for all* $x_0 \in \mathbb{Z}_{N_1}$ *in time* $O(\delta^6 \log^2 M)$ *provided that*

$$\sum_{i=1}^{k} \frac{1}{\delta_i} \ge 1. \tag{3}$$

Proof. Let x_0 be a common solution to all the equations. An application of Theorem 3 gives us $|x_0| < M^{\frac{1}{\delta}} := (\prod_{i=1}^{k} N_i^{\frac{\delta}{\delta_i}})^{\frac{1}{\delta}}$ as an upper bound for all roots that can be computed in time $O(\delta^6 \log^2 M)$. As $(\prod_{i=1}^{k} N_i^{\frac{\delta}{\delta_i}})^{\frac{1}{\delta}} \ge \prod_{i=1}^{k} N_1^{\frac{1}{\delta_i}} = N_1^{\sum_{i=1}^{k} \frac{1}{\delta_i}} \ge N_1$ all solutions $x_0 \in \mathbb{Z}_{N_1}$ can be found. □

This gives us an algorithm to solve the SMUPE-problem with running time polynomial in the bitsize of the N_i, $i = 1, \ldots, k$, if δ is polynomial in the bitsize of the N_i.

Comparing this to the result due to Håstad and Coppersmith we observe that in the case $\delta := \delta_1 = \ldots = \delta_k$ the sufficient condition is $k \geq \delta$ with both methods. For different δ_i however, our method is always superior. Taking e.g. the illustrating example with public exponents $(3, 3, 5, 5)$ from the beginning of this section, we see that our new condition $\frac{1}{3} + \frac{1}{3} + \frac{1}{5} + \frac{1}{5} = \frac{16}{15} \geq 1$ is fulfilled.

4   Application: RSA with Polynomially Related Messages

A typical example in which polynomially related messages occur is an RSA broadcast scenario. Assume a user wants to broadcast a message m to k different users using an RSA encryption scheme with public exponents $e_1, \ldots, e_k$ and co-prime public moduli $N_1 < \ldots < N_k$. From the ciphertexts $c_1 \pmod{N_1}, \ldots, c_k \pmod{N_k}$ an attacker can compute the message m if m is smaller than the upper bound given in Theorem 3. He sets $f_i(x) = x^{e_i} - c_i \pmod{N_i}$ and applies Theorem 3.

In order to avoid sending various encryptions of the same message, a user might add some randomness r_i and then encrypt the linearly related messages $(m + r_i)$, $i = 1, \ldots, k$, instead of m. However, if the attacker gets to know the randomness, he can calculate $F_i(x) := f_i(x + r_i) \pmod{N_i}$ and analyze the system of equations $F_i(x) \equiv 0 \pmod{N_i}$, $i = 1, \ldots, k$. As degree, modulus and leading coefficient are the same for $F_i(x)$ and $f_i(x)$, the upper bound on m, up to which m can be recovered efficiently, also remains unchanged. More generally, taking polynomially related messages instead of linearly related ones, the degree of $F_i(x)$, $i = 1, \ldots, k$, changes from e_i to $e_i \gamma_i$, where γ_i is the degree of the known polynomial relation.

Theorem 4. *Let $k \in \mathbb{N}$, (e_i, N_i), $i = 1, \ldots, k$, be RSA public keys with $N_1 < N_2 < \ldots < N_k$ and co-prime N_i. Furthermore, let $m \in \mathbb{Z}_{N_1}$ and let $g_i(x) \in \mathbb{Z}[x]$ be polynomials of degree $\gamma_i \in \mathbb{N}$ with $a_{i\gamma_i}$ the coefficient of x^{γ_i} for $i = 1, \ldots, k$. Let $c_1, \ldots, c_k$ be the RSA-encryptions of $g_i(m)$ under the public key (e_i, N_i).*

Define $\delta_i := e_i \gamma_i$ and $M := \prod_{i=1}^{k} N_i^{\frac{\delta}{\delta_i}}$ with $\delta := lcm\{\delta_i, i = 1, \ldots, k\}$.

Then an adversary can recover the message m in time $O(\delta^6 \log^2 M)$ provided that

$$\sum_{i=1}^{k} \frac{1}{\delta_i} \geq 1.$$

Proof. Without loss of generality we assume that all $a_{i\gamma_i}$ are invertible modulo N_i. (Otherwise $\gcd(a_{i\gamma_i}, N_i)$ and $\frac{N_i}{\gcd(a_{i\gamma_i}, N_i)}$ will give us the factorization of N_i for at least one $i \in \{1, \ldots, k\}$. We can then compute m modulo the prime factors. This can be done efficiently (see [1])).

We are looking for a solution m of $f_i(x) := g_i(x)^{e_i} - c_i \equiv 0 \pmod{N_i}$, $i = 1, \ldots, k$. However, the polynomials $f_i(x)$ are not necessarily monic. Therefore, we modify them slightly to be able to apply Corollary 1. Let $F_i(x) := a_{i\gamma_i}^{-e_i}(g_i(x)^{e_i} - c_i) \pmod{N_i}$, $i = 1, \ldots, k$. Hence, $F_i(x)$ is a monic polynomial of degree $\delta_i = e_i \gamma_i$. The theorem then directly follows as an application of Corollary 1. $\square$

5   Optimality of Our Bound for Solving SMUPE

In this section, we will see that the condition $|x_0| < M^{\frac{1}{\delta}}$ for efficiently solving the SMUPE-problem given in Theorem 3 is optimal if the moduli N_i are prime powers. This implies that the condition cannot be improved in general, unless we make use of the structure of the moduli or of the specific polynomials occuring in the system. Thus, our argument does not exclude the existence of superior conditions for special moduli, e.g. square-free N_i. Moreover, our formula captures the intuition that equations of low degree δ_i comprise more information since they contribute to the sum in (3) with a larger term $\frac{1}{\delta_i}$ than equations with higher degree.

The counting argument that we use is a generalization of the argument in [5] to systems of polynomial equations instead of a single equation.

Let $k \in \mathbb{N}$. Let $p_1, \ldots, p_k$ be different prime numbers, $\delta_1, \ldots, \delta_k \in \mathbb{N}$ and $N_1 := p_1^{\delta_1}, \ldots, N_k := p_k^{\delta_k}$. Suppose $N_1 < \ldots < N_k$. Let us look at the following system of polynomial equations.

$$
\begin{aligned}
f_1(x) &:= x^{\delta_1} \equiv 0 \pmod{N_1} \\
f_2(x) &:= x^{\delta_2} \equiv 0 \pmod{N_2} \\
&\vdots \\
f_k(x) &:= x^{\delta_k} \equiv 0 \pmod{N_k}
\end{aligned}
\tag{4}
$$

We would like to determine all solutions x_0 of this system with $|x_0| < N_1 = p_1^{\delta_1}$. An application of Theorem 1 to a single equation $f_i(x) \equiv 0 \pmod{N_i}$ efficiently yields all solutions x_0 with $|x_0| < (N_i)^{\frac{1}{\delta_i}} = p_i$. Furthermore, each multiple of p_i is a solution of $f_i(x) \equiv 0 \pmod{N_i}$. Thus, if x_0 is a multiple of $\prod_{i=1}^{k} p_i$, then x_0 is a common zero of all the polynomials.

Let $\delta := \operatorname{lcm}\{\delta_i, i = 1, \ldots, k\}$. We apply the same method as in the proof of Theorem 3 to the polynomial equations in system (4). Namely, we take their $\frac{\delta}{\delta_i}$th powers and combine them by Chinese Remaindering (Theorem 2). This gives us an equation $f(x) \equiv x^{\delta} \pmod{M}$ with $M := \prod_{i=1}^{k} N_i^{\frac{\delta}{\delta_i}} = \prod_{i=1}^{k} p_i^{\delta}$ with the same roots as in (4).

We assume that $M^{\frac{1}{\delta}} < N_1$. Otherwise $M^{\frac{1}{\delta}} \geq N_1 > |x_0|$, i.e. the condition of Theorem 3 is fulfilled and there is nothing to be shown. Therefore, let $\epsilon > 0$ such that $M^{\frac{1}{\delta}+\epsilon} < N_1$. Suppose now we could calculate all simultaneous solutions x_0 of the system such that $|x_0| < M^{\frac{1}{\delta}+\epsilon} = (\prod_{i=1}^{k} p_i)^{1+\delta\epsilon}$. Since we know that every integer multiple of $\prod_{i=1}^{k} p_i$ is a root of (4), the number of roots is roughly $2(\prod_{i=1}^{k} p_i)^{\delta\epsilon}$. This implies that we have exponentially many roots x_0 with $|x_0| < M^{\frac{1}{\delta}+\epsilon}$, which we cannot even output in polynomial time. Consequently, there is no polynomial time algorithm that improves upon the exponent in the condition $|x_0| < M^{\frac{1}{\delta}}$ of Theorem 3.

Acknowledgments

We thank the anonymous reviewers of PKC 2008 for their helpful comments.

References

1. Bach, E., Shallit, J.: Algorithmic Number Theory, vol. 1, efficient algorithms. MIT Press, Cambridge (1996)
2. Boneh, D.: Twenty years of attacks on the RSA cryptosystem. Notices of the AMS (1999)
3. Boneh, D., Venkatesan, R.: Breaking RSA May Not Be Equivalent To Factoring. In: Nyberg, K. (ed.) EUROCRYPT 1998. LNCS, vol. 1403, pp. 59–71. Springer, Heidelberg (1998)
4. Brown, D.: Breaking RSA May Be As Difficult As Factoring., Cryptology ePrint Archive Report 2005/380 (2005)
5. Coppersmith, D.: Finding Small Solutions to Small Degree Polynomials. In: Silverman, J.H. (ed.) CaLC 2001. LNCS, vol. 2146, pp. 20–31. Springer, Heidelberg (2001)
6. Coppersmith, D.: Small solutions to polynomial equations and low exponent vulnerabilities. Journal of Cryptology 10(4), 223–260 (1997)
7. Coppersmith, D., Franklin, M., Patarin, J., Reiter, M.: Low-exponent RSA with related messages. In: Maurer, U.M. (ed.) EUROCRYPT 1996. LNCS, vol. 1070, pp. 1–9. Springer, Heidelberg (1996)
8. Håstad, J.: On Using RSA with Low Exponent in a Public Key Network. In: Williams, H.C. (ed.) CRYPTO 1985. LNCS, vol. 218, pp. 403–408. Springer, Heidelberg (1986)
9. Håstad, J.: Solving Simultaneous Modular Equations of Low Degree. SIAM Journal on Computing 17(2), 336–341 (1988)
10. Leander, G., Rupp, A.: On the Equivalence of RSA and Factoring Regarding Generic Ring Algorithms. In: Lai, X., Chen, K. (eds.) ASIACRYPT 2006. LNCS, vol. 4284, pp. 241–251. Springer, Heidelberg (2006)
11. Lenstra, A.K., Lenstra, H.W., Lovász, L.: Factoring polynomials with rational coefficients. Mathematische Annalen 261, 513–534 (1982)
12. May, A.: Using LLL-Reduction for Solving RSA and Factorization Problems: A Survey. LLL+25 Conference in honour of the 25th birthday of the LLL algorithm (2007), http://www.cits.rub.de/personen/may.html
13. Nguyen, P.Q., Stehlé, D.: Floating Point LLL Revisited. In: Cramer, R.J.F. (ed.) EUROCRYPT 2005. LNCS, vol. 3494, pp. 215–233. Springer, Heidelberg (2005)
14. Rivest, R., Shamir, A., Adleman, L.: A Method for Obtaining Digital Signatures and Public-Key Cryptosystems. Communications of the ACM 21(2), 120–126 (1978)
15. Shoup, V.: A Computational Introduction to Number Theory and Algebra. Cambridge University Press, Cambridge (2005)
16. Simmons, G.: A "Weak" Privacy Protocol Using the RSA Crypto Algorithm. Cryptologia 7(2), 180–182 (1983)

Relations Among Notions of Plaintext Awareness

James Birkett and Alexander W. Dent

Information Security Group,
Royal Holloway, University of London,
Egham, TW20 0EX, UK
{j.m.birkett,a.dent}@rhul.ac.uk

Abstract. We introduce a new simplified notion of plaintext awareness, which we term PA2I, and show that this is equivalent to the standard definition of PA2 plaintext awareness for encryption schemes that satisfy certain weak security and randomness requirements. We also show that PA2 plaintext awareness is equivalent to PA2+ plaintext awareness under similar security and randomness requirements. This proves a conjecture of Dent that, for suitably random public-key encryption schemes, PA2 plaintext awareness implies PA1+ plaintext awareness.

1 Introduction

Loosely speaking, a public-key encryption scheme is plaintext aware if it is impossible for any reasonable attacker to create a ciphertext without knowing the underlying message. This is an interesting concept, but one that has proven difficult to formalise. The first formal notion of plaintext awareness was introduced by Bellare and Rogaway [3] and later refined by Bellare et al. [1]. However, this notion of plaintext awareness could only be achieved in the random oracle model.

Later, Bellare and Palacio [2] introduced a new definition for plaintext awareness. This new notion could be achieved without recourse to the random oracle methodology, yet was consistent with the earlier definitions in the sense that a schemes proven secure under the earlier definition were also secure under the new definition. These new definitions were slightly extended by Dent [4].

In the formal definition, for every ciphertext creator (algorithm) that can output a ciphertext, there should exist a plaintext extractor (algorithm) that can extract the underlying message given all of the inputs of the ciphertext creator (i.e. the explicit inputs and the random coins that the ciphertext creator uses). This is meant to represent the idea that the plaintext extractor can "observe" every action that the ciphertext creator makes when constructing the ciphertext it finally outputs. The plaintext extractor should be able to extract the underlying message of a ciphertext even if the ciphertext creator can query an encryption oracle that provides the ciphertext creator with the encryption of messages that have been drawn from some arbitrary and unknown (polynomial-time) distribution. This is known as PA2 plaintext awareness.

R. Cramer (Ed.): PKC 2008, LNCS 4939, pp. 47–64, 2008.

We may also consider a weaker definition in which the ciphertext creator does not have the ability to obtain ciphertexts from the encryption oracle. This is known as PA1 plaintext awareness. Furthermore, the ciphertext creator may also have access to a randomness oracle which returns random bits (PA1+/PA2+ plaintext awareness). This has the effect of making the actions of the ciphertext creator unpredictable in advance. The complexity of these definitions, and the difficulty in achieving the definition using standard computational assumptions, are the two main barriers to the use of plaintext awareness in cryptography.

However, the concept of plaintext awareness has several uses. First, it can be used to show that an encryption scheme is IND-CCA2 secure. It has been proven that an encryption scheme that is PA2 plaintext aware and IND-CPA secure is necessarily IND-CCA2 secure [2]. Second, there are some cryptographic applications which require a scheme to be plaintext aware; for example, the deniable authentication protocol of Di Raimondo, Gennaro and Krawczyk [6]. Lastly, the concept provides an insight into why some public-key encryption schemes are secure, while others are not. We therefore believe that it is an interesting and useful notion to study.

Our Contributions

We attempt to simplify the definition of plaintext awareness. In particular, we introduce a new notion of plaintext awareness in which the ciphertext creator cannot obtain the encryption of messages drawn from an arbitrary and unknown distribution, but only the encryption of messages drawn from a simple, fixed distribution. This distribution is defined by the plaintext creator $\mathcal{P}_I$ which takes two messages as input and chooses one of those messages at random. We term this new notion of plaintext awareness PA2I as this is precisely the distribution of messages that one considers when proving IND security.

We show that for encryption schemes meeting certain weak security and randomness requirements (IND-CPA security, OW-CPA security and γ-uniformity) the notions of PA2, PA2I and PA2+ plaintext awareness are equivalent. This equivalence proves a conjecture of Dent [4] that a suitably random PA2 plaintext aware encryption scheme is necessarily PA1+ plaintext aware. As a by-product of these theorems, we also show that an encryption scheme that is IND-CPA and PA2 plaintext aware must satisfy the stronger property that an adversary cannot distinguish between encryptions of messages of different lengths, a property not required by the standard definition of indistinguishability. In particular, this implies that the scheme has a finite message space. Finally, we show that PA2I plaintext awareness is not equivalent to PA2 plaintext awareness if the encryption scheme is only OW-CPA secure and γ-uniform.

2 Definitions

2.1 Notation

We will use the following notation in this paper. If S is a set, then $x \xleftarrow{\text{R}} S$ means x is sampled uniformly at random from the set S. If S is a distribution, then

$x \xleftarrow{\text{R}} S$ means that x is sampled according to the distribution. For a deterministic algorithm $\mathcal{A}$, we write $x \leftarrow \mathcal{A}^{\mathcal{O}}(y, z)$ to mean that x is assigned the output of running $\mathcal{A}$ on inputs y and z, with access to oracle $\mathcal{O}$. If $\mathcal{A}$ is a probabilistic algorithm, we may write $x \leftarrow \mathcal{A}^{\mathcal{O}}(y, z; R)$ to mean the output of $\mathcal{A}$ when run on inputs y and z with oracle access to $\mathcal{O}$ and using the random coins R. If we do not specify R then we implicitly assume that the coins are selected uniformly at random from $\{0, 1\}^{\infty}$. This is denoted $x \xleftarrow{\text{R}} \mathcal{A}^{\mathcal{O}}(y, z)$. We let $R[\mathcal{A}]$ denote the coins of an algorithm $\mathcal{A}$.

2.2   Public-Key Encryption Schemes

An encryption scheme is a triple $(\mathcal{G}, \mathcal{E}, \mathcal{D})$ of probabilistic polynomial-time algorithms. The algorithm $\mathcal{G}(1^{\lambda})$ outputs a key pair (pk, sk). The public key pk implicitly defines a message space $\mathcal{M}$ and a ciphertext space $\mathcal{C}$. The encryption algorithm takes as input a public key pk and a message $m \in \mathcal{M}$, and outputs a ciphertext $C \in \mathcal{C}$. The decryption algorithm takes as input a private key sk and a ciphertext $C \in \mathcal{C}$, and outputs either a message $m \in \mathcal{M}$ or the unique 'reject' symbol $\perp$. We require that if $(pk, sk) \xleftarrow{\text{R}} \mathcal{G}(1^{\lambda})$, then for all $m \in \mathcal{M}$

$$\Pr[\mathcal{D}(sk, \mathcal{E}(pk, m)) = m] = 1 \, .$$

where the probability is taken over the random coins of the encryption algorithm.

We will refer to a public-key encryption scheme as having either a finite or infinite message space. A public-key encryption scheme Π has an infinite message space if $\mathcal{M}$ is an infinite set for all values of the security parameter λ. Π has a finite message space if $\mathcal{M}$ is a finite set for all values of the security parameter λ. For simplicity, we will assume that all public-key encryption schemes either have the infinite message space $\mathcal{M} = \{0, 1\}^{*}$ (as with most hybrid encryption schemes) or the finite message space $\mathcal{M} = \{0, 1\}^{\ell(\lambda)}$. We will assume that all encryption schemes run in time that is polynomially bounded in the size of their inputs (i.e. λ and $|m|$).

Note that if $\ell(\lambda)$ is polynomially bounded then we may equivalently define a finite message space as $\mathcal{M} = \{0, 1\}^{<\ell}$, i.e. the set of all bit strings of length less than ℓ, as there is a trivial polynomial-time map from $\{0, 1\}^{<\ell}$ into $\{0, 1\}^{\ell}$.

2.3   Indistinguishability of Ciphertexts

We first describe the IND-ATK (where ATK is either CPA or CCA2) game for an adversary $\mathcal{A} = (\mathcal{A}_1, \mathcal{A}_2)$, where $\mathcal{A}_1$ and $\mathcal{A}_2$ are probabilistic polynomial-time algorithms:

$(pk, sk) \xleftarrow{\text{R}} \mathcal{G}(1^{\lambda})$
$(m_0, m_1, \text{STATE}) \xleftarrow{\text{R}} \mathcal{A}_1^{\mathcal{O}}(pk)$
$b \xleftarrow{\text{R}} \{0, 1\}$
$C^* \xleftarrow{\text{R}} \mathcal{E}(pk, m_b)$
$b' \xleftarrow{\text{R}} \mathcal{A}_2^{\mathcal{O}}(C^*, \text{STATE})$

In the above, $\mathcal{A}_1$ outputs two messages (m_0, m_1) such that $|m_0| = |m_1|$ and some state information. The challenger chooses a bit b at random and encrypts m_b to give a challenge ciphertext C^*. $\mathcal{A}_2$ takes C^* and the state information as input and outputs a guess for b. We define the advantage of $\mathcal{A}$ as

$$\mathbf{Adv}_{\mathcal{A}}^{\text{IND-ATK}} = |\Pr[b' = 1 | b = 1] - \Pr[b' = 1 | b = 0]|.$$

We consider two attack models. In the chosen plaintext attack (CPA) model, $\mathcal{A}$ does not have access to any oracles. In the adaptive chosen ciphertext attack (CCA2) model, $\mathcal{A}$ may query a decryption oracle $\mathcal{D}$, which takes a ciphertext C as input and returns $\mathcal{D}(sk, C)$. The only restriction is that $\mathcal{A}_2$ may not query the decryption oracle on C^*.

Definition 1 (IND-ATK). *A public key encryption scheme $\Pi = (\mathcal{G}, \mathcal{E}, \mathcal{D})$ is IND-ATK secure if for any probabilistic, polynomial-time IND-ATK adversary $\mathcal{A}$, the advantage $\mathbf{Adv}_{\mathcal{A}}^{IND\text{-}ATK}$ is negligible as a function of λ.*

Frequently, where it will not cause undue confusion, we will suppress the state information STATE and simply assume that all necessary information is passed from $\mathcal{A}_1$ to $\mathcal{A}_2$.

2.4   One-Wayness

We also require a notion of one-wayness (OW-CPA) for an encryption scheme with an infinite message space. For simplicity we assume that $\mathcal{M} = \{0,1\}^*$. One-wayness is assessed via the following game:

$$(pk, sk) \xleftarrow{\text{R}} \mathcal{G}(1^\lambda)$$
$$m \xleftarrow{\text{R}} \{0,1\}^\lambda$$
$$C^* \xleftarrow{\text{R}} \mathcal{E}(pk, m)$$
$$m' \xleftarrow{\text{R}} \mathcal{A}(pk, C^*)$$

We define the attacker $\mathcal{A}$'s success probability to be $\Pr[m' = m]$.

Definition 2 (OW-CPA). *A public key encryption scheme $\Pi = (\mathcal{G}, \mathcal{E}, \mathcal{D})$ is OW-CPA secure if for any probabilistic polynomial-time OW-CPA adversary $\mathcal{A}$, the success probability of $\mathcal{A}$ is negligible as a function of λ.*

2.5   Plaintext Awareness

The formal definition of plaintext awareness in the standard model was proposed by Bellare and Palacio [2]. A scheme is plaintext aware if for every probabilistic polynomial-time algorithm (ciphertext creator) $\mathcal{A}$ there exists a probabilistic polynomial-time algorithm (plaintext extractor) $\mathcal{A}^*$ which can simulate a decryption oracle for $\mathcal{A}$ when given the random coins that $\mathcal{A}$ uses (in the sense that the output of $\mathcal{A}$ when interacting with $\mathcal{A}^*$ is computationally indistinguishable from the output of $\mathcal{A}$ when interacting with a real decryption oracle). In

order to model the attacker's ability to obtain ciphertexts for which it does
not know the underlying decryption, the ciphertext creator is equipped with
an oracle that will return the encryption of a randomly chosen message $m \overset{\text{R}}{\leftarrow}$
$\mathcal{P}(s)$ where $\mathcal{P}$ is an arbitrary probabilistic polynomial-time algorithm (plaintext
creator) and s is supplied by the ciphertext creator $\mathcal{A}$. Note that both $\mathcal{P}$ and
$\mathcal{A}^*$ are considered to be stateful algorithms.

Formally, we consider two games. In both cases, the ciphertext creator $\mathcal{A}$ is
given a public key pk from a correctly generated public-key pair $(pk, sk) \overset{\text{R}}{\leftarrow} \mathcal{G}(1^\lambda)$
and outputs a bitsting x. In both cases, the ciphertext creator has access to an
"encryption oracle" that will, on input s, generate a message $m \overset{\text{R}}{\leftarrow} \mathcal{P}(s)$, compute
$C \overset{\text{R}}{\leftarrow} \mathcal{E}(pk, m)$, add C to a list of returned ciphertexts CLIST and return C to the
ciphertext creator. The games are distinguished by the "decryption oracle" to
which $\mathcal{A}$ has access. In the REAL game, $\mathcal{A}$ can query a decryption oracle on any
ciphertext $C \notin$ CLIST and the oracle will return $\mathcal{D}(sk, C)$. In the FAKE game, $\mathcal{A}$
can query a decryption oracle on any ciphertext $C \notin$ CLIST and the oracle will
execute $\mathcal{A}^*(pk, C, R[\mathcal{A}], \text{CLIST})$ and return the result. We stress again that $\mathcal{A}^*$
and $\mathcal{P}$ are stateful algorithms. We can summarise these two games as follows:

REAL GAME:

$(pk, sk) \overset{\text{R}}{\leftarrow} \mathcal{G}(1^\lambda)$

$x_{\text{Real}} \overset{\text{R}}{\leftarrow} \mathcal{A}^{\mathcal{D}(sk, \cdot), \mathcal{E}(pk, \mathcal{P}(\cdot))}(pk)$

FAKE GAME:

$(pk, sk) \overset{\text{R}}{\leftarrow} \mathcal{G}(1^\lambda)$

$x_{\text{Fake}} \overset{\text{R}}{\leftarrow} \mathcal{A}^{\mathcal{A}^*(pk, \cdot, R[\mathcal{A}], \text{CLIST}), \mathcal{E}(pk, \mathcal{P}(\cdot))}(pk)$

Definition 3 (PA2). *A public key encryption scheme $\Pi = (\mathcal{G}, \mathcal{E}, \mathcal{D})$ is PA2
plaintext aware if for all polynomial-time ciphertext creators $\mathcal{A}$, there exists a
polynomial-time plaintext extractor $\mathcal{A}^*$ such that for all polynomial-time plaintext
creators $\mathcal{P}$ and polynomial-time distinguishing algorithms D, the advantage*

$$\mathbf{Adv}^{PA2}_{\mathcal{A}, \mathcal{A}^*, \mathcal{P}, D} = |\Pr[D(x_{\text{Real}}) = 1] - \Pr[D(x_{\text{Fake}}) = 1]|$$

*is negligible as a function of the security parameter (where x_{Real} is the output of
$\mathcal{A}$ in the REAL game and x_{Fake} is the output of $\mathcal{A}$ in the FAKE game).*

Definition 4 (PA1). *A public key encryption scheme $\Pi = (\mathcal{G}, \mathcal{E}, \mathcal{D})$ is PA1
plaintext aware if it is PA2 plaintext aware for all ciphertext creators $\mathcal{A}$ that
do not make any queries to the encryption oracle. In other words, Π is PA1
plaintext aware if for all polynomial-time ciphertext creators $\mathcal{A}$, there exists a
polynomial-time plaintext extractor $\mathcal{A}^*$ such that for all polynomial-time distinguishing algorithms D, the advantage*

$$\mathbf{Adv}^{PA1}_{\mathcal{A}, \mathcal{A}^*, D} = |\Pr[D(x_{\text{Real}}) = 1] - \Pr[D(x_{\text{Fake}}) = 1]|$$

is negligible as a function of the security parameter.

Dent [4] extended these definitions to allow the ciphertext creator $\mathcal{A}$ to take
actions that are unpredictable to the plaintext extractor $\mathcal{A}^*$ in advance by allowing the ciphertext creator $\mathcal{A}$ to repeatedly query a "randomness oracle" which
returns a single random bit.

Definition 5 (PA+). *For any plaintext awareness definition PA (PA1, PA2I, PA2), we define a new condition PA+ (PA1+, PA2I+, PA2+) by adding a randomness oracle, which takes no input and returns a random bit. The plaintext extractor is altered so that it takes a list* RLIST *of all such bits queried so far as one of its inputs, i.e.* $\mathcal{A}^*(pk, C, R[\mathcal{A}], \text{RLIST}, \text{CLIST})$.

Note that any such PA+ definition implies the corresponding PA definition, since an adversary may simply not use the randomness oracle.

Bellare and Palacio proved that [2] any scheme that was PA2 plaintext aware and IND-CPA secure was IND-CCA2 secure. The proof of this fact makes use of a particular plaintext creator $\mathcal{P}_I$ which takes as input two messages (m_0, m_1) and outputs a randomly chosen message m_b. We call this the IND plaintext creator and define a scheme to be PA2I plaintext aware if it is PA2 plaintext aware for the IND plaintext creator.

Definition 6 (PA2I). *A public key encryption scheme* $\Pi = (\mathcal{G}, \mathcal{E}, \mathcal{D})$ *is PA2I plaintext aware if for all polynomial-time ciphertext creators* $\mathcal{A}$, *there exists a polynomial-time plaintext extractor* $\mathcal{A}^*$ *such that for all polynomial-time distinguishing algorithms D, the advantage*

$$\mathbf{Adv}^{PA2I}_{\mathcal{A}, \mathcal{A}^*, D} = \mathbf{Adv}^{PA2}_{\mathcal{A}, \mathcal{A}^*, \mathcal{P}_I, D}$$

is negligible as a function of the security parameter.

The paper of Bellare and Palacio [2] actually proves that a scheme which is PA2I plaintext aware and IND-CPA secure is IND-CCA2 secure. We note that a theorem of Teranishi and Ogata [8] shows that any scheme which is one-way and PA2 plaintext aware is IND-CCA2 secure. We stress that the proof of Teranishi and Ogata requires the use of the arbitrary plaintext creator $\mathcal{P}$ provided by the full definition of PA2 plaintext awareness.

3   Theoretical Results about Plaintext Awareness

3.1   Connection between PA2I and PA2

One of the more complex aspects of plaintext awareness is the fact that the encryption oracle returns an encryption of a message that has been chosen from some arbitrary distribution defined by $\mathcal{P}$. The order of the quantifiers in the definition of PA2 plaintext awareness means that neither the ciphertext creator $\mathcal{A}$, nor the plaintext extractor $\mathcal{A}^*$, know the distribution from which messages are chosen, although the ciphertext creator does have the ability to affect this distribution via its input s to the encryption oracle. In this section, we show that for IND-CPA encryption schemes it is sufficient to consider the fixed plaintext creator $\mathcal{P}_I$. We note that PA2 plaintext awareness trivially implies PA2I plaintext awareness, so we will concentrate on proving the converse theorem.

Theorem 1. *If an encryption scheme with the finite message space* $\mathcal{M} = \{0, 1\}^{\ell(\lambda)}$ *is IND-CPA secure and PA2I plaintext aware, and* $\ell(\lambda)$ *is polynomially bounded in* λ, *then it is PA2.*

Note that we could have equivalently chosen the message space to be $\{0,1\}^{<\ell}$, i.e. the set of bitstrings of length less than ℓ, as we can trivially map one set onto the other. Note also that ℓ may depend on the security parameter λ but for each value of λ we have that $\ell(\lambda)$ is finite.

Proof. Consider an arbitrary plaintext creator $\mathcal{P}$. We prove that the output of $\mathcal{A}$ interacting with $\mathcal{P}$ is computationally indistinguishable from the output of $\mathcal{A}$ interacting with $\mathcal{P}_I$ and therefore, if there exists a plaintext extractor $\mathcal{A}^*$ for the ciphertext creator $\mathcal{A}$ in the PA2I model, then $\mathcal{A}^*$ is also a plaintext extractor for the ciphertext creator $\mathcal{A}$ in the PA2 model. We prove this through a sequence of four games. Let x_i be the output of $\mathcal{A}$ in Game i. Fix a distinguishing algorithm D and let S_i be the event that $D(x_i) = 1$.

Game 0: Let Game 0 be the FAKE game with plaintext creator $\mathcal{P}$. In other words, the encryption oracle computes messages $m \stackrel{\text{R}}{\leftarrow} \mathcal{P}(s)$ and returns $C \stackrel{\text{R}}{\leftarrow} \mathcal{E}(pk, m)$. The decryption oracle returns $\mathcal{A}^*(pk, C, R[\mathcal{A}], \text{CLIST})$.

Game 1: We replace $\mathcal{P}$ with the $\mathcal{P}_I$. Since $\mathcal{A}$ expects to be interacting with $\mathcal{P}$, and will not explicitly format its queries as (m_0, m_1), we will define $\mathcal{P}_I$ so that it truncates or pads s with zeros to 2ℓ bits if necessary, and then splits the result into two ℓ bit messages, chooses one of them at random and returns it. Since $\ell(\lambda)$ is polynomially bounded, this action can be computed in polynomial time. The oracle then encrypts this message, then returns the ciphertext to $\mathcal{A}$ and adds it to CLIST.

If $|\Pr[S_1] - \Pr[S_0]|$ is non-negligible, then we can construct an adversary $\mathcal{B}$ that breaks the IND-CPA security of the scheme. We use a simple hybrid argument. Suppose $\mathcal{A}$ makes at most q_e queries to the encryption oracle. $\mathcal{B}_1$ takes as input the public key pk and runs $\mathcal{A}$ and $\mathcal{A}^*$ exactly as described in the Game 0. $\mathcal{B}$ responds to the first $q_e - 1$ encryption oracle queries as in Game 0 (i.e. by computing a message $m \stackrel{\text{R}}{\leftarrow} \mathcal{P}(s)$ and returning $C \stackrel{\text{R}}{\leftarrow} \mathcal{E}(pk, m)$). For the q_e-th query to the encryption oracle, $\mathcal{B}_1$ generates both $m_0 \stackrel{\text{R}}{\leftarrow} \mathcal{P}(s)$ and $m_1 \stackrel{\text{R}}{\leftarrow} \mathcal{P}_I(s)$ and outputs (m_0, m_1) as the messages on which it wishes to be challenged.

The challenger will pick one of these messages and encrypt it, the result will be returned to $\mathcal{B}_2$. $\mathcal{B}_2$ handles any decryption oracle queries by $\mathcal{A}$ in the same way as before (i.e. by using $\mathcal{A}^*$). Eventually $\mathcal{A}$ terminates and outputs a bitstring x. $\mathcal{B}_2$ terminates by outputting the bit $D(x)$.

Since Π is IND-CPA, $\mathcal{B}$'s advantage is bounded by $\mathbf{Adv}_{\mathcal{B}}^{\text{IND-CPA}}$. It is clear that if the challenger chose to encrypt message m_0, then $\mathcal{A}$ was playing Game 0. It also clear that if the challenger chose to encrypt message m_1 then $\mathcal{A}$ was playing a hybrid game in which the first $q_e - 1$ queries were answered as in Game 0 and the last query was answered as in Game 1. Hence, the probability that the ciphertext creator $\mathcal{A}$ outputs a bitstring x such that $D(x) = 1$ can only change by at most $\mathbf{Adv}_{\mathcal{B}}^{\text{IND-CPA}}$ if the final encryption is computed using $\mathcal{P}_I$ rather than $\mathcal{P}$.

We now repeat this "trick" q_e times, until all the encryption oracle queries are handled as in Game 1. Hence,

$$|Pr[S_1] - Pr[S_0]| \le q_e \mathbf{Adv}_{\mathcal{B}}^{\text{IND-CPA}}.$$

Game 2: We replace $\mathcal{A}^*$ with a real decryption oracle. By definition, we have that

$$|\Pr[S_2] - \Pr[S_1]| \leq \mathbf{Adv}_{\mathcal{A},\mathcal{A}^*,D}^{\text{PA2I}}$$

Game 3: We replace $\mathcal{P}_I$ by $\mathcal{P}$. We can prove that $|\Pr[S_3] - \Pr[S_2]|$ is negligible by much the same argument as in Game 1, except that this time we construct an IND-CCA2 adversary $\mathcal{B}$, which uses its own decryption oracle to answer decryption queries. We may assume that Π is IND-CCA2 secure as it is both IND-CPA secure and PA2I plaintext aware. Hence, after q_e rounds, we have that

$$|\Pr[S_3] - \Pr[S_2]| \leq q_e \mathbf{Adv}_C^{\text{IND-CCA}}$$

Note that Game 3 is identical to the REAL game with plaintext creator $\mathcal{P}$. We can therefore conclude that

$$\mathbf{Adv}_{\mathcal{A},\mathcal{A}^*,\mathcal{P},D}^{\text{PA2}} = |Pr[S_0] - Pr[S_3]|$$
$$\leq q_e \mathbf{Adv}_{\mathcal{B}}^{\text{IND-CPA}} + \mathbf{Adv}_{\mathcal{A},\mathcal{A}^*,D}^{\text{PA2I}} + q_e \mathbf{Adv}_{\mathcal{B}}^{\text{IND-CCA}}$$

Since the scheme is PA2I and IND-CPA, we see that

$$\mathbf{Adv}_{\mathcal{B}}^{\text{IND-CCA}} \leq \mathbf{Adv}_C^{\text{IND-CPA}} + q_d \mathbf{Adv}_{\mathcal{F},\mathcal{F}^*,D'}^{\text{PA2I}}$$

for some probabilistic polynomial time algorithms $\mathcal{C}, \mathcal{F}, \mathcal{F}^*$ and D'. Thus

$$\mathbf{Adv}_{\mathcal{A},\mathcal{A}^*,\mathcal{P},D}^{\text{PA2}} \leq q_e \mathbf{Adv}_{\mathcal{B}}^{\text{IND-CPA}} + \mathbf{Adv}_{\mathcal{A},\mathcal{A}^*,D}^{\text{PA2I}} + q_e(\mathbf{Adv}_C^{\text{IND-CPA}} + q_d \mathbf{Adv}_{\mathcal{F},\mathcal{F}^*,D'}^{\text{PA2I}})$$

which is negligible as required.   □

Corollary 1. *If an encryption scheme Π is IND-CPA secure and PA2I+ plaintext aware then it is PA2+ plaintext aware.*

Proof. The proof of this theorem mirrors the proof of Theorem 1.   □

The fact that we may be substitute an arbitrary plaintext creator $\mathcal{P}$ with the specific plaintext creator $\mathcal{P}_I$ will be crucial in proving the relationship between PA2 and PA2+ in Section 3.3.

For schemes that have already been shown to be IND-CCA2 secure, but about which their plaintext awareness may be in doubt, we can prove a stronger result. Let $\mathcal{P}_m$ be the plaintext creator that constantly outputs the message $m \in \mathcal{M}$.

Corollary 2. *If an encryption scheme Π is IND-CCA2 secure and PA2 (resp. PA2+) plaintext aware with respect to the specific plaintext creator $\mathcal{P}_m$, then it is PA2 (resp. PA2+) plaintext aware.*

Proof. The proof of this theorem mirrors the proof of Theorem 1 except we explicitly use the fact that Π is IND-CCA2 secure in the third game hop, rather than deriving the fact that Π is IND-CCA2 secure from the fact that it is IND-CPA secure and PA2I plaintext aware.   □

This corollary may have some applications in situations where public key encryption schemes are known to be IND-CCA2 secure, but need to be shown to be PA2 plaintext aware in order that they might be used in some specific protocol, e.g. the deniable authentication protocol of Di Raimondo, Gennaro and Krawczyk [6].

3.2   PA2 and One-Wayness Implies a Finite Message Space

In the previous section, we introduced an extra condition into our proof – we required the encryption scheme to have a finite message space. This may seem like an unreasonable restriction. Far from being unreasonable, particularly when one considers hybrid encryption schemes; however, we will show in this section that a finite message space is necessary in order for a one-way scheme to achieve PA2 plaintext awareness. Hence, we can conclude that many hybrid encryption schemes, are unable to achieve this level of security, at least if we define the message space to be $\{0,1\}^*$, the set of all bitstrings. Our proof will not preclude the possibility that a scheme is PA2I plaintext aware, OW-CPA secure and has an infinite message space.

Theorem 2. *Let $\Pi = (\mathcal{G}, \mathcal{E}, \mathcal{D})$ be an encryption scheme. If Π is PA2 and has an infinite message space, then it is not OW-CPA.*

In order to prove this theorem, we use the proof technique of Teranishi and Ogata [8]. The technique involves using a specific plaintext creator $\mathcal{P}$ to leak the value of a ciphertext C^* to the ciphertext creator $\mathcal{A}$ bit-by-bit in such a way that C^* does not appear on CLIST. The plaintext creator can then query the decryption oracle on C^* to obtain the underlying message (the validity of which it can check using one further query to the plaintext creator). Now, since this system allows the ciphertext creator to decrypt an arbitrary ciphertext by interacting with only the polynomial-time plaintext extractor, the encryption scheme cannot be one-way. Our proof differs from Teranishi and Ogata in that we will leak the value of the challenge ciphertext C^* by outputting short ciphertexts if a bit of C^* is zero and long ciphertexts if a bit of C^* is one. We can produce ciphertexts which are recognisably short or long due to the infinite size of the message space.

Proof. We will prove that if $\Pi = (\mathcal{G}, \mathcal{E}, \mathcal{D})$ is PA2 and has an infinite message space then Π is not OW-CPA secure. For simplicity, we assume $\mathcal{M} = \{0,1\}^*$.

Note that the length of any ciphertext must be bounded by a polynomial $f(\lambda, |m|)$ in the security parameter λ and length of the corresponding plaintext. An upper bound for f is simply the running time of $\mathcal{E}$. Let $l_0 = f(\lambda, \lambda) + \lambda + 1$, $l_1 = f(\lambda, l_0) + \lambda + 1$, and $l_2 = f(\lambda, l_1) + \lambda + 1$.

Let Encode be an algorithm which takes input $i \in \{0,1,2\}$ outputs a message $m \xleftarrow{\text{R}} \{0,1\}^{l_i}$. Let Decode be an algorithm which takes a ciphertext C and returns

$$
\text{Decode}(C) = \begin{cases}
0 & \text{if } f(\lambda, \lambda) < |C| \leq f(\lambda, l_0) \\
1 & \text{if } f(\lambda, l_0) < |C| \leq f(\lambda, l_1) \\
2 & \text{if } f(\lambda, l_1) < |C| \leq f(\lambda, l_2) \\
\bot & \text{otherwise}
\end{cases}
$$

If $C \xleftarrow{\text{R}} \mathcal{E}(pk, \text{Encode}(0))$, then we would like $\text{Decode}(C) = 0$. However, since we only know that $|C| \leq f(\lambda, l_0)$, it is possible that $|C| \leq f(\lambda, \lambda)$ and so the decode algorithm will fail. But, since there exists only $2^{f(\lambda,\lambda)+1} - 1$ ciphertexts of length at most $f(\lambda, \lambda)$ and $2^{l_0} - 1$ messages of length l_0, the probability that a randomly chosen message will encrypt to give a ciphertext of length less than or equal to $f(\lambda, \lambda)$ is bounded by $2^{-\lambda}$. Similarly, the probability that $\mathsf{Decode}(C) \neq i$ when $C \stackrel{R}{\leftarrow} \mathcal{E}(pk, \mathsf{Encode}(i))$ for $i \in \{1, 2\}$ is bounded by $2^{-\lambda}$.

Next we construct a ciphertext creator $\mathcal{A}$ and a specific plaintext creator $\mathcal{P}$. The plaintext creator $\mathcal{P}$ works in a series of phases:

1. The first time the plaintext creator is initialised it picks a random message $m^* \stackrel{R}{\leftarrow} \{0, 1\}^\lambda$ and computes $C^* \stackrel{R}{\leftarrow} \mathcal{E}(pk, m)$.
2. For the i-th query, where $1 \leq i \leq |C^*|$, the plaintext creator returns $\mathsf{Encode}(b_i)$, where b_i is the i-th bit of C^*. Hence, the ciphertext creator will receive $\mathcal{E}(pk, \mathsf{Encode}(b_i))$. This leaks the value of the ciphertext C^* to the ciphertext creator.
3. For the next query the plaintext creator returns $\mathsf{Encode}(2)$. This signifies the end of the ciphertext.
4. For the next query the plaintext creator uses the input s provided by the ciphertext creator. If $s = m^*$ then the ciphertext creator returns $\mathsf{Encode}(1)$; otherwise it returns $\mathsf{Encode}(0)$. This is a validity check.
5. For all subsequent queries the plaintext creator outputs 0.

The ciphertext creator $\mathcal{A}$ works as follows:

1. The ciphertext creator queries the plaintext creator repeatedly, each time receiving a ciphertext C and computing the bit $b \leftarrow \mathsf{Decode}(C)$. If $b \in \{0, 1\}$ then the ciphertext creator stores this bit and repeats the query. If $b = 2$ then the ciphertext creator continues to the next phase.
2. The ciphertext creator reconstructs the ciphertext C^* from the bits recovered in the first phase.
3. The ciphertext creator submits the ciphertext C^* to the decryption oracle and receives a message m.
4. Next, the ciphertext creator submits m to the encryption oracle and receives back a ciphertext C.
5. The ciphertext creator outputs the bit $\mathsf{Decode}(C)$

Let S_{real} be the event that $\mathcal{A}$ returns 1 in the REAL game, and S_{fake} be the event that $\mathcal{A}$ returns 1 in the FAKE game. We note that if the decode algorithm always returned the correctly encoded bit, then $C^* \notin \mathrm{CLIST}$ as every ciphertext C that the encryption oracle returns is of size greater than $f(\lambda, \lambda)$. Furthermore, if the decode algorithm always returned the correctly encoded bit, the $\mathcal{A}$ will always return 1 in the REAL game. Hence,

$$\Pr[S_{real}] \geq 1 - (|C^*| + 2) \cdot 2^{-\lambda}.$$

Since, Π is PA2 plaintext aware, there exists a plaintext extractor $\mathcal{A}^*$ for the ciphertext creator $\mathcal{A}$ with the property that

$$Pr[S_{fake}] \geq 1 - (|C^*| + 2) \cdot 2^{-\lambda} - \mathbf{Adv}^{\mathrm{PA2}}_{\mathcal{A}, \mathcal{A}^*, \mathcal{P}, D}$$

where D is the trivial distinguishing algorithm that outputs the single bit which it takes as input. Due to the validity check, this means that $\mathcal{A}^*$ must return the correct decryption of C^* with probability $Pr[S_{fake}]$.

We use the functionality of $\mathcal{A}$ and $\mathcal{A}^*$ to create an adversary $\mathcal{B}$ against the OW-CPA security of Π as follows:

1. $\mathcal{B}$ receives a ciphertext C^* and sets n to be $|C^*|$.
2. $\mathcal{B}$ generates a simulation of $\text{CLIST} \leftarrow \{C_0, C_1, \dots, C_{n+1}\}$ in which $C_i \overset{\text{R}}{\leftarrow} \mathcal{E}(pk, \text{Encode}(b_i))$, for $1 \leq i \leq n$ and where b_i is the i-th bit of C^*, and $C_{n+1} \overset{\text{R}}{\leftarrow} \mathcal{E}(pk, \text{Encode}(2))$.
3. $\mathcal{B}$ generates a suitably large random tape $R[\mathcal{A}]$. The useable tape length can be polynomially bounded by the runtime of $\mathcal{A}^*$; hence, the construction of such a tape is polynomial time.
4. $\mathcal{B}$ computes $m \overset{\text{R}}{\leftarrow} \mathcal{A}^*(pk, C^*, R[\mathcal{A}], \text{CLIST})$ and returns m.

Since $\mathcal{B}$ exactly simulates the environment in which $\mathcal{A}^*$ runs, $\mathcal{B}$ correctly decrypts C^* with probability $Pr[S_{fake}] \geq 1 - (|C^*| + 2) \cdot 2^{-\lambda} - \mathbf{Adv}^{\text{PA2}}_{\mathcal{A}, \mathcal{A}^*, \mathcal{P}, D}$ which is non-negligible as required. $\qquad \square$

This proof actually shows that any PA2 plaintext-aware encryption scheme which a message space $M = \{0,1\}^{<\ell(\lambda)}$ cannot be OW-CPA if $\ell(\lambda)$ grows faster than any polynomial. This is because we only require that the message space be able to cope with messages up to length $l_2(\lambda)$ for the proof to work.

We may also conclude that any public-key encryption scheme Π which is IND-CPA secure, PA2I plaintext aware and has an infinite message space cannot be PA2 plaintext aware (as in such a case IND-CPA security implies OW-CPA security and this contradicts the previous theorem). Hence, the condition that the message space be finite in Theorem 1 is necessary.

3.3 Connection between PA2 and PA2+

Clearly, a scheme which is PA2+ must necessarily be PA2, since an adversary may simply not use its randomness oracle, but the converse is not obviously true. We now show that it is true for a sufficiently randomised encryption scheme, since an adversary may use randomness inherent in a ciphertext generated by the encryption oracle to simulate a randomness oracle. This in turn implies that a suitably random PA2 encryption scheme is PA1+, thus giving a formal proof to the conjecture of Dent [4].

The proof essentially involves constructing a randomness oracle by taking ciphertexts created by a γ-uniform encryption algorithm and hashing them onto a single bit using a randomly chosen universal$_2$ hash function. The resulting distribution on $\{0,1\}$ is only a small statistical distance from the uniform distribution on $\{0,1\}$ and the result follows from the Leftover Hash Lemma [5]. One subtlety of the proof is that we will require the ciphertext creator $\mathcal{A}^*$ that we construct to know the functionality of the plaintext creator $\mathcal{P}$. Hence, we actually prove that a suitably random PA2I plaintext aware encryption scheme is PA2+, and appeal to Theorem 1 to finish the proof.

Definition 7 (γ-Uniformity). *An encryption scheme is γ-uniform if for all public keys pk, messages m and ciphertexts C, $\Pr[\mathcal{E}(pk, m) = C] \leq \gamma$, where the probability is taken over the choice of random coins used by the encryption algorithm.*

Definition 8 (Universal$_2$ Hash Family). *A family $\mathbf{H} = (H, K, A, B)$ of functions $(H_k)_{k \in K}$ where each H_k maps A to B is universal$_2$ if for all $x \neq y$ in A, $\Pr[H_k(x) = H_k(y) | k \xleftarrow{R} K] \leq 1/|B|$.*

We will use a universal$_2$ function family $\mathbf{H} = (H_k)_{k \in K}$ where H_k is a function from $\{0, 1\}^* \to \{0, 1\}$ for all $k \in K$. For simplicity, we will assume $K = \{0, 1\}^n$. Such families are known to exist without any computational assumptions [9].

Definition 9 (Statistical Distance). *Let x and y be random variables taking values on a finite set S. We define the statistical distance between x and y as*

$$\Delta[x, y] = \frac{1}{2} \sum_{s \in S} |\Pr[x = s] - \Pr[y = s]|.$$

Note that if $\mathcal{A}$ is a predicate on the set S, then the following inequalities holds:

$$\Delta[x, y] \geq |\Pr[\mathcal{A}(x)] - \Pr[\mathcal{A}(y)]| \tag{1}$$

We give the version of Leftover Hash Lemma given in Theorem 6.21 of [7].

Lemma 1 (Leftover Hash Lemma). *Let $\mathbf{H}$ be a family of universal$_2$ hash functions from A to B where B is of size β. Let V denote any distribution on A which is independent of the choice of k. Let $\hat{U}$ and $\hat{V}$ denote the distributions given by*

$$\hat{U} = \{(k, y) : k \xleftarrow{R} K, y \xleftarrow{R} B\} \qquad \hat{V} = \{(k, y) : k \xleftarrow{R} K, x \xleftarrow{R} V, y \leftarrow H_k(x)\}$$

and let

$$\kappa = \sum_{a \in A} Pr[V = a]^2.$$

Then $\Delta[\hat{U}, \hat{V}] \leq \sqrt{\beta \kappa}/2$.

This allows us to prove the following lemma.

Lemma 2. *Let Π be a γ-uniform encryption scheme, then, for any fixed message $m \in \mathcal{M}$ and public key pk, we have*

$$|\Pr[H_k(\mathcal{E}(pk, m)) = 1] - \frac{1}{2}| \leq \sqrt{\gamma/2},$$

where the probability is taken over the choice of $k \xleftarrow{R} \{0, 1\}^n$ and the random coins used by the encryption algorithm.

Proof. Let V be the distribution of $C \xleftarrow{\text{R}} \mathcal{E}(pk, m)$. By the γ-uniformity of Π we have

$$\max_{v \in \{0,1\}^*} \Pr[C = v] \leq \gamma$$

So

$$\kappa(V) \quad \leq \quad \sum_{v \in \{0,1\}^*} \Pr[C = v]\gamma \quad = \quad \gamma \sum_{v \in \{0,1\}^*} \Pr[C = v] \quad = \quad \gamma$$

and so by the Leftover Hash Lemma we have

$$\Delta[(k, H_k(C)), (k, y)] \leq \sqrt{2\gamma}/2,$$

where $y \xleftarrow{\text{R}} \{0, 1\}$. However,

$$\Delta[(k, H_k(C)), (k, y)] \geq |Pr[H_k(C) = 1] - 1/2|$$

which gives the required result. □

Theorem 3. *Suppose a public key encryption scheme Π is γ-uniform (for a negligible value of γ) and PA2I plaintext aware. Then it is PA2I+ plaintext aware.*

Proof. Let **H** be as above. Let $\mathcal{A}$ be a PA2I+ ciphertext creator that makes at most q_r queries to the randomness oracle. We construct a PA2I ciphertext creator $\mathcal{B}$ as follows: $\mathcal{B}$ takes input pk. We designate the first q_r n-bit chunks of the random tape of $\mathcal{B}$ as $(k_1, \ldots, k_{q_r})$ and the rest $R[\mathcal{A}]$. $\mathcal{B}$ runs $\mathcal{A}(pk; R[\mathcal{A}])$. $\mathcal{B}$ answers $\mathcal{A}$'s encryption and decryption queries by passing them to its own oracle and returning the result. To answer the ith randomness query, it queries the encryption oracle on the input 0 and receives a ciphertext C. It then computes $b_i \leftarrow H_{k_i}(C)$ and returns b_i.

Since $\mathcal{B}$ is a valid PA2I ciphertext creator, there exists a plaintext extractor $\mathcal{B}^*$. We use $\mathcal{B}^*$ to construct a plaintext extractor $\mathcal{A}^*$ for $\mathcal{A}$.

Recall that $\mathcal{A}^*$ takes input $(pk, C, R[\mathcal{A}], \text{RLIST}, \text{CLIST})$. We will assume that when $\mathcal{A}^*$ is first initialised it chooses hash keys $(k_1, \ldots, k_{q_r}) \xleftarrow{\text{R}} (\{0, 1\}^n)^{q_r}$ and stores these keys. If $\mathcal{A}^*$ is queried with a ciphertext C, then it runs as follows:

1. If the randomness oracle has been queried since $\mathcal{A}^*$ was last executed, i.e. RLIST has grown, then for each new bit b_i that has been returned $\mathcal{A}^*$ generates a ciphertext C_i by running $\mathcal{E}(pk, \mathcal{P}_I(0))$ repeatedly until it finds C_i such that $H_{k_i}(C_i) = b_i$, then adds C_i to CLIST in the appropriate place. We note that, by Lemma 2, the probability that $Pr[H_{k_i}(C) \neq b_i] \leq \frac{1}{2} + \sqrt{\gamma/2}$. We limit $\mathcal{A}^*$ to running λ trials; hence, $\mathcal{A}^*$ will run in polynomial time, but fail with the negligible probability $(\frac{1}{2} + \sqrt{\gamma/2})^\lambda$.

2. $\mathcal{A}^*$ then computes $m \xleftarrow{\text{R}} \mathcal{B}^*(pk, C, R, \text{CLIST})$ where $R = k_1 || \ldots || k_{q_r} || R[\mathcal{A}]$.

We now show that $\mathcal{A}^*$ is a valid plaintext extractor for $\mathcal{A}$, i.e. the output $x \xleftarrow{\text{R}} \mathcal{A}^{\mathcal{O}}(pk)$ is computationally indistinguishable in the REAL and FAKE games.

Fix a distinguishing algorithm D, let x_i be the output of $\mathcal{A}$ in Game i and let S_i be the event that $D(x_i) = 1$.

Game 0: Let Game 0 be the REAL game for $\mathcal{A}$. In other words, the encryption oracle takes as input s, computes $m \xleftarrow{\text{R}} \mathcal{P}_I(s)$ and returns $C \xleftarrow{\text{R}} \mathcal{E}(pk, m)$. The decryption oracle returns $\mathcal{D}(sk, C)$.

Game 1: We modify the randomness oracle so that on the ith query it computes $C_i \xleftarrow{\text{R}} \mathcal{E}(pk, \mathcal{P}_I(0))$ and sets $b_i \leftarrow H_{k_i}(C_i)$, where $1 \leq i \leq q_r$, rather than simply returning a random bit. In order to prove that $|\Pr[S_0] - \Pr[S_1]|$ is negligible, we use a hybrid argument. Suppose we consider changing the response of the first query to the randomness oracle from the random bit b to the bit $b' \xleftarrow{\text{R}} H_{k_1}(\mathcal{E}(pk, \mathcal{P}_I(0)))$ and let S^* be the event that $D(x) = 1$ in this new game. By Lemma 2 and Equation 1 we have that

$$|\Pr[S_0] - \Pr[S^*]| \quad \leq \quad \Delta[(k_1, b), (k_1, b')] \quad \leq \quad \sqrt{\gamma/2}$$

We may repeat this argument for all q_r randomness oracle queries to obtain

$$|\Pr[S_0] - \Pr[S_1]| \leq q_r \sqrt{\gamma/2}$$

Game 2: We modify the randomness oracle so that it adds each ciphertext $C_i \xleftarrow{\text{R}} \mathcal{P}_I(0)$ it generates to CLIST. Since the ciphertext creator $\mathcal{A}$ does not have access to CLIST and the ciphertext creator $\mathcal{A}$ has access to a real decryption oracle, the view of $\mathcal{A}$ is identical in the two games unless it submits one of these ciphertexts to the decryption oracle. The probability that a specific ciphertext involved in a decryption oracle query matches a specific ciphertext created by the randomness oracle is bounded by γ due to the γ-uniformity property. Since $\mathcal{A}$ makes at most q_r randomness oracle queries such ciphertexts and at most q_d decryption queries, we have

$$|\Pr[S_2] - \Pr[S_1]| \leq q_r q_d \gamma$$

Game 3: We modify the decryption oracle so that it uses the plaintext extractor $\mathcal{A}^*$ to answer decryption oracle queries. Game 3 exactly simulates the environment of $\mathcal{B}^*$ providing that the $\mathcal{B}^*$ finds a suitable ciphertext C_i for each random bit b_i on RLIST, so if D is an arbitrary distinguishing algorithm for $\mathcal{B}$,

$$|\Pr[S_3] - \Pr[S_2]| \leq \mathbf{Adv}^{\text{PA2I}}_{\mathcal{B}, \mathcal{B}^*, \mathcal{P}, D} + q_r (\frac{1}{2} + \sqrt{\gamma/2})^\lambda$$

However, Game 3 is the FAKE game for $\mathcal{A}$, so

$$\mathbf{Adv}^{\text{PA2I+}}_{\mathcal{A}, \mathcal{A}^*, \mathcal{P}, D} = |\Pr[S_3] - \Pr[S_0]|$$
$$\leq \mathbf{Adv}^{\text{PA2I}}_{\mathcal{B}, \mathcal{B}^*, \mathcal{P}, D} + q_r q_e \gamma + q_r \sqrt{\gamma/2} + q_r (\frac{1}{2} + \sqrt{\gamma/2})^\lambda.$$

which is negligible as required. $\square$

Corollary 3. *Suppose a public key encryption scheme Π is PA2 plaintext aware, OW-CPA secure, and γ-uniform. Then Π is PA2+ plaintext aware.*

Proof. Since Π is PA2 plaintext aware and OW-CPA secure, we have that it is PA2I plaintext aware, IND-CPA secure and that it has a finite message space $\mathcal{M} = \{0,1\}^{\ell(\lambda)}$ where $\ell(\lambda)$ is polynomially bounded (Theorem 2). Since Π is PA2I plaintext aware and γ-uniform, we have that it is PA2I+ plaintext aware (Theorem 3). Since Π has a finite message space and is both PA2I+ plaintext aware and IND-CPA secure, we have that it is PA2+ plaintext aware (Corollary 1).   □

3.4   PA2I+ and OW-CPA Do Not Guarantee IND-CPA Security

We have shown that for IND-CPA encryption schemes, the notions of PA2I plaintext awareness and PA2 plaintext awareness are equivalent. It might be hoped that this equivalence also holds for schemes with fewer security guarantees – in particular, it might be hoped that one can find an analogue of the Teranishi and Ogata theorem [8] which would prove that a scheme which was PA2I plaintext aware and OW-CPA secure was IND-CCA2 secure.

In this section we give evidence that this is not the case by proving that there exist schemes that are PA2I+ plaintext aware and OW-CPA secure, but which are not IND-CPA secure. Alternatively, by Theorem 3, we have that there exists a scheme which is PA2I plaintext aware, OW-CPA secure and γ-uniform, but not IND-CPA secure. We leave the question of showing that there exists schemes that are PA2I plaintext aware and OW-CPA secure, but not IND-CPA secure, as an open problem.

Theorem 4. *Suppose there exists a public key encryption encryption scheme $\Pi = (\mathcal{G}, \mathcal{E}, \mathcal{D})$ which is OW-CPA, IND-CPA, and PA2I+. Then there exists another encryption scheme $\Pi' = (\mathcal{G}, \mathcal{E}', \mathcal{D}')$ which is OW-CPA and PA2I+ but not IND-CPA.*

Proof. We assume that the message space $\mathcal{M}$ for Π is such that it is easy to find messages m_0 and m_1 which differ in the final bit and let $F(m)$ denote the final bit of message m. We now describe a new encryption scheme $\Pi' = (\mathcal{G}, \mathcal{E}', \mathcal{D}')$ as follows:

$\mathcal{E}'(pk, m):$
   $C' \overset{\text{R}}{\leftarrow} \mathcal{E}(pk, m)$
   $b \leftarrow F(m)$
   $C \leftarrow (C', b)$
   Return C

$\mathcal{D}'(sk, C):$
   Parse C as (C', b)
   $m \leftarrow \mathcal{D}(sk, C')$
   If $b = F(m):$
      Return m
   Else
      Return $\perp$

Clearly, Π' is OW-CPA, since if there is an adversary against the OW-CPA security of Π' with advantage ϵ, there is an adversary against Π with advantage $\epsilon/2$ which just guesses the final bit at random. It is also clear that Π' is not IND-CPA, since an adversary may simply choose two messages (m_0, m_1) that differ in the final bit.

We now show that Π' is PA2I+. Let $\mathcal{A}$ be a PA2I+ ciphertext creator against Π'. We construct a PA2I+ ciphertext creator $\mathcal{B}$ against Π. $\mathcal{B}$ runs $\mathcal{A}(pk; R[\mathcal{B}])$ and handles queries as follows:

- If $\mathcal{A}$ makes an encryption oracle query on (m_0, m_1), $\mathcal{B}$ queries its own encryption oracle on (m_0, m_1) and receives a ciphertext C'. It then checks if $F(m_0) = F(m_1)$. If so, $\mathcal{B}$ then returns $C = (C', F(m_0))$ to $\mathcal{A}$. If not, $\mathcal{B}$ queries its randomness oracle to get a bit b', and returns $C = (C', b')$.
- If $\mathcal{A}$ makes a decryption query on $C = (C', b')$, $\mathcal{B}$ checks whether $(C', b' \oplus 1)$ is on CLIST. If so, $\mathcal{B}$ returns $\perp$ to $\mathcal{A}$. Otherwise, $\mathcal{B}$ queries its own decryption oracle on C' to get a message m, and returns m if $F(m) = b'$ or $\perp$ otherwise.

Finally, when $\mathcal{A}$ outputs x and terminates, $\mathcal{B}$ does the same.

By the PA2I+ property of Π there exists a plaintext extractor $\mathcal{B}^*$ for the ciphertext creator $\mathcal{B}$. We use $\mathcal{B}^*$ to construct a plaintext extractor $\mathcal{A}^*$ for the ciphertext creator $\mathcal{A}$. $\mathcal{A}^*$ takes input $(pk, C, R[\mathcal{A}], \text{RLIST}, \text{CLIST})$ and runs as follows:

1. When it is first initialised, $\mathcal{A}^*$ creates two empty lists RLIST' and CLIST' which will be used to simulate the inputs to the plaintext extractor $\mathcal{B}^*$.
2. $\mathcal{A}^*$ checks to see if the encryption oracle or decryption oracle has been used since it was last activated. It does this by executing $\mathcal{A}$ on all the appropriate inputs (using pk, $R[\mathcal{A}]$ and the values on CLIST and RLIST).
   - For each new bit b' returned by the randomness oracle, $\mathcal{A}^*$ appends b' to RLIST'.
   - For each new ciphertext (C', b') returned by the encryption oracle, $\mathcal{A}^*$ examines the two messages (m_0, m_1) that $\mathcal{A}$ submitted to the encryption oracle (which $\mathcal{A}^*$ knows because it has executed $\mathcal{A}$). If $F(m_0) = F(m_1)$, then $\mathcal{A}^*$ appends C' to CLIST'. If $F(m_0) \neq F(m_1)$, then $\mathcal{A}^*$ appends b' to RLIST' and C' to CLIST'.
3. If $C \in \text{CLIST}'$ then $\mathcal{A}^*$ returns $\perp$.
4. Otherwise, $\mathcal{A}^*$ computes $m \xleftarrow{\text{R}} \mathcal{B}^*(pk, C, R[\mathcal{A}], \text{RLIST}', \text{CLIST}')$.
5. If $F(m) = b'$ then $\mathcal{A}^*$ returns m; otherwise $\mathcal{A}^*$ returns $\perp$.

We must now show that $\mathcal{A}^*$ is a valid plaintext extractor for $\mathcal{A}$. We do this by showing that $\mathcal{A}$ and $\mathcal{A}^*$ almost perfectly simulates the output of $\mathcal{B}$ and $\mathcal{B}^*$. Fix a distinguishing algorithm D, let x_i be the output of $\mathcal{A}$ in Game i and let S_i be the event that $D(x_i) = 1$ in Game i.

Game 0: Let Game 0 be the REAL game for $\mathcal{A}$. In other words, the encryption oracle takes as input two messages (m_0, m_1), chooses a bit $b \xleftarrow{\text{R}} \{0, 1\}$ and returns $(C', b') \xleftarrow{\text{R}} \mathcal{E}'(pk, m_b)$. The decryption oracle returns $\mathcal{D}'(sk, C)$.

Game 1: We let Game 1 be identical to Game 0 except that for each ciphertext (C', b') returned by the encryption oracle, the bit b' is chosen in the same way that $\mathcal{B}$ does – i.e. if $F(m_0) = F(m_1)$ then the oracle chooses $b' = F(m_0)$, otherwise b' is chosen uniformly at random $\{0, 1\}$ independently of the message that is encrypted.

Game 1 exactly simulates the REAL game for $\mathcal{B}$. We claim that

$$|\Pr[S_1] - \Pr[S_0]| \leq q_e \mathbf{Adv}_{\mathcal{B}'}^{\text{IND-CCA2}}$$

for some IND-CCA2 adversary $\mathcal{B}'$ against Π, since if the outputs of $\mathcal{A}$ are distinguishable in these two games, we can construct an adversary which distinguishes ciphertexts. Note that we may assume Π is IND-CCA2 secure as it is IND-CPA secure and PA2I+ plaintext aware.

Game 2: Let Game 2 be the same as Game 1, except that $\mathcal{A}$'s $\mathcal{D}$ queries are handled by $\mathcal{A}^*$. We note that Game 2 exactly simulates the FAKE game for $\mathcal{B}$. Thus by the PA2I+ property of Π,

$$|\Pr[S_2] - \Pr[S_1]| \leq \mathbf{Adv}_{\mathcal{B},\mathcal{B}^*,D}^{\text{PA2I+}}.$$

Game 3: Let Game 3 be as Game 2, except with the original behaviour of the encryption oracle restored, i.e. the final bit of the ciphertext is the final bit of the message. Hence,

$$|\Pr[S_3] - \Pr[S_2]| \leq q_e \mathbf{Adv}_{\mathcal{B}'}^{\text{IND-CPA}}$$

for some IND-CPA adversary $\mathcal{B}'$ for the same reasoning as in Game 1.

However, Game 3 is identical to the FAKE game for $\mathcal{A}$. Hence,

$$\begin{aligned}
\mathbf{Adv}_{\mathcal{A},\mathcal{A}^*,D}^{\text{PA2I+}} &= |\Pr[S_0] - \Pr[S_3]| \\
&\leq q_e \mathbf{Adv}_{\mathcal{B}'}^{\text{IND-CCA}} + \mathbf{Adv}_{\mathcal{B},\mathcal{B}^*,D}^{\text{PA2I+}} + q_e \mathbf{Adv}_{\mathcal{B}'}^{\text{IND-CPA}}
\end{aligned}$$

which is negligible as required. □

4   Conclusion

In this paper we have discussed the relationship between several notions of computational plaintext awareness, most notably the relationship between PA2 and the newly introduced notion of PA2I. The relationships between PA2I and PA2 are summarised in the diagram below:

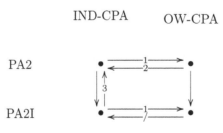

IND-CPA   OW-CPA

PA2

PA2I

The downwards arrows in the diagram follow trivially, since PA2I is a weaker notion than PA2. The arrows numbered 1 follow trivially if the message space is super-polynomial sized in the security parameter, since in this case any scheme which is IND-CPA is also OW-CPA. The arrow numbered 2 follows from the result of Teranishi and Ogata [8]. The arrow numbered 3 is a result of Theorem 1 and the separation is a result of Theorem 4 (under the added assumption that the encryption scheme is γ-uniform). Note that the diagram also demonstrates that there exist schemes that are OW-CPA, γ-uniform and PA2I, but not PA2. We believe that in almost all practical cases, the PA2I notion of plaintext awareness suffices.

We also explored some of the properties of encryption schemes that are PA2 plaintext aware, γ-uniform, OW-CPA secure and IND-CPA secure. We demonstrated that these schemes must have a finite message space and that they are necessarily PA2+. This latter result proves the conjecture of Dent [4].

Acknowledgements

The work described in this paper has been supported in part by the European Commission through the IST Programme under Contract IST-2002-507932 ECRYPT. The information in this document reflects only the authors' views, is provided as is and no guarantee or warranty is given that the information is fit for any particular purpose. The user thereof uses the information at its sole risk and liability. The first author was also funded in part by the EPSRC.

References

1. Bellare, M., Desai, A., Pointcheval, D., Rogaway, P.: Relations among notions of security for public-key encryption schemes. In: Krawczyk, H. (ed.) CRYPTO 1998. LNCS, vol. 1462, pp. 26–45. Springer, Heidelberg (1998)
2. Bellare, M., Palacio, A.: Towards plaintext-aware public-key encryption without random oracles. In: Lee, P.J. (ed.) ASIACRYPT 2004. LNCS, vol. 3329, pp. 48–62. Springer, Heidelberg (2004)
3. Bellare, M., Rogaway, P.: Optimal asymmetric encryption. In: De Santis, A. (ed.) EUROCRYPT 1994. LNCS, vol. 950, pp. 92–111. Springer, Heidelberg (1995)
4. Dent, A.W.: The Cramer-Shoup encryption scheme is plaintext aware in the standard model. In: Vaudenay, S. (ed.) EUROCRYPT 2006. LNCS, vol. 4004, pp. 289–307. Springer, Heidelberg (2006)
5. Impagliazzo, R., Levin, L.A., Luby, M.: Pseudo-random generation from one-way functions (extended abstracts). In: STOC, pp. 12–24. ACM, New York (1989)
6. Di Raimondo, M., Gennaro, R., Krawczyk, H.: Deniable authentication and key exchange. In: Juels, A., Wright, R.N., De Capitani di Vimercati, S. (eds.) ACM Conference on Computer and Communications Security, pp. 400–409. ACM, New York (2006)
7. Shoup, V.: A Computational Introduction to Number Theory and Algebra. Cambridge University Press, Cambridge (2005)
8. Teranishi, I., Ogata, W.: Relationship between standard model plaintext awareness and message hiding. In: Lai, X., Chen, K. (eds.) ASIACRYPT 2006. LNCS, vol. 4284, pp. 226–240. Springer, Heidelberg (2006)
9. Wegman, M.N., Carter, L.: New classes and applications of hash functions. In: Foundations Of Computer Science, pp. 175–182. IEEE, Los Alamitos (1979)

Completely Non-malleable Encryption Revisited

Carmine Ventre and Ivan Visconti

Dipartimento di Informatica ed Applicazioni
Università di Salerno, 84084 Fisciano (SA), Italy
{ventre,visconti}@dia.unisa.it

Abstract. Several security notions for public-key encryption schemes have been proposed so far, in particular considering the powerful adversary that can play a so called "man-in-the-middle" attack.

In this paper we extend the notion of completely non-malleable encryption introduced in [Fischlin, ICALP 05]. This notion immunizes a scheme from adversaries that can generate related ciphertexts under new public keys. This notion is motivated by its powerful features when encryption schemes are used as subprotocols. While in [Fischlin, ICALP 05] the only notion of *simulation-based* completely non-malleable encryption with respect to CCA2 adversaries was given, we present new *game-based* definitions for completely non-malleable encryption that follow the standard separations among NM-CPA, NM-CCA1 and NM-CCA2 security given in [Bellare et al., CRYPTO 98]. This is motivated by the fact that in several cases, the simplest notion we introduce (i.e., NM-CPA*) in several cases suffices for the main application that motivated the introduction of the notion of NM-CCA2* security, i.e., the design of non-malleable commitment schemes. Further the game-based definition of NM-CPA* security actually implies the simulation-based one.

We then focus on constructing encryption schemes that satisfy these strong security notions and show: 1) an NM-CCA2* secure encryption scheme in the shared random string model; 2) an NM-CCA2* secure encryption scheme in the plain model; for this second result, we use interaction and non-black-box techniques to overcome an impossibility result.

Our results clarify the importance of these stronger notions of encryption schemes and show how to construct them without requiring random oracles.

1 Introduction

The study of the relations among security notions for public-key encryption is a central question in Cryptography. Several notions for encryption schemes have been defined in order to construct schemes that are secure against strong adversaries. One of the most general and accepted concept is that of non-malleability formalized with the notion of adaptive chosen ciphertext security (shortly referred to as CCA2). Intuitively, a man-in-the-middle adversary should not be able given a public key pk and a ciphertext c, relative to a message m sampled from a distribution of its choice, to output a relation R and a ciphertext

R. Cramer (Ed.): PKC 2008, LNCS 4939, pp. 65–84, 2008.
© International Association for Cryptologic Research 2008

c' whose plaintext m' is related through R with m. This task has to be hard even in case that the adversary has access to a decryption oracle. Important constructions (see [1,2]) as well as relations among security notions [3] currently clarify the power of CCA2 security with respect to the weaker notions of CCA1 (where the decryption oracles can be accessed only before the challenge is received) and CPA (where no access to a decryption oracle is possible) security.

Recently, Fischlin presented in [4] a new security notion for public-key encryption, referred to as complete non-malleability. This notion, requires that non-malleability has to be preserved even in case that the man-in-the-middle adversary can also choose a new public key (that thus could be related to the original one). The goal of the adversary is to compute a ciphertext (under the new public key) that corresponds to a plaintext that is related to the original plaintext. Notice that in this more general case the relation considers also the new public key.

The main motivation for considering this new notion is that encryption schemes are often used as building blocks for larger protocols and in [4] it is stressed that completely non-malleable security has much more applications than the standard non-complete security notions for public-key encryption schemes. In particular, in [4] Fischlin discusses possible approaches for the design of non-malleable commitment schemes on top of completely non-malleable encryption schemes.

This new security notion is strong but unfortunately also impossible to achieve in the standard model when non-interactive encryption with simulation-based black-box security is considered (see [4]). Constructions are instead possible [4] in the random oracle model.

1.1   Our Results

In this paper we revisit the study of the concept of completely non-malleable encryption schemes initiated in [4]. First we notice that the idea behind complete non-malleability can be extended also to the notions of CPA and CCA1 security, while the original notion of Fischlin only considered CCA2 security. In order to motivate these new definitions, we present separating examples (see Theorem 1) showing that such notions seem to capture more than what the older non-complete definitions actually do. We will refer to these new notions of security for encryption schemes as NM-CPA*, NM-CCA1* and NM-CCA2* respectively.

The importance of the new definitions (and thus of our study of the relations among the different notions) follows from the following observation. The main motivation given in [4] for NM-CCA2* security concerned the possibility of constructing non-malleable commitments on top of NM-CCA2* secure encryption schemes[1]. This could be done (under some additional assumption that however

---

[1] Additionally, in [4] similar powerful attacks are discussed with respect to signature schemes.

we do not stress here) by assuming that the committer selects a public key, encrypts the message and sends the encryption as commitment. Then the opening is performed by sending the randomness used for the encryption. Obviously a man-in-the-middle could select a related public key in order to compute a related encryption and thus a related commitment. NM-CCA2* security should guarantee the failure of the above attack of the man-in-the-middle.

We observe that the role of a decryption oracle is not clear in this context and in particular could not be required in many applications. Indeed, for non-malleable commitments, the man-in-the-middle $\mathcal{A}$ does not have access to oracles that can open challenge commitments, therefore the NM-CCA2* security requirement in some cases can be relaxed to NM-CPA* security. Therefore, in this work we consider the possible variants for complete non-malleability, considering also the potential presences of a decryption oracle.

We stress that while the definitions of [4] follow the simulation-based approach already used in [1], we give definitions that follow the game-based approach of [3]. The choice of this formulation follows from the fact that the game-based definition of NM-CPA* security (our motivating notion) implies its simulation-based variant. Thus, we give a simpler formulation for NM-CPA* security and also show that for a large set of relations, the game-based formulations of NM-CCA1* and NM-CCA2* security imply the simulation-based ones. This implication shows that the impossibility result proved by Fischlin [4] about the design (in the plain model) of public-key encryption schemes that are completely non-malleable can be adapted to the game-based version of the definition of NM-CCA2* security.

We next focus on feasibility results with the goal of overcoming known impossibility results as well as improving the assumptions needed by previous constructions.

1. We first consider the shared random string model. By starting from any IND-CPA secure encryption scheme and by using the non-malleable NIZK proof of knowledge of [5] we obtain an NM-CCA2* secure encryption schemes in the shared random string model. In this construction we enrich the known technique due to [2] in which every ciphertext of the underlying IND-CPA secure encryption scheme is augmented with a NIZK proof of knowledge of the corresponding plaintext. In our construction we also need a proof that the new public key is indeed valid (i.e., the output of the honest key generation algorithm of the underlying encryption scheme). We stress that such a construction improves the assumption (i.e., the existence of random oracles) needed by Fischlin's constructions. Moreover we show that by using robust NIZK [5] (thus strengthening the non-malleable NIZK proof of knowledge), the construction also satisfies the simulation-based notion of NM-CCA2* security.

2. We show a construction of an interactive non-black-box completely non-malleable encryption scheme that works by assuming that oracle queries are asked sequentially. We stress that even this second construction satisfies the simulation-based notion of NM-CCA2* security. Since the impossibility

results proved by Fischlin in [4] only concerned black-box adversaries and non-interactive encryption, the possibility of further improving our construction by relaxing either the non-black-box requirement or the interactiveness of the encryption or the concurrency issue for oracle queries is an interesting open problem. The techniques of [1,6] would potentially avoid the non-black-box techniques, but would produce a non-constant round complexity. We finally stress that the potential drawback due to the interaction could not be an issue when encryption is used as subprotocol in an interactive protocol.

The motivation behind the constructions we present in this work is the proved failure of the random oracle proved in several papers [7,8,9,10]. We therefore show (constructively) that without a random oracle complete non-malleability is achievable in at least two settings.

2   New Definitions for Encryption Schemes

In this section we give the first contribution of this work by giving new definitions for completely non-malleable encryption schemes.

2.1   Completely Non-malleable Encryption

We define stronger notions of security against man-in-the-middle attacks following the lead of [4]. Indeed, Fischlin in [4] defined complete non-malleability as a stronger notion of NM-CCA2 security. We will refer to these stronger encryption schemes as NM-CCA2* secure encryption schemes. We here generalize that notion with respect to all the three main variants of security: namely NM-CPA, NM-CCA1 and NM-CCA2.

An important ingredient that we take from the framework introduced in [4] is that of a *complete relation*. A complete relation R is a (probabilistic) algorithm that takes as inputs: a public key $\mathbf{pk}$, a message m, a public key $\mathbf{pk}^*$, a ciphertext vector (under $\mathbf{pk}^*$) $\mathbf{c}^*$ and a plaintext vector $\mathbf{m}^*$ (the decryption of $\mathbf{c}^*$). R returns either **false** or **true**.

In our definition we will use the notation introduced in [3] based on indistinguishability rather than on the simulation paradigm (used in [4]) as the game-based paradigm simplifies the task of working with non-malleability, moreover it implies the simulation-based approach for the case of NM-CPA* security.

Definition 1 (NM-CPA*, NM-CCA1*, NM-CCA2*). *Let* $\mathcal{PE} = (\mathcal{G}, \mathcal{E}, \mathcal{D})$ *be a public-key encryption scheme, let* $\mathcal{A} = (\mathcal{A}_1, \mathcal{A}_2)$ *be an adversary. For* atk $\in \{\mathrm{cpa}, \mathrm{cca1}, \mathrm{cca2}\}$ *and* $k \in \mathbb{N}$ *let*

$$\mathbf{Adv}_{\mathcal{PE}, \mathcal{A}}^{\mathrm{nm-atk}^*}(k) = \left| \mathrm{Prob}\left[\mathbf{Expt}_{\mathcal{PE}, \mathcal{A}}^{\mathrm{nm-atk}^*}(k) \right] - \mathrm{Prob}\left[\mathbf{Expt}_{\mathcal{PE}, \mathcal{A}, \$}^{\mathrm{nm-atk}^*}(k) \right] \right|$$

where, the experiments $\text{Expt}_{\mathcal{PE}, \mathcal{A}}^{\text{nm}-\text{atk}^*}(k)$, *and* $\text{Expt}_{\mathcal{PE}, \mathcal{A}, \$}^{\text{nm}-\text{atk}^*}(k)$ *are defined as follows:*

$\text{Expt}_{\mathcal{PE}, \mathcal{A}}^{\text{nm}-\text{atk}^*}(k)$:	$\text{Expt}_{\mathcal{PE}, \mathcal{A}, \$}^{\text{nm}-\text{atk}^*}(k)$:
$(\text{pk}, \text{sk}) \leftarrow \mathcal{G}(r)$ where $r \leftarrow \{0,1\}^k$	$(\text{pk}, \text{sk}) \leftarrow \mathcal{G}(r)$ where $r \leftarrow \{0,1\}^k$
$(M, s) \leftarrow \mathcal{A}_1^{\mathcal{O}_1}(\text{pk})$	$(M, s) \leftarrow \mathcal{A}_1^{\mathcal{O}_1}(\text{pk})$
$x \leftarrow M$	$x, \tilde{x} \leftarrow M$
$c = \mathcal{E}_{\text{pk}}(x)$	$c = \mathcal{E}_{\text{pk}}(x)$
$(R, \text{pk}^*, \mathbf{c}^*) \leftarrow \mathcal{A}_2^{\mathcal{O}_2}(M, \text{pk}, s, c)$	$(R, \text{pk}^*, \mathbf{c}^*) \leftarrow \mathcal{A}_2^{\mathcal{O}_2}(M, \text{pk}, s, c)$
return true *iff* $\exists\, \mathbf{m}^*$ *such that*	**return true** *iff* $\exists\, \mathbf{m}^*$ *such that*
$\quad(\mathbf{c}^* = \mathcal{E}_{\text{pk}^*}(\mathbf{m}^*))\ \wedge$	$\quad(\mathbf{c}^* = \mathcal{E}_{\text{pk}^*}(\mathbf{m}^*))\ \wedge$
$\quad(c \notin \mathbf{c}^* \vee \text{pk} \neq \text{pk}^*)\ \wedge$	$\quad(c \notin \mathbf{c}^* \vee \text{pk} \neq \text{pk}^*)\ \wedge$
$\quad(\mathbf{m}^* \neq \perp)\ \wedge$	$\quad(\mathbf{m}^* \neq \perp)\ \wedge$
$\quad(R(x, \mathbf{m}^*, \text{pk}, \text{pk}^*, \mathbf{c}^*) = \text{true})$	$\quad(R(\tilde{x}, \mathbf{m}^*, \text{pk}, \text{pk}^*, \mathbf{c}^*) = \text{true})$

Above

$$\text{if atk} = \text{cpa} \quad \text{then } \mathcal{O}_1(\cdot) = \epsilon \qquad \text{and } \mathcal{O}_2(\cdot) = \epsilon,$$
$$\text{if atk} = \text{cca1} \text{ then } \mathcal{O}_1(\cdot) = \mathcal{D}_{\text{sk}}(\cdot) \text{ and } \mathcal{O}_2(\cdot) = \epsilon,$$
$$\text{if atk} = \text{cca2} \text{ then } \mathcal{O}_1(\cdot) = \mathcal{D}_{\text{sk}}(\cdot) \text{ and } \mathcal{O}_2(\cdot) = \mathcal{D}_{\text{sk}}^{(c)}(\cdot),$$

with $\mathcal{D}_{\text{sk}}^{(c)}(\cdot)$ *meaning that the oracle decrypts any ciphertext except c. We insist, above, that the message space M is valid:* $|x| = |x'|$ *for any* x, x' *with non-zero probability in the message space M. Moreover, we let* $\mathbf{m}^* \neq \perp$ *meaning that at least one of the ciphertexts in* $\mathbf{c}^*$ *is valid, i.e., in* $\mathbf{m}^*$ *there is at least one message that is different from a special symbol* $\perp$.

We say that $\mathcal{PE}$ *is NM-ATK* secure if for every probabilistic polynomial-time adversary* $\mathcal{A}$, $\mathbf{Adv}_{\mathcal{PE}, \mathcal{A}}^{\text{nm}-\text{atk}^*}(\cdot)$ *is negligible.*

In the definition above we assume (as in [4,3]) that any a priori information of the adversary, i.e. the history, is in the message space M.

Insecurity of known schemes with respect to complete non-malleability. In order to motivate his definitions Fischlin showed in [4] that two encryption schemes, namely Cramer-Shoup [11] and RSA-OAEP [12,13], are not NM-CCA2* secure though they are NM-CCA2 secure. We first note that both separations trivially work also under our game-based definitions and further motivate both our definitions and Fischlin's security notion by providing the next two theorems. Below, we let ATK $\in \{\text{cpa}, \text{cca1}, \text{cca2}\}$.

Theorem 1. *For any NM-ATK secure encryption scheme* $\mathcal{PE} = (\mathcal{G}, \mathcal{E}, \mathcal{D})$ *there exists an NM-ATK secure encryption scheme* $\mathcal{PE}' = (\mathcal{G}', \mathcal{E}', \mathcal{D}')$ *which is not NM-ATK* secure.*

The proof of above result is based on the following simple observation. A bit is appended to the public key of an NM-ATK secure encryption scheme and it is ignored by the encryption and decryption algorithms. Obviously the resulting scheme is still NM-ATK secure but it is not NM-ATK* secure as the adversary can simply change the appended bit of the public key, thus obtaining a new encryption of the same message with respect to a new public key. It is also possible to show that the NM-CCA2 secure encryption schemes known in literature [2,5] are not NM-CCA2* secure even under our game-based definition.

Game-Based vs Simulation-Based Definitions. We next study the relation between the game-based definitions and the simulation-based ones. We start by giving the simulation-based definition for NM-CCA2* [4] security.

Definition 2 (SNM-CCA2*). ([4]) *Let $\mathcal{PE} = (\mathcal{G}, \mathcal{E}, \mathcal{D})$ be a public key encryption scheme, let R be a complete relation, let $\mathcal{A} = (\mathcal{A}_1, \mathcal{A}_2)$ be an adversary and let $\mathcal{S} = (\mathcal{S}_1, \mathcal{S}_2)$ be a pair of algorithms that we call simulator. For $k \in \mathbb{N}$ we define*

$$\mathbf{Adv}_{\mathcal{PE}, \, \mathcal{A}, \, \mathcal{S}, \, R}^{\mathrm{snm-cca2}^*}(k) = \left| \mathrm{Prob}\left[\mathbf{Expt}_{\mathcal{PE}, \, \mathcal{A}, \, R}^{\mathrm{snm-cca2}^*}(k) \right] - \mathrm{Prob}\left[\mathbf{Expt}_{\mathcal{PE}, \, \mathcal{S}, \, R}^{\mathrm{snm-cca2}^*}(k) \right] \right|$$

where, the experiments $\mathbf{Expt}_{\mathcal{PE}, \, \mathcal{A}, \, R}^{\mathrm{snm-cca2}^*}(k)$, *and* $\mathbf{Expt}_{\mathcal{PE}, \, \mathcal{S}, \, R}^{\mathrm{snm-cca2}^*}(k)$ *are defined as follows:*

$\mathbf{Expt}_{\mathcal{PE}, \, \mathcal{A}, \, R}^{\mathrm{snm-cca2}^*}(k)$:	$\mathbf{Expt}_{\mathcal{PE}, \, \mathcal{S}, R}^{\mathrm{snm-cca2}^*}(k)$:
$(\mathrm{pk}, \mathrm{sk}) \leftarrow \mathcal{G}(1^k)$	$(\mathrm{pk}, \mathrm{sk}) \leftarrow \mathcal{G}(1^k)$
$(M, s) \leftarrow \mathcal{A}_1^{\mathcal{D}\mathrm{sk}(\cdot)}(\mathrm{pk})$	$(M, s) \leftarrow \mathcal{S}_1(\mathrm{pk})$
$m \leftarrow M; \ c = \mathcal{E}_{\mathrm{pk}}(m)$	$m \leftarrow M$
$(\mathrm{pk}^*, c^*) \leftarrow \mathcal{A}_2^{\mathcal{D}_{\mathrm{sk}}^{(c)}(\cdot)}(c, s)$	$(\mathrm{pk}', c') \leftarrow \mathcal{S}_2(s)$
return true *iff* $\exists \ m^*$ *such that*	**return true** *iff* $\exists m'$ *such that*
$(c^* = \mathcal{E}_{\mathrm{pk}^*}(m^*)) \wedge$	$(c' = \mathcal{E}_{\mathrm{pk}'}(m')) \wedge$
$((\mathrm{pk}, c) \neq (\mathrm{pk}^*, c^*)) \wedge$	
$(R(m, m^*, \mathrm{pk}, \mathrm{pk}^*, c^*) = \mathbf{true})$	$(R(m, m', \mathrm{pk}, \mathrm{pk}', c') = \mathbf{true})$

where $\mathcal{D}_{\mathrm{sk}}^{(c)}(\cdot)$ *means the oracle that decrypts any ciphertext except c. We insist, above, that the message space M is valid: $|x| = |x'|$ for any x, x' with non-zero probability in the message space M.*

We say that $\mathcal{PE}$ is SNM-CCA2 secure if for every probabilistic polynomial-time adversary $\mathcal{A}$ and complete relation R computable in polynomial time, there exists a polynomial-time simulator $\mathcal{S}$ such that $\mathbf{Adv}_{\mathcal{PE}, \, \mathcal{A}, \, \mathcal{S}, \, R}^{\mathrm{snm-cca2}^*}(\cdot)$ is negligible.*

We remark that if we remove both oracle accesses to the adversary $\mathcal{A}$ in the above definition then we have a simulation-based definition of NM-CPA* security (we refer to this notion as SNM-CPA*). To be consistent with Fischlin's definition we slightly change our game-based definitions by not asking for the condition $\mathrm{m}^* \neq \perp$ (see Definition 1). We are now in the position to show that our game-based definition of NM-CPA* security implies the corresponding simulation-based one (see Definition 2).

Theorem 2. *If an encryption scheme $\mathcal{PE} = (\mathcal{G}, \mathcal{E}, \mathcal{D})$ is NM-CPA* secure according to the game-based definition then $\mathcal{PE}$ is SNM-CPA* secure according to simulation-based definition.*

Proof. We next show that given a relation R and an adversary $\mathcal{A} = (\mathcal{A}_1, \mathcal{A}_2)$ we are able to construct a simulator $\mathcal{S} = (\mathcal{S}_1, \mathcal{S}_2)$. The simulator simply runs the adversary $\mathcal{A}$. More formally:

$S_1(\text{pk})$:	$S_2(\tilde{s})$ where $\tilde{s} = (M, s, \text{pk})$:
	$x \leftarrow M$
$(M, s) \leftarrow \mathcal{A}_1(\text{pk})$	$c \leftarrow \mathcal{E}_{\text{pk}}(x)$
$\tilde{s} \leftarrow (M, s, \text{pk})$	$(\text{pk}^*, c^*) \leftarrow \mathcal{A}_2(c, s)$
return $(M, \tilde{s})$	**return** (pk^*, c^*)

A key point is that the simulator can indeed run $\mathcal{A}$ as $\mathcal{A}$ has not oracle access (and therefore $\mathcal{S}$ does not need to know the secret key corresponding to pk). Now we want to show that $\mathbf{Adv}^{\text{snm}-\text{cpa}^*}_{\mathcal{PE}, \mathcal{A}, \mathcal{S}, \text{R}}(\cdot)$ is negligible. We do this using the hypothesis that $\mathcal{PE}$ is secure in the sense of NM-CPA*. To that end, we consider the following adversary $\mathcal{B} = (\mathcal{B}_1, \mathcal{B}_2)$ attacking $\mathcal{PE}$ in the sense of NM-CPA* security:

$\mathcal{B}_1(\text{pk})$:	$\mathcal{B}_2(M, \text{pk}, s, c)$:
$(M, s) \leftarrow \mathcal{A}_1(\text{pk})$	$(\text{pk}^*, c^*) \leftarrow \mathcal{A}_2(c, s)$
return (M, s)	**return** $(\text{R}, \text{pk}^*, c^*)$

It is clear from the definition of $\mathcal{B}$ that

$$\text{Prob}\left[\text{Expt}^{\text{nm}-\text{cpa}^*}_{\mathcal{PE}, \mathcal{B}}(k) \right] = \text{Prob}\left[\text{Expt}^{\text{snm}-\text{cpa}^*}_{\mathcal{PE}, \mathcal{A}, \text{R}}(k) \right]$$

for all $k \in \mathbb{N}$. Now, let us expand the definition of $\text{Expt}^{\text{snm}-\text{cpa}^*}_{\mathcal{PE}, \mathcal{S}, \text{R}}(k)$, substituting in the definition of $\mathcal{S}$ given above.

$\text{Expt}^{\text{snm}-\text{cpa}^*}_{\mathcal{PE}, \mathcal{S}, \text{R}}(k)$:
$(\text{pk}, \text{sk}) \leftarrow \mathcal{G}(1^k)$
$(M, s) \leftarrow \mathcal{A}_1(\text{pk})$
$\tilde{s} \leftarrow (M, s, \text{pk})$
$m \leftarrow M$
$x \leftarrow M$
$c \leftarrow \mathcal{E}_{\text{pk}}(x)$
$(\text{pk}^*, c^*) \leftarrow \mathcal{A}_2(c, s)$
return true iff there exists m^* such that
$(c^* = \mathcal{E}_{\text{pk}^*}(m^*)) \wedge$
$(\text{R}(m, m^*, \text{pk}, \text{pk}^*, c^*) = \text{true})$

Examining the code above we notice that we can drop instructions $\tilde{s} \leftarrow (M, s, \mathrm{pk})$ (as $\tilde{s}$ is never referred to). The resulting code is equivalent to that of $\mathrm{Expt}_{\mathcal{PE},\ \mathcal{B},\ \$}^{\mathrm{nm-cpa}^*}(k)$ so that:

$$\mathrm{Prob}\left[\mathrm{Expt}_{\mathcal{PE},\ \mathcal{B},\ \$}^{\mathrm{nm-cpa}^*}(k)\right] = \mathrm{Prob}\left[\mathrm{Expt}_{\mathcal{PE},\ \mathcal{S},\ \mathrm{R}}^{\mathrm{snm-cpa}^*}(k)\right]$$

for all $k \in \mathbb{N}$. Thus for all $k \in \mathbb{N}$ we have:

$$\mathbf{Adv}_{\mathcal{PE},\ \mathcal{A},\ \mathcal{S},\ \mathrm{R}}^{\mathrm{snm-cpa}^*} = \mathbf{Adv}_{\mathcal{PE},\ \mathcal{B}}^{\mathrm{nm-cpa}^*}.$$

But $\mathcal{PE}$ is assumed to be secure in the sense of NM-CPA*, so $\mathbf{Adv}_{\mathcal{PE},\ \mathcal{B}}^{\mathrm{nm-cpa}^*}$ is negligible. The above implies that $\mathbf{Adv}_{\mathcal{PE},\ \mathcal{A},\ \mathcal{S},\ \mathrm{R}}^{\mathrm{snm-cpa}^*}$ is negligible too. Therefore, $\mathcal{PE}$ is secure in the sense of SNM-CPA*. $\square$

Using the same technique we can show that the game-based definitions of NM-CCA1* and NM-CCA2* security imply the corresponding simulation-based definitions for a large set of relations. Below we just present discussion for the NM-CCA2* security notion.

We say that an encryption scheme is (S)NM-CCA2* secure with respect to a set of complete relations $\mathcal{R}$ if in Definitions 1 and 2 we require $\mathrm{R} \in \mathcal{R}$ (we require that the scheme is resistant to a set of relations – and not to all relations as demanded by the definition). Further, we call a relation R *lacking* if R is a complete relation that ignores the input of the challenge public key: R is lacking if and only if $\mathrm{R}(m, m^*, pk, pk^*, c^*) = \mathrm{R}(m, m^*, pk^*, c^*)$ where pk is the challenge public key.

Theorem 3. *Let $\mathcal{R}$ be the set of lacking relations. If an encryption scheme $\mathcal{PE} = (\mathcal{G}, \mathcal{E}, \mathcal{D})$ is NM-CCA2* secure (Definition 1) with respect to $\mathcal{R}$ then $\mathcal{PE}$ is SNM-CCA2* secure with respect to $\mathcal{R}$ (Definition 2).*

The proof is similar in spirit to that we gave above (and to the one in [14] where it is shown that the game-based formulation of [3] implies the simulation-based formulation of [1]). However, there is the following technical problem. The proof in [14] consists in designing a simulator that on input a challenge public key pk, runs an adversary $\mathcal{A}$ of the simulation-based notion. The simulator generates a new pair of public and private keys and runs $\mathcal{A}$ on input the new public key. The simulator computes an encryption of a randomly chosen message and uses it as challenge for the adversary $\mathcal{A}$. The simulator uses the secret key to answer to all decryption queries of $\mathcal{A}$ and can decrypt the final ciphertext produced by $\mathcal{A}$. The plaintext obtained is then encrypted under the challenge public key pk and returned by the simulator. The assumption that the original encryption scheme is secure under the game-based notion is crucially used in [14] as it is possible to show that the simulator has the same probability of succeeding as the adversary $\mathcal{A}$.

In our case, when $\mathcal{A}$ is a completely non-malleable adversary it generates the final ciphertexts under a new public key. Moreover, $\mathcal{A}$'s success depends also on this new public key and the fake public key generated by the simulator (i.e., the outcome of complete relations does not depend just on plaintexts). This means that such a success of $\mathcal{A}$ does not seem to be easily reproducible by the simulator with respect to the challenge public key pk. Thus the technique exploited in [14] fails, in our case, because we are considering complete relations. Therefore, if we restrict $\mathcal{R}$ to relations that ignore the challenge public key pk, the simulator can use his own pair of keys. Consequently, it can answer to decryption queries of the underlying adversary $\mathcal{A}$ (knowing the secret key) and can return the new public key and ciphertexts given in output by $\mathcal{A}$. If the relation ignores the challenge public key pk in input to the simulator (as we assume) then such a simulator is successful whenever $\mathcal{A}$ is.

Theorem 6 in [15] shows the impossibility result for simulation-based black-box NM-CCA2* security with respect to a set of relation that contains relations R_{msg-eq}: $R \in R_{msg-eq}$ means that $R(m, m^*, pk, pk^*, c^*) = 1$ if and only if $m = m^*$. Since R_{msg-eq} is lacking, we have the following corollary.

Corollary 1. *Encryption schemes which are game-based NM-CCA2* secure according to black-box adversaries do not exist.*

3   NM-CCA2* Secure Encryption with Shared Random Strings

In this section we show an NM-CCA2* secure encryption scheme in the shared random string model.

We stress that the NM-CCA2* security definition easily adapts to the shared random string model by simply feeding each algorithm (and the relation) with the shared random string Σ as extra input. We remark that such a string is not under the control of the adversary and is known to all players in the game.

IND-CPA Secure Encryption Schemes. In our construction we will make use of encryption scheme satisfying the following classical security notions (see [3]).

Definition 3 (IND-CPA).   *Let* $\mathcal{PE} = (\mathcal{G}, \mathcal{E}, \mathcal{D})$ *be a public-key encryption scheme, let* $\mathcal{A} = (\mathcal{A}_1, \mathcal{A}_2)$ *be an adversary. For* $k \in \mathbb{N}$ *let*

$$\mathbf{Adv}_{\mathcal{PE},\,\mathcal{A}}^{ind-cpa}(k) = \left|\mathrm{Prob}\left[\mathbf{Expt}_{\mathcal{PE},\,\mathcal{A}}^{indcpa-0}(k) = 0\right] - \mathrm{Prob}\left[\mathbf{Expt}_{\mathcal{PE},\,\mathcal{A}}^{indcpa-1}(k) = 0\right]\right|$$

where, for $b \in \{0, 1\}$,

$$
\begin{aligned}
&\mathbf{Expt}_{\mathcal{PE},\,\mathcal{A}}^{indcpa-b}(k): \\
&(\mathrm{pk}, \mathrm{sk}) \leftarrow \mathcal{G}(r) \text{ where } r \leftarrow \{0,1\}^k \\
&(x_0, x_1, s) \leftarrow \mathcal{A}_1(\mathrm{pk}) \\
&c = \mathcal{E}_{\mathrm{pk}}(x_b) \\
&d \leftarrow \mathcal{A}_2(x_0, x_1, s, c) \\
&\mathbf{return}\ d
\end{aligned}
$$

Above it is mandatory that $|x_0| = |x_1|$. We say that $\mathcal{PE}$ is IND-CPA secure if $\mathcal{A}$ being polynomial-time implies $\mathbf{Adv}_{\mathcal{PE}, \, \mathcal{A}}^{\mathrm{ind-cpa}}(\cdot)$ is negligible.

Non-Malleable NIZK proof of knowledge. An important tool of our construction is the following notion defined in [5].

Definition 4 (Non-Malleable NIZK). *Let $\Pi = (\ell, \mathcal{P}, \mathcal{V}, \mathcal{S})$ be an unbounded NIZK proof system for the $\mathcal{NP}$ language L with witness relation W. We say that Π is a* non-malleable (in the explicit witness sense) *NIZK proof system for L if there exists a probabilistic polynomial-time oracle machine $\mathcal{M} = (\mathcal{M}_0, \mathcal{M}_1, \mathcal{M}_2)$ such that:*

For all non-uniform probabilistic polynomial-time adversaries $\mathcal{A}$ and for all non-uniform polynomial-time relations R, there exists a negligible function $\nu(k)$ such that

$$\left| \mathrm{Prob}\left[\mathrm{Expt}_{\mathcal{A},R}^{\mathcal{S}}(k) \right] - \mathrm{Prob}\left[\mathrm{Expt}'_{\mathcal{A},R}(k) \right] \right| \leq \nu(k)$$

where $\mathrm{Expt}_{\mathcal{A},R}^{\mathcal{S}}(k)$ and $\mathrm{Expt}'_{\mathcal{A},R}$ are the following experiments:

$\mathrm{Expt}_{\mathcal{A},R}^{\mathcal{S}}(k)$:	$\mathrm{Expt}'_{\mathcal{A},R}(k)$
$(\Sigma, \tau) \leftarrow \mathcal{S}_1(1^k)$	
$(x, \pi, \mathbf{aux}) \leftarrow \mathcal{A}^{\mathcal{S}_2(\cdot, \Sigma, \tau)}(\Sigma)$	
Let Q be list of pairs (x, π) given by $\mathcal{S}_2$ above	$(x, w, \mathbf{aux}) \leftarrow \mathcal{M}^{\mathcal{A}}(1^k)$
return true iff	
$\quad ((x, \pi) \notin Q) \wedge$	**return true** iff
$\quad (\mathcal{V}(x, \pi, \Sigma) = \mathbf{true}) \wedge$	$\quad ((x, w) \in W) \wedge$
$\quad (R(x, \mathbf{aux}) = \mathbf{true})$	$\quad (R(x, \mathbf{aux}) = \mathbf{true})$

We focus our attention to the construction given in [5] and thus we can rewrite the non-malleability machine $\mathcal{M}$ of the non-malleable NIZK proof of knowledge of [5] as follows. We can state that $\mathcal{M}$ is actually composed of three different algorithms $(\mathcal{G}_\Sigma, \mathcal{M}_1, \mathcal{M}_2)$. In particular we can rewrite $\mathrm{Expt}'_{\mathcal{A},R}(k)$ above as follows:

$\mathrm{Expt}'_{\mathcal{A},R}(k)$
Make reference string Σ
$\quad (\Sigma, \tau) \leftarrow \mathcal{G}_\Sigma(1^k)$
Interact with $\mathcal{A}(\Sigma)$. When asked for a proof of x, do:
$\quad \pi_x \leftarrow \mathcal{M}_1(\Sigma, x, \tau)$
Extract witness from some proof π
$\quad (x, w, \mathbf{aux}) \leftarrow \mathcal{M}_2(\Sigma, \tau, x, \pi)$
return true *iff* $((x, w) \in W) \wedge (R(x, \mathbf{aux}) = \mathbf{true})$

Ingredients of the Construction. Our scheme $(\mathcal{G}', \mathcal{E}', \mathcal{D}')$ is based on:

1. Any IND-CPA secure encryption scheme $\mathcal{PE} = (\mathcal{G}, \mathcal{E}, \mathcal{D})$ in the standard model.
2. A non-malleable NIZK proof of knowledge $\Pi = (\ell, \mathcal{P}, \mathcal{V}, \mathcal{S})$ for the following languages:

$$L_1 = \{\mathrm{pk} : \exists\, r \text{ s.t. } |r| = k, (\mathrm{pk}, \mathrm{sk}) \leftarrow \mathcal{G}(r)\},$$
$$L_2 = \{(c, \mathrm{pk}) : \exists\, r, m \text{ s.t. } c = \mathcal{E}_{\mathrm{pk}}(m; r)\}.$$

We observe that both languages are in $\mathcal{NP}$. Indeed, for L_1, r witnesses the membership in the language, and further, the length of r is polynomial in the size of pk. For L_2, r and m witness the membership in the language; the size of r and m is polynomial in the sizes of c and pk.

Construction 4. *The scheme $(\mathcal{G}', \mathcal{E}', \mathcal{D}')$ is defined as follows:*

- $\mathcal{G}'(1^k)$: *randomly pick $r \leftarrow \{0,1\}^*$, call $\mathcal{G}(r)$ to obtain a valid pair of keys $(\mathrm{pk}, \mathrm{sk})$. Use $\mathcal{P}, r$ and Σ to generate a proof of knowledge π_1 that $\mathrm{pk} \in L_1$ using r as witness. The public key is $PK = (\mathrm{pk}, \pi_1)$. The private key is $SK = \mathrm{sk}$.*
- $\mathcal{E}'_{PK}(m)$: *Use $\mathcal{V}$ to verify the correctness of the proof π_1 in PK. If π_1 is valid then compute (using randomness r) $c = \mathcal{E}_{\mathrm{pk}}(m)$. Use $\mathcal{P}, r, m$ and Σ to generate a proof of knowledge π_2 that $(c, \mathrm{pk}) \in L_2$ using r and m as witnesses. Output (c, π_2).*
- $\mathcal{D}'_{SK}(c)$: *Use $\mathcal{V}$ to verify the correctness of the proof π_2 in c. If π_2 is valid then output $\mathcal{D}_{\mathrm{sk}}(c)$.*

We next give an informal argument supporting the complete non-malleability of our scheme. Since the component encryption scheme is IND-CPA in the standard model then every IND-CPA adversary for $\mathcal{PE}$ has a negligible advantage. We define one of such IND-CPA adversaries $\mathcal{A}$ in the standard model by means of an NM-CCA2* adversary $\mathcal{B}$ in the shared random string model. The adversary $\mathcal{A}$, on input the challenge ciphertext c, starts by creating a random string using the algorithm $\mathcal{G}_\Sigma$ (thus allowing $\mathcal{A}$ to know a trapdoor for Σ). $\mathcal{B}$, with such a random string and on input the challenge c returns a relation R, a new public key PK^* (i.e., a component public key pk^* and the proof of knowledge of a corresponding secret key sk^*) and a vector of ciphertexts $\mathbf{c}^*$ under the new public key PK^*. If $\mathcal{B}$ is a winning adversary then the probability that the plaintext encrypted in c, the ciphertext vector $\mathbf{c}^*$ and the corresponding plaintexts are in relation R is noticeable. The adversary $\mathcal{A}$ then uses the trapdoor to extract the secret key sk^* and then evaluates the relation R. This leads to a noticeable advantage for $\mathcal{A}$ distinguishing the plaintext behind the challenge c contradicting the IND-CPA security of $\mathcal{PE}$. Since we augmented the encryption of a message m by a proof of knowledge of m, $\mathcal{A}$ can answer the decryption queries the NM-CCA2* adversary $\mathcal{B}$ will ask for, due to the fact that $\mathcal{A}$ knows the trapdoor for Σ.

Theorem 5. *The encryption scheme* $(\mathcal{G}', \mathcal{E}', \mathcal{D}')$ *above is NM-CCA2* secure in the shared random string model.*

Proof. The main idea is to transform a strong NM-CCA2* attack against the new encryption scheme $\mathcal{PE}' = (\mathcal{G}', \mathcal{E}', \mathcal{D}')$ into an IND-CPA attack against the component encryption scheme $\mathcal{PE}$. In particular, let $\mathcal{B} = (\mathcal{B}_1, \mathcal{B}_2)$ be an NM-CCA2* adversary attacking the new encryption scheme. We must show that $\mathbf{Adv}_{\mathcal{PE}', \mathcal{B}}^{\mathrm{nm-cca2^*}}(\cdot)$ is negligible. Towards this end we describe an IND-CPA adversary $\mathcal{A} = (\mathcal{A}_1, \mathcal{A}_2)$ attacking the component encryption scheme $\mathcal{PE}$.

$\mathcal{A}_1(\mathrm{pk})$:
$(\Sigma, \tau) \leftarrow \mathcal{G}_\Sigma(1^k)$
$\pi \leftarrow \mathcal{M}_1(\Sigma, \mathrm{pk}, \tau)$
Run $B_1^{\mathcal{D}_{\mathrm{sk}}(\cdot)}$ on input $((\mathrm{pk}, \pi), \Sigma)$:
  When B_1 asks $\mathcal{D}_{\mathrm{sk}}(\cdot)$ for a ciphertext (c', π'), do:
    If $\mathcal{V}((c', \mathrm{pk}), \pi', \Sigma) = \mathtt{false}$ **return** $\perp$ to $\mathcal{B}_1$
    $(r, m) \leftarrow \mathcal{M}_2(\Sigma, \tau, (c', \mathrm{pk}), \pi')$
    return m to $\mathcal{B}_1$
  Let (M, s) the output of $\mathcal{B}_1$
$x_0, x_1 \leftarrow M$
return $(x_0, x_1, (s, \tau, (\mathrm{pk}, \pi), \Sigma, M))$

$\mathcal{A}_2(x_0, x_1, s', c)$: where $s' = (s, \tau, PK, \Sigma, M)$
Run $B_2^{\mathcal{D}_{\mathrm{sk}}^{(c)}(\cdot)}$ on input (M, PK, s, c, Σ):
  When B_2 asks $\mathcal{D}_{\mathrm{sk}}^{(c)}(\cdot)$ for a ciphertext (c', π'), do:
    If $\mathcal{V}((c', \mathrm{pk}), \pi', \Sigma) = \mathtt{false}$ **return** $\perp$ to $\mathcal{B}_2$
    $(r, m) \leftarrow \mathcal{M}_2(\Sigma, \tau, (c', \mathrm{pk}), \pi')$
    return m to $\mathcal{B}_2$
  Let $(\mathtt{R}, (\mathrm{pk}^*, \pi^*), \mathbf{c}^*)$ the output of $\mathcal{B}_2$
$r^* \leftarrow \mathcal{M}_2(\Sigma, \tau, \mathrm{pk}^*, \pi^*)$
$(\mathrm{pk}^*, \mathrm{sk}^*) \leftarrow \mathcal{G}(r^*)$; $\mathbf{x} = \mathcal{D}_{\mathrm{sk}^*}(\mathbf{c}^*)$
$f = (c \notin \mathbf{c}^* \vee \mathrm{pk} \neq \mathrm{pk}^*)$
if $(f \wedge (\mathbf{x} \neq \perp) \wedge \mathtt{R}(x_0, \mathbf{x}, (\mathrm{pk}, \pi), (\mathrm{pk}^*, \pi^*), \mathbf{c}^*, \Sigma))$ **then** $d \leftarrow 0$
else $d \leftarrow \{0, 1\}$
return d

Notice $\mathcal{A}$ is polynomial time given that the running time of $\mathcal{B}$, the time to compute $\mathtt{R}$, the time to sample from M and the running time of $\mathcal{M}$ are all bounded by a fixed polynomial.

Observe that in the adversary above we use three different kind of proofs: π is the (non-malleable NIZK) proof (of knowledge) that $\mathrm{pk} \in L_1$, π' is the (non-malleable NIZK) proof (of knowledge) that the ciphertext c' for which $\mathcal{B}_j$

$(j = 1, 2)$ is asking for the decryption is valid – i.e., $(c', \mathbf{pk}) \in L_2$ –, and π^* is the (non-malleable NIZK) proof (of knowledge) that $\mathbf{pk}^* \in L_1$. We use the proofs π' along with the trapdoor τ to allow $\mathcal{A}$ to answer to the decryption queries. Indeed, up to a negligible factor, $\mathcal{M}_2$ extracts the witnesses r, m and therefore $\mathcal{A}$ can correctly return m to the NM-CCA2* adversary.

Moreover, observe that since we are using a non-malleable NIZK PoK proof system then $\mathcal{M}_2(\cdot, \cdot, \cdot, \cdot)$ must extract (up to a negligible factor) the plaintext used by $\mathcal{B}_2(\cdot, \cdot, \cdot, \cdot)$ in the proof π^*. If it was not the case, then we could use $\mathcal{B}_2(\cdot, \cdot, \cdot, \cdot)$ to break the properties of the non-malleable NIZK proof system. Thus the operation of using the output of $\mathcal{M}_2(\cdot, \cdot, \cdot, \cdot)$ to generate the secret key $\mathbf{sk}^*$ corresponding to $\mathbf{pk}^*$ is well defined. The decryption with $\mathbf{sk}^*$ will thus give the actual plaintext vector behind $\mathbf{c}^*$.

The advantage of $\mathcal{A}$ is given by $\mathbf{Adv}_{\mathcal{PE}, \mathcal{A}}^{\text{ind}-\text{cpa}}(k) = |p_k(0) - p_k(1)|$ where, for $b \in \{0, 1\}$, we let

$$p_k(b) = \text{Prob}\left[(\mathbf{pk}, \mathbf{sk}) \leftarrow \mathcal{G}(1^k); (x_0, x_1, s') \leftarrow \mathcal{A}_1(\mathbf{pk}); c \leftarrow \mathcal{E}_{\mathbf{pk}}(x_b) : \right.$$

$$\left. \mathcal{A}_2(x_0, x_1, s', c) = 0 \right].$$

Also for $b \in \{0, 1\}$ we let[2]

$$p_k'(b) = \text{Prob}\left[(\mathbf{pk}, \mathbf{sk}) \leftarrow \mathcal{G}(1^k); (\Sigma, \tau) \leftarrow \mathcal{G}_\Sigma(1^k); \pi \leftarrow \mathcal{M}_1(\Sigma, \mathbf{pk}, \tau); \right.$$

$$(M, s) \leftarrow \mathcal{B}_1^{\mathcal{D}^{\mathbf{sk}(\cdot)}}((\mathbf{pk}, \pi), \Sigma); x_0, x_1 \leftarrow M; c \leftarrow \mathcal{E}_{\mathbf{pk}}(x_b);$$

$$(R, (\mathbf{pk}^*, \pi^*), \mathbf{c}^*) \leftarrow \mathcal{B}_2^{\mathcal{D}^{(c)}{\mathbf{sk}}(\cdot)}(M, PK, s, c, \Sigma); r^* \leftarrow \mathcal{M}_2(\Sigma, \tau, \mathbf{pk}^*, \pi^*);$$

$$(\mathbf{pk}^*, \mathbf{sk}^*) \leftarrow \mathcal{G}(r^*); \mathbf{x} = \mathcal{D}_{\mathbf{sk}^*}(\mathbf{c}^*); f = (c \notin \mathbf{c}^* \vee \mathbf{pk} \neq \mathbf{pk}^*) :$$

$$\left. f \wedge (\mathbf{x} \neq \perp) \wedge R(x_0, \mathbf{x}, (\mathbf{pk}, \pi), (\mathbf{pk}^*, \pi^*), \mathbf{c}^*, \Sigma) \right].$$

Now observe that $\mathcal{A}_2$ may return 0 either when $\mathbf{x}$ is R-related to x_0 or as a result of the coin flip. Thus we have:

$$\mathbf{Adv}_{\mathcal{PE}, \mathcal{A}}^{\text{ind}-\text{cpa}}(k) = |p_k(0) - p_k(1)| = \frac{1}{2}\left|p_k'(0) - p_k'(1)\right|.$$

We now observe that the experiment of $\mathcal{B}_2$ being given a ciphertext of x_1 and R-relating $\mathbf{x}$ to x_0 is exactly $\text{Expt}_{\mathcal{PE}', \mathcal{B}, \$}^{\text{nm}-\text{cca2}^*}(k)$. On the other hand, in the case in which $\mathcal{B}_2$ works on the ciphertext of x_0, we are looking at the experiment $\text{Expt}_{\mathcal{PE}', \mathcal{B}}^{\text{nm}-\text{cca2}^*}(k) = 1$. Therefore we obtain the following.

$$\mathbf{Adv}_{\mathcal{PE}', \mathcal{B}}^{\text{nm}-\text{cca2}^*}(k) = |p_k'(0) - p_k'(1)| = 2 \cdot \mathbf{Adv}_{\mathcal{PE}, \mathcal{A}}^{\text{ind}-\text{cpa}}(k).$$

---

[2] To simplify our notation, in the definition of $p_k'(b)$ we do not specify that the decryption queries of $\mathcal{B}$ are replied as in the description of the IND-CPA adversary $\mathcal{A}$.

Since $\mathcal{PE}$ is IND-CPA secure then $\mathbf{Adv}^{\text{ind}-\text{cpa}}_{\mathcal{PE},\,\mathcal{A}}(\cdot)$ is negligible. It follows that $\mathbf{Adv}^{\text{nm}-\text{cca2}^*}_{\mathcal{PE'},\,\mathcal{B}}(\cdot)$ is negligible.   □

We stress that we cannot use just one of the two languages above. Indeed, L_2 is needed because it allows an IND-CPA adversary to answer to the queries of an NM-CCA2* adversary. Moreover, we need L_1 to enforce the NM-CCA2* adversary to output a valid new public key $\mathbf{pk}^*$ (i.e., $\mathbf{pk}^*$ is the output of the key generation algorithm of $\mathcal{PE}$) for the component IND-CPA secure encryption scheme. One would be tempted to use the proof of knowledge contained in $\mathbf{c}^*$ – the ciphertext output of the NM-CCA2* adversary – to extract the corresponding plaintext and use it to evaluate the relation. This approach fails when $\mathbf{pk}^*$ is not valid since the NM-NIZK PoK extractor returns one of the messages for which $\mathbf{c}^*$ is the corresponding encryption but not necessarily the one that satisfies the relation.

Simulation-based NM-CCA2* security. We now discuss that our construction can be adapted to achieve the simulation-based notion of NM-CCA2* security. In particular, we will consider the following tool. We start by giving the definition of same-string ZK.

Definition 5 (Same-String Zero Knowledge). *We say that an NIZK argument system is* same-string *NIZK if the (unbounded) zero knowledge requirement above is replaced with the following requirement: there exists a negligible function ν such that for all k the following property holds.*

Same-string Zero Knowledge: *For all non-uniform probabilistic polynomial-time adversaries $\mathcal{A}$ we have that*
$|\text{Prob}\,[\,X = 1\,] - \text{Prob}\,[\,Y = 1\,]| \leq \nu(k)$, *where X and Y are as defined in (and all probabilities are taken over) the experiment $\texttt{Expt}(k)$ below:*

$$
\boxed{
\begin{array}{l}
\texttt{Expt}(k): \\
(\Sigma, \tau) \leftarrow \mathcal{S}_1(1^k) \\
X \leftarrow \mathcal{A}^{\mathcal{P}(\cdot,\cdot,\Sigma)}(\Sigma) \\
Y \leftarrow \mathcal{A}^{\mathcal{S}'(\cdot,\cdot,\Sigma,\tau)}(\Sigma)
\end{array}
}
$$

where $\mathcal{S}'(x, w, \Sigma, \tau) \overset{\text{def}}{=} \mathcal{S}_2(x, \Sigma, \tau)$. The distribution on Σ produced by $\mathcal{S}_1(1^k)$ is the uniform distribution over $\{0,1\}^{\ell(k)}$.

We refer to NIZK arguments that are both non-malleable and same-string as *robust NIZK* (as in [5]). We denote a robust NIZK Π as the following tuple: $\Pi = (\ell, \mathcal{P}, \mathcal{V}, \mathcal{S})$. We remark that the authors of [5] give a construction of a robust NIZK starting from a same-string NIZK proof of knowledge given that one-way functions exist.

The construction. We now show that in the above scheme by simply replacing the non-malleable NIZK proof of knowledge $\Pi = (\ell, \mathcal{P}, \mathcal{V}, \mathcal{S})$ by a robust NIZK $\Pi' = (\ell', \mathcal{P}', \mathcal{V}', \mathcal{S}')$ we obtain a scheme that satisfies the simulation-based definition of [4] (see Definition 2) adapted to the shared random string model.

First of all we argue why Construction 4 does not seem to be sufficient. The simulator S receives as input a pair $(\text{pk} = (\text{pk}', \pi), \Sigma)$ generates a fake SRS Σ' along with a trapdoor τ', and computes a new proof π' so that $\text{pk}'' = (\text{pk}', \pi')$ is a valid public key with respect to Σ'. Then S runs $\mathcal{A}$ on input (pk'', Σ') and can obviously answer to all its queries since knowledge of τ' allows S to decrypt all valid ciphertexts. Moreover S feeds to $\mathcal{A}$ the encryption c of a random message m as challenge. Finally $\mathcal{A}$ outputs a pair $(c^\star, \text{pk}^\star)$ that corresponds to the encryption of a messages $\tilde{m}$ related to m. However, the relation R receives as input also the public keys $\text{pk}'', \text{pk}^\star$ and Σ'. S could obviously decrypt the message $\tilde{m}$ encrypted in $c^\star$ and could compute an encryption of $\tilde{m}$ with respect to a new public key $\tilde{\text{pk}}$ and shared random string Σ (notice that S can not simply output the pair $(c^\star, \text{pk}^\star)$ since this is valid only with respect to Σ' while S needs to output a valid pair with respect to Σ). However even though the same message has been encrypted, the relation could not be satisfied as $\Sigma \neq \Sigma'$ and $\text{pk}^\star \neq \tilde{\text{pk}}$.

We fix this problem by strengthening the ingredient that we use in the construction: we replace the non-malleable NIZK by a robust NIZK. Robust NIZK considers non-malleable zero-knowledge arguments (i.e., computationally sound proofs) of knowledge where the simulator works using the same shared random string of the real game, still having a trapdoor that will allow it to compute simulated proofs and to extract witnesses from accepting proofs.

Concretely, S will run $\mathcal{A}$ precisely on input (pk, Σ) and will feed it the encryption c of a random message m. S decrypts A's queries by using τ and finally outputs the pair $(c^\star, \text{pk}^\star)$ given in output by $\mathcal{A}$. The indistinguishability of the output of the stand-alone S with respect to the man-in-the-middle $\mathcal{A}$ can be proved by using standard hybrid arguments.

We finally stress that the above simulator does not require access to a decryption oracle, therefore it satisfies the stronger notion of stand-alone simulation discussed in [4].

4   Interactive Non-black-box Complete Non-malleability

In this section we present a completely non-malleable encryption scheme using interaction and non-black-box techniques. Our construction can be compared to Fischlin's impossibility result. Indeed, that impossibility proof holds for black-box non-interactive encryption schemes, therefore it is still possible to relax either the need of interaction or the need of non-black-box techniques[3]. The construction we give is NM-CCA2* secure under both our game-based definition and under the simulation-based definition. Moreover, it is *stand-alone* (i.e., the simulator does not access to a decryption oracle) and requires sequential decryption queries (i.e., the decryption oracle sends its answers one-by-one, sequentially). We construct a non-black-box constant-round interactive completely non-malleable encryption scheme in the standard model using the recent technique by Pass and Rosen [16,17] that produced a constant-round NMZK argument of knowledge in the standard

---

[3] We stress that the techniques of [1,6] would potentially avoid the non-black-box techniques, but would produce a non-constant round complexity.

model. On top of this tool they showed also how to construct constant-round concurrent non-malleable commitments in the standard model by composing a commitment scheme with the NMZK argument of knowledge of the committed message. The same approach has been recently used in [18] where non-malleable witness indistinguishable argument systems are achieved by committing to an $\mathcal{NP}$ witness and then using the NMZK argument of knowledge to prove that the committed message satisfies an $\mathcal{NP}$ relation. We notice that by following the same approach, it is possible to first encrypt a message using an IND-CPA encryption scheme and then prove knowledge of the encrypted message with the NMZK argument of knowledge. While this gives NM-CPA* security, extra work is required to claim NM-CCA1* and NM-CCA2* security as in these last two cases, queries to a decryption oracle have to be taken into account.

Definitions for interactive encryption. The definitions for NM-ATK*-secure encryption for ATK $\in$ {CPA, CCA1, CCA2} given in Section 2 assume that an encryption and a decryption (oracle answer) is computed non-interactively by an efficient algorithm. An interactive encryption is instead a two-party protocol. Therefore, in order to recycle all the previous definitions we have to specify the role of the parties in all the steps described in Definition 1.

An *interactive encryption* is a protocol played between a sender sen and a receiver rec. At the end of the protocol, if both parties behave correctly, the exchanged transcript corresponds to an encryption of a message computed by sen for rec under a public key pk.

Non-malleable interactive encryption concerns a man-in-the-middle adversary $\mathcal{A}$ that controls the communication between sen and rec (e.g., he can delay, discard, scramble, and update the messages, as defined for non-malleable protocols in [1]). $\mathcal{A}$ aims at computing encryptions for rec of messages that are related to the message encrypted by sen. The goal of a non-malleable interactive encryption scheme is to preserve security against such man-in-the-middle attacks, thus making useless the attack of $\mathcal{A}$. Different definitions of interactive non-malleable encryption can be given by possibly giving to $\mathcal{A}$ access to decryption oracles, thus producing the variations CPA, CCA1 and CCA2. In order to have a definition of interactive encryption following the standard non-interactive Definition 1, we consider the framework used by Katz in [19,20]. We sketch here the setting on which we base our protocol, more details can be in the full version of the paper.

$\mathcal{A}$ has access to an encryption oracle $\mathcal{O}_E = \mathcal{E}_{pk}(\cdot)$ that plays as sender while $\mathcal{A}$ plays as receiver. The goal of $\mathcal{A}$ is to produce the description of a relation R, a new public key pk* and encryptions of messages that are related through R to the message encrypted by $\mathcal{O}_E$. In order to do that, $\mathcal{A}$ plays the protocol with honest receivers potentially interleaving (even concurrently) these interactions and the one with $\mathcal{O}_E$.

The above sketched discussion only concerns NM-CPA* security given in Definition 1 but adapted for interactive encryption. Instead, for the notions of NM-CCA1* and NM-CCA2* security the adversary $\mathcal{A}$ has to include the capability of accessing to a decryption oracle. Such accesses (e.g., oracle queries) are interactive encryptions where the adversary acts as a sender and the decryption oracle $\mathcal{O}_D = \mathcal{D}_{\mathbf{sk}}(\cdot)$ plays the role of a receiver. Indeed, an oracle query is an encryption sent by the adversary (and thus the interactive encryption protocol is played) plus an answer of the oracle. Each time a given interactive encryption with $\mathcal{O}_D$ is completed, the decryption oracle computes the decryption (using the secret key) and sends the resulting message (or a special symbol, if the transcript was invalid) to the adversary.

The definition of NM-CCA1* security assumes that $\mathcal{A}$ has first access to the decryption oracle $\mathcal{O}_D$ and then, once all interactions with $\mathcal{O}_D$ have been completed, $\mathcal{A}$ starts the game above, choosing the messages distribution M and receiving an encryption from $\mathcal{O}_E$ while computing encryptions for honest receivers. For the case of NM-CCA1* security we therefore assume a time barrier between all decryption queries and the remaining protocols. These accesses to $\mathcal{O}_D$ correspond to queries to $\mathcal{O}_1$ in Definition 1.

The definition of NM-CCA2* security instead allows $\mathcal{A}$ to run decryption queries even during and/or after receiving the challenge encryption from $\mathcal{O}_E$. Obviously some limitations must be placed on the adversary access to the decryption oracle or else the adversary may simply forward messages between $\mathcal{O}_E$ and $\mathcal{O}_D$ and therefore trivially succeeds in computing encryptions of messages that are related to the challenge plaintext. We therefore require that the transcript of the encryptions of $\mathcal{O}_E$ must be different from the ones of the decryption queries. These additional accesses to $\mathcal{O}_D$ correspond to queries to $\mathcal{O}_2$ in Definition 1.

The above definition gives to the adversary $\mathcal{A}$ the power of controlling the communication channel and thus of deciding the schedule of the messages of different interactions involving different parties (different honest receivers, the encryption oracle and the decryption oracle). It is therefore obvious to assume that interactions with different parties can be run concurrently. The only restriction we have is on the interactions with the decryption oracle that we required to be sequential. Notice that this is also applicable in practice since $\mathcal{O}_D$ is a stateful algorithm that can simply manage a queue of requests to satisfies them one by one.

We finally say that an encryption scheme is self-certifiable, if there exists an efficient algorithm that on input a public key outputs 1 if it holds that any valid ciphertext corresponds to only one plaintext and 0 otherwise.

Theorem 6. *Under the assumption that there exists a family of claw-free permutations and that self-certifiable IND-CPA secure encryption schemes exist, there exists an interactive (constant-round) non-black-box NM-CCA2* secure encryption scheme with sequential decryption queries.*

For lack of space we show the construction in Fig. 1 (where we let $\Pi_{\mathsf{tag}} = \langle P_{\mathsf{tag}}, V_{\mathsf{tag}} \rangle$ be the tag-based constant-round one-left many-right concurrent non-malleable statistical zero-knowledge argument of knowledge of [16,17] and $SS = (\mathsf{SG}, \mathsf{Sig}, \mathsf{SVer})$ be a one-time secure signature scheme of [21]). The proof can be found in the full version of the paper, where we also show in a separate theorem that the same protocol also satisfies the simulation-based notion of complete non-malleability. We remark that the proof exploits the power of the simulator and the extractor of the statistical non-malleable zero knowledge argument of knowledge of [17,16]. In particular the extractor will be used for answering to the decryption queries, and, since it requires rewinds, we assume that decryption queries are answered sequentially, so that we do not need to face the known problems of concurrent zero knowledge [22].

We stress that a public key of our scheme is the public key of a self-certifiable IND-CPA secure encryption scheme.

---

1. **sen** sets $c \leftarrow \mathcal{E}_{pk}(w)$ where w is the k-bit message to encrypt.
2. **sen** sets $(ssk, spk) \leftarrow SG(1^n)$.
3. **sen** sends the pair (c, spk) to **rec**.
4. **sen** and **rec** run protocol $\Pi_{spk} = \langle P_{spk}, V_{spk} \rangle$ where **sen** proves knowledge of w such that $c \leftarrow \mathcal{E}_{pk}(w)$.
5. **sen** computes a signature $\tau \leftarrow Sig(pk \circ trans, ssk)$ where **trans** is the transcript exchanged so far and sends it to **rec**.
6. **rec** accepts the encryption iff $SVer(pk \circ trans, \tau, spk) = 1$ and V_{spk} outputs 1.

Fig. 1. Constant-Round Completely Non-Malleable Encryption

We now only give an intuition of the proof.

Proof's sketch. Assume by contradiction that an adversary $\mathcal{A}$ succeeds in computing encryptions of related messages under a new public and a new relation of its choice. Therefore $\mathcal{A}$ has non-negligible success of generating an encryption $c_0^\star$ of a message $m_0^\star$ related to m_0 on input an encryption c_0 of m_0 and an encryption $c_1^\star$ of a message $m_1^\star$ related to m_1 on input an encryption c_1 of m_1.

Let Expt_0 and Expt_3 the two above experiments, we can consider two hybrid experiments $\text{Expt}_1, \text{Expt}_2$ where instead of running $\mathcal{A}$, we run the simulator S associated to the statistical non-malleable zero knowledge argument of knowledge of [17,16] giving it access to $\mathcal{A}$ and c_0 in Expt_1 and access to $\mathcal{A}$ and c_1 in Expt_2.

By the statistical zero-knowledge property of this tool, we have that experiment Expt_1 in indistinguishable with respect to Expt_0.

A distinguisher between Expt_1 and Expt_2 can be used for breaking the semantic security of the (non-interactive) encryption scheme used as subprotocol. This can be done by feeding to $\mathcal{A}$ a challenge c that can be either an encryption of m_0 or an encryption of m_1 under the encryption scheme used as subprotocol. Then the extractor of [17,16] obtains the encrypted message and can therefore be used to break with non-negligible advantage the semantic security of the encryption scheme.

Finally, Expt_2 and Expt_3 are indistinguishable for the same reason that make indistinguishable Expt_0 and Expt_1.

The full proof considers other issues as concurrency and adaptiveness. Moreover it is shown that the protocol satisfies also the simulation-based definition, as a simulator can be designed by simply sending an encryption of any message (say 0^k) and then using the simulator of the NMZK argument of knowledge. □

Concluding Remarks. In this paper we explored the notion of complete non-malleability for public-key encryption schemes. We have given new definitions and proved relations among these notions. Finally, we have shown new constructions that achieve these security notions without using random oracles.

Acknowledgments

We wish to thank Alex Dent for his useful comments on an early draft of this paper. Moreover we thank the anonymous reviewers for their accurate suggestions and Pino Persiano for useful discussions about non-malleability.

The work of the authors has been supported in part through the FP6 program under contract FP6-1596 AEOLUS and in part by the European Commission through the IST program under Contract IST-2002-507932 ECRYPT.

References

1. Dolev, D., Dwork, C., Naor, M.: Non-malleable cryptography. In: Proc. of STOC, pp. 542–552 (1991)
2. Sahai, A.: Non-Malleable Non-Interactive Zero Knowledge and Adaptive Chosen-Ciphertext Security. In: 40th Symposium on Foundations of Computer Science (FOCS 1999), 1109 Spring Street, Suite 300, Silver Spring, MD 20910, USA, pp. 543–553. IEEE Computer Society Press, Los Alamitos (1999)
3. Bellare, M., Desai, A., Pointcheval, D., Rogaway, P.: Relations among notions of security for public-key encryption schemes. In: Krawczyk, H. (ed.) CRYPTO 1998. LNCS, vol. 1462, pp. 26–45. Springer, Heidelberg (1998)
4. Fischlin, M.: Completely non-malleable schemes. In: Caires, L., et al. (eds.) ICALP 2005. LNCS, vol. 3580, pp. 779–790. Springer, Heidelberg (2005)
5. De Santis, A., Di Crescenzo, G., Ostrovsky, R., Persiano, G., Sahai, A.: Robust non-interactive zero knowledge. In: Kilian, J. (ed.) CRYPTO 2001. LNCS, vol. 2139, pp. 566–598. Springer, Heidelberg (2001)
6. Barak, B., Prabhakaran, M., Sahai, A.: Concurrent non-malleable zero knowledge. In: 47th, IEEE Computer Society Press, Los Alamitos (2006)
7. Bellare, M., Boldyreva, A., Palacio, A.: An uninstantiable random-oracle-model scheme for a hybrid-encryption problem. In: Cachin, C., Camenisch, J.L. (eds.) EUROCRYPT 2004. LNCS, vol. 3027, pp. 171–188. Springer, Heidelberg (2004)
8. Canetti, R., Goldreich, O., Halevi, S.: The random oracle methodology, revisited (preliminary version). In: STOC, pp. 209–218 (1998)
9. Nielsen, J.B.: Separating random oracle proofs from complexity theoretic proofs: The non-committing encryption case. In: Yung, M. (ed.) CRYPTO 2002. LNCS, vol. 2442, pp. 111–126. Springer, Heidelberg (2002)
10. Goldwasser, S., Kalai, Y.T.: On the (in)security of the fiat-shamir paradigm. In: FOCS (2003)
11. Cramer, R., Shoup, V.: A Practical Public-Key Cryptosystem Provably Secure Against Adaptive Chosen Ciphertext Attack. In: Krawczyk, H. (ed.) CRYPTO 1998. LNCS, vol. 1462, pp. 13–25. Springer, Heidelberg (1998)

12. Bellare, M., Rogaway, P.: Optimal asymmetric encryption. In: Helleseth, T. (ed.) EUROCRYPT 1993. LNCS, vol. 765, pp. 92–111. Springer, Heidelberg (1994)
13. Fujisaki, E., Okamoto, T., Pointcheval, D., Stern, J.: Rsa-oaep is secure under the rsa assumption. In: Kilian, J. (ed.) CRYPTO 2001. LNCS, vol. 2139, pp. 260–274. Springer, Heidelberg (2001)
14. Bellare, M., Sahai, A.: Non-malleable encryption: Equivalence between two notions, and an indistinguishability-based characterization. In: Wiener, M.J. (ed.) CRYPTO 1999. LNCS, vol. 1666, pp. 519–536. Springer, Heidelberg (1999)
15. Fischlin, M.: Completely non-malleable schemes. Technical report, Full version of [4] (2005)
16. Pass, R., Rosen, A.: New and improved constructions of non-malleable cryptographic protocols. In: Proc. of STOC, pp. 533–542 (2005)
17. Pass, R., Rosen, A.: Concurrent non-malleable commitments. In: Proc. of FOCS, pp. 563–572 (2005)
18. Ostrovsky, R., Persiano, G., Visconti, I.: Concurrent non-malleable witness indistinguishability and its applications. Technical Report TR06-095, ECCC (2006)
19. Katz, J.: Efficient Cryptographic Protocols Preventing Man-in-the-Middel Attacks, Ph.D. Thesis. Columbia University (2002)
20. Katz, J.: Efficient and Non-Malleable Proofs of Plaintext Knowledge and Applications. In: Biham, E. (ed.) EUROCRYPT 2003. LNCS, vol. 2656, pp. 211–228. Springer, Heidelberg (2003)
21. Rompel, J.: One-way functions are necessary and sufficient for secure signatures. In: Proc. of STOC, pp. 387–394 (1990)
22. Dwork, C., Naor, M., Sahai, A.: Concurrent Zero-Knowledge. In: 30th ACM Symposium on Theory of Computing (STOC 1998), pp. 409–418. ACM Press, New York (1998)

Cryptographic Test Correction

Eric Levieil and David Naccache

École normale supérieure
Département d'informatique, Équipe de cryptographie
45 rue d'Ulm, F-75230, Paris CEDEX 05, France
{eric.levieil,david.naccache}@ens.fr

Abstract. Multiple choice questionnaires (MCQs) are a widely-used assessment procedure where examinees are asked to select one or more choices from a list.

This invited talk[1] explores the possibility of transferring a part of the MCQ's correction burden to the *examinee* when sophisticated technological means (*e.g.* optical character recognition systems) are unavailable. Evidently, such schemes must make cheating difficult or at least conspicuous.

We did not manage to devise a fully satisfactory solution (cheating strategies do exist) – but our experiments with a first clumsy system encouraged us to develop alternative MCQ formats and analyze their performance and security.

1 Foreword

Three years ago I moved from industry to academia.

At the first staff meeting, I discovered that the university's policy[2] was to assign first-year amphitheater courses to the newest staff members. I was delighted by the perspective of lecturing computer science to 600 students.

A day later, I got a call from the Reprography Department. The reprographer wanted to ascertain that the test's camera-ready copy will reach him at least a month before the test. I suddenly realized that my Ph.D. students and I will have to spend our winter vacations correcting a heap of 600 multiple choice questionnaires (MCQs).

While designing the MCQ, an intriguing question started taunting my mind: Could the freshmen "chip-farm" help correcting the heap of copies?

After all – since twenty years we routinely witness all sorts of miracles in cryptography: Alice and Bob regularly prove knowledge without revealing secrets, anonymously say "no", flip coins over the phone, transfer bits obliviously and so on.

Could any of these wonderful tools help?

I challenged my Ph.D. students to imagine methods for safely delegating to the examinees the burden of MCQ correction.

The result is the cryptographic curiosity presented here.

David Naccache

---

[1] This *is not* a refereed research paper.

[2] Université Paris II Panthéon-Assas.

R. Cramer (Ed.): PKC 2008, LNCS 4939, pp. 85–100, 2008.

2   Introduction

MCQs are an assessment procedure, invented in 1914 by Frederick J. Kelly, where examinees are asked to select one or more choices from a list. MCQs are widely used in education, opinion polls, elections, and many other areas.

This paper explores the possibility of safely transferring a part of the MCQ's correction burden to the *examinee*, when sophisticated technological means, such as optical character recognition (OCR) systems, are unavailable.

We regard an MCQ as a list of n questions $\{\texttt{question}_1, \ldots, \texttt{question}_n\}$.

Each $\texttt{question}_i$ is associated to two potential choices $\texttt{answer}_{i,0}$ and $\texttt{answer}_{i,1}$, of which only one is correct. We denote by c the MCQ's answer-vector, namely:

$$c_i = 1 \text{ iff } \texttt{answer}_{i,1} \text{ is correct.}$$

The student is required to generate an answer-vector $\tilde{c}$:

$$\tilde{c}_i = 1 \text{ iff the student thinks that } \texttt{answer}_{i,1} \text{ is correct.}$$

And the corrector, usually the newest member of the faculty staff, computes the mark:

$$m = n - \sum_{i=1}^{n} (c_i \oplus \tilde{c}_i)$$

2.1   Cryptographic Test Correction

To transfer the correction burden to the examinee, the MCQ designer generates a secret key k and computes, using an *encoding algorithm* $\mathcal{E}$, a set of $2n$ public values $v_{i,j}$ where $1 \le i \le n$, $j \in \{0,1\}$:

$$\{v_{i,j}\} = \mathcal{E}(c, k)$$

Students are instructed to:

- Generate $\tilde{c}$ as before but, in addition, apply an easily computable *accumulation algorithm* $\mathcal{M}$ to $\{v_{i,j}\}$ and $\tilde{c}$.
- Write down the result $t = \mathcal{M}(\{v_{i,j}\}, \tilde{c})$ on the questionnaire.

The examiner uses a (potentially complex) *scoring algorithm* $\mathcal{C}$ to compute the student's final mark m:

$$m = \mathcal{C}(t, k) = \begin{cases} n - \sum_{i=1}^{n}(c_i \oplus \tilde{c}_i) & \text{if } \exists \tilde{c} \text{ such that } t = \mathcal{M}(\{v_{i,j}\}, \tilde{c}) \\ \bot & \text{otherwise} \end{cases}$$

We call $\{\mathcal{E}, \mathcal{M}, \mathcal{C}\}$ a *Cryptographic Test Correction* (CTC) scheme.

2.2   Desirable Features

Ideally, we would like $\{\mathcal{E}, \mathcal{M}, \mathcal{C}\}$ to have the following features:

Security: We say that an algorithm $\mathcal{A}$ has a CTC *cheating advantage* ϵ if:

$$\left| \Pr[\mathcal{C}(\mathcal{A}(\{v_{i,j}\}, \tilde{c}), k) > n - \sum_{i=1}^{n} c_i \oplus \tilde{c}_i] - \frac{1}{2} \right| \geq \epsilon$$

$\{\mathcal{E}, \mathcal{M}, \mathcal{C}\}$ is $\{w, \epsilon\}$-*secure* if no algorithm requiring w basic calculator operations (*i.e.* $+, -, \times, \div$) has a CTC cheating advantage ϵ.

In other words, we require that even if a cheating student knows the correct answers to all the questions but one, inferring the missing answer from $\{v_{i,j}\}$, or (more generally) manipulating t to artificially increase m is unfeasible given the simple calculator authorized by the university's regulations (Figure 1) and the test's limited duration.

Unlike e-cash or e-voting protocols, CTC does not seem to require protection against colluding parties (examinees cannot communicate). However, we do need some form of limited resistance against adaptive attacks as students knowing u correct answers can potentially generate 2^u valid t-values corresponding to marks expectedly[3] ranging between zero and $\frac{(n+u)}{2}$.

Efficiency: Trivially, one can design a secure CTC by assigning to the $v_{i,j}$ successive powers of two or zeros. *i.e.*:

$$v_{i,j} = \begin{cases} 0 & \text{if } j = 0 \\ 2^{i-1} & \text{if } j = 1 \end{cases}$$

The encoding $v_{i,j} = j \times 2^i$ is secure but inefficient. The size of t, *i.e.* n bits, is obviously an *overkill* as we do not need to convey to the examiner the *precise* answer vector $\tilde{c}$ but only the Hamming distance between c and $\tilde{c}$ (a quantity of information encodable in $\log_2 n$ bits).

Denoting by T the maximal bit length of t we require that $T < n$.

T measures the CTC's efficiency as it represents the number of digits that the corrector will need to key into his computer per corrected form.

As the theoretical foundations were ready, we started thinking about implementing CTCs.

3   Practical Experiments with an Insecure and Clumsy CTC

A simplified CTC was tested on 550 economics freshmen[4]. To avoid unresolvable complaints and computational errors, students were requested to both tick the correct answers and use the CTC. Ticked answers were used whenever $\mathcal{C}$ returned $\perp$ (27 cases), when a statistical alert occurred (unrecorded number of cases) or when the student didn't sum up the $v_{i,j}$ at all (79 cases).

---

[3] The student can *force* part of the MCQ to contribute any precise number of points $\leq u$. Answers to the rest of the MCQ will result in an expected contribution of $\frac{(n-u)}{2}$ points.

[4] Examinees were given additional thirty minutes to account for the extra computational burden.

Fig. 1. Authorized Calculator (10-Digit Precision, Restricted to $+, -, \times, \div$)

We made the following *risk management* assumptions:

- As modular arithmetic was not part of the students' curriculum we assumed that the theoretical tools necessary for cheating were not at the average student's command.
- No parameters or specifications were revealed and a form of psychological warfare was used: we subtly hinted that the scheme is "...probably very resilient to cheating...".
- A cheater who would have discovered[5] one of the (many) existing cheating strategies would have anyway obtained an excellent mark given the course's subject matter[6].

3.1 Description

Generate five integers $\{\rho, k, g > nk, p > (n+1)g, e\}$ such that $\gcd(e, p) = 1$.

The authorized pocket-calculator must be able to handle at least the number $(\rho + 1)np$.

Prepare the following values:

- Pick n random bits $\{b_1, \ldots, b_n\}$ and define $\epsilon_{i,b_i} = 0$ and $\epsilon_{i,1-b_i} = 1$.
- For $1 \le i \le n$ and $j \in \{0, 1\}$ generate randomly $0 \le r_{i,j} \le \rho$.
- For $1 \le i \le n$ generate randomly $0 \le a_i < p$.

---

[5] *E.g.* given the scheme's additive nature.

[6] Introduction to Computer Science.

We denote by $\tau_i = (\neg c_i \oplus \tilde{c}_i)k$, in other words:

$$\tau_i = \begin{cases} k & \text{if the student's answer to question } i \text{ is correct} \\ 0 & \text{if the student's answer to question } i \text{ is incorrect} \end{cases}$$

and define:

$$v_{i,j} = ((a_i + (\neg c_i \oplus j)k + g\epsilon_{i,j})\, e \mod p) + r_{i,j} \times p$$

Students were instructed to sum the $v_{i,j}$ corresponding to their answers and *answer randomly* whenever they don't know the answer[7].

The examiner computes: $(t \times e^{-1} - (\sum_{i=1}^{n} a_i) \mod p)$ which is $\sum_{i=1}^{n}(\tau_i + g\epsilon_{i,\tilde{c}_i}) \in \mathbb{N}$.

This is easily checked by bounding:

$$0 < \sum_{i=1}^{n}(\tau_i + g\epsilon_{i,\tilde{c}_i}) < n(k+g) = g + n \times g < p$$

We therefore recover the exact value:

$$t' = t \times e^{-1} - \left(\sum_{i=1}^{n} a_i\right) \mod p = \sum_{i=1}^{n}(\tau_i + g\epsilon_{i,\tilde{c}_i}) = mk + g\sum_{i=1}^{n}\epsilon_{i,\tilde{c}_i} = mk + gq$$

where:

$$0 \le q = \sum_{i=1}^{n}\epsilon_{i,\tilde{c}_i} \le n$$

but $mk \le nk < g$ hence we can retrieve mk and q with no ambiguity.

$$q = \left\lfloor \frac{t'}{g} \right\rfloor \quad \text{and} \quad m = \frac{t' - qg}{k}$$

If $m \notin \mathbb{N}$ or $m \notin [0, n]$ or $q \notin [0, n]$ return $\bot$ (*i.e.* trigger a manual form verification). The odds to hit a multiple of k by picking t at random are $\frac{1}{k}$.

Implementation values and a marking example are given in Appendix A.

3.2   Statistical Analysis

Unfortunately, this scheme is insecure. Namely, if a student knows the algorithm's specifications, then several efficient cheating strategies exist. For instance the cheater may identify one correct answer, say i, subtract the incorrect $v_{i,j}$ from the correct one and obtain a "clean" encoding of $+k$:

$$\Delta = (k + \epsilon g)e + \alpha p \quad \text{where} \quad \epsilon \in \{-1, 1\}$$

---

[7] The rationale is both the need to collect all the a_is for decryption to work, and preventing "the cryptanalyst" from generating t-values corresponding to *precisely* chosen marks.

Fig. 2. 550 Distrusted Correctors (Right) Filling 550 Cryptographic MCQs (Left)

Fig. 3. The University's Grand Amphithéatre

The cheater will then pick random answers to the entire questionnaire, thereby reaching an expected average mark of $\frac{n}{2}$ and artificially improve it by adding a multiple of Δ.

To overcome this (to some extent) we used a basic statistical test on q. Namely, if q does not exceed a given likelihood threshold, we treat the form as suspicious and verify it manually. Indeed, if the cheater brutally adds $\mu\Delta$ to t the additional $\pm\mu g$ will start showing up as a statistical bias in the distribution of q.

Evidently, a very good student could use much smarter cheating strategies based on the linear combination of several Δ values derived from different questions weighted by moderate coefficients but we considered such a strategy unlikely given our risk management assumptions.

A given $v_{i,j}$ has a $\frac{1}{2}$ probability to contain no g and a $\frac{1}{2}$ probability to contain g. Thus, the probability that q takes a given value $0 \le d \le n$ is simply:

$$\Pr[q = d] = \binom{n}{d} \times \frac{1}{2^n}$$

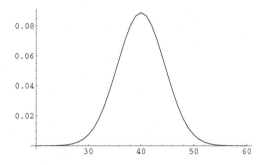

Fig. 4. $\Pr[q = d] = \binom{80}{d} \times 2^{-80}$

That is, for $n = 80$:

Table 1. $\Pr[q = d] = \binom{80}{d} \times 2^{-80}$

d	$\Pr[\,|q - n/2| \le d\,]$	d	$\Pr[\,|q - n/2| \le d\,]$	d	$\Pr[\,|q - n/2| \le d\,]$
0	0.08893	7	0.90709	14	0.99895
1	0.26245	8	0.94334	15	0.99955
2	0.42357	9	0.96701	16	0.99982
3	0.56596	10	0.98168	17	0.99993
4	0.68569	11	0.99032	18	0.99997
5	0.78148	12	0.99513	19	0.99999
6	0.85436	13	0.99768	20	1.00000

We hence triggered, in addition, a manual verification whenever $|q - 40| \ge 7$.

We conjecture that no student tried to cheat but the scheme's clumsiness and poor security performances motivated the quest for alternative CTC mechanisms – some of which we describe in the next section.

4   Alternative CTC Mechanisms

An alternative line of research is the development of new MCQ mechanisms. This section describes such a scheme – called *Interval Estimation* MCQs (IEMCQs).

Again, question$_i$ is associated to two potential choices answer$_{i,0}$ and answer$_{i,1}$, of which only one is correct. answer$_{i,0}$ is printed in *blue* while answer$_{i,1}$ is printed in *red*[8].

The test's idea consists in having the student determine the (correct) number of (correct) red answers.

In other words, the student's output is a sequence of three digits: the number of red answers, the number of blue answers and (implicitly) the difference between n and the sum of the previous two, *i.e.* the number of unsolved questions. This output can be encoded using only two integers – we choose to ask for an interval containing the number of red answers.

---

[8] The use of colors is not mandatory. Any form of distinction between answers will do (*e.g.* preceding answers by symbols such as ♡ or ♠ *etc.*).

Assume, for example, that $n = 9$ and that the examinee identified 2 reds and 3 blues, the student's answer will be $[2, 6]$. This notation means that the student thinks that there are at least 2 reds and at most $6 = 9 - 3$ reds. The low and high bounds will be denoted by a and c (here $a = 2$ and $c = 6$) while b will denote the correct answer, *i.e.* the precise number of reds. In other words, $[a, c]$ reads as "*I hope that $a \leq b \leq c$*". The interval's narrowness reflects the examinee's knowledge.

Evidently, if questions are independent, we would expect $b \simeq \frac{n}{2}$. Hence, we must first pick b randomly in $[0, n]$ and color the IEMCQ accordingly. In practice, we recommend $n = 9$, as this shrinks answers to two decimal digits (compact notation) and allows approaching 100 points using eleven question-packs. Note that, unlike additive CTCs, filling an IEMCQ does not require a pocket calculator.

Mapping $[a, c]$ to a mark (scoring) is the most delicate part, as the scoring function must:

- faithfully reflect the student's knowledge.
- be fairly resilient to statistical attacks.
- and have a small standard deviation.

In addition – we would like IEMCQs to allow students who know answers with sufficiently high probability (say 80%) to continue benefiting from this knowledge.

As these objectives are independent and incomparable, an "ideal" scoring function might not exist. We hence looked for functions that *reasonably comply* with the above objectives. The following proposals are thus examples and not reference designs.

We will start with a basic scoring function $\mathcal{C}_1$ and refine it progressively, explaining at each step the rationale of our successive refinements. To simplify calculations we assume that a correct answer is rewarded by a point while an incorrect answer is penalized by a point.

4.1   Notations and Definitions

We denote by $\chi_{a,c}(x)$ the Heaviside function:

$$\chi_{a,c}(x) = \begin{cases} 1 & \text{if } x \in [a, c] \\ 0 & \text{otherwise} \end{cases}$$

and by $d_{a,c}(x)$ the distance between x and the interval $[a, c]$, *i.e.*:

$$d_{a,c}(x) = (1 - \chi_{a,c}(x)) \max(a - x, x - c)$$

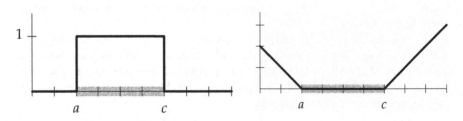

Fig. 5.A. The Heaviside Function $\chi_{a,c}(x)$ **Fig. 5.B.** The Distance Function $d_{a,c}(x)$

We also define two auxiliary variables:

$$\Delta = n + a - c \quad \text{and} \quad \delta = \begin{cases} \left| \frac{a}{\Delta} - \frac{b}{n} \right| & \text{if } \Delta \neq 0 \\ 0 & \text{if } \Delta = 0 \end{cases}$$

Δ is the number of possibilities that the student has ruled out.

δ expresses the difference between the ratio of reds estimated by the student ($\frac{a}{\Delta}$) and the *actual* ratio of reds ($\frac{b}{n}$) in the IEMCQ.

4.2 Heaviside Scoring

Heaviside scoring is defined as:

$$\mathcal{C}_1(n, a, b, c) = \Delta + (\chi_{a,c}(b) - 1)(n + 1)$$

Intuitively, $\mathcal{C}_1$ correlates the student's mark to the number of possibilities ruled-out. The role of the *penalty component* $(\chi_{a,c}(b) - 1)(n + 1)$ is to equate the expectation of random guessing to zero.

$\mathcal{C}_1$ complies with all criteria but resilience to statistical attacks. Indeed, a cheater could use the proportion of reds he spots as an estimate (sample) of the actual ratio of reds in the IEMCQ (IEMCQ "redness") and narrow his interval accordingly. This might significantly optimize his mark (*e.g.* by +20%).

For example, if the cheater successfully detected 3 reds and no blues amongst $n = 9$, the risk taken by betting that the unknown answers contain 2 more reds is moderate. We call such cheaters "narrowers".

4.3 Distance Scoring

In addition, $\mathcal{C}_1$'s penalty component is insensitive to the *magnitude of mistakes*. After all, it would be desirable to penalize a $\{[a, c] = [1, 4], b = 5\}$ less than a $\{[a, c] = [1, 4], b = 9\}$.

While it seems clear that gradual penalty implies using $d_{a,c}(x)$, there seems to be no obvious way to tune the penalty function (other than increasing penalty as $d_{a,c}(x)$ grows). We therefore used the probability $\varphi(d)$ to miss b by d to fine-tune a linear penalty coefficient γ_1:

$$\mathcal{C}_2(n, a, b, c) = \Delta - \gamma_1 (n + 1) d_{a,c}(b)$$

Note that $\varphi(x)$ reflects the test's hardness (*i.e.* depending on *pedagogic* factors).

Typically, the configurations $\varphi(1) = \varphi(2) = \frac{1}{2}$ or $\{\varphi(1) = \frac{6}{10}, \varphi(2) = \frac{3}{10}, \varphi(3) = \frac{1}{10}\}$ are $\mathcal{C}_1$-compatible when $\gamma_1 = \frac{2}{3}$. We recommend to adopt this value of γ_1 – a value we used in our simulations hereafter.

A second design objective is to discourage narrowers. Indeed, an examinee's answer is not only an interval. It also expresses a redness approximation.

In general a (non exaggerating) narrower will score the same Δ as an honest examinee, however, the narrower's redness estimate will be less accurate. In other words, his δ will be *expectedly bigger*. We thus use δ to damp Δ:

$$\mathcal{C}_3(n, a, b, c) = \Delta(1 - \delta) - \gamma_1 (n + 1) d_{a,c}(b)$$

4.4   Father Christmas Scoring

During the French revolution, different strategies for abolishing birth privileges were debated. Proposals ranged from forbidding titles to exiling noblemen or... making titles available to anybody *i.e.* eliminate distinctions by devaluation.

All our scoring functions allow cheaters to estimate the IEMCQ's redness. While endeavoring to limit the cheaters' redness estimation abilities (using δ) we also reduce the cheaters' advantage by devaluation: namely, we award automatically to any examinee the cheaters' redness approximation advantage. We call this "*Father Christmas Scoring*", as we distribute extra points to all examinees.

$$\mathcal{C}_4(n,a,b,c) = \begin{cases} \mathcal{C}_3(n,a,b,c) + \gamma_2(c-a) & \text{if } b = c = n \text{ or } a = b = 0 \\ \mathcal{C}_3(n,a,b,c) & \text{otherwise} \end{cases}$$

$\mathcal{C}_4$'s side-effect is an increase in standard deviation, but this increase can be controlled by γ_2. We propose to use $\gamma_2 = \frac{1}{2}$.

4.5   Features

Accuracy. Table 2 shows the correlation between the mark obtained by considering a test as a traditional MCQ and as an IEMCQ scored with $\mathcal{C}_\ell$ (for $\ell = 1, 3, 4$).
The quantity:

$$\mu_{k,n} = \sum_{a=0}^{k} \sum_{b=0}^{n} \binom{b}{a}\binom{n-b}{k-a} = (k+1)\binom{n+1}{k+1}$$

counts the number of different ways in which k correct answers can be potentially distributed between a reds and $k - a$ blues[9]. We can hence compute $\text{Av}[\mathcal{C}_\ell, k, n]$, the average mark of an examinee knowing k answers out of n in an IEMCQ scored with $\mathcal{C}_\ell$:

$$\text{Av}[\mathcal{C}_\ell, k, n] = \frac{1}{n \times \mu_{k,n}} \sum_{a=0}^{k} \sum_{b=0}^{n} \binom{b}{a}\binom{n-b}{k-a} \mathcal{C}_\ell(n, a, b, n-k+a)$$

Note that for $\mathcal{C}_1$ averaging is unnecessary as $\mathcal{C}_1$ coincides with scores obtained using a traditional MCQ.

It appears that all scoring functions approximate quite faithfully a traditional MCQ (plain black line).

Narrowers' Advantage. Table 3 lists $\text{Ad}[\mathcal{C}_\ell, k, n]$, the average advantage of a narrower over an honest examinee assuming that both know k answers (of which a are red).

---

[9] μ_k is the denominator of the k-th element in line n in Leibniz's Harmonic triangle.

Table 2. Average Accuracy for $n = 9$ and $n = 12$

k	$\mathrm{Av}[\mathcal{C}_1, k, 9]$	$\mathrm{Av}[\mathcal{C}_3, k, 9]$	$\mathrm{Av}[\mathcal{C}_4, k, 9]$
0	0.000	0.000	0.100
1	0.111	0.078	0.167
2	0.222	0.180	0.257
3	0.333	0.286	0.353
4	0.444	0.394	0.450
5	0.556	0.505	0.550
6	0.667	0.620	0.653
7	0.778	0.735	0.757
8	0.889	0.856	0.867
9	1.000	1.000	1.000

k	$\mathrm{Av}[\mathcal{C}_1, k, 12]$	$\mathrm{Av}[\mathcal{C}_3, k, 12]$	$\mathrm{Av}[\mathcal{C}_4, k, 12]$
0	0.000	0.000	0.077
1	0.083	0.058	0.128
2	0.167	0.133	0.197
3	0.250	0.212	0.269
4	0.333	0.292	0.343
5	0.417	0.373	0.418
6	0.500	0.457	0.496
7	0.583	0.540	0.572
8	0.667	0.626	0.651
9	0.750	0.712	0.731
10	0.833	0.800	0.813
11	0.917	0.891	0.898
12	1.000	1.000	1.000

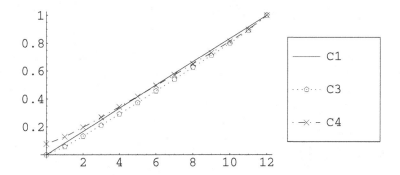

Fig. 6. $\mathrm{Av}[\mathcal{C}_1, k, 12]$, $\mathrm{Av}[\mathcal{C}_3, k, 12]$ and $\mathrm{Av}[\mathcal{C}_4, k, 12]$

The cheater's strategy will depend on $\{a, k\}$ – whose values he knows. As b is unknown to the cheater, we exhaust all the possible fraudulent answers $[\tilde{a}, \tilde{c}]$ (given $\{a, k\}$), select the best-performing (over $[\tilde{a}, \tilde{c}]$) cheating advantage:

$$\mathcal{F}_\ell(n, \tilde{a}, \tilde{c}, a, b, k) = \mathcal{C}_\ell(n, \tilde{a}, b, \tilde{c}) - \mathcal{C}_\ell(n, a, b, n - k + a)$$

and average[10] over b:

$$\mathrm{Ad}[\mathcal{C}_\ell, k, n] = \frac{1}{n \times \mu_{k,n}} \sum_{a=0}^{k} \left(\max_{\substack{0 \le \tilde{a} \le n \\ \tilde{a} \le \tilde{c} \le n}} \left(\sum_{b=0}^{n} \binom{b}{a} \binom{n-b}{k-a} \mathcal{F}_\ell(n, \tilde{a}, \tilde{c}, a, b, k) \right) \right)$$

Table 2 reads as follows: Under $\mathcal{C}_1$ and $n = 9$, an honest examinee knowing $k = 2$ answers will score 0.22 (*cf.* to Table 1). Table 2 shows that under identical circumstances a cheater could hope to score $0.22 + 0.198 \simeq 0.42$.

Naturally, an ideal scoring function $\mathcal{C}_\ell$ will feature an $\mathrm{Ad}[\mathcal{C}_\ell, k, n] = 0$. Note that, for $n = 9$ and $n = 12$, we nearly always have:

$$\mathrm{Ad}[\mathcal{C}_4, k, n] \le \mathrm{Ad}[\mathcal{C}_3, k, n] \le \mathrm{Ad}[\mathcal{C}_1, k, n]$$

---

[10] The $\sum_{b=0}^{n}$ in the following formula can be simplified into a $\sum_{b=a}^{n-k+a}$.

Table 3. Narrower's Advantage for $n = 9$ and $n = 12$

k	0	1	2	3	4	5	6	7	8	9
$\text{Ad}[\mathcal{C}_1, k, 9]$	0.000	0.198	0.198	0.175	0.147	0.102	0.069	0.031	0.000	0.000
$\text{Ad}[\mathcal{C}_3, k, 9]$	0.012	0.091	0.145	0.144	0.134	0.102	0.074	0.038	0.008	0.000
$\text{Ad}[\mathcal{C}_4, k, 9]$	0.000	0.068	0.111	0.110	0.101	0.078	0.052	0.027	0.000	0.000

k	0	1	2	3	4	5	6	7	8	9	10	11	12
$\text{Ad}[\mathcal{C}_1, k, 12]$	0.000	0.208	0.225	0.216	0.205	0.177	0.151	0.113	0.082	0.049	0.020	0.000	0.000
$\text{Ad}[\mathcal{C}_3, k, 12]$	0.011	0.081	0.144	0.167	0.163	0.156	0.136	0.110	0.086	0.054	0.028	0.005	0.000
$\text{Ad}[\mathcal{C}_4, k, 12]$	0.000	0.066	0.118	0.142	0.136	0.131	0.111	0.091	0.068	0.042	0.022	0.000	0.000

Table 4. $\text{Pa}[\mathcal{C}_\ell, \omega, 12]$ for $n = 9$ and $n = 12$

ω	1.00	0.90	0.80	0.70	0.60	0.50
$\text{Pa}[\mathcal{C}_1, \omega, 9]$	1.00	0.64	0.47	0.31	0.15	0.00
$\text{Pa}[\mathcal{C}_3, \omega, 9]$	1.00	0.60	0.38	0.18	0.05	0.01
$\text{Pa}[\mathcal{C}_4, \omega, 9]$	1.00	0.60	0.40	0.22	0.11	0.10
$\text{Pa}[\text{MCQ}, \omega, 9]$	1.00	0.80	0.60	0.40	0.20	0.00

ω	1.00	0.90	0.80	0.70	0.60	0.50
$\text{Pa}[\mathcal{C}_1, \omega, 12]$	1.00	0.67	0.50	0.33	0.17	0.00
$\text{Pa}[\mathcal{C}_3, \omega, 12]$	1.00	0.61	0.40	0.20	0.05	0.01
$\text{Pa}[\mathcal{C}_4, \omega, 12]$	1.00	0.62	0.42	0.22	0.10	0.08
$\text{Pa}[\text{MCQ}, \omega, 12]$	1.00	0.80	0.60	0.40	0.20	0.00

Partial Knowledge. Another interesting benchmark is $\text{Pa}[\mathcal{C}_\ell, \omega, n]$, the mark expected by an examinee who knows the answer to each question with probability ω.

We regard the experiment as a vision test where the student – standing at a distance from the corrector's answer form – tries to identify (and count) the colors of the IEMCQ's answers. As distance increases, ω tends to $\frac{1}{2}$, i.e. reds and blues become less and less distinguishable.

Having stared at the distant form for long enough, the student finally makes his mind and bets that the form contains s red answers and $n - s$ blue answers. The probability ω applies to each individual answer.

For each $\{\mathcal{C}_\ell, \omega, s, n\}$ there exists an optimal answer $[a, c]$ that we discover by exhausting all intervals $[\tilde{a}, \tilde{c}]$. The frequency-weighted score-contribution of these *optima* when the student's blind shot hits x reds amongst b reds and $s - x$ reds amongst $n - b$ blues gives:

$$\text{Pa}[\mathcal{C}_\ell, \omega, n] = \frac{1}{n \times \nu_n} \sum_{s=0}^{n} \max_{\substack{0 \leq \tilde{a} \leq n \\ \tilde{a} \leq \tilde{c} \leq n}} \sum_{x=0}^{s} \sum_{b=0}^{n} \omega^{n-b-s+2x} (1 - \omega)^{b+s-2x} \binom{b}{x} \binom{n-b}{s-x} \mathcal{C}_\ell(n, \tilde{a}, b, \tilde{c})$$

The normalization factor ν_n is:

$$\nu_n = \sum_{s=0}^{n} \sum_{x=0}^{s} \sum_{b=0}^{n} \omega^{n-b-s+2x} (1 - \omega)^{b+s-2x} \binom{b}{x} \binom{n-b}{s-x}$$

Note that $\text{Pa}[\mathcal{C}_\ell, \omega, n] = \text{Pa}[\mathcal{C}_\ell, 1-\omega, n]$ and $\text{Pa}[\text{usual MCQ}, \omega, n] = \omega - (1-\omega) = 2\omega - 1$.

Standard Deviation. To assess the typical standard deviation of the different $\mathcal{C}_\ell$s the following simulation was performed: We generated one million random 99-question IEMCQs. Each IEMCQ contained 11 groups of $n = 9$ questions.

For each IEMCQ we generated a random binary vector $e_1, \ldots, e_{99}$. If $e_i = 1$ we considered that the examinee answered the i-th question correctly. If $e_i = 0$ the question was not answered. The IEMCQ was then corrected as a traditional MCQ and as an IEMCQ scored with $\mathcal{C}_1$, $\mathcal{C}_3$ and $\mathcal{C}_4$.

The experiment's means, μ and standard deviations, σ, are reported here:

Table 5. Experimental Results

	MCQ	$\mathcal{C}_1$	$\mathcal{C}_3$	$\mathcal{C}_4$
σ	0.050	0.050	0.052	0.060
μ	0.500	0.500	0.453	0.503

Efficiency. Table 5 allows to estimate efficiency, *i.e.* the number of decimal digits that the examiner needs to key into his computer per corrected form.

The examiner starts by setting a target σ' and multiplies the number of questions by:

$$\left(\frac{\sigma}{\sigma'}\right)^2$$

The following table assumes binary encoding for the traditional MCQ and the compressed answer encoding of Appendix B for $n = 12$:

Table 6. Efficiency

	MCQ	$\mathcal{C}_1$	$\mathcal{C}_3$	$\mathcal{C}_4$
$n = 9$	31	24	24	32
$n = 12$	31	18	18	24

5   Further Research

It seems that homomorphism, necessary for mark accumulation, is the root-cause of the security problems encountered while designing all additive CTCs we could think of. The design of an additive CTC which is simultaneously practical, secure and efficient remains an open problem. Potential solutions could involve the use of non commutative operations such as moderate-size matrix multiplications or vector products[11]. Unfortunately, the cost of 80 matrix multiplications or vector products is prohibitive and so are the foreseeable error odds. The use of simple physical accessories (scratch cards [1], tables, envelopes, etc) also seems a promising idea.

The generalization of IEMCQs and scoring functions to more than two colors, attacks on the IEMCQs proposed in this paper or the development of better scoring functions are also welcome – as these might find practical applications during the 2008-2009 academic year...

---

[11] Taking advantage of the fact that $\vec{u} \wedge (\vec{v} \wedge \vec{w}) \neq (\vec{u} \wedge \vec{v}) \wedge \vec{w}$.

Acknowledgments

The authors wish to warmly thank Nora Dabbous, Vanessa Gratzer, Hervé Leplat and Gueorgui Tzotchev for their comments and suggestions during the design of the schemes proposed in this work.

Reference

1. Moran, T., Naor, M.: Polling with Physical Envelopes: A Rigorous Analysis of a Human-Centric Protocol. In: Vaudenay, S. (ed.) EUROCRYPT 2006. LNCS, vol. 4004, pp. 88–108. Springer, Heidelberg (2006)

A   Implementation Details

Fix $\{n = 80, g = 9189, k = 54, p = 3931231, e = 2032603\}$ and generate:

i	a_i	$v_{i,0}$	student	$v_{i,1}$
1	5498	50178050	•	18103810 ✓
2	19893	61139595	•	09409200 ✓
3	6294	✓ 32424036	•	04908839
4	6545	71173575	•	39099335 ✓
4	5441	✓ 32286548	•	67671047
5	9189	28139589	•	55033814 ✓
7	17580	✓ 68719202	•	81137287
8	13388	✓ 19850231	•	79443088
9	14708	✓ 61409445	•	49619172
10	19321	14960283	•	69373125 ✓
11	6861	44856367	•	72371564 ✓
12	1571	71821899	•	60024786 ✓
13	13903	✓ 05518892	•	09453543
14	18627	66751733	•	26815031 ✓
15	11471	23445338	•	62754228 ✓
16	14564	47835434	•	43900783 ✓
17	2659	42802779	•	61834542 ✓
18	11202	19495495	•	66045875 ✓
19	13374	70642801	•	34637330 ✓
20	10978	✓ 39557468	•	51354581
21	18810	61319906	•	21383204 ✓
22	13683	57926475	•	21921004 ✓
23	13811	78294568	•	26564173 ✓
24	12734	43495725	•	19283947 ✓
25	9648	60541981	•	01570096 ✓
26	12917	✓ 64958123	•	53788822
27	3219	72142831	•	09239715 ✓
28	8971	17157059	•	21084870 ✓
29	4619	✓ 67330650	•	67955042
30	1482	✓ 63890976	•	16719624
31	13212	✓ 24095841	•	35892954
32	11850	15728623	•	58347772 ✓
33	9833	31656743	•	31653323 ✓
34	5271	09108400	•	01242518 ✓
35	9059	✓ 54187901	•	19431214
36	10894	02794576	•	61138649 ✓
37	1410	07965293	•	39411721 ✓
38	6456	31796224	•	15446908 ✓
39	6519	06532204	•	49151353 ✓
40	5459	✓ 49217247	•	41358205
41	4395	✓ 36600526	•	49018611
42	2457	✓ 48613553	•	76135590
43	6430	37606525	•	80846646 ✓
44	18139	14405678	•	68818520 ✓
45	9341	61598589	•	81251324 ✓
46	3423	26839816	•	58286244 ✓
47	13508	75687895	•	78994734 ✓
48	4543	✓ 38652214	•	82520147
49	18648	15086852	•	49843539 ✓
50	10242	✓ 09910823	•	25639167
51	3981	✓ 32765573	•	72081303
52	4790	57477648	•	22093149 ✓
53	10402	68117501	•	43905723 ✓
54	13061	35916405	•	51016937 ✓
55	5825	22942575	•	65561724 ✓
56	1062	✓ 47239433	•	59657518
57	18333	11676329	•	81814095 ✓
58	19114	✓ 69576507	•	38130079
59	3226	63094152	•	42813605 ✓
60	15857	✓ 53546130	•	69895446
61	10718	73560627	•	69005004 ✓
62	7214	✓ 58360971	•	03948129
63	4281	13552933	•	17480744 ✓
64	18135	41656345	•	68550570 ✓
65	2170	27736431	•	27112039 ✓
66	4245	✓ 34725349	•	58316155
67	849	03800769	•	43109659 ✓
68	10077	32276769	•	12617194 ✓
69	927	✓ 24436812	•	25061204
70	7304	25391442	•	25388022 ✓
71	8668	73518851	•	34203121 ✓
72	18606	24067070	•	47030064 ✓
73	10119	82265016	•	78330365 ✓
74	7537	✓ 70480342	•	27240221
75	5030	42415286	•	49653356 ✓
76	18830	✓ 03377285	•	46624246
77	3049	✓ 76476460	•	48961263
78	17663	60833762	•	21518032 ✓
79	15458	✓ 40577426	•	17614432
80	6769	15416617	•	22654687 ✓

i	$\epsilon_{i,0}$	$r_{i,0}$	$r_{i,1}$	i	$\epsilon_{i,0}$	$r_{i,0}$	$r_{i,1}$	i	$\epsilon_{i,0}$	$r_{i,0}$	$r_{i,1}$	i	$\epsilon_{i,0}$	$r_{i,0}$	$r_{i,1}$
1	1	12	4	21	1	15	5	41	0	9	12	61	1	18	17
2	1	15	2	22	1	14	5	42	1	12	19	62	0	14	1
3	1	8	1	23	1	19	6	43	0	9	20	63	0	3	4
4	1	18	9	24	1	11	4	44	1	3	17	64	1	10	17
5	1	8	17	25	0	15	0	45	0	15	20	65	1	7	6
6	1	7	13	26	0	16	13	46	0	6	14	66	1	8	14
7	0	17	20	27	0	18	2	47	1	19	20	67	0	0	10
8	0	5	20	28	0	4	5	48	0	9	20	68	0	8	3
9	1	15	12	29	0	17	17	49	1	3	12	69	0	6	6
10	1	3	17	30	1	16	4	50	1	2	6	70	0	6	6
11	0	11	18	31	1	6	9	51	1	8	18	71	0	18	8
12	0	18	15	32	1	4	14	52	0	14	5	72	1	6	11
13	1	1	2	33	0	8	8	53	1	17	11	73	0	20	19
14	1	16	6	34	0	2	0	54	1	9	12	74	1	17	6
15	0	5	15	35	0	13	4	55	1	5	16	75	1	10	12
16	0	12	11	36	1	0	15	56	0	12	15	76	1	0	11
17	1	10	15	37	0	2	10	57	1	2	20	77	1	19	12
18	1	4	16	38	1	8	3	58	1	17	9	78	0	15	5
19	1	17	8	39	1	1	12	59	1	16	10	79	0	10	4
20	1	10	13	40	1	12	10	60	1	13	17	80	1	3	5

As $\epsilon_{i,1} = 1 - \epsilon_{i,0}$ we only list here $\epsilon_{i,0}$.

The MCQ included $n = 80$ questions. To reduce computational errors, examinees were provided with a form in which they had to report five groups of four numbers. Examinees were instructed to add four consecutive $v_{i,j}$ values[12] using the M+ key and subtract the $v_{i,j}$s again to control that no addition error occurred. If no error occurred, the result would be recalled using the MRC key and copied into the table. In the table, the 20 numbers were divided into five groups of four and added, again, using the same procedure. Finally, the five partial sums were added to get t.

To ease the students' task, a lookup table was also given in the test's appendix. The table gave, for each group of four consecutive questions, sixteen possible sums. Hence – all in all – students could compute t by adding (and controlling the addition of) only 25 integers.

Example: The student's choice (materialized by •s) results in $t = 3355519689$. The examiner computes:

$$t' = \left(t \times e^{-1} - \left(\sum_{i=1}^{n} a_i \right) \mod p \right) = 388206$$

Hence:

$$q = \left\lfloor \frac{t'}{g} \right\rfloor = \left\lfloor \frac{388206}{9189} \right\rfloor = 42 \quad \text{and} \quad m = \frac{t' - qg}{k} = \frac{388206 - 42 \times 9189}{54} = 42$$

As $0 \leq m \leq n$ and $m \in \mathbb{N}$ we accept $m = 42$ as the student's mark and do not trigger a manual form verification because $\Pr[\, |q - 40| \leq 2 \,] \simeq 0.42$.

---

[12] For instance $\texttt{table}_1 = v_{1,0} + v_{2,1} + v_{3,1} + v_{4,0} + v_{5,1}$ etc.

B   Compressed Answer Encoding

This appendix describes a way to compress IEMCQ answers for $n = 12$. Despite the fact that, in principle, $0 \leq a \leq 12$ and $0 \leq c \leq 12$, we compress the answer into a couple of decimal digits by "reusing" impossible interval notations such as $[7, 3]$.

This is achieved by asking the student to write on the form:

$$
\begin{array}{lll}
[c - 7, a] & \text{if } a \leq 3 & \text{and} \quad c \geq 10 \\
[c - 3, a - 4] & \text{if } a \geq 4 & \text{and} \quad c \geq 10 \\
[a, c] & \text{otherwise}
\end{array}
$$

$n = 12$ is particularly suitable both in terms of answer compactness and standard deviation.

Off-Line/On-Line Signatures: Theoretical Aspects and Experimental Results[*]

Dario Catalano[1], Mario Di Raimondo[1], Dario Fiore[1], and Rosario Gennaro[2]

[1] Dipartimento di Matematica e Informatica – Università di Catania
{catalano,diraimondo,fiore}@dmi.unict.it
[2] IBM Research – Yorktown Heights, NY, USA
rosario@watson.ibm.com

Abstract. This paper presents some theoretical and experimental results about off-line/on-line digital signatures. The goal of this type of schemes is to reduce the time used to compute a signature using some kind of preprocessing. They were introduced by Even, Goldreich and Micali and constructed by combining regular digital signatures with efficient one-time signatures. Later Shamir and Tauman presented an alternative construction (which produces shorter signatures) by combining regular signatures with chameleon hash functions.

We first unify the Shamir-Tauman and Even *et al.* approaches by showing that they can be considered different instantiations of the same paradigm. We do this by showing that the one-time signatures needed in the Even *et al.* approach only need to satisfy a weak notion of security. We then show that chameleon hashing are in effect a type of one-time signatures which satisfy this weaker security notion.

In the process we study the relationship between one-time signatures and chameleon hashing, and we prove that a special type of chameleon hashing (which we call *two-trapdoor*) is a fully secure one-time signature.

Finally we ran experimental tests using OpenSSL libraries to test the difference between the two approaches. In our implementation we make extensive use of the observation that off-line/on-line digital signatures do not require collision-resistant hash functions to compress the message, but can be safely implemented with universal one-way hashing in both the off-line and the on-line step. The main application of this observation is that both the steps can be applied to shorter digests. This has particular relevance if block-ciphers or hash functions based one-time signatures are used since these are very sensitive to the length of the message. Interestingly, we show that (mostly due to the above observation about hashing), the two approaches are comparable in efficiency and signature length.

1 Introduction

Off-line/On-line digital signatures were introduced by Even, Goldreich and Micali in [12]. In these signatures the signing process is divided in two parts. First

---

[*] The full version of the article is available at http://www.dmi.unict.it/~fiore

R. Cramer (Ed.): PKC 2008, LNCS 4939, pp. 101–120, 2008.

a computationally intensive part is performed off-line, i.e. before the message being signed is known. This off-line part produces some temporary data which is stored and then used at the time the message to be signed is known. At that point, the computation of the actual signature requires very little effort.

The original construction in [12] was based on combining two different types of digital signatures: many-times (or "regular") signatures and one-time signatures [24,21,2,22,26]. While the former can be used to sign a polynomial number of messages, in the latter a private key can be used to sign only a single message. Because of this limitation, one-time signatures can be constructed more efficiently. The construction in [12] goes as following. The signer generates a pair (VK, SK) of keys for a regular signature scheme: she publishes VK and keeps SK as a secret. In the off-line part she generates vk a one-time public verification key, and signs it with SK: let S be the resulting signature. Then when the message m is available, the signer computes its signature s with the one-time signing key sk. The final signature is (vk, S, s).

The construction in [12] utilizes one-way functions based one-time signatures, such as the ones introduced by Lamport [20]. While these signatures are very fast to compute and verify, the signature string can be very long, and it grows quadratically with the length of the message being signed.

To address these issues Shamir and Tauman in [27] offered an alternative construction which combines regular signatures with chameleon hashing [18]. A chameleon hash function is defined by a public key pk and a secret trapdoor tk. The function $C_{pk}(\cdot, \cdot)$ takes two arguments a message m and a random string r. The function is collision-resistant, unless one knows the trapdoor tk. But knowledge of tk allows to find arbitrary collisions, i.e. given $c = C_{pk}(m, r)$ and an arbitrary different message m', the holder of the trapdoor can find r' such that $c = C_{pk}(m', r')$. For many chameleon hash functions, this collision-finding procedure is very efficient, requiring only a single modular multiplication. The Shamir-Tauman idea is to construct off-line/on-line signatures as follows. The signer's public key is VK, like before, and pk. The off-line part would consists of computing $c = C_{pk}(a, r')$ for some arbitrary a, r' and then computes S the signature of c using SK. On input the actual message m the signer (who knows the trapdoor tk as part of the signing key) computes r such that $c = C_{pk}(m, r)$ and outputs (S, r). The verifier re-computes c as $C_{pk}(m, r)$ and verifies S on it. As we will see later in the examples of chameleon hashing, the length of r grows only linearly in the length of the message m, so the Shamir-Tauman approach provides shorter signatures.

1.1 Our Contributions

This work was motivated by two basic questions:

1. Is the Shamir-Tauman approach conceptually different from the Even *et al.* approach, or are they really two different instantiations of the same paradigm?
2. In practical implementations, for today's security levels, which approach is preferable, in terms of speed, memory and ease of implementation?

This paper presents some theoretical and experimental results about off-line/on-line digital signatures which are aimed at answering the above questions.

We first show that conceptually the Shamir-Tauman construction is not different from the Even *et al.* one. Indeed we present a unifying paradigm which encompasses both the Shamir-Tauman and the Even *et al.* approaches. We do this by showing that a chameleon hash function can also be seen as a one-time signature with a very weak security property. As already observed in [12], this weak property is sufficient to prove the security of the Even *et al.* approach. In the process of exploring the relationship between one-time signatures and chameleon hashing, we discovered that fully secure one-time signatures can be obtained from a special type of chameleon hashing that we call *two-trapdoor chameleon hashing*.

Finally we ran experimental tests using OpenSSL libraries to test the difference between the two approaches. In our implementation we make extensive use of the observation that off-line/on-line digital signatures do not require collision-resistant hash functions to compress the message, but can be safely implemented with universal one-way hashing in both the off-line and the on-line step. The main application of this observation is that both the steps can be applied to shorter digests. This has particular relevance if block-ciphers or hash functions based one-time signatures are used since these are very sensitive to the length of the message. Surprisingly, we show that (mostly due to the above observation about hashing), the two approaches are comparable in efficiency and signature length.

RELATED WORK. As we pointed out, Even *et al.* introduced the notion of off-line/on-line signatures in [12] and constructed them combining regular signatures with efficient one-time signatures. However the length of the signatures is an issue in this approach. Shorter signatures can be obtained by using chameleon hashing [18] combined with regular signatures as pointed out by Shamir and Tauman [27]. Off-line/On-Line digital signatures can also be obtained by applying the Fiat-Shamir heuristic to a variety of identification protocols known as Σ-protocols. Example of such schemes are [13,30,11,28]. However such schemes are proved secure in the random oracle model [3,23]; our paper is focused on schemes which are secure in the standard model.

2   Preliminaries

In the following, with $\mathbb{N}$ we denote the set of integers and with $\mathbb{R}$ the set of real numbers. We denote the security parameter with ℓ. A function $f : \mathbb{N} \to \mathbb{R}$ is said to be negligible if for any $c > 0$, there exists an index $\ell_c \in \mathbb{N}$ such that $f(\ell) < \ell^{-c}$ for all $\ell > \ell_c$.

2.1   Hash Functions

For lack of space the definitions of Collision resistant hash functions and Target collision resistant hash functions, are deferred to the full version.

Target Division Intractable (TDI) hash functions: Consider a family $\mathcal{H} = \{h^{\mathsf{tdi}}(k, \cdot)\}_k$ (we are making explicit the fact that an element of the family is parametrized by a key k) with $poly(\ell)$-bit input and ℓ bit output. We say that $\mathcal{H}$ is *target division intractable* if it is hard for the attacker to win the following game:

1. the attacker chooses polynomially many inputs $x_1, x_2, \ldots$;
2. a random key k is chosen;
3. the attacker outputs $y \neq x_i$ such that $h^{\mathsf{tdi}}(k, y)$ divides the product of the $h^{\mathsf{tdi}}(k, x_i)$'s.

This notion was introduced in a stronger variant[1] by Gennaro *et al.* [14]. They conjectured that a random oracle with approximately 600 bits of output would be a safe choice for a DI function. Later, Coron and Naccache [7] described an attack that disproves such a conjecture and forces one to use functions with much longer outputs (see [7] for details).

Recently, Kurosawa and Schmidt-Samoa [19] introduced the notion of *weak division intractability* (wDI). Informally, wDI formalizes a weaker (i.e. with respect to the notions discussed above) notion of division intractability. Here, the adversary A should be unable to find $y \neq x_1, \ldots x_n$, such that $h^{\mathsf{tdi}}(k, y)$ divides the product of the $h^{\mathsf{tdi}}(k, x_i)$'s, when the x_i's are chosen at random (i.e. and thus are not of A's choice). Kurosawa and Schmidt-Samoa showed that this property is sufficient to prove the random-message security (see Section 2.3) of the GHR signature scheme. Very informally, this is because the attack of Coron and Naccache crucially relies on the attacker choosing the x_i's.

Notice that, by a similar reasoning, the same attack cannot be applied if one uses a TDI function. This is because, in such a case, the adversary does not know the key (of the hash function) when choosing the x_i's. This is why in our constructions we only require the GHR scheme to be obliviously secure and the underlying hash function to be target division intractable.

2.2   Chameleon Hashing

Definition 1. *A chameleon hash function (also known as trapdoor commitment scheme) is a triplet of polynomial-time algorithms:*

$\mathsf{CKG}(1^\ell)$: *a probabilistic algorithm which, on input a security parameter 1^ℓ, outputs a pair of matching public/private keys (pk, tk);*

$\mathsf{C}_{pk}(m, r)$: *the evaluation algorithm which, on input the public key pk, a message m and a random nonce r, outputs a hashed value;*

$\mathsf{Coll}(tk, m, m', r)$: *the collision finding algorithm which, on input the private trapdoor key tk, two messages m, m' and a nonce r, outputs a nonce r' such that $\mathsf{C}_{pk}(m, r) = \mathsf{C}_{pk}(m', r')$.*

---

[1] In such a variant, called division intractability (DI), the adversary is allowed to choose the x_i's after having seen the hash function.

As required in [18], the public key defines a particular hash function which, however, takes a random input additionally to the message. The security properties of this function are as follows:

Collision Resistance. Without knowledge of the associated trapdoor, this function is collision resistant, i.e. it is infeasible to find two different pairs (m, r), (m', r') such that $C_{pk}(m, r) = C_{pk}(m', r')$;

Distribution of Collisions. For every m, m', and a random r, the distribution of $r' = \text{Coll}(tk, m, m', r)$ is uniform, even when given $pk, c = C_{pk}(m, r)$, m and m'. This implies that the chameleon hashing function is also a information-theoretically hiding commitment.

Two efficient constructions of chameleon hash function follow: the first is due to Boyar *et al.* [4] and its security is based on the Discrete Log problem difficulty; the second [8,10] relies on the RSA assumption.

2.3   Signature Schemes

We recall the definition of secure signature scheme from [15].

Definition 2. *A signature scheme is a triplet* (KG, Sign, Ver) *of PPT algorithms:*

- *the key generation algorithm* $KG(1^\ell)$ *outputs a pair* (vk, sk) *of matching public/private keys;*
- *the signing algorithm* $Sign(sk, m)$ *takes as input the private key and a message* m *and produces a signature* σ;
- *the verification algorithm* $Ver(vk, m, \sigma)$ *takes as input the public key, a message and an alleged signature* σ *and outputs a single bit.*

For every possible output (vk, sk) of KG, and every m, it is required that $Ver(vk, m, Sign(sk, m)) = 1$. We say that a signature scheme is secure against adaptive chosen message attack (or in short "secure") if a forger after asking for the signature on several adaptively chosen messages will not be able to produce a valid signature on a message he had not previously requested.

Definition 3. (KG, Sign, Ver) *is a* secure signature scheme *if for every efficient forger* $\mathcal{F}$, *the following*

$$\Pr \begin{bmatrix} (vk, sk) \leftarrow KG(1^\ell) \; ; \\ \textbf{for } i = 1 \textbf{ to } k \\ \qquad M_i \leftarrow \mathcal{F}(vk, M_1, \sigma_1, \ldots, M_{i-1}, \sigma_{i-1}) \; ; \\ \qquad \sigma_i \leftarrow Sign(sk, M_i) \; ; \\ (M, \sigma) \leftarrow \mathcal{F}(vk, M_1, \sigma_1, \ldots, M_k, \sigma_k) \; ; \\ Ver(vk, M, \sigma) = 1 \ \text{ and } \ M \neq M_i \end{bmatrix}$$

is negligible in ℓ.

We say that a signature scheme is *obliviously secure* if in the game above the adversary chooses the messages M_i before seeing the public key. Also we say that a signature scheme is *random-message secure* if the above holds for messages M_i chosen randomly in the message space, rather than adaptively and adversarially chosen. Similar security definitions apply to one-time signatures if the above hold for $k = 1$.

Examples of One-Time Signatures. Lamport *et al.* [20] proposed a method to construct a one-time signature scheme from one-way functions. Later Even, Goldreich and Micali [12] suggested an improved method to shorten the length of keys and signatures. In the follow we recall their ideas and also describe a technique due to Jakobsson [17] to speedup the signature phase.

- **Lamport's scheme:** let M be the m-bit message to sign and $f : \{0,1\}^\ell \to \{0,1\}^\ell$ be a one-way function. We choose $2m$ ℓ-bit strings $x_1^0, x_1^1, \ldots, x_m^0, x_m^1$ at random as the signing key. The verification key is computed applying f to each x_i^0, x_i^1 for $i = 1, \ldots, m$: $f(x_1^0), f(x_1^1), \ldots, f(x_m^0), f(x_m^1)$.

  To sign a message $M = \mu_1, \cdots, \mu_m$ the signer reveals $x_1^{\mu_1}, \ldots, x_m^{\mu_m}$. Given a message M and its signature $s = s_1, \cdots, s_m$, the verifier applies f to the values $s_1, \cdots, s_m$ from the signature and checks if they are equal to the corresponding images in the verification key.

  This simple scheme is proved to be secure if f is a one-way function; it is really fast but has the drawback of quite large keys and signatures.

- **Shortening length of keys and signatures (Even *et al.*'s):** let M be the m-bit message, we partition the message in blocks of t bits, where $t|m$. Let f be a one-way function as before[2]. We choose at random $\frac{m}{t} + 1$ ℓ-bit strings $x_0, x_1, \ldots, x_{m/t}$ as the signing key. The corresponding verification key is:

$$y_0 = f^{(2^t-1)m/t}(x_0); \quad y_1 = f^{2^t-1}(x_1), \ldots, y_{m/t} = f^{2^t-1}(x_{m/t})$$

  To sign a message $M = \mu_1, \ldots, \mu_{m/t}$, whose t-bit blocks μ_i are interpreted as integers, the signer outputs:

$$s_0 = f^{\sum_{i=1}^{m/t} \mu_i}(x_0), \; s_1 = f^{2^t-1-\mu_1}(x_1), \ldots, s_{m/t} = f^{2^t-1-\mu_{m/t}}(x_{m/t})$$

  Given a message $M = \mu_1, \ldots, \mu_{m/t}$ and a signature $s_0, s_1, \ldots, s_{m/t}$ the verifier applies f to each signature component the proper times and compares the resulting values with the verification key elements. Namely, it checks:

$$y_0 \stackrel{?}{=} f^{(2^t-1)m/t - \sum_{i=1}^{m/t} \mu_i}(s_0); \quad y_1 \stackrel{?}{=} f^{\mu_1}(s_1), \ldots, y_{m/t} \stackrel{?}{=} f^{\mu_{m/t}}(s_{m/t})$$

  It is interesting to note the trade-off: a small t makes the signature computation more efficient (because the hash chains are shorter), but makes the signature longer (because the number of blocks m/t is bigger).

- **Speedup the signature step (Jakobsson's):** in the previous scheme the length of the hash chains is exponential in the size of the block; this makes the signature and verification steps computationally expensive for big blocks. The optimization for one-way hash chains traversal proposed by Jakobsson [17] can be applied here: the idea is to store not only the first and last value of the chains, but also some intermediate elements (called *pebbles*) that

---

[2] As explained in Appendix A, the proof of security requires a stronger assumption than the inverting infeasibility: the *quasi-inverting assumption* has to hold on f. Also in Appendix A we make a concrete security analysis of this assumption compared to the assumption of basic one-wayness.

permit in the signature procedure to speedup the traversal originating the iterative computation from the nearer pebble in the chain. In [17] it is stated that keeping $O(\log n)$ number of pebbles, where n is the chain length, the traversal time becomes $O(\log n)$; in our case, the storage and the running time become $O(t)$, where t is the size of the block.

Examples of Obliviously Secure Signatures. In this section we recall two signature schemes: one is due to Gennaro *et al.* [14] and the other to Cramer and Shoup [10]. Their security is based on the Strong RSA Assumption, and they are the most efficient signature schemes in the literature whose security can be proved without using the random oracle model.

We present simplified versions of these schemes which can be proved to be obliviously secure since that's all we need later.

- **Simplified GHR Signature:** This scheme uses a target division-intractable hash function $h^{\mathsf{tdi}}(\cdot, \cdot)$.
  - **Key generation:** let $N = pq$ be an RSA modulus where p, q are safe primes of identical sizes; select a random element s in $\mathbb{Z}_N^*$ and a key k for the TDI hash function $h^{\mathsf{tdi}}(\cdot, \cdot)$; the public key is (N, s, k) and the secret key is $\phi(N) = (p-1)(q-1)$.
  - **Signature algorithm:** given a message m to sign, compute $e = h^{\mathsf{tdi}}(k, m)$ and $d = e^{-1} \bmod \phi(N)$ and outputs the signature $\sigma = s^d \bmod N$.
  - **Verification algorithm:** on input the public key (N, s, k) and the message/signature pair m, σ, compute the value $e = h^{\mathsf{tdi}}(k, m)$ and check if $\sigma^e = s \bmod N$.
- **Simplified CS Signature:**
  - **Key generation:** generate an RSA modulus $N = pq$ as in GHR (safe primes), select two random elements s, t in $\mathbb{Z}_N^*$ and draw a random key k for a TCR hash function $h^{\mathsf{tcr}}(\cdot, \cdot)$; the public key is (N, s, t, k) and the secret key is $\phi(N)$.
  - **Signature algorithm:** given an arbitrary long message m to sign, generate a random 161-bit prime e and compute $d = e^{-1} \bmod \phi(N)$ and $\sigma = (st^{h^{\mathsf{tcr}}(k,m)})^d \bmod N$. The signature is (e, σ).
  - **Verification algorithm:** on input the public key (N, s, t, k) and the message/signature pair $m, (e, \sigma)$, check if $\sigma^e = st^{h^{\mathsf{tcr}}(k,m)} \bmod N$.

Cramer and Shoup in [10] suggest an efficient method for the generation of small primes of 161 bits. This operation is critical for the performance of the scheme since a fresh 161 bit prime number is necessary to sign a message.

2.4   Off-Line/On-Line Digital Signatures

In this section we recall the Even *et al.* and Shamir-Tauman approaches to construct off-line/on-line signatures.

Using one-time signatures. The idea is to combine a random-message secure signature scheme with a one-time signature. In the off-line step a pair of keys for a one-time signature is generated and the public key of this scheme is signed using the long-term signing key. During the on-line phase, given the message to sign, its signature is computed using the one-time secret key.

We call this scheme the EGM scheme. A more detailed description follows: let $(\mathsf{KG}, \mathsf{Sign}, \mathsf{Ver})$ be a signature scheme, $(\mathsf{KG}^{ot}, \mathsf{Sign}^{ot}, \mathsf{Ver}^{ot})$ a one-time signature scheme. The combined off-line/on-line signature works as follows:

- **Key generation:** this step coincides with the key generation of the ordinary scheme; run $\mathsf{KG}(1^\ell)$ to obtain a pair of long-term keys (VK, SK); the public component VK is announced, while SK is kept secret.
- **Off-line Signature:** in this phase a fresh pair of keys (vk, sk) for a one-time signature is generated using $\mathsf{KG}^{ot}(1^\ell)$. The verification key vk is signed with the long-term signing key SK as $\pi = \mathsf{Sign}(SK, vk)$. The token (vk, sk, π) is kept as part of the signer's state.
- **On-line Signature:** given the message m to sign, a precomputed token (vk, sk, π) is retrieved; the message m is signed using the one-time scheme as $\sigma = \mathsf{Sign}^{ot}(sk, m)$ and the complete signature is the triple (vk, π, σ).
- **Verification:** given a message m and its purported signature (vk, π, σ), the master verification key VK is used as follows. First, the algorithm Ver is used to check that π is indeed a valid signature of vk with respect of the long-term verification key VK. Next, the tag σ is verified to be a (one-time) signature of m using vk; namely, the verification consists in evaluating the following predicate:

$$\mathsf{Ver}(VK, vk, \pi) \wedge \mathsf{Ver}^{ot}(vk, m, \sigma)$$

The following Theorem appears in [12].

Theorem 1 (EGM [12]). *If* $(\mathsf{KG}, \mathsf{Sign}, \mathsf{Ver})$ *is a "regular" signature scheme and* $(\mathsf{KG}^{ot}, \mathsf{Sign}^{ot}, \mathsf{Ver}^{ot})$ *is a one-time signature scheme and both the schemes are secure (as in Definition 3) then the EGM scheme described above is secure in the standard sense.*

Using Chameleon hash functions. This construction is also known as the "hash-sign-switch" paradigm: in the off-line phase, the signer hashes an arbitrary message m' with a chameleon hash. It then signs the results. When, during the on-line phase, he is given the message m the signer uses its knowledge of the chameleon hash trapdoor to find a second preimage and "switches" m with the arbitrary m' used in the off-line phase.

We call this the ST scheme. Let $(\mathsf{KG}, \mathsf{Sign}, \mathsf{Ver})$ be a signature scheme and $(\mathsf{CKG}, \mathsf{C}, \mathsf{Coll})$ a chameleon hash function family. Given a security parameter ℓ, an off-line/on-line signature scheme can be constructed as follows:

- **Key generation:** a pair of keys (VK, SK) is generated using the signature key generation algorithm $\mathsf{KG}(1^\ell)$; furthermore, a specific chameleon hash function is selected in the family using the trapdoor key generation algorithm as $(pk, tk) = \mathsf{CKG}(1^\ell)$. The signing key is (SK, tk) and the verification key is (VK, pk).

- **Off-line Signature:** an arbitrary message m' is chosen together with a random string r'. The hash value $\delta = \mathsf{C}_{pk}(m', r')$ is computed and signed with SK, to compute $\sigma = \mathsf{Sign}(SK, \delta)$; the token (m', r', σ) is kept in the signer's internal state.
- **On-line Signature:** given the message m to sign, a precomputed token (m', r', σ) is retrieved; use Coll with the trapdoor key tk to find r such that $\mathsf{C}_{pk}(m, r) = \delta = \mathsf{C}_{pk}(m', r')$; the signature given in output is (r, σ).
- **Verification:** given a message m and a signature (r, σ), first compute $\delta = \mathsf{C}_{pk}(m, r)$ and then verify the signature σ on it using $\mathsf{Ver}(VK, \mathsf{C}_{pk}(m, r))$.

Theorem 2 (ST [**27**]). *If* $(\mathsf{CKG}, \mathsf{C}, \mathsf{Coll})$ *is a chameleon hash function and* $(\mathsf{KG}, \mathsf{Sign}, \mathsf{Ver})$ *is an obliviously secure signature scheme then the* ST *scheme described above is a secure signature scheme.*

3   A Unifying Paradigm

In this section we show that the Even, Goldreich, Micali [12] construction and the Shamir, Tauman [27] solution can be seen as two special cases of the same methodology. This would be immediate if we could show that chameleon hashing is a form of secure one-time signatures. Unfortunately that is not true in general, though in the next subsection, we describe a sufficient condition on chameleon hashing to be a secure one-time signature. Nevertheless, for a general statement, we must follow a different approach.

Our starting point, is the observation (originally made in [12]) that the Even, Goldreich, Micali construction remains secure even if the underlying one-time and regular signature schemes are obliviously secure. Next, we show that chameleon hash functions are a form of oblivious one-time signatures. This shows an unifying paradigm that encompasses both the Even *et al.* and the Shamir-Tauman approach.

Informally an oblivious one-time signature is guaranteed to be secure only against an adversary which chooses the (one) message for which she is allowed to see a valid signature, *before* seeing the public key. Notice that this level of security is indeed sufficient for the EGM approach since, in the off-line/on-line EGM signature, the keys of the one-time signatures are chosen *independently* from the message being signed (i.e. the adversary does not see the keys of the one-time signature when she submits a message to be signed).

Definition 4. $(\mathsf{KG}, \mathsf{Sign}, \mathsf{Ver})$ *is an* oblivious secure one-time signature *if for every efficient forger* $\mathcal{F}$, *the following probability is negligible in* ℓ.

$$\Pr \begin{bmatrix} (M, \mathsf{state}) \leftarrow \mathcal{F}; \ (vk, sk) \leftarrow \mathsf{KG}(1^\ell); \ \sigma \leftarrow \mathsf{Sign}(sk, M) \ ; \\ (M', \sigma') \leftarrow \mathcal{F}(vk, M, \sigma, \mathsf{state}) \ : \\ \mathsf{Ver}(vk, M', \sigma') = 1 \ \ and \ \ M' \neq M \end{bmatrix}$$

We state the following

Theorem 3 (EGM [12]). *If* (KG, Sign, Ver) *is an obliviously secure signature scheme and* (KG^{ot}, Sign^{ot}, Ver^{ot}) *is an obliviously secure one-time signature scheme then the* EGM *scheme described above is a secure signature scheme.*

Now we show that an oblivious one-time signature scheme can be implemented using a chameleon hash function. The construction Cham-Sig is as follows.

KEY GENERATION. On input a security parameter ℓ, run CKG(1^{ℓ}). Then it chooses a message α and a nonce r and computes $c = C_{pk}(\alpha, r)$. The public key is (pk, c), the signing key is (tk, α, r).

SIGNATURE ALGORITHM. On input a message m the signer uses his knowledge of the trapdoor to compute a nonce s such that, $c = C_{pk}(m, s)$. The signature is then (m, s).

VERIFICATION. On input a purported signature (m, s), the verifier checks whether $c = C_{pk}(m, s)$. If this is the case the signature is accepted as valid, otherwise it is rejected.

Theorem 4. *The scheme presented above is an obliviously secure one-time signature scheme assuming that the underlying primitive is a chameleon hash function.*

The proof is very simple. For lack of space it is deferred to the full version of the paper.

3.1   Double Trapdoor Chameleon Hash Function

In the previous section we showed that a chameleon hash function is an obliviously secure one-time signature. It is not hard to see why it fails to be a (fully) secure one-time signature. In the oblivious case, the adversary commits to the message she wants to be signed before seeing the public key: this allows us to "prepare" the public key as a commitment to that specific message. In the adaptive case, when we prepare the public key we do not know the message, so when the adversary asks us for a signature we do not know how to produce it.

In order to get a fully adaptively secure one-time signature from chameleon hashing, a possible way is to compose two different hash functions (i.e. apply one function over the output of the other). Conceptually this is not surprising as it corresponds to a chain of length two in the [15] signature scheme (in that scheme a chain of length two, instead of a full binary tree, gives a one-time signature).

In some cases we can do better. If a chameleon hashing admits the "double trapdoor" property (described below) then we can obtain the same effect as composing two hash functions, but more efficiently.

A double trapdoor chameleon hash function scheme generalizes the notion of chameleon hash by allowing the existence of two independent trapdoors. Knowing either of the two trapdoors, one can can easily find collisions. More formally:

Definition 5. *Let ℓ be a security parameter. A double trapdoor chameleon hash function is composed of the following, polynomial-time, algorithms:*

$\mathsf{CKG}(1^\ell)$: *a probabilistic algorithm which, on input the security parameter 1^ℓ, outputs a triplet of public/private keys (pk, tk_0, tk_1)*

$\mathsf{TCKG}(1^\ell, i)$: *a probabilistic algorithm which, on input the security parameter 1^ℓ and a bit i outputs a pair of public/private keys (pk, tk).*

$\mathsf{C}_{pk}(m, r)$: *the evaluation algorithm which, on input the public key pk, a message $m \in M$ and a random nonce $r \in R$, outputs a hashed value;*

$\mathsf{Coll}(tk_i, m, m', r)$: *the collision finding algorithm which, on input one of the two private trapdoor keys tk_i, two messages m, m' and a nonce r, outputs a nonce r' such that $\mathsf{C}_{pk}(m, r) = \mathsf{C}_{pk}(m', r')$.*

We make the following security requirements

Distribution of Keys. Let $\overline{\mathsf{CKG}}(1^\ell, i)$ the algorithm that executes $\mathsf{CKG}(1^\ell)$ and restricts its output to (pk, tk_i). We require that the distribution of the output of $\mathsf{TCKG}(1^\ell, i)$ is identical to the distribution of the output of $\overline{\mathsf{CKG}}(1^\ell, i)$.

Collision Resistance. Let $(pk, tk_0, tk_1) = \mathsf{CKG}(1^\ell)$.
    1. For every $i = 0, 1$, given pk and tk_i it is infeasible to find $tk_{i\oplus 1}$.
    2. Moreover there exists an, efficient, algorithm A that on input the public key pk and a collision m, r, m', r' finds at least one of the trapdoors tk_i.
As a consequence, it is infeasible to find collisions without at least one of the trapdoors tk_i.

Distribution of Collisions. For every m, m', and a random r, and for every $i = 0, 1$, the distribution of $r' = \mathsf{Coll}(tk_i, m, m', r)$ is uniform, even when given pk, $c = \mathsf{C}_{pk}(m, r)$, m and m'. As in the case of the 'regular' chameleon hashing, this implies that the function is an information-theoretically hiding commitment. Moreover it implies that the distributions of the openings are the same no matter what trapdoor one uses.

Double trapdoor chameleon hashing leads to a very simple construction of a fully secure one-time signature scheme (rather than just an obliviously secure signature scheme as it is the case when using standard chameleon hash functions). The construction given a two-trapdoor chameleon hash $(\mathsf{CKG}, \mathsf{C}, \mathsf{Coll})$ is as follows.

KEY GENERATION. On input a security parameter ℓ, run $\mathsf{CKG}(1^\ell) = (pk, tk_0, tk_1)$. Then it chooses a message α and a nonce r and computes $c = \mathsf{C}_{pk}(\alpha, r)$. The public key is (pk, c), the signing key is (tk_0, tk_1, α, r).

SIGNATURE ALGORITHM. On input a message m the signer uses his knowledge of either trapdoor to compute a nonce s such that, $c = \mathsf{C}_{pk}(m, s)$. The signature is then (m, s).

VERIFICATION. On input a purported signature (m, s), the verifier checks whether $c = \mathsf{C}_{pk}(m, s)$. If this is the case the signature is accepted as valid, otherwise it is rejected.

Theorem 5. *If* (CKG, C, Coll) *is a two-trapdoor chameleon hash function then the scheme presented above is a secure one-time signature scheme.*

For lack of space the proof is deferred to the full version of the paper.

CONSTRUCTION. The notion of double trapdoor commitment scheme was proposed (even though not explicitly defined) in [6]. There they present a scheme based on the discrete logarithm problem and they show how to use such a construction to build threshold on-line off-line digital signature schemes. In Appendix B we briefly recall the double trapdoor commitment scheme given in [6]

4   Experimental Results

As we said in the introduction, this work was motivated by two basic questions about the relationship between the EGM and the Shamir-Tauman approach to build off-line/on-line signatures. In the previous section we showed that, at least conceptually, the Shamir-Tauman approach is really an instantiation of the EGM paradigm. In this section we set out to discuss a *practical* comparison between the two approaches in terms of their efficiency. To achieve that, an extensive work of implementation was carried out. We implemented all the schemes presented in the previous sections, in order to directly measure their real efficiency. To get objective values, all the implementations share the same level of optimization and all the tests were iterated hundreds of times on a reference hardware: an Intel Pentium 4 CPU running at 2.80 GHz. We implemented the algorithms in C using OpenSSL[29] as the underlying library for large number manipulations[3].

4.1   Implementation Details

The different types of hash functions (see Section 2.1) required in our constructions were implemented as follows:

- **FCR hashing:** we use SHA-1 [9] with its full 160-bit output;
- **TCR hashing:** it is implemented using SHA-1 as follows[16]: given a message x and the key k, the function is computed as $h^{\text{tcr}}(k, x) = Trunc_\ell(\text{SHA-1}(x \oplus k'))$, where k' is the concatenation of copies of k until k' and x have the same length. $Trunc_\ell(\cdot)$ is a function that outputs the first ℓ bits of its input.
- **TDI hashing:** as practical construction we use the one suggested in [14] with SHA-1 as the underling tool, but with an additional randomizing key. Given a message x and a key k:

$$h^{\text{tdi}}(k, x) = Set_{msb}(Set_{lsb}(\text{SHA-1}(x \circ 1 \oplus k') \circ \cdots \circ \text{SHA-1}(x \circ 4 \oplus k')))$$

where $\circ$ is the concatenation operator, k' is the concatenation of copies of k until k' and x have the same length and $Set_{msb}(\cdot)$, $Set_{lsb}(\cdot)$ are functions that force the most-significant-bit (resp. least-significant-bit) to be 1; this function takes arbitrarily long inputs and outputs of 640-bit integers.

---

[3] The sources of the tests are available upon request to the authors.

One-Time Signatures. In our tests we implemented the one-time signature proposed by Even *et al.* with the option to apply Jakobsson's speedup (see Section 2.3). The one-way function used in the implementation is:

$f(x) = Trunc_\ell(\mathsf{SHA}\text{-}1(x))$ with different values for the security parameter ℓ.

The public key in this scheme is composed of m/t strings $y_0, y_1, \ldots, y_{m/t}$, but it can also be replaced with its hash value $y = h^{\mathsf{fcr}}(y_0, y_1, \ldots, y_{m/t})$, which is what we do in our implementation, in order to keep keys shorter (the price to pay is an extra computation of h^{fcr} at verification time).

4.2 Using Target-Collision Resistant Hash

USING TCR HASHING IN THE ON-LINE STEP. When signing messages one usually hashes them down with a FCR function to shorten them. It is well known that one can uses a TCR function provided that the key of the hash function is signed together with the message digest and sent as part of the signature. One of the advantages of using TCR functions is that the message digest may be shorter, but this advantage is usually off-set by the need to sign the key as well.

However in the case of off-line/on-line signatures, the advantage of using TCR functions can be substantial. Indeed one can 'prepare in advance' the key k for the TCR function to be used in the on-line step, and sign it during the off-line step with the "regular" signature scheme.

In the EGM construction, this results in a substantial efficiency gain, since the one-way functions based one-time signatures are very sensitive to the length of the message being signed. Indeed the size of the signature grows quadratically in the length. Since the key k of the TCR function is signed in the off-line step, the one-time signature is only applied to the digest, resulting in a substantially shorter signature.

Similarly in the Shamir-Tauman approach, using a TCR function to hash the message in the online case can improve the efficiency. For example if we use the RSA-based chameleon hash it will be possible to use a shorter public exponent e.

USING TCR HASH IN THE OFF-LINE STEP. As we pointed in the previous section, the quantities signed in the off-line step are *not* under the control of the adversary, and they are actually random quantities (the verification key of the one-time signature or of the chameleon hashing, and the key of the TCR function). For this reason it is also possible to use a TCR function to compress them, rather than a FCR one. In this case the key k is chosen once and for all and made part of the public key.

4.3 Test Settings

As we said above we performed implementation of all the schemes described above. With OTS we denote the "one-time signature" based on one-way functions described in Section 2.3.

GHR-OTS **setting**: This implementation uses the GHR scheme for the off-line step, and the OTS scheme for the on-line case. As pointed above we use TCR hashing to compress the message, the key is signed in the off-line part. The GHR-OTS setting can be configured with various parameters. In all our experiments we set the size of the RSA modulus to 1024. We varied the other parameters as you can see in the Table. These parameters are: ots_l = 80, 96, 112 the size of the TCR output, i.e. the size of the digest being signed in the OTS scheme; ots_t = 4, 8, 10, 12, 16 the size of the blocks in the OTS scheme; and ots_p = 1, 5, 8, 10, 12, 16 the number of memorized pebbles in Jakobsson's optimization (1 means that it is disabled).

GHR-DL setting: This implementation uses the GHR scheme for the off-line step, and the discrete-log based chameleon hashing for the on-line case. Here we use FCR hashing to compress the message in the on-line step. We implemented the group G as the subgroup of order q in Z_p^* where p, q are primes such that $q|(p-1)$. The parameters of the GHR-DL setting are: the size of the GHR modulus N and the sizes of the primes p and q. We only ran experiments with $|N| = |p| = 1024$ and $|q| = 160$.

GHR-RSA setting: This implementation uses the GHR scheme for the off-line step, and the RSA based chameleon hashing for the on-line case. Here we use FCR hashing to compress the message in the on-line step. The parameters of the GHR-RSA setting are: the size of the GHR modulus N (which can be used also as the modulus for the chameleon hash) and the size of the exponent e for the chameleon hash. We only ran experiments with $|N| = 1024$ and $|e| = 160$.

GHR-DL2 setting: This the same as GHR-DL but use TCR hashing to compress the message in the on-line step. The key of the TCR hash is signed in the off-line step. This results in the shortening of some of the exponents used to compute the chameleon hash. The parameters are the same of GHR-DL with an extra one: tcr_bits = 80, 96 the length of the output of the TCR hash function.

GHR-RSA2 setting: the same as GHR-RSA but using TCR hashing to compress the message in the on-line step. The key of the TCR hash is signed in the off-line step. This results in the shortening of the public exponent e used to compute the chameleon hash. In this case the parameter tcr_bits = 80, 96 denotes the length of the output of the TCR hash function and of the exponent e (actually $|e| = $ tcr_bits $+ 1$).

CS-OTS, CS-DL, CS-RSA, CS-DL2 and CS-RSA2 settings: they are analogous to the previous settings, but here we use the CS signature scheme instead of the GHR one. As before the CS signature modulus was always chosen as a 1024-bit one. The other parameters are the same, as in the above cases.

4.4 Analysis of the Results

In this section we summarize what we learned from our experimental results.

EGM construction *vs.* ST construction. The use of TCR hashing in the EGM settings, results in experimental results which are comparable to the ST measurements. For example if we focus on the time to perform the on-line step (arguably the most important measure in off-line/on-line signatures), we see that for the ST construction this is minimized with a time of about 0.03 ms by using the Discrete Log based chameleon hashing (no matter if the GHR and CS signature is used in the off-line step, of course) Nevertheless the setting GHR-OTS reaches a comparable on-line signing time of 0.47 ms when istantiated with similar security levels. The drawback is a longer signature, though the difference is not huge: 2944 bits versus the 1184 bits of GHR-DL. It is possible to shrink the EGM signature size to 2144 using bigger blocks and applying Jakobsson's technique. The on-line signature time continues to be competitive (1.27 ms) at the cost of a bigger temporary storage (8304 bits). It is important to note that the hash chain traversals in the verification step do not enjoy the benefit of the Jakobsson's technique as the pebbles must be kept secret.

GHR *vs.* CS. The GHR signature scheme outperforms the CS signature scheme in almost all parameters: off-line and on-line signature time, and signature size. The CS scheme is faster only in verification time, as to be expected since the GHR must use a longer public exponent, because of the division-intractability assumptions.

Chameleon hashing: DL-based *vs.* RSA-based. The time required for the hash evaluation step is comparable in both the schemes but the DL-based one has a notable advantage in the collision finding step. This operation is fundamental in the off-line/on-line signature construction, so it is the optimal choice for the ST construction.

Use of TCR hashing. As we pointed out above the use of TCR hashing has a dramatic impact on the efficiency of the OTS schemes. The experiments also point out that TCR hashing improves also the Shamir-Tauman approach, as it reduces the size of some of the exponents used in the exponentiations. A more pronounced improvement is obtained when using the RSA-based chameleon hashing: as in this construction the use of TCR hashing reduces the size of two exponents, rather than one as in the Discrete Log based one.

5   Conclusions

This paper presents some theoretical results about off-line/on-line digital signatures. We showed that the Shamir-Tauman approach is conceptually just a different instantiation of the generic EGM paradigm. We did this by proving that the EGM paradigm requires weaker security properties from its components and then showing that such properties are satisfied by chameleon hash functions. We also showed that some type of chameleon hash functions can be used as full-fledged one-time signatures. We performed extensive implementation results to see what approach is preferable. Surprisingly we found that for appropriate choices of security parameters the ST and EGM approaches are comparable. Our experiments also showed that the Gennaro-Halevi-Rabin signature scheme is preferable to the Cramer-Shoup one on all respects except verification time.

Acknowledgments. We thank the anonymous reviewers for their useful comments.

References

1. Barić, N., Pfitzmann, B.: Collision-free Accumulators and Fail-stop Signature Schemes without Trees. In: Fumy, W. (ed.) EUROCRYPT 1997. LNCS, vol. 1233, pp. 480–494. Springer, Heidelberg (1997)
2. Bellare, M., Micali, S.: How To Sign Given Any Trapdoor Function. In: Proceedings of STOC 88, pp. 32–42. ACM, New York (1988)
3. Bellare, M., Rogaway, P.: Random Oracles Are Practical: a Paradigm for Designing Efficient Protocols. In: proceedings of 1st ACM Conference on Computer and Communications Security (CCS 1993), pp. 62–73. ACM Press, New York (1993)
4. Boyar, J.F., Kurtz, S.A., Krentel, M.W.: A Discrete Logarithm Implementation of Perfect Zero-Knowledge Blobs. Journal of Cryptology 2(2), 63–76 (1990)
5. Brassard, G., Chaum, D., Crépeau, C.: Minimum disclosure proofs of knowledge. Journal of Computer and System Sciences 37(2), 156–189 (1988)
6. Bresson, E., Catalano, D., Gennaro, R.: Improved On-Line/Off-Line Threshold Signatures. In: Okamoto, T., Wang, X. (eds.) PKC 2007. LNCS, vol. 4450, pp. 217–232. Springer, Heidelberg (2007)
7. Coron, J., Naccache, D.: Security analysis of the Gennaro-Halevi-Rabin Signature Scheme. In: Preneel, B. (ed.) EUROCRYPT 2000. LNCS, vol. 1807, pp. 91–101. Springer, Heidelberg (2000)
8. Cramer, R., Damgard, I.: New Generation of Secure and Practical RSA-based Signatures. In: Koblitz, N. (ed.) CRYPTO 1996. LNCS, vol. 1109, pp. 173–185. Springer, Heidelberg (1996)
9. Eastlake, D., Jones, P.: US Secure Hash Algorithm 1 (SHA1), RFC, RFC Editor
10. Cramer, R., Shoup, V.: Signature Scheme based on the Strong RSA Assumption. In: Proceedings of 6th ACM Conference on Computer and Communications Security (CCS 1999), pp. 46–51. ACM Press, New York (1999)
11. ElGamal, T.: A public key cryptosystem and a signature scheme based on discrete logarithms. IEEE Transactions on Information Theory 31(4), 469–472 (1985)
12. Even, S., Goldreich, O., Micali, S.: On-Line/Off-Line Digital Signatures. Journal of Cryptology 9(1), 35–67 (1996)
13. Fiat, A., Shamir, A.: How to Prove Yourself: Practical Solutions of Identification and Signature Problems. In: Odlyzko, A.M. (ed.) CRYPTO 1986. LNCS, vol. 263, pp. 187–194. Springer, Heidelberg (1987)
14. Gennaro, R., Halevi, S., Rabin, T.: Secure Hash-and-Sign Signatures without the Random Oracle. In: Stern, J. (ed.) EUROCRYPT 1999. LNCS, vol. 1592, pp. 123–139. Springer, Heidelberg (1999)
15. Goldwasser, S., Micali, S., Rivest, R.L.: A Digital Signature Scheme Secure Against Adaptive Chosen-Message Attacks. SIAM Journal on Computing 17(2), 281–308 (1988)
16. Halevi, S., Krawczyk, H.: Strengthening Digital Signatures Via Randomized Hashing. In: Dwork, C. (ed.) CRYPTO 2006. LNCS, vol. 4117, pp. 41–59. Springer, Heidelberg (2006)
17. Jakobsson, M.: Fractal Hash Sequence Representation and Traversal. In: Jakobsson, M. (ed.) Proceedings of IEEE International Symposium on Information Theory (ISIT 2002), p. 437 (2002)

18. Krawczyk, H., Rabin, T.: Chameleon Hashing and Signatures. In: Proceedings of Network and Distributed Systems Security Symposium (NDSS 2000), pp. 143–154. Internet Society (2000)
19. Kurosawa, K., Schmidt-Samoa, K.: New Online/Offline Signature Schemes Without Random Oracles. In: Yung, M., et al. (eds.) PKC 2006. LNCS, vol. 3958, pp. 330–346. Springer, Heidelberg (2006)
20. Lamport, L.: Constructing digital signatures from a one-way function, Technical Report SRI-CSL-98, SRI International Computer Science Laboratory (October 1979)
21. Merkle, R.C.: A digital signature based on a conventional encryption function. In: Pomerance, C. (ed.) CRYPTO 1987. LNCS, vol. 293, pp. 369–378. Springer, Heidelberg (1988)
22. Naor, M., Yung, M.: Universal One-Way Hash Functions and Their Cryptographic Application. In: Proceedings of STOC 1989, pp. 33–43. ACM Press, New York (1989)
23. Pointcheval, D., Stern, J.: Security Arguments for Digital Signatures and Blind Signatures. Journal of Cryptology 13(3), 361–396 (2000)
24. Rabin, M.O.: Digital Signatures. In: DeMillo, R.A., et al. (eds.) Foundations of Secure Computation, pp. 155–168. Academic Press, London (1978)
25. Rivest, R., Shamir, A., Adelman, L.: A Method for Obtaining Digital Signature and Public Key Cryptosystems. Communications of the ACM 21(2), 120–126 (1978)
26. Rompel, J.: One-Way Functions Are Necessary and Sufficient for Secure Signatures. In: Proceedings of STOC 1990, pp. 387–394 (1990)
27. Shamir, A., Tauman, Y.: Improved On-line/Off-line Signature Schemes. In: Kilian, J. (ed.) CRYPTO 2001. LNCS, vol. 2139, pp. 355–367. Springer, Heidelberg (2001)
28. Schnorr, C.P.: Efficient Signature Generation by Smart Cards. Journal of Cryptology 4(3), 161–174 (1991)
29. OpenSSL Project, http://www.openssl.org
30. National Institute for Standards and Technology, Digital Signature Standard (DSS), Technical Report 169, August 30 (1991)

A   On One-Time Signatures

In Section 2.3 we presented two one-time signature schemes: Lamport's and Even *et al.*'s. The former is faster, but produces long signatures and keys. The latter allows for an efficiency trade-off between the signature/key sizes and time required to generate and to verify a signature tag.

SECURITY. Lamport's scheme is proved secure under the assumption that one way functions exist. Even *et al.* solution relies on a seemingly stronger assumption:

Definition 6 (Quasi-Inverting). *Let* $f : \{0,1\}^* \to \{0,1\}^*$ *be a polynomial-time computable function. Given an image,* y*, the task of quasi-inverting* f *on* y *is to find an* x *and an* $i = poly(|y|)$ *so that* $f^{i+1}(x) = f^i(y)$*. (For* $i = 0$*, the standard notion of inverting is regained.)*

CONCRETE SECURITY ANALYSIS. Here we focus on the security of the two one-time signature schemes presented in Section 2.3. In particular we analyze the efficiency (in terms of signature/key length) of Even *et al.*'s scheme with respect to Lamport's one, under the additional requirement that the two schemes should achieve the same security level.

Let $f : \{0,1\}^\ell \to \{0,1\}^\ell$ be a one-way function. In both schemes we assume to sign messages of length m. In the scheme of Even *et al.*, t represents the block length.

Let $\mathcal{A}$ be an adversary that breaks Lamport's one-time signature scheme with probability ϵ. It is possible to prove that this leads to an adversary $\mathcal{B}$ that inverts f with probability $\frac{\epsilon}{2m}$.

Similarly, if $\mathcal{A}'$ is an adversary that breaks Even *et al.* scheme with probability ϵ', this leads to an adversary $\mathcal{B}'$ that quasi-inverts f with probability $\frac{\epsilon'}{(m/t)2^{t+1}}$ (see [12], for details).

In what follows, we restrict to the case where f is a one way permutation (so that quasi-inverting f is equivalent to inverting f). We assume that no adversary can invert f with probability better than $1/2^\ell$. For the case of Lamport's scheme, this leads to $\frac{\epsilon}{2m} = \frac{1}{2^\ell}$ which means that one cannot forge signatures with probability better than $\epsilon = \frac{2m}{2^\ell}$. Similarly for Even *et al.*'s scheme we have that $\frac{\epsilon'}{(m/t)2^{t+1}} = \frac{1}{2^{\ell'}}$, implies a security for the signature scheme which is $\epsilon' = \frac{m2^{t+1-\ell'}}{t}$. Thus, in order for the two schemes to achieve the same security level, it has to be the case that $\epsilon' = \epsilon$, which means $\frac{2m}{2^\ell} = \frac{m2^{t+1-\ell'}}{t}$.

Thus, to achieve the same security level, for the two schemes, one has to consider a larger security parameter for the Even *et al.* scheme.

$$\ell' = \ell + t - log(t) \tag{1}$$

SIGNATURE LENGTH. In Lamport's scheme signatures have length $d = m\ell$. In Even *et al.*'s, on the other hand, the signature length is $d' = ((m/t)+1)\ell'$. From Equation (1) we get:

$$d' = \frac{m\ell}{t} + m + \ell + t - (\frac{m}{t} + 1)log(t) \tag{2}$$

Now, we want to establish for which choice of t we have $d' < d$. That is, for which choice of t Even *et al.* signatures are shorter than Lamport's ones.

From $\frac{m\ell}{t} + m + \ell + t - (\frac{m}{t} + 1)log(t) < m\ell$ one easily derives that if $m, \ell > 2$ then $t > 1$ is the required condition.

EXPERIMENTAL RESULTS. The relation among the variables involved in Equation (2) is analyzed through the tabulation of realistic values. We fix the security parameter for the Lamport's scheme $\ell = 80$ and we assume to deal with messages of $m = 2\ell$ bits length. For different values of t we determine the corresponding values for the Even *et al.*'s parameters ℓ', d' using the above relations. All these values are reported in Table A; the signature length gain $(d - d')$ obtained using the EGM scheme instead of the Lamport's one is emphasized too (a negative value means that the use of the EGM construction is self-defeating).

We observe that the EGM solution is a winning solution for each real cases: the necessary augment of the security parameter ℓ' is minimal.

Table 1. Experimental results with parameters $\ell = 80, m = 2\ell$

t	ℓ'	d'	d	gain $(d - d')$
1	81	13041	12800	-241
2	81	6561	12800	6239
3	81.4150	4423.6	12800	8376.4
4	82	3362	12800	9438
5	82.6781	2728.4	12800	10071.6

B   A Discrete Log-Based Double Trapdoor Commitment Scheme

Here we briefly recall the double trapdoor commitment scheme given in [6] and then we discuss further applications of such a scheme.

KEY GENERATION. Consider a cyclic group G of prime order q (with $|q| = \ell$ the security parameter) like before. Next, denoting with g a generator of G, choose two random values $x, y \in \mathbb{Z}_q$ and sets $h_1 = g^x$ and $h_2 = g^y$. The public key is (G, q, g, h_1, h_2) the private key is (x, y).

THE COMMITMENT FUNCTION. To commit to a message $m \in \mathbb{Z}_q$, we use two random values $r, s \in_R \mathbb{Z}_q^*$ and set $\mathsf{C}(m, r, s) = g^m h_1^r h_2^s$

Theorem 6. *Under the assumption that computing discrete logarithms is hard, the above function* C *is a double trapdoor commitment scheme.*

Proof. We prove this theorem by showing that the three main properties of double trapdoor chameleon hash functions are satisfied.

Distribution of keys.. Here we show the details of the TCKG algorithm. On input 1^ℓ and a bit i, it chooses two random generators $g, h_{i\oplus 1} \in G$, a random $tk_i \in \mathbb{Z}_q^*$ and sets, $h_i = g^{tk_i}$. The public key is set as (G, q, g, h_1, h_2) the trapdoor is tk_i. It is trivial to verify that all the required properties are satisfied.

Collision resistance. We prove this by contradiction. We assume there exists an adversary $\mathcal{A}$ that can find a collision in the proposed double trapdoor commitment scheme with non-negligible probability ϵ. Then we show how to build a simulator $\mathcal{B}$ that can solve the Discrete Logarithm (DLog) problem with non-negligible probability at least $\epsilon/6$. $\mathcal{A}$ finds a collision if, given the public key pk, it outputs two triples $(m, r, s), (m', r', s')$ with $m \neq m'$ such that $\mathsf{C}_{pk}(m, r, s) = \mathsf{C}_{pk}(m', r', s')$. We observe that at least one of the following conditions must hold: (1) $r \neq r'$ or (2) $s \neq s'$. We can distinguish between three types of collisions:

Type I $m \neq m', r \neq r', s \neq s'$
Type II $m \neq m', r = r', s \neq s'$
Type III $m \neq m', r \neq r', s = s'$

Thus $\mathcal{A}$ outputs a collision of either type I, type II or type III with probability at least $\epsilon/3$. Now we describe a simulator $\mathcal{B}$ that uses such collisions to solve the DLog problem.

In the first phase $\mathcal{B}$ receives in input two primes p, q such that $q|p - 1$, a generator g of a cyclic subgroup G of $\mathbb{Z}_p^*$ of order q and an element $X \in G$. The aim of $\mathcal{B}$ is to output $x \in \mathbb{Z}_q^*$ such that $g^x = X$.

$\mathcal{B}$ has to construct the public key for the double trapdoor commitment scheme. First it flips a binary coin β. If $\beta = 0$ $\mathcal{B}$ bets on the fact that $\mathcal{A}$ will provide a collision of type I or III (where condition 1 holds true). Otherwise if $\beta = 1$ it bets on the fact that the received collision is of type I or II (it satisfies condition 2). $\mathcal{B}$ chooses random $y \xleftarrow{\$} \mathbb{Z}_q^*$. If $\beta = 0$ it sets $h_1 = X, h_2 = g^y$, otherwise it sets $h_1 = g^y, h_2 = X$. It gives $PK = (G, q, g, h_1, h_2)$ to $\mathcal{A}$. Then $\mathcal{A}$ produces a collision $(m, r, s), (m', r', s')$. Now we distinguish between the three types of collisions described above.

TYPE I COLLISION. In this case $\mathcal{B}$ can solve the DLog problem with non-negligible probability $\epsilon/3$. Indeed if $\beta = 0$ $\mathcal{B}$ outputs $x = \frac{m'-m+y(s'-s)}{r-r'}$ mod q as the discrete logarithm of X. Otherwise if $\beta = 1$ $\mathcal{B}$ outputs $x = \frac{m'-m+y(r'-r)}{s-s'}$ mod q.

TYPE II COLLISION. In this case if $\beta = 0$ $\mathcal{B}$ loses its initial bet and fails. Otherwise if $\beta = 1$ it computes $x = \frac{m'-m}{s-s'}$ mod q. Thus with probability at least $\frac{\epsilon}{3}\frac{1}{2}$ $\mathcal{B}$ solves the DLog problem.

TYPE III COLLISION. This case is similar to the previous. If $\beta = 1$ $\mathcal{B}$ loses its initial bet and fails. Otherwise if $\beta = 0$ it computes $x = \frac{m'-m}{r-r'}$ mod q. Thus with probability at least $\frac{\epsilon}{3}\frac{1}{2}$ the simulator can find the discrete logarithm of X.

Distributions of Collisions. We consider the two distributions:

$$\{m, m', r, s \leftarrow \mathbb{Z}_q^*, : \mathsf{Coll}(tk_1, m, m', r, s)\}$$

$$\{m, m', r, s \leftarrow \mathbb{Z}_q^*, : \mathsf{Coll}(tk_2, m, m', r, s)\}$$

In the first distribution Coll outputs a value (r', s) such that $r' = \frac{m-m'}{x} + r$ mod q. We observe that s is uniformly distributed in $\mathbb{Z}_q^*$ and if r is uniformly distributed in $\mathbb{Z}_q^*$, then also r' is uniformly distributed in $\mathbb{Z}_q^*$. In the second distribution Coll outputs a pair (r, s') such that $s' = \frac{m-m'}{y} + s$ mod q. If s is uniform in $\mathbb{Z}_q^*$, then also s' is uniform in $\mathbb{Z}_q^*$. Thus, both the two distributions are perfectly indistinguishable from uniform in $\mathbb{Z}_q^*$.

Construction of Universal Designated-Verifier Signatures and Identity-Based Signatures from Standard Signatures

Siamak F. Shahandashti[1] and Reihaneh Safavi-Naini[2]

[1] School of Comp. Sci. and Soft. Eng., University of Wollongong, Australia
http://www.uow.edu.au/~sfs166
[2] Department of Computer Science, University of Calgary, Canada
http://www.cpsc.ucalgary.ca/~rei

Abstract. We give a generic construction for universal designated-verifier signature schemes from a large class, $\mathbb{C}$, of signature schemes. The resulting schemes are efficient and have two important properties. Firstly, they are provably DV-unforgeable, non-transferable and also non-delegatable. Secondly, the signer and the designated verifier can independently choose their cryptographic settings. We also propose a generic construction for identity-based signature schemes from any signature scheme in $\mathbb{C}$ and prove that the construction is secure against adaptive chosen message and identity attacks. We discuss possible extensions of our constructions to universal multi-designated-verifier signatures, hierarchical identity-based signatures, identity-based universal designated verifier signatures, and identity-based ring signatures from any signature in $\mathbb{C}$.

1 Introduction

Universal Designated-Verifier Signatures (UDVS). UDVS schemes were first proposed by Steinfeld et al. [1], based on ideas of Jakobsson et al. [2], with the goal of protecting users' privacy when using certificates. In such a scheme, a user Alice has a certificate that is signed by a certificate issuer. If Alice wants to present her certificate to a verifier Bob, she will use Bob's public key to transform the issuer's signature into a *designated signature* for Bob. Bob can verify the issuer's signature by verifying the validity of the designated signature. However, he cannot convince a third party that the certificate was signed by the issuer because he can use his secret key to construct the same designated signature.

Steinfeld et al. proposed security definitions for UDVS schemes and gave a concrete scheme based on bilinear group pairs [1]. In [3] Lipmaa et al. argued that the original security definition in [1] did not sufficiently capture the verifier-designation property and introduced a new security notion, called *non-delegability*. Authors showed that in some UDVS schemes including Steinfeld et al's [1], the issuer can delegate his signing ability - with respect to a fixed designated verifier - to a third party, without revealing his secret key or even enabling the third party to sign with respect to other designated verifiers. They

R. Cramer (Ed.): PKC 2008, LNCS 4939, pp. 121–140, 2008.

argue that, in many scenarios, such delegation property is undesirable and must be prevented.

As an example, consider the following scenario. A university uses a digital signature scheme to issue student cards. Alice, a student, wants to prove herself a student in a gym to get a discount. To protect her privacy, she converts the university's signature on her card to a designated signature first and then presents the designated signature as a proof of studentship. Now if the UDVS in use is delegatable, the university, without having to issue a card for Alex, a non-student, will be able to publish a value that enables him (and anybody) to compute a designated signature for himself get the discount at the gym. This value does not enable Alex to compute university's private key, sign other documents on behalf of the university, or even compute a designated signature of the university to use other services. Besides, since the university has not actually issued any fraudulent student cards, it cannot be held responsible for any malicious activity. These two facts provide enough safety margin for the university to abuse such delegation ability.

None of the UDVS schemes proposed to date, except a recent scheme of Huang et al. [4], has treated non-delegatability as a security requirement. Furthermore, the results of Lipmaa et al. [3] and later results of Li et al. [5] show that many of the proposed UDVS schemes are delegatable, including the scheme from [1] and one of the schemes from [6].

Our Contributions on UDVS. We give a generic construction for secure UDVS schemes from a large class of signature schemes. The class is defined by requiring certain properties from signature schemes. We use a definition of security that includes the original security notions of Steinfled et al, i.e. *unforgeability* and *non-transferability privacy*, and also the notion of *non-delegatability* inspired by the work of Lipmaa et al. [3] and adapted to UDVS.

To construct non-delegatable UDVS schemes, we will use Jakobsson et al's approach to providing verifier designation [2]: *"Instead of proving Θ, Alice will prove the statement: Either Θ is true, or I am Bob."* In UDVS schemes, Alice wants to prove validity of her certificate to Bob. A natural construction of UDVS is a non-interactive version of a proof of the following statement by Alice: *"Either my certificate is valid, or I am Bob."* Such a signature can be constructed as follows: first pick a protocol for proof of knowledge of Alice's certificate and another for the proof of knowledge of Bob's secret key; then construct a protocol for proof of knowledge of Alice's certificate *or* Bob's secret key by combining the two protocols via e.g. techniques of Cramer et al. [7]; finally make the resulting protocol non-interactive via e.g. Fiat-Shamir transform [8]. It is intuitively clear that such a construction yields a secure UDVS scheme, assuming both the underlying protocols are honest-verifier zero-knowledge (HVZK) proofs of knowledge. However, efficient protocols for HVZK proof of knowledge of a signature on a message are only known for a small group of signature schemes.

We propose a construction for UDVS schemes that works for any combination of a signature in class $\mathbb{C}$ of signature schemes and all verifier key pairs that belong to a class $\mathbb{K}$, and prove its security in the above sense, in the *Random*

Oracle Model (ROM) [9]. The class $\mathbb{C}$ of signatures that can be used in our construction includes signature schemes such as RSA-FDH [10], Schnorr [11], modified ElGamal [12], BLS [13], BB [14], Cramer-Shoup [15], and both schemes proposed by Camenisch and Lysyanskaya [16,17]. Class $\mathbb{K}$ is the set of all key pairs for which there exist protocols for HVZK proofs of knowledge of the secret key corresponding to a public key and includes public and private key pairs of RSA cryptosystem, GQ identification scheme [18], and discrete-log based public and private key pairs.

Our construction are generic and security proofs guarantee security of a large class of UDVS schemes that are obtained from standard signature schemes that are members of the class $\mathbb{C}$. We note that the only other known non-delegatable UDVS due to Huang et al. [4] is in fact an instance of our construction. Secondly, the construction does not limit the signer and the verifier to have 'compatible' settings: the construction works for any choice of signer and verifier settings as long as the signature scheme is a member of class $\mathbb{C}$ and the verifier key belongs to the class $\mathbb{K}$. All previous constructions only work for a specific combination of signature schemes and verifier key pairs.

Identity-Based Signatures. Identity-based cryptography was proposed by Shamir in [19], where he also proposed an *identity-based signature* (IBS) scheme. There are two known generic constructions of IBS. The first is due to Bellare et al. [20], which generalizes an earlier construction of Dodis et al. [21]. They show that a large number of previously proposed schemes are in fact instances of their generic construction. However, as noted by the authors, there are some IBS schemes, including Okamoto's discrete logarithm based IBS [22] (called OkDL-IBS by Bellare et al.) and a new IBS scheme proposed in [20] (called BNN-IBS), that are not instances of their generic construction.

The other generic construction is the one of Kurosawa and Heng [23]. Their construction requires an efficient zero-knowledge protocol for proof of knowledge of a signature, which makes their construction applicable to only a few schemes such as RSA-FDH and BLS.

Our Contributions on IBS. We propose a construction of IBS schemes from any signature in the aforementioned class $\mathbb{C}$ and prove the construction secure against adaptive chosen message and identity attacks. In our construction, a user's secret key is basically a signature of the authority on the user's identity. An identity-based signature is generated as follows: the user constructs a proof of knowledge of her secret key (i.e. the authority's signature on her identity) and then transforms it into a signature on a message using the Fiat-Shamir transform. For signature schemes with efficient zero-knowledge protocols for proof of knowledge of a signature, our constructions will become the same as those of Kurosawa and Heng [23]. Thus, our constructions can be seen as a generalization of theirs.

Many previous IBS schemes can be seen as instances of our generic construction; this includes the schemes of Fiat and Shamir [8], Guillou and Quisquater [18], Shamir [19], pairing-based schemes from [24,25,26,27,28,29] and basically all the convertible IBS schemes constructed in [20]. Both OkDL-IBS and BNN-IBS, which are not captured by generic constructions of Bellare et al, fit as instances of our generic construction as well. However, all the IBS schemes that we construct are proved secure in ROM. Thus, ROM-free constructions such as the folklore *certificate-based* IBS schemes formalized in [20] and the scheme of Paterson and Schuldt [30] are not captured by our framework.

Further Contributions. Our constructions of UDVS schemes can be naturally extended to (non-delegatable) *universal multi-designated-verifier signatures*. Furthermore, we observe that our identity-based constructions support a *nesting-like* property in the sense that a user can act as a new key generation authority and issue keys for other users. This fact enables extensions of our IBS constructions to *hierarchical identity-based signatures* out of any signature scheme in the class ℂ. We will also point out the possibility of generic construction of (non-delegatable) *identity-based universal designated verifier signatures* and *identity-based ring signatures* from any signature in ℂ using our techniques.

1.1 Related Work

UDVS schemes were first proposed by Steinfeld et al. in [1]. The proposed security definitions and a concrete scheme based on bilinear group pairs. In [6] authors proposed extensions of Schnorr and RSA signatures to UDVS schemes. Other pairing-based schemes were proposed in [31] and [32], and Laguillaumie et al. introduced 'Random Oracle free' constructions [33].

Our constructions are very close to Goldwasser and Waisbard's generic constructions of *designated confirmer signatures* in [34]. They also use protocols for proof of knowledge of a signature as a tool for their constructions. They also present such protocols for a number of signature schemes including Goldwasser-Micali-Rivest [35], Gennaro-Halevi-Rabin [36], and Cramer-Shoup [15]. This shows that the above signatures are in class ℂ.

A closely related area is that of *ring signatures*. Generic constructions of ring signatures as Fiat-Shamir transformed proofs of knowledge of one-out-of-n secret keys were previously known. Our techniques deal with a similar but different concept of proofs of knowledge of signatures on known messages. Although protocols for proof of knowledge of a secret key corresponding to a public key are more studied and well-known, proof of knowledge of a signature on a message with respect to a known public key has been less studied.

It is worth noting that the previous constructions of identity-based universal deignated verifier signatures by Zhang et al. [37] and universal multi-designated-verifier signatures by Ng et al. [38] are both delegatable. Our generic constructions of the above schemes, as mentioned before, guarantee non-delegatability.

2 Preliminaries

2.1 Notation

We use different fonts to denote **Algorithms**, SECURITY NOTIONS, and *Oracles*, respectively. By '$x \leftarrow a$' we denote that a is assigned to x and by '$x \leftarrow \mathsf{X}(a)$'

we denote that X with input a is run and the output is assigned to x. $\|$ and $\triangle$ denote concatenation and definition, respectively.

2.2   Proofs of Knowledge

Let P be ab *NP problem* and *Rel* be the corresponding *NP relation*. Let Rel be the corresponding (poly-time) membership deciding algorithm, i.e. $(Pub, Sec) \in Rel$ iff Rel (Pub, Sec). Following the works of Camenisch and Stadler [39], we will use the notation PoK $\{Sec : \text{Rel}\,(Pub, Sec)\}$ for showing a protocol for *proof of knowledge* where the prover proves knowledge of her secret *Sec* corresponding to a publicly known *Pub*, s.t. $(Pub, Sec) \in Rel$.

A *public-coin* protocol is a protocol in which the verifier chooses all its messages during the protocol run randomly from publicly known sets. A three-move public-coin protocol can be written in a *canonical* form in which the messages sent in the three moves are often called *commitment, challenge,* and *response,* denoted here by Cmt, Chl, and Rsp, respectively. The challenge Chl is drawn randomly from a set, called the *challenge space*. The protocol is said to have the *honest-verifier zero-knowledge* property (HVZK) [40], if there exists an algorithm that is able to *simulate* transcripts that are indistinguishable from the ones of the real protocol runs without the knowledge of the secret. The protocol is said to have the *special soundness* property (SpS from now on) as described in [7], if there also exists an algorithm that is able to *extract* the secret from two transcripts of the protocol with the same commitment and different challenges. A three-move public-coin protocol with both the HVZK and SpS properties is usually called a Σ protocol.

2.3   Proofs of Disjunctive Knowledge

Cramer et al. showed how to extend Σ protocols to *witness indistinguishable* (WI) Σ protocols for proving knowledge of (at least) t out of n values using secret sharing schemes [7]. They called such protocols *proofs of partial knowledge.* Witness indistinguishability guarantees that even a cheating verifier will not be able to tell which t-subset of the n values is known by the prover. Thus, the transcripts of different runs of the protocol with different t-subsets as prover input will be indistinguishable from one another.

An instance of such partial proofs of knowledge that we find useful here is a WI proof of knowledge of one out of two, which we call a *proof of disjunctive knowledge.* These proofs were also observed by Camenisch and Stadler [41] for discrete logarithms. In line with the above, we will use the following notation to show such proofs: to show a protocol for proof of knowledge of a value Sec_1 such that Rel$_1$ (Pub_1, Sec_1) or a value Sec_2 such that Rel$_2$ (Pub_2, Sec_2), we use the notation PoK $\{(Sec_1 \vee Sec_2) : \text{Rel}_1\,(Pub_1, Sec_1)$, Rel$_2\,(Pub_2, Sec_2)$ $\}$. The Σ protocol for proof of knowledge of Sec_1 or Sec_2 corresponding to $Pub = (Pub_1, Pub_2)$ can be constructed in the canonical form using simple techniques. Both HVZK and SpS properties are also inherited by the constructed proof of disjunctive knowledge.

2.4   The Fiat-Shamir Transform

Fiat and Shamir proposed a method for transforming (interactive) three-move public-coin protocols into non-interactive schemes [8]. The idea is to replace the verifier with a hash function. The rationale is that in such a protocols, all the verifier does is providing an unpredictable challenge that can be replaced by a Random Oracle hash function. This idea has been applied in two different ways depending on what is included in the hash function argument. Firstly, the challenge can be set to the hash of the concatenation of the public inputs and the commitment, i.e. $Chl \leftarrow H(Pub \parallel Cmt)$. This will result in a *non-interactive proof of knowledge*. We will denote the resulting algorithms for non-interactive proof and verification of knowledge by NIPoK and NIVoK, respectively. Note that the output of the former, denoted by π, is a non-interactive proof that can be publicly verified. HVZK and SpS properties for non-interactive proofs are defined similar to their counterparts in interactive proofs. Pointcheval and Stern's *Forking Lemma* [12] can be used to easily prove in the Random Oracle Model that if the original interactive proof has HVZK and SpS properties then the Fiat-Shamir construction will have these properties too.

A second way of applying the Fiat-Shamir method is to set the challenge as the hash of the concatenation of the public inputs, the commitment, and an arbitrary message m, i.e. $Chl \leftarrow H(Pub \parallel Cmt \parallel m)$. This will give us a *signature scheme*. Let Sign and Verify denote the resulting algorithms for signing and verification, respectively. Similarly, a signature, denoted by σ, can be verified publicly. The resulting signature scheme will be existentially unforgeable under chosen message attack if the original protocol is a Σ protocol [12,42,43].

We use the phrase *signature of knowledge* (SoK) for both the NIPoK and Sign algorithms, and the phrase *verification of knowledge* (VoK) for both the NIVoK and Verify algorithms resulting from applying Fiat-Shamir transform to a Σ protocol as above. Assuming the original protocol is $\mathsf{PoK}\{Sec : \mathsf{Rel}(Pub, Sec)\}$, we denote the corresponding SoK and VoK by,

$$\mathsf{SoK}\{Sec : \mathsf{Rel}(Pub, Sec)\} \triangleq \mathsf{NIPoK}(Pub, Sec)$$
$$\mathsf{VoK}\{Sec : \mathsf{Rel}(Pub, Sec)\}(\pi) \triangleq \mathsf{NIVoK}(Pub, \pi)$$
$$\mathsf{SoK}\{Sec : \mathsf{Rel}(Pub, Sec)\}(m) \triangleq \mathsf{Sign}(Pub, Sec, m)$$
$$\mathsf{VoK}\{Sec : \mathsf{Rel}(Pub, Sec)\}(m, \sigma) \triangleq \mathsf{Verify}(Pub, m, \sigma).$$

2.5   On Public-Private Key Pairs

Key pairs are generated by a *key generation* algorithm KeyGen that takes a security parameter as input and outputs the key pair. In public key systems it must be hard to compute the secret key corresponding to a given public key. We call the hard problem of computing the secret key from a given public key for a key pair, the *underlying problem* of that key pair. A public key thus gives an *instance* of the underlying problem and the corresponding secret key is the *solution* to that problem. If key pairs are poly-time verifiable, i.e. one can efficiently verify if a given secret key corresponds to a given public key, the key generation algorithm KeyGen defines an NP relation $Pair$ consisting of all the possible key pairs. We are interested in key pairs for which there exists a Σ protocol to prove knowledge of a secret key corresponding to a given public key. Let us call the set of these key pairs $\mathbb{K}$. A Σ protocol for a key pair in $\mathbb{K}$ can be shown as PoK $\{sk : \mathsf{Pair}\,(pk, sk)\}$. Some key pairs that have Σ protocols as above are listed in [44]. These include key pairs such as GQ identification scheme, discrete-log-like key pairs, and key pairs of the RSA cryptosystem. We will use the phrase *key type* to refer to the types of the keys. For instance, we denote the keys for the GQ identification scheme by the term 'GQ-type key pairs'.

3   Defining the Class $\mathbb{C}$ of Signatures

Let $\mathsf{SS} = \mathsf{SS.}\,(\mathsf{KeyGen}, \mathsf{Sign}, \mathsf{Verify})$ be a provably-secure (standard) signature scheme. Security of the scheme, i.e. its existential unforgeability under chosen message attack (EUF-CMA) [35], is based on the hardness of an *underlying* problem denoted here by $\mathsf{P_{SS}}$. We use $PKSp$ and MSp to denote the *public key space* (i.e. the set of all possible public keys) and the *message space* of a standard signature scheme, respectively. We define a class $\mathbb{C}$ of standard signature schemes as follows.

Definition 1. $\mathbb{C}$ *is the set of all signature schemes* SS *for which there exists a pair of algorithms,* Convert *and* Retrieve, *where* Convert *gets the public key* pk, *a message* m, *and a valid signature* σ *on the message as input and* converts *the signature to a pair* $\tilde{\sigma} = (\tilde{\sigma}_{\mathrm{aux}}, \tilde{\sigma}_{\mathrm{pre}})$ *called* converted signature *as follows:*

$$\tilde{\sigma} = (\tilde{\sigma}_{\mathrm{aux}}, \tilde{\sigma}_{\mathrm{pre}}) \leftarrow \mathsf{Convert}\,(pk, m, \sigma) \ , \ such \ that:$$

- *there exists an algorithm* AuxSim *such that for every* $pk \in PKSp$ *and* $m \in MSp$ *the output of* AuxSim (pk, m) *is (information-theoretically) indistinguishable from* $\tilde{\sigma}_{\mathrm{aux}}$,
- *there exists an algorithm* Compute *that on input* pk, m, *and* $\tilde{\sigma}_{\mathrm{aux}}$ *computes a description of a one-way function* $f\,(\cdot)$ *and an* I *in the range of* f, *such that* I *is the image of* $\tilde{\sigma}_{\mathrm{pre}}$ *under the one-way function* f, *i.e. for a converted signature the output of the following algorithm is* `true`.

$$\begin{aligned}
&\text{Algorithm } \mathsf{Valid}\,(pk, m, \tilde{\sigma}) \\
&\quad (f, I) \leftarrow \mathsf{Compute}\,(pk, m, \tilde{\sigma}_{\mathrm{aux}}) \\
&\quad d \leftarrow (f\,(\tilde{\sigma}_{\mathrm{pre}}) = I) \\
&\quad \texttt{return } d
\end{aligned}$$

- *there exists a* Σ *protocol for proof of knowledge of a* $Sec = \tilde{\sigma}_{\mathrm{pre}}$ *corresponding to a* $Pub = (pk, m, \tilde{\sigma}_{\mathrm{aux}})$ *such that* $\tilde{\sigma}$ *is valid with respect to* pk *and* m, *i.e. there exist a* Σ *protocol for the following proof of knowledge*

$$\mathsf{PoK}\,\{\tilde{\sigma}_{\mathrm{pre}} : \mathsf{Valid}\,(pk, m, (\tilde{\sigma}_{\mathrm{aux}}, \tilde{\sigma}_{\mathrm{pre}}))\} \ ,$$

and for any candidate converted signature satisfying Valid $(pk, m, (\tilde{\sigma}_{\text{aux}}, \tilde{\sigma}_{\text{pre}}))$, *a valid signature on the message m can be* retrieved *via the* Retrieve *algorithm as follows:*

$$\sigma \leftarrow \text{Retrieve}(pk, m, \tilde{\sigma}) \ .$$

The properties required by the definition enables the holder of a signature on a message, that is known to a verifier, to efficiently prove the knowledge of the signature, by first converting the signature and then revealing the simulatable part of the converted signature; this will enable the verifier to determine I and f. Finally, the protocol for proof of knowledge of the pre-image of I under f is carried out by the two parties. Note that since any NP relation has a Σ protocol [45] ensures that for any signature scheme there is a protocol that proves the knowledge of the signature although such protocols are not in general efficient.

Many of the signature schemes in use today fall into the class $\mathbb{C}$. Examples are RSA-FDH [10], Schnorr [11], Modified ElGamal [12], BLS [13], BB [14], Cramer-Shoup [15], Camenisch-Lysyanskaya-02 [16], and Camenisch-Lysyanskaya-04 [17] signatures. In the full version of this paper [44] we briefly show why each of these schemes belongs to $\mathbb{C}$.

4 Universal Designated Verifier Signatures

In this section, we first review the definitions of UDVS schemes and their security. We then propose our generic construction of UDVS schemes from signature schemes in $\mathbb{C}$, and prove its security.

4.1 Definition

A UDVS is a signature scheme with an extra functionality: a holder of a signature can designate the signature to a particular verifier, using the verifier's public key. A UDVS can be described by adding extra algorithms to the ones needed for the the underlying signature scheme. Here, we briefly recall the definitions from Steinfeld et al. [1]. A UDVS has eight algorithms: a *Common Parameter Generation* algorithm CPGen that on input 1^k, where k is the security parameter, outputs a string consisting of common parameters cp publicly shared by all users; a *Signer (resp. Verifier) Key Generation* algorithms SKeyGen (resp. VKeyGen) that on input cp, output a secret/public key-pair (sk_s, pk_s) (resp. (sk_v, pk_v)) for the signer (resp. verifier); a *Signing* and a *Public Verification* algorithm Sign and PVer, where the former takes as input sk_s and a message m and outputs a signer's publicly-verifiable (PV) signature σ and the latter takes as input pk_s and (m, σ) and outputs a boolean variable for versification result; a *Designation* and a *Designated Verification* algorithm Desig and DVer, where the former on input pk_s, pk_v, and (m, σ), outputs a designated-verifier (DV) signature $\hat{\sigma}$ and the latter on input pk_s, sk_v, and $(m, \hat{\sigma})$, outputs a boolean verification decision; finally a *Verifier Key-Registration* VKeyReg algorithm, which is a protocol between a *Key Registration Authority* (KRA) and a verifier to register verifier's public key.

4.2   Security

Steinfeld et al. identified two security requirements for UDVS schemes: *DV-unforgeability* and *non-transferability privacy*. We consider a third property proposed by Lipmaa et al. called *non-delegatability*. Intuitively, *DV-unforgeability* captures the inability of the adversary to forge designated signatures on new messages even if it can have signatures on chosen messages and can verify chosen pairs of messages and designated signatures, *non-transferability privacy* captures the inability of the designated verifier to produce evidence to convince a third party that the message has actually been signed by the signer, and finally *non-delegatability* captures the inability of everyone else (everyone except the signature holder and the designated verifier) to generate designated signatures, hence effectively preventing the signer, the signature holder and the designated verifier to delegate their ability to generate designated signatures without revealing their corresponding secrets.

DV-Unforgeability. We use Steinfeld et al's definition of security of UDVS schemes [20] against existential designated signature unforgeability under chosen message attack, denoted by DV-EUF-CMA-attack. For the formal definition refer to [20] or [44].

Non-transferability Privacy. Steinfeld et al. have formalized this property in detail and proposed a definition capturing the fact that possessing a designated signature does not add to the computational ability of the designated verifier [1]. In their formalization, they require that whatever a designated verifier who has been given a designated signature can leak to a third party (even at the expense of disclosing his secret key), he would have been able to leak without the designated signature. One can easily see that if designated signatures are simulatable by the verifier himself then a designated signature adds no computational ability to the verifier and thus, without going into details of the formal definition for non-transferability privacy, we will state and use the following lemma to prove our schemes secure.

Lemma 1. *A scheme* UDVS *achieves* perfect *non-transferability privacy if there exists an efficient forgery algorithm* Forge, *such that for any two pairs of keys* (sk_s, pk_s) *and* (sk_v, pk_v) *generated by the key generation algorithms of* UDVS, *and for any message m, the following two random variables have the same distribution:*

$$\mathsf{Forge}\,(pk_s, sk_v, pk_v, m) \quad and \quad \mathsf{Desig}\,(pk_s, pk_v, m, \mathsf{Sign}\,(sk_s, m)) \ .$$

Other flavors of non-transferability privacy, i.e. *statistical* and *computational* non-transferability privacy can be analogously defined by requiring the two distributions to be statistically or computationally indistinguishable, respectively.

Non-delegatability. Lipmaa et al. defined non-delegatability property of designated-verifier signatures [3]. Their definition of κ-non-delegatability requires the designated signature to be a non-interactive *proof of knowledge* with knowledge error κ [46], of the signer's or the designated verifier's secret key. The reason for such a definition is to guarantee that only the signer or the designated verifier are able to produce a designated signature, thus preventing them from being able to delegate their ability without revealing their secret key. In a UDVS scheme, we want only the person who holds a signature or the designated verifier be able to produce a designated signature. Lipmaa et al's definition can be extended to the UDVS case as follows. κ-non-delegatability for UDVS schemes requires the designated signature to be a non-interactive proof of knowledge, with knowledge error κ, of a signature or the designated verifier's secret key.

We use an observation of Cramer et al. [47, p. 359] to simplify the non-delegatability proofs of our constructions. Cramer et al. noted that is that a three-move public-coin protocol with SpS property and challenge space $ChSp$ is a proof of knowledge with knowledge error $\kappa = |ChSp|^{-1}$. Using Forking Lemma, it can be easily seen that the non-interactive version of this observation holds in the Random Oracle Model. That is, a Fiat-Shamir non-interactive proof of knowledge (i.e. our NIPoK) with SpS property and challenge space $ChSp$ is a non-interactive κ-proof of knowledge in the the Random Oracle Model with knowledge error $\kappa = |ChSp|^{-1}$. Based on these observations, we have the following lemma:

Lemma 2. *A scheme* UDVS *is κ-non-delegatable if a designated signature is a Fiat-Shamir non-interactive proof of knowledge of a signature or the secret key of the verifier, with SpS property and $|ChSp| \geq \frac{1}{\kappa}$.*

4.3 Construction of UDVS Schemes from Standard Signatures

We show how to construct a universal designated verifier signature from any signature scheme in $\mathbb{C}$, assuming the verifier has a key pair with key type in $\mathbb{K}$. We use the building blocks introduced before, i.e. proof of disjunctive knowledge and the Fiat-Shamir transform, to construct the UDVS schemes. Our construction has the distinctive property that the verifier's key pair type can be chosen *independently* from the signer's signature. That is the construction works for any combination of a signature in class $\mathbb{C}$ and a verifier key pair type in $\mathbb{K}$. Let SS = (KeyGen, Sign, Verify) be a standard signature scheme in class $\mathbb{C}$ and KT be a verifier-chosen key type in $\mathbb{K}$ with key generation algorithm KeyGen and pair deciding algorithm Pair. The construction is as follows:

- CPGen gets as input 1^k, and returns $cp = 1^k$ as the common parameter. The signer and the verifiers choose their own signature scheme and key pair type, respectively, i.e.

$$\text{GUDVS. (SKeyGen, Sign, PVer)} \triangleq \text{SS. (KeyGen, Sign, Verify)}$$
$$\text{and} \quad \text{VKeyGen} \triangleq \text{KeyGen .}$$

- To designate, the signature-holder first converts the signature and then constructs a signature of disjunctive knowledge of $\tilde{\sigma}_{\mathrm{pre}}$ or sk_{v}. The DV-signature is a pair consisting of $\tilde{\sigma}_{\mathrm{aux}}$ and this signature of knowledge, i.e.

```
Algorithm GUDVS.Desig (pk_s, pk_v, m, σ)
    (σ̃_aux, σ̃_pre) ← Convert (pk_s, m, σ)
    δ ← SoK {(σ̃_pre ∨ sk_v) : Valid (pk_s, m, (σ̃_aux, σ̃_pre)), Pair (pk_v, sk_v)}
    σ̂ ← (σ̃_aux, δ)
    return σ̂
```

- To verify the DV-signature, one verifies the validity of the signature of knowledge δ according to the message, the public keys of the signer and the verifier, and the value $\tilde{\sigma}_{\mathrm{aux}}$ provided, i.e.

```
Algorithm GUDVS.DVer (pk_s, pk_v, m, σ̂)
    d ← VoK {(σ̃_pre ∨ sk_v) : Valid (pk_s, m, (σ̃_aux, σ̃_pre)), Pair (pk_v, sk_v)} (δ)
    return d
```

4.4 Security Analysis

DV-Unforgeability. We use the *Forking Lemma* to prove DV-Unforgeability of the construction. The Forking Lemma was originally proposed by Pointcheval and Stern [12]. Recently, Bellare and Neven proposed a general version of the Forking Lemma in [48]. We use the results and formulations from the latter in our proof. Basically, our *SoK*-type constructions guarantees the ability to extract a signature or the verifier's secret key from a DV-forger through forking. The extracted signature or secret key is later used to solve the underlying problem of the signature scheme or that of the verifier key pair, respectively. Thus, given a successful DV-forger, we will be able to solve at least one of the above underlying problems and we have the following theorem. The proof is given in the full version of this paper [44].

Theorem 1. *Let* SS *be a standard signature in* $\mathbb{C}$ *and* P_{SS} *be its underlying problem. Also, let* KT *be a key type in* $\mathbb{K}$ *and* P_{KT} *be its underlying problem. The construction* GUDVS *based on the combination of the signature* SS *and the verifier key-type* KT *is DV-unforgeable if* P_{SS} *and* P_{KT} *are both hard.*

Non-transferability Privacy. Non-transferability privacy for GUDVS is due to the very concept behind our construction. The designated signature consists of two values, a publicly-simulatable value $\tilde{\sigma}_{\mathrm{aux}}$ and a *witness indistinguishable* signature of knowledge of a valid converted signature or the verifier's secret key. Both values are generateable by the designated verifier, indistinguishably from the real designated signatures. To forge a designated signature, the verifier will first simulate $\tilde{\sigma}_{\mathrm{aux}}$ via the algorithm AuxSim and then, similar to the prover, he will be able to construct a non-interactive proof of disjunctive knowledge of $\tilde{\sigma}_{\mathrm{pre}}$ or the verifier's secret key (knowing the latter, of course). The forged designated signature will be consisting of the simulated $\tilde{\sigma}_{aux}$ along with this signature of knowledge, i.e. we have the following forge algorithm:

> Algorithm GUDVS.Forge (pk_s, sk_v, pk_v, m)
> $\tilde{\sigma}_{aux} \leftarrow$ AuxSim (pk_s, m)
> $\delta \leftarrow$ SoK $\{(\tilde{\sigma}_{pre} \vee sk_v) :$ Valid $(pk_s, m, (\tilde{\sigma}_{aux}, \tilde{\sigma}_{pre})),$ Pair $(pk_v, sk_v)\}$
> $\hat{\sigma} \leftarrow (\tilde{\sigma}_{aux}, \delta)$
> return $\hat{\sigma}$

AuxSim's ability to simulate $\tilde{\sigma}_{aux}$ and witness indistinguishability of the signature of knowledge together, will imply that the output of the algorithm GUDVS.Forge is indistinguishable from real designated signatures. The existence of AuxSim and a Σ protocol for the proof of knowledge of a converted signature is guaranteed if SS belongs to $\mathbb{C}$. Furthermore, the existence of a Σ protocol for proof of knowledge of the verifier's secret key is guaranteed if KT belongs to $\mathbb{K}$. Thus, GUDVS.Forge will be successful in forging designated signatures for any combination of a signature in $\mathbb{C}$ and a verifier key type in $\mathbb{K}$. Combining this with Lemma 1, we will have the following theorem.

Theorem 2. *The construction* GUDVS *achieves non-transferability privacy for any combination of a signature in $\mathbb{C}$ and a verifier key type in $\mathbb{K}$.*

Non-delegatability. The very design of our UDVS construction is geared towards providing non-delegatability through the use of signatures of knowledge. However, to meet the requirements of Lemma 2, we must first prove that a designated signature in our scheme is a signatures of knowledge of a *signature* or the secret key of the verifier with SpS property. All we know now is that a designated signature in our scheme consists of a $\tilde{\sigma}_{aux}$ and a signature of knowledge of $\tilde{\sigma}_{pre}$ or the secret keys of the verifier, with both HVZK and SpS properties.

It can be seen that a designated signature $(\tilde{\sigma}_{aux}, \delta)$ as a signature of knowledge has the SpS property in the Random Oracle Model. The reason is that two designated signatures with the same first-move message (i.e. Random Oracle query, which includes $\tilde{\sigma}_{aux}$ along with the commitment) and different challenges (i.e. Random Oracle responses) will provide two δs with the same commitment and different challenges. This will give us the secret, i.e. $\tilde{\sigma}_{pre}$ or sk_v. If the former is given, then one can retrieve a valid signature by running the Retrieve algorithm on input $(\tilde{\sigma}_{aux}, \tilde{\sigma}_{pre})$. Thus, two designated signatures with the same Random Oracle query and different Random Oracle responses will give us a signature or the verifier's secret key. Hence, the designated signature will have the SpS property as well and by Lemma 2 we will have the following theorem:

Theorem 3. *The construction* GUDVS *is κ-non-delegatable for any combination of a signature in $\mathbb{C}$ and a verifier key type in $\mathbb{K}$ for which $|ChSp| \geq \frac{1}{\kappa}$.*

Note that although a designated signature is an HVZK signature of knowledge of a $\tilde{\sigma}_{pre}$ or the verifier's public key, it may *not* be an HVZK signature of knowledge of a *signature* or the verifier's public key, since it reveals $\tilde{\sigma}_{aux}$ which might include some information about the signature. However, Lemma 2 does not require the designated signature to have the HVZK property.

4.5   Further Constructions

Our constructions can be easily extended to *universal multi-designated-verifier signatures*, where a signature is designated to more than one verifier. This can be done by setting the designated signature to be a one-out-of-$(n+1)$ disjunctive signature of knowledge of the (converted) signature and the secret keys of the n verifiers. Again, these schemes allow the signer and the verifiers to choose their settings independently, thus the verifiers might have different types of keys.

The construction can also be extended to designate more than one signature at a time. This is useful in situations where a user wishes to show more than one certificate to a verifier and does not want the verifier to be able to convince a third party of the validity of her certificate. For instance, consider a situation where a user must show at least k out of n certificates to a verifier to obtain a service from the verifier. The user will construct the designated signature by constructing a $(k+1)$-out-of-$(n+1)$ signature of knowledge of the n (converted) signatures and the secret key of the verifier. This construction offers an extra privacy property in that the verifier, after seeing a designated signature, can not determine which k certificates is used by the user.

4.6   Comparison

We use constructions in [1,6] as benchmarks for our constructions. We choose instances of our constructions that match the signature scheme and verifier key type of the benchmark schemes. Similar to [6], we assume the cost of computing a product $a^x \cdot b^y \cdot c^z$ and $O(\alpha)$ low exponent exponentiations both, are equivalent to a single exponentiation. We use the same typical parameters for lengths of members of different groups, namely 1.024 kb for DL groups and RSA modules and 0.16 kb for $ChSp$. To further simplify the comparison, we only consider the dominant term for the costs of computation assuming that a pairing (pair.) $\succ$ an exponentiation (exp.) $\succ$ a multiplication (mult.) $\succ$ an addition, with "$\succ$" standing for "costs (much) more than". We note that designation of a certificate has two phases: before choosing the designated verifier and after that and so computation can be carried out in accordingly. We *off-line* and *on-line* to denote the two phases, respectively. An interesting property of our construction is that cost of on-line phase is relatively low (one multiplication). This makes our constructions suitable for systems in which certificates must be frequently verified by (and hence designated to) multiple different verifiers. Table 1 summarizes the comparisons, with "Typ. $\hat{\sigma}$ len." and "ND" standing for "Typical $\hat{\sigma}$ length" and "Non-Delegatability", respectively and comparatively more desirable values in bold. The table shows, our schemes generally have more (yet comparable) costs of off-line designation and designated verification and result in longer designated signatures. However, our schemes have less online designation cost and provide provable non-delegatabilty. Our schemes are also (almost) generic and provide the desirable property of *signer-verifier setting independence*. A side effect of using the Forking Lemma for proof of security is that security reductions are not *tight*.

Table 1. Comparison of the properties of Steinfeld et al's schemes with those of their corresponding GUDVS counterparts

Scheme	Hard problem	Desig cost		DVer cost	Typ. $\hat{\sigma}$ len.	ND
		off-line	on-line			
DVSBM [1]	BDH	none	1 pair.	1 pair.	1.0 kb	✗
GUDVS (BLS+DL)	**CDH**	2 pair.	**1 mult.**	2 pair.	5.3 kb	✓
SchUDVS$_1$ [6]	SDH	1 exp.	1 exp.	1 exp.	2.0 kb	✗
SchUDVS$_2$ [6]	**DL**	2 exp.	1 exp.	2 exp.	**1.5 kb**	?
GUDVS (Schnorr+DL)	DL	4 exp.	**1 mult.**	3 exp.	5.3 kb	✓
RSAUDVS [6]	**RSA**	1 exp.	2 exp.	2 exp.	11.6 kb	?
GUDVS (RSA-FDH+DL)	RSA & DL	2 exp.	**1 mult.**	2 exp.	**4.3 kb**	✓

5   Identity-Based Signatures

In this section, we first review the definitions of the IBS scheme and its security. Then we propose a generic construction of IBS schemes from any signature scheme in $\mathbb{C}$ and prove it secure.

5.1   Definition and Security

Identity-based cryptosystems were proposed by Shamir [19] in an attempt to remove the need for a public-key infrastructure. In such systems, the users' identities are used as their public keys. However, users lose their ability to choose their own secret keys and must ask a *key-generation center* (KGC) to provide them with their respective private keys.

An identity-based signature is a tuple of four algorithms as follows: a *master key generation* algorithm MKeyGen, which on input 1^k, where k is a security parameter, outputs a pair of master secret key and master public key (msk, mpk), a *user key generation* algorithm UKeyGen, which on input msk and a user identity id, outputs a user secret key usk, a *signing* algorithm Sign, which on input usk and a message m, outputs a signature σ on the message, and finally a *verification* algorithm Verify, which on input mpk, id, and (m, σ), outputs a binary decision indicating whether or not σ is a valid signature on m with respect to mpk and id.

We use Bellare and Neven's definition for the security of an IBS scheme [20] against existential unforgeability under chosen message and identity attacks, denoted by ID-EUF-CMA-attack. For the formal definition refer to [20] or [44].

5.2   Generic Construction of IBS and Its Security

In this section we show how to extend a signature in $\mathbb{C}$ to an IBS scheme. The idea is to use the key pair of the signature scheme as the master key pair of KGC, and use the signing algorithm as the users' key generation algorithm in the following way: a user's secret key corresponding to her public identity, is obtained by signing the user's identity using the KGC's secret key. The secret key is securely given to the user. Now, the user is able to prove her identity, since she can prove the knowledge of a converted signature on her identity. The Fiat-Shamir transform can be used to transform this proof into a signature scheme. The resulting signature would be an identity-based signature.

The concrete description of the generic construction is as follows. Let that the standard signature SS = (KeyGen, Sign, Verify) be in $\mathbb{C}$. The generic IBS scheme GIBS is constructed as follows:

To generate a master key pair, the KCG runs the key generation algorithm of the signature scheme and outputs the public and secret key pair as the master public and secret key pair for the identity based signature scheme. To generate a user's key pair, the KCG simply signs the user's identity using his master secret key and outputs the generated signature (together with the master public key and the user's identity) as the user's secret key, i.e.

Algorithm GIBS.MKeyGen (k)	**Algorithm** GIBS.UKeyGen (msk, id)
$(msk, mpk) \leftarrow$ SS.KeyGen (k)	$\sigma \leftarrow$ SS.Sign (msk, id)
return (msk, mpk)	$usk \leftarrow (mpk, id, \sigma)$
	return usk

An identity-based signature is constructed as a signature of knowledge of KGC's signature on the identity of the signer by, first running the corresponding conversion algorithm on input σ (which is contained in the user secret key of the signer) to obtain $(\tilde{\sigma}_{\mathrm{aux}}, \tilde{\sigma}_{\mathrm{pre}})$, then constructing a proof of knowledge of $\tilde{\sigma}_{\mathrm{pre}}$ and, finally transforming the result into a signature of knowledge on m via the Fiat-Shamir transform. The signature is a pair consisting of $\tilde{\sigma}_{\mathrm{aux}}$ and this signature of knowledge, i.e.

$$\begin{aligned}
&\textbf{Algorithm } \mathsf{GIBS.Sign}\,(usk, m)\\
&\quad (\tilde{\sigma}_{\mathrm{aux}}, \tilde{\sigma}_{\mathrm{pre}}) \leftarrow \mathsf{Convert}\,(mpk, id, \sigma)\\
&\quad \delta \leftarrow \mathsf{SoK}\,\{\tilde{\sigma}_{\mathrm{pre}} : \mathsf{Valid}\,(mpk, id, (\tilde{\sigma}_{\mathrm{aux}}, \tilde{\sigma}_{\mathrm{pre}}))\}\,(m)\\
&\quad \sigma \leftarrow (\tilde{\sigma}_{\mathrm{aux}}, \delta)\\
&\quad \textbf{return } \sigma
\end{aligned}$$

To verify an identity-based signature σ, one verifies the validity of the signature of knowledge δ according to the identity of the signer, the master public key, and the value $\tilde{\sigma}_{\mathrm{aux}}$ provided, i.e.

$$\begin{aligned}
&\textbf{Algorithm } \mathsf{IBS.Verify}\,(mpk, id, m, \sigma)\\
&\quad d \leftarrow \mathsf{VoK}\,\{\tilde{\sigma}_{\mathrm{pre}} : \mathsf{Valid}\,(mpk, id, (\tilde{\sigma}_{\mathrm{aux}}, \tilde{\sigma}_{\mathrm{pre}}))\}\,(m, \delta)\\
&\quad \textbf{return } d
\end{aligned}$$

This construction is a generalized version of Kurosawa and Heng's construction [23]. They required a stronger requirement on their signature schemes. We note the similarities between the ideas behind Kurosawa and Heng's and our constructions, and that of Naor's observation on transforming any identity-based encryption to a standard signature scheme [49, p. 226]. In both, a user's secret key is a signature of the KGC on the user's identity. Our constructions can be seen as the Naor's observation in the reverse direction, i.e. from the non-identity-based world to the identity-based world. A possible result of combining the two ideas is the construction of identity-based signatures from identity-based encryptions.

We propose the following theorem for the security of our construction. A sketch of the proof is given in the full version of this paper [44].

Theorem 4. *Let* SS *be a standard signature in* $\mathbb{C}$ *and* P_{SS} *be its underlying problem. The construction* GIBS *based on the signature* SS *is* ID-EUF-CMA-*secure if* P_{SS} *is hard.*

5.3   Further Constructions

We observe that the above generic construction of IBS schemes has kind of a *nesting* property in the sense that if one extends the definition of class $\mathbb{C}$ to identity-based signature schemes, then the construction GIBS will belong to the class $\mathbb{C}$ itself. This is due to the fact that a GIBS signature in the form $\sigma = (\tilde{\sigma}_{\text{aux}}, (Cmt, Rsp))$ can be converted to the converted signature bellow:

$$\tilde{\tilde{\sigma}} = \left(\tilde{\tilde{\sigma}}_{\text{aux}}, \tilde{\tilde{\sigma}}_{\text{pre}}\right) = \left((\tilde{\sigma}_{\text{aux}}, Cmt), Rsp\right) \ .$$

For all the signatures listed above, knowledge of Rsp can be proved via a Σ protocol. Hence, for all the constructions of IBS schemes from these signatures, the GIBS can be *nested* in the way that an identity based signer can act as a new KGC for a new user. This enables construction of *hierarchical* identity-based signature schemes [50].

An extension of the GIBS construction that follows from the nesting property is the construction of *identity-based universal designated verifier signatures* from any signature in $\mathbb{C}$. In such a scheme, a designator wishes to designate a certificate signed by an identity-based signature, and the designated verifier is also identity-based. The designated verifier's secret key is a signature on his identity by the KGC. To designate, the designator will simply construct a disjunctive proof of knowledge of (a converted version of) her certificate *or* (a converted version of) the verifier's secret key. Proofs of security of the scheme can be constructed by combining the ideas used to prove the generic UDVS and IBS schemes secure.

Another possible extension of the GIBS schemes is the construction of *identity-based ring signatures* from any signature scheme in $\mathbb{C}$. To generate such a signature, the signer will construct a one-out-of-n signature of knowledge of the n user secret keys in the chosen ring, where each user secret key is a signature of the KGC on the corresponding user identity.

6   Concluding Remarks

We proposed generic constructions of UDVS and IBS schemes from a large class of signatures. Our constructions result in schemes which have comparable efficiency to those with similar properties. The generic UDVS construction is provably non-delegatable and offers a desirable property, which is independence of the signer's and the verifier's setting. Many IBS schemes can be seen as instances of our generic IBS construction. It is possible to use our techniques to construct generic universal multi-designated-verifier signatures, hierarchical identity-based signatures, identity-based universal designated verifier signatures, and identity-based ring signatures

Acknowledgments

Authors would like to thank Shaoquan Jiang and the anonymous reviewers of PKC '08 for fruitful discussions and comments. The first author extends his thanks to the iCORE Information Security Lab of the University of Calgary for hosting him during part of this work.

References

1. Steinfeld, R., Bull, L., Wang, H., Pieprzyk, J.: Universal Designated-Verifier Signatures. In: Laih, C.-S. (ed.) ASIACRYPT 2003. LNCS, vol. 2894, pp. 523–542. Springer, Heidelberg (2003)
2. Jakobsson, M., Sako, K., Impagliazzo, R.: Designated Verifier Proofs and Their Applications. In: Maurer, U.M. (ed.) EUROCRYPT 1996. LNCS, vol. 1070, pp. 143–154. Springer, Heidelberg (1996)
3. Lipmaa, H., Wang, G., Bao, F.: Designated Verifier Signature Schemes: Attacks, New Security Notions and a New Construction. In: Caires, L., Italiano, G.F., Monteiro, L., Palamidessi, C., Yung, M. (eds.) ICALP 2005. LNCS, vol. 3580, pp. 459–471. Springer, Heidelberg (2005)
4. Huang, X., Susilo, W., Mu, Y., Wu, W.: Universal Designated Verifier Signature Without Delegatability. In: Ning, P., Qing, S., Li, N. (eds.) ICICS 2006. LNCS, vol. 4307, pp. 479–498. Springer, Heidelberg (2006)
5. Li, Y., Lipmaa, H., Pei, D.: On Delegatability of Four Designated Verifier Signatures. In: Qing, S., Mao, W., López, J., Wang, G. (eds.) ICICS 2005. LNCS, vol. 3783, pp. 61–71. Springer, Heidelberg (2005)
6. Steinfeld, R., Wang, H., Pieprzyk, J.: Efficient Extension of Standard Schnorr/RSA Signatures into Universal Designated-Verifier Signatures. In: Bao, F., Deng, R., Zhou, J. (eds.) PKC 2004. LNCS, vol. 2947, pp. 86–100. Springer, Heidelberg (2004)
7. Cramer, R., Damgård, I., Schoenmakers, B.: Proofs of Partial Knowledge and Simplified Design of Witness Hiding Protocols. In: Desmedt, Y.G. (ed.) CRYPTO 1994. LNCS, vol. 839, pp. 174–187. Springer, Heidelberg (1994)
8. Fiat, A., Shamir, A.: How to Prove Yourself: Practical Solutions to Identification and Signature Problems. In: Odlyzko, A.M. (ed.) CRYPTO 1986. LNCS, vol. 263, pp. 186–194. Springer, Heidelberg (1987)
9. Bellare, M., Rogaway, P.: Random Oracles are Practical: A Paradigm for Designing Efficient Protocols. In: ACM Conference on Computer and Communications Security, pp. 62–73 (1993)
10. Bellare, M., Rogaway, P.: The Exact Security of Digital Signatures - How to Sign with RSA and Rabin. In: Maurer, U.M. (ed.) EUROCRYPT 1996. LNCS, vol. 1070, pp. 399–416. Springer, Heidelberg (1996)
11. Schnorr, C.P.: Efficient Signature Generation by Smart Cards. J. Cryptology 4, 161–174 (1991)

12. Pointcheval, D., Stern, J.: Security Arguments for Digital Signatures and Blind Signatures. J. Cryptology 13, 361–396 (2000)
13. Boneh, D., Lynn, B., Shacham, H.: Short Signatures from the Weil Pairing. In: Boyd, C. (ed.) ASIACRYPT 2001. LNCS, vol. 2248, pp. 514–532. Springer, Heidelberg (2001)
14. Boneh, D., Boyen, X.: Short Signatures Without Random Oracles. In: Cachin, C., Camenisch, J.L. (eds.) EUROCRYPT 2004. LNCS, vol. 3027, pp. 56–73. Springer, Heidelberg (2004)
15. Cramer, R., Shoup, V.: Signature Schemes Based on the Strong RSA Assumption. ACM Trans. Inf. Syst. Secur. 3, 161–185 (2000)
16. Camenisch, J., Lysyanskaya, A.: A Signature Scheme with Efficient Protocols. In: Cimato, S., Galdi, C., Persiano, G. (eds.) SCN 2002. LNCS, vol. 2576, pp. 268–289. Springer, Heidelberg (2003)
17. Camenisch, J., Lysyanskaya, A.: Signature Schemes and Anonymous Credentials from Bilinear Maps. In: Franklin, M. (ed.) CRYPTO 2004. LNCS, vol. 3152, pp. 56–72. Springer, Heidelberg (2004)
18. Guillou, L.C., Quisquater, J.J.: A "Paradoxical" Indentity-Based Signature Scheme Resulting from Zero-Knowledge. In: Goldwasser, S. (ed.) CRYPTO 1988. LNCS, vol. 403, pp. 216–231. Springer, Heidelberg (1990)
19. Shamir, A.: Identity-Based Cryptosystems and Signature Schemes. In: Blakely, G.R., Chaum, D. (eds.) CRYPTO 1984. LNCS, vol. 196, pp. 47–53. Springer, Heidelberg (1985)
20. Bellare, M., Namprempre, C., Neven, G.: Security Proofs for Identity-Based Identification and Signature Schemes. In: Cachin, C., Camenisch, J.L. (eds.) EUROCRYPT 2004. LNCS, vol. 3027, pp. 268–286. Springer, Heidelberg (2004)
21. Dodis, Y., Katz, J., Xu, S., Yung, M.: Strong Key-Insulated Signature Schemes. In: Desmedt, Y.G. (ed.) PKC 2003. LNCS, vol. 2567, pp. 130–144. Springer, Heidelberg (2002)
22. Okamoto, T.: Provably Secure and Practical Identification Schemes and Corresponding Signature Schemes. In: Brickell, E.F. (ed.) CRYPTO 1992. LNCS, vol. 740, pp. 31–53. Springer, Heidelberg (1993)
23. Kurosawa, K., Heng, S.-H.: From Digital Signature to ID-based Identification/Signature. In: Bao, F., Deng, R., Zhou, J. (eds.) PKC 2004. LNCS, vol. 2947, pp. 248–261. Springer, Heidelberg (2004)
24. Sakai, R., Ohgishi, K., Kasahara, M.: Cryptosystems based on pairing. In: Sympoium on Cryptography and Information Security (SCIS), Okinawa, Japan, pp. 26–28 (2000)
25. Hess, F.: Efficient Identity Based Signature Schemes Based on Pairings. In: Nyberg, K., Heys, H.M. (eds.) SAC 2002. LNCS, vol. 2595, pp. 310–324. Springer, Heidelberg (2003)
26. Cha, J.C., Cheon, J.H.: An Identity-Based Signature from Gap Diffie-Hellman Groups. In: Desmedt, Y.G. (ed.) PKC 2003. LNCS, vol. 2567, pp. 18–30. Springer, Heidelberg (2002)
27. Yi, X.: An Identity-Based Signature Scheme from the Weil Pairing. Communications Letters, IEEE 7, 76–78 (2003)
28. Barreto, P.S.L.M., Libert, B., McCullagh, N., Quisquater, J.J.: Efficient and Provably-Secure Identity-Based Signatures and Signcryption from Bilinear Maps. In: Roy, B. (ed.) ASIACRYPT 2005. LNCS, vol. 3788, pp. 515–532. Springer, Heidelberg (2005)

29. Huang, Z., Chen, K., Wang, Y.: Efficient Identity-Based Signatures and Blind Signatures. In: Desmedt, Y.G., Wang, H., Mu, Y., Li, Y. (eds.) CANS 2005. LNCS, vol. 3810, pp. 120–133. Springer, Heidelberg (2005)
30. Paterson, K.G., Schuldt, J.C.N.: Efficient Identity-Based Signatures Secure in the Standard Model. In: Batten, L.M., Safavi-Naini, R. (eds.) ACISP 2006. LNCS, vol. 4058, pp. 207–222. Springer, Heidelberg (2006)
31. Zhang, R., Furukawa, J., Imai, H.: Short Signature and Universal Designated Verifier Signature Without Random Oracles. In: Ioannidis, J., Keromytis, A.D., Yung, M. (eds.) ACNS 2005. LNCS, vol. 3531, pp. 483–498. Springer, Heidelberg (2005)
32. Vergnaud, D.: New Extensions of Pairing-Based Signatures into Universal Designated Verifier Signatures. In: Bugliesi, M., Preneel, B., Sassone, V., Wegener, I. (eds.) ICALP 2006. LNCS, vol. 4052, pp. 58–69. Springer, Heidelberg (2006)
33. Laguillaumie, F., Libert, B., Quisquater, J.-J.: Universal Designated Verifier Signatures Without Random Oracles or Non-black Box Assumptions. In: De Prisco, R., Yung, M. (eds.) SCN 2006. LNCS, vol. 4116, pp. 63–77. Springer, Heidelberg (2006)
34. Goldwasser, S., Waisbard, E.: Transformation of Digital Signature Schemes into Designated Confirmer Signature Schemes. In: Naor, M. (ed.) TCC 2004. LNCS, vol. 2951, pp. 77–100. Springer, Heidelberg (2004)
35. Goldwasser, S., Micali, S., Rivest, R.L.: A Digital Signature Scheme Secure Against Adaptive Chosen-Message Attacks. SIAM J. Comput. 17, 281–308 (1988)
36. Gennaro, R., Halevi, S., Rabin, T.: Secure Hash-and-Sign Signatures Without the Random Oracle. In: Stern, J. (ed.) EUROCRYPT 1999. LNCS, vol. 1592, pp. 123–139. Springer, Heidelberg (1999)
37. Zhang, F., Susilo, W., Mu, Y., Chen, X.: Identity-Based Universal Designated Verifier Signatures.. In: Enokido, T., Yan, L., Xiao, B., Kim, D.Y., Dai, Y.-S., Yang, L.T. (eds.) EUC-WS 2005. LNCS, vol. 3823, pp. 825–834. Springer, Heidelberg (2005)
38. Ng, C.Y., Susilo, W., Mu, Y.: Universal Designated Multi Verifier Signature Schemes.. In: ICPADS, 2nd edn., pp. 305–309. IEEE Computer Society, Los Alamitos (2005)
39. Camenisch, J., Stadler, M.: Efficient Group Signature Schemes for Large Groups (Extended Abstract). In: Kaliski Jr., B.S. (ed.) CRYPTO 1997. LNCS, vol. 1294, pp. 410–424. Springer, Heidelberg (1997)
40. Goldwasser, S., Micali, S., Rackoff, C.: The Knowledge Complexity of Interactive Proof Systems. SIAM J. Comput. 18, 186–208 (1989)
41. Camenisch, J., Stadler, M.: Proof Systems For General Statements about Discrete Logarithms. Technical Report 260, Dept. of Computer Science, ETH Zurich (1997)
42. Ohta, K., Okamoto, T.: On Concrete Security Treatment of Signatures Derived from Identification. In: Krawczyk, H. (ed.) CRYPTO 1998. LNCS, vol. 1462, pp. 354–369. Springer, Heidelberg (1998)
43. Abdalla, M., An, J.H., Bellare, M., Namprempre, C.: From Identification to Signatures via the Fiat-Shamir Transform: Minimizing Assumptions for Security and Forward-Security. In: Knudsen, L.R. (ed.) EUROCRYPT 2002. LNCS, vol. 2332, pp. 418–433. Springer, Heidelberg (2002)
44. Shahandashti, S.F., Safavi-Naini, R.: Construction of Universal Designated-Verifier Signatures and Identity-Based Signatures from Standard Signatures. Cryptology ePrint Archive, Report 2007/462 (2007), http://eprint.iacr.org/
45. Catalano, D., Dodis, Y., Visconti, I.: Mercurial Commitments: Minimal Assumptions and Efficient Constructions. In: Halevi, S., Rabin, T. (eds.) TCC 2006. LNCS, vol. 3876, pp. 120–144. Springer, Heidelberg (2006)

46. Bellare, M., Goldreich, O.: On Defining Proofs of Knowledge. In: Brickell, E.F. (ed.) CRYPTO 1992. LNCS, vol. 740, pp. 390–420. Springer, Heidelberg (1993)
47. Cramer, R., Damgård, I., MacKenzie, P.D.: Efficient Zero-Knowledge Proofs of Knowledge Without Intractability Assumptions. In: Imai, H., Zheng, Y. (eds.) PKC 2000. LNCS, vol. 1751, pp. 354–372. Springer, Heidelberg (2000)
48. Bellare, M., Neven, G.: Multi-Signatures in the Plain Public-Key Model and a General Forking Lemma. In: Juels, A., Wright, R.N., di Vimercati, S.D.C. (eds.) ACM Conference on Computer and Communications Security, pp. 390–399. ACM, New York (2006)
49. Boneh, D., Franklin, M.K.: Identity-Based Encryption from the Weil Pairing. In: Kilian, J. (ed.) CRYPTO 2001. LNCS, vol. 2139, pp. 213–229. Springer, Heidelberg (2001)
50. Gentry, C., Silverberg, A.: Hierarchical ID-Based Cryptography. In: Zheng, Y. (ed.) ASIACRYPT 2002. LNCS, vol. 2501, pp. 548–566. Springer, Heidelberg (2002)

Proxy Signatures Secure Against Proxy Key Exposure

Jacob C.N. Schuldt[1], Kanta Matsuura[1], and Kenneth G. Paterson[2,*]

[1] Institute of Industrial Science, University of Tokyo,
4-6-1 Komaba, Meguro-ku, Tokyo 153-8505, Japan
{schuldt,kanta}@iis.u-tokyo.ac.jp
[2] Information Security Group,
Royal Holloway, University of London,
Egham, Surrey, TW20 0EX, UK
kenny.paterson@rhul.ac.uk

Abstract. We provide an enhanced security model for proxy signatures that captures a more realistic set of attacks than previous models of Boldyreva *et al.* and of Malkin *et al.*. Our model is motivated by concrete attacks on existing schemes in scenarios in which proxy signatures are likely to be used. We provide a generic construction for proxy signatures secure in our enhanced model using sequential aggregate signatures; our construction provides a benchmark by which future specific constructions may be judged. Finally, we consider the extension of our model and constructions to the identity-based setting.

Keywords: proxy signatures, provable security.

1   Introduction

A proxy signature scheme allows an entity, the *delegator*, to delegate his signing capabilities to another entity, the *proxy*, which can then construct signatures on behalf of the delegator. A signature constructed by the proxy, called a *proxy signature*, will not only convince a verifier that the signature was indeed constructed by the proxy, but also that the proxy was delegated the signing rights of the delegator. In a *multi level* scheme, the proxy has the option of re-delegating the signing rights obtained from the delegator, to another proxy.

The concept of proxy signatures was first proposed by Mambo, Usuda and Okamoto in [24]. Among the ideas presented in [24], the concept of *delegation by warrant*, in which a signed warrant is used to describe the delegation, has received the most attention. Kim, Park and Won [16] expanded on this idea and suggested that a proxy key could be generated from the warrant. One of the main advantages of the use of warrants is that it is possible to include any type of security policy in the warrant to describe the restrictions under which the delegation is valid. Most proxy signature schemes uses a variant of this approach

---

* This author's research was supported by the European Commission under contract IST-2002- 507932 (ECRYPT).

R. Cramer (Ed.): PKC 2008, LNCS 4939, pp. 141–161, 2008.

and it is often expected that new proxy signature schemes will implement the functionality of warrants.

Since their introduction, many proxy signature schemes have been proposed (e.g. see [24,27,18,19,2,35,26]) and many extensions (e.g. see [32,36,29,17,30]) have been considered. However, the initial security notion introduced by Mambo, Usuda and Okamoto (slightly expanded by Lee, Kim and Kim [18]), was based on a list of security aims, and no security model in which schemes could be analysed was given. The lack of formal security definitions had a huge impact on the security of the initially proposed schemes. Many constructions were shown to be insecure, then fixed, only to be shown insecure again (e.g. see [24,18,19,31]). This not only illustrates the need for well defined security models and a rigorous security analysis, but also indicates that the security of proxy signatures is more subtle than was initially assumed.

Security models for proxy signatures. Boldyreva, Palacio and Warinschi [2] were the first to introduce a proper security model for proxy signatures and to propose a provably secure proxy signature scheme. These results provided a significant improvement over previous treatments of proxy signatures in terms of security analysis and also highlighted security concerns with the trivial scheme in which the delegator signs the public key of the proxy and proxy signatures are constructed with the private key of the proxy. Malkin, Obana and Yung [22] later proposed an extended security model, allowing multi-level proxy signatures, and showed that proxy signatures are equivalent to key-insulated signatures [8]. However, if we consider the typical environments in which proxy signatures will be used, then these models do not capture all desired properties of proxy signatures. We expand on this next.

The use of warrants demands special attention in both the definition and security model of proxy signatures. If warrants are not explicitly modeled, it might be possible for an adversary to alter the warrant under which a proxy has made a signature on the delegator's behalf, even though the scheme has been proved secure. This is clearly an undesirable property, since users of proxy signatures should be able to rely on warrants not being mutable once a proxy signature has been created. Even though the schemes presented in [2] use warrants, these are not a part of the presented security model. However, the model presented in [22] rectifies this and explicitly models the warrants.

The security models of [2,22] are both in the registered key model, meaning that the adversary is required to submit both the public and the private key of all users used in the security game, except the challenge user. Although this might be convenient when constructing proofs of security, it does not capture attacks where the adversary derives and registers a public key for which he cannot compute the corresponding private key. These types of attacks are also known from multi- and aggregate signatures (e.g. see [1,5]), and are relevant in practice since users may not be required to prove knowledge of their private key when registering a public key (for example, due to efficiency concerns). Furthermore, the attacks seem to pose a real threat to some proxy signature schemes. As an example of this, consider the construction proposed by Zhang, Safavi-Naini and Lin [35]. This construction efficiently combines the Boneh-Lynn-Shacham signature scheme [6] with the identity-based signature scheme of Hess [15] to create a proxy signature scheme. But the construction is insecure in a security model which does not use the registered key model. In this case, an adversary will be able to produce proxy signatures on behalf of a user, without that user having delegated his signing rights (details of this are given in Appendix A). This illustrates the need for a security model which can guarantee security of a proxy signature scheme when used in the more practical setting where the registered key model is not required.

Proxy signatures are often proposed for use in applications where signing is done in a potentially hostile environment. In this setting, it is assumed that secure storage is available for a long term key pair (e.g. key storage in a TPM within a laptop), but that it is not possible to perform all signature computations within the fully trusted device due to the number of signature requests or the amount of data that needs to be signed. Hence, these computations are performed on a less trusted device (e.g. by the operating system on a laptop which might become infected with malware). To limit the potential damage resulting from compromise of the less trusted device, a limited set of signing rights for the long term key pair can be delegated to this device, which can then act as a signing proxy. Thereby, only the limited proxy key is exposed in a compromise. However, this raises the concern that compromised proxy keys might somehow leak information about the long term key. This is relevant not only in the case where delegation is performed to protect a long term key, but also in the general case of delegation of signing rights from one entity to another. The security model of [2] does not model this possibility, since an adversary is not allowed to gain access to any proxy keys. The model of [22] has only limited support for proxy key exposure, since an adversary is only allowed access to proxy keys which a user has obtained by *self-delegation*, i.e. by delegating his signing rights to himself. However, this is not sufficient to guarantee security in an environment where any proxy key can potentially be exposed, and the assumption that only self-delegated proxy keys are at risk of being exposed seems unnatural and restrictive. Indeed, systems that rely on proxy key material (of any type) not revealing information about long term keys are already in use today (e.g. in applications such as the Grid Security Infrastructure [9]). So it is important to extend the adversarial capabilities to allow a richer set of proxy key exposures in order to correctly model the threats against these systems. However, if the adversary gains access to arbitrary proxy keys, many of the existing proxy signature schemes become insecure. In particular, the scheme proposed by Malkin *et al.* [22,23] will be insecure, since private keys double as proxy keys in an ordinary delegation (i.e. a non-self-delegation). Schemes where this is not the case might also be vulnerable. For example, the triple Schnorr scheme whose security is analyzed by Boldyreva *et al.* [2] has the weakness that an adversary can compute the (long term) private key of a user upon exposure of a proxy key for a delegation procedure for which the adversary has a transcript (details of this attack are given in Appendix B). Lastly, we emphasize that to model the compromise of a proxy correctly, the adversary should be given access to *all* information held by the proxy. For example, a closer look at [22,23] reveals that the adversary there is given access to an oracle that returns a single self-delegated proxy key, but that the proxy information in the concrete scheme can potentially contain many keys (the scheme generates all keys used as self-delegated proxy keys in the initial key generation phase, and therefore should include any keys needed for further delegation in the proxy information). We argue that the approach taken in [22] is not sufficient to model the threat posed by a proxy compromise.

Our contributions. First and foremost, we define a refined security model for proxy signatures along with the security notion *Proxy Signature Unforgeability Under an Adaptive Chosen Message Attack with Proxy Key Exposure* (ps-uf-pke). In addition to more accurately capturing the threats against proxy signatures, we claim that our model and security notion are more direct and clear when compared to the model given in [22]. Hence they more easily allow proposed schemes to be proven secure. Our model is strictly stronger than the models of [2] and [22] in that our model allows an adversary to gain access to any proxy key and does not require the registered key model. Hence, a scheme secure in our model will also be secure in the models of [2] and [22], whereas the converse does not necessarily hold (in fact, as mentioned above, the schemes proposed in [2] and [22] will be insecure in our model).

We then present a simple generic construction for proxy signatures using sequential aggregate signatures. This is closely related to the delegation-by-certificate and aggregate-based constructions of [2], but our security proof is in our enhanced security model. We discuss how the construction can be instantiated (in the random oracle model) to give efficient proxy signature schemes with security relying on either the bilinear Diffie-Hellman assumption or the assumption that RSA is a claw-free permutation. We also discuss how a scheme secure in the standard model can be obtained.

Lastly, we sketch how to extend our security model to the identity-based setting and give a fairly simple generic construction that is secure in the extended model. We also discuss the possibilities for instantiating this construction.

Since our constructions are relatively simple and easy to prove secure, they provide a performance benchmark, both in terms of security and efficiency, for any new proxy signature schemes.

2   Preliminaries

Notation. Let $PK = (pk_1, \ldots, pk_n)$ be a list of public keys (or any other strings). We use the notation $PK_{i\ldots j}$ with $i \leq j$ to indicate the sublist of keys from the i-th key to the j-th key in PK, e.g. $PK_{2\ldots4} = (pk_2, pk_3, pk_4)$. By $PK.(pk_{n+1})$ we mean that the key pk_{n+1} is appended to the end of PK. Lastly we will use the notation $m_1 \| m_2$ to mean the concatenation of the strings m_1 and m_2. When elements that are not strings appear in a concatenation, we will assume that they will be encoded as a string before the actual concatenation takes place.

Signature schemes. We briefly recall the definitions of an ordinary signature scheme and a sequential aggregate signature scheme.

A signature scheme, $\mathcal{S}$, is given by the following algorithms:

- Setup which on input a security parameter 1^k generates a set of global system parameters params. We assume that params are made publicly available and will not write params as an explicit argument to the functions defined below.
- KeyGen which generates a public/private key pair (pk, sk).
- Sign which on input (sk, m), where m is a message to be signed, generates a signature σ on m.
- Verify which on input (pk, m, σ), outputs either accept or reject.

A signature scheme is said to be *sound* if for all $(pk, sk) \leftarrow$ KeyGen and all messages m, we have that

$$\Pr[\text{Verify}(pk, m, \text{Sign}(sk, m)) = \text{accept}] = 1$$

where the probability is taken over all random coin tosses made in the KeyGen, Sign and Verify algorithms. A signature σ is said to be *valid* on m under public key pk if Verify$(pk, m, \sigma) = $ accept.

The standard notion of security for signature schemes is *Existential Unforgeability under a Chosen Message Attack* (euf-cma) [11].

A sequential aggregate signature scheme, $\mathcal{AS}$, is given by the following algorithms:

- Setup and KeyGen which are similar to the corresponding algorithms of a ordinary signature scheme.
- AggSign which takes as input (sk, m, σ_{agg}), where sk is a private key, m is a message to be signed and σ_{agg} is a sequential aggregate signature on messages $(m_1, \ldots, m_n)$ under public keys $(pk_1, \ldots, pk_n)$, constructed by previous calls to AggSign. The output of AggSign is a sequential aggregate signature σ'_{agg} on messages $(m_1, \ldots, m_n, m)$ under public keys $(pk_1, \ldots, pk_n, pk)$ where pk is the public key corresponding to sk. Note that we can construct an ordinary signature scheme by using an "empty" sequential aggregate signature as part of the input to AggSign.
- AggVerify takes as input $((pk_1, \ldots, pk_n), (m_1, \ldots, m_n), \sigma_{agg})$ and outputs accept or reject.

A sequential aggregate signature scheme is said to be *sound* if for all $n \geq 1$, all $(pk_i, sk_i) \leftarrow$ KeyGen $i \subset \{1, \ldots, n\}$, all messages $(m_1, \ldots, m_n)$ and all sequential aggregated signatures constructed as $\sigma_i \leftarrow$ AggSign$(sk_i, m_i, \sigma_{i-1}), i \in \{1, \ldots, n\}$ with $\sigma_0 = \emptyset$, we have that

$$\Pr[\text{AggVerify}((pk_1, \ldots, pk_n), (m_1, \ldots, m_n), \sigma_n) = \text{accept}] = 1$$

where the probability is taken over all random coin tosses used in the KeyGen, AggSign and AggVerify algorithms. Validity of sequential aggregate signatures is defined as one would expect.

There exist two different security notions for sequential aggregate signatures, introduced by Lysyanskaya *et al.* [21] and Lu *et al.* [20], respectively. The difference between the two notions is that the latter requires the registered key model whereas the former does not. In this paper we will insist that the registered key model is not required and use the notion defined in [21], referred to as *Existential Unforgeability in the Sequential Aggregate Chosen-Key Model.*

3   Proxy Signatures

Before formally defining a proxy signature scheme, we will briefly discuss a few basic assumptions and the format of a proxy signature.

We will assume that users can be uniquely identified by their public keys. So a delegation chain consisting of an original delegator and a number of proxies will be uniquely identified by an ordered list of their public keys. This requirement can be met in practice by requiring the certification authority not to issue certificates for two different users on the same public key. This simple expedient is much simpler to realise than relying on proofs of knowledge (that are implicit in the registered key model).

A proxy signature scheme is required to implement a *proxy identification* algorithm, which, when given a valid proxy signature, outputs the identities (i.e. public keys) of the proxies in the delegation chain. Since we require this function to be publicly available (i.e. no secret information is required to run the algorithm), we have chosen to explicitly include a list PK of the public keys in the proxy signature itself. This does not represent a restriction, since the requirement of a public identification algorithm forces the keys to be part of a proxy signature anyway. For simplicity, we will also require the original delegator to add his public key to PK, making a proxy signature "self-verifiable", i.e. only the signature and a message is required for verification.

It will also be required that a proxy signature contains a list of warrants W for the delegation chain. It is common not to specify the format of warrants since a concrete security policy might depend on the particular usage of the proxy signatures. However, it is also common to assume that some information about the delegation is a part of the warrant to prevent trivial attacks against the scheme. We consider the combination of these two assumptions to be bad practice and suggest that the definition of a proxy scheme should explicitly include all elements which are required for the scheme to be secure. This will help prevent implementation flaws from the use of non-standard or perhaps empty warrants.

A multi-level proxy signature scheme is an extension of an ordinary signature scheme $\mathcal{S} = \{\texttt{Setup}, \texttt{Keygen}, \texttt{Sign}, \texttt{Verify}\}$ with the following additional algorithms:

- (`Delegate`, `ProxyKeyGen`) which is a pair of randomized interactive algorithms for delegation of signing rights.
  - `Delegate` is run by the delegator with input $(PK, W, pk_d, pk_p, sk, w)$, where PK and W are lists of (public keys of) previous delegators and previous warrants in the delegation chain, pk_d and pk_p are the public keys

of the delegator and the proxy, sk is the private key for which signing rights are delegated, and w is the warrant for the current delegation. If the delegator is delegating his own signing rights (i.e. the lists PK and W are empty), we will set $sk = sk_d$ where sk_d is the private key of the delegator itself. However, if the delegator is delegating signing rights for a proxy key psk he has obtained playing the role of a proxy in a previous delegation, we will set $sk = psk$. Delegate will interact with ProxyKeyGen to perform the delegation, but will have no local output.

- ProxyKeyGen is run by the proxy and takes as input (pk_d, pk_p, sk_p) where pk_d is the public key of the delegator and (pk_p, sk_p) is the public/private key pair of the proxy. Upon completion of the interaction with Delegate, ProxyKeyGen returns the local output (PK', W', psk), where PK' and W' are lists of public keys of the delegators and warrants in the delegation chain, extended with the public key of the proxy and the warrant of the current delegation, and psk is a private proxy key which can be used to create proxy signatures on behalf of the delegator.

- ProxySign is run by the proxy and takes as input (PK, W, psk, m) where PK and W are the delegators and warrants in the delegation chain, psk is a proxy key and m is a message to be signed. The output of ProxySign is a proxy signature $(PK, W, p\sigma)$ where $p\sigma$ is a signature on the message m created with the proxy key psk. We say that the proxy signature is generated by the proxy on behalf of the delegator.

- ProxyVerify is run by the verifier and takes as input $(m, (PK, W, p\sigma))$ where m is a message and $(PK, W, p\sigma)$ is a proxy signature as generated by the ProxySign algorithm. The output of ProxyVerify is either accept or reject. Note that ProxyVerify does not take any public keys as input since these are assumed to be part of PK in the proxy signature itself.

Note that a properly generated proxy signature will have one more element in PK than in W since no warrant will be added by the signing proxy. From the explicit inclusion of both PK and W in the proxy signature, it is clear that the public keys of the delegators and the warrants in the delegation chain can be extracted from a proxy signature. Hence, there is no need to define functions which provides this functionality.

The above definition can be seen as a multi-level extension of the definition given in [2], but with explicit modeling of warrants. Compared to the definition given in [22], there are only minor differences which do not impact the functionality of the scheme.

Notation for delegation. To make the notation more clear, we will write

$$(PK', W', psk) \leftarrow \begin{bmatrix} \texttt{Delegate}(PK, W, pk_d, pk_p, sk, w); \\ \texttt{ProxyKeyGen}(pk_d, pk_p, sk_p); \end{bmatrix}$$

for the interaction between the algorithms Delegate and ProxyKeyGen with the inputs $(PK, W, pk_d, pk_p, sk, w)$ and (pk_d, pk_p, sk_p) respectively, and let psk be the proxy key output by ProxyKeyGen.

Soundness. We say that a proxy signature scheme is sound if, firstly, the basic signature scheme $\mathcal{S}$ is sound, and secondly, for all $n \geq 1$, for all possible delegation chains of users with public/private key pairs and proxy keys generated as

$$(pk_i, sk_i) \leftarrow \texttt{KeyGen} \quad \text{for } i \in \{1, \dots, n\}, \qquad psk_1 \leftarrow sk_1 \quad \text{and}$$

$$(PK_i, W_i, psk_i) \leftarrow \begin{bmatrix} \texttt{Delegate}(PK_{i-1}, W_{i-1}, pk_{i-1}, pk_i, psk_{i-1}, w_{i-1}); \\ \texttt{ProxyKeyGen}(pk_{i-1}, pk_i, sk_i); \end{bmatrix}$$

$$\text{for } i \in \{2, \dots n\},$$

and all messages m satisfying the warrants $W_n = (w_1, \dots, w_{n-1})$, we have that

$$\Pr\left[\texttt{ProxyVerify}(m, \texttt{ProxySign}(PK_n, W_n, psk_n, m)) = \texttt{accept}\right] = 1,$$

where the above probability is taken over all random coins used by the $\texttt{KeyGen}$, $\texttt{Delegate}$, $\texttt{ProxyKeyGen}$ and $\texttt{ProxySign}$ algorithms.

4   Security Model

We define the security notion *Existential Unforgeability under an Adaptive Chosen Message Attack with Proxy Key Exposure* ($\texttt{ps-uf-pke}$) for multi-level proxy signature schemes. The security notion is based on the security game defined below, played between a challenger $\mathcal{C}$ and an adversary $\mathcal{A}$. We first introduce some notation and features of the security model, and then give formal definitions.

In the game, $\mathcal{A}$ will control all but a single user, u^*, whose public/private key pair (pk^*, sk^*) will be generated by the challenger, and only pk^* will be made available to $\mathcal{A}$. The public/private key pairs of all the other users will be generated by $\mathcal{A}$, and it will not be required of $\mathcal{A}$ to register generated keys or prove knowledge of the private keys corresponding to the public keys used in the game. This means that $\mathcal{A}$ is allowed to generate and use public keys for which he cannot compute the private key.

The goal of the adversary in the game is to produce a forgery. In this case, a forgery is one of the following: (*i*) an ordinary signature which verifies under u^*'s public key, (*ii*) a proxy signature that appears to be constructed by u^* on behalf of one of the users controlled by the adversary, or (*iii*) a proxy signature on behalf of u^* that is computed by one of the users controlled by the adversary which has not been delegated the signing rights of u^*. We will of course have some requirements on the forgeries to exclude trivial cases, e.g. it is required for a type (*i*) or type (*ii*) forgery that the signature was not obtained in a query to the challenger. However, when considering a message/proxy signature pair $(m, (PK, W, p\sigma))$ produced by the adversary as a type (*ii*) forgery, we will treat any query on a different m or with a different PK or W list, as being unrelated. By this we mean that a forgery will be considered to be valid even if the adversary, for example, has received a proxy signature on the same message m from the same delegation chain PK, but with a different set of warrants W'.

Lastly, in a type (iii) forgery we will allow the adversary to place u^* anywhere in the delegation chain except as the last proxy, which would make the forgery a type (ii) forgery (i.e. we will not restrict u^* to be the original delegator).

For convenience, during the game the challenger will maintain two sets of lists: $pskList(*,*)$ and $delList(*,*,*)$. Each list $pskList(PK, W)$ holds all proxy keys generated by u^* in delegations from the delegation chain with the public keys in the list PK and with the warrants in the list W. This list will be used by the challenger to respond to the various queries made by the adversary during the game. Each list $delList(PK, W, w)$ holds the public keys of users to whom u^* has re-delegated the signing rights of one of the keys in $pskList(PK, W)$ with the warrant w. This list is only used to define valid type (iii) forgeries. If u^* delegates the signing rights of his own private key under the warrant w, the public key of the proxy will be stored in $delList(\{\}, \{\}, w)$ using empty lists, $\{\}$, as the previous public key and warrant lists.

The security game is formally defined as follows:

Setup. The challenger C runs Setup with input 1^k and generates the public/private key pair of u^* by running $(pk^*, sk^*) \leftarrow$ KeyGen. C then passes pk^* to the adversary A and stores sk^*.

Queries. While A is running, it can adaptively make any of the following queries which are answered by C:

1. *Ordinary signature.* On input m from A, C runs $\sigma \leftarrow$ Sign(sk^*, m) and returns σ to A.

2. *Delegation to u^*.* On input pk_d from A, C interacts with A through the delegation protocol by running ProxyKeyGen(pk_d, pk^*, sk^*). Upon completion, C will obtain the proxy information (PK', W', psk). If no $pskList(PK', W')$ list exists, C creates one and adds psk to it. Otherwise, C just adds psk to the existing $pskList(PK', W')$ list.

3. *Delegation from u^*.* For clarity, we will define an oracle for each of the three different types of delegation the adversary can request u^* to perform:

   (a) *Delegation of sk^*.* On input (pk_p, w) from A, C interacts with A by running Delegate$(\{\}, \{\}, pk^*, pk_p, sk^*, w)$. Upon completion of the delegation protocol, C adds pk_p to the list $delList(\{\}, \{\}, w)$.

   (b) *Re-delegation of psk.* On input (PK, W, j, pk_p, w) where $j \in \mathbb{N}$, C looks up the j-th proxy key, psk_j, in $pskList(PK, W)$. If no such key exists, C returns $\perp$ to A. Otherwise, C interacts with A by running Delegate$(PK, W, pk^*, pk_p, psk_j)$. When the delegation is complete, C adds pk_p to $delList(PK, W, w)$.

   (c) *Self-delegation.* On input (PK, W, j, w), C sets $sk = sk^*$ if $PK = W = \{\}$ and $j = 1$. Otherwise, C sets sk to be the j-th proxy key in $pskList(PK, W)$ (if this proxy key does not exist, C returns $\perp$ to A). Then C interacts with itself by running

$$(PK', W', psk) \leftarrow \begin{bmatrix} \text{Delegate}(PK, W, pk^*, pk^*, sk, w); \\ \text{ProxyKeyGen}(pk^*, pk^*, sk^*); \end{bmatrix}$$

When the delegation is complete, $\mathcal{C}$ adds psk to $pskList(PK', W')$ and send the transcript of the delegation to $\mathcal{A}$.

4. *Proxy signature.* On input (PK, W, j, m), $\mathcal{C}$ looks up the j-th proxy key, psk_j, in $pskList(PK, W)$ and returns $\perp$ to $\mathcal{A}$ if no such key exists. Otherwise, $\mathcal{C}$ computes $(PK', W, p\sigma) \leftarrow \texttt{ProxySign}(PK, W, psk_j, m)$ and sends $(PK', W, p\sigma)$ to $\mathcal{A}$.

5. *Proxy key exposure.* On input (PK, W, j), $\mathcal{C}$ returns the j-th proxy key in $pskList(PK, W)$ if such a key exists. Otherwise, $\mathcal{C}$ returns $\perp$ to $\mathcal{A}$.

Forgery. The adversary outputs a forgery and halts. The forgery can be of one of the following forms:

(i) *Ordinary signature of u^*.* The adversary outputs (m, σ). This forgery is said to be *valid* if $\texttt{Verify}(pk^*, m, \sigma) = \texttt{accept}$ and m has not been submitted in an ordinary signature query.

(ii) *Proxy signature of u^*.* The adversary outputs a message/signature tuple, $(m, (PK, W, p\sigma))$, where the last key in PK is pk^*. This forgery is said to be *valid* if $\texttt{ProxyVerify}(m, (PK, W, p\sigma)) = \texttt{accept}$, $(PK, W, *, m)$ has not been submitted in a proxy signature query and $(PK, W, *)$ has not been submitted in a proxy key exposure query.

(iii) *Proxy signature on behalf of u^*.* The adversary outputs a message/signature tuple, $(m, (PK, W, p\sigma))$, as a forgery, where the last key in PK is different from pk^*. Let $PK = (pk_1, \ldots, pk_n)$. The forgery is said to be *valid* if $\texttt{ProxyVerify}(m, (PK, W, p\sigma)) = \texttt{accept}$ and there exists an $1 \leq i^* \leq n-1$ such that $pk_{i^*} = pk^*$, $pk_{i^*+1} \notin delList(PK_{1\ldots i^*}, W_{1\ldots i^*-1}, w_{i^*})$ and $(PK_{1\ldots i^*}, W_{1\ldots i^*-1}, *)$ has not been submitted in a proxy key exposure query.

If the forgery output by the adversary is valid, return 1 as a result of the game. Otherwise, return 0.

Note that a type (ii) forgery $(m, (PK, W, p\sigma))$ is not considered to be valid in our model if the adversary has exposed *any* of the proxy keys generated by u^* in a delegation from the users PK with the warrants W, or requested a signature on m with one of these keys. Multiple keys can exists if the delegation is randomized and the adversary makes identical delegation requests multiple times. However, since all signatures created with these proxy keys will verify under the same conditions, a compromise of just one of them should be considered as a complete compromise of the delegation from the users PK under warrants W.

Let $\mathbf{Gm}_{\mathcal{PS},\mathcal{A}}^{\text{ps-uf-pke}}(k)$ be the outcome of running the above security game with proxy signature scheme $\mathcal{PS}$, adversary $\mathcal{A}$ and security parameter k. We then define the advantage of the adversary in the security game as

$$\mathbf{Adv}_{\mathcal{PS},\mathcal{A}}^{\text{ps-uf-pke}}(k) = \Pr[\mathbf{Gm}_{\mathcal{PS},\mathcal{A}}^{\text{ps-uf-pke}}(k) = 1]$$

where the probability is taken over all random coins tosses made by the adversary and the challenger.

Definition 1. *An adversary $\mathcal{A}$ is said to be a (ϵ, t, q_d, q_s)-forger of a proxy signature scheme if $\mathcal{A}$ has advantage at least ϵ in the above game, runs in time at most* *t and makes at most q_d and q_s delegation and signing queries to the challenger. A proxy signature scheme is said to be (ϵ, t, q_d, q_s)-secure if no (ϵ, t, q_d, q_s)-forger exists.*

5 Proxy Schemes Based on Sequential Aggregation

We will now present a generic proxy signature construction that satisfy the security definition given in Section 4, using a sequential aggregate signature scheme that is existentially unforgeable in the sequential aggregate chosen-key model. To guarantee that no information about a user's long term secret key is leaked if proxy keys are exposed, we will let a proxy generate a fresh independent key pair (pk, sk) in a delegation, create a certificate for pk and keep sk as the proxy key. The generated public keys will be stored in a separate list FK. To avoid trivial attacks against the scheme, we will use the idea of Boldyreva *et al.* [2], and introduce symbols dlg, sgn and prx, which will be attached to the content being signed in, respectively, a delegation, an ordinary signature and a proxy signature.

Construction 1. Let $\mathcal{AS} = \{\texttt{Setup}', \texttt{KeyGen}', \texttt{AggSign}, \texttt{AggVerify}\}$ be a sequential aggregate signature scheme and let the symbols dlg, sgn and prx be defined as different strings. Then a multi-level proxy signature scheme can be constructed as follows:

- **Setup, KeyGen.** Same as the corresponding algorithms from the sequential aggregate signature scheme.
- **Sign**(sk, m) Compute $\sigma \leftarrow \texttt{AggSign}(sk, \texttt{sgn}\|m, \emptyset)$, where $\emptyset$ indicates an "empty" sequential aggregate signature, and return σ as a signature.
- **Verify**(pk, m, σ) Return the output of $\texttt{AggVerify}(pk, \texttt{sgn}\|m, \sigma)$.
- **Delegate**$(PK, W, pk_d, pk_p, sk, w)$ Depending on (PK, W), take one of the following actions:
  - If PK and W are empty lists (i.e. sk is an ordinary private key), construct the lists $PK' = (pk_d, pk_p)$, $FK = ()$ and $W' = (w)$. Compute $\sigma_{del} \leftarrow \texttt{AggSign}(sk, \texttt{dlg}\|PK'\|FK\|W', \emptyset)$ and send the delegation message $(PK', FK, W', \sigma_{del})$ to the proxy.
  - If PK and W are not empty (i.e. sk is a proxy key), construct $PK' = PK.(pk_p)$ and $W' = W.(w)$. Parse sk as $(FK, \sigma_{del}, sk_{prx})$, compute

$$\sigma'_{del} \leftarrow \texttt{AggSign}(sk_{prx}, \texttt{dlg}\|PK'\|FK\|W', \sigma_{del})$$

  and send the delegation message $(PK', FK, W', \sigma'_{del})$ to the proxy.
- **ProxyKeyGen**(pk_d, pk_p, sk_p) When $(PK', FK, W', \sigma_{del})$ is received from the delegator, generate a fresh proxy key pair $(pk'_p, sk'_p) \leftarrow \texttt{KeyGen}$ and construct $FK' = FK.(pk'_p)$. Compute $\sigma''_{del} \leftarrow \texttt{AggSign}(sk_p, \texttt{dlg}\|PK'\|FK'\|W', \sigma_{del})$, set $psk = (FK', \sigma''_{del}, sk'_p)$ and output (PK', W', psk).
- **ProxySign**(PK, W, psk, m) Parse the proxy key psk as (FK, σ_{del}, sk_p) and compute $p\sigma \leftarrow \texttt{AggSign}(sk_p, \texttt{prx}\|PK\|FK\|W\|m, \sigma_{del})$. Return the tuple $(PK, W, (FK, p\sigma))$ as a proxy signature.

- ProxyVerify$(m, (PK, W, (FK, p\sigma)))$ Assume that PK contains $n + 1$ elements. Construct

$$m_i = \texttt{dlg}\|PK_{1...i+1}\|FK_{1...i}\|W_{1...i} \quad \text{for } i \in \{1, \ldots, n\} \quad \text{and}$$
$$\overline{m} = (m_1, \ldots, m_n, \texttt{prx}\|PK\|FK\|W\|m).$$

Return the output of AggVerify$(PK, \overline{m}, p\sigma)$.

Theorem 2. *Let $\mathcal{AS}$ be a (t, q_s, ϵ)-unforgeable sequential aggregate signature scheme. Then Construction 1 yields a $(t', q'_s, q'_d, \epsilon')$-unforgeable proxy signature scheme where $\epsilon = \epsilon'/2q_d$, $t = t'$ and $q_s = q'_s + q'_d$.*

The proof of this theorem is given in Appendix C.

The above construction can be instantiated with a number of different sequential aggregate signature schemes to give proxy signature schemes with various security properties. For example, if the (fully aggregate) scheme of Boneh *et al.* [5] is used, we obtain a proxy signature scheme which is secure in the random oracle model under the Computational co-Diffie-Hellman assumption, a natural generalization of the CDH assumption suited to bilinear groups. Notice, however, that since a proxy signature will potentially include many public keys, but only one aggregate signature, the most efficient scheme (in terms of proxy signature size) is achieved by minimizing the size of the public keys and not the size of the aggregate signature. The scheme of [5] easily allows this modification, and using this we obtain a very efficient scheme, even if only single-level delegations are considered. Instantiating the scheme with the MNT elliptic curves [25], we can achieve a public key size of 168 bits and an aggregate signature size of 1008 bits, giving a proxy signature size of 1512 bits, all for a security level of approximately 80 bits. Hence, the scheme provides proxy signatures which are less than half the size of the triple Schnorr signatures as they are presented in [2], while satisfying a stronger definition of security and providing self-verifiability and multi-level capabilities. Note, however, that the triple Schnorr scheme allows faster verification.

To achieve an RSA-based proxy signature scheme, we can use the sequential aggregate signature technique proposed by Lysyanskaya *et al.* [21], which is secure in the random oracle model given that a claw-free permutation family is used in the construction. Note that the RSA-based instantiation proposed in [21] has the disadvantage that the aggregate signature will grow with one bit for each signer. To avoid this expansion, the slightly more computationally expensive RSA-family of trap-door permutations with common domain proposed by Hayashi *et al.* [13] can be used. It should be mentioned that to avoid the need for key certification, a few extra properties are needed to guarantee that each public key does define a permutation over the common domain; details are in [21]. However, with these minor changes, we obtain a scheme at the 80-bit security level having an aggregate signature size of 1024 bits and, assuming that all users use the same encryption exponent, a public key size of 1024 bits, giving a proxy signature size of 4096 bits for a single-level delegation.

Lastly, it is also possible to construct a scheme which is secure in the standard model. However, the sequential aggregate scheme proposed by Lu *et al.* [20] cannot be used for this purpose since this scheme is dependent on the registered key model for security. In fact, to our knowledge, it is still an open problem to construct an efficient sequential aggregate signature scheme which is secure in the standard model and which does not require the registered key model. This leaves only the "trivial" construction from an ordinary signature scheme (in which the aggregate signature is simply a concatenation of ordinary signatures). Using this together with, for example, the signature scheme of Boneh and Boyen [3], gives a scheme which is secure, albeit somewhat inefficient, in the standard model under the q-Strong Diffie-Hellman assumption. Instantiating the scheme with an elliptic curve similar to the one suggested above, it is possible to achieve a public key size of 336 bits (assuming all users use the same group generator and that redundant parts of the public key are left out), a signature size of 1176 bits, and a proxy signature size of 4536 bits for a single-level delegation, all at a security level of 80 bits. We note that if one is willing to downgrade the security requirements and use the registered key model, the scheme of Lu *et al.* [20] can be used, but a direct application will not be efficient due to the large size of the public keys.

6   Identity-Based Constructions

Identity-based cryptography was originally proposed by Shamir [28] more than two decades ago, but identity-based encryption was first efficiently instantiated recently by Boneh and Franklin [4]. The construction methods presented in [4] inspired the extension of many existing cryptographic primitives to the identity-based setting along with efficient constructions. Among these, specific identity-based proxy signatures were also constructed (see, for example, [34,33,12]).

Both our definition of a proxy signature scheme given in Section 3 and the security model presented in Section 4, can easily be extended to the identity-based setting. However, due to space restrictions, we will not give the full definitions here, but only briefly discuss the changes needed to obtain the identity-based formulations.

Identity-based proxy signatures. First of all, in an identity-based setting, the presence of a *master entity* is assumed. The role of the master entity is to initially generate a set of public system parameters and a *master key*, which the master entity will use to generate private keys corresponding to identities in the scheme. An identity-based signature scheme is given by the algorithms $\mathcal{IBS} = \{\texttt{Setup}, \texttt{Extract}, \texttt{Sign}, \texttt{Verify}\}$, where $\texttt{Setup}$ generates the system parameters and the master key, $\texttt{Extract}$ generates a private key for an identity and $\texttt{Sign}$ and $\texttt{Verify}$ implement similar functionality to the corresponding algorithms of an ordinary signature scheme, with the exception that public keys are replaced by identities. An identity-based proxy signature scheme extends an identity-based signature scheme with the algorithms $\{\texttt{Delegate}, \texttt{ProxyKeyGen},$

ProxySign, ProxyVerify}, which implement similar functionality to the corresponding algorithms for an ordinary proxy signature scheme, with the exception that all public keys are replaced by identities.

Security model. The security notion *Identity-Based Proxy Signature Unforgeability Under an Adaptive Chosen Message Attack with Proxy Key Exposure* (id-ps-uf-pke) can be defined by introducing the following changes to the security game in Section 4:

Setup The adversary is no longer given a public key pair, but only the system parameters.

Queries The adversary is allowed to make similar queries to those in the ordinary security game, using identities instead of public keys. The adversary will furthermore be allowed to adaptively request the private keys of identities.

Forgery The adversary is allowed to choose an identity ID^* for which he will produce a forgery (in the ordinary game the adversary was forced to produce a forgery for pk^* chosen by the challenger), but it is required that he has not requested the private key of ID^* during the game. Besides this, the restrictions on the forgery from the ordinary game apply.

With the above changes to the security game, the advantage of the adversary can be defined exactly as in the ordinary security game and (ϵ, t, q_d, q_s)-security for an identity-based proxy signature scheme can be formulated exactly as in Definition 1.

Construction Having defined the identity-based security model, it remains to be seen if Construction 1 will yield a secure identity-based proxy signature scheme, using an identity-based sequential aggregate signature scheme [14]. Looking at the definition of ProxyKeyGen reveals one problem though: a proxy is required to generate a fresh key pair in a delegation. This represents a limitation in the identity-based setting, since only the master entity can generate a private key corresponding to a given identity[1]. However, note that it is not necessary for the key pair generated in ProxyKeyGen to be identity-based (i.e. consist of an identity and a private key) for the overall scheme to maintain its identity-based properties. In fact, a key pair from an ordinary sequential aggregate signature scheme will suffice. Since signatures from an ordinary and an identity-based sequential aggregate signature scheme cannot generally be aggregated in the same signature, σ_{del} and $p\sigma$ in Construction 1 will have to be split into two parts – one part containing aggregated identity-based signatures and the other containing aggregated ordinary signatures. However, with these small changes, a secure identity-based proxy signature scheme can be obtained.

Theorem 3. *Let a* (t', q'_s, ϵ')*-unforgeable sequential aggregate signature scheme and a* (t'', q''_s, ϵ'')*-unforgeable identity-based sequential aggregate signature scheme*

---

[1] We note that a user can generate private keys for new identities if a hierarchical identity-based signature scheme is used, but due to space limitations, we will not discuss this alternative approach here.

be given. Then the above modifications to Construction 1 yields a (t, q_s, q_d, ϵ)-unforgeable identity-based proxy signature scheme where $\epsilon = q_d \epsilon' + \epsilon''$, $t = \min(t', t'')$ and $q_s + q_d = \min(q_s', q_s'')$.

The proof of this theorem is very similar to that of the proof of Theorem 2 and will not be given here. The main difference from the proof of Theorem 2 is that a successful forgery against the identity-based proxy signature scheme will potentially lead to either a forgery of the identity-based or the ordinary signature scheme, depending on the type of the proxy signature forgery. However, these different types of proxy signature forgeries are already considered in the proof of Theorem 2 although only a forgery for the single underlying scheme is produced.

When instantiating the above construction, all of the options for an ordinary sequential aggregate signature scheme discussed in Section 5 can be used. However, the choice of an identity-based sequential aggregate signature scheme is less obvious. One would imagine that the scheme by Gentry and Ramzan [10] would be an ideal candidate, but this scheme is based on all users agreeing on a random string w, which is used in the signing process, before signatures can be aggregated, and the scheme will become insecure if the same w is used for different aggregate signatures[2]. The latter property means that the Gentry-Ramzan scheme does not have the full flexibility of a sequential aggregate signature scheme, since an existing aggregate signature cannot be aggregated with two different signatures to yield two new aggregate signatures. In our construction, this would mean that a proxy could only delegate the signing rights of a proxy key once. To our knowledge, no other identity-based sequential aggregate signature scheme (which provides full aggregation) has been proposed, and it remains an open problem to construct such a scheme. However, schemes that provide partial aggregation (i.e. the size of the aggregate signature is not independent of the number of signers) have been proposed and can be used to instantiate our construction. For example, the scheme proposed by Herranz [14], which is secure in the random-oracle model under the Computational co-Diffie-Hellman assumption, can be used to achieve a fairly efficient scheme.

7   Conclusion

In this paper, we have motivated the introduction of a new security model for proxy signatures that enhances the existing models of [2,22]. The new model incorporates warrants, allows unregistered public keys, and lets the attacker recover proxy private keys. These extensions were motivated by practical considerations as well as attacks on existing schemes. We showed how our new security definition could be achieved through a generic construction involving sequential aggregate signatures, and considered concrete and efficient instantiations of the construction. Finally, we sketched how our models and constructions can be extended to the identity-based setting.

---

[2] This is not just a property of the security proof given in [10], but will enable an adversary to construct selective forgeries.

In the full version, we complete the routine investigation of the security and performance trade-offs of our schemes and provide the full details of the identity-based setting. We also consider how hierarchical identity-based signatures can be used to construct efficient identity-based proxy signatures.

References

1. Bellare, M., Neven, G.: Multi-signatures in the plain public-key model and a general forking lemma. In: ACM Conference on Computer and Communications Security, pp. 390–399. ACM, New York (2006)
2. Boldyreva, A., Palacio, A., Warinschi, B.: Secure proxy signature schemes for delegation of signing rights. Cryptology ePrint Archive, Report 2003/096 (2003), http://eprint.iacr.org/
3. Boneh, D., Boyen, X.: Short signatures without random oracles. In: Cachin, C., Camenisch, J.L. (eds.) EUROCRYPT 2004. LNCS, vol. 3027, Springer, Heidelberg (2004)
4. Boneh, D., Franklin, M.K.: Identity-based encryption from the Weil pairing. In: Kilian, J. (ed.) CRYPTO 2001. LNCS, vol. 2139, pp. 213–229. Springer, Heidelberg (2001)
5. Boneh, D., Gentry, C., Lynn, B., Shacham, H.: Aggregate and verifiably encrypted signatures from bilinear maps. In: Biham, E. (ed.) EUROCRYPT 2003. LNCS, vol. 2656, pp. 416–432. Springer, Heidelberg (2003)
6. Boneh, D., Lynn, B., Shacham, H.: Short signatures from the Weil pairing. J. Cryptology 17(4), 297–319 (2004)
7. Cachin, C., Camenisch, J.L. (eds.): EUROCRYPT 2004. LNCS, vol. 3027. Springer, Heidelberg (2004)
8. Dodis, Y., Katz, J., Xu, S., Yung, M.: Strong key-insulated signature schemes. In: Desmedt, Y.G. (ed.) PKC 2003. LNCS, vol. 2567, pp. 130–144. Springer, Heidelberg (2002)
9. Foster, I.T., Kesselman, C., Tsudik, G., Tuecke, S.: A security architecture for computational grids. In: ACM Conference on Computer and Communications Security, pp. 83–92 (1998)
10. Gentry, C., Ramzan, Z.: Identity-based aggregate signatures. In: Yung, M., Dodis, Y., Kiayias, A., Malkin, T.G. (eds.) PKC 2006. LNCS, vol. 3958, pp. 257–273. Springer, Heidelberg (2006)
11. Goldwasser, S., Micali, S., Rivest, R.L.: A digital signature scheme secure against adaptive chosen-message attacks. SIAM J. Comput. 17(2), 281–308 (1988)
12. Gu, C., Zhu, Y.: An efficient id-based proxy signature scheme from pairings. Cryptology ePrint Archive, Report 2006/158 (2006), http://eprint.iacr.org/
13. Hayashi, R., Okamoto, T., Tanaka, K.: An RSA family of trap-door permutations with a common domain and its applications. In: Bao, F., Deng, R., Zhou, J. (eds.) PKC 2004. LNCS, vol. 2947, pp. 291–304. Springer, Heidelberg (2004)
14. Herranz, J.: Deterministic identity-based signatures for partial aggregation. Cryptology ePrint Archive, Report 2005/313 (2005), http://eprint.iacr.org/
15. Hess, F.: Efficient identity based signature schemes based on pairings. In: Nyberg, K., Heys, H.M. (eds.) SAC 2002. LNCS, vol. 2595, pp. 310–324. Springer, Heidelberg (2003)

16. Kim, S., Park, S., Won, D.: Proxy signatures, revisited. In: Han, Y., Quing, S. (eds.) ICICS 1997. LNCS, vol. 1334, pp. 223–232. Springer, Heidelberg (1997)
17. Lal, S., Awasthi, A.K.: Proxy blind signature scheme. Cryptology ePrint Archive, Report 2003/072 (2003), http://eprint.iacr.org/
18. Lee, B., Kim, H., Kim, K.: Strong proxy signature and its application. In: SCIS, pp. 603–608 (2001)
19. Lee, J.-Y., Cheon, J.H., Kim, S.: An analysis of proxy signatures: Is a secure channel necessary? In: Joye, M. (ed.) CT-RSA 2003. LNCS, vol. 2612, pp. 68–79. Springer, Heidelberg (2003)
20. Lu, S., Ostrovsky, R., Sahai, A., Shacham, H., Waters, B.: Sequential aggregate signatures and multisignatures without random oracles. Cryptology ePrint Archive, Report 2006/096 (2006), http://eprint.iacr.org/
21. Lysyanskaya, A., Micali, S., Reyzin, L., Shacham, H.: Sequential aggregate signatures from trapdoor permutations. In: Cachin, C., Camenisch, J.L. (eds.) EURO-CRYPT 2004. LNCS, vol. 3027, pp. 74–90. Springer, Heidelberg (2004)
22. Malkin, T., Obana, S., Yung, M.: The hierarchy of key evolving signatures and a characterization of proxy signatures. In: Cachin, C., Camenisch, J.L. (eds.) EU-ROCRYPT 2004. LNCS, vol. 3027, pp. 306–322. Springer, Heidelberg (2004)
23. Malkin, T., Obana, S., Yung, M.: The hierarchy of key evolving signatures and a characterization of proxy signatures. Cryptology ePrint Archive, Report 2004/052 (2004), http://eprint.iacr.org/
24. Mambo, M., Usuda, K., Okamoto, E.: Proxy signatures for delegating signing operation. In: Proceedings of the 3st ACM conference on Computer and Communications Security, pp. 48–57 (1996)
25. Miyaji, A., Nakabayashi, M., Takano, S.: New explicit conditions of elliptic curve traces for FR-reduction. IEICE Transactions, Fundamentals E84-A(5), 1234–1243 (2001)
26. Okamoto, T., Inomata, A., Okamoto, E.: A proposal of short proxy signature using pairing. In: ITCC, vol. 1, pp. 631–635. IEEE Computer Society, Los Alamitos (2005)
27. Okamoto, T., Tada, M., Okamoto, E.: Extended proxy signatures for smart cards. In: Zheng, Y., Mambo, M. (eds.) ISW 1999. LNCS, vol. 1729, pp. 247–258. Springer, Heidelberg (1999)
28. Shamir, A.: Identity-based cryptosystems and signature schemes. In: Blakely, G.R., Chaum, D. (eds.) CRYPTO 1984. LNCS, vol. 196, pp. 47–53. Springer, Heidelberg (1985)
29. Sun, H.-M.: An efficient nonrepudiable threshold proxy signature scheme with known signers. Computer Communications 22(8), 717–722 (1999)
30. Wang, G.: Designated-verifier proxy signature schemes. In: Sasaki, R., Qing, S., Okamoto, E., Yoshiura, H. (eds.) SEC, pp. 409–424. Springer, Heidelberg (2005)
31. Wang, G., Bao, F., Zhou, J., Deng, R.H.: Security analysis of some proxy signatures. In: Lim, J.-I., Lee, D.-H. (eds.) ICISC 2003. LNCS, vol. 2971, pp. 305–319. Springer, Heidelberg (2004)
32. Wang, H., Pieprzyk, J.: Efficient one-time proxy signatures. In: Laih, C.-S. (ed.) ASIACRYPT 2003. LNCS, vol. 2894, pp. 507–522. Springer, Heidelberg (2003)
33. Xu, J., Zhang, Z., Feng, D.: ID-based proxy signature using bilinear pairings. Cryptology ePrint Archive, Report 2004/206 (2004), http://eprint.iacr.org/
34. Zhang, F., Kim, K.: Efficient ID-based blind signature and proxy signature from bilinear pairings. In: Safavi-Naini, R., Seberry, J. (eds.) ACISP 2003. LNCS, vol. 2727, pp. 312–323. Springer, Heidelberg (2003)

35. Zhang, F., Safavi-Naini, R., Lin, C.-Y.: New proxy signature, proxy blind signature and proxy ring signature schemes from bilinear pairing. Cryptology ePrint Archive, Report 2003/104 (2003), http://eprint.iacr.org/
36. Zhang, K.: Threshold proxy signature schemes. In: Proc. 1st International Information Security Workshop, pp. 282–290 (1997)

A   Key Registration Attack on ZSL-Scheme

We briefly illustrate how an adversary can mount an attack on the proxy signature scheme proposed by Zhang, Safavi-Naini and Lin [35], if key registration is not required as a part of the security model.

In the construction presented in [35], delegation is done by letting the delegator construct a Boneh-Lynn-Shacham signature [6] on the warrant w, i.e. by computing $\sigma_d = s_d H(w)$ (where $s_d \in \mathbb{Z}_q$ is the private key of the delegator and H is a hash function onto a bilinear group $\mathbb{G}$ of prime order q), and then sending σ_d to the proxy. Upon receiving σ_d, the proxy generates a private proxy key psk by computing his own signature on the warrant, $\sigma_p = s_p H(w)$, where $s_p \in \mathbb{Z}_q$ is the private key of the proxy, and setting $psk = \sigma_d + \sigma_p = (s_d + s_p)H(w)$.

A proxy signature is then created by using the identity-based signature scheme of Hess [15], letting w act as the signing identity and psk as the private key for this identity. A verifier can construct a master public key for the Hess signature scheme in which psk is the private key of w, by summing the public keys for the delegator and the proxy, i.e. by setting $pk_d + pk_p = (s_d + s_p)P$ where P generates $\mathbb{G}$, and then verify the proxy signature as a signature by the identity w.

However, this construction is insecure if the registered key model is not used. This can easily be seen as follows: let $pk^* = s^* P$ be the public key of the challenge user and let the adversary choose the public key $pk = s_a P - pk^*$ for a malicious proxy (note that the adversary cannot compute the private key corresponding to this public key). Then, for any warrant w, the adversary can compute $s_a H(w) = (s_a - s^* + s^*)H(w) = \sigma^* + \sigma_a$ and thereby construct the private key needed for creating proxy signatures on behalf of the challenge user, without the challenge user having delegated his signing rights.

B   Proxy Key Exposure Attack on BPW-Scheme

We briefly illustrate how an adversary can recover the private key of the user in the triple Schnorr proxy signature scheme analyzed by Boldyreva, Palacio and Warinschi [2], if a proxy key is exposed.

The key observation is that the value $t = G(0||pk_d||pk_p||w, Y) \cdot sk_p + s \mod q$ is a part of the proxy key, where G is a hash function, pk_d and pk_p are the public keys of the delegator and the proxy, w is a warrant, (Y, s) are values sent by the delegator to the proxy in a delegation, and sk_p is the private key of the proxy. Since it is not assumed that there is a secure channel between the delegator and the proxy, (Y, s) can be observed by the adversary, and if a proxy key is exposed, the adversary can recover the private key sk_p of the proxy, simply by computing $sk_p = (t - s) \cdot G(0||pk_d||pk_p||w, Y)^{-1} \mod q$.

C   Proof of Theorem 2

Proof. The proof is by contradiction: we will assume that an adversary $\mathcal{A}$ that $(t', q_s', q_d', \epsilon')$-breaks Construction 1 exists, and from this, construct an adversary $\mathcal{B}$ that (t, q_s, ϵ)-breaks the underlying sequential aggregate signature scheme.

Initially, $\mathcal{B}$ will be given a challenge public key pk' and access to a sequential aggregate signing oracle $\mathcal{O}_{sig}(m, \sigma_{agg})$ for the secret key sk' corresponding to pk'. Firstly, $\mathcal{B}$ flips a fair coin c. If $c = 0$, $\mathcal{B}$ sets $pk^* = pk'$ and $sk^* = \emptyset$. Otherwise, $\mathcal{B}$ generates a fresh key pair $(pk^*, sk^*) \leftarrow$ KeyGen, and chooses $i^* \in \{1, \ldots, q_d'\}$ ($\mathcal{B}$ will later use pk' instead of a fresh key in the i^*-th delegation query by $\mathcal{A}$). For ease of notation, we define the following function for signature generation by $\mathcal{B}$:

$$\texttt{Sign}_{\mathcal{B}}(sk, m, \sigma_{agg}) = \begin{cases} \mathcal{O}_{sig}(m, \sigma_{agg}) & \text{if } sk = \emptyset \\ \texttt{AggSign}(sk, m, \sigma_{agg}) & \text{otherwise} \end{cases}$$

$\mathcal{B}$ runs $\mathcal{A}$ with input pk^*. As the challenger in the security game, $\mathcal{B}$ will maintain a set of lists $pskList(*, *)$ while $\mathcal{A}$ is running. Each list $pskList(PK, W)$ will hold all proxy keys generated by $\mathcal{B}$ for the delegation chain with the public keys PK and the warrants W. While running, $\mathcal{A}$ can make various queries which $\mathcal{B}$ will answer as follows (note that, to answer the queries, $\mathcal{B}$ simply implements the challenger by using his access to the signing oracle and taking into account the value of c):

- *Ordinary signature.* On input m from $\mathcal{A}$, $\mathcal{B}$ returns $\texttt{Sign}_{\mathcal{B}}(sk^*, \texttt{sgn}\|m, \emptyset)$.
- *Delegation to u^*.* $\mathcal{A}$ submits the delegation message $(PK, FK, W, \sigma_{del})$. If $c = 0$, or $c = 1$ and this is *not* the i^*-th delegation query, $\mathcal{B}$ generates a fresh key pair $(pk, sk) \leftarrow KeyGen$, constructs $FK' = FK.(pk)$ and sets $sk_{prx} = sk$. If $c = 1$ and this *is* the i^*-th delegation query, $\mathcal{B}$ constructs $FK' = FK.(pk^*)$ and sets $sk_{prx} = \emptyset$. Then $\mathcal{B}$ computes $\sigma_{del}' \leftarrow \texttt{Sign}_{\mathcal{B}}(sk_{prx}, \texttt{dlg}\|PK\|FK'\|W, \sigma_{del})$ and stores $psk = (FK', \sigma_{del}', sk_{prx})$ in $pskList(PK, W)$.
- *Delegation from u^*.* There are three different types of queries $\mathcal{A}$ can make:
  1. *Delegation of sk^** On input (pk_p, w) from $\mathcal{A}$, $\mathcal{B}$ constructs the lists $PK' = (pk^*, pk_p)$, $FK = ()$ and $W' = (w)$. Then $\mathcal{B}$ computes the signature $\sigma_{del} \leftarrow \texttt{Sign}_{\mathcal{B}}(sk^*, \texttt{dlg}\|PK'\|FK'\|W', \emptyset)$ and sends the delegation message $(PK', FK, W', \sigma_{del})$ to $\mathcal{A}$.
  2. *Re-delegation of psk.* On input (PK, W, j, pk_p, w) from $\mathcal{A}$, where $j \in \mathbb{N}$, $\mathcal{B}$ looks up the j-th proxy key in $pskList(PK, W)$ and parses it as $(FK, \sigma_{del}, sk_{prx})$. Then $\mathcal{B}$ constructs $PK' = PK.(pk_p)$ and $W' = W.(w)$, computes $\sigma_{del}' \leftarrow \texttt{Sign}_{\mathcal{B}}(sk_{prx}, \texttt{dlg}\|PK'\|FK\|W', \sigma_{del})$, and sends the delegation message $(PK', FK, W', \sigma_{del}')$ to $\mathcal{A}$.
  3. *self-delegation.* Depending on the input (PK, W, j, w) submitted by $\mathcal{A}$, $\mathcal{B}$ will do one of the following:
     - If PK and W are empty (self-delegation of sk^*), $\mathcal{B}$ constructs the lists $PK' = (pk^*, pk^*)$, $FK = ()$ and $W' = (w)$, and sets $sk_{self} = sk^*$ and $\sigma_{self} = \emptyset$.

- If PK and W are not empty (delegation of psk), $\mathcal{B}$ looks up the j-th proxy key in $pskList(PK, W)$ and parses it as $(FK, \sigma_{del}, sk_{prx})$. Then $\mathcal{B}$ constructs $PK' = PK.(pk^*)$ and $W' = W.(w)$, and sets $sk_{self} = sk_{prx}$ and $\sigma_{self} = \sigma_{del}$

  Then $\mathcal{B}$ computes $\sigma'_{del} \leftarrow \text{Sign}_{\mathcal{B}}(sk_{self}, \text{dlg}\|PK'\|FK\|W', \sigma_{self})$. Now, if $c = 0$, or $c = 1$ and this is *not* the i^*-th delegation query, $\mathcal{B}$ generates $(pk, sk) \leftarrow \text{KeyGen}$ and constructs $FK' = FK.(pk)$. Otherwise, $\mathcal{B}$ just constructs $FK' = FK.(pk^*)$ and sets $sk = \emptyset$. Finally, $\mathcal{B}$ computes $\sigma''_{del} \leftarrow \text{Sign}_{\mathcal{B}}(sk_{self}, \text{dlg}\|PK'\|FK'\|W', \sigma'_{del})$, stores the proxy key $psk = (FK', \sigma''_{del}, sk)$ in $pskList(PK', W')$ and sends the transcript $(PK', FK, W', \sigma'_{del})$ to $\mathcal{A}$.

- *Proxy signature.* On input (PK, W, j, m) from $\mathcal{A}$, $\mathcal{B}$ looks up the j-th proxy key, in $pskList(PK, W)$ and parses it as $(FK, \sigma_{del}, sk_{prx})$. Then $\mathcal{B}$ computes the signature $p\sigma \leftarrow \text{Sign}_{\mathcal{B}}(sk_{prx}, \text{prx}\|PK\|FK\|W\|m, \sigma_{del})$ and returns $(PK, W, (FK, p\sigma))$ to $\mathcal{A}$.

- *Proxy key exposure.* On input (PK, W, j), $\mathcal{B}$ looks up the j-th proxy key in $pskList(PK, W)$ and parses it as $(FK, \sigma_{del}, sk_{prx})$. If $sk_{prx} = \emptyset$, $\mathcal{B}$ aborts. Otherwise, $\mathcal{B}$ returns $(FK, \sigma_{del}, sk_{prx})$ to $\mathcal{A}$.

Note that pk^* will be drawn from the same distribution as public keys generated by KeyGen and that $\mathcal{B}$'s choice of c will be completely hidden from $\mathcal{A}$, unless an abort occurs.

If $\mathcal{B}$ is not forced to abort, $\mathcal{A}$ will eventually output a forgery. We will classify forgeries into two different categories:

Category A forgeries are either a valid type (i) forgery (m, σ), a valid type (ii) forgery $(m, (PK, W, (FK, p\sigma)))$ where the last key in FK was not generated by $\mathcal{B}$, or a valid type (iii) forgery $(m, (PK, W, (FK, p\sigma)))$ where the $(i^* - 1)$-th key in FK was not generated by $\mathcal{B}$.

Category B forgeries are all valid forgeries that are not in Category A, i.e. a type (ii) or type (iii) forgery where $\mathcal{B}$ has generated the public key in FK which corresponds to u^*'s position in the delegation chain of the forgery.

Informally, Category A forgeries correspond to forgeries where $\mathcal{A}$ has forged a signature under u^*'s long term key, and Category B forgeries correspond to forgeries where $\mathcal{A}$ has forged a signature under one of the keys generated by u^* in a delegation, but for which $\mathcal{A}$ has not received the corresponding private key.

Consider the case where $c = 0$. In this case, $\mathcal{B}$ sets $pk^* = pk'$. If $\mathcal{A}$ constructs a valid Category A forgery, then

- if the forgery is of type (i) i.e. (m, σ), then $\mathcal{A}$ will not have requested a signature on m (since the forgery is valid), and $\mathcal{B}$ will therefore not have submitted $(\text{sgn}\|m, \emptyset)$ to his own signing oracle. Hence, σ is a valid forgery of a sequential aggregate signature of length 1 on the message $\text{sgn}\|m$ under the the the public key $pk^* = pk'$.

- if the forgery is of type (ii) i.e. $(m, (PK, W, (FK, p\sigma)))$, where the last key $pk_n \in PK$ is equal to $pk^* = pk'$, then $\mathcal{B}$ will not have submitted

($\texttt{dlg}||PK||FK||W, \sigma_{del}$) for any σ_{del} to his own signing signing oracle (since this is a Category A forgery). Hence, $p\sigma$ will be a valid forgery of a sequential aggregate signature containing a signature on the message $\texttt{dlg}||PK||FK||W$ under $pk^* = pk'$.

– if the forgery is of type (iii) i.e. $(m, (PK, W, (FK, p\sigma)))$, $p\sigma$ will be a valid forgery for the same reasons as in a type (ii) forgery, just having pk^* appearing at a different position in PK.

If $\mathcal{A}$, on the other hand, constructs a Category B forgery, $\mathcal{B}$ will abort.

Now consider the case where $c = 1$. In this case $\mathcal{B}$ inserts pk' as a fresh key in a delegation query. If $\mathcal{A}$ outputs a Category A forgery, $\mathcal{B}$ will abort. However, if $\mathcal{A}$ outputs a category B forgery $(m, (PK, W, (FK, p\sigma)))$, which will be of either type (ii) or type (iii), $p\sigma$ will be a sequential aggregate signature containing a signature under a key pk generated by $\mathcal{B}$ in a delegation query (i.e. pk will appear as the last key in FK' for a proxy key $(FK', \sigma_{del}, sk_{prx}) \in pskList(PK_{1...i}, W_{1...i-1})$ for some i), and for which $\mathcal{A}$ has not asked for the proxy key containing the corresponding private key. With probability $1/q_d$, $\mathcal{B}$ will have chosen $pk = pk'$. In this case, $\mathcal{B}$ outputs $p\sigma$ as a valid forgery for the underlying sequential aggregate signature scheme. Otherwise, $\mathcal{B}$ will abort.

Note that if $c = 0$, $\mathcal{B}$ provides a perfect simulation for $\mathcal{A}$ and does not need to abort before $\mathcal{A}$ outputs a forgery. Also note that if $c = 1$, $\mathcal{A}$ is constructing a Category B forgery and $\mathcal{B}$ has guessed the correct value of i^* (i.e. guessed the key pk_{i^*} which $\mathcal{A}$ will use in a forgery and inserted $pk_{i^*} = pk'$), $\mathcal{B}$ will not have to abort either since $\mathcal{A}$ will not compromise the key pk_{i^*} in order to produce a valid forgery.

Let E_1 be the event that $\mathcal{A}$ produces a Category A forgery, E_2 be the event that $\mathcal{A}$ produces a Category B forgery, and E_3 be the event that $\mathcal{B}$ guesses the correct value of i^* in a Category B forgery. The success probability ϵ' of $\mathcal{A}$ can be expressed as $\epsilon' = \Pr[E_1] + \Pr[E_2]$. The success probability of $\mathcal{B}$ can be expressed as

$$
\begin{aligned}
\epsilon &= \Pr[c = 0 \wedge E_1] + \Pr[c = 1 \wedge E_2 \wedge E_3] \\
&= 1/2 \Pr[E_1] + \Pr[E_3|c = 1 \wedge E_2] \Pr[c = 1|E_2] \Pr[E_2] \\
&= 1/2 \Pr[E_1] + 1/q_d \cdot 1/2 \cdot \Pr[E_2] \\
&\geq \epsilon'/2q_d
\end{aligned}
$$

Hence, the theorem follows.

Lattice-Based Identification Schemes Secure Under Active Attacks*

Vadim Lyubashevsky

University of California, San Diego
9500 Gilman Drive, La Jolla, CA 92093-0404, USA
vlyubash@cs.ucsd.edu

Abstract. There is an inherent difficulty in building 3-move ID schemes based on combinatorial problems without much algebraic structure. A consequence of this, is that most standard ID schemes today are based on the hardness of number theory problems. Not having schemes based on alternate assumptions is a cause for concern since improved number theoretic algorithms or the realization of quantum computing would make the known schemes insecure. In this work, we examine the possibility of creating identification protocols based on the hardness of lattice problems. We construct a 3-move identification scheme whose security is based on the worst-case hardness of the shortest vector problem in all lattices, and also present a more efficient version based on the hardness of the same problem in *ideal* lattices.

1 Introduction

Public key identification (ID) protocols allow a party holding a secret key to prove its identity to any other entity holding the corresponding public key. The minimum security of such protocols should be that a passive observer who sees the interaction should not then be able to perform his own interaction and successfully impersonate the prover. In a more realistic model, the adversary should first be allowed to interact with the prover in a "dishonest" way in hopes of extracting some information, and then try to impersonate the prover. Identification schemes resistant to such impersonation attempts are said to be secure in the active attack model [7], and this is currently the *de facto* security notion.

Since Fiat and Shamir's seminal paper [9], there have been many proposals for constructing secure ID protocols. With a few notable exceptions, most of these protocols (e.g. [11,26,21,29,23,10]) are based on problems from number theory, and as such, they require fairly costly multiplication and exponentiation operations. Another potential problem is that the security of these protocols is based on problems that are easy if (when) practical quantum computers become reality [28]. Thus it is prudent to have viable alternative schemes based on different hardness assumptions.

The identification protocols not based on number theory problems (e.g. [27,30]) are generally combinatorial in nature. Because of this lack of algebraic structure,

---

* Supported by NSF grant CCF-0634909.

R. Cramer (Ed.): PKC 2008, LNCS 4939, pp. 162–179, 2008.

these combinatorial schemes all seem to have an inherent shortcoming in that they require a lot more rounds of communication than their algebraic counterparts. This problem arises because the proof of security is established by showing that the schemes are zero-knowledge proofs of knowledge. It is shown that the prover (or adversary) who successfully proves his identity, actually "knows" the secret (as defined in [7]), yet the protocol is zero-knowledge, and as such, the prover doesn't reveal anything about his secret key. The problem is that in order for the protocol to have negligible soundness error, it must be repeated a polynomial number of times. But zero-knowledge is not preserved under parallel-repetition, and so the protocol has to be run sequentially in order for it to maintain the claimed security.

In recent years, lattices have emerged as a possible alternative to number theory. Cryptography based on lattices was pioneered by Ajtai [1], who showed a fascinating connection between solving random instances of a certain problem and solving *all* instances of certain lattice problems. This opened up a way to base cryptographic functions on the hardness of worst-case problems. Since then, there has been a lot of work on improving the average case/worst-case reduction [19], building cryptographic primitives [3,24,25], and using similar techniques to build more efficient cryptographic primitives [17,22,15,16] based on similar worst-case assumptions. Additionally, there are currently no efficient quantum algorithms for solving lattice problems.

1.1 This Work

In this work, we present an ID scheme whose security is based on the worst-case hardness of lattice problems. In addition, we present a more efficient version of the scheme that is based on the hardness of problems on *ideal* lattices (see section 2.5). We prove security by showing that an adversary who successfully attacks our scheme can be used to solve random instances of problems defined in [19] and [17], which were proven to be as hard as lattice problems in the worst case. Thus, in this work, we do not deal with average-case/worst-case reductions directly.

We believe that the technical details of our ID protocol may also be of independent interest. While our scheme has the structure of a standard 3-move commit-challenge-response protocol, for security reasons, an honest prover sometimes "refuses" to respond to the verifier's challenge. It can be shown that if the prover always responds to the verifier, then his secret key is leaked to even a passive observer. On the other hand, by strategically refusing to reply, each round of the protocol can be shown to be *witness-indistinguishable*. And since witness-indistinguishability is preserved under parallel-composition, all the rounds can be performed in parallel.

1.2 Related Work

The one place in the literature that mentions constructions of lattice-based identification schemes is the work of Micciancio and Vadhan [20] on statistical zero knowledge relating to lattice problems. In this work, the authors show an efficient-prover SZK proof system for certain lattice problems and mention that one can convert the proof system into an identification scheme. The conversion is non-trivial (due to the problem of zero-knowledge not being closed under parallel-composition), and many details remain to be filled in.

2   Preliminaries

2.1   Notation

We will represent vectors by bold letters. By $x \xleftarrow{\$} X$, we mean that x is chosen uniformly at random from the set X. The notation $\tilde{O}(n^k)$ is equivalent to $O(n^k \log^c n)$ for some constant c.

2.2   Statistical Distance

Informally, statistical distance is a measure of how far apart two distributions are. Formally, if X and Y are random variables over a countable set A, then the statistical distance between X and Y, denoted $\Delta(X, Y)$, is defined as

$$\Delta(X, Y) = \frac{1}{2} \sum_{a \in A} |Pr[X = a] - Pr[Y = a]|$$

From the definition, it's easy to see that

$$\Delta(X, Z) \leq \Delta(X, Y) + \Delta(Y, Z)$$

2.3   Identification Schemes

An identification scheme consists of a key-generation algorithm and a description of an interactive protocol between a prover, possessing the secret key, and verifier possessing the corresponding public key. In general, it is required that the verifier accepts the interaction with a prover who behaves honestly with probability one. In this work, though, we need to relax this definition, and only require that the verifier accepts an honest prover with probability negligibly close to one (i.e $1 - 2^{-\omega(\log n)}$).

The standard active attack model against identification schemes proceeds in two phases [7]. In the first phase, the adversary interacts with the prover in an effort to obtain some information. In the second stage, the adversary plays the role of the prover and tries to make a verifier accept the interaction. We remark that in the second stage, the adversary no longer has access to the honest prover. We will say that the adversary has advantage adv, if the verifier accepts the interaction with the adversary with probability adv (where the probability is over the randomness of the prover, verifier, and the adversary).

2.4   Witness Indistinguishability

The concept of *witness indistinguishability* was introduced by Feige and Shamir in [8]. For a string x and relation R, a witness set $W_R(x)$ consists of all strings w such that $R(w, x) = 1$. For example, x could be a boolean formula and the relation R could be defined as $R(x, w) = 1$ iff w is an assignment that makes x evaluate to 1. Then the set $W_R(x)$ is the set of all assignments that make x evaluate to 1. In our case, the witness will correspond to the secret key and the string x is the public key.

Let $\mathcal{P}$ and $\mathcal{V}$ be two randomized interactive Turing machines and $(\mathcal{P}, \mathcal{V})$ be a protocol between $\mathcal{P}$ and $\mathcal{V}$. We denote by $\mathcal{V}_{\mathcal{P}(x,w)}(x, y)$ the output of $\mathcal{V}$ after participating in the protocol $(\mathcal{P}, \mathcal{V})$. We say that $(\mathcal{P}, \mathcal{V})$ is statistically witness-indistinguishable if for all $\mathcal{V}'$, all large enough x, any y, and any two $w, w' \in W_R(x)$,

$$\Delta\left(\mathcal{V}'_{\mathcal{P}(x,w)}(x, y), \mathcal{V}'_{\mathcal{P}(x,w')}(x, y)\right) < 2^{-\omega(\log |x|)}.$$

In other words, every cheating verifier $\mathcal{V}'$ with any auxiliary input y, cannot distinguish whether the witness that $\mathcal{P}$ is using in the protocol is w or w'. An important feature of witness indistinguishability is that it is closed under parallel composition.

2.5   Lattices

General Lattices. An integer lattice $\mathcal{L}$ of dimension n is simply an additive subgroup of $\mathbb{Z}^n$. A fundamental set of parameters associated with a lattice $\mathcal{L}$ is the set of successive minima $\lambda_i(\mathcal{L})$ for $1 \leq i \leq n$. For every i, $\lambda_i(\mathcal{L})$ is defined as the minimal radius of a sphere centered at the origin that contains i linearly independent lattice vectors. For example, $\lambda_1(\mathcal{L})$ corresponds to the length of the shortest vector in $\mathcal{L}$, and finding a vector of length $\lambda_1(\mathcal{L})$ is known as the Shortest Vector Problem (SVP). Likewise, the problem of finding n independent vectors all of length at most $\lambda_n(\mathcal{L})$ is known as the Shortest Independent Vector Problem (SIVP). Approximation versions of SVP and SIVP are defined in the natural way. That is, an approximate solution to SVP within some factor γ is a vector in the lattice that is of length at most $\gamma\lambda_1(\mathcal{L})$. Similarly, an approximate solution to SIVP within a factor γ is a set of n linearly independent lattice vectors each having length at most $\gamma\lambda_n(\mathcal{L})$

The shortest vector problem was shown to be NP-hard by Ajtai [2] and NP-hard to approximate to within any constant factor by Khot [13]. The best known algorithm to find the exact shortest vector, or even some polynomial in n factor approximation of it, takes time $2^{O(n)}$ [4,14]. As far as SIVP is concerned, it is known that this problem is NP-hard to approximate for any constant factor [6], and finding the exact solution takes time approximately $n!$ [18] (although finding a $(1 + \epsilon)$ approximation takes time $2^{O(n)}$ for any constant ϵ [5]).

The aspect that makes lattices interesting in cryptography is that one can build collision-resistant hash function families that are as hard to break on the average, as solving approximate SIVP in the worst case. This work began with the seminal paper by Ajtai [1], and the currently tightest reduction is due to

Micciancio and Regev [19]. Below, we restate the main result of [19] in a way that will be convenient for our proof. [1]

Definition 1. *(The small integer solution SIS(A) problem) Given a matrix $A \in \mathbb{Z}_p^{n \times m}$, find two distinct vectors $z, z' \in \mathbb{Z}^m$ such that $Az \bmod p = Az' \bmod p$ and $\|z\|, \|z'\| \leq 10m^{1.5}$.*

Theorem 2. *[19, Theorem 5.9] For integer $m = \lceil 4n \log n \rceil$ and some integer $p = \tilde{\Theta}(n^3)$, if there exists a polynomial-time algorithm that solves SIS(A) for uniformly random $A \in \mathbb{Z}_p^{n \times m}$, then the SIVP problem can be approximated in polynomial time to within a factor of $\tilde{O}(n^2)$ in every n-dimensional lattice.*

Ideal Lattices. Ideal lattices were first studied in the context of cryptography by Lyubashevsky and Micciancio in [15]. Such lattices are a special class of general lattices and a generalization of cyclic lattices [17]. Their usefulness is attributed to the fact that very efficient and practical collision-resistant hash functions can be built based on the hardness of finding an approximate shortest vector in such lattices. Roughly speaking, ideal lattices are lattices corresponding to ideals in rings of the form $\mathbb{Z}[x]/\langle f \rangle$ for some irreducible polynomial f of degree n. For simplicity we will only concentrate on rings of the form $\mathbb{Z}[x]/\langle x^n + 1 \rangle$, as they have proved to be the most useful for practical applications [16]. An n-dimensional ideal lattice in the ring $\mathbb{Z}[x]/\langle x^n + 1 \rangle$ is a lattice with the additional restriction that for every vector $(a_1, \ldots, a_{n-1}, a_n)$ in the lattice, the rotated vector with the first coordinate negated $(-a_n, a_1, \ldots, a_{n-1})$ must also be in the lattice. It was shown in [15] that efficient collision resistant hash functions could be built based on the hardness of finding the shortest vector in ideal lattices. The average-case hard problem in [15] is essentially the SIS problem in Definition 1, with the one difference being (and this is what gives the hash function its efficiency) that the matrix $A \in \mathbb{Z}_p^{n \times m}$ is no longer chosen from the entire domain $\mathbb{Z}_p^{n \times m}$. Instead, it is chosen as follows: first pick any vector $a_1 \in \mathbb{Z}_p^n$ and make it the first column of A. The next $n - 1$ columns of A consist of consecutive rotations (while always negating the coordinate that gets rotated to the beginning of the vector) of a_1. For column $n + 1$, we choose another random vector a_2 and then fill the next $n - 1$ columns with its rotations. We continue repeating this process until all m columns are filled (we assume that m is a multiple of n). We will call this domain of all such matrices ROT(n, m, p), and selecting a random $A \in$ ROT(n, m, p) corresponds to performing the above procedure while choosing $a_1, a_2, \ldots a_{m/n}$ randomly from $\mathbb{Z}_p^n$.

Notice that because of the repetition, it is not necessary to store all m columns of matrices chosen from ROT(n, m, p). Another extremely important feature is that multiplying such matrices by any vector in $\mathbb{Z}_p^m$ requires only $\tilde{O}(m \log n)$ time rather than $\tilde{O}(mn)$. This is because the multiplication can be done using the Fast Fourier Transform (see [17,15] for details).

---

[1] We point out that the below result is weaker than what was proved in [19]. Unfortunately, in this paper we cannot construct an identification scheme with security based on the strongest results from [19].

We will now state a convenient form of the main result of [15] [2].

Theorem 3. *[15, Theorem 2] For integer $m = \lceil 4n \log n \rceil$ and some integer $p = \tilde{\Theta}(n^3)$, if there exists a polynomial-time algorithm that solves $SIS(\boldsymbol{A})$ for uniformly random $\boldsymbol{A} \in ROT(n, m, p)$, then SIVP (and also SVP^3) can be approximated in polynomial time to within a factor of $\tilde{O}(n^2)$ in every n-dimensional lattice corresponding to an ideal in $\mathbb{Z}[x]/\langle x^n + 1 \rangle$.*

2.6   Leftover Hash Lemma

In this section, we review the leftover hash lemma [12]. This lemma will be crucial in proving the witness-indistinguishability property of our protocol.

Lemma 4. *(Leftover Hash Lemma) Let X and Y be two finite sets and U be the uniform distribution over Y. If $\mathcal{H}$ is a universal family of hash functions[4] from X to Y, then for all but a $2^{\frac{\log |Y| - \log |X|}{4}}$ fraction of the possible $h_i \in \mathcal{H}$, $\Delta(h_i(x), U) \le 2^{\frac{\log |Y| - \log |X|}{4}}$ where x is chosen uniformly at random from X.*

The following lemma is a straightforward consequence of the leftover hash lemma.

Lemma 5. *Let X be some subset of $\mathbb{Z}_p^m$. Then for all but a $2^{\frac{n \log p - \log |X|}{4}}$ fraction of all $\boldsymbol{A} \in \mathbb{Z}_p^{n \times m}$, we have*

$$\Delta(\boldsymbol{A}\boldsymbol{x} \bmod p, \boldsymbol{u}) \le 2^{\frac{n \log p - \log |X|}{4}},$$

where $\boldsymbol{x}$ is a random variable distributed uniformly in X and $\boldsymbol{u}$ is a random variable distributed uniformly in $\mathbb{Z}_p^n$.

Proof. We consider a family of hash functions $\mathcal{H}$ consisting of functions $h_{\boldsymbol{A}}$ indexed by $\boldsymbol{A} \in \mathbb{Z}_p^{n \times m}$, where $h_{\boldsymbol{A}}(\boldsymbol{x})$ is defined as $\boldsymbol{A}\boldsymbol{x} \bmod p$. The domain of these functions is any subset of $\mathbb{Z}_p^m$ and the range is $\mathbb{Z}_p^n$. To apply the Leftover Hash Lemma, we need to show that $\mathcal{H}$ is a universal family of hash functions. In other words, for any distinct $\boldsymbol{x}, \boldsymbol{x}' \in X$, we need to show that for a randomly chosen $\boldsymbol{A} \in \mathbb{Z}_p^{n \times m}$,

$$Pr[h_{\boldsymbol{A}}(\boldsymbol{x}) = h_{\boldsymbol{A}}(\boldsymbol{x}')] = \frac{1}{2^{n \log p}}.$$

In other words, we need to show that for a randomly chosen $\boldsymbol{A} \in \mathbb{Z}_p^{n \times m}$,

$$\frac{1}{2^{n \log p}} = Pr[\boldsymbol{A}\boldsymbol{x} \bmod p = \boldsymbol{A}\boldsymbol{x}' \bmod p]$$

$$= Pr[\boldsymbol{A}(\boldsymbol{x} - \boldsymbol{x}') \bmod p = \boldsymbol{0}] = Pr[\boldsymbol{A}\boldsymbol{y} \bmod p = \boldsymbol{0}]$$

where $\boldsymbol{y}$ is some non-zero vector. Without loss of generality, assume that the last coefficient of $\boldsymbol{y}$ is non-zero, and let $\boldsymbol{y}'$ be the first $m - 1$ coefficients of $\boldsymbol{y}$.

---

[2] As for general lattices, the below result is weaker than what was proved in [15].

[3] This is because lattices of this form have the property that $\lambda_1(\mathcal{L}) = \ldots = \lambda_n(\mathcal{L})$.

[4] Recall that a hash function family $\mathcal{H} : X \to Y$ is called universal if for every two distinct elements $x, x' \in X$, we have $Pr_{h \xleftarrow{\$} \mathcal{H}}[h(x) = h(x')] = 1/|Y|$.

Similarly, let a be the last column of A and let A' be the first $m - 1$ columns of A. Then,

$$Pr[Ay \bmod p = 0] = Pr[A'y' + ay_m \bmod p = 0]$$
$$= Pr[a \equiv y_m^{-1}(-A'y')(\bmod p)] = \frac{1}{2^{n \log p}}$$

Since p is prime and y_m is non-zero, the multiplicative inverse of y_m modulo p exists. And since a is chosen uniformly at random from $\mathbb{Z}_p^n$, the probability that it is equal to any specific value is $\frac{1}{2^{n \log p}}$. And now that we have shown that $\mathcal{H}$ is a family of universal hash functions, the claim of the lemma follows from the Leftover Hash Lemma. $\square$

The below corollary is obtained by applying Lemma 5 twice, and using the triangular inequality property of statistical distance.

Corollary 6. *Let X and Y be any two subsets of $\mathbb{Z}_p^m$. Then for all but a $2^{\frac{n \log p - \log |X|}{4}} + 2^{\frac{n \log p - \log |Y|}{4}}$ fraction of all $A \in \mathbb{Z}_p^{n \times m}$, we have*

$$\Delta(Ax \bmod p, Ay \bmod p) \leq 2^{\frac{n \log p - \log |X|}{4}} + 2^{\frac{n \log p - \log |Y|}{4}},$$

where x is a random variable distributed uniformly in X and y is a random variable distributed uniformly in Y.

3   The Identification Scheme

We will first describe one round of our identification scheme (Figure 1). The prover picks a secret key $\tilde{w} \in \{0, 1\}^m$, and publishes the public keys $A \xleftarrow{\$} \mathbb{Z}_p^{n \times m}$ and $w \leftarrow A\tilde{w} \bmod p$, where $m = \lceil 4n \log n \rceil$ and p is some integer of order $\tilde{\Theta}(n^3)$.[5] We note that the matrix A may either be created by the prover or be created by a trusted third party. In fact, all users may share the same matrix A. In the first step of the protocol, the prover picks a uniformly random vector $\tilde{y}$ from the set of vectors $\{0, 1, \ldots, 5m - 1\}^m$, and sends $y \leftarrow A\tilde{y} \bmod p$ to the verifier. The verifier then sends a challenge $c \leftarrow \{0, 1\}$. If $c = 0$, the prover simply sends $z \leftarrow \tilde{y}$ as the response. If, on the other hand, $c = 1$, the prover first checks whether the quantity $\tilde{w} + \tilde{y}$ is in the set SAFE=$\{1, 2, \ldots, 5m - 1\}^m$. If it is, then the prover sends $z \leftarrow \tilde{w} + \tilde{y}$, and if it is not, then the prover sends $z \leftarrow \perp$ which signifies that he refuses to answer. If the prover sends $\perp$, then the verifier obviously rejects the interaction. Otherwise, the verifier checks whether $\|z\| \leq 5m^{1.5}$ and $Az \bmod p = cw + y$. The verifier accepts if and only if those two conditions are satisfied.

Some comments are in order about the somewhat unusual way in which the prover picks his response z when the challenge is $c = 1$. Notice that if the prover

---

[5] For the reader's convenience, we will make the convention of putting tildes over the variables which are kept "secret" by the prover (e.g. $\tilde{w}, \tilde{y}$).

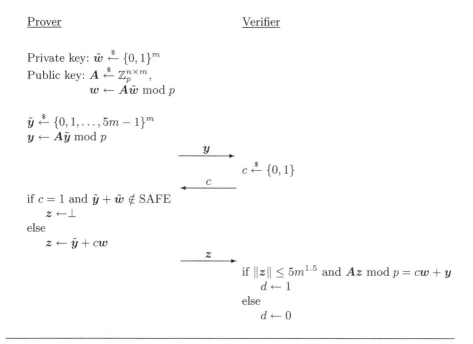

Fig. 1. One round of our identification scheme. The parameters are $p = \tilde{O}(n^3)$, $m = \lceil 4n \log n \rceil$, and the set SAFE is defined as $\{1, \ldots, 5m - 1\}^m$.

always sends $z \leftarrow \tilde{w} + \tilde{y}$ for $c = 1$, then even a passive observer can deduce the secret $\tilde{w}$ after he sees enough rounds. This is because if any coordinate of z is ever 0, the observer knows that the corresponding bit of $\tilde{w}$ must also be 0. Similarly, if any coordinate of z is $5m$, then the corresponding bit of $\tilde{w}$ must be 1. One might think that a way to resolve this problem would be to choose $\tilde{y}$ in a way such that seeing $\tilde{w} + \tilde{y}$ will not give anything away about $\tilde{w}$. The problem with this approach is that when the verifier sends $c = 0$, the prover will have to reveal $\tilde{y}$, and the distribution of the $\tilde{y}$'s may actually end up revealing the secret $\tilde{w}$. (Consider the naïve idea of never setting any coordinates of $\tilde{y}$ to 0 if the corresponding bits of $\tilde{w}$ are 0. Then the fact that some coordinates of $\tilde{y}$ are never 0 will give away the fact that those bits of $\tilde{w}$ were themselves 0's.) At the present, the only way that we know of to "fix" this, is to make the integers m of order $n^{\omega(1)}$. This way, with high probability, the coefficients of $\tilde{y}$ will never be 0 or $5m - 1$, and so $\tilde{w}$ will potentially be safe. Unfortunately, setting m to such a large number significantly weakens the result of the security proof.

A consequence of the prover sometimes refusing to answer is that the verifier may end up rejecting an honest prover. So it is important that the honest prover is not rejected too often in each round. This way, if the protocol is repeated enough times, the prover will answer correctly enough times so that the verifier will be able to distinguish between an honest prover and an impersonator.

We will now outline the rest of this section. We first show that an honest prover will able to get the verifier to accept with a "high enough" probability (Lemma 7). We then show that every round of the protocol is statistically *witness-indistinguishable* (Theorem 9). Since witness indistinguishability is preserved under parallel composition, we can repeat the protocol in Figure 1 many times in parallel. The result of this is the identification protocol in Figure 2. In Theorem 13, we show that this protocol is secure in the active attack model by showing that an adversary who successfully attacks the protocol can be used to solve the SIS problem from Definition 1, which by Theorem 2 implies being able to solve the approximate Shortest Independent Vector Problem in every lattice.

Lemma 7. *For $m \geq 10$, the probability that the verifier will accept (i.e. set $d = 1$) an interaction with an honest prover during a round is at least .81.*

Proof. Notice that if $c = 0$, then the verifier will always accept because the prover will always send $z = \tilde{y}$ and thus $Az \equiv A\tilde{y} \equiv y \pmod{p}$. Similarly, if $c = 1$ and $\tilde{w} + \tilde{y} \in \text{SAFE}$, then the verifier will always accept because the prover sends $z = \tilde{w} + \tilde{y}$ and so $Az \equiv A(\tilde{w} + \tilde{y}) \equiv w + y \pmod{p}$. Thus the probability that the verifier accepts is at least the probability that $\tilde{w} + \tilde{y} \in \text{SAFE}$.

$$Pr[d = 1] \geq Pr[\tilde{w} + \tilde{y} \in \text{SAFE}] = \left(1 - \frac{1}{5m}\right)^m \geq .81 \text{ for } m \geq 10 \quad (1)$$

The equality is true because for every i, only one of $5m$ possibilities for the coefficient $\tilde{y}_i$ of $\tilde{y}$ will lead to $\tilde{w} + \tilde{y}$ to be not in the set SAFE. That is, if $\tilde{w}_i = 0$, then $\tilde{y}_i$ can be anything except 0, and if $\tilde{w}_i = 1$, then $\tilde{y}_i$ can be anything except $5m - 1$. □

Before showing that every round of the protocol is witness-indistinguishable, we need to show that with extremely high probability over the choices of the public key, there does indeed exist more than one possible secret key.

Lemma 8. *For any matrix $A \in \mathbb{Z}_p^{n \times m}$ and a randomly chosen $\tilde{w} \overset{\$}{\leftarrow} \{0,1\}^m$, the probability that there exists another $\tilde{w}' \in \{0,1\}^m \setminus \tilde{w}$ such that $A\tilde{w} \bmod p = A\tilde{w}' \bmod p$ is at least $1 - 2^{n \log p - m}$.*

Proof. The result of $A\tilde{w} \bmod p$ falls into $\mathbb{Z}_p^n$, and thus there can be at most $|\mathbb{Z}_p^n| = 2^{n \log p}$ elements $\tilde{w} \in \{0,1\}^m$ such that $A\tilde{w} \bmod p$ leads to a unique element in $\mathbb{Z}_p^n$. Thus the probability that a randomly chosen $\tilde{w} \in \{0,1\}^m$ collides with some other $\tilde{w}' \in \{0,1\}^m$ is at least $1 - 2^{n \log p - m}$. □

We now move to showing witness indistinguishability. The proof will roughly proceed as follows. First, we observe that when the challenge is $c = 0$, the protocol is trivially witness indistinguishable because the secret key is completely uninvolved in the response. So we concentrate on the case where $c = 1$. In that case, two things can happen. In one case, $\tilde{w} + \tilde{y}$ will be in the set SAFE and the prover sends $z \leftarrow \tilde{w} + \tilde{y}$. In this case, we will show that the protocol is *perfectly* witness-indistinguishable. In the case that $\tilde{w} + \tilde{y}$ is not in SAFE and the prover sends $z \leftarrow \bot$, we will show that the protocol is *statistically* witness indistinguishable.

The below theorem actually proves witness indistinguishability of the protocol for all but a $2^{-\Omega(n \log^2 n)}$ fraction of $A \in \mathbb{Z}_p^{n \times m}$. Since the matrix A is chosen at random, there is only a $2^{-\Omega(n \log^2 n)}$ chance that it is one of the "bad" A's that doesn't result in the protocol being witness indistinguishable.

Theorem 9. *For all but a $2^{-\Omega(n \log^2 n)}$ fraction of $A \in \mathbb{Z}_p^{n \times m}$, the following holds true. For any two vectors $\tilde{w}, \tilde{w}' \in \{0,1\}^m$ where $A\tilde{w} \bmod p = A\tilde{w}' \bmod p = w$, any cheating verifier $\mathcal{V}$, and auxiliary input string r,*

$$\Delta \left(\mathcal{V}_{\mathcal{P}(A,\tilde{w})}(A, w, r), \mathcal{V}_{\mathcal{P}(A,\tilde{w}')}(A, w, r) \right) \leq 2^{-\Omega(n \log^2 n)}.$$

Since the protocol is clearly witness indistinguishable when the verifier sends $c = 0$, we will assume that $c = 1$. We will show that

$$\Delta \left(\mathcal{V}_{\mathcal{P}(A,\tilde{w})}(A, w, r), \mathcal{V}_{\mathcal{P}(A,\tilde{w}')}(A, w, r) \right) \leq 2^{-n \log^2 n}$$

by showing that the distribution of the messages that the prover sends to the verifier is almost independent of whether the witness is $\tilde{w}$ or $\tilde{w}'$.

The messages that the prover sends to the verifier consist of the elements y and z. For convenience, in the case that the witness is $\tilde{w}$, we will use the variables y, z and when the witness is $\tilde{w}'$, we will use the variables y', z'.

$$\Delta \left(\mathcal{V}_{\mathcal{P}(A,\tilde{w})}(A, w, r), \mathcal{V}_{\mathcal{P}(A,\tilde{w}')}(A, w, r) \right) \tag{2}$$

$$\leq \frac{1}{2} \sum_{(\alpha,\beta)} |Pr[(y, z) = (\alpha, \beta)] - Pr[(y', z') = (\alpha, \beta)]| \tag{3}$$

$$= \frac{1}{2} \sum_{(\alpha,\beta \neq \bot)} |Pr[(y, z) = (\alpha, \beta)] - Pr[(y', z') = (\alpha, \beta)]| \tag{4}$$

$$+ \frac{1}{2} \sum_{(\alpha,\beta = \bot)} |Pr[(y, z) = (\alpha, \bot)] - Pr[(y', z') = (\alpha, \bot)]| \tag{5}$$

In the above equations, the sums are over all $\alpha \in \{0, 1, \ldots, 5m - 1\}^m$ and $\beta \in \{1, 2, \ldots, 5m - 1\}^m \cup \{\bot\}$.

We will finish the proof of the theorem by showing that (4) is 0 for all matrices $A \in \mathbb{Z}_p^{n \times m}$ (Lemma 10), and (5) is negligibly small for all but a $2^{-\Omega(n \log^2 n)}$ fraction of $A \in \mathbb{Z}_p^{n \times m}$ (Lemma 11).

Lemma 10

$$\frac{1}{2} \sum_{(\alpha,\beta \neq \bot)} |Pr[(y, z) = (\alpha, \beta)] - Pr[(y', z') = (\alpha, \beta)]| = 0$$

Proof. We will show that for every α and $\beta \neq \bot$,

$$Pr[(y, z) = (\alpha, \beta)] = Pr[(y', z') = (\alpha, \beta)]. \tag{6}$$

We rewrite $Pr[(y, z) = (\alpha, \beta)]$ as

$$Pr[(y, z) = (\alpha, \beta)] = Pr[A\tilde{y} \bmod p = \alpha \wedge \tilde{y} + \tilde{w} = \beta]$$
$$= Pr[A\tilde{y} \bmod p = \alpha | \tilde{y} + \tilde{w} = \beta] Pr[\tilde{y} + \tilde{w} = \beta]$$

And similarly,

$$Pr[(y', z') = (\alpha, \beta)] = Pr[A\tilde{y}' \bmod p = \alpha | \tilde{y}' + \tilde{w}' = \beta] Pr[\tilde{y}' + \tilde{w}' = \beta].$$

Notice that the probability $Pr[A\tilde{y} \bmod p = \alpha | \tilde{y}+\tilde{w} = \beta]$ is being conditioned on $\tilde{y}$, which is the only random variable in the expression, and thus the probability evaluates to either 1 or 0. It is 1 whenever $A(\beta - \tilde{w}) \bmod p = \alpha$ and it is 0 otherwise. Similarly, $Pr[A\tilde{y}' \bmod p = \alpha | \tilde{y}' + \tilde{w}' = \beta] = 1$ whenever $A(\beta - \tilde{w}') \bmod p = \alpha$ and 0 otherwise. The important thing is that $A(\beta - \tilde{w}) \bmod p = A(\beta - \tilde{w}') \bmod p$ (because $A\tilde{w} \bmod p = A\tilde{w}' \bmod p$) and thus

$$Pr[A\tilde{y} \bmod p = \alpha | \tilde{y} + \tilde{w} = \beta] = Pr[A\tilde{y}' \bmod p = \alpha | \tilde{y}' + \tilde{w}' = \beta].$$

So all that remains to show to prove the equality in equation (6) is to show that

$$Pr[\tilde{y} + \tilde{w} = \beta] = Pr[\tilde{y}' + \tilde{w}' = \beta].$$

This is done by observing that since $\beta \neq \perp$, it must be in the set SAFE, which means that all coefficients of β are between 1 and $5m - 1$. And since the coefficients of $\tilde{w}$ are all 0 or 1, the coefficients of $\beta - \tilde{w}$ are between 0 and $5m - 1$, which is exactly the range that $\tilde{y}$ is chosen uniformly from. Thus,

$$Pr[\tilde{y} + \tilde{w} = \beta] = Pr[\tilde{y} = \beta - \tilde{w}] = 1/(5m)^m$$

for all values of β and any secret key $\tilde{w}$. And by the same reasoning, we have $Pr[\tilde{y}' = \beta - \tilde{w}'] = 1/(5m)^m$. □

Lemma 11. *For all but a $2^{-\Omega(n \log^2 n)}$ fraction of possible $A \in \mathbb{Z}_p^{n \times m}$,*

$$\frac{1}{2} \sum_{(\alpha, \beta = \perp)} |Pr[(y, z) = (\alpha, \perp)] - Pr[(y', z') = (\alpha, \perp)]| \leq 2^{-\Omega(n \log^2 n)}$$

Proof. Define the set $S_{\tilde{w}} = \{\tilde{y} \in \{0, \ldots, 5m - 1\}^m$ such that $\tilde{y} + \tilde{w} \notin$ SAFE$\}$. The two important characteristics of the sets $S_{\tilde{w}}$ and $S_{\tilde{w}'}$, for any two secret keys $\tilde{w}$ and $\tilde{w}'$, is that their sizes are equivalent and "large enough". Both of these are implicit from equation (1) in Lemma 7. More precisely,

$$|S_{\tilde{w}}| = |S_{\tilde{w}'}| = (5m)^m - (5m)^m \left(1 - \frac{1}{5m}\right)^m \tag{7}$$

$$\geq (5m)^m - (5m)^m \left(\frac{1}{e}\right)^{1/5} \geq \frac{(5m)^m}{6} \tag{8}$$

We now proceed with the proof of the lemma.

$$\frac{1}{2} \sum_{(\boldsymbol{\alpha},\boldsymbol{\beta}=\perp)} |Pr[(\boldsymbol{y},\boldsymbol{z}) = (\boldsymbol{\alpha},\perp)] - Pr[(\boldsymbol{y}',\boldsymbol{z}') = (\boldsymbol{\alpha},\perp)]| \tag{9}$$

$$= \frac{1}{2} \sum_{\boldsymbol{\alpha}} |Pr[\boldsymbol{A}\tilde{\boldsymbol{y}} \bmod p = \boldsymbol{\alpha} \ \wedge \ \tilde{\boldsymbol{y}} \in S_{\tilde{\boldsymbol{w}}}] \tag{10}$$

$$- Pr[\boldsymbol{A}\tilde{\boldsymbol{y}}' \bmod p = \boldsymbol{\alpha} \ \wedge \ \tilde{\boldsymbol{y}}' \in S_{\tilde{\boldsymbol{w}}'}]| \tag{11}$$

$$= \frac{1}{2} \sum_{\boldsymbol{\alpha}} |Pr[\boldsymbol{A}\tilde{\boldsymbol{y}} \bmod p = \boldsymbol{\alpha}|\tilde{\boldsymbol{y}} \in S_{\tilde{\boldsymbol{w}}}]Pr[\tilde{\boldsymbol{y}} \in S_{\tilde{\boldsymbol{w}}}] \tag{12}$$

$$- Pr[\boldsymbol{A}\tilde{\boldsymbol{y}}' \bmod p = \boldsymbol{\alpha}|\tilde{\boldsymbol{y}}' \in S_{\tilde{\boldsymbol{w}}'}]Pr[\tilde{\boldsymbol{y}}' \in S_{\tilde{\boldsymbol{w}}'}]| \tag{13}$$

$$\leq \frac{1}{2} \sum_{\boldsymbol{\alpha}} |Pr[\boldsymbol{A}\tilde{\boldsymbol{y}} \bmod p = \boldsymbol{\alpha}|\tilde{\boldsymbol{y}} \in S_{\tilde{\boldsymbol{w}}}] - Pr[\boldsymbol{A}\tilde{\boldsymbol{y}}' \bmod p = \boldsymbol{\alpha}|\tilde{\boldsymbol{y}}' \in S_{\tilde{\boldsymbol{w}}'}]| \tag{14}$$

$$= \frac{1}{2} \sum_{\boldsymbol{\alpha}} \left| Pr_{\tilde{\boldsymbol{y}} \xleftarrow{\$} S_{\tilde{\boldsymbol{w}}}}[\boldsymbol{A}\tilde{\boldsymbol{y}} \bmod p = \boldsymbol{\alpha}] - Pr_{\tilde{\boldsymbol{y}}' \xleftarrow{\$} S_{\tilde{\boldsymbol{w}}'}}[\boldsymbol{A}\tilde{\boldsymbol{y}}' \bmod p = \boldsymbol{\alpha}] \right| \tag{15}$$

The inequality in equation (14) is true because $|S_{\tilde{\boldsymbol{w}}}| = |S_{\tilde{\boldsymbol{w}}'}|$, and so $Pr[\tilde{\boldsymbol{y}} \in S_{\tilde{\boldsymbol{w}}}] = Pr[\tilde{\boldsymbol{y}}' \in S_{\tilde{\boldsymbol{w}}'}] < 1$. We now notice that equation (15) is the statistical distance between the distributions $\boldsymbol{A}\tilde{\boldsymbol{y}} \bmod p$ and $\boldsymbol{A}\tilde{\boldsymbol{y}}' \bmod p$ where $\tilde{\boldsymbol{y}}$ and $\tilde{\boldsymbol{y}}'$ are chosen uniformly from the sets $S_{\tilde{\boldsymbol{w}}}$ and $S_{\tilde{\boldsymbol{w}}'}$ respectively. Using the fact that $|S_{\tilde{\boldsymbol{w}}}| = |S_{\tilde{\boldsymbol{w}}'}| = \Omega(m \log m) = \Omega(n \log^2 n)$ and $p = \tilde{O}(n^3)$, we apply Corollary 6 to obtain the claim of the lemma. $\qquad \square$

Having shown that one round of the protocol is witness indistinguishable, we move on to building the full identification scheme (see Figure 2). As we alluded to earlier, the scheme will not have perfect completeness since an honest prover will sometimes have to refuse to answer and thus get rejected by the verifier. Nevertheless, by having enough rounds, an adversary will reject an honest adversary with negligible probability.

Lemma 12. *The identification protocol in Figure 2 has completeness error less than $2^{-t/14}$.*

Proof. By Lemma 7, we know that the honest prover will respond correctly to challenge c_i with probability at least .81. Since the prover is honest, the probabilities of success are independent for all the challenges, and so using the Chernoff bound, we obtain:

$$Pr[\text{REJECT}] = Pr[sum < .65t] = Pr[sum < (.81 - .16)t] \leq e^{-2t(.16^2)} < 2^{-t/14}$$

$$\square$$

Thus setting $t = \omega(\log n)$ results in the protocol having negligible completeness error.

We now move to proving the security of the ID scheme. We will show that an adversary who successfully attacks the protocol can be used to successfully solve

Prover   Verifier

Private key: $\tilde{w} \xleftarrow{\$} \{0,1\}^m$
Public key: $A \xleftarrow{\$} \mathbb{Z}_p^{n \times m}$
$\qquad w \leftarrow A\tilde{w} \bmod p$

for $i = 1$ to t
$\quad \tilde{y}_i \xleftarrow{\$} \{0, 1, \ldots, 5m - 1\}^m$
$\quad y_i \leftarrow A\tilde{y}_i \bmod p$

$\xrightarrow{\quad y_1, \ldots, y_t \quad}$

$\qquad\qquad\qquad\qquad\qquad\qquad$ for $i = 1$ to t
$\qquad\qquad\qquad\qquad\qquad\qquad\quad c_i \xleftarrow{\$} \{0,1\}$

$\xleftarrow{\quad c_1, \ldots, c_t \quad}$

for $i = 1$ to t
$\quad$ if $c_i = 1$ and $\tilde{y}_i + \tilde{w}_i \notin \text{SAFE}$
$\qquad z_i \leftarrow \perp$
$\quad$ else
$\qquad z_i \leftarrow \tilde{y}_i + cw_i$

$\xrightarrow{\quad z_1, \ldots, z_t \quad}$

$\qquad\qquad\qquad\qquad\qquad\qquad$ for $i = 1$ to t
$\qquad\qquad\qquad\qquad\qquad\qquad\quad$ if ($\|z_i\| \le 5m^{1.5}$ and
$\qquad\qquad\qquad\qquad\qquad\qquad\qquad A z_i \bmod p = c_i w + y_i$)
$\qquad\qquad\qquad\qquad\qquad\qquad\qquad d_i \leftarrow 1$
$\qquad\qquad\qquad\qquad\qquad\qquad\quad$ else
$\qquad\qquad\qquad\qquad\qquad\qquad\qquad d_i \leftarrow 0$
$\qquad\qquad\qquad\qquad\qquad\qquad sum = d_1 + \ldots + d_t$
$\qquad\qquad\qquad\qquad\qquad\qquad$ if $sum \ge 0.65t$ then ACCEPT
$\qquad\qquad\qquad\qquad\qquad\qquad$ else REJECT

Fig. 2. The identification scheme. The parameters are $p = \tilde{O}(n^3)$, $m = \lceil 4n \log n \rceil$, $t = \omega(\log n)$, and the set SAFE is defined as $\{1, \ldots, 5m - 1\}^m$.

the SIS problem for random A. By Theorem 2, this implies that this adversary can be used to approximate the length of the Shortest Vector to within a factor of $\tilde{O}(n^2)$ in every lattice.

Theorem 13. *If there exists a polynomial-time adversary who can break the ID protocol in Figure 2 with probability adv in the active attack model, then there exists a polynomial-time algorithm that solves the SIS(A) problem with success probability $\Omega\left((adv)^2 - 2 \cdot 2^{-t/18}\right)$ when A is chosen uniformly at random from $\mathbb{Z}_p^{n \times m}$.*

Proof. We explain how to build an algorithm that solves the SIS(A) problem using an adversary attacking the identification scheme. Given a random matrix $A \xleftarrow{\$} \mathbb{Z}_p^{n \times m}$, we create a random secret key $\tilde{w} \xleftarrow{\$} \{0,1\}^m$, and output A and $w \leftarrow A\tilde{w} \bmod p$ as the public key of the identification scheme. Since we know the secret key, we can perfectly simulate the identification scheme with an adversary who is acting as the verifier. If the adversary wishes to interact with more than one prover, we can easily accommodate him by creating more secret keys $\tilde{w}_i$ and public keys $w_i \leftarrow A\tilde{w}_i \bmod p$ and perfectly simulate those interactions as well.

After the adversary finishes his interaction with the prover(s), it's now his turn to perform an impersonation of the prover whose public key is (A, w). We will use this impersonation to extract a solution to the SIS(A) problem. In the first step of the protocol, the adversary sends us t vectors $y_1, \ldots, y_t$. We reply by sending t random challenges $c_1, \ldots, c_t$. The adversary replies with vectors $z_1, \ldots, z_t$. We then rewind the adversary, and send another set of independently random challenges $c'_1, \ldots, c'_t$ and receive responses $z'_1, \ldots, z'_t$. We then find an i such that $c_i \neq c'_i$, $Az_i \bmod p = c_i w + y_i$, and $Az'_i \bmod p = c'_i w + y_i$ (the fact that such an i exists will be shown later). Without loss of generality, suppose that $c_i = 1$ and $c'_i = 0$. We thus obtain that

$$A(z_i - z'_i) \bmod p = w = A\tilde{w} \bmod p. \tag{16}$$

Since our identification scheme is witness-indistinguishable, and there is at least one other $\tilde{w}' \in \{0, 1\}^m$ such that $A\tilde{w} \bmod p = A\tilde{w}' \bmod p$ (Lemma 8), the probability that $z_i - z'_i = \tilde{w}$ is at most $1/2$. Also, $\|z_i - z'_i\| \leq \|z_i\| + \|z'_i\| \leq 10m^{1.5}$. Thus, with probability at least $1/2$, the values $z_i - z'_i$ and $\tilde{w}$ are a solution to the SIS(A) problem.

What we now need to show that with high probability, there indeed will exist an i such that $c_i \neq c'_i$, $Az_i \bmod p = c_i w + y_i$, and $Az'_i \bmod p = c'_i w + y_i$. We will call this condition ($\star$). We will say that a pair of challenge sequences $c_1, \ldots, c_t$ and $c'_1, \ldots, c'_t$ is *good* if $\sum_i |c_i - c'_i| > .35t$ (they differ on more than $.35t$ coordinates). Notice that if the adversary succeeds in impersonating on both sequences of a *good* pair, then by the pigeonhole principle, ($\star$) will be satisfied[6]. By the Chernoff bound, the probability that a random pair of sequences is not *good* is

$$Pr\left[\sum_{i=1}^{t} |c_i - c'_i| < .36t\right] \leq e^{-2t(.14^2)} < 2^{-t/18}$$

The adversary succeeds on a random challenge sequence with probability adv, and thus succeeds on a pair of independently random sequences with probability $(adv)^2$. Since we just showed that at most a $2^{-t/18}$ fraction of all pairs is not *good*, we know that the adversary must be able to answer correctly on a randomly chosen *good* pair of sequences with probability at least $(adv)^2 - 2^{-t/18}$. Multiplying this by the probability that the pair of sequences we randomly chose is *good*, we get

$$Pr[(\star)] > \left((adv)^2 - 2^{-t/18}\right)\left(1 - 2^{-t/18}\right) > (adv)^2 - 2 \cdot 2^{-t/18} \qquad \square$$

---

[6] Recall that an adversary is allowed to answer incorrectly up to $.35t$ times and still be accepted, and this is why having just one i for which $c_i \neq c'_i$ is not enough.

Algorithm 1. $\big($Attack on ID scheme given public keys $\boldsymbol{A} \in \mathbb{Z}_p^{n \times m}, \boldsymbol{w} \in \mathbb{Z}_p^n\big)$

1: Find $\tilde{\boldsymbol{w}}' \in \{-5m, \ldots, -1, 0, 1, \ldots, 5m-1\}^m$ such that $\boldsymbol{A}\tilde{\boldsymbol{w}}' \bmod p = \boldsymbol{w}$
2: **for** $i = 1$ to t (performed concurrently for all i) **do**
3:    Pick random $\tilde{\boldsymbol{y}}_i' \in \{0, 1\}^m$. Set $\boldsymbol{y}_i \leftarrow \boldsymbol{A}\tilde{\boldsymbol{y}}_i' \bmod p$
4:    Send $\boldsymbol{y}_i$ to the Verifier
5:    Receive $c_i \in \{0, 1\}$ from the Verifier
6:    Set $\boldsymbol{z}_i \leftarrow c\tilde{\boldsymbol{w}}_i' + \tilde{\boldsymbol{y}}_i'$
7:    Send $\boldsymbol{z}_i$ to the Verifier
8: **end for**

---

4   Ideal Lattices

In this section, we discuss how the identification scheme can be sped up by almost a factor n if we base its security on the hardness of finding the shortest vector in *ideal* lattices. The main savings in efficiency, and the only difference in the protocol, is that the matrix $\boldsymbol{A} \in \mathbb{Z}_p^{n \times m}$ will no longer be chosen at random from $\mathbb{Z}_p^{n \times m}$, but instead from $\mathrm{ROT}(n, m, p)$. Everything else in the identification scheme in Figure 2 remains exactly the same. Notice that the most expensive operation in the protocol is the multiplication $\boldsymbol{A}\tilde{\boldsymbol{y}} \bmod p$ for the prover and $\boldsymbol{A}\boldsymbol{z} \bmod p$ for the verifier, which involves $O(mn)$ multiplications of integers of bit length $\log p = O(\log n)$. But it's possible to exploit the algebraic structure of $\boldsymbol{A} \in \mathrm{ROT}(n, m, p)$, and perform that same matrix-vector multiplication by using the Fast Fourier Transform, and thus require only $O(m \log n)$ operations. The proof of security for the new protocol is extremely similar to the one already provided for general lattices. Thus, rather than providing complete proofs, we briefly sketch the necessary modifications.

It is still be true that each round of the protocol remains witness indistinguishable, and the proof of witness indistinguishability is almost the same. The only difference is that we have to be careful to make sure that Corollary 6 remains valid when the matrix $\boldsymbol{A}$ is chosen from $\mathrm{ROT}(n, m, p)$ rather than from all of $\mathbb{Z}_p^{n \times m}$. A condition that is sufficient for this is that we choose the parameter p in a way that makes the ring $\mathbb{Z}_p[x]/\langle x^n + 1 \rangle$ a field (i.e. every element in the ring should have an inverse). We point out that it's also possible to prove witness-indistinguishability when $\mathbb{Z}_p[x]/\langle x^n + 1 \rangle$ is not a field, but then we can no longer use the leftover hash lemma, and we would instead need to use a lemma very similar to Micciancio's regularity lemma [17, Theorem 4.2].

5   Attacks

We have shown that our identification schemes are provably secure in an asymptotic sense, but as we'll show in this section, they unfortunately cannot yet be put into practice because they are insecure for parameters that one might conceivably use in applications. The core issue behind our schemes' vulnerabilities is that lattice-reduction algorithms seem to work better in practice than in theory. See Algorithm 1 for the description of the attack.

Notice that the vectors z_i will always have coordinates in the range between $-5m$ and $5m$, and so $\|z_i\| \leq 5m^{1.5}$. Also notice that the adversary has no need to hide his "secret key" and so he never has to respond with $\bot$, and thus the verifier will always accept this interaction. The hard part is performing step 1 of the above attack. In fact, performing this step is as hard as approximating the shortest vector in all lattices to within a factor of $\tilde{O}(n^{1.5})$. As n grows large, this is believed to be a hard problem, but for small parameters, it is feasible to solve and we will explain this next.

The problem of finding the $\tilde{w}'$ in step 1 is the problem of finding a vector x with small coefficients such that $Ax \bmod p = y$ where A is random matrix in $\mathbb{Z}_p^{n \times m}$ (or in $\mathrm{ROT}(n, m, p)$) and y is a random vector in $\mathbb{Z}_p^n$. We want to phrase this problem as a lattice reduction, and so we first construct the matrix $A' = [A|y]$ and consider the problem of finding a vector $x' \in \mathbb{Z}^{m+1}$ such that $A'x' \bmod p = 0$. Notice that if we are able to find such an x' all of whose coefficients are small and the last coefficient is -1, then we are able to find an x that solves the original problem. Also notice that all the $x' \in \mathbb{Z}^{m+1}$ that satisfy $A'x' \bmod p = 0$ form an additive subgroup of $\mathbb{Z}^{m+1}$, and thus an integer lattice of dimension $m+1$. So what we need to do is first construct a basis of this lattice and then find a vector in it with coordinates between $-5m$ and $5m - 1$ (and have the last coordinate be -1).

Constructing a basis for this lattice can be done in polynomial time by viewing A' as a linear function mapping $\mathbb{Z}^{m+1}$ to $\mathbb{Z}_p^n$ and computing the basis for its kernel. This basis is exactly the basis of the lattice we referred to above. It's not hard to see that by the pigeonhole principle the lattice has a vector all of whose coefficients are either $-1, 0$, or 1, and so finding a vector that has coefficients between $-5m$ and $5m-1$ roughly equates to finding a short vector within a factor of m of the shortest one. This becomes a hard problem as m gets large, but for small and medium-sized m that could potentially be used in practice (around 1000), lattice reduction algorithms can find such vectors fairly efficiently. And finding such a vector whose last coordinate is -1 is heuristically feasible.

6   Conclusions and Open Problems

We have presented a framework for constructing identification schemes that are secure in the active attack model based on the worst-case hardness of lattice problems. A lot of open questions remain, though. The most significant of these is whether the ideas presented in this paper can be used for the construction of an identification protocol that can be instantiated with practical-sized parameters. Recent results that provide practical instantiations [16] of collision resistant lattice-based hash functions based on theoretical ideas in [22,15] makes us optimistic that with some new ideas the same could be done for the identification schemes presented here.

A possible approach would be to see whether it is somehow plausible to pick the values $\tilde{y}$ from a smaller set. Notice that the set that $\tilde{y}$'s got picked from was designed so that for a random $\tilde{y}$, the value of $\tilde{y} + \tilde{w}$ could be safely revealed with a high enough probability. Since the size of this set played a critical role in the attack, reducing it would make the attack more difficult to mount. Another open problem is to somehow modify the ID scheme so that it has perfect completeness. Having perfect completeness would allow us to reduce the number of rounds t in the protocol.

References

1. Ajtai, M.: Generating hard instances of lattice problems. In: STOC, pp. 99–108 (1996)
2. Ajtai, M.: The shortest vector problem in ℓ_2 is NP-hard for randomized reductions. In: STOC, pp. 10–19 (1998)
3. Ajtai, M., Dwork, C.: A public-key cryptosystem with worst-case/average-case equivalence. In: STOC, pp. 284–293 (1997)
4. Ajtai, M., Kumar, R., Sivakumar, D.: A sieve algorithm for the shortest lattice vector problem. In: STOC, pp. 601–610 (2001)
5. Blömer, J., Naewe, S.: Sampling methods for shortest vectors, closest vectors and successive minima. In: Arge, L., Cachin, C., Jurdziński, T., Tarlecki, A. (eds.) ICALP 2007. LNCS, vol. 4596, pp. 65–77. Springer, Heidelberg (2007)
6. Blömer, J., Seifert, J.-P.: On the complexity of computing short linearly independent vectors and short bases in a lattice. In: STOC, pp. 711–720 (1999)
7. Feige, U., Fiat, A., Shamir, A.: Zero-knowledge proofs of identity. J. Cryptology 1(2), 77–94 (1988)
8. Feige, U., Shamir, A.: Witness indistinguishable and witness hiding protocols. In: STOC, pp. 416–426 (1990)
9. Fiat, A., Shamir, A.: How to prove yourself: Practical solutions to identification and signature problems. In: Odlyzko, A.M. (ed.) CRYPTO 1986. LNCS, vol. 263, pp. 186–194. Springer, Heidelberg (1987)
10. Girault, M., Poupard, G., Stern, J.: On the fly authentication and signature schemes based on groups of unknown order. J. Cryptology 19(4), 463–487 (2006)
11. Guillou, L., Quisquater, J.J.: A "paradoxical" indentity-based signature scheme resulting from zero-knowledge. In: Goldwasser, S. (ed.) CRYPTO 1988. LNCS, vol. 403, pp. 216–231. Springer, Heidelberg (1990)
12. Impagliazzo, R., Zuckerman, D.: How to recycle random bits. In: FOCS, pp. 248–253 (1989)
13. Khot, S.: Hardness of approximating the shortest vector problem in lattices. In: FOCS, pp. 126–135 (2004)
14. Kumar, R., Sivakumar, D.: On polynomial-factor approximations to the shortest lattice vector length. SIAM J. Discrete Math. 16(3), 422–425 (2003)
15. Lyubashevsky, V., Micciancio, D.: Generalized compact knapsacks are collision resistant. In: Bugliesi, M., Preneel, B., Sassone, V., Wegener, I. (eds.) ICALP 2006. LNCS, vol. 4052, pp. 144–155. Springer, Heidelberg (2006)
16. Lyubashevsky, V., Micciancio, D., Peikert, C., Rosen, A.: SWIFFT: A modest proposal for FFT hashing. In: Fast Software Encryption (FSE) (2008); Preliminary version appeared at the 2nd NIST Cryptographic Hash Function Workshop (to appear)

17. Micciancio, D.: Generalized compact knapsacks, cyclic lattices, and efficient one-way functions from worst-case complexity assumptions. In: Computational Complexity (2002); Preliminary version in FOCS 2002 (to appear)

18. Micciancio, D.: Efficient reductions among lattice problems. In: SODA (to appear, 2008)

19. Micciancio, D., Regev, O.: Worst-case to average-case reductions based on Gaussian measures. SIAM J. on Computing 37(1), 267–302 (2007)

20. Micciancio, D., Vadhan, S.: Statistical zero-knowledge proofs with efficient provers: Lattice problems and more. In: Boneh, D. (ed.) CRYPTO 2003. LNCS, vol. 2729, pp. 282–298. Springer, Heidelberg (2003)

21. Okamoto, T.: Provably secure and practical identification schemes and corresponding signature schemes. In: Brickell, E.F. (ed.) CRYPTO 1992. LNCS, vol. 740, pp. 31–53. Springer, Heidelberg (1993)

22. Peikert, C., Rosen, A.: Efficient collision-resistant hashing from worst-case assumptions on cyclic lattices. In: Halevi, S., Rabin, T. (eds.) TCC 2006. LNCS, vol. 3876, Springer, Heidelberg (2006)

23. Pointcheval, D.: The composite discrete logarithm and secure authentication. In: Public Key Cryptography, pp. 113–128 (2000)

24. Regev, O.: New lattice based cryptographic constructions. In: STOC, pp. 407–416 (2003)

25. Regev, O.: On lattices, learning with errors, random linear codes, and cryptography. In: STOC (2005)

26. Schnorr, C.P.: Efficient signature generation by smart cards. J. Cryptology 4(3), 161–174 (1991)

27. Shamir, A.: An efficient identification scheme based on permuted kernels (extended abstract). In: Brassard, G. (ed.) CRYPTO 1989. LNCS, vol. 435, pp. 606–609. Springer, Heidelberg (1990)

28. Shor, P.: Polynomial-time algorithms for prime factorization and discrete logarithms on a quantum computer. SIAM J. Comput. 26(5), 1484–1509 (1997)

29. Shoup, V.: On the security of a practical identification scheme. J. Cryptology 12(4), 247–260 (1999)

30. Stern, J.: A new paradigm for public key identification. IEEE Transactions on Information Theory 42 (1996)

Efficient Simultaneous Broadcast

Sebastian Faust[1], Emilia Käsper[1], and Stefan Lucks[2]

[1] K.U.Leuven ESAT-COSIC, Kasteelpark Arenberg 10,
3001 Leuven-Heverlee, Belgium
[2] Bauhaus-Universität Weimar,
99421 Weimar, Germany
{sebastian.faust,emilia.kasper}@esat.kuleuven.be,
stefan.lucks@medien.uni-weimar.de

Abstract. We present an efficient *simultaneous broadcast* protocol ν-SimCast that allows n players to announce independently chosen values, even if up to $t < \frac{n}{2}$ players are corrupt. Independence is guaranteed in the partially synchronous communication model, where communication is structured into rounds, while each round is asynchronous. The ν-SimCast protocol is more efficient than previous constructions. For repeated executions, we reduce the communication and computation complexity by a factor $\mathcal{O}(n)$. Combined with a deterministic extractor, ν-SimCast provides a particularly efficient solution for distributed coin-flipping. The protocol does not require any zero-knowledge proofs and is shown to be secure in the standard model under the Decisional Diffie Hellman assumption.

1 Introduction

1.1 The Simultaneous Broadcast Problem

Simultaneous broadcast allows n participants to simultaneously announce independently chosen values. It is useful in many applications such as auctions or coin-flipping, and is in fact a generic building block for any distributed protocol with an honest majority [16]. While this goal is trivial to achieve in a perfectly synchronous network where messages from all participants are broadcast at exactly the same moment, such a communication model itself is infeasible in practice. Instead, it is common to assume a partially synchronous network [6,14,15], where communication is divided into synchronized rounds, while every round is asynchronous, i.e., messages in a given round may arrive at any given moment within a time frame allocated to that round. Thus, in a partially synchronous network, every announced message may be chosen depending on all previously broadcast messages, including earlier messages received in the same round.

Consider the example of contract bidding where n players participating in a sealed bid auction wish to announce their bids in a "blind" way, such that the bids are revealed only once the auction is closed. In the partially synchronous model, simply announcing the messages in cleartext violates the requirement of blind bidding and allows the player speaking last to place the winning bid. At first sight, it seems sufficient to commit to a bid and only open the commitment after the bidding period has elapsed. However,

R. Cramer (Ed.): PKC 2008, LNCS 4939, pp. 180–196, 2008.

if Alice and Bob are competing players, then after seeing Alice's message, Bob may be able to create a related bid even if the commitment scheme is hiding. For example, Bob may simply copy Alice's message and thus guarantee that their bids are equal. In cryptography, such an (often undesirable) property is called *malleability* [9], and the attack is known as a *rushing attack*.

Secondly, it is often desirable that participants are bound to their commitments. If Alice and Bob use non-malleable commitments, Bob is not able to use the rushing attack to create a related bid.[1] He could, however, decide not to decommit at all after seeing Alice's bid, if the outcome is not to his favour. Thus, we need a simultaneous broadcast protocol that is both non-malleable—participants cannot choose their contribution based on other players' choices—and robust—nobody can pull out their contribution. Combined, this property is known as *independence*. Simultaneous broadcast protocols have many applications beyond contract bidding (see Sect. 4), and several solutions have been proposed to achieve independence in partially synchronous communication [6,14]. However, previous protocols require each party to broadcast $\mathcal{O}(n)$ messages and perform $\mathcal{O}(n^2)$ computation, so some authors use more efficient custom protocols for specific tasks such as coin-flipping [10]. In contrast, we propose a new *generic* simultaneous broadcast protocol that is particularly efficient in repeated runs.

1.2   Previous Work

The notion of non-malleability in cryptographic primitives was put forth by Dolev et al. [9]. In particular, non-malleable commitment schemes exhibit the property that, given a commitment $\mathsf{Com}(a)$, it is difficult to produce a commitment $\mathsf{Com}(b)$ to a related value b. More precisely, we require that if an adversary is capable of creating a commitment $\mathsf{Com}(b)$ satisfying some relation $R(a, b)$ then he is equally successful in creating such commitments without seeing $\mathsf{Com}(a)$ at all. Liskov et al. also introduced the notion of mutually independent commitments [19]; however, they propose a solution for the two-party setting, whereas we are interested in the multi-party case.

Recall that non-malleability alone does not provide independence since, after seeing honest players' values, malicious players may refuse to open their commitments. To ensure robustness in distributed computations, several authors have proposed to use verifiable secret sharing (VSS) to "back up" values. Rabin [21] and Gennaro et al. [15] propose to use *additive* (n-out-of-n) sharings of a joint secret key. Such an approach yields particularly efficient protocols for distributed signatures. For example, if an RSA signing key d is shared amongst n players as $d = d_1 + \cdots + d_n$, then each player's contribution to the signature $m^d \bmod N$ on message m is computed simply as $m^{d_i} \bmod N$. The novelty lies in the clever use of VSS to obtain robustness. Namely, they have every player verifiably share d_i of the key according to a (t, n)-threshold scheme. This assures that honest players can restore the contributions of failed players.

The idea of using VSS as back-up has since become quite well known. Returning to the case of commitments, the simple auction protocol can be made robust by having every participant VSS the committed value, as put forth by Gennaro [14]. We can thus enforce that all commitments are opened in the second round: if some player aborts, other

---

[1] The traditional notion of non-malleability does not, however, preclude exact copying of the commitment, so extra care must be taken to thwart the "copycat" attack.

players can open his commitment by reconstructing the shared value. Notice though that as opposed to the case of threshold signatures, Gennaro's broadcast protocol requires a new run of VSS for every round of broadcast, and additional zero-knowledge (ZK) proofs to ensure that the value under the non-malleable commitment is identical to the secret-shared value. We note that Pedersen's verifiable secret sharing [20] could also be used to provide simultaneous broadcast. This solution would eliminate ZK-proofs but not the communication overhead induced by verifiable secret sharing, and would be computationally heavier due to the use of Pedersen commitments.

1.3   Our Contribution

In many applications, the same set of parties need to perform multiple simultaneous broadcasts. For example, distributed statistical databases [10] require simultaneous broadcast for every database query. We present the first simultaneous broadcast protocol that significantly optimizes communication and computation cost for multiple invocations. Namely, in all previous solutions, verifiable secret sharing is required in every invocation of the protocol, even if the previous run was error-free. This means that each party has to broadcast more than t verification values and perform about tn exponentiations for verification. In contrast, we propose a new broadcast protocol ν-SimCast that requires one run of VSS in the initialization phase, after which multiple (ν) runs of broadcast can be carried out extremely efficiently. An error-free execution requires only two rounds, during which each party broadcasts only one ciphertext and its decryption. Consequently, computation cost drops by $t/2$, since each party now needs to compute only $2n$ exponentiations. For $t \approx n/2$, we have order n gain in both computation and communication. In particular, even though ν-SimCast is optimized for repeated execution, 1-SimCast (a single execution of the protocol with $\nu = 1$) is no less efficient than previous solutions. Table 1 (Section 3.5) compares the performance of simultaneous broadcast protocols.

Our protocol does not require any zero-knowledge proofs and is thus proven secure in the *standard model* (Thm. 1). This makes ν-SimCast suitable for coin-flipping, since players do not need common (known in advance) randomness for non-interactive ZK-proofs to produce common (unpredictable) randomness as protocol output. We achieve this by combining Gennaro's idea of using semantically secure encryption for commitment with Rabin's idea of backing up secret keys through VSS. Our protocol achieves independence of outputs (following the definition by Gennaro [14]) with a reduction to the semantic security of ElGamal. We note that ElGamal can be substituted with any other semantically secure encryption scheme under somewhat stronger assumptions (the common random string model, or trusted setup).

In Section 3.4, we argue that ν-SimCast allows participants to broadcast multiple announcements in parallel. In addition to the broadcast function, we show how ν-SimCast can be used to generate random values (Cor. 1 in Sect. 3.3). In Section 4, we discuss how to optimize ν-SimCast even further to efficiently obtain random *bits* rather than random group elements. These results provide a particularly efficient coin-flipping algorithm for e.g. the distributed databases example described above.

2 Preliminaries

2.1 Communication and Adversary Model

We consider a network of n players $\mathcal{P} = \{P_1, \ldots, P_n\}$. The players are pairwise connected through private point-to-point links and have access to a reliable public broadcast channel. Messages sent via this channel are reliably delivered to all participants, i.e. all parties receive the same message. The existence of reliable broadcast channels is a common assumption for cryptographic protocols [6,14].

Private point-to-point links can be simulated by using encryption on the public channel. If physical broadcast channels are not available, they can be implemented with special broadcast protocols [3,18]. However, reliable broadcast is costly when implemented on realistic networks such as the Internet. The protocol of Cachin et al. has message complexity $O(n^2)$ when run amongst a group of n parties and is "only" probabilistic, i.e., it introduces a small error probability.

In our setting we allow the adversary $\mathcal{A}$ to corrupt an arbitrary set of $t < n/2$ players. Corrupt players can act in any way during protocol execution, including protocol violation and early abort. The adversary is considered to be static, i.e., the set of corrupt players is fixed before the protocol execution. A special broadcast protocol further restricts the corruption tolerance to $t < n/3$, although it is possible to keep the resilience at $t < n/2$ under certain additional assumptions (e.g., the existence of a PKI) [18].

We structure the communication in rounds, and model delay in the transmission of messages by assuming partially synchronous communication. In contrast to the perfectly synchronous model where all messages in a given round are delivered simultaneously, the partially synchronous model allows an arbitrary delay within each round. In practice, such a model can be implemented by using synchronized clocks: if a participant does not finish its operations during a predefined time frame, he is disqualified from further processing. In a way, the partially synchronous communication model augments the adversary's power by allowing to fix the delay of messages sent by corrupt parties. As a consequence, a protocol that claims to be secure in the partially synchronous model has to withstand an adversary that speaks last in each round and incorporates all information learned from *all* honest parties in the same as well as previous rounds.

2.2 Cryptographic Components

In the following, we use the concept of a negligible function $\varepsilon(k)$ to express that for every constant $c \geq 0$ there exists an integer k_c such that $\varepsilon(k) < k^{-c}$ for all $k \geq k_c$.

Semantically Secure Encryption. We model public key encryption as a triple of probabilistic polynomial-time algorithms Gen, Enc and Dec for key generation, encryption and decryption, respectively. Intuitively, a public key encryption scheme is said to be semantically secure if a ciphertext does not reveal any information on the encrypted message other than what is known *a priori*. This is formalized as a game Sem-Sec where the adversary $\mathcal{A}$ has to guess a bit b corresponding to the correct plaintext. Let $\mathcal{R}$ be the appropriate domain of randomness:

Sem-Sec$[k]$:
    $(\mathsf{pk}, \mathsf{sk}) \leftarrow \mathsf{Gen}(1^k)$;
    $(\mathsf{state}, m_0, m_1) \leftarrow \mathcal{A}(\mathsf{pk})$;
    $b \leftarrow \{0, 1\}; r \leftarrow \mathcal{R}$;
    $c \leftarrow \mathsf{Enc}_{\mathsf{pk}}(m_b, r)$;
    output $\mathcal{A}(\mathsf{state}, c)$;

The semantic security of the scheme is then quantified by the adversary's success probability.

Definition 1. *A public-key encryption scheme* (Gen, Enc, Dec) *is said to be semantically secure if for any probabilistic, polynomial-time bounded adversary $\mathcal{A}$ the advantage $\varepsilon(k) = \Pr[\mathsf{Sem\text{-}Sec}[k] = b] - \frac{1}{2}$ is negligible in the security parameter k.*

In our construction, we explicitly require that the encryption scheme is *committing*, i.e., no two different messages encrypt to the same ciphertext under the same public key.

ElGamal Encryption. Let p and $q|p - 1$ be primes. Let $g \in \mathbb{Z}_p^*$ be the generator of a cyclic group G of prime order q. Recall that given a secret key $x \in \mathbb{Z}_q$ and the corresponding public key $y = g^x$, a (randomized) ElGamal encryption of a message $m \in G$ is a tuple $c = (g^r, y^r m)$, where $r \in \mathbb{Z}_q$ is chosen uniformly at random. The semantic security of the ElGamal scheme is equivalent to the Decisional Diffie-Hellman assumption [23]. ElGamal is a committing encryption scheme: given an ElGamal public key y, one can commit to a message m by $\mathsf{Com}(m) = c = (g^r, y^r m)$ and decommit by revealing (r, m). Naturally, the same commitment can also be opened by anyone who knows the secret exponent x. This property will be crucial for us in achieving robustness.

Verifiable Secret Sharing. In a (t, n)-threshold secret sharing scheme, a dealer D shares a secret s amongst a group of players $\mathcal{P} = \{P_1, \ldots, P_n\}$ during the Share phase by sending a share s_i to P_i. In the Recover phase, a group of at least $t + 1$ players can reconstruct the secret s, using their shares s_i. Unfortunately, simple secret sharing suffers from two drawbacks: first, a corrupt dealer can easily distribute inconsistent shares. Second, other share-holders cannot detect a corrupt share-holder P_j presenting a fake share s_j' in the Recover-phase. A verifiable secret sharing scheme (VSS) solves both problems by adding a third primitive Verify that allows parties to verify the consistency of sharing and recovery. As an inherent property, VSS guarantees that if D is not disqualified during the sharing process, then any set of $t + 1$ shares of honest parties define the same unique secret s (except with possibly a neglible error probability). Unless mentioned otherwise, we assume that the reconstruction error is zero.

Feldman VSS. Feldman's VSS scheme [11] builds on Shamir secret sharing [22] and consists of the following phases (omitting some details of error handling):

- Share: Let G be a cyclic subgroup of prime order q with generator g. To share a secret s, the dealer chooses a polynomial $f(x) = a_0 + a_1 x + \cdots + a_t x^t, a_{i>0} \in_R \mathbb{F}_q$

over the field $\mathbb{F}_q$ with $a_0 = s$ and degree t. The dealer sends each party P_i the share $s_i = f(i)$.

- Verify: The dealer broadcasts commitments $A_0 = g^{a_0}, A_1 = g^{a_1}, \ldots, A_t = g^{a_t}$ and each player P_i verifies $g^{s_i} \stackrel{?}{=} \prod_{j=0}^{t}(A_j)^{i^j}$.
- Recover: Given a set of $t+1$ shares $s_i = f(i)$, one can reconstruct the polynomial and find the secret free coefficient s by employing Lagrange interpolation. The validity of each submitted share can be verified as above.

In Feldman's VSS, a cheating dealer will always be caught. Finally, we will need the following result, stating that the scheme is perfectly simulatable:

Proposition 1. *Given any t shares of a secret s and the public value g^s, there exists an efficient simulator S that produces an outcome of the* Share *phase that is identical to the real execution of the* Share *phase.*

The simulation property shows that an adversary, controlling up to t participants, can compute consistent verification values A_i, $i = 1, \ldots, t$ himself. Thus, Feldman's VSS leaks no information about the secret beyond what is implied by the public value g^s.

Note that it is not know how to construct such a simulator for an adaptive adversary that may only corrupt some players at a later point. Thus, we present all security claims in the static adversary setting. In order for our protocol to achieve security against an adaptive adversary, one would first have to address the adaptive security of Feldman VSS [1].

Pedersen VSS. Compared to Feldman's VSS, Pedersen's scheme requires an additional element $h \in G$ (presumably generated by a trusted party during parameter setup) such that the discrete logarithm $\log_g h$ is kept secret. The sharing goes as follows:

- Share: To share a secret s, the dealer D now generates two degree t polynomials $f(x) = a_0 + a_1 x + \cdots + a_t x^t$ and $g(x) = b_0 + b_1 x + \cdots + b_t x^t$, where $a_0 = s$, and hands each participant two shares $s_i = f(i)$ and $s_i' = g(i)$.
- Verify: The dealer broadcasts commitments $A_i = g^{a_i} h^{b_i}$ for $i = 0, \ldots, t$. and each player P_i verifies $g^{s_i} h^{s_i'} \stackrel{?}{=} \prod_{j=0}^{t}(A_j)^{i^j}$.
- Recover: Given a set of $t+1$ shares $s_i = f(i)$, one can reconstruct the polynomial f and find the secret free coefficient s by employing Lagrange interpolation. The validity of each share can be verified as above, by having parties broadcast both shares s_i and s_i'.

Pedersen VSS assumes that a cheating dealer cannot solve the discrete logarithm problem. On the other hand, the next result shows that it guarantees unconditional privacy of the secret (while the privacy of Feldman's scheme is computational). More precisely, the adversary's view and thus actions are independent of the secret [20]:

Proposition 2. *For any (computationally unbounded) adversary $\mathcal{A}$ corrupting at most t parties and any view* view$_\mathcal{A}$,

$$\Pr[D \text{ has secret } s | \text{view}_\mathcal{A}] = \Pr[D \text{ has secret } s].$$

3   The Simultaneous Broadcast Protocol ν-SimCast

3.1   The Basic Protocol

Our n-party protocol ν-SimCast allows each player P_i to announce a value u_i, such that the values announced by corrupt players are independent of the values announced by honest players. We divide the protocol into two phases: the Setup phase is executed only once, after which the SimCast phase can be iterated ν times sequentially or in parallel to announce ν values (where $\nu = \nu(k)$ is polynomial in the security parameter). The protocol has maximum possible fault tolerance: it remains secure if up to $t < n/2$ players are controlled by an adversary.

We first present a version of ν-SimCast using ElGamal encryption and Feldman's VSS. For simplicity, we also assume that all players use the same cyclic subgroup G of prime order q with generator g. In Section 3.2, we discuss other possible instantiations.

ν-SimCast$[t, n, G, g, k]$

I. Setup:
  1. Share: Each party P_i generates an ElGamal key pair (x_i, y_i) and verifiably shares the secret key x_i using (t, n) Feldman-VSS. The public key $y_i = g^{x_i}$ is broadcast as a verification value during the Share phase.
  2. Verify: Each party P_j verifies each share. If verification fails for some party P_i, P_j broadcasts a complaint against P_i.
  3. For each complaint, P_i (as a dealer) reveals the correct share. Parties who receive more than t complaints or fail to deliver correct shares are disqualified. Each party builds the set of qualified parties $QUAL \subseteq P$.

II. SimCast (ν **iterations**):
  Each party $P_i \in QUAL$ publishes an announcement u_i:
  1. Encrypt: Each party $P_i \in QUAL$ wishing to announce u_i chooses a random value $r_i \leftarrow \mathbb{Z}_q$ and broadcasts a ciphertext

  $$c_i = (g^{r_i}, y_i^{r_i} u_i).$$

  If some party P_i does not broadcast a ciphertext, he is disqualified and his output is set to $u_i = \bot$.
  2. Decrypt: For every published c_i, the party P_i broadcasts the decryption (u_i', r_i').
  3. Recover: Each party P_j verifies the decryption values of each other party P_i by checking that $c_i \overset{?}{=} (g^{r_i'}, y_i^{r_i'} u_i')$. If verification fails for some P_i, parties run Recover to reconstruct the secret key x_i and compute the decryption $u_i = \text{Dec}_{x_i}(c_i)$. Players who failed to deliver a valid decryption message are disqualified from the next iterations and the set $QUAL$ is updated.

Fig. 1. Simultaneous broadcast protocol ν-SimCast

Informally, the protocol works as follows. In the Setup phase, each player generates a key pair (x_i, y_i) for ElGamal and shares the secret key x_i amongst all players using (t, n) Feldman VSS. The SimCast phase consists of only two rounds of broadcast followed by fault handling:

1. Each player P_i broadcasts an ElGamal encryption $c_i = (g^{r_i}, y_i^{r_i} u_i)$, where $u_i \in G$ and $r_i \leftarrow \mathbb{Z}_q$ is the encryption randomizer;
2. Each player P_i reveals (u'_i, r'_i). If the revealed values do not match, i.e., $c_i \neq (g^{r'_i}, y_i^{r'_i} u'_i)$, players run the Recover phase of the VSS scheme to recover u_i.

Notice that it is also possible to decrypt the contribution of a corrupt player P_i without revealing his personal secret key x_i by using standard threshold decryption techniques. This may be useful if the adversary model includes *fail-corruptions* [12], where players are simply unavailable from time to time. As a drawback, ElGamal threshold decryption requires additional ZK-proofs to verify the validity of decryption shares.

For efficiency reasons, we may also allow parties not to contribute an announcement in an iteration of SimCast, as long as they faithfully participate in verification and reconstruction. Such a behavior can easily be integrated in our security analysis. Some applications such as coin-flipping do however require everyone to participate (see Cor. 1).

3.2 Generalizing ν-SimCast for other Cryptosystems

The instantiation of the ν-SimCast protocol using ElGamal encryption and Feldman VSS is particularly efficient: it does not require any zero-knowledge proofs and can be proven secure in the standard model. The fact that verifiably shared keys are never combined to a single threshold encryption/signing key allows us to use simple Feldman verifiable secret sharing in the Setup phase instead of the less efficient Pedersen VSS.

In principle, one could instantiate ν-SimCast, using any semantically secure committing encryption scheme and any suitable VSS scheme. However, the efficiency of ν-SimCast relies on the discrete-log setting in one intricate detail: we must ensure that the verifiably shared secret key indeed corresponds to the player's public key. Feldman VSS for ElGamal keys solves this problem automatically, since the public key g^{x_i} is broadcasted as a verification value during the Share phase and all players check that their received shares are consistent shares of the secret key x_i. This may require additional zero-knowledge proofs, and thus we may have to give up the standard model. Alternatively, one may assume trusted setup, which is a reasonable assumption in settings where malicious faults are expected to be relatively rare. Even under those assumptions, our scheme is likely to be more efficient than the previous protocol [14], which requires complex zero-knowledge proofs during every iteration (see Section 3.5 for details).

3.3 The Security of ν-SimCast

First, a secure simultaneous broadcast protocol should satisfy the basic properties of broadcast: the protocol outcome is *consistent* for all honest parties and each honest party *correctly* receives the announcement of each other honest party. In addition, we require *independence*: for each iteration of SimCast, there should be no correlation between the announcements of corrupt parties and the announcements of honest parties.

Let $\mathcal{A}$ be a static polynomially bounded adversary that corrupts at most t out of the n parties and coordinates their action. Denote by $\mathcal{B}$ the subset of corrupt parties and set $\mathcal{G} = \mathcal{P} \backslash \mathcal{B}$. Consider one iteration of SimCast. Let $u_j \in G$ be the group element that P_j announces and let $u_{i,j} \in \mathcal{M} = G \cup \{\bot\}$ be the value that P_i receives as P_j's announcement. Set $\overrightarrow{U_i} = (u_{i,1}, \ldots, u_{i,n})$, i.e., $\overrightarrow{U_i}$ is the announcement vector received by P_i in one iteration of SimCast.

Our security definition of a simultaneous broadcast protocol is based on the definition introduced by Gennaro [14]. The latter requires that the output of any single corrupt party should be uncorrelated with the output of honest parties. Hevia and Micciancio [17] note that this definition does not capture the *collaboration* of corrupt parties, and bring an (admittedly artificial) example of a protocol that satisfies Gennaro's definition, but allows two corrupt parties to output values whose XOR is correlated to the output of honest parties. Thus, we modify the definition of independence to require that not only the output of a *single* corrupt party should be independent of the output of honest parties but also that there is no correlation between the announcement vector of *any* subset of corrupt and honest parties.

For each iteration of SimCast the following properties have to hold:

Consistency: For any $\mathcal{A}$, and for any pair of honest players P_i, P_j the probability $Pr[\overrightarrow{U}_i \neq \overrightarrow{U}_j]$ is negligible in the security parameter k.

Correctness: For any $\mathcal{A}$ and for any pair of honest players P_i, P_j the probability $Pr[u_{i,j} \neq u_j]$ is negligible in k.

Independence: For any $\mathcal{A}$, for any subset of corrupt players $Q \subseteq \mathcal{B}$, for all $\overrightarrow{m} \in \mathcal{M}^{|Q|}$ and all $\overrightarrow{u}, \overrightarrow{v} \in G^{n-t}$, we have that

$$|p_{\overrightarrow{m}, \overrightarrow{u}}^Q - p_{\overrightarrow{m}, \overrightarrow{v}}^Q| \leq \epsilon(k), \tag{1}$$

where $\overrightarrow{u}, \overrightarrow{v}$ are the announcements of honest players, ϵ is a negligible function of k and

$$p_{\overrightarrow{m}, \overrightarrow{u}}^Q = \Pr[\text{Players in } Q \text{ announce } \overrightarrow{m} \mid \overrightarrow{u}]$$

denotes the probability that corrupt players in Q announce vector $\overrightarrow{m}$, given that honest players have announced $\overrightarrow{u}$.

Intuitively, the independence property of ν-SimCast follows from the fact that each player P_i *must know* the value u_i he chose to broadcast. Indeed, since P_i has verifiably shared his secret key x_i, he can always compute the decryption of the published value c_i. In approaches that combine non-malleable commitments with VSS-ing the value under commitment, complex ZK-proofs are required to ensure that the shared value is identical to the one under commitment. In contrast, knowledge of the secret key acts as an implicit proof of knowledge of the encrypted value and no additional proofs are required. We proceed to give a formal security proof.

Theorem 1. *Let $t < \frac{n}{2}$. If the Decisional Diffie-Hellman assumption holds in group G, then ν-SimCast$[t, n, G, g, k]$ is a simultaneous broadcast protocol.*

Proof. First, notice that in each iteration all honest parties use the same set $QUAL$, as disqualification of parties is done solely based on public information. In the following we set $\mathcal{B} = (\mathcal{P} \cap QUAL) \backslash \mathcal{G}$. It is easy to see that honest players are never disqualified.

Let $P_i, P_j \in \mathcal{G}$. If $P_\ell \in \mathcal{G}$, then $u_{i,\ell} = u_{j,\ell} = u_\ell$, since P_ℓ publishes the correct unique opening of c_ℓ. If $P_\ell \in \mathcal{B}$ then there are two options. First, P_ℓ does not broadcast c_ℓ. In this case $u_{i,\ell} = u_{j,\ell} = \bot$. Second, P_ℓ publishes a ciphertext c_ℓ but fails to decrypt it in Step 2. Since there are at least $t + 1$ honest parties, the Recover-procedure of Feldman-VSS allows to reconstruct the unique value u_ℓ corresponding to c_ℓ, so $u_{i,\ell} = u_{j,\ell} = u_\ell$. This shows *consistency* and *correctness*.

The *independence* property is proven by reduction to the DDH assumption, or equivalently, the semantic security of ElGamal. Suppose that an adversary $\mathcal{A}$, given a security parameter k, achieves advantage $\varepsilon = \varepsilon(k)$. We build a second adversary $\mathcal{A}'$ that wins the semantic security game Sem-Sec$[k]$ with a related advantage ε', showing that $\varepsilon(k)$ must be negligible in k.

Assume that $\mathcal{A}$ corrupts t parties (wlog $\mathcal{B} = \{P_{n-t+1}, \ldots, P_n\}$) and that for at least one iteration $s \in [1, \nu]$ there exist two vectors $\overrightarrow{u}, \overrightarrow{v} \in G^{n-t}$, a subgroup $Q \subseteq \mathcal{B}$, and an announcement of corrupt parties $\overrightarrow{m} \in \mathcal{M}^{|Q|}$ such that $|p^Q_{\overrightarrow{m}, \overrightarrow{u}} - p^Q_{\overrightarrow{m}, \overrightarrow{v}}| > \varepsilon$ in iteration s. We use a similar hybrid argument as in [14]. Namely, for the vectors $\overrightarrow{u}$ and $\overrightarrow{v}$ in iteration s, define hybrids $\overrightarrow{u}^{(\ell)} = (v_1, \ldots, v_\ell, u_{\ell+1}, \ldots u_{n-t})$ for $\ell \in [0, n-t]$. Clearly, $\overrightarrow{u}^{(0)} = \overrightarrow{u}$ and $\overrightarrow{u}^{(n-t)} = \overrightarrow{v}$. Now,

$$\left| p^Q_{\overrightarrow{m}, \overrightarrow{u}} - p^Q_{\overrightarrow{m}, \overrightarrow{v}} \right| = \left| \sum_{\ell=1}^{n-t} (p^Q_{\overrightarrow{m}, \overrightarrow{u}^{(\ell-1)}} - p^Q_{\overrightarrow{m}, \overrightarrow{u}^{(\ell)}}) \right| \leq \sum_{\ell=1}^{n-t} \left| p^Q_{\overrightarrow{m}, \overrightarrow{u}^{(\ell-1)}} - p^Q_{\overrightarrow{m}, \overrightarrow{u}^{(\ell)}} \right|,$$

so there must exist an index j for which

$$|p^Q_{\overrightarrow{m}, \overrightarrow{u}^{(j-1)}} - p^Q_{\overrightarrow{m}, \overrightarrow{u}^{(j)}}| > \frac{\varepsilon}{n-t}. \tag{2}$$

Wlog assume that $p^Q_{\overrightarrow{m}, \overrightarrow{u}^{(j-1)}} - p^Q_{\overrightarrow{m}, \overrightarrow{u}^{(j)}} > \frac{\varepsilon}{(n-t)}$ (otherwise we simply modify $\mathcal{A}'$ such that it flips the output of $\mathcal{A}$). Note that the hybrids $\overrightarrow{u}^{(j-1)}$ and $\overrightarrow{u}^{(j)}$ differ only in position j, where the corresponding values are u_j and v_j.

As specified in the game Sem-Sec, $\mathcal{A}'$ gets as input a challenge public key $\hat{y}$. We let $\mathcal{A}'$ choose $m_0 = u_j$ and $m_1 = v_j$ as the two messages. $\mathcal{A}'$ then obtains the challenge $c = \text{Enc}_{\hat{y}}(m_b, r)$, where $b \leftarrow \{0, 1\}$ and r is a random value. Now, $\mathcal{A}'$ runs $\mathcal{A}$. In the following, $\mathcal{A}'$ has to perform the steps of the protocol on behalf of the honest players $\mathcal{G}$ and simulate the view of $\mathcal{A}$:

1. For the simulation of the Setup phase, $\mathcal{A}'$ follows the protocol instructions for each player $P_i \in \mathcal{G} \backslash \{P_j\}$, i.e., he generates a key pair (x_i, y_i) and shares x_i. For P_j, $\mathcal{A}'$ deals t random shares to $\mathcal{A}$ and runs the simulator $\mathcal{S}$ from Proposition 1 on input $y_j = \hat{y}$ to publish the challenge public key $\hat{y}$ and appropriate verification values.
2. For iterations $1, \ldots, s - 1, s + 1, \ldots \nu$ of SimCast, $\mathcal{A}'$ simply follows protocol instructions. That is, for all honest players $P_i \in \mathcal{G}$, $\mathcal{A}'$ broadcasts a ciphertext c_i and its decryption.
3. For iteration s, $\mathcal{A}'$ follows the protocol instructions for all parties $P_i \in \mathcal{G} \backslash \{P_j\}$ using as announcement the appropriate value from the hybrid vector $\overrightarrow{u}^{(j)}$. For P_j, it publishes the challenge ciphertext c.

Since $\mathcal{A}'$ controls more than t parties, for all $P_i \in \mathcal{B}$ that have not been disqualified it has received $t + 1$ shares of x_i in the Setup phase. This allows $\mathcal{A}'$ to decrypt P_i's encrypted announcements c_i and obtain u_i. Let $\overrightarrow{u}_Q$ be the announcements of the parties in Q. If $\overrightarrow{u}_Q = \overrightarrow{m}$ then $\mathcal{A}'$ outputs $b' = 0$; otherwise it outputs $b' = 1$.

First, we have to show that the simulation is indistinguishable from a real run of ν-SimCast.

Ad. 1: For all parties $P_i \in \mathcal{G}\backslash\{P_j\}$ our adversary $\mathcal{A}'$ follows exactly the protocol description. For P_j, $\mathcal{A}'$ uses the simulator $\mathcal{S}$ of Proposition 1 which produces a distribution that is identical to the distribution of a real execution.

Ad. 2: The simulation of iterations $1, \ldots, s - 1, s + 1, \ldots \nu(k)$ of SimCast is done as described in the protocol. Thus, both distributions are identical.

Ad. 3: $\mathcal{A}'$ simply follows the protocol, using announcements from hybrid $j - 1$ (if $b = 0$) or hybrid j (if $b = 1$).

It remains to show that $\mathcal{A}'$ breaks the semantic security with a sufficiently large advantage ε':

$$\varepsilon' = Pr[\text{Sem-Sec}[k] = b] - 1/2 = Pr[b' = b] - 1/2$$
$$= \frac{Pr[b' = 0|b = 0] + Pr[b' = 1|b = 1]}{2} - \frac{1}{2}.$$

Notice that $Pr[b' = 0|b = 0] = p^Q_{\overrightarrow{m}, \overrightarrow{u}(j-1)}$ and $Pr[b' = 1|b = 1] = 1 - p^Q_{\overrightarrow{m}, \overrightarrow{u}(j)}$, so from above we get

$$\varepsilon' = \frac{p^Q_{\overrightarrow{m}, \overrightarrow{u}(j-1)} + 1 - p^Q_{\overrightarrow{m}, \overrightarrow{u}(j)}}{2} - \frac{1}{2} > \frac{\varepsilon}{2(n - t)}. \qquad \square$$

The following corollary shows that ν-SimCast can be used for fair coin-flipping. We discuss this application in detail in Section 4.

Corollary 1. *Let $\mathcal{A}$ corrupt at most $t < n/2$ parties. If ν-SimCast$[t, n, G, g, k]$ is used to announce values $u_i \leftarrow G$ chosen uniformly at random, then the product $u = \prod_{i=1}^{n} u_i$ is also random in G.*

Proof. The product $u = \prod_{i=1}^{n} u_i$ contains the random announcement u_j of at least one honest party P_j, which by Thm. 1 is independent from the announcements of corrupt parties. Thus, u is a random group element. $\qquad \square$

3.4 Parallel Execution of SimCast

Up to this point, we have considered the security of ν-SimCast in a strictly sequential communication model. This means that parties first execute the Setup phase and then sequentially execute ν iterations of SimCast. However, when our protocol is executed in a real-world network such as the Internet, it is often advantageous when instances of the protocol can be run in parallel. Unfortunately, parallel execution of protocols often makes the security analysis more subtle or even allows new attacks. Mostly, this is due to the need to rewind protocol execution in the simulation.

Table 1. Performance of simultaneous broadcast protocols with n participants and threshold t

	rounds	comm.	broad.	exponent.	rand. elem.	model	sec.
Gennaro-00 [14]	5	$\approx n + t + 160$	$\approx t + 160$	$\approx nt + 160n$	$t + 1$	CRS	DDH
Pedersen-VSS [20]	3	$2n + t + 1$	$t + 1$	$\approx nt$	$2t + 1$	standard	DL
SimCast (setup)	2	$n + t$	$t + 1$	$\approx nt$	t		
SimCast (iter)	2	4	4	**2n**	1	standard	DDH
1-SimCast	4	$n + t + 4$	$t + 5$	$\approx nt$	$t + 1$		

Our protocol can be simulated without rewinding. Additionally, we do not require a full parallelization of ν-SimCast and rather focus on a simpler case where Setup is executed once after which the participants run iterations of SimCast in parallel, i.e. for all parallel instances, the Encrypt step of SimCast has to be completed before a single decryption takes place. Such a scenario is sufficient to decrease the running-time for many practical purposes (see Section 4). It is easy to see that the independence of non-decrypted announcements is still guaranteed, with a factor $1/\nu$ loss in the tightness of the reduction.

We believe that full concurrency of SimCast iterations is also possible but requires a more thorough analysis.

3.5   Performance Comparison for Simultaneous Broadcasts

We compare the performance of ν-SimCast with Gennaro's simultaneous broadcast protocol [14] and an approach based on Pedersen's verifiable secret sharing [20], which to the best of our knowledge are the most efficient solutions for simultaneous broadcast. For explicit comparison, we present all protocols in the same familiar discrete-log setting.

Table 1 summarizes the key properties. We count communication and computation cost in terms of group elements for a single player. For simplicity, we only consider exponentiations, as they dominate the computation cost. Additionally, we analyze the number of privately generated random group elements, the number of rounds and the number of broadcasts, as for practical implementations they are the most expensive factor.

All three protocols under comparison employ exactly the same mechanism—verifiable secret sharing—for error handling. Thus, we describe all protocols in the optimistic scenario, where all parties follow the protocol. Notice that since in the fault-free scenario no errors occur, no additional communication and computation is needed in the protocols' complaint phases. Also, in all our evaluations, we assume that polynomial evaluation does not require any exponentiations, i.e., that the values x^j are precomputed for all $x = 1, \ldots, n$ and $j = 0, \ldots, t$.

We start by briefly reviewing Gennaro's protocol, which we call Gennaro-00. The protocol consists of the following steps (note that we omit steps for verifying the zero-knowledge proofs):

1. Each party P_i publishes its own public key y_i.
2. P_i, wishing to announce u_i, publishes an ElGamal encryption $\mathsf{Enc}_{y_i}(u_i, r_i)$ and proves knowledge of u_i.

3. P_i verifiably shares u_i and proves in zero-knowledge that the VSS-ed value is identical to the encrypted value.
4. The parties process complaints.
5. Each P_i reveals the values u_i and r_i.

In the discrete-log setting, the proof in Step 2—knowledge of a value u_i encrypted under $y_i = g^{x_i}$ as $(g^{r_i}, y_i^{r_i} u_i)$—can be done efficiently by proving knowledge of the discrete logarithm of $\log_g y_i$.[2] The equivalence of the value under commitment and the value under VSS (Step 3) can be proven, using standard cut-and-choose techniques [2,4]. However, in order to guarantee that a cheating prover cannot succeed with probability greater than 2^{-n}, roughly n iterations are required. In other words, in order to achieve error probability 2^{-80}, the prover has to compute 80 ElGamal encryptions. Recently, Camenisch et al. proposed a practical verifiable encryption scheme that avoids cut-and-choose techniques altogether [5]. However, to guarantee soundness, the secret key of the encryption scheme has to be unknown to the prover. Thus, the scheme cannot be employed here, unless we assume trusted setup in Step 1.

To sum it up, Gennaro-00 runs in five rounds: in the first two rounds, each party publishes a public key, an ElGamal ciphertext and a (short) ZK-proof. Round 3 requires each party to privately send $n - 1$ shares, and broadcast $t + 1$ verification values for the polynomial together with a non-interactive ZK-proof involving 80 ElGamal ciphertexts. In Round 4 no extra work has to be done in the fault-free case. The last round adds two more broadcasted values. The total communication cost for one player is about $n + t + 160$ group elements including the $t + 3$ expensive reliable broadcasts. Computation cost is dominated by verification of shares and ZK-proofs—each party needs to compute about t exponentiations for each received share and 160 exponentiations for each proof, resulting in about $n(t + 160)$ exponentiations for each player.

Second, we note that Pedersen's verifiable secret sharing (Pedersen-VSS) can also be employed for simultaneous broadcast. The security of the scheme follows from Proposition 2 and the hardness of the discrete logarithm (refer to [15] for a similar proof). It also requires an additional element $h \in G$ such that the discrete logarithm $\log_g h$ is kept secret. Ignoring malicious faults, Pedersen-VSS then runs in three rounds, where in the first round each party P_i runs Share to announce a value $a_{i0} = u_i$, followed by a complaint phase and, finally, P_i opens the announcement by revealing a_{i0} and b_{i0}.

Compared to Gennaro's protocol, Pedersen-VSS does not require any zero-knowledge proofs and is thus also secure in the standard model. On the other hand, the VSS increases the amount of communication and computation, and each player needs to generate twice as many random elements for the coefficients of the polynomials. Both ν-SimCast and Gennaro-00 can employ the more efficient Feldman VSS scheme, even though standalone Feldman VSS is malleable [15].

The ν-SimCast protocol is comparable to Gennaro-00 and Pedersen-VSS in the setup phase, where verifiable secret sharing dominates the cost. However, each subsequent error-free iteration is much cheaper, requiring only 4 broadcast elements (one ElGamal ciphertext and its decryption from each player), $2n$ exponentiations for verifying the

---

[2] It is not guaranteed that each party actually knows the secret key corresponding to the public key y_i, and thus we indeed need an additional proof here.

decryption, and only a single random element for the ciphertext. To model the worst-case scenario when faults are frequent, we may look at the cost of 1-SimCast. We see that 1-SimCast still clearly outperforms Gennaro-00, and is slightly more efficient than Pedersen-VSS, at the cost of one extra round. However, in most applications that require simultaneous broadcast frequently, one does not expect malicious faults at every iteration, and thus ν-SimCast is clearly more practical than Pedersen-VSS. We discuss applications in detail in the next section.

4   Applications

The ν-SimCast protocol is a generic protocol that can be employed whenever players need to simultaneously announce independent values. As we have seen, this allows for the so-called sealed envelope auctions: non-malleability of SimCast guarantees that players cannot choose their bids to be higher than (or related in any other way to) previously announced bids; robustness further enforces that all "sealed" bids can later be opened.

Moreover, Corollary 1 shows that ν-SimCast can be used for joint generation of random values, opening up many applications beyond auction protocols. In particular, as our protocol does not employ zero-knowledge proofs, it can be used for the distributed generation of challenges for ZK-proofs without contradiction. We present some of the most prominent examples, and discuss efficiency matters.

4.1   Multi-Party Computation

The ν-SimCast protocol can be applied whenever a multi-party computation (MPC) protocol requires publicly known random values. As a prominent example, we present the Commitment Multiplication Protocol (CMP) [7,8] that is widely used in secure multi-party computation. Namely, in order to add verifiability to an MPC protocol and thus protect against active adversaries, players start by broadcasting commitments to their inputs. In order to detect malicious behaviour, each player then needs to create commitments to his output in a verifiable manner after every operation. Using a homomorphic commitment scheme, addition and multiplication with a public constant are straightforward operations: given a constant m, and P's commitments $\mathsf{Com}(a)$ and $\mathsf{Com}(b)$ to inputs a and b, everyone can compute commitments $\mathsf{Com}(a + b) = \mathsf{Com}(a) \cdot \mathsf{Com}(b)$ and $\mathsf{Com}(ma) = m\mathsf{Com}(a)$. Verifying the correctness of a commitment $\mathsf{Com}(c) \overset{?}{=} \mathsf{Com}(ab)$ is done interactively, using the following protocol:

1. P chooses a random β and broadcasts commitments $\mathsf{Com}(c)$, $\mathsf{Com}(\beta)$, $\mathsf{Com}(\beta b)$.
2. Other players jointly generate a random challenge r using 1-SimCast.
3. P opens commitment $\mathsf{Com}(ra+\beta)$ to reveal r' and commitment $\mathsf{Com}(r'b-\beta b-rc)$ to reveal 0.
4. Other players accept the commitment $\mathsf{Com}(c)$ iff all openings succeed.

Thus, such a protocol allows P to convince others that he has correctly generated a commitment to the product of two inputs without revealing anything about his inputs or output. More specifically, the protocol can be used to add verifiability to any MPC protocol based on multiplicative secret sharing schemes (SSS). Namely, given shares of two secrets, any linear SSS allows participants to locally compute shares of their sum, and a multiplicative SSS allows to locally compute shares of their product. CMP then adds verifiability to the computations, since every participant can prove that he has correctly generated commitments to the new shares.

4.2 Coin Flipping

Our protocol can also be used in situations where random *bits* are required, rather than random group values. In practice, it is common to apply a hash function to the group element to obtain, say, a symmetric key from Diffie-Hellman key exchange. For a more rigorous approach, a recent result by Fouque et al. implies that in subgroups of $\mathbb{Z}_p^*$, efficient deterministic extractors exist in the standard model [13]. More precisely, the authors bound the distance from uniform of the k least significant bits of a random group element. For example, if p is a 2048-bit prime, then one can extract 128 bits with a bias $\varepsilon < 2^{-80}$ in a suitably sized prime order subgroup of Z_p^*.

Dwork et al. consider distributed noise generation for privacy-preserving statistical databases [10]. In order to guarantee a particular (Gaussian) distribution of the noise, their protocol requires n public random bits (where n is the number of participants). They obtain those bits by having each participant verifiably share out 2 bits, and then applying a deterministic extractor to the $2n$ low-quality bits to obtain n bits from a "close-to-uniform" distribution. Using 1-SimCast, we can directly obtain (a constant number of) random bits with a provably small bias in two rounds (excluding setup). Compared to the VSS-based solution, we again have a factor t gain. If one requires more random bits or stronger randomness guarantees than one execution of 1-SimCast can provide, we can run ν-SimCast with $\nu > 1$ *parallel* executions in two rounds.

5   Conclusion

ν-SimCast is an efficient protocol for simultaneous broadcasting that allows n parties to announce independently chosen values, even if up to $t < \frac{n}{2}$ players are corrupted. In contrast to previous solutions, our protocol only requires one run of verifiable secret sharing in the initialization phase, after which an arbitrary number of broadcasts can be carried out. During each broadcast, each party broadcasts only one ElGamal ciphertext and its opening, and verifies $n - 1$ encryptions, which gives a factor $t \approx n$ improvement in communication and computation, compared to previous protocols. Also, our security properties do not rely on the usage of any ZK-proofs. Instead, we combine semantically secure encryption with backing up secret keys through VSS and obtain security in the standard model. Simultaneous broadcasting has various applications in distributed computations: for instance, ν-SimCast can be used to jointly generate random values. Multiple random bits can efficiently be extracted from the output of a single execution of 1-SimCast, making it practical in coin-flipping applications.

Acknowledgements. The authors thank Gregory Neven for many helpful comments. Emilia Käsper did part of this research while visiting the Computer Laboratory in the University of Cambridge, UK.

This work was supported in part by the Concerted Research Action (GOA) Ambiorics 2005/11 of the Flemish Government, by the European Commission through the IST Programme under Contract IST-2002-507932 ECRYPT and the IAPP–Belgian State–Belgian Science Policy BCRYPT. Sebastian Faust is supported in part by a research grant of the IBBT (Interdisciplinary institute for BroadBand Technology) of the Flemish Government. Emilia Käsper is also partially supported by the FWO-Flanders project nr. G.0317.06 *Linear Codes and Cryptography*.

References

1. Abe, M., Fehr, S.: Adaptively secure Feldman VSS and applications to universally-composable threshold cryptography. In: Franklin, M. (ed.) CRYPTO 2004. LNCS, vol. 3152, pp. 317–334. Springer, Heidelberg (2004)
2. Asokan, N., Shoup, V., Waidner, M.: Optimistic fair exchange of digital signatures (extended abstract). In: Nyberg, K. (ed.) EUROCRYPT 1998. LNCS, vol. 1403, pp. 591–606. Springer, Heidelberg (1998)
3. Cachin, C., Kursawe, K., Petzold, F., Shoup, V.: Secure and efficient asynchronous broadcast protocols. In: Kilian, J. (ed.) CRYPTO 2001. LNCS, vol. 2139, pp. 524–541. Springer, Heidelberg (2001)
4. Camenisch, J., Damgård, I.: Verifiable encryption, group encryption, and their applications to separable group signatures and signature sharing schemes. In: Okamoto, T. (ed.) ASIACRYPT 2000. LNCS, vol. 1976, pp. 331–345. Springer, Heidelberg (2000)
5. Camenisch, J., Shoup, V.: Practical verifiable encryption and decryption of discrete logarithms. In: Boneh, D. (ed.) CRYPTO 2003. LNCS, vol. 2729, pp. 126–144. Springer, Heidelberg (2003)
6. Chor, B., Rabin, M.O.: Achieving independence in logarithmic number of rounds. In: PODC 1987: Proceedings of the sixth annual ACM Symposium on Principles of distributed computing, Vancouver, British Columbia, Canada, pp. 260–268. ACM Press, New York (1987)
7. Cramer, R., Damgård, I., Dziembowski, S., Hirt, M., Rabin, T.: Efficient multiparty computations secure against an adaptive adversary. In: Stern, J. (ed.) EUROCRYPT 1999. LNCS, vol. 1592, pp. 311–326. Springer, Heidelberg (1999)
8. Cramer, R., Damgård, I., Maurer, U.M.: General secure multi-party computation from any linear secret-sharing scheme. In: Preneel, B. (ed.) EUROCRYPT 2000. LNCS, vol. 1807, pp. 316–334. Springer, Heidelberg (2000)
9. Dolev, D., Dwork, C., Naor, M.: Non-malleable cryptography (extended abstract). In: Annual ACM Symposium on Theory of Computing (STOC 1991), pp. 542–552 (1991)
10. Dwork, C., Kenthapadi, K., McSherry, F., Mironov, I., Naor, M.: Our data, ourselves: Privacy via distributed noise generation. In: Vaudenay, S. (ed.) EUROCRYPT 2006. LNCS, vol. 4004, pp. 486–503. Springer, Heidelberg (2006)
11. Feldman, P.: A practical scheme for non-interactive verifiable secret sharing. In: Proceedings of the 28th Annual Symposium on Foundations of Computer Science (FOCS 1987), pp. 427–437 (1987)
12. Fitzi, M., Hirt, M., Maurer, U.M.: Trading correctness for privacy in unconditional multiparty computation (extended abstract). In: Krawczyk, H. (ed.) CRYPTO 1998. LNCS, vol. 1462, pp. 121–136. Springer, Heidelberg (1998)
13. Fouque, P.-A., Pointcheval, D., Stern, J., Zimmer, S.: Hardness of distinguishing the MSB or LSB of secret keys in Diffie-Hellman schemes. In: Bugliesi, M., Preneel, B., Sassone, V., Wegener, I. (eds.) ICALP 2006. LNCS, vol. 4052, pp. 240–251. Springer, Heidelberg (2006)

14. Gennaro, R.: A protocol to achieve independence in constant rounds. IEEE Trans. Parallel Distrib. Syst. 11(7), 636–647 (2000)

15. Gennaro, R., Jarecki, S., Krawczyk, H., Rabin, T.: Secure distributed key generation for discrete-log based cryptosystems. In: Stern, J. (ed.) EUROCRYPT 1999. LNCS, vol. 1592, pp. 295–310. Springer, Heidelberg (1999)

16. Goldreich, O., Micali, S., Wigderson, A.: How to play any mental game or a completeness theorem for protocols with honest majority. In: Annual ACM Symposium on Theory of Computing (STOC 1987), pp. 218–229 (1987)

17. Hevia, A., Micciancio, D.: Simultaneous broadcast revisited. In: 24th Annual ACM SIGACT-SIGOPS Symposium on Principles of Distributed Computing (PODC 2005), pp. 324–333 (2005)

18. Katz, J., Koo, C.-Y.: On expected constant-round protocols for Byzantine agreement. In: Dwork, C. (ed.) CRYPTO 2006. LNCS, vol. 4117, pp. 445–462. Springer, Heidelberg (2006)

19. Liskov, M., Lysyanskaya, A., Micali, S., Reyzin, L., Smith, A.: Mutually independent commitments. In: Boyd, C. (ed.) ASIACRYPT 2001. LNCS, vol. 2248, pp. 385–401. Springer, Heidelberg (2001)

20. Pedersen, T.P.: Non-interactive and information-theoretic secure verifiable secret sharing. In: Feigenbaum, J. (ed.) CRYPTO 1991. LNCS, vol. 576, pp. 129–140. Springer, Heidelberg (1992)

21. Rabin, T.: A simplified approach to threshold and proactive RSA. In: Krawczyk, H. (ed.) CRYPTO 1998. LNCS, vol. 1462, pp. 89–104. Springer, Heidelberg (1998)

22. Shamir, A.: How to share a secret. Commun. ACM 22(11), 612–613 (1979)

23. Tsiounis, Y., Yung, M.: On the security of ElGamal based encryption. In: Imai, H., Zheng, Y. (eds.) PKC 1998. LNCS, vol. 1431, pp. 117–134. Springer, Heidelberg (1998)

SAS-Based Group Authentication
and Key Agreement Protocols

Sven Laur[1,*] and Sylvain Pasini[2,**]

[1] Helsinki University of Technology, Finland
slaur@tcs.hut.fi
[2] EPFL, Lausanne, Switzerland
sylvain.pasini@epfl.ch

Abstract. New trends in consumer electronics have created a strong demand for fast, reliable and user-friendly key agreement protocols. However, many key agreement protocols are secure only against passive attacks. Therefore, message authentication is often unavoidable in order to achieve security against active adversaries. Pasini and Vaudenay were the first to propose a new compelling methodology for message authentication. Namely, their two-party protocol uses short authenticated strings (SAS) instead of pre-shared secrets or public-key infrastructure that are classical tools to achieve authenticity. In this article, we generalise this methodology for multi-party settings. We give a new group message authentication protocol that utilises only limited authenticated communication and show how to combine this protocol with classical key agreement procedures. More precisely, we describe how to transform any group key agreement protocol that is secure against passive attacks into a new protocol that is secure against active attacks.

Keywords: Groups, multi-party, message authentication, key agreement.

1 Introduction

Recently, Pasini and Vaudenay [18] analysed a peer-to-peer Voice over IP (VoIP) protocol and deduced that two users starting an (insecure) call through the Internet can build an authenticated channel thanks to their ability to recognise the voice and behaviour of the other speaker. This channel can thus be used to exchange authenticated data. In particular, exchanging Diffie-Hellman [10] public values leads to a shared secret key. As such messages are very long, they proposed to use a message cross-authentication (MCA) protocol instead of authenticating them directly. Indeed, an MCA protocol sends messages through an insecure channel and then authenticates them by using *short authenticated strings* (SAS), e.g. 20 bits. Similar protocols are used in Bluetooth and WUSB

---

* Partially supported by Finnish Academy of Sciences and by Estonian Doctoral School in Information and Communication Technologies.
** Supported by the Swiss National Science Foundation, 200021-113329.

R. Cramer (Ed.): PKC 2008, LNCS 4939, pp. 197–213, 2008.

standards for authentication [14]. Different from other approaches such as certificate chains and password-based authentication, the security can be introduced as an afterthought—there is no need for a supporting infrastructure, the mere presence of limited authentic communication is sufficient.

The main aim of this article is to extend the SAS-based methodology previously outlined in [21] from a two-party setting to a group setting. Namely, manual authentication can be used to secure group key agreement protocols, i.e., group members can establish a shared secret over an insecure network. Afterwards, the group can use standard cryptographic methods to establish secure communication. The corresponding group formation protocol significantly simplifies common key establishment and works even if the participants of the group are not known ahead. Although the group structure is often predetermined, e.g. participants of the conference calls know to whom they want to talk, ad hoc group formation is quite common, too. The most obvious example is automatic device detection in wireless networks. In particular, a user may form a secure piconet from all accessible Bluetooth devices. Ad hoc formation of secure WLAN groups is another natural example both in the military and civil context.

In principle, two party protocols are sufficient to establish message authentication for groups. On the other hand, such an approach requires a lot of user-interaction that diminishes usability of the corresponding solutions in practical applications. It is clearly more convenient to join 10 guest computers into a WLAN network together, than repeat the same procedure over and over again. Motivated by this concern, we propose a new SAS-based group authentication protocol that significantly minimises the required user interaction, see Section 3. Essentially, the amount of user interaction for the pairwise and group authentication coincides—user has to remember only single test value. The latter is significantly more convenient than operating with 10 different test values that are needed when we iterate pairwise authentication protocol.

The security of our SAS-based protocol is based on the non-malleability of a commitment scheme. Each user chooses a secret key, then commits to it while revealing the input message to be authenticated. When all participants have committed, then the secrets are opened. Next, each party uses an almost universal hash function to compute a test value from the received messages and secrets and then compares it with the others using authenticated communication. Thus, an adversary that wants to modify input messages has to find a "collision" on the hash function or break the commitment scheme. The corresponding security proof itself is straightforward but technical due to the complicated nature of non-malleability. All definitions that are needed for the formal proof are given in Sections 2 and 3 and the proof itself is presented in Section 4.

Section 6 provides a solution to the group key agreement problem. Shortly put, we can achieve immunity against active attacks if we first run a standard group key agreement protocol over the insecure channel and then authenticate the corresponding protocol transcript. Moreover, if we additionally authenticate some long term public keys, then we can form separate subgroups without relying on authenticated communication. In other words, there is no need for additional user interaction when we decide to expel some group members. Such an "authenticate once" philosophy is particularly useful in the context of wireless home networks, as it provides a simple and provably secure method for hosting guest computers in the network for limited time.

2 Cryptographic Preliminaries

All of our results are stated in the framework of exact security, i.e., our main goal is to construct protocols that are secure against all t-time adversaries. In particular, all security properties are formally specified by a game or a game pair between an adversary $\mathcal{A}$ and a challenger $\mathcal{C}$. For a single game $\mathcal{G}$, the advantage is defined by $\mathrm{Adv}(\mathcal{A}) = \Pr[\mathcal{G}^{\mathcal{A}} = 1]$. For a game pair $\mathcal{G}_0, \mathcal{G}_1$, the advantage is defined $\mathrm{Adv}(\mathcal{A}) = |\Pr[\mathcal{G}_0^{\mathcal{A}} = 1] - \Pr[\mathcal{G}_1^{\mathcal{A}} = 1]|$. Typically, one requires that for all t-time adversaries $\mathcal{A}$ the advantage $\mathrm{Adv}(\mathcal{A})$ is upper bounded by ε. Of course, all results can be translated back to the non-uniform polynomial security model by considering asymptotics.

Keyed Hash Functions. A keyed hash function $h : \mathcal{M} \times \mathcal{R} \to \mathcal{T}$ takes two arguments: a message $m \in \mathcal{M}$ and a key $r \in \mathcal{R}$, and outputs a digest $t \in \mathcal{T}$. A hash function h is ε_u-*almost universal*, if for any two inputs $x_0 \neq x_1$,

$$\Pr[r \in_u \mathcal{R} : h(x_0, r) = h(x_1, r)] \leq \varepsilon_u .$$

The notion can be extended to handle n sub-keys of the same domain, i.e., $h : \mathcal{M} \times \mathcal{R}^n \to \mathcal{T}$. A hash function h is ε_u-*almost universal w.r.t. the sub-key pairs*, if for any two inputs $x_0 \neq x_1$, indices i, j and $r_1, \ldots, r_n, \hat{r}_1, \ldots, \hat{r}_n \in \mathcal{R}$:

$$\Pr[r_* \in_u \mathcal{R} : h(x_0, \boldsymbol{r}) = h(x_1, \hat{\boldsymbol{r}})] \leq \varepsilon_u ,$$

where $\boldsymbol{r} = (r_1, \ldots, r_{i-1}, r_*, r_{i+1}, \ldots, r_n)$, $\hat{\boldsymbol{r}} = (\hat{r}_1, \ldots, \hat{r}_{j-1}, r_*, \hat{r}_{j+1}, \ldots, \hat{r}_n)$ and $i = j$ is allowed. That is, output values are likely to be different if the corresponding hash functions share at least one correctly formed sub-key $r_* \in_u \mathcal{R}$. A function h is ε_r-*almost regular w.r.t. to the sub-key* r_i, if for any $x, \hat{r}_1, \ldots, \hat{r}_n, y$:

$$\Pr[r_i \in_u \mathcal{R}_i : h(x_1, \hat{r}_1, \ldots, \hat{r}_{i-1}, r_i, \hat{r}_{i+1}, \ldots, \hat{r}_n) = y] \leq \varepsilon_r .$$

We need a hash function that is ε_u-almost universal and ε_r-almost regular and could handle variable number of sub-keys at the same time. A priori it is not clear that such hash functions exist. Therefore, we give one possible explicit construction. Let all sub-keys be from $\{0,1\}^{2s}$ and messages from $\{0,1\}^s$ for a certain integer s which bound the message space. To hash a message x, we first compute an intermediate key $a \leftarrow r_1 \oplus \cdots \oplus r_n$; split a into two halves a_1, a_2; interpret x, a_1, a_2 as elements of the Galois field $\mathsf{GF}(2^s)$ and define $h(x, r_1, \ldots, r_n) = a_1 x + a_2$ over $\mathsf{GF}(2^s)$. If $x_0 \neq x_1$ then it is straightforward to verify that a pair $h(x_0, \boldsymbol{r}), h(x_1, \hat{\boldsymbol{r}})$ is uniformly distributed over $\{0,1\}^{2s}$ in the universality experiment. To get shorter hash values, we can output ℓ lowest bits. Then the hash function has optimal bounds $\varepsilon_r = \varepsilon_u = 2^{-\ell}$.

Common Reference String Model. In the *common reference string* (CRS) model, a trusted third party generates system wide initial parameters pk and automatically transfers them to all participants. Most of the communication and computation efficient commitment schemes are specified for the CRS model.

Although such a model seems quite restrictive at first glance, all communication standards provide system-wide public parameters such as specifications of hash functions or a bit length of public keys. In other words, the CRS model is not problem in practise. Nevertheless, one should make a trade-off between computational efficiency and reusability and the size of system-wide public parameters pk. Also, there are theoretic constructions that allow generation of a common reference string in the standard model.

Commitment Schemes. A *commitment scheme Com* is specified by a triple (setup, commit, open). The setup algorithm setup generates public parameters pk for the commitment scheme. The randomised commitment algorithm $\mathsf{commit}_{\mathsf{pk}}$: $\mathcal{M} \to \mathcal{C} \times \mathcal{D}$ maps messages $m \in \mathcal{M}$ into a commitment string $c \in \mathcal{C}$ of fixed length and a decommitment value $d \in \mathcal{D}$. Usually the decommitment value is a pair $d = (m, r)$, where r is the randomness used to compute c. A commitment scheme is functional if for all $(c, d) \leftarrow \mathsf{commit}_{\mathsf{pk}}(m)$ the equality $\mathsf{open}_{\mathsf{pk}}(c, d) = m$ holds. Incorrect decommitment values should yield a special abort value $\perp$.

Proofs usually rely on three cryptographic properties of commitment schemes: hiding, binding and non-malleability. Non-malleability is the strongest property, as binding and hiding properties directly follow from non-malleability and not vice versa. Many notions of non-malleable commitments have been proposed in cryptographic literature [11,9,12,7,14]. All these definitions try to capture requirements that are necessary to defeat man-in-the-middle attacks. We adopt the modernised version of non-malleability w.r.t. opening. The corresponding definition [14] mimics the framework of non-malleable encryption [5] and leads to more natural security proofs compared to the simulation based definitions [9,7].

Non-malleability and security against chosen ciphertext attacks (CCA) are known to be tightly coupled. In fact, these notions coincide if the adversary is allowed to make decryption queries throughout the entire attack [1] and thus usage of decryption oracles can simplify many proofs without significantly increasing the security requirements. Unfortunately, a similar technique is not applicable to commitment schemes as there can be several different valid decommitment values d_i for a single commitment c. Thus, we must use explicit definitions of binding and non-malleability properties in our proofs. A commitment scheme Com is $(t, \varepsilon_{\mathsf{b}})$-*binding* if for any t-time adversary $\mathcal{A}$:

$$\mathrm{Adv}_{Com}^{\mathsf{bind}}(\mathcal{A}) = \Pr \left[\begin{array}{l} \mathsf{pk} \leftarrow \mathsf{setup}, (c, d_0, d_1) \leftarrow \mathcal{A}(\mathsf{pk}) : \\ \perp \neq \mathsf{open}_{\mathsf{pk}}(c, d_0) \neq \mathsf{open}_{\mathsf{pk}}(c, d_1) \neq \perp \end{array} \right] \leq \varepsilon_{\mathsf{b}} \ ,$$

The non-malleability property is defined by complicated games, and thus we use an illustrative pictorial style to specify security games, see Fig. 1. Intuitively, the goal is: given a valid commitment c, it is infeasible to generate related commitments $\hat{c}_1, \ldots, \hat{c}_n$ that can be successfully opened after seeing a decommitment

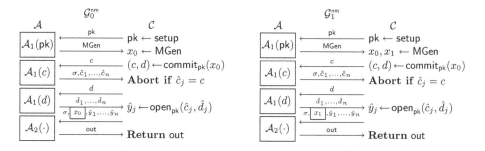

Fig. 1. Non-malleability games $\mathcal{G}_0^{nm}$ and $\mathcal{G}_1^{nm}$

value d. More formally, the adversary $\mathcal{A}$ consists of two parts: $\mathcal{A}_1$ corresponds to the *active* part of the adversary that tries to create and afterwards open commitments related to c while $\mathcal{A}_2$ captures a desired *target relation*. Note that $\mathcal{A}_1$ is a stateful algorithm and can pass information from one stage to the other but no information can be passed from $\mathcal{A}_1$ to $\mathcal{A}_2$ except σ. By convention, a game is ended with the output $\perp$ if any operation leads to $\perp$.

Fig. 1 should be read as follows. In $\mathcal{G}_0^{nm}$, a challenger $\mathcal{C}$ first generates the public parameters pk. Given pk, the adversary outputs a message generator MGen. Next, the challenger $\mathcal{C}$ selects $x_0 \leftarrow$ MGen and computes (c, d). Given c, the adversary outputs some commitment values $\hat{c}_i$ and an advice σ for $\mathcal{A}_2$ and then, given d he generates some decommitment values $\hat{d}_i$. Finally, $\mathcal{C}$ opens all commitments $\hat{y}_i \leftarrow \mathsf{open}_{pk}(\hat{c}_i, \hat{d}_i)$ and tests whether $\mathcal{A}_1$ won or not by computing $\mathcal{A}_2(\sigma, x_0, \hat{y}_1, \ldots, \hat{y}_n)$. The condition $\hat{c}_j \neq c$ eliminates trivial attacks. The game $\mathcal{G}_1^{nm}$ is almost the same, except the challenger tests a relation $\mathcal{A}_2(\sigma, x_1, \hat{y}_1, \ldots, \hat{y}_n)$ instead, where $x_1 \leftarrow$ MGen is chosen independently from the rest of the game. A commitment scheme is (t, ε_{nm})-*non-malleable* w.r.t. to opening if for any adversary $\mathcal{A}$ such that the working times of $\mathcal{G}_0^{nm}$ and $\mathcal{G}_1^{nm}$ are less than t, the advantage

$$\mathrm{Adv}_{Com}^{nm}(\mathcal{A}) = |\Pr\left[\mathcal{G}_0^{nm} = 1\right] - \Pr\left[\mathcal{G}_1^{nm} = 1\right]| \leq \varepsilon_{nm} \ .$$

Note that $\mathcal{A}_2$ can be any computable relation that is completely fixed after seeing c. For instance, we can define $\mathcal{A}_2(\sigma, x, y) = [x = y]$. Hence, it must be infeasible to construct a commitment $\hat{c}$ that can be opened later to the same value as c.

Non-malleable commitments schemes can be easily constructed based on simulation-sound trapdoor commitments from Mac-Kenzie and Yang [16] as detailed by Vaudenay [21]. They can also be built using a CCA2 secure encryption scheme, or by using a hash function as detailed by Laur and Nyberg [14].

3   Manual Group Message Authentication

Although our final goal is to establish a secure group key agreement protocol, we start from the group message authentication. Since active attacks can be detected by group authentication, any cryptographic key agreement protocol secure against passive attacks can be made fully-secure, see Theorem 1 in [18] and Section 6.

Communication Model. As usual, the communication is asynchronous. Participants can send two types of messages. Insecure in-band communication is routed via an active adversary $\mathcal{A}$ who can drop, delay, modify and insert messages. But participants can also send *short authenticated strings* (SAS) aka *out-of-band messages*. Out-of-band communication is authentic: the adversary can only read and possibly delay SAS messages.

Note that there are no *true* broadcast channels in our model. Although several networks such as WLAN in ad hoc mode offer physical broadcast channels, there are no guarantees that the signal actually reaches all nodes. If we can guarantee this by physical means, then the authentication task becomes trivial. Otherwise, different recipients can receive different broadcast messages and there is no difference between broadcasting and standard messaging except for efficiency. Similarly, broadcasting authenticated messages does not change the security analysis, although in practise, broadcasting can significantly reduce the necessary human interaction and make the protocol more user-friendly. For instance, considering the Bluetooth pairing, a human entering the same PIN on each mobile device is considered a broadcast primitive. Considering a VoIP-based conference, when participants are talking together, they use an (insecure) authenticated channel that broadcasts messages. The authentication comes from the ability of other users to recognise the speaker, e.g. by its voice and behaviour.

It is hard to formalise desired security properties for group authentication, as there are many different attack scenarios and security goals. Hence, we first consider a simple stand-alone security model and then gradually extend our definitions to cover more complex settings including key agreement protocols.

Idealised Functionality. Consider a network $\mathcal{P}_1, \ldots, \mathcal{P}_N$ of N nodes. A node name is a label $\mathsf{id} \in \{1, \ldots, N\}$ that uniquely determines the corresponding node $\mathcal{P}_{\mathsf{id}}$. In principle, node names can be non-consecutive such as hardware addresses, i.e., $\{1, \ldots, N\}$ is only a set of potential group members. A *group message authentication* (GMA) protocol for an n-element subgroup $\mathcal{G} = \{\mathsf{id}_1, \ldots, \mathsf{id}_n\}$ works as follows: each participant $\mathcal{P}_{\mathsf{id}}$, $\mathsf{id} \in \mathcal{G}$ starts with inputs m_{id} and ends with outputs $\mathcal{G}$ and $\boldsymbol{m}$, where $\boldsymbol{m} = (m_{\mathsf{id}_1}, \ldots, m_{\mathsf{id}_n})$ is ordered w.r.t. the sender identities $\mathsf{id}_1 < \mathsf{id}_2 < \cdots < \mathsf{id}_n$. In other words, given $\mathcal{G}$ and $\boldsymbol{m}$ it is trivial to restore who participated in the protocol and what was its input.

Stand-Alone Security. There are several important aspects to note. First, a group may be dynamically formed based on the participation in a GMA protocol, for example fast setup of ad hoc military networks. But then an adversary can always split the group into several subgroups and block the traffic between the subgroups. As a result, each subgroup agrees on a different output. Such attacks cannot be defeated unless parties know the description of $\mathcal{G}$ in advance, i.e., there is some authenticated way to broadcast $\mathcal{G}$. Second, an adversary may set up several dummy network nodes in order to corrupt communication or secretly shuffle different groups. Thus, we consider a scenario where a subset $\mathcal{G}$ of all network nodes wants to establish a common message m. At the end of the protocol, either all participants halt or each $\mathcal{P}_{id}$, $id \in \mathcal{G}$ obtains values $\hat{\mathcal{G}}_{id}$ and $\hat{m}_{id}$. We allow adaptive malicious corruption[1] of group participants, i.e., at any time during the protocol execution $\mathcal{A}$ can take total control over any node $\mathcal{P}_{id}$.

Let $\mathcal{H} \subseteq \mathcal{G}$ be the set of uncorrupted participants at the end of the protocol. Then the adversary $\mathcal{A}$ *succeeds in deception* if at least two uncorrupted group members $\alpha, \beta \in \mathcal{H}$ have different outputs $(\hat{\mathcal{G}}_\alpha, \hat{m}_\alpha) \neq (\hat{\mathcal{G}}_\beta, \hat{m}_\beta)$ and the group was not trivially split, i.e., $\mathcal{G} \subseteq \hat{\mathcal{G}}_\gamma$ for some $\gamma \in \mathcal{H}$. In other words, at least one honest participant gets messages from all members of $\mathcal{G}$. Formally, it is impossible to assure $\mathcal{G} = \hat{\mathcal{G}}_\gamma$, as an honest party cannot distinguish whether a node freely joined or was forced to join by $\mathcal{A}$. If the question of free will is irrelevant, then we can postulate that after the successful execution honest participants obtain $\mathcal{G}$. This is the maximum achievable security level, as honest members cannot detect corruption and missing messages caused by the splitting of the network. An alternative is to state correctness for each subgroup separately, but then protocol instances are run in parallel and this is covered by Section 5.

Since commitment schemes are often defined only for common reference string model, we give the security definition in the CRS model. To assure reusability of public parameters, we must consider chosen input attacks. More precisely, an adversary $\mathcal{A}$ can choose the group members $\mathcal{G}$ and their contributed messages m_{id} depending on the shared authentic common reference string $\mathsf{pk} \leftarrow \mathsf{setup}$. The advantage of $\mathcal{A}$ against a protocol instance π is defined as

$$\mathrm{Adv}_\pi^{\mathrm{forge}}(\mathcal{A}) = \Pr\left[\mathsf{pk} \leftarrow \mathsf{setup}, (m, \mathcal{G}) \leftarrow \mathcal{A}(\mathsf{pk}) : \mathcal{A} \text{ succeeds in deception}\right] \ .$$

A protocol instance π is (t, ε)-secure in the stand-alone model if for any t-time adversary $\mathcal{A}$, the corresponding advantage is bounded $\mathrm{Adv}_\pi^{\mathrm{forge}}(\mathcal{A}) \leq \varepsilon$.

Note that stand-alone security model covers only the case where no other protocols are executed together with π. In particular, it is not clear whether parallel execution of several different instances of π remains secure. We will return to this issue in Section 5 and show that parallel composition remains secure if some natural assumptions are satisfied. Still, for many cases where GMA is used once, the stand-alone security is sufficient. For example, many ad hoc groups use GMA to share a common secret to establish secure channels.

4   A SAS-Based Group Message Authentication Protocol

Our new group message authentication protocol SAS-GMA (See Fig. 2) borrows ideas from Vaudenay's cross-authentication protocol SAS-MCA [21, App. A] and MANA IV [14,19]. Both aforementioned protocols use commitments to temporarily hide certain keys. Similarly to SAS-MCA, all sub-keys are released after the adversary has delivered all messages. And similarly to MANA IV, messages m_i are sent in the clear and authenticated test values are ℓ-bit hash codes.

---

[1] In many cases, adaptive corruption is impossible, but with our new protocol being secure against adaptive corruption, it makes no sense to consider weaker models.

As the SAS-GMA protocol is symmetric, Fig. 2 only specifies the behaviour of a single party $\mathcal{P}_i$ who wants to participate in the protocol. Here $\hat{\mathcal{G}}_i$ denotes the group of participants who joined $\mathcal{P}_i$ during the first round before the timeout. Of course, if the group $\hat{\mathcal{G}}_i$ is known beforehand then $\mathcal{P}_i$ can wait until all other group members have sent their first messages. For clarity, variables $\hat{m}_{ji}, \hat{c}_{ji}, \hat{d}_{ji}$ denote the values from $\mathcal{P}_j$ that are received by $\mathcal{P}_i$. The hats indicate a possible modification by an adversary. The output vector $\hat{\boldsymbol{m}} = (\hat{m}_{ji})$ and the sub-key vector $\hat{\boldsymbol{r}}_i = (\hat{r}_{ji})$ are ordered w.r.t. sender identities, see Section 3. To be exact, $\hat{m}_{ii} = m_i$, $\hat{r}_{ii} = r_i$ and j ranges over $\hat{\mathcal{G}}_i$. Also note that (i, r_i) and $(\hat{\mathcal{G}}_i, \hat{\boldsymbol{m}}_i)$ are shorthands for binary strings that uniquely encode the corresponding elements.

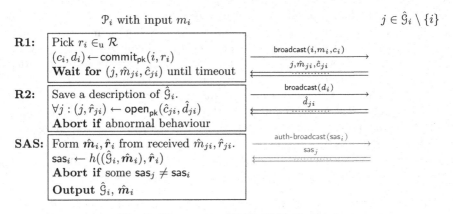

Fig. 2. The proposed SAS-GMA Protocol

Implementation Details. The cryptographic requirements for the hash function h and the commitment scheme $\mathcal{C}om$ are formally specified by Theorem 1, but there are many other minor details that are not covered by Fig. 2.

Assume that the final output $(\hat{\mathcal{G}}_i, \hat{\boldsymbol{m}}_i)$ can be always encoded as s-bit string. Then the hash function $h : \{0,1\}^s \times \mathcal{R}^* \to \mathcal{T}$ must support variable number of sub-keys r_j, since the size of the group can vary. For example, we can use a single keyed hash function h_1 and some sort of secure combiner to derive a new master key from sub-keys, as described in Section 2. The restriction $(\hat{\mathcal{G}}_i, \hat{\boldsymbol{m}}_i) \in \{0,1\}^s$ is not limiting in practise, as we can use collision resistant hash functions like SHA-256 to compress an encoding of any length to 256-bit string.

Secondly, we assume that the description of h and the public parameters of $\mathcal{C}om$ are fixed and distributed by a trusted authority. Thirdly, we assume that a participant $\mathcal{P}_i$ halts if there is any hint of an attack: (a) some group member halts; (b) there are duplicates $(j, \hat{m}_{ji}, \hat{c}_{ji}) \neq (j, \hat{m}'_{ji}, \hat{c}'_{ji})$; (c) a sub-key is in invalid form $(j, \star) \neq \mathsf{open}_{\mathsf{pk}}(\hat{c}_{ji}, \hat{d}_{ji})$; (d) some SAS messages do not match.

Another important aspect is secure comparison of SAS messages. In principle, it is sufficient to deliver minimal amount of messages so that participants can detect $\mathsf{sas}_\alpha \neq \mathsf{sas}_\beta$ for $\alpha, \beta \in \mathcal{G}$, where $\mathcal{G}$ is the set of all active participants of the protocol. If it is possible to detect all these active nodes, then a single node can broadcast the SAS message so that the remaining nodes can compare to their SAS messages. For many applications such as securing conference calls over VoIP, forming Bluetooth piconets and other wireless device networks, the group is known in advance and thus broadcast of a single SAS message is a viable option. Also note that the group formation can be combined with node detection in the Bluetooth networks and thus the timeout effect is marginal.

Stand-Alone Security. The security proof for SAS-GMA is straightforward but quite technical. Hence, we present the proof of Theorem 1 in smaller chunks to make it more comprehensible. Note that the security level depends linearly on $|\mathcal{G}|$ but the constant term $\max\{\varepsilon_u, \varepsilon_r\} \approx 1/|\mathcal{T}| \approx 2^{-\ell}$ dominates over the term $n \cdot \varepsilon_{nm} + \varepsilon_b$. Therefore, the deception probability asymptotically approaches the theoretical lower bound $2^{-\ell}$.

Theorem 1. *Let n be the maximal size of the group $\mathcal{G}$ and h be ε_u-almost universal w.r.t. each sub-key pair and ε_r-almost regular w.r.t. each sub-key. Then for any t there exists $\tau = t + \mathcal{O}(1)$ such that if the commitment scheme is (τ, ε_b)-binding and (τ, ε_{nm})-non-malleable, then the SAS-GMA protocol is $(t, n \cdot \varepsilon_{nm} + \varepsilon_b + \max\{\varepsilon_u, \varepsilon_r\})$-secure in the stand-alone model.*

Proof. For a sake of contradiction, assume that t-time adversary $\mathcal{B}$ violates the bound on the deception probability. Then we transform $\mathcal{B}$ to an adversary against the non-malleability games $\mathcal{G}_0^{nm}$, $\mathcal{G}_1^{nm}$ depicted in Fig. 1. The exact reduction is depicted on Fig. 3 and explained further in Lemma 1 and 2. Here, we just note that $\mathcal{A}_1$ simulates an instance π of the SAS-GMA protocol for $\mathcal{B}$ so that $\mathcal{A}_2$ can compute the predicate '$\mathcal{B}$ succeeds in deception' in the non-malleability game.

More precisely, $\mathcal{A}_1$ replaces the commitment c_k of $\mathcal{P}_k$ by the challenge commitment $c \leftarrow \mathsf{commit}_{pk}(k, r)$ for $r \in_u \mathcal{R}$. As $\mathcal{A}_1$ can pass information to $\mathcal{A}_2$ only via the commitment vector $\hat{c}$ and the advice σ, then the predicate '$\mathcal{B}$ succeeds in deception' must be computable from σ, $\hat{c}$ and corresponding decommitment vector $\hat{d}$. The latter is possible only if $\mathcal{P}_k$ is the last honest party to release his decommitment value d_k, see Lemma 2. Thus, $\mathcal{A}_1$ must choose k randomly from the group $\mathcal{G}$ provided by $\mathcal{B}$ after seeing pk. Lemma 1–3 establish

$$\mathrm{Adv}^{nm}(\mathcal{A}) = \Pr[\mathcal{A}_1 \neq \bot] \cdot |\Pr[\mathcal{G}_0^{nm} = 1|\mathcal{A}_1 \neq \bot] - \Pr[\mathcal{G}_1^{nm} = 1|\mathcal{A}_1 \neq \bot]|$$

$$\geq \frac{1}{n}(\mathrm{Adv}^{forge}(\mathcal{B}) - \varepsilon_b) - \frac{1}{n} \cdot \max\{\varepsilon_u, \varepsilon_r\} > \varepsilon_{nm} .$$

As the working time of $(\mathcal{A}_1, \mathcal{A}_2)$ is $\tau = t + 2t_\pi + \mathcal{O}(n) = t + \mathcal{O}(1)$ where t_π is the working time of the honest parties, we have reached a desired contradiction. $\square$

Lemma 1. *The sub-adversary $\mathcal{A}_1$ described below satisfies $\Pr[\mathcal{A}_1 \neq \bot] \geq \frac{1}{n} \cdot (\mathrm{Adv}^{forge}(\mathcal{A}) - \varepsilon_b)$ and the challenger $\mathcal{C}$ never halts unless $\mathcal{A}_1 = \bot$.*

Proof. The sub-adversary $\mathcal{A}_1$ sketched by Fig. 3 first forwards pk to $\mathcal{B}$ that replies $\mathcal{G}$ and $\boldsymbol{m}$. Hence, $\mathcal{A}_1(pk)$ can choose $k \in_u \mathcal{G}$ and return a description of the uniform distribution over $\{k\} \times \mathcal{R}$ as MGen. Given $c \leftarrow \mathsf{commit}_{pk}(k, r_k)$,

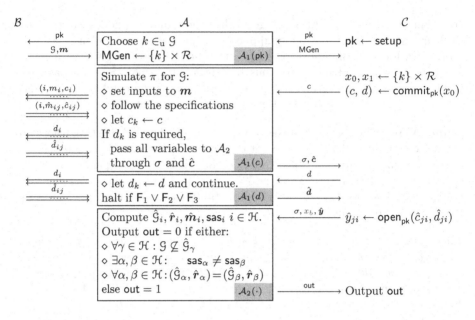

Fig. 3. Reduction to the NM game $\mathcal{G}_b^{nm}$ for $b \in \{0,1\}$

the sub-adversary $\mathcal{A}_1$ can continue simulation of π so that $c_k \leftarrow c$ and collect all messages received by all nodes in $\mathcal{G}$. To be precise, the simulation follows the specification of SAS-GMA except for computing c_k, d_k. In particular, if $\mathcal{B}$ corrupts $\mathcal{P}_i$, then $\mathcal{A}_1$ gives the control over $\mathcal{P}_i$ to $\mathcal{B}$ as in the real execution of π (If $\mathcal{P}_k$ is corrupted then d_k must be released). The simulation continues until $\mathcal{P}_k$ must release d_k. To proceed, $\mathcal{A}_1$ passes all variables that are needed to compute the predicate '$\mathcal{B}$ succeeds in deception' to $\mathcal{C}$:

1. Compute sets $\mathcal{I} = \{(j,i) : \hat{c}_{ji} \neq c\}$ and $\mathcal{J} = \{(j,i) : \hat{c}_{ji} = c\}$.
2. Send sets $\mathcal{I}, \mathcal{J}, \mathcal{G}$, all observed $\hat{m}_{ji}$, and current value of $\mathcal{H}$ as σ to $\mathcal{C}$.
3. Send all plausible commitments $\hat{c} = (\hat{c}_{ji})$ for $(j,i) \in \mathcal{I}$ to $\mathcal{C}$.

Then the challenger $\mathcal{C}$ releases d, and $\mathcal{A}_1$ continues the simulation of π with $d_k \leftarrow d$ until the end and halts if one of the following conditions is satisfied:

F_1: The adversary $\mathcal{B}$ fails in deception.
F_2: A double opening is revealed: $\mathsf{open}_{pk}(c,d) \neq \mathsf{open}_{pk}(c, \hat{d}_{ji}) \neq \bot$.
F_3: The node $\mathcal{P}_k$ is not the last honest node to reveal the decommitment.

By this construction, $\Pr[\neg\mathsf{F}_1] = \mathrm{Adv}_\pi^{\mathrm{forge}}(\mathcal{B})$ and $\Pr[\mathsf{F}_2] \leq \varepsilon_b$ or otherwise $\mathcal{A}_1$ can be used to defeat the binding property of the commitment scheme. Note that the simulation is perfect and thus $\mathcal{P}_k$ is the last honest node that releases d_k with probability[2] $\frac{1}{|\mathcal{G}|}$. The latter is true even if $\neg\mathsf{F}_1$ and $\neg\mathsf{F}_2$ and we obtain

$$\Pr[\mathcal{A}_1 \neq \bot] = \Pr[\neg\mathsf{F}_3 | \neg\mathsf{F}_1 \wedge \neg\mathsf{F}_2] \cdot \Pr[\neg\mathsf{F}_1 \wedge \neg\mathsf{F}_2] \geq \frac{1}{n} \cdot (\mathrm{Adv}_\pi^{\mathrm{forge}}(\mathcal{B}) - \varepsilon_b) \ .$$

---

[2] Note that $\mathcal{B}$ cannot succeed if it corrupts all nodes and thus w.l.o.g. that $\mathcal{H} \neq \emptyset$.

Finally, note that $\mathcal{C}$ halts only if some $\hat{d}_{ji}$ is an invalid decommitment value but then $\mathcal{B}$ fails also in the simulation of π and $\mathcal{A}_1 = \perp$. $\square$

Lemma 2. *If $\mathcal{A}_1 \neq \perp$ in the game $\mathcal{G}_0^{nm}$, then $\mathcal{A}_2$ described below correctly recovers the end state of the simulation and thus $\Pr\left[\mathcal{G}_0^{nm} = 1 | \mathcal{A}_1 \neq \perp\right] = 1$.*

Proof. Assuming that $\mathcal{A}_1 \neq \perp$, then the simulation conducted by $\mathcal{A}_1$ ended with a successful deception. As $\mathcal{P}_k$ was indeed the last honest node to release d_k, then $\hat{m}_{ji}, \hat{r}_{ji}$ for indices $(j, i) \in \mathcal{I} \cup \mathcal{J}$ are sufficient to recover all SAS messages computed by $\mathcal{H}$. By the construction, $(j, \hat{r}_j) = \mathsf{open}_{\mathsf{pk}}(\hat{c}_{ji}, \hat{d}_{ji}) = \hat{y}_{ji}$ for $(j, i) \in \mathcal{I}$ and $\mathsf{open}_{\mathsf{pk}}(\hat{c}_{ji}, \hat{d}_{ji}) = \mathsf{open}_{\mathsf{pk}}(c, d) = x_0$ for $(j, i) \in \mathcal{J}$ since F_2 cannot happen. As a result, $\mathcal{A}_2$ can compute all $\hat{m}_i$ and $\hat{r}_i$ for $i \in \mathcal{H}$ by setting $(k, r_{kk}) \leftarrow x_b$ and replacing $\mathsf{open}_{\mathsf{pk}}(\hat{c}_{ji}, \hat{d}_{ji})$ calls with appropriate values specified above. Then it remains to restore $\mathsf{sas}_i \leftarrow h((\hat{\mathcal{G}}_i, \hat{m}_i), \hat{r}_i)$ for $i \in \mathcal{H}$ and test $\mathsf{sas}_\alpha = \mathsf{sas}_\beta$ for $\alpha, \beta \in \mathcal{H}$ and output 1 in case of deception. Recall that deception happens only if the test values sas_α match but some $(\hat{\mathcal{G}}_\alpha, \hat{m}_\alpha) \neq (\hat{\mathcal{G}}_\beta, \hat{m}_\beta)$ and $\mathcal{G} \subseteq \hat{\mathcal{G}}_\alpha$.

As $\mathcal{A}_2$ computes the predicate '$\mathcal{B}$ succeeds in deception' and since $\mathcal{A}_1 \neq \perp$ implies $\neg\mathsf{F}_1$, we have $\Pr\left[\mathcal{G}_0^{nm} = 1 | \mathcal{A}_1 \neq \perp\right] = 1$. $\square$

Lemma 3. *Let $\mathcal{A}_2$ be as described in Lemma 2. Then we can bound the conditional probability $\Pr\left[\mathcal{G}_1^{nm} = 1 | \mathcal{A}_1 \neq \perp\right] \leq \max\{\varepsilon_{\mathsf{u}}, \varepsilon_{\mathsf{r}}\}$.*

Proof. Assuming that $\mathcal{A}_1 \neq \perp$, then the simulation conducted by $\mathcal{A}_1$ ended with a successful deception. Consequently, $c = \mathsf{commit}_{\mathsf{pk}}(k, r_k)$ could have been broadcast only as $\hat{c}_{ki}$, otherwise $\mathcal{B}$ would have failed in deception. Therefore, $\mathcal{I} \subseteq \{k\} \times \mathcal{H}$ and $\hat{\mathcal{G}}_i, \hat{m}_i$ and all components of $\hat{r}_i$ except $\hat{r}_{ki}$ for $i \in \mathcal{H}$ are fixed when $\mathcal{A}_2$ starts. Next, we bound the probability $\mathsf{sas}_\alpha = \mathsf{sas}_\beta$ for $\alpha, \beta \in \mathcal{H}$.

Consider the authentic broadcast of c_k first, i.e., the case $\mathcal{I} = \{k\} \times \mathcal{H}$. The condition $\neg\mathsf{F}_1$ implies $(\hat{\mathcal{G}}_\alpha, \hat{m}_\alpha) \neq (\hat{\mathcal{G}}_\beta, \hat{m}_\beta)$ for some $\alpha, \beta \in \mathcal{H}$. As $x_1 \in_{\mathsf{u}} \{k\} \times \mathcal{R}$ the universality of h w.r.t. to all sub-key pairs[3] yields

$$\Pr\left[\hat{r}_k \in_{\mathsf{u}} \mathcal{R} : h((\hat{\mathcal{G}}_\alpha, \hat{m}_\alpha), \ldots, \hat{r}_k, \ldots) = h((\hat{\mathcal{G}}_\beta, \hat{m}_\beta), \ldots, \hat{r}_k, \ldots)\right] \leq \varepsilon_{\mathsf{u}}$$

where $\ldots$ denote the fixed components of $\hat{r}_\alpha$ and $\hat{r}_\beta$. So, we have obtained $\Pr\left[\mathcal{A}_2 = 1 | \mathcal{I} = \{k\} \times \mathcal{H}\right] \leq \Pr\left[\mathsf{sas}_\alpha = \mathsf{sas}_\beta | \mathcal{I} = \{k\} \times \mathcal{H}\right] \leq \varepsilon_{\mathsf{u}}$.

In the remaining case, let $\mathcal{H}_0$ be the set of honest nodes that receive c_k, i.e., $\mathcal{I} = \{k\} \times \mathcal{H}_0$. Since there is a compulsory node γ such $\mathcal{H} \subseteq \mathcal{G} \subseteq \hat{\mathcal{G}}_\gamma$ there are nodes $\alpha \in \mathcal{H}_0$ and $\beta \in \mathcal{H} \backslash \mathcal{H}_0$ such that $\mathcal{A}_2$ compares sas_α and sas_β. Moreover, α, β and sas_β are fixed before x_1 and almost regularity w.r.t. all sub-keys provides

$$\Pr\left[\hat{r}_k \in_{\mathsf{u}} \mathcal{R} : h((\hat{\mathcal{G}}_\alpha, \hat{m}_\alpha), \ldots, \hat{r}_k, \ldots) = \mathsf{sas}_\beta\right] \leq \varepsilon_{\mathsf{r}}$$

where $\ldots$ denote the fixed components of $\hat{r}_\alpha$. Therefore, we have proved the desired claim, i.e. $\Pr\left[\mathcal{G}_1^{nm} = 1 | \mathcal{A}_1 \neq \perp\right] \leq \max\{\varepsilon_{\mathsf{u}}, \varepsilon_{\mathsf{r}}\}$. $\square$

---

[3] Note that the varying components $\hat{r}_{k\alpha} = \hat{r}_{k\beta}$ can be in different locations of $\hat{r}_\alpha$, $\hat{r}_\beta$.

5   Security of Parallel Compositions

The parallel composition of message authentication protocols is often insecure although a single instance of the protocol is secure in a stand-alone setting. The phenomenon is caused by shared long term secrets. Bellare and Rogaway formalised a corresponding security model [3,4] where an adversary can execute several protocol instances concurrently and succeeds in deception if at least one protocol reaches an accepting state with incorrect outputs. The model was later extended to capture security of key agreement protocols [2] and then used in the context of manual authentication [21,20,17,18].

The possible security drop emerges only if two protocol instances are not statistically independent, i.e., share long-term keys. Clearly, an independent protocol instance cannot help the adversary, as the adversary can generate the protocol transcript himself. Therefore, the SAS-GMA protocol can be securely composed with any other protocol, provided that the following restrictions hold:

$\mathcal{R}_1$: Randomness used in the SAS-GMA instance is freshly generated.
$\mathcal{R}_2$: The output $(\mathcal{G}, \boldsymbol{m})$ is never used before all parties reach accepting state.
$\mathcal{R}_3$: The SAS messages determine unique instance of SAS-GMA.
$\mathcal{R}_4$: All group members have different identities, i.e., $\mathcal{G}$ is indeed a set.

The claim itself is valid for any protocol but we prove only that the SAS-GMA protocol is self-composable. The proof for the general case is analogous but requires a very fine-grained formalism similar to [15, p. 394–396] and provides no additional insight. Due to the space limitations, we omit such dubious details.

Bellare-Rogaway Model. Similarly to the stand-alone setting, an adversary $\mathcal{A}$ has complete control over the protocol participants $\mathcal{G}$ and their inputs $\boldsymbol{m}$ and in addition adaptive corruption is allowed. However, as opposed to the stand-alone model, $\mathcal{A}$ can adaptively launch[4] new instances $\pi^{(i)}$ of the protocol for $\mathcal{G}^{(i)}$ and $\boldsymbol{m}^{(i)}$. The adversary $\mathcal{A}$ succeeds in deception if the end state of at least one protocol instance $\pi^{(i)}$ is invalid, i.e., honest parties accept different outputs. Since a single instance of SAS-GMA has non-negligible deception probability we must bound the number of protocol instances that can be launched. A protocol π is (t, q, ε)-*self-composable* if any t-time adversary $\mathcal{A}$ that can launch up to q instances of π succeeds in deception with probability less than ε.

The SAS-GMA protocol in the original form is not suitable for parallel execution, as a party $\mathcal{P}_i$ who receives two first round messages from $\mathcal{P}_j$ cannot decide whether $\mathcal{P}_i$ invites him to participate in two separate group authentication protocols or an adversary tries to attack a single protocol instance. There must be a legitimate way to divide message between several protocols. As a solution, we assume that each protocol has an initiator $\mathcal{P}_i$ who first broadcasts or sends directly to group members a unique tag **tag** for the GMA protocol and **tag** is appended as an identifier to each protocol message. We emphasise that an adversary can alter **tag**. To assure condition $\mathcal{R}_3$, no participant $\mathcal{P}_i$ can have two parallel runs of SAS-GMA with the same set of participants $\hat{\mathcal{G}}_i$.

---

[4] See [2] for the thorough formalisation of the Bellare-Rogaway model.

Theorem 2. *Let the parameters of SAS-GMA protocol be such that a SAS-GMA instance is (t, ε)-secure in the stand-alone model. Then the protocol instances are also $(\tau, q, q\varepsilon)$-self-composable for $\tau = t - \mathcal{O}(1)$ if restrictions $\mathcal{R}_1$–$\mathcal{R}_4$ are satisfied.*

Proof. Let $\mathcal{B}$ be such a τ-time adversary that contradicts the claim. W.l.o.g. we can assume that an adversary launches the protocol instances in the following way. First, it chooses the initiator $\mathcal{P}_i$ and then the set of participants that get the introduction message tag from $\mathcal{P}_i$ and decide to reply. Second it provides the corresponding inputs to the participants. For simplicity, assume that tag $\in \{1, \ldots, q\}$ and let $\varepsilon_{\mathsf{tag}}$ denote the probability that $\mathcal{B}$ succeeds in deception w.r.t. the instance $\pi^{(\mathsf{tag})}$. By the assumption $\varepsilon_1 + \cdots + \varepsilon_q > q\varepsilon$. Hence, we have the following simple reduction strategy $\mathcal{A}$. Given pk from $\mathcal{C}$:

1. Choose a protocol instance $k \in_{\mathrm{u}} \{1, \ldots, q\}$.
2. Simulate the Bellare-Rogaway model until $\mathcal{B}$ specifies $\mathcal{G}_k$ and $\hat{m}_k$.
3. Send $\mathcal{G}_k$ and $\hat{m}_k$ to the challenger $\mathcal{C}$ in the stand-alone model.
4. Continue the simulation by generating all messages tagged by tag $\neq k$.
5. Obtain other messages with tag $= k$ from the stand-alone environment.
6. If required by $\mathcal{B}$, corrupt the true nodes in the stand-alone environment.

Clearly, $\mathcal{A}$ provides a perfect simulation of the Bellare-Rogaway model, thus

$$\Pr\left[\mathcal{A} \text{ succeeds in deception}\right] = \frac{\varepsilon_1 + \cdots + \varepsilon_q}{q} > \varepsilon$$

and we have a desired contradiction.   □

Note 1. Recall that we had a problem in the stand-alone model if an adversary decided to split the group. The latter cannot happen anymore as the initiator is always in $\hat{\mathcal{G}}_i$ and thus all nodes in the group must have same SAS test values.

6   Manually Authenticated Group Key Agreements

The main application of manual group message authentication (MGMA) is to establish a commonly shared secret key among the group members. We show how to combine MGMA with any group key agreement (GKA) protocol so that the resulting group key agreement protocol is secure against active attacks.

There is a trade-off between the security and the amount of authenticated communication. For many practical applications, the SAS message consists of 6 digits and thus has only 20 bits of entropy. So, an adversary can always succeed in deception with probability 2^{-20}. On the other hand, 2^{-20} is also the probability of not noticing an active attack. The latter is small enough to demotivate most of the possible attackers. Consequently, the subjective security level can be much higher, for example 2^{-40} if the probability of an active attack is below 10^{-6}.

Of course, the cryptographic security levels can be achieved only with sufficiently long SAS messages. Therefore, it is important to minimise the amount of manually authenticated communication in scenarios where nodes can form many subgroups. In particular, it should be easy to exclude corrupted nodes from the group without transferring any additional SAS messages.

Idealised Functionality. A *group key agreement* protocol π between n participants $\mathcal{G} = \{\mathsf{id}_1, \ldots, \mathsf{id}_n\}$ starts with no input, is independent from the current state, and outputs $\mathcal{G}$ and a shared common secret key $\mathsf{key} \in_{\mathrm{u}} \mathcal{K}$.

Immunity Against Active Attacks. A group key agreement protocol π is (t, ε)-*immune against active attacks* if for any t-time adversary $\mathcal{A}$ that can choose a group $\mathcal{G} = \{\mathsf{id}_1, \ldots, \mathsf{id}_n\}$ then the probability that uncorrupted parties $\mathcal{H}$ do not detect active attack is less than ε. Obviously, any GKA protocol that is (t, ε_1)-immune against active attacks and (t, ε_2)-secure against passive attacks is also $(t, \varepsilon_1 + \varepsilon_2)$-secure, as long as both definitions are given in the same attack model. For many practical cases, stand-alone security is sufficient.

Burmester-Desmedt Key Agreement Protocol. The Burmester-Desmedt (BD) key agreement protocol [8] is provably secure against passive attacks [6] and thus is a perfect starting point for a manually authenticated GKA. Though the Burmester-Desmedt GKA protocol is a generalisation of the Diffie-Hellman key agreement protocol, it can also be generalised for other two-party key agreement protocols, see the compiler of Just and Vaudenay [13]. For simplicity, consider a group of n participants[5] $\mathcal{P}_0, \ldots, \mathcal{P}_{n-1}$ arranged in a ring, see Fig. 4. The protocol has two rounds over an authenticated channel, while most of the schemes requires $\mathcal{O}(n)$ rounds. Here, let g be a generator of a q-element secure Diffie-Hellman Decision Group $\mathbb{G}$. At the end of the protocol, each participant $\mathcal{P}_i$ obtains $\widehat{\mathsf{key}}_i = g^{k_1 k_2 + k_2 k_3 + \ldots + k_n k_1}$, see Appendix A.

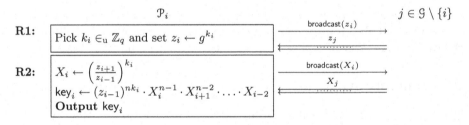

Fig. 4. The BD Group Key Agreement Protocol

New Manually Authenticated Group Key Agreement. Ideally, group members should run manually authenticated GKA only once to obtain a common group key key and long-term pairwise authentication keys, which provides possibility to re-run ordinary GKA protocols without additional SAS messages. The long-term pairwise authentication keys are formed based on Diffie-Hellman key exchange and the group key key generated by the BD GKA, see Fig. 5.

As the transcript of the BD GKA is authenticated with the SAS-GMA, the protocol is immune against active attacks with the same guarantees as Theorem 1 and Theorem 2 specify. Moreover, any two parties $\alpha, \beta \in \mathcal{H}$ can establish a pairwise secret key $\mathsf{key}_{\alpha, \beta} = f(g^{x_\alpha x_\beta})$, as they both know the corresponding

---

[5] The protocol can be trivially generalised to any n-element group $\mathcal{G}$.

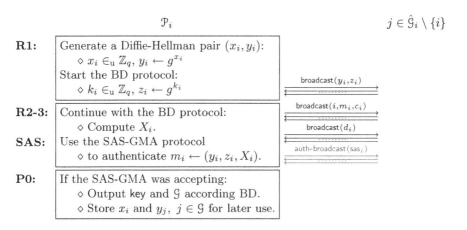

$$\mathcal{P}_i \qquad\qquad j \in \hat{\mathcal{G}}_i \setminus \{i\}$$

Fig. 5. The final SAS-based AKA Protocol with simplified notations

long-term public keys $y_i = g^{x_i}$ for all group members $i \in \mathcal{G}$. Hence, they can use any classical authentication protocol to protect new instances of GKA against active attacks. In particular, we can merge small groups $\mathcal{G}_1, \mathcal{G}_2$, if there is an honest party $\mathcal{P}_i \in \mathcal{G}_1 \cap \mathcal{G}_2$, by sending all intergroup communication through $\mathcal{P}_i$.

Of course, if the formed group is known to have a static nature, then one can skip the setup of long-term Diffie-Hellman keys $\mathsf{key}_{\alpha,\beta}$.

7 Applications and Conclusion

As shown in this article, our new SAS-based group message authentication protocol is provably secure in any computational context, provided that simple and natural restrictions $\mathcal{R}_1$–$\mathcal{R}_4$ are fulfilled. We also provided proofs under the natural non-malleability requirement that must be satisfied for all protocols that use commitments to temporarily hide sub-keys of hash function.

It allows building of secure SAS-based group key agreements, as presented in the last section. Such a key agreement protocol has the advantage that it does not require any trusted third party, any public-key infrastructure, nor any pre-shared key. Security is ensured peer-to-peer by using an authentication primitive, e.g. voice recognition for VoIP or string copy for devices. Therefore, consumers can establish and reconfigure security associations for electronic devices with minimal effort. In a certain sense, security can be provided as an add-on feature.

References

1. Bellare, M., Desai, A., Pointcheval, D., Rogaway, P.: Relations Among Notions of Security for Public-Key Encryption Schemes. In: Krawczyk, H. (ed.) CRYPTO 1998. LNCS, vol. 1462, pp. 26–45. Springer, Heidelberg (1998)
2. Bellare, M., Pointcheval, D., Rogaway, P.: Authenticated Key Exchange Secure against Dictionary Attacks. In: Preneel, B. (ed.) EUROCRYPT 2000. LNCS, vol. 1807, pp. 139–155. Springer, Heidelberg (2000)

3. Bellare, M., Rogaway, P.: Entity Authentication and Key Distribution. In: Stinson, D.R. (ed.) CRYPTO 1993. LNCS, vol. 773, pp. 232–249. Springer, Heidelberg (1994)

4. Bellare, M., Rogaway, P.: Provably secure session key distribution: the three party case. In: STOC 1995: Proceedings of the Twenty-Seventh Annual ACM Symposium on Theory of Computing, Las Vegas, Nevada, U.S.A, pp. 57–66. ACM press, New York (1995)

5. Bellare, M., Sahai, A.: Non-malleable encryption: Equivalence between two notions, and an indistinguishability-based characterization. In: Wiener, M.J. (ed.) CRYPTO 1999. LNCS, vol. 1666, pp. 519–536. Springer, Heidelberg (1999)

6. Burmester, M., Desmedt, Y.: A secure and scalable Group Key Exchange system. Information Processiong Letter 94(3), 137–143 (2005)

7. Damgård, I., Groth, J.: Non-interactive and reusable non-malleable commitment schemes. In: STOC 2003: Proceedings of the Thirty-Fifth Annual ACM Symposium on Theory of Computing, San Diego, California, U.S.A., pp. 426–437. ACM Press, New York (2003)

8. Desmedt, Y., Burmester, M.: A secure and efficient conference key distribution system (extended abstract). In: De Santis, A. (ed.) EUROCRYPT 1994. LNCS, vol. 950, pp. 275–286. Springer, Heidelberg (1995)

9. Di Crescenzo, G., Ishai, Y., Ostrovsky, R.: Non-interactive and non-malleable commitment. In: STOC 1998: Proceedings of the Thirtieth Annual ACM Symposium on Theory of Computing, Dallas, Texas, USA, pp. 141–150. ACM Press, New York (1998)

10. Diffie, W., Hellman, M.E.: New Directions in Cryptography. IEEE Transactions on Information Theory IT–22(6), 644–654 (1976)

11. Dolev, D., Dwork, C., Naor, M.: Non-malleable cryptography (extended abstract). In: STOC 1991: Proceedings of the Twenty Third Annual ACM Symposium on Theory of Computing, New Orleans, Louisiana, U.S.A., pp. 542–552. ACM Press, New York (1991)

12. Fischlin, M., Fischlin, R.: Efficient non-malleable commitment schemes. In: Bellare, M. (ed.) CRYPTO 2000. LNCS, vol. 1880, pp. 413–431. Springer, Heidelberg (2000)

13. Just, M., Vaudenay, S.: Authenticated Multi-Party Key Agreement. In: Kim, K.-c., Matsumoto, T. (eds.) ASIACRYPT 1996. LNCS, vol. 1163, pp. 36–49. Springer, Heidelberg (1996)

14. Laur, S., Nyberg, K.: Efficient Mutual Data Authentication Using Manually Authenticated Strings. In: Pointcheval, D., Mu, Y., Chen, K. (eds.) CANS 2006. LNCS, vol. 4301, pp. 90–107. Springer, Heidelberg (2006)

15. Lindell, Y.: General composition and universal composability in secure multi-party computation. In: FOCS 2003, pp. 394–403. IEEE Computer Society, Los Alamitos (2003)

16. MacKenzie, P., Yang, K.: On Simulation-Sound Trapdoor Commitments. In: Cachin, C., Camenisch, J.L. (eds.) EUROCRYPT 2004. LNCS, vol. 3027, pp. 382–400. Springer, Heidelberg (2004)

17. Pasini, S., Vaudenay, S.: An Optimal Non-interactive Message Authentication Protocol. In: Pointcheval, D. (ed.) CT-RSA 2006. LNCS, vol. 3860, pp. 280–294. Springer, Heidelberg (2006)

18. Pasini, S., Vaudenay, S.: SAS-based Authenticated Key Agreement. In: Yung, M., Dodis, Y., Kiayias, A., Malkin, T.G. (eds.) PKC 2006. LNCS, vol. 3958, pp. 395–409. Springer, Heidelberg (2006)

19. Valkonen, J., Asokan, N., Nyberg, K.: Ad hoc security association for groups. In: Buttyán, L., Gligor, V.D., Westhoff, D. (eds.) ESAS 2006. LNCS, vol. 4357, pp. 150–164. Springer, Heidelberg (2006)
20. Vaudenay, S.: On Bluetooth repairing: Key agreement based on symmetric-key cryptography. In: Feng, D., Lin, D., Yung, M. (eds.) CISC 2005. LNCS, vol. 3822, pp. 1–9. Springer, Heidelberg (2005)
21. Vaudenay, S.: Secure communications over insecure channels based on short authenticated strings. In: Shoup, V. (ed.) CRYPTO 2005. LNCS, vol. 3621, pp. 309–326. Springer, Heidelberg (2005)

A   Burmester Desmedt Key Derivation Proof

$$\text{key}_i = (z_{i-1})^{nk_i} \cdot X_i^{n-1} \cdot X_{i+1}^{n-2} \cdot \ldots \cdot X_{i-2}$$
$$= \left[z_{i-1}^{k_i} \right] \cdot \left[z_{i-1}^{k_i} \cdot X_i \right] \cdot \left[z_{i-1}^{k_i} \cdot X_i \cdot X_{i+1} \right] \cdot \ldots \cdot \left[z_{i-1}^{k_i} \cdot X_i \cdot X_{i+1} \cdots X_{i-2} \right]$$
$$= \left[g^{k_{i-1}k_i} \right] \cdot \left[g^{k_i k_{i+1}} \right] \cdot \left[g^{k_{i+1}k_{i+2}} \right] \cdot \ldots \cdot \left[g^{k_{i-2}k_{i-1}} \right]$$
$$= g^{k_1 k_2 + k_2 k_3 + \ldots + k_n k_1}$$

An Optimized Hardware Architecture for the Montgomery Multiplication Algorithm

Miaoqing Huang[1], Kris Gaj[2], Soonhak Kwon[3], and Tarek El-Ghazawi[1]

[1] The George Washington University, Washington, DC 20052, USA
{mqhuang,tarek}@gwu.edu
[2] George Mason University, Fairfax, VA 22030, USA
kgaj@gmu.edu
[3] Sungkyunkwan University, Suwon 440-746, Korea
shkwon@skku.edu

Abstract. Montgomery modular multiplication is one of the fundamental operations used in cryptographic algorithms, such as RSA and Elliptic Curve Cryptosystems. At CHES 1999, Tenca and Koç introduced a now-classical architecture for implementing Montgomery multiplication in hardware. With parameters optimized for minimum latency, this architecture performs a single Montgomery multiplication in approximately $2n$ clock cycles, where n is the size of operands in bits. In this paper we propose and discuss an optimized hardware architecture performing the same operation in approximately n clock cycles with almost the same clock period. Our architecture is based on pre-computing partial results using two possible assumptions regarding the most significant bit of the previous word, and is only marginally more demanding in terms of the circuit area. The new radix-2 architecture can be extended for the case of radix-4, while preserving a factor of two speed-up over the corresponding radix-4 design by Tenca, Todorov, and Koç from CHES 2001. Our architecture has been verified by modeling it in Verilog-HDL, implementing it using Xilinx Virtex-II 6000 FPGA, and experimentally testing it using SRC-6 reconfigurable computer.

Keywords: Montgomery Multiplication, MWR2MM Algorithm, Field Programmable Gate Arrays.

1 Introduction

Since the introduction of the RSA algorithm [1] in 1978, high-speed and space-efficient hardware architectures for modular multiplication have been a subject of constant interest for almost 30 years. During this period, one of the most useful advances came with the introduction of Montgomery multiplication algorithm due to Peter L. Montgomery [2]. Montgomery multiplication is the basic operation of the modular exponentiation, which is required in the RSA public-key cryptosystem. It is also used in Elliptic Curve Cryptosystems, and several methods of factoring, such as ECM, p-1, and Pollard's "rho" method, as well as in many other cryptographic and cryptanalytic transformations [3].

R. Cramer (Ed.): PKC 2008, LNCS 4939, pp. 214–228, 2008.

At CHES 1999, Tenca and Koç introduced a scalable word-based architecture for Montgomery multiplication, called a Multiple-Word Radix-2 Montgomery Multiplication (MWR2MM) [4,5]. Several follow-up designs based on the MWR2MM algorithm have been published to reduce the computation time [6,7,8]. In [6], a high-radix word-based Montgomery algorithm (MWR2^{k}MM) was proposed using Booth encoding technique. Although the number of scanning steps was reduced, the complexity of control and computational logic increased substantially at the same time. In [7], Harris $et\ al.$ implemented the MWR2MM algorithm in a quite different way and their approach was able to process an n-bit precision Montgomery multiplication in approximately n clock cycles, while keeping the scalability and simplicity of the original implementation. In [8], Michalski and Buell introduced a MWRkMM algorithm, which is derived from $The\ Finely\ Integrated\ Operand\ Scanning\ Method$ described in [9]. MWRkMM algorithm requires the built-in multipliers to speed up the computation and this feature makes the implementation expensive. The systolic high-radix design by McIvor $et\ al.$ described in [10] is also capable of very high speed operation, but suffers from the same disadvantage of large requirements for fast multiplier units. A different approach based on processing multi-precision operands in carry-save form has been presented in [11]. This architecture is optimized for the minimum latency and is particularly suitable for repeated sequence of Montgomery multiplications, such as the sequence used in modular exponentiations (e.g., RSA).

In this paper, we focus on the optimization of hardware architectures for MWR2MM and MWR4MM algorithms in order to minimize the number of clock cycles required to compute an n-bit precision Montgomery multiplication. We start with the introduction of Montgomery multiplication in Section 2. Then, the classical MWR2MM architecture is discussed and the proposed new optimized architecture is demonstrated in Section 3. In Section 4, the high-radix version of our architecture is introduced. In Section 5, we first compare our architecture with three earlier architectures from the conceptual point of view. Then, the hardware implementations of all discussed architectures are presented and contrasted with each other. Finally, in Section 6, we present the summary and conclusions for this work.

2   Montgomery Multiplication Algorithm

Let $M > 0$ be an odd integer. In many cryptosystems, such as RSA, computing $X \cdot Y \pmod{M}$ is a crucial operation. Taking the reduction of $X \cdot Y \pmod{M}$ is a more time consuming step than the multiplication $X \cdot Y$ without reduction. In [2], Montgomery introduced a method for calculating products $\pmod{M}$ without the costly reduction $\pmod{M}$, since then known as Montgomery multiplication. Montgomery multiplication of X and $Y \pmod{M}$, denoted by $MP(X, Y, M)$, is defined as $X \cdot Y \cdot 2^{-n} \pmod{M}$ for some fixed integer n.

Table 1. Conversion between Ordinary Domain and Montgomery Domain

Ordinary Domain	$\Longleftrightarrow$	Montgomery Domain
X	$\leftrightarrow$	$X' = X \cdot 2^n \pmod{M}$
Y	$\leftrightarrow$	$Y' = Y \cdot 2^n \pmod{M}$
XY	$\leftrightarrow$	$(X \cdot Y)' = X \cdot Y \cdot 2^n \pmod{M}$

Algorithm 1. Radix-2 Montgomery Multiplication

Require: odd $M, n = \lfloor \log_2 M \rfloor + 1, X = \sum_{i=0}^{n-1} x_i \cdot 2^i$, with $0 \le X, Y < M$
Ensure: $Z = MP(X, Y, M) \equiv X \cdot Y \cdot 2^{-n} \pmod{M}, 0 \le Z < M$
1: $S[0] = 0$
2: **for** $i = 0$ to $n - 1$ step 1 **do**
3:     $q_i = S[i]_0 \oplus x_i \cdot Y_0$
4:     $S[i+1] = (S[i] + x_i \cdot Y + q_i \cdot M)$ div 2
5: **end for**
6: **if** $(S[n] > M)$ **then**
7:     $S[n] = S[n] - M$
8: **end if**
9: **return** $Z = S[n]$

Since Montgomery multiplication is not an ordinary multiplication, there is a process of conversion between the ordinary domain (with ordinary multiplication) and the Montgomery domain. The conversion between the ordinary domain and the Montgomery domain is given by the relation $X \longleftrightarrow X'$ with $X' = X \cdot 2^n$ (mod M), and the corresponding diagram is shown in Table 1.

The Table 1 shows that the conversion is compatible with multiplications in each domain, since

$$MP(X', Y', M) \equiv X' \cdot Y' \cdot 2^{-n} \equiv (X \cdot 2^n) \cdot (Y \cdot 2^n) \cdot 2^{-n} \tag{1a}$$

$$\equiv X \cdot Y \cdot 2^n \equiv (X \cdot Y)' \pmod{M}. \tag{1b}$$

The conversion between each domain can be done using the same Montgomery operation, in particular $X' = MP(X, 2^{2n}(\text{mod } M), M)$ and $X = MP(X', 1, M)$, where $2^{2n}(\text{mod } M)$ can be precomputed. Despite the initial conversion cost, if we do many Montgomery multiplications followed by an inverse conversion, as in RSA, we obtain an advantage over ordinary multiplication.

Algorithm 1 shows the pseudocode for radix-2 Montgomery multiplication, where we choose $n = \lfloor \log_2 M \rfloor + 1$, which is the precision of M.

The verification of the above algorithm is given below: Let us define $S[i]$ as

$$S[i] \equiv \frac{1}{2^i} \left(\sum_{j=0}^{i-1} x_j \cdot 2^j \right) \cdot Y \pmod{M} \tag{2}$$

Algorithm 2. The Multiple-Word Radix-2 Montgomery Multiplication Algorithm

---

Require: odd $M, n = \lfloor \log_2 M \rfloor + 1$, word size w, $e = \lceil \frac{n+1}{w} \rceil$, $X = \sum_{i=0}^{n-1} x_i \cdot 2^i$,
$\quad Y = \sum_{j=0}^{e-1} Y^{(j)} \cdot 2^{w \cdot j}$, $M = \sum_{j=0}^{e-1} M^{(j)} \cdot 2^{w \cdot j}$, with $0 \le X, Y < M$

Ensure: $Z = \sum_{j=0}^{e-1} S^{(j)} \cdot 2^{w \cdot j} = MP(X, Y, M) \equiv X \cdot Y \cdot 2^{-n} \pmod{M}, 0 \le Z < 2M$

1: $S = 0$ *— initialize all words of S*
2: **for** $i = 0$ to $n - 1$ step 1 **do**
3:     $q_i = (x_i \cdot Y_0^{(0)}) \oplus S_0^{(0)}$
4:     $(C^{(1)}, S^{(0)}) = x_i \cdot Y^{(0)} + q_i \cdot M^{(0)} + S^{(0)}$
5:     **for** $j = 1$ to $e - 1$ step 1 **do**
6:        $(C^{(j+1)}, S^{(j)}) = C^{(j)} + x_i \cdot Y^{(j)} + q_i \cdot M^{(j)} + S^{(j)}$
7:        $S^{(j-1)} = (S_0^{(j)}, S_{w-1..1}^{(j-1)})$
8:     **end for**
9:     $S^{(e-1)} = (C_0^{(e)}, S_{w-1..1}^{(e-1)})$
10: **end for**
11: return $Z = S$

---

with $S[0] = 0$. Then, $S[n] \equiv X \cdot Y \cdot 2^{-n} \pmod{M} = MP(X, Y, M)$. Thus, $S[n]$ can be computed iteratively using dependence:

$$S[i+1] \equiv \frac{1}{2^{i+1}} \left(\sum_{j=0}^{i} x_j \cdot 2^j \right) \cdot Y \equiv \frac{1}{2^{i+1}} \left(\sum_{j=0}^{i-1} x_j \cdot 2^j + x_i \cdot 2^i \right) \cdot Y \qquad (3a)$$

$$\equiv \frac{1}{2} \left(\frac{1}{2^i} \left(\sum_{j=0}^{i-1} x_j \cdot 2^j \right) \cdot Y + x_i \cdot Y \right) \equiv \frac{1}{2} (S[i] + x_i \cdot Y) \pmod{M}. \tag{3b}$$

Therefore depending on the parity of $S[i] + x_i \cdot Y$, we compute $S[i+1]$ as

$$S[i+1] = \frac{S[i] + x_i \cdot Y}{2} \quad \text{or} \quad \frac{S[i] + x_i \cdot Y + M}{2}, \tag{4}$$

to make the numerator divisible by 2. Since $Y < M$ and $S[0] = 0$, one has $0 \le S[i] < 2M$ for all $0 \le i < n$. Thus only one conditional subtraction is necessary to bring $S[n]$ to the required range $0 \le S[n] < M$. This subtraction will be omitted in the subsequent discussion since it is independent of the specific algorithm and architecture and can be treated as a part of post processing.

3   Optimizing MWR2MM Algorithm

In [4], Tenca and Koç proposed a scalable architecture based on the Multiple-Word Radix-2 Montgomery Multiplication Algorithm (MWR2MM), shown as Algorithm 2.

In Algorithm 2, the operand Y (multiplicand) is scanned word-by-word, and the operand X is scanned bit-by-bit. The operand length is n bits, and the

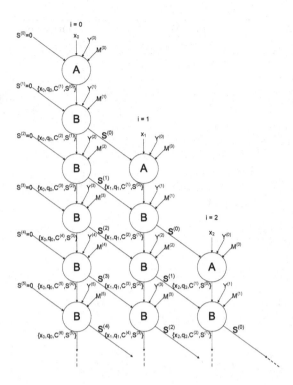

Fig. 1. The data dependency graph for original architecture of the MWR2MM Algorithm

wordlength is w bits. $e = \lceil \frac{n+1}{w} \rceil$ words are required to store S since its range is $[0, 2M - 1]$. The original M and Y are extended by one extra bit of 0 as the most significant bit. Presented as vectors, $M = (M^{(e-1)}, \ldots, M^{(1)}, M^{(0)})$, $Y = (Y^{(e-1)}, \ldots, Y^{(1)}, Y^{(0)})$, $S = (S^{(e-1)}, \ldots, S^{(1)}, S^{(0)})$, $X = (x_{n-1}, \ldots, x_1, x_0)$. The carry variable $C^{(j)}$ has two bits, as shown below. Assuming $C^{(0)} = 0$, each subsequent value of $C^{(j+1)}$ is given by $(C^{(j+1)}, S^{(j)}) = C^{(j)} + x_i \cdot Y^{(j)} + q_i \cdot M^{(j)} + S^{(j)}$. Assuming that $C^{(j)} \leq 3$, we obtain $(C^{(j+1)}, S^{(j)}) = C^{(j)} + x_i \cdot Y^{(j)} + q_i \cdot M^{(j)} + S^{(j)} \leq 3 + 3 \cdot (2^w - 1) = 3 \cdot 2^w \leq 2^{w+2} - 1$, and thus $C^{(j+1)} \leq 3$. Thus, by induction, $C^{(j)} \leq 3$ for any $0 \leq j \leq e$.

The dependency graph for the MWR2MM algorithm is shown in Figure 1. Each circle in the graph represents an atomic computation and is labeled according to the type of action performed. Task A consists of computing lines 2 and 2 in Algorithm 2. Task B consists of computing lines 2 and 2 in Algorithm 2. The computation of each column ends with Task C consisting of line 2 of Algorithm 2.

The data dependencies between operations within the loop for j makes it impossible to execute the steps in a single j loop in parallel. However, parallelism is possible among executions in different i loops. In [4], Tenca and Koç suggested that each column in the graph may be computed by a separate processing element

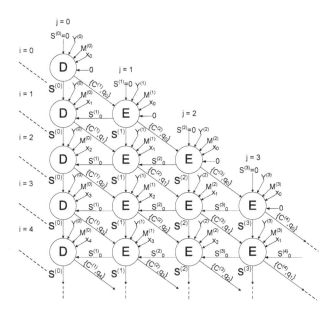

Fig. 2. The data dependency graph of the proposed new architecture of MWR2MM Algorithm

(PE), and the data generated from one PE may be passed into another PE in a pipelined fashion. Following this way, all atomic computations represented by circles in the same row can be processed concurrently. The processing of each column takes $e + 1$ clock cycles (1 clock cycle for Task A, $e - 1$ clock cycles for Task B, and 1 clock cycle for Task C). Because there is a delay of 2 clock cycles between processing a column for x_i and a column for x_{i+1}, the minimum computation time T (in clock cycles) is $T = 2n + e - 1$ given $P_{max} = \lceil \frac{e+1}{2} \rceil$ PEs are implemented to work in parallel. In this configuration, after $e + 1$ clock cycles, PE#0 switches from executing column 0 to executing column P_{max}. After additional two clock cycles, PE#1 switches from executing column 1 to executing column $P_{max} + 1$, etc.

The only option for improving the performance of Algorithm 2 seems to reduce the delay between the processing of two i loops that are next to each other. Here we present a new data dependency graph of MWR2MM algorithm in Figure 2. The circle in the graph represents an atomic computation. Task D consists of three steps, the computation of q_i corresponding to line 2 of Algorithm 2, the calculation of Equations 5a and 5b with $j = 0$ and $C^{(0)} = 0$, and the selection between two sets of results from Equations 5a and 5b using an additional input $S_0^{(j+1)}$ which becomes available at the end of the processing time for Task D.

$$(CO^{(j+1)}, SO_{w-1}^{(j)}, S_{w-2..0}^{(j)}) = (1, S_{w-1..1}^{(j)}) + C^{(j)} + x_i \cdot Y^{(j)} + q_i \cdot M^{(j)} \quad (5a)$$
$$(CE^{(j+1)}, SE_{w-1}^{(j)}, S_{w-2..0}^{(j)}) = (0, S_{w-1..1}^{(j)}) + C^{(j)} + x_i \cdot Y^{(j)} + q_i \cdot M^{(j)} \quad (5b)$$

Algorithm 3. Pseudocode of the processing element PE#j of type E

Require: Inputs: q_i, x_i, $C^{(j)}$, $Y^{(j)}$, $M^{(j)}$, $S_0^{(j+1)}$

Ensure: Output: $C^{(j+1)}$, $S_0^{(j)}$

1: $(CO^{(j+1)}, SO_{w-1}^{(j)}, S_{w-2..0}^{(j)}) = (1, S_{w-1..1}^{(j)}) + C^{(j)} + x_i \cdot Y^{(j)} + q_i \cdot M^{(j)}$

2: $(CE^{(j+1)}, SE_{w-1}^{(j)}, S_{w-2..0}^{(j)}) = (0, S_{w-1..1}^{(j)}) + C^{(j)} + x_i \cdot Y^{(j)} + q_i \cdot M^{(j)}$

3: **if** $(S_0^{(j+1)} = 1)$ **then**

4:     $C^{(j+1)} = CO^{(j+1)}$

5:     $S^{(j)} = (SO_{w-1}^{(j)}, S_{w-2..0}^{(j)})$

6: **else**

7:     $C^{(j+1)} = CE^{(j+1)}$

8:     $S^{(j)} = (SE_{w-1}^{(j)}, S_{w-2..0}^{(j)})$

9: **end if**

Task E corresponds to the calculation of Equations 5a and 5b, and the selection between two sets of results using an additional input $S_0^{(j+1)}$. The feedback in the new graph is used for making the selection in the last step of Tasks D and E, and will be discussed in detail as we proceed. Similar to the previous graph, the computation of each column in Figure 2 can be processed by one separate PE. However there is only one clock cycle latency between the processing of two adjacent columns in the new data dependency graph.

The two data dependency graphs map the Algorithm 2 following different strategies. In Figure 1, each column maps to one single i loop and covers all the internal j loops corresponding to this i loop. In contrast, each column in Figure 2 maps to one single j loop and covers this particular part of all external i loops.

Following the data dependency graph in Figure 2, we present a new hardware architecture of MWR2MM algorithm in Figure 3, which can finish the computation of Montgomery multiplication of n-bit precision in $n + e - 1$ clock cycles. Furthermore, our design is simpler than the approach given in [4] in terms of control logic and data path logic.

As shown in Figure 3(d), the architecture consists of e PEs that form a computation chain. Each PE focuses on the computation of a specific word in vector S, i.e., PE #j only works on $S^{(j)}$. In other words, each PE corresponds to one fixed round in loop for j in Algorithm 2. Meanwhile, all PEs scan different bits of operand X at the same time.

In order to avoid an extra clock cycle delay due to the right shift, each PE#j first computes two versions of $C^{(j+1)}$ and $S_{w-1}^{(j)}$ simultaneously, as shown in Equations 5a and 5b. One version assumes that $S_0^{(j+1)}$ is equal to one, and the other assumes that this bit is equal to zero. Both results are stored in registers, and the bit $S_0^{(j)}$ is forwarded to the previous stage, $j - 1$. At the same moment, the bit $S_0^{(j+1)}$ becomes available and PE#j can output the correct $C^{(j+1)}$ and use the correct $S^{(j)}$. These computations are summarized by the pseudocode given in Algorithm 3.

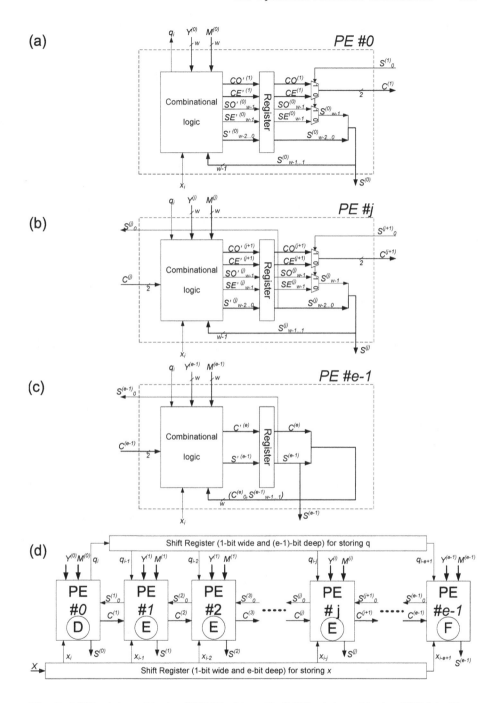

Fig. 3. (a)The internal logic of PE#0 of type D. (b)The internal logic of PE#j of type E. (c)The internal logic of PE#$e - 1$ of type F. (d)New hardware architecture of the MWR2MM algorithm.

The internal logic of all PEs is same except the two PEs residing at the head and tail of the chain. PE#0, shown in Figure 3(a) as the cell of type D, is also responsible for computing q_i and has no $C^{(j)}$ input. PE#$(e-1)$, shown in Figure 3(c) as type F, has only one branch inside because the most significant bit of $S^{(e-1)}$ is equivalent to $C_0^{(e)}$ and is known already at the end of the previous clock cycle (see line 2 of Algorithm 2).

Two shift registers parallel to PEs carry x_i and q_i, respectively, and do a right shift every clock cycle. Before the start of multiplication, all registers, including the two shift registers and the internal registers of PEs, should be reset to zeros. All the bits of X will be pushed into the shift register one by one from the head and followed by zeros. The second shift register will be filled with values of q_i computed by PE#0 of type D. All the registers can be enabled at the same time after the multiplication process starts because the additions of $Y^{(j)}$ and $M^{(j)}$ will be nullified by the zeros in the two shift registers before the values of x_0 and q_0 reach a given stage.

Readers must have noticed that the internal register of PE #j keeps the value of $S^{(j)}$ that should be shifted one bit to the right for the next round calculation. This feature gives us two options to generate the final product.

1. We can store the contents of $S_{w-1..0}^{(j)}$ clock cycle by clock cycle after PE #0 finishes the calculation of the most significant bit of X, i.e. after n clock cycles, and then do a right shift on them, or

2. We can do one more round of calculation right after the round with the most significant bit of X. To do so, we need to push one bit of "0" into two shift registers to make sure that the additions of $Y^{(j)}$ and $M^{(j)}$ are nullified. Then we go to collect the contents of $S_{w-1..0}^{(j)}$ clock cycle by clock cycle after PE #0 finishes its extra round of calculation. We concatenate these words to form the final product.

After the final product is generated, we have two methods to collect them. If the internal registers of PEs are disabled after the end of computation, the entire result can be read in parallel after $n + e - 1$ clock cycles. Alternatively, the results can be read word by word in e clock cycles by connecting internal registers of PEs into a shift register chain.

The exact way of collecting the results depends strongly on the application. For example in the implementation of RSA, a parallel output would be preferred, while in the ECC computations, reading results word by word may be more appropriate.

4   High-Radix Architecture of Montgomery Multiplication

The concepts illustrated in Figure 2 and 3 can be adopted to design high-radix hardware architecture of Montgomery multiplication. Instead of scanning one bit of X, several bits of X can be scanned together for high-radix cases. Assuming we

---

Algorithm 4. The Multiple-Word Radix-4 Montgomery Multiplication Algorithm

---

Require: odd $M, n = \lfloor \log_2 M \rfloor + 1$, word size w, $e = \lceil \frac{n+1}{w} \rceil$, $X = \sum_{i=0}^{\lceil \frac{n}{2} \rceil - 1} x^{(i)} \cdot 4^i$,
$Y = \sum_{j=0}^{e-1} Y^{(j)} \cdot 2^{w \cdot j}$, $M = \sum_{j=0}^{e-1} M^{(j)} \cdot 2^{w \cdot j}$, with $0 \leq X, Y < M$

Ensure: $Z = \sum_{j=0}^{e-1} S^{(j)} \cdot 2^{w \cdot j} = MP(X, Y, M) \equiv X \cdot Y \cdot 2^{-n} \pmod{M}, 0 \leq Z < 2M$

1: $S = 0$ — *initialize all words of S*
2: **for** $i = 0$ to $n - 1$ step 2 **do**
3:      $q^{(i)} = Func(S_{1..0}^{(0)}, x^{(i)}, Y_{1..0}^{(0)}, M_{1..0}^{(0)})$ — $q^{(i)}$ *and* $x^{(i)}$ *are 2-bit long*
4:      $(C^{(1)}, S^{(0)}) = S^{(0)} + x^{(i)} \cdot Y^{(0)} + q^{(i)} \cdot M^{(0)}$ — *C is 3-bit long*
5:      **for** $j = 1$ to $e - 1$ step 1 **do**
6:         $(C^{(j+1)}, S^{(j)}) = C^{(j)} + S^{(j)} + x^{(i)} \cdot Y^{(j)} + q^{(i)} \cdot M^{(j)}$
7:         $S^{(j-1)} = (S_{1..0}^{(j)}, S_{w-1..2}^{(j-1)})$
8:      **end for**
9:      $S^{(e-1)} = (C_{1..0}^{(e)}, S_{w-1..2}^{(e-1)})$
10: **end for**
11: return $Z = S$

---

want to scan k bits of X at one time, 2^k branches should be covered at the same time to maximize the performance. Considering the value of 2^k increases exponentially as k increments, the design will become impractical beyond radix-4.

Following the same definitions regarding words as in Algorithm 2, we have the radix-4 version of Montgomery multiplication shown as Algorithm 4. We scan two bits in one step this time instead of one bit as in Algorithm 2. The radix-4 version design still has e PEs working parallel but it takes $\frac{n}{2} + e - 1$ clock cycles to process n-bit Montgomery multiplication.

The value of $q^{(i)}$ at line 4 of Algorithm 4 is defined by a function involving $S_{1..0}^{(0)}$, $x^{(i)}$, $Y_{1..0}^{(0)}$ and $M_{1..0}^{(0)}$ such that the Equation 6 is satisfied. The carry variable C has 3 bits, which can be proven in a similar way to the proof for the size of $C^{(j)}$ for the case of radix 2.

$$S_{1..0}^{(0)} + x^{(i)} \cdot Y_{1..0}^{(0)} + q^{(i)} \cdot M_{1..0}^{(0)} = 0 \pmod{4} \tag{6}$$

Since M is odd, $M_0^{(0)} = 1$. From Equation 6, we can derive

$$q_0^{(i)} = S_0^{(0)} \oplus (x_0^{(i)} \cdot Y_0^{(0)}) \tag{7}$$

where $x_0^{(i)}$ and $q_0^{(i)}$ denote the least significant bit of $x^{(i)}$ and $q^{(i)}$ respectively. The bit $q_1^{(i)}$ is a function of only seven one-bit variables and can be computed using a relatively small look-up table.

The multiplication by 3, necessary to compute $x^{(i)} \cdot Y^{(j)}$ and $q^{(i)} \cdot M^{(j)}$ can be done on the fly or avoided by using Booth recoding as discussed in [6]. Using the Booth recoding would require adjusting the algorithm and architecture to deal with signed operands.

Furthermore we can generalize Algorithm 4 to handle MWR2^{k}MM algorithm. In general, $x^{(i)}$ and $q^{(i)}$ are both k-bit variables. $x^{(i)}$ is a k-bit digit of X, and $q^{(i)}$ is defined by Equation 8.

$$S^{(0)} + x^{(i)} \cdot Y^{(0)} + q^{(i)} \cdot M^{(0)} = 0 \quad (\mathrm{mod}\ 2^k) \tag{8}$$

Nevertheless the implementation of this architecture for $k > 2$ would be impractical in majority of applications.

5   Hardware Implementation and Comparison of Different Architectures

In this section, we compare and contrast four major types of architectures for Montgomery multiplication from the point of view of the number of PEs and latency in clock cycles. In the architecture by Tenca and Koç, the number of PEs can vary between one and $P_{max} = \lceil \frac{e+1}{2} \rceil$. The larger the number of PEs the smaller the latency, but the larger the circuit area, which allows the designer to choose the best possible trade-off between these two requirements. The architecture of Tenca and Koç is often referred as a scalable architecture. Nevertheless, the scalability of this architecture is not perfect. In order to process operands with different number of bits, the sizes of shift registers surrounding processing units must change, and the operation of the internal state machines must be modified, which makes it impractical to utilize the same circuit for different operand sizes.

The architecture by Harris et al. [7] has the similar scalability as the original architecture by Tenca and Koç [4]. Instead of making right-shift of the intermediate $S^{(j)}$ values, their architecture left-shifts the Y and M to avoid the data dependency between $S^{(j)}$ and $S^{(j-1)}$. For the number of processing elements optimized for minimum latency, the architecture by Harris reduces the number of clock cycles from $2n + e - 1$ (for Tenca and Koç [4]) to $n + 2e - 1$. Similar to the original architecture, changing n or w requires changes in the sizes of shift registers and/or memories surrounding processing units, and the operation of the internal state machines, which makes it impractical to utilize the same circuit for different operand sizes.

Our architecture and the architecture of McIvor et al. both have fixed size, optimized for minimum latency. Our architecture consists of e processing units, each operating on operands of the size of a single word. The architecture of McIvor et al. consists of just one type of the processing unit, operating on multi-precision numbers represented in the carry-save form. The final result of the McIvor architecture, obtained after n clock cycles is expressed in the carry-save form. In order to convert this result to the non-redundant binary representation, additional e clock cycles are required, which makes the total latency of this architecture comparable to the latency of our architecture. In the sequence of modular multiplications, such as the one required for modular exponentiation, the conversion to the non-redundant representation can be delayed to the very end of computations, and thus each subsequent Montgomery multiplication can start every n clock cycles. The similar property can be implemented in our architecture by starting a new multiplication immediately after the first processing unit, PE#0, has released the first least significant word of the final result.

Our architecture is scalable in terms of the value of the word size w. The larger w, the smaller the maximum clock frequency. The latency expressed in the number of clock cycles is equal to $n + \lceil((n + 1)/w)\rceil - 1$, and is almost independent of w for $w \geq 16$. Since actual FPGA-based platforms, such as SRC-6 used in our implementations, have a fixed target clock frequency, this target clock frequency determines the optimum value of w. The area of the circuit is almost independent of w (for sufficiently large w, e.g., $w \geq 16$), as the size of each cell is proportional to w, and the number of cells is inversely proportional to w. Additionally, the same HDL code can be used for different values of the operand size n and the parameter w, with only a minor change in the values of respective constants.

The new architecture has been implemented in Verilog HDL and its code verified using reference software implementation. The results matched perfectly.

We have selected Xilinx Virtex-II6000FF1517-4 FPGA device used in the SRC-6 reconfigurable computer for a prototype implementation. The synthesis tool was Synplify Pro 8.1 and the Place and Route tool was Xilinx ISE 8.1.

We have implemented four different sizes of multipliers, 1024, 2048, 3072 and 4096 bits, respectively, in the radix-2 case using Verilog-HDL to verify our approach. The resource utilization on a single FPGA is shown in Table 2. For comparison, we have implemented the multipliers of these four sizes following the hardware architectures described in [4] as well. In both approaches, the word length is fixed at 16 bits. Because the frequency of FPGA on SRC-6 platform is fixed at 100MHz, we targeted this frequency when we implemented the design. At first, we selected 32 bits as the word length and it turned out the max frequency of the multiplier was 87.7 MHz. So, we halved the word length to meet the timing on SRC-6 platform. In order to maximize the performance, we used the maximum number of PEs in both approaches.

Additionally, we have implemented the approach based on CSA (Carry Save Addition) from [11] as a reference, showing how the MWR2MM architecture compares to other types of architectures in terms of resource utilization and performance.

Compared to the design by Harris *et al.* in [7], our architecture accomplishes the same objective, however, using a totally different and never published before approach. The exact quantitative comparison between our architecture and the architecture by Harris [7] would require implementing both architectures using exactly the same FPGA device, environment and design style.

From Table 2, we can see that our architecture gives a speed up by a factor of almost two compared to the architecture by Tenca *et al.* [4] in terms of latency expressed in the number of clock cycles. The minimum clock period is comparable in both cases and the extra propagation delay in our architecture is introduced by the multiplexers directly following the Registers, as shown in Figures 3(a) and (b). At the same time both architectures almost tie in terms of resource

Table 2. Comparison of hardware resource utilization and performance for the implementations using Xilinx Virtex-II6000FF1517-4 FPGA

		1024-bit	2048-bit	3072-bit	4096-bit
Architecture of	Max Freq.(MHz)	110.1			
Tenca & Koç [4]	Min Latency (clks)	2113	4225	6337	8449
(radix-2)	Min Latency (μs)	19.186	38.363	57.540	76.717
(with the # of	Area (Slices)	3,937	7,756	11,576	15,393
PEs optimized for	MinLatency×Area	75,535	297,543	666,083	1,180,905
minimum latency)	(μs×slices)				
	Max Freq.(MHz)	123.6	110.6	116.7	92.81
	Min Latency (clks)	1025	2049	3073	4097
Architecture of	Min Latency (μs)	8.294	18.525	26.323	44.141
McIvor *et al.* [11]	Area (Slices)	6,241	12,490	18,728	25,474
(radix-2)	MinLatency×Area (μs×slices)	51,763	231,377	492,977	1,124,448
	Latency×Area Gain vs. Tenca & Koç (%)	31.47	22.24	25.99	4.78
	Max Freq.(MHz)	100.0			
	Min Latency (clks)	1088	2176	3264	4352
Our Proposed	Min Latency (μs)	10.880	21.760	32.640	43.520
Architecture	Area (Slices)	4,178	8,337	12,495	16,648
(radix-2)	MinLatency×Area (μs×slices)	45,457	181,413	407,837	724,521
	Latency×Area Gain vs. Tenca & Koç (%)	39.82	39.03	38.77	38.65

utilization expressed in the number of CLB slices, in spite of our architecture using almost twice as many processing elements (PEs). This result is caused by the fact that our processing element shown in Figure 3(b) is substantially simpler than processing element in the architecture by Tenca *et al.* [4]. The major difference is that PE in [4] is responsible for calculating not only one, but multiple columns of the dependency graph shown in Figure 1, and it must switch among Tasks A, B and C, depending on the phase of calculations. In contrast, in our architecture, each processing element is responsible for only one column of the dependency graph in Figure 2, and is responsible for only one Task, either D or E or F. Additionally in [4], the words $Y^{(j)}$ and $M^{(j)}$ must rotate with regard to PEs, which further complicates the control logic.

Compared to the architecture by McIvor *et al.* [11], our architecture has a latency (expressed in the number of clock cycles) comparable for radix-2, and almost twice as low for radix-4. At the same time, the resource utilization, expressed in the number of CLB slices, is smaller in our design with radix-2 by about 33%.

For radix-4 case, we only have implemented a 1024-bit precision Montgomery multiplier as a showcase. The word-length is the same as in radix-2 case, 16 bits. One radix-4 1024-bit precision core takes 9,471(28%) slices and has a latency of

Table 3. Comparison of the radix-2 and radix-4 versions of our architecture (n=1024, w=16) for the implementation using Xilinx Virtex-II6000FF1517-4 FPGA

	Max Freq. (MHz)	Min Latency (clocks)	Min Latency (μs)	Slices
radix-2	100	1088	10.880	4,178(12%)
radix-4	94	576	6.128	9,471(28%)

576 clock cycles. Further, the max frequency of the radix-4 case drops to 94MHz. These figures fall within our expectations because radix-4 PE has 4 internal branches, which doubles the quantity of branches of radix-2 version, and some small design tweaks were required to redeem the propagation delay increase caused by more complicated combinational logic. Some of these optimization techniques are listed below,

1. At line 4 of Algorithm 4 there is an addition of three operands whose length is w-bit or larger. To reduce the propagation delay of this step, we precomputed the value of $x^{(i)} \cdot Y^{(j)} + q^{(i)} \cdot M^{(j)}$ one clock cycle before it arrives at the corresponding PE.
2. For the first PE in which the update of $S^{(0)}$ and the evaluation of $q^{(i)}$ happen in the same clock cycle, we can not precompute the value of $x^{(i)} \cdot Y^{(0)} + q^{(i)} \cdot M^{(0)}$ in advance. To overcome this difficulty, we precompute four possible values of $x^{(i)} \cdot Y^{(0)} + q^{(i)} \cdot M^{(0)}$ corresponding to $q^{(i)} = 0, 1, 2, 3$, and make a decision at the end of the clock cycle based on the real value of $q^{(i)}$.

As mentioned at the beginning of Section 4, the hardware implementation of our architecture beyond radix-4 is no longer viable considering the large resource cost for covering all the 2^k branches in one clock cycle, and the need to perform multiplications of words by numbers in the range $0..2^k - 1$.

6   Conclusion

In this paper, we present an optimized hardware architecture to implement the word-based MWR2MM and MWR4MM algorithms for Montgomery multiplication. The structure is scalable to fit multi-precision Montgomery multipliers, the approach is easy to be realized in hardware, and the design is space efficient. One n-bit precision Montgomery multiplication takes $n + e - 1$ clock cycles for the radix-2 version, and $\frac{n}{2} + e - 1$ clock cycles for the radix-4 version. These latencies amount to almost a factor of two speed-up over now-classical designs by Tenca, Koç, and Todorov presented at CHES 1999 (radix-2) [4] and CHES 2001 (radix-4) [6]. This speed-up in terms of latency in clock cycles has been accomplished with comparable maximum clock frequencies and less than 10% area penalty, when both architectures have been implemented using Xilinx Virtex-II 6000 FPGA. Although our architecture is not scalable in the same sense as architecture by Tenca and Koç, it performs better when both architectures are optimized for minimum latency. It is also easily parameterizable, so the same generic code with different values of parameters can be easily used for multiple operand sizes. Our radix-2 architecture guarantees also almost the same latency as the recent design by McIvor *et al.* [11], while outperforming this design in terms of the circuit area by at least 30% when implemented in Xilinx Virtex-II FPGA. Our architecture has been fully verified by modeling it in Verilog-HDL, and comparing its function vs. reference software implementation based on GMP. The code has been implemented using Xilinx Virtex-II 6000 FPGA and experimentally tested using SRC-6 reconfigurable computer.

Acknowledgements

The authors would like to acknowledge the contributions of Hoang Le and Ramakrishna Bachimanchi from George Mason University who provided results for their implementation of the Montgomery multiplier from [11].

References

1. Rivest, R.L., Shamir, A., Adleman, L.: A method for obtaining digital signatures and public-key cryptosystems. Communications of the ACM 21(2), 120–126 (1978)
2. Montgomery, P.L.: Modular multiplication without trial division. Mathematics of Computation 44(170), 519–521 (April 1985)
3. Gaj, K., et al.: Implementing the elliptic curve method of factoring in reconfigurable hardware. In: Goubin, L., Matsui, M. (eds.) CHES 2006. LNCS, vol. 4249, pp. 119–133. Springer, Heidelberg (2006)
4. Tenca, A.F., Koç, Ç.K.: A scalable architecture for Montgomery multiplication. In: Koç, Ç.K., Paar, C. (eds.) CHES 1999. LNCS, vol. 1717, pp. 94–108. Springer, Heidelberg (1999)
5. Tenca, A.F., Koç, Ç.K.: A scalable architecture for modular multiplication based on Montgomery's algorithm. IEEE Trans. Comput. 52(9), 1215–1221 (2003)
6. Tenca, A.F., Todorov, G., Koç, Ç.K.: High-radix design of a scalable modular multiplier. In: Koç, Ç.K., Naccache, D., Paar, C. (eds.) CHES 2001. LNCS, vol. 2162, pp. 185–201. Springer, Heidelberg (2001)
7. Harris, D., Krishnamurthy, R., Anders, M., Mathew, S., Hsu, S.: An improved unified scalable radix-2 Montgomery multiplier. In: Proc. the 17th IEEE Symposium on Computer Arithmetic (ARITH 17), June 2005, pp. 172–178 (2005)
8. Michalski, E.A., Buell, D.A.: A scalable architecture for RSA cryptography on large FPGAs. In: Proc. International Conference on Field Programmable Logic and Applications (FPL 2006), August 2006, pp. 145–152 (2006)
9. Koç, Ç.K., Acar, T., Kaliski Jr., B.S.: Analyzing and comparing Montgomery multiplication algorithms. IEEE Micro 16(3), 26–33 (1996)
10. McIvor, C., McLoone, M., McCanny, J.V.: High-radix systolic modular multiplication on reconfigurable hardware. In: Proc. IEEE International Conference on Field-Programmable Technology 2005 (FPT 2005), December 2005, pp. 13–18 (2005)
11. McIvor, C., McLoone, M., McCanny, J.V.: Modified Montgomery modular multiplication and RSA exponentiation techniques. IEE Proceedings – Computers and Digital Techniques 151(6), 402–408 (2004)

New Composite Operations and Precomputation Scheme for Elliptic Curve Cryptosystems over Prime Fields

Patrick Longa[1] and Ali Miri[2]

[1] Department of Electrical and Computer Engineering
University of Waterloo, Canada
plonga@uwaterloo.ca
[2] School of Information Technology and Engineering (SITE)
University of Ottawa, Canada
Ali.Miri@uottawa.ca

Abstract. We present a new methodology to derive faster composite operations of the form $dP + Q$, where d is a small integer ≥ 2, for generic ECC scalar multiplications over prime fields. In particular, we present an efficient Doubling-Addition (DA) operation that can be exploited to accelerate most scalar multiplication methods, including multiscalar variants. We also present a new precomputation scheme useful for window-based scalar multiplication that is shown to achieve the lowest cost among all known methods using only one inversion. In comparison to the remaining approaches that use none or several inversions, our scheme offers higher performance for most common I/M ratios. By combining the benefits of our precomputation scheme and the new DA operation, we can save up to 6.2% on the scalar multiplication using fractional wNAF.

Keywords: Elliptic curve cryptosystem, scalar multiplication, point operation, composite operation, precomputation scheme.

1 Introduction

Elliptic curve cryptography (ECC) was independently introduced by Koblitz and Miller in 1985. Since then, this public-key cryptosystem has attracted increasing attention due to its shorter key size requirement in comparison with other established systems such as RSA and DL-based cryptosystems. For instance, it is widely accepted that 160-bit ECC offers equivalent security to 1024-bit RSA. This significant difference makes ECC especially attractive for applications in constrained environments as shorter key sizes are translated to less power and storage requirements, and reduced computing times.

Scalar multiplication, denoted by kP, where k is the secret key (scalar) and P is a point on the elliptic curve, is the central operation of elliptic curve cryptosystems. Methods to efficiently compute such operation have traditionally exploited the binary expansion of numbers (e.g., NAF and wNAF). This is mainly due to

R. Cramer (Ed.): PKC 2008, LNCS 4939, pp. 229–247, 2008.

the fact that the binary expansion directly translates to computations using the simplest elementary ECC point operations, namely point doubling and addition.

However, recent developments in the field suggest that it is possible to use more complex operations to accelerate the scalar multiplication [4,7,8,24]. For instance, Ciet *et al* [4] introduced the ternary/binary method using radices 2 and 3 for the representation of the scalar. Dimitrov *et al* [7] proposed the double-base number system for the scalar multiplication using mixed powers of 2 and 3. Radix 5 was added to the previous approach by Mishra *et al* [21] to represent scalars with mixed powers of 2, 3 and 5. More recently, Longa and Miri [18] have proposed the multibase non-adjacent form (mbNAF) method, which uses a very efficient representation of integers using multiple bases. Efficiency of the previous methods strongly depends on the costs of such operations as tripling ($3P$, denoted by T) or quintupling ($5P$, denoted by Q) of a point, unified doubling-addition ($2P + Q$, denoted by DA), unified tripling-addition ($3P + Q$, denoted by TA), unified quintupling-addition ($5P + Q$, denoted by QA), among others. Thus, it is a critical task to reduce the computing cost of these operations, which are referred to as composite operations since they are inherently based on basic doubling and addition, to further speed up the execution time of the scalar multiplication.

In the first part, we propose a new technique to derive faster composite operations of the form $dP + Q$, where d is a small integer ≥ 2 and P, Q are points on the elliptic curve in Jacobian and affine coordinates, respectively. As pointed out, operations of this form are highly common in all known scalar multiplication methods, including multiscalar versions which are used in the ECDSA signature verification [12]. For instance, DA is a recurrent operation in NAF, wNAF and Shamir's trick, where each mixed Jacobian-affine addition is always computed right after a doubling. In addition to DA, TA is used in the double-base method [7], and TA and QA in the triple-base method [21] and mbNAF methods [16,18].

Our technique makes use of Meloni's idea of adding two points with the same z coordinates [19] (which we will refer to as special addition with identical z-coordinate) to have an iterative computation of the form $dP + Q = P + \ldots + P + P + (P+Q)$, which is computed backwards and where only the first addition shown in parentheses is computed with a traditional mixed addition. Every extra addition can then be efficiently computed with the addition with identical z-coordinate. We show that our new composite operations are more efficient than formulas using the cheapest operations existent in current literature. See [17] for the state-of-the-art point formulas in Jacobian coordinates.

In the second part, we modify the previous methodology to yield a new scheme for the precomputation of points in window-based methods such as wNAF and fractional wNAF (denoted by Frac-wNAF). Using pre-stored points is a practical technique to accelerate the scalar multiplication when there is extra memory available. However, for scalar multiplications kP with P unknown, the precomputation of such points is necessarily done on-line and its time execution included in the whole time estimation of the scalar multiplication. Examples of this case can be found during decryption in the ElGamal encryption scheme or in the Diffie-Hellman key exchange. Thus, it is crucial to reduce the time for the pre-computation to boost the savings achieved by window-based methods.

Given that precomputations follow the form $d_i P$, where d_i are the odd integers in the range $[3, m]$ with $m \geq 3$, we modify our original approach to the iterative computation of the form $d_i P = 2P + \ldots + 2P + 2P + 2P + P$, which is again computed backwards, and requires one point doubling followed by cheaper additions with identical z-coordinate. Following, and to keep advantage of the efficient mixed addition during the scalar multiplication, points are converted to affine representation using the well-known Montgomery's method which permits to reduce the number of expensive inversions to only one. Moreover, this method is further sped up by efficiently using values computed during the first stage of our methodology. For the latter, two variants with different memory requirements are presented, which will be shown to be suitable for different window widths.

Our precomputation scheme is compared with the best previous approaches using only one inversion, and shown to deliver the lowest cost. In comparison to methods using none or several inversions, our scheme is shown to offer the highest performance for most common I/M ratios.

Our work is organized as follows. In Section 2, we detail some background about ECC over prime fields. Then, we present our methodology based on the special addition with identical z-coordinate, and apply it to derive efficient composite operations of the form $dP + Q$, whose costs are compared to previous formulae right after. In Section 4, a variant of the previous methodology is used to build a new precomputation scheme for window-based scalar multiplications. The cost and memory requirements of our scheme are then discussed and compared with previous efforts. Some conclusions summarizing the contributions of this work are presented at the end.

2   Preliminaries

An elliptic curve E over a prime field $\mathbb{F}_p$ (denoted by $E(\mathbb{F}_p)$) is defined by the reduced Weierstrass equation [12]:

$$E : \ y^2 = x^3 + ax + b. \tag{1}$$

Where: $a, b \in \mathbb{F}_p$ and $\triangle = 4a^3 + 27b^2 \neq 0$.

The set of pairs (x, y) that solves (1), where $x, y \in \mathbb{F}_p$, and the point at infinity $\mathcal{O}$, which is the identify for the group law, form an *abelian* group $(E(\mathbb{F}_p), +)$, over which the ECC computations are performed.

The main operation in ECC is known as scalar multiplication, which is denoted by $Q = kP$, where P and Q are points in $E(\mathbb{F}_p)$, and k is the secret scalar.

The simplest representation of points on the elliptic curve E with two coordinates (x, y) , namely affine coordinates (denoted by $\mathcal{A}$), introduces field inversions into the computation of point doubling and addition. Inversions over prime fields are the most expensive field operation and are avoided as much as possible.

Although their relative cost depends on the characteristics of a particular implementation, it has been observed that, especially in the case of efficient forms for the prime p as recommended by [11], the inversion can result as computationally expensive as $1I > 30M$. For instance, benchmarks presented by [15] and [2,12] show I/M ratios between 30-40 and 50-100, respectively.

Projective coordinates (X, Y, Z) solve the previous problem by adding the third coordinate Z to replace inversions with a few other field operations. The foundation of these inversion-free coordinate systems can be explained by the concept of *equivalence class*, which is defined in the following in the context of Jacobian coordinates $\mathcal{J}$, a special case of projective coordinates that has yielded very efficient point formulae [10].

Given a prime field $\mathbb{F}_p$, there is an equivalence relation $\equiv$ among non-zero triplets over $\mathbb{F}_p$, such that [1]:

$$(X_1, Y_1, Z_1) \equiv (X_2, Y_2, Z_2) \Leftrightarrow X_1 = \lambda^2 X_2, \ Y_1 = \lambda^3 Y_2 \text{ and } Z_1 = \lambda Z_2, \text{ for some } \lambda \in \mathbb{F}_p^*.$$

Thus, the equivalence class of a *(Jacobian) projective point*, denoted by $(X : Y : Z)$, is:

$$(X, Y, Z) = \{\lambda^2 X, \lambda^3 Y, \lambda Z) : \lambda \in \mathbb{F}_p^*\}. \tag{2}$$

It is important to remark that any (X, Y, Z) in the equivalence class (2) can be used as a representative of a given projective (Jacobian) point.

In the following, we succinctly summarize costs of the improved formulae in $\mathcal{J}$ introduced by [17], which applied an effective technique to speed up the traditional point operations. The improved formulae will be later used for comparison with our new composite operations in Section 3. For further details about point formulae the reader is referred to [17].

The cost of using the Jacobian representation for the doubling formula has been found to be $2M + 8S$ (reduced from the traditional $4M + 6S$). When w successive executions of several doublings are used, the cost is $(3w)M + (5w+2)S$ by combining the strategy in [17] to accelerate operations with the approach by [14], which means that doublings are performed with only $3M + 5S$, with exception of the first one that costs $3M + 7S$.

Also, it is important to note that it has been suggested that the parameter a (see (1)) be fixed at -3 for efficiency purposes. In fact, most curves recommended by public-key standards [13] use $a = -3$, which has been shown to not impose significant restrictions to the cryptosystem [3]. In this case, the cost of point doubling is reduced to only $3M + 5S$.

In the remainder of this work, we will refer to the *special case* when $a = -3$, and the *general case* when the parameter is not fixed and can be any value in the field.

In the case of addition, representing one of the points in $\mathcal{J}$ and the other in $\mathcal{A}$ has yielded the most efficient addition formula, which is known as mixed Jacobian-affine addition and presents a cost of $8M + 3S$ [5]. In [17], the cost of this operation was reduced further to only $7M + 4S$. If one considers both points to be added in $\mathcal{J}$, then the cost is $12M + 4S$ (reduced to $11M + 5S$ by [17]). We will refer to the latter as general addition in $\mathcal{J}$.

In the case of the tripling, Longa and Miri improved the formula proposed by [7] and reduced its cost from $10M + 6S$ to $6M + 10S$ in the general case, and to only $7M + 7S$ if one fixes $a = -3$ [17]. Similarly, an efficient quintupling was presented by the same authors [18] with costs of $10M + 14S$ in the general case and only $11M + 11S$ when $a = -3$, improving the formulae by [21] that cost $15M + 10S$ and $15M + 8S$ for the corresponding cases.

Variants to the $\mathcal{J}$ have also been proposed. In particular, the four-tuple (X, Y, Z, aZ^4) and five-tuple (X, Y, Z, Z^2, Z^3), known as modified Jacobian $(\mathcal{J}^m)$ and Chudnovsky $(\mathcal{C})$ coordinates, respectively, permit to save some operations by passing recurrent values between point operations. Also, a technique that combines different representations (known as mixed coordinates) to yield efficient schemes for the scalar multiplication including precomputation was presented by [5]. We discuss the application of these mixed representations in Section 4. The reader is referred to [1,5] for further details.

3   Composite Operations $dP + Q$

Our strategy to yield cheaper composite operations of the form $dP + Q$ is based on the efficient use of the new addition formula with identical z-coordinate introduced by Meloni [19], which is described in the following.

Let $P = (X_1, Y_1, Z)$ and $Q = (X_2, Y_2, Z)$ be two points with the same z coordinates in $\mathcal{J}$ on the elliptic curve E. The addition $P + Q = (X_3, Y_3, Z_3)$ can be obtained as follows:

$$
\begin{aligned}
X_3 &= (Y_2 - Y_1)^2 - (X_2 - X_1)^3 - 2X_1(X_2 - X_1)^2 \\
Y_3 &= (Y_2 - Y_1)(X_1(X_2 - X_1)^2 - X_3) - Y_1(X_2 - X_1)^3 \\
Z_3 &= Z(X_2 - X_1).
\end{aligned}
\tag{3}
$$

This new addition only costs $5M + 2S$, which represents a significant reduction in comparison with $7M + 4S$ corresponding to the mixed Jacobian-affine addition. Sadly, it is not possible to directly replace traditional additions with this special operation since, obviously, it is expected that additions are computed over operands with different z coordinates during the scalar multiplication.

The author in [19] applied his formula to the context of scalar multiplication with star addition chains, where the particular sequence of operations allows the replacement of each traditional addition by (3). However, we noticed that the new addition can in fact be applied to a wider context with traditional scalar multiplication methods. In the following, we develop faster composite operations by exploiting the advantages of this special addition on ECC using generic scalar multiplications over prime fields.

3.1 Our Methodology

We propose to compute $dP + Q$ as follows:

$$dP + Q = P + \ldots + P + P + (P + Q), \qquad (4)$$

where d is a small integer ≥ 2, and P, Q are points in $\mathcal{J}$ and $\mathcal{A}$ on $E(\mathbb{F}_p)$, respectively.

Strategy (4) would lead to high costs if computed with mixed and general additions. However, we will show in the following that only the first addition in parentheses needs to be computed with a mixed addition. Then, every extra addition can be computed with (3).

First, we compute $P + Q = (X_1, Y_1, Z_1) + (X_2, Y_2) = (X_3, Y_3, Z_3)$ as mixed Jacobian-affine addition with the following [17]:

$$X_3 = 4(Z_1^3 Y_2 - Y_1)^2 - 4(Z_1^2 X_2 - X_1)^3 - 8X_1(Z_1^2 X_2 - X_1)^2$$
$$Y_3 = 2(Z_1^3 Y_2 - Y_1)(4X_1(Z_1^2 X_2 - X_1)^2 - X_3) - 8Y_1(Z_1^2 X_2 - X_1)^3$$
$$Z_3 = 2Z_1(Z_1^2 X_2 - X_1) = (Z_1 + Z_1^2 X_2 - X_1)^2 - Z_1^2 - (Z_1^2 X_2 - X_1)^2. \quad (5)$$

The main observation from (5) is that if we assume the next new representation for P:

$$(X_1^{(1)}, Y_1^{(1)}, Z_1^{(1)}) = (4X_1(Z_1^2 X_2 - X_1)^2, 8Y_1(Z_1^2 X_2 - X_1)^3, 2Z_1(Z_1^2 X_2 - X_1)) \equiv (X_1, Y_1, Z_1) \quad (6)$$

we can use the special addition (3) to perform the next addition between P and $(P + Q)$ because both points would have the same z coordinate. It is important to note that the equivalence relation in (6) holds by fixing $\lambda = Z_1^2 X_2 - X_1$ in the equivalence class for $\mathcal{J}$ given in (2). Most importantly, the equivalent point $(X_1^{(1)}, Y_1^{(1)}, Z_1^{(1)})$ does not require any extra computation because its coordinates have already been computed in (5).

Similarly, every extra addition with P according to (4) can be performed with the special addition (3) as P always has an equivalent point with the same z coordinate as the resultant point of the previous computation. In fact, we observe that every addition outside the parentheses in (4) adjusts to the next generic formulae for $j = 1$ to $(d - 1)$:

$$P + \underbrace{(P + \ldots + P}_{(j-1)-\text{terms}} + (P + Q)) = (X_1^{(j)}, Y_1^{(j)}, Z_1^{(j)}) + (X_{j+2}, Y_{j+2}, Z_{j+2}) = (X_{j+3}, Y_{j+3}, Z_{j+3}) :$$

$$X_{j+3} = (Y_{j+2} - Y_1^{(j)})^2 - (X_{j+2} - X_1^{(j)})^3 - 2X_1^{(j)}(X_{j+2} - X_1^{(j)})^2$$
$$Y_{j+3} = (Y_{j+2} - Y_1^{(j)})(X_1^{(j)}(X_{j+2} - X_1^{(j)})^2 - X_{j+3}) - Y_1^{(j)}(X_{j+2} - X_1^{(j)})^3$$
$$Z_{j+3} = Z_1^{(j)}(X_{j+2} - X_1^{(j)}). \qquad (7)$$

where $(X_1^{(j)}, Y_1^{(j)}, Z_1^{(j)})$ denotes the equivalent point to P for the jth addition.

As we can see in (7) it holds true that one always gets an equivalent point to P for the following addition by fixing:

$$(X_1^{(j+1)}, Y_1^{(j+1)}, Z_1^{(j+1)}) = (X_1^{(j)}(X_{j+2} - X_1^{(j)})^2, Y_1^{(j)}(X_{j+2} - X_1^{(j)})^3, Z_1^{(j)}(X_{j+2} - X_1^{(j)}))$$

which is equivalent to $(X_1^{(j)}, Y_1^{(j)}, Z_1^{(j)})$ according to (2), and has the same z coordinate as (7).

The cost of (4) is given by $1A + (d-1)A'$, where $d \in \mathbb{Z}^+$, $d \geq 2$, and A and A' denote the cost of the mixed and special additions, respectively. Thus, strategy (4) would cost $(7M + 4S) + (d-1)(5M + 2S)$. However, in the following section we will show that by merging the mixed addition between parentheses (see (4)) with the first special addition it is possible to achieve additional savings.

Unified Doubling-Addition (DA) Operation

When $d = 2$, the strategy (4) can be used to perform a doubling-addition (DA) operation as $P + (P + Q)$. We can reduce further the cost of this operation by unifying the first two point additions (i.e., mixed and special additions) into the following unified DA formulae:

$$X_4 = \omega^2 - \theta^3 - 2X_1^{(1)}\theta^2, \ Y_4 = \omega(X_1^{(1)}\theta^2 - X_4) - Y_1^{(1)}\theta^3, \ Z_4 = Z_1^{(1)}\theta. \quad (8)$$

Where: $\alpha = Z_1^3 Y_2 - Y_1$, $\beta = Z_1^2 X_2 - X_1$,
$$X_1^{(1)} = 4X_1\beta^2, \ Y_1^{(1)} = 8Y_1\beta^3, \ Z_1^{(1)} = (Z_1 + \beta)^2 - Z_1^2 - \beta^2,$$
$$\theta = X_3 - X_1^{(1)} = 4\left[\alpha^2 - \beta^3 - 3X_1\beta^2\right],$$
$$\omega = Y_3 - Y_1^{(1)} = \alpha^2 + \theta^2 - (\alpha + \theta)^2 - 16Y_1\beta^3.$$

Note that we directly compute $\theta = X_3 - X_1^{(1)}$ and $\omega = Y_3 - Y_1^{(1)}$ to avoid the intermediate computations of X_3, Y_3 and Z_3 from the first addition (5), saving some field additions and trading *one* multiplication for *one* squaring. Thus, the cost of the unified DA is fixed at only $(6M + 5S) + (5M + 2S) = 11M + 7S$.

Based on this formula, we can now define the total cost of our methodology for computing composite operations of the form $dP + Q$.

Using (8) to perform the mixed addition and the first special addition, the methodology (4) costs:

$$(6M + 5S) + (d-1)(5M + 2S). \quad (9)$$

where $d \geq 2 \in \mathbb{Z}^+$ for a composite operation of the form $dP + Q$.

Note that, after executing the DA operation as $P + (P + Q)$, the procedure described in Section 3.1 still applies. Hence, the cost of a special addition (i.e., $5M + 2S$) is added at every extra addition with P in (4).

Let us now compare the cost of the methodology (4) with previous formulae. For instance, when $d = 2$, (4) computes the DA operation with a cost of $11M + 7S$, which is superior to the traditional execution consisting of a doubling followed by a mixed addition: $12M + 7S$ if $a = -3$. In this case, the proposed DA reduces the cost in one multiplication. The new operation is even superior to the improved formulas by [17]: $(3M + 5S) + (7M + 4S) = 10M + 9S$, trading *one* multiplication for *two* squarings.

Remarkably, because our strategy does not involve a traditional doubling, the same aforementioned cost for DA is achieved when the parameter a in (1) is randomly chosen. In contrast, a general doubling followed by a mixed addition costs $12M + 9S$, or $(2M + 8S) + (7M + 4S) = 9M + 12S$ with the formulas by [17]. In this case, the new DA reduces the cost in *one* multiplication and *two* squarings (or trades *two* multiplications for *five* squarings, in the second case).

We remark that $2P + Q$ is a recurrent operation in efficient scalar multiplications. Thus, the new DA can be used to speed up well-known methods such as NAF, wNAF and the Shamir's trick [12] by directly replacing every doubling followed by a mixed addition.

Also, it is important to remark that, as expected, adding one point P at a time in the methodology (4) results efficient for small values of d, specifically when $d = 2$ and 3. For higher values of d it is better to take advantage of the already efficient doubling, tripling and quintupling operations. In this case, we propose to first perform some computation on the point P using these operations and then apply our approach to the result. For instance, for $d = 4, 6, 7$ and 8, $dP + Q$ would be computed as follows:

- $4P + Q = 2P + (2P + Q)$, which involves a point doubling followed by a DA.
- $6P + Q = 3P + (3P + Q)$, which involves a point tripling followed by a DA.
- $7P + Q = P + (3P + (3P + Q))$, which involves a point tripling followed by DA and a general addition.
- $8P + Q = 4P + (4P + Q)$, which involves two point doublings followed by DA.

3.2   Performance Comparison

Cost estimates using our strategy (4) and the traditional formulae for different composite operations of the form $dP + Q$ are summarized in Table 1. Since we could not find in the literature any effort to accelerate composite operations of the form $dP+Q$ in the case of projective (Jacobian) coordinates over prime fields, new composite operations are compared against operations combining the fastest point operations of form dP (i.e., improved doubling, tripling and quintupling by [17,18]) with addition, in the most efficient way. Thus, $2P+Q$, $3P+Q$ and $5Q+P$ are computed by a doubling, tripling and quintupling, respectively, followed by a mixed addition; $4P + Q$ and $8P + Q$, by two and three consecutive doublings, respectively, and a mixed addition; $6P + Q$, by one doubling, one tripling and one mixed addition; and $7P+Q$, by three doublings, one general addition (with $-P$) and one mixed addition. Note that approaches in Table 1 have been slightly improved for the general case by saving some operations during computation of consecutive doublings ($d = 4, 8$), as detailed in Section 2. Also, for the general case, $d = 6$, we have reduced the cost further by saving two squarings during computation of a doubling followed by a tripling (see details in Appendix A).

In the case of the proposed composite operations, we show performance when applying the methodology (4) in cases $d = 2, 3$ and 5, whose cost is given by (9) as detailed in Section 3.1. For $d = 4, 6, 7$ and 8, we use the already efficient

Table 1. Performance of proposed composite operations of the form $dP + Q$ in comparison with previous formulae. (a) Parameter a is fixed to -3, (b) Using tripling [17], (c) Using quintupling by [18].

Method	$2P + Q$	$3P + Q$	$4P + Q$	$5P + Q$	$6P + Q$
Ours (5)	$11M + 7S$	$16M + 9S$	$14M + 12S^{(a)}$	$26M + 13S$	$18M + 14S^{(a,b)}$
			$13M + 15S$		$17M + 17S^{(b)}$
Previous	$10M + 9S^{(a)}$	$14M + 11S^{(a,b)}$	$13M + 14S^{(a)}$	$18M + 15S^{(a,c)}$	$17M + 16S^{(a)}$
[17,18]	$9M + 12S$	$13M + 14S^{(b)}$	$13M + 16S$	$17M + 18S^{(c)}$	$16M + 19S$

Method	$7P + Q$	$8P + Q$
Ours (5)	$29M + 19S^{(a)}$	$17M + 17S^{(a)}$
	$28M + 22S$	$16M + 20S$
Previous	$28M + 21S^{(a)}$	$16M + 19S^{(a)}$
[17,18]	$27M + 24S$	$16M + 21S$

DA in combination with the fast doubling, tripling or quintupling by [17,18], as described in Section 3.1.

As we can see, our methodology reduces costs in comparison with the best implementations using previous operation formulae. The only exception is when $d = 3$ (special case) or 5, where the efficient tripling and quintupling formulas previously presented in [17] and [18], respectively, permit to achieve the lowest costs. In most frequent scenario, our new composite operations introduce some savings by trading *one* multiplication for *two* squarings (special case, $d = 2, 4, 8$; both cases, $d = 6, 7$). In other cases, we trade up to five squarings for only *two* multiplications (general case, $d = 2$), or save *one* squaring (general case, $d = 4, 8$). The reader must note that the savings are more dramatic if we compare the presented cases with the traditional formulae [12] or the composite operations by [7,21].

4   New Method for Precomputation

Precomputed points are extensively used to accelerate the scalar multiplication in applications where extra memory is available. Well-known methods in this category are wNAF and Frac-wNAF, which rely on precomputations to reduce the Hamming weight of the binary expansion of the scalar, and thus, reduce the cost of the scalar multiplication. In particular, Frac-wNAF requires building the following table with digits d_i [22]:

$$d_i \in D_i = \{1, 3, 5, \ldots, m\}. \tag{10}$$

Using the digit set (10), the average non-zero density $\mathcal{D}$ for Frac-wNAF is [22]:

$$\mathcal{D} = \left[\lfloor \log_2 m \rfloor + \frac{(m+1)}{2^{\lfloor \log_2 m \rfloor}} + 1 \right]^{-1}. \tag{11}$$

It is important to remark that Frac-wNAF is a generalization of wNAF and covers all the possibilities in terms of memory requirements.

We propose a variation to strategy (4) and compute the precomputed table as follows:

$$d_i P = \ldots + 2P + 2P + 2P + P. \tag{12}$$

We will show that all the additions in (12) can be computed with the special addition with identical z-coordinate (3), reducing costs in comparison with previous approaches. Further, some values computed during the mentioned additions are efficiently exploited to minimize costs. In this regard, we present two schemes with different memory requirements that achieve high performance. For the remainder of this work, we refer to them as Schemes 1 and 2.

Our method can be summarized in the following two steps.

Step 1: Computation of precomputed points in Jacobian coordinates

Point P is assumed to be originally in $\mathcal{A}$. Thus, if we want to use the special addition, we should translate computations to $\mathcal{J}$.

By applying the mixed coordinates approach proposed in [5], we can compute the doubling $2P$ in (12) in $\mathcal{A}$ and yield the result in $\mathcal{J}$ as follows:

$$X_2 = (3x_1^2 + a)^2 - 2\alpha, \ Y_2 = (3x_1^2 + a)(\alpha - X_2) - 8y_1^4, \ Z_2 = 2y_1 \tag{13}$$

with $\alpha = 4x_1 y_1^2 = 2[(x_1 + y_1^2)^2 - x_1^2 - y_1^2]$, where the input and result are $P = (x_1, y_1)$ and $2P = (X_2, Y_2, Z_2)$, respectively.

Formula (13) is easily derived from the doubling formula in $\mathcal{A}$ [12] by applying (2) with $\lambda = 2y_1$, and has a cost of only $1M + 5S$. Note that we have reduced the cost of (13) by replacing the multiplication $4x_1 \cdot y_1^2$ by one squaring and other cheaper operations.

Then, by fixing $\lambda = 2y_1$ in (2) we can assume the following equivalent point to P:

$$P^{(1)} = (X_1^{(1)}, Y_1^{(1)}, Z_1^{(1)}) = (4x_1 y_1^2, 8y_1^4, 2y_1) \equiv (X_1, Y_1, Z_1), \tag{14}$$

which does not introduce extra costs since its coordinates have already been computed in (13). Following additions to compute digits d_i would be performed using (4) as follows:

1st $3P = 2P + P^{(1)} = (X_2, Y_2, Z_2) + (X_1^{(1)}, Y_1^{(1)}, Z_1^{(1)}) = (X_3, Y_3, Z_3)$:
$X_3 = (Y_1^{(1)} - Y_2)^2 - (X_1^{(1)} - X_2)^3 - 2X_2(X_1^{(1)} - X_2)^2$
$Y_3 = (Y_1^{(1)} - Y_2)(X_2(X_1^{(1)} - X_2)^2 - X_3) - Y_2(X_1^{(1)} - X_2)^3$
$Z_3 = Z_2(X_1^{(1)} - X_2)$.

2nd Having $2P^{(1)} = (X_2^{(1)}, Y_2^{(1)}, Z_2^{(1)}) = \left(X_2(X_1^{(1)} - X_2)^2, Y_2(X_1^{(1)} - X_2)^3, Z_2(X_1^{(1)} - X_2) \right) \equiv$
(X_2, Y_2, Z_2),
$5P = 2P^{(1)} + 3P = (X_2^{(1)}, Y_2^{(1)}, Z_2^{(1)}) + (X_3, Y_3, Z_3) = (X_4, Y_4, Z_4)$:
$X_4 = (Y_3 - Y_2^{(1)})^2 - (X_3 - X_2^{(1)})^3 - 2X_2^{(1)}(X_3 - X_2^{(1)})^2$

$$Y_4 = (Y_3 - Y_2^{(1)})(X_2^{(1)}(X_3 - X_2^{(1)})^2 - X_4) - Y_2^{(1)}(X_3 - X_2^{(1)})^3$$
$$Z_4 = Z_2^{(1)}(X_3 - X_2^{(1)}), A_4 = (X_3 - X_2^{(1)}), B_4 = (X_3 - X_2^{(1)})^2, C_4 = (X_3 - X_2^{(1)})^3$$

$$\vdots$$

$((m-1)/2)^{th}$ Having $2P^{((m-3)/2)} = (X_2^{((m-3)/2)}, Y_2^{((m-3)/2)}, Z_2^{((m-3)/2)}) = (X_2^{((m-5)/2)}(X_{(m-1)/2}-$
$X_2^{((m-5)/2)})^2, \ldots, Y_2^{((m-5)/2)}(X_{(m-1)/2}-X_2^{((m-5)/2)})^3, Z_2^{((m-5)/2)}(X_{(m-1)/2}-X_2^{((m-5)/2)})) \equiv$
$(X_2^{((m-5)/2)}, Y_2^{((m-5)/2)}, Z_2^{((m-5)/2)})$,
$mP = 2P^{((m-3)/2)} + (m-2)P = (X_2^{((m-3)/2)}, Y_2^{((m-3)/2)}, Z_2^{((m-3)/2)}) + (X_{(m+1)/2}, Y_{(m+1)/2}, Z_{(m+1)/2})$
$mP = 2P^{((m-3)/2)} + (m-2)P = (X_{(m+3)/2}, Y_{(m+3)/2}, Z_{(m+3)/2})$:

$$X_{(m+3)/2} = (Y_{(m+1)/2}-Y_2^{((m-3)/2)})^2 - (X_{(m+1)/2}-X_2^{((m-3)/2)})^3 - 2X_2^{((m-3)/2)}(X_{(m+1)/2}-$$
$X_2^{((m-3)/2)})^2$,
$$Y_{(m+3)/2} = (Y_{(m+1)/2}-Y_2^{((m-3)/2)})(X_2^{(m-3)/2}(X_{(m+1)/2}-X_2^{((m-3)/2)})^2 - X_{((m-3)/2)}) -$$
$Y_2^{(m-3)/2}(X_{(m+1)/2} - X_2^{((m-3)/2)})^3$,
$$Z_{(m+3)/2} = Z_2^{(m-3)/2}(X_{(m+1)/2} - X_2^{((m-3)/2)}),$$
$A_{(m+3)/2} = (X_{(m+1)/2}-X_2^{((m-3)/2)}), B_{(m+3)/2} = (X_{(m+1)/2}-X_2^{((m-3)/2)})^2, C_{(m+3)/2} =$
$(X_{(m+1)/2} - X_2^{((m-3)/2)})^3$.

Values A_i and (B_i, C_i), for $i = 4$ to $(m+3)/2$, are stored for Schemes 1 and 2, respectively, and used in *Step 2* to save some computations when converting points to $\mathcal{A}$.

Step 2: Conversion to affine coordinates

Points (X_i, Y_i, Z_i) from *Step 1*, for i from 3 to $(m+3)/2$, have to be converted back to $\mathcal{A}$ since this would allow the use of the efficient mixed addition during the scalar multiplication. This can be achieved by means of the following:

$$(X_i/Z_i^2, Y_i/Z_i^3, 1). \tag{15}$$

To avoid the computation of several expensive inversions when using (15) for each point in the case $m > 3$ (10), we use the method due to Montgomery, called simultaneous inversion [12], to limit the requirement to only *one* inversion.

In Scheme 1, we first compute the inverse $r = Z_{(m+3)/2}^{-1}$, and then recover every point using (15) as follows:

$$mP : x_{(m+3)/2} = r^2 \cdot X_{(m+3)/2}, \ y_{(m+3)/2} = r^3 \cdot Y_{(m+3)/2}$$
$$(m-2)P : r = r \cdot A_{(m+3)/2}, \ x_{(m+1)/2} = r^2 \cdot X_{(m+1)/2}, \ y_{(m+1)/2} = r^3 \cdot Y_{(m+1)/2}$$

$$\vdots$$

$$3P : r = r.A_4, \ x_3 = r^2.X_3, \ y_3 = r^3.Y_3.$$

It is important to observe that $Z_j = Z_3 \times \prod_{i=4}^{j} A_i$ for $j = 4$ to $(m+3)/2$, according to Step 1, and hence, for $i = (m-2)$ down to 3, $Z_{(i+3)/2}^{-1}$ for each point iP is recovered at every multiplication $r.A_{(i+5)/2}$.

For Scheme 2, we first compute $r_1 = \left(Z_{(m+3)/2}^{-1}\right)^2$ and $r_2 = \left(Z_{(m+3)/2}^{-1}\right)^3$, and then recover every point using (15) as follows:

$mP : x_{(m+3)/2} = r_1 \cdot X_{(m+3)/2}, \; y_{(m+3)/2} = r_2 \cdot Y_{(m+3)/2}$
$(m-2)P : r_1 = r_1 \cdot B_{(m+3)/2}, \; r_2 = r_2 \cdot C_{(m+3)/2}, \; x_{(m+1)/2} = r_1 \cdot X_{(m+1)/2}, \; y_{(m+1)/2} = r_2 \cdot Y_{(m+1)/2}$

$\vdots$

$3P : r_1 = r_1 \cdot B_4, \; r_2 = r_2 \cdot C_4, \; x_3 = r_1 \cdot X_3, \; y_3 = r_2 \cdot Y_3.$

In this case $Z_j^2 = Z_3^2 \times \prod_{i=4}^{j} B_i$ and $Z_j^3 = Z_3^3 \times \prod_{i=4}^{j} C_i$ for $j = 4$ to $(m+3)/2$, according to Step 1, and hence, for $i = (m-2)$ down to 3, the pair $(Z_{(i+3)/2}^{-2}, Z_{(i+3)/2}^{-3})$ for each point iP is recovered at every multiplication $r_1 \cdot B_{(i+5)/2}$ and $r_2 \cdot C_{(i+5)/2}$.

4.1 Cost Analysis

In total, Scheme 1 has the following cost when computing the precomputed table (10):

$$\text{Cost}_{\text{Scheme 1}} = 1I + (9L)M + (3L+5)S, \qquad (16)$$

where $L = (m-1)/2$ represents the number of points. In terms of memory usage, Scheme 1 requires $(3L+3)$ registers for temporary calculations and storing the precomputed points. We will show later that this requirement does not exceed the number of available registers for the scalar multiplication for practical values of L.

In the case of Scheme 2, the cost is as follows:

$$\text{Cost}_{\text{Scheme 2}} = 1I + (9L)M + (2L+6)S. \qquad (17)$$

For this scheme, we require $(4L+1)$ registers when $L > 1$. For $L = 1$, the requirement is fixed at 6 registers. It will be shown that this requirement does not exceed the memory allocated for scalar multiplication for small values of L. For a detailed description of the estimation of costs and memory requirements for Schemes 1/2, we refer to Appendix B.

As we can see from (16) and (17), Scheme 2 reduces further the cost to compute the precomputed table at the expense of some extra memory. In the following, we analyze the memory requirements for the scalar multiplication and determine if our method adjusts to such constrains.

Considering that the precomputed table requires $2L$ registers for storing L points, the total requirement of the scalar multiplication is given by $(2L+R)$ registers, where R is the number of registers needed by the most memory-consuming point operation in a given implementation. On scalar multiplications using solely radix 2, addition is usually such operation. Depending on the used coordinates and/or implementation details, point addition can require from 7/8 registers in $\mathcal{J}$ [17] and $\mathcal{J}^m$, respectively, to 8 registers for an SSCA-protected version [20]. If the scalar multiplication includes radix 3 in its expansion, then tripling becomes the most expensive operation with a requirement of up to 9/10 registers [7,17]. Consequently, Scheme 2 adjusts to the previous requirements for small precomputed tables with $L = 1$ to 3 if addition is the main operation. If we also consider tripling, Scheme 2 is suitable for values $L = 1$ to 4. In the case of Scheme 1, it follows the memory constrains for values $L = 1$ to 5 and $L = 1$ to 7 for radix-2 and radix-3 cases, respectively, which demonstrates that this scheme is efficient for practical Frac-wNAF implementations. The reader must note that, in general, values $L > 7$ are not efficient since the cost of computing the precomputed table results more expensive than the savings achieved by precomputation during the scalar multiplication.

In the following section, we analyze the performance of our method in comparison with previous efforts.

4.2   Performance Comparison

There are different efficient schemes to compute precomputed points in the literature. The simplest approaches suggest performing computations in $\mathcal{A}$ or $\mathcal{C}$ using the chain $P \to 3P \to 5P \to \ldots \to mP$. The latter requires one doubling and $L = (m-1)/2$ additions, which can be expressed as follows in terms of field operations for the mentioned cases:

$$\text{Cost}_{\mathcal{A}} = (L+1)I + (2L+2)M + (L+2)S \tag{18}$$
$$\text{Cost}_{\mathcal{C}} = (10L-1)M + (4L+5)S \tag{19}$$

Note that (19) shows a better performance than the estimated cost given by [6] since we are considering that the doubling $2P$ is computed as $2\mathcal{A} \to \mathcal{C}$ with a cost of $2M + 5S$, the first addition $P + 2P$ computed with a mixed addition as $\mathcal{A}+\mathcal{C} \to \mathcal{C}$ ($7M+4S$), and the following $(L-1)$ additions as $\mathcal{C}+\mathcal{C} \to \mathcal{C}$ ($10M+4S$). The new operation costs are obtained by applying the technique of replacing multiplications by squarings introduced in [17]. The memory requirements of the $\mathcal{A}-$ and $\mathcal{C}-$based methods are $2L + R$ and $5L + R$ registers, respectively.

Other methods that achieve better performance in scenarios where inversion is relatively expensive, perform computations in Projective $\mathcal{P}$, $\mathcal{J}$ or $\mathcal{C}$ coordinates and, then, convert the points to $\mathcal{A}$ by using the Montgomery's method to reduce the number of required inversions to only one. Cost for these methods are shown in the following [6,9], considering the general assumption $1S \approx 0.8M$:

$$\text{Cost}_{\mathcal{P} \to \mathcal{A}} = 1I + (16L-3)M + (3L+5)S = 1I + (18.4L+1)M \tag{20}$$
$$\text{Cost}_{\mathcal{J} \to \mathcal{A}} = 1I + (16L-5)M + (5L+5)S = 1I + (20L-1)M \tag{21}$$
$$\text{Cost}_{\mathcal{C} \to \mathcal{A}} = 1I + (16L-4)M + (5L-5)S = 1I + (20L)M. \tag{22}$$

Recently, Dahmen et al. [6] proposed a new scheme, whose computations were efficiently performed using solely formulae in $\mathcal{A}$. Also, the number of inversions was limited to only one by means on the Montgomery's method. This scheme costs:

$$\text{Cost}_{[6]} = 1I + (10L - 1)M + (4L + 4)S = 1I + (13.2L + 2.2)M, \qquad (23)$$

that shows its superiority when compared with all the previous methods requiring only one inversion. However, our method achieves even lower costs as shown in Section 4.1:

$$\text{Cost}_{\text{Scheme 1}} = 1I + (11.4L + 4)M, \quad \text{Cost}_{\text{Scheme 2}} = 1I + (10.6L + 4.8)M.$$

which make our approach, and specifically Scheme 2, the fastest in the literature when the number of inversions is limited to one.

For comparing with the approach (18), which includes several field inversions in their computation, it is better to specify the range of I/M ratios for which each method is superior. Table 2 shows the I/M values for which our schemes and the $\mathcal{A}$-based scheme are the most efficient for a given number of precomputed points. To present a fair comparison, methods are compared according to the memory constrains for the scalar multiplication using radix-2. As analyzed in Section 4.1, Schemes 1 and 2 are suitable for values $L = 1$ to 5 and $L = 1$ to 4, respectively.

Table 2. I/M ranges for which each method achieves the lowest cost

# Points	1	2	3	4	5
Scheme 1	-	-	-	≥ 8.1	≥ 8.7
Scheme 2	≥ 9	≥ 8.4	≥ 8.2	-	-
Affine (18)	≤ 9	≤ 8.4	≤ 8.2	≤ 8.1	≤ 8.7

As it can be seen, our schemes outperform the $\mathcal{A}$-based approach for the most commonly found I/M ratios, where inversion is relatively expensive. In average, Schemes 1 and 2 are superior when inversion is more than 9 times the cost of multiplication. As discussed in Section 2, it is usually expected that $I/M > 30$.

Finally, we compare performance of our schemes with the $\mathcal{C}$-based approach, whose cost is given by (19). In this case, we should also consider the scalar multiplication cost in our comparisons since precomputations in $\mathcal{C}$ require different computing and memory requirements to the $\mathcal{A}$ case. When precomputations are in $\mathcal{C}$, [5] proposed the use of $\mathcal{J} + \mathcal{C} \rightarrow \mathcal{J}^m$ to perform additions $(10M + 6S)$, $2\mathcal{J}^m \rightarrow \mathcal{J}$ to every doubling preceding an addition $(2M + 5S)$, and $2\mathcal{J}^m \rightarrow \mathcal{J}^m$ $(3M + 5S)$ to the rest of doublings. Note that we have reduced further the cost of the mentioned operations by applying the same technique introduced in [17] to replace multiplications by squarings. Following this scheme, the scalar multiplication cost including precomputations is as follows:

$$[nD((10M + 6S) + (2M + 5S)) + n(1 - D)(3M + 5S)] + [(10L - 1)M + (4L + 5)S] \qquad (24)$$

where $\mathcal{D}$ represents the Hamming weight as expressed in (11).

For our approach, we consider an improved scheme taking advantage of the faster DA operation proposed in Section 3.1. Thus, we use $\mathcal{J} + (\mathcal{J} + \mathcal{A}) \rightarrow \mathcal{J}$ to perform doubling-addition operations following the form $P + (P + Q)$ with a cost of $11M + 7S$, and the fast point operations by [17]. With this scheme, the scalar multiplication cost including precomputations is as follows:

$$[n\mathcal{D}(11M + 7S) + n(1 - \mathcal{D})(3M + 5S)] + \text{Cost}_{\text{Scheme}1/2}. \qquad (25)$$

We also include in our comparison a traditional scheme using $\mathcal{J}$ and only one inversion to assess the advantages of our improved scheme (25). By using (21) and the point operations by [17], the cost of the scalar multiplication including precomputations is given by:

$$[n\mathcal{D}(7M + 4S) + n(3M + 5S)] + [1I + (20L - 1)M] \qquad (26)$$

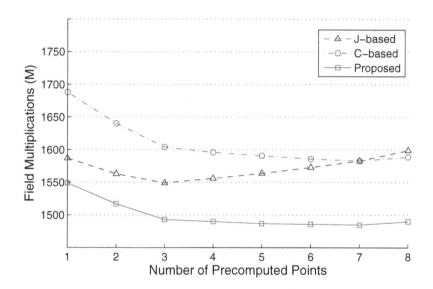

Fig. 1. Cost performance of the proposed scheme and previous methods to perform the scalar multiplication including precomputation ($1I = 30M, 1S = 0.8M, n = 160$ bits)

Figure 1 plots the costs of our scheme (25), and the $\mathcal{C}-$ and $\mathcal{J}$-based approaches as given by (24) and (26), assuming $1I = 30M, 1S = 0.8M$ and $n = 160$ bits. As we can see, our proposed scheme outperforms both methods, introducing an improvement of up to 6.2% in comparison with the already optimized $\mathcal{J}$-based approach, when assuming unrestricted availability of memory (optimal case when using the Frac-wNAF method with 7 precomputed points). We remark that the given estimation is a lower bound as additions and other operations are not included in the cost. The new DA offers a reduced number of these operations, and thus, a real implementation would achieve a higher performance improvement. Also, it is important to note that the improvement would be even more significant in implementations where a hardware multiplier executes both squarings and multiplications (i.e., $1S = 1M$).

The previous analysis does not take into consideration memory consumption when comparing the $\mathcal{C}$-based approach and our method. Recalling that the former has a memory requirement of $(5L + R)$ and assuming $R = 8$, Table 3 summarizes the I/M break even points at which both methods perform equivalently for a given number of available registers. Similarly, costs have been derived according to (24) and (25). Notice that our method is superior in any case the I/M ratio is below the displayed numbers, which makes it superior for typical I/M ratios, as discussed in Section 2.

Table 3. I/M break even points for which our schemes and the $\mathcal{C}$-based approach perform equivalently for a given number of registers ($n = 160$ bits). (1) Scheme 1 and (2) Scheme 2.

# Registers	≤ 10	12	13	14-16	17	18-20	21-23
Break point	$337^{(1,2)}$	$369^{(2)}$	$201^{(2)}$	$224^{(2)}$	$228^{(2)}$	$180^{(2)}$	$182^{(2)}$
# Registers	24	25-28	29-32	33-37	38-42	≥ 43	
Break point	$144^{(1)}$	$149^{(2)}$	$141^{(2)}$	$136^{(2)}$	$131^{(2)}$	$128^{(2)}$	

5   Conclusions

We have described an innovative methodology to derive composite operations of the form $dP + Q$ by applying the special addition with identical z-coordinate to the setting of generic scalar multiplications over prime fields. These new operations are shown to be faster than operations built on top of previous formulae, which would potentially speed up computations in all known binary methods and in new scalar multiplications using other radices beside 2 such as double-base [7], triple-base [21] or mbNAF [18].

In the second part of this work, we presented two variants of a new precomputation scheme for window-based scalar multiplications, and showed that our methods offer the lowest costs, given by $1I + (9L)M + (3L + 5)S$ and $1I + (9L)M + (2L + 6)S$, when using only one inversion. For the rest of cases, we demonstrated that they achieve superior performance for most common I/M ratios found in practical implementations.

References

1. Avanzi, R., Cohen, H., Doche, C., Frey, G., Lange, T., Nguyen, K., Vercauteren, F.: Handbook of Elliptic and Hyperelliptic Curve Cryptography. CRC Press, Boca Raton (2005)
2. Brown, M., Hankerson, D., Lopez, J., Menezes, A.: Software Implementation of the NIST elliptic curves over prime fields. In: Naccache, D. (ed.) CT-RSA 2001. LNCS, vol. 2020, pp. 250–265. Springer, Heidelberg (2001)

3. Billet, O., Joye, M.: Fast Point Multiplication on Elliptic Curves through Isogenies. In: Fossorier, M.P.C., Høholdt, T., Poli, A. (eds.) AAECC 2003. LNCS, vol. 2643, pp. 43–50. Springer, Heidelberg (2003)
4. Ciet, M., Joye, M., Lauter, K., Montgomery, P.L.: Trading Inversions for Multiplications in Elliptic Curve Cryptography. Designs, Codes and Cryptography 39(2), 189–206 (2006)
5. Cohen, H., Miyaji, A., Ono, T.: Efficient Elliptic Curve Exponentiation using Mixed Coordinates. In: Ohta, K., Pei, D. (eds.) ASIACRYPT 1998. LNCS, vol. 1514, pp. 51–65. Springer, Heidelberg (1998)
6. Dahmen, E., Okeya, K., Schepers, D.: Affine Precomputation with Sole Inversion in Elliptic Curve Cryptography. In: Pieprzyk, J., Ghodosi, H., Dawson, E. (eds.) ACISP 2007. LNCS, vol. 4586, pp. 245–258. Springer, Heidelberg (2007)
7. Dimitrov, V., Imbert, L., Mishra, P.K.: Efficient and Secure Elliptic Curve Point Multiplication using Double-Base Chains. In: Roy, B. (ed.) ASIACRYPT 2005. LNCS, vol. 3788, pp. 59–78. Springer, Heidelberg (2005)
8. Doche, C., Icart, T., Kohel, D.: Efficient Scalar Multiplication by Isogeny Decompositions. In: Yung, M., Dodis, Y., Kiayias, A., Malkin, T.G. (eds.) PKC 2006. LNCS, vol. 3958, pp. 191–206. Springer, Heidelberg (2006)
9. Eisentraeger, K., Lauter, K., Montgomery, P.: Fast Elliptic Curve Arithmetic and Improved Weil Pairing Evaluation. In: Joye, M. (ed.) CT-RSA 2003. LNCS, vol. 2612, pp. 343–354. Springer, Heidelberg (2003)
10. Elmegaard-Fessel, L.: Efficient Scalar Multiplication and Security against Power Analysis in Cryptosystems based on the NIST Elliptic Curves over Prime Fields, Master Thesis, University of Copenhagen (2006)
11. FIPS PUB 186-2. Digital Signature Standard (DSS). National Institute of Standards and Technology (NIST) (2000)
12. Hankerson, D., Menezes, A., Vanstone, S.: Guide to Elliptic Curve Cryptography. Springer, Heidelberg (2004)
13. IEEE Std 1363-2000. IEEE Standard Specifications for Public-Key Cryptography. The Institute of Electrical and Electronics Engineers (IEEE) (2000)
14. Itoh, K., Takenaka, M., Torii, N., Temma, S., Kurihara, Y.: Fast Implementation of Public-Key Cryptography on a DSP TMS320C6201. In: Koç, Ç.K., Paar, C. (eds.) CHES 1999. LNCS, vol. 1717, pp. 61–72. Springer, Heidelberg (1999)
15. Lim, C.H., Hwang, H.S.: Fast implementation of Elliptic Curve Arithmetic in GF(pn). In: Imai, H., Zheng, Y. (eds.) PKC 2000. LNCS, vol. 1751, pp. 405–421. Springer, Heidelberg (2000)
16. Longa, P.: Accelerating the Scalar Multiplication on Elliptic Curve Cryptosystems over Prime Fields, Master's Thesis, University of Ottawa (June 2007)
17. Longa, P., Miri, A.: Fast and Flexible Elliptic Curve Point Arithmetic over Prime Fields. IEEE Transactions on Computers (to appear, 2007), http://doi.ieeecomputersociety.org/10.1109/TC.2007.70815
18. Longa, P., Miri, A.: New Multibase Non-Adjacent Form Scalar Multiplication and its Application to Elliptic Curve Cryptosystems (submitted, 2007)
19. Meloni, N.: Fast and Secure Elliptic Curve Scalar Multiplication over Prime Fields using Special Addition Chains. Cryptology ePrint Archive, Report 2006/216 (2006)
20. Mishra, P.: Scalar Multiplication in Elliptic Curve Cryptosystems: Pipelining with Precomputations. Cryptology ePrint Archive, Report 2004/191 (2004)
21. Mishra, P., Dimitrov, V.: Efficient Quintuple Formulas for Elliptic Curves and Efficient Scalar Multiplication using Multibase Number Representation. Cryptology ePrint Archive, Report 2007/040 (2007)

22. Moller, B.: Improved Techniques for Fast Exponentiation. In: Lee, P.J., Lim, C.H. (eds.) ICISC 2002. LNCS, vol. 2587, pp. 298–312. Springer, Heidelberg (2003)
23. Solinas, J.: Generalized Mersenne Numbers, Technical Report CORR-99-39, Dept. of C&O, University of Waterloo (1999)
24. Takagi, T., Yen, S.-M., Wu, B.-C.: Radix-r Non-Adjacent Form. In: Zhang, K., Zheng, Y. (eds.) ISC 2004. LNCS, vol. 3225, pp. 99–110. Springer, Heidelberg (2004)

A Doubling-Tripling formulae

Having $P = (X_1, Y_1, Z_1)$ on the elliptic curve E, the doubling $2P = (X_2, Y_2, Z_2)$ in Jacobian coordinates is computed by [17]:

$$X_2 = A^2 - 2B, \ Y_2 = A \cdot (B - X_2) - 8D, \ Z_2 = (Y_1 + Z_1)^2 - C - E,$$

$$A = 3G + H, \ B = 2\left[(X_1 + C)^2 - G - D\right], \ C = Y_1^2, \ D = C^2, \ E = Z_1^2, \ F = E^2,$$

$$G = X_1^2, \ H = a \cdot F,$$

and followed by the next revised tripling formulae to yield $6P = (X_3, Y_3, Z_3)$, which derives from the fast tripling in [17]:

$$X_3 = I \cdot T + X, \ Y_3 = 8Y_2 \cdot (V - W), \ Z_3 = 2Z_2 \cdot P,$$

$$I = Y_2^2, \ J = I^2, \ K = 16D \cdot H, \ L = X_2^2, \ M = 3L + K, \ N = P^2,$$

$$P = 6\left[(X_1 + I)^2 - L - J\right] - N, \ R = P^2, \ S = (M + P)^2 - N - R, \ T = 16J - S,$$

$$U = 16J + T, \ V = -T \cdot U, \ W = P \cdot R, \ X = 4X_2 \cdot R.$$

The general doubling still requires $2M + 8S$, but the tripling reduces its cost to $7M + 7S$ by using previously computed values D and H to compute aZ_2^4 as $16Y_1^4 \cdot aZ_1^4$. Thus, the total cost of a Doubling-Tripling operation when the parameter a is randomly chosen is $9M + 15S$.

B Cost Analysis of Precomputation Scheme

Scheme 1 has the following cost:

$$\text{Cost}_{\text{Scheme 1}} = 1I + (9L)M + (3L + 5)S,$$

and requires $(3L + 3)$ registers, where L is the number of points in the precomputed table.

Proof: The doubling (13) of *Step 1*, Section 4, cost $1M + 5S$ and requires 6 temporary registers. The first addition $2P + P$ in (12) using the special addition with identical z-coordinates costs $5M + 2S$ and requires 6 temporary registers if the precomputed table contains only one point. Otherwise, it would require 6 temporary registers for calculations, and 2 extra registers to store the (X, Y)

coordinates of $3P$. Following additions in (12) using the special addition with identical z-coordinates cost $5M + 2S$ per extra point, and 6 temporary registers for calculations, and 3 / 4 extra registers per each point for Schemes 1 / 2, respectively to store the values (X, Y, A, B, C). In the last iteration of *Step 1* (Section 4) the memory requirement is reduced to storing (X, Y, B) values in temporary registers. Thus, Schemes 1 and 2 only require the previous 6 registers plus 1 extra register in this case. Finally, the modified Montgomery's method corresponding to *Step 2* costs $1I + (3M + 1S) + (4M + 1S)(L - 1)$ and $1I + (3M + 1S) + 4M(L - 1)$ for Schemes 1 and 2 respectively, and requires 4 / 5 temporary registers for calculations, in addition to registers for storing the affine coordinates (x, y) of the precomputed points. Thus, Steps 1 and 2 cost $(1M+5S)+(5M+2S)+(5M+2S)(L-1)$ and $1I+(3M+1S)+(4M+1S)(L-1)$, respectively. By adding these values, we obtain the cost of Scheme 1 as presented above.

Regarding memory requirements, the doubling (13) needs 6 temporary registers $T_1, \ldots, T_6$. The same registers can be reused by the first special addition. Additionally, it needs 2 extra registers to store (X, Y) coordinates corresponding to $3P$, making a total of 8 registers. Following additions also reuses temporary registers $T_1, \ldots, T_6$, and requires 3 registers per point, excepting the last one, to store (X, Y, A) values. For the last iteration, we only require registers $T_1, \ldots, T_6$ and 1 extra register to store A since the last (X, Y) coordinates are store in T_1 and T_2. That makes an accumulated requirement of $6 + 3(L - 1) = 3L + 3$ at the end of Step 1, for $L \geq 2$. If $L = 1$, we only require the first special addition, fixing the requirement at only 6 registers (note that in this case (X, Y) coordinates are stored in T_1 and T_2). Step 2 only requires 4 registers for calculations, two of which store the first pair (x, y). The rest of points require $3(L - 1)$ registers, making a total requirement of $4 + 3(L - 1) = 3L + 1$. In conclusion, Scheme 1 requires $3L + 3$ registers.

The cost and memory estimation for Scheme 2 easily follows.

Online-Untransferable Signatures

Moses Liskov[1] and Silvio Micali[2]

[1] Computer Science Department,
The College of William and Mary
Williamsburg, VA 23187, USA
mliskov@cs.wm.edu
[2] CSAIL,
Massachusetts Institute of Technology
Cambridge, MA 02139, USA
silvio@csail.mit.edu

Abstract. Non-transferability of digital signatures is an important security concern, traditionally achieved via interactive verification protocols. Such protocols, however, are vulnerable to "online transfer attacks" — i.e., attacks mounted during the protocols' executions.

In this paper, we show how to guarantee *online untransferability* of signatures, via a reasonable public-key infrastructure and general assumptions, without random oracles. Our untransferable signatures are as efficient as prior ones that provably provide weaker types of untransferability.

1   Introduction

Berkeley wishes to make a signed job offer to Alice. In this scenario, the ability of Alice to show the signature to others is a negative for Berkeley: for instance, Alice could use that ability to leverage a better offer from another university (e.g., Stanford). The transferability of digital signatures is indeed a well recognized concern. The focus of this paper is to make digital signatures as untransferable as possible. Let us start by recalling prior solutions to this problem.

A first solution to the problem of transferability in signatures was offered by Chaum and Van Antwerpen[10]. Their "undeniable signatures" cannot ever be verified without the signer's cooperation. The idea, therefore, is that the signature recipient should be unable to transfer a signature to a third party, because the signer would refuse to interact with that party.

Undeniable signatures, however, suffer from another drawback: the signer can effectively repudiate even a valid signature by refusing to cooperate. In the job offer scenario, this allows Berkeley to escape from the contract, leaving Alice no recourse.

Jakobsson, Sako, and Impagliazzo proposed *designated verifier signatures* [19], in which only a particular party, chosen by the signer, can verify without the signer's help. The untransferability of this solution is effectively the same as in undeniable signatures. Recent extensions allow a signature holder other than the original signer to designate a separate verifier [26,1]. However, this still falls short

R. Cramer (Ed.): PKC 2008, LNCS 4939, pp. 248–267, 2008.

of the solution we need for the job offer scenario: the designated verifier will have to be the recipient, since she must be convinced of the validity of the signature, but this implies that the recipient will be unable to establish its validity in court, should the signer be uncooperative.

Designated Confirmer Signatures. A solution to these repudiation problems has been provided by Chaum [9]. In a designated confirmer signature scheme (or DCS scheme for short), there are three parties: the signer, the recipient, and a trusted party called the *designated confirmer*. The idea is that the signer will produce a signature of an arbitrary message m in a way such that the recipient can be convinced of the validity of the signature in an interactive protocol. If such a signature of m is valid then either the confirmer or the signer will be able to prove its validity with respect to m, and will also be able to deny its validity with respect to any other message. Further, the confirmer and the signer should each be able to transform a valid signature of a message m into a traditional signature of m that can be verified by (and transferred to) anyone. Valuable variants of DCS schemes have been provided by Okamoto [22], Michels and Stadler [20], Camenisch and Michels [5], Goldwasser and Waisbard [16], Monnerat and Vaudenay [21], and Gentry, Molnar, and Ramzan [15].

The problem of online transferability. In prior solutions, the key to achieving untransferability is to make signature verification an interactive process between the sender and the receiver. Such untransferability, however, is guaranteed only after a certain time, namely, when the protocol completes. When Berkeley uses a DCS scheme to sign Alice's job offer, she will be unable to convince Stanford that the DCS signature she received was valid, but assuming that Alice attempts to convince Stanford of the validity of the signature only *after* completing the verification protocol. We call such an attack an *offline transfer*. On the other hand, Alice and Stanford could be actively communicating *during* the protocol Alice engages in with Berkeley, in which case, Alice may attempt to convince Stanford interactively of the validity of the signature. We call such an attack an *online transfer*.

All prior solutions to the problem of preventing transfer of signatures are vulnerable to online transfer.[1] Consider the following common paradigm to guarantee untransferability. The sender produces a signature σ of the message m and encrypts σ under a public encryption key to obtain a ciphertext c. Then, to prove that the signature is valid, the sender provides a zero-knowledge proof that c is an encryption of a valid signature of m. Here, it is then apparent that if Alice merely acts as a passive conduit for a conversation that is really taking place between Berkeley and Stanford, Stanford necessarily will be convinced that the job offer is genuine, because the legitimate recipient ought to be convinced, and there is no difference between a transferee and the legitimate recipient in this attack. Notice that even replacing the general zero-knowledge

---

[1] Steinfeld et al. [26] show how to prevent the transfer of a proof of ownership of a signature in a way that is online-untransferable. However, there is no confirmer, so the recipient of such a proof cannot trust that it will not be repudiated.

proof with a stronger form of zero-knowledge (e.g. nonmalleable [14] or reset-table zero-knowledge proofs [8]) does not appear to help. Whether relying on zero-knowledge proofs, or using some other type of protocol, if the (illegitimate) transferee and the (legitimate) recipient of the signature cannot be meaningfully distinguished, this attack remains viable.

Our Model. In our job offer example, Alice is merely an entity who makes some random choices in order to be convinced by Berkeley that the signature is valid. To prevent online transferability, therefore, we put forward a reasonable model that ensures some kind of distinction between Alice and Stanford.

The distinction we propose to build upon is this: although Alice and Stanford may be colluding at present, if they are separate entities at all, Alice and Stanford will not have been colluding at some point in the past. We thus plan to solve the online untransferability problem via a model that in essence *forces* part of the signature process to take place when Alice and Stanford are not colluding.

Our model is very simple. It consists of a public-key infrastructure (PKI) in which not only signers and confirmers have registered public keys, but signature verifiers have them as well. In a variant of our model—guaranteeing a stronger version of online untransferability— verifiers can register their public keys only after providing a proof of knowledge of their corresponding secret keys.

First of all, our basic model is very *reasonable:* in fact, some form of PKI is necessary for signatures to be meaningful. In addition, even our variant model is realistic. Indeed, PKI requiring proofs of knowledge of secret keys have been considered in the past and proved to possess many attractive properties. In particular, plaintext-aware encryption can be realized without random oracles [17] in this model, resettable zero-knowledge can be achieved [8], and this model is favorable for universally composable security [2]. In addition, Steinfeld et al. rely on this same model in order to establish proofs of signature knowledge that cannot be transferred. Thus, not only are such PKIs feasibly implemented, but actually have many independent and valid reasons to be used.

There must be a crucial point in time in the past at which Alice was honest (or at least, that she was not colluding with Stanford). It is by leveraging this past point that online untransferability can be guaranteed in the present. Our model assumes that the time at which Alice registers her key is such a time in the past. This provides a meaningful version of online untransferability.

Our Solution. Our model provides only a framework in which online untransferability is *plausible*. It is, however, quite far from guaranteeing the existence of a solution, let alone a *reasonably efficient* solution.

The high-level structure of our solution (like that of Gentry et al. [15]) is that the signer produces (1) an encryption c that specifies the message m, (2) a zero-knowledge proof that c specifies m appropriately, and (3) a signature of c, along with certain elements of the proof transcript.

It is a crucial property for the security of our solution that the proof in point 2 is a full-fledged zero-knowledge proof, and that can be simulated without rewinding. Due to the result of [8], this guarantees that this proof is concurrently zero-knowledge. While this does not in itself imply online untransferability, it will imply that we do not need to worry whether our separately proven online untransferability will apply in a concurrent setting. (The concurrent setting is very natural, where we may imagine multiple verifiers, multiple third parties, et cetera.)

Most prior protocols for achieving (just) offline untransferability achieved a reasonable level of efficiency by either relying on unusually strong assumptions (e.g. the random oracle assumption) [5,20], or provided weaker security by relying on protocols that are not fully zero-knowledge (e.g. the solution of Goldwasser and Waisbard [16] at TCC 2004). A second crucial property of our solution is that it be reasonably efficient for the provable security it delivers, and does not rely on the random oracle assumption.

Most known constructions of DCS schemes fall under the following paradigm. To create a confirmer signature, the signer creates a traditional signature σ, and encrypts it under the confirmer's public encryption key to produce c. Thus, the extraction requirement is guaranteed by the fact that both the signer and the confirmer can produce σ. To verify that c is a designated confirmer signature of m, one proves in zero-knowledge that c is indeed an encryption of a valid traditional signature of m relative to the proper public keys. Similarly, zero-knowledge proofs are used to disavow invalid signatures.

Goldwasser and Waisbard [16] were the first to give practical and efficient schemes in the plain model by using strong witness-hiding proofs instead of fully zero-knowledge ones. This achieves a weaker, but reasonable, level of security: in their scheme, transfer is only prevented when the transferee is honest. Gentry, Molnar, and Ramzan [15] give a practical and efficient scheme based on the Paillier cryptosystem [23], and their proofs of confirmation and disavowal are fully zero-knowledge, so they prevent all offline transfer.

One drawback of our solution is that, in order to prevent the transfer of signatures, the signer must be willing to issue invalid signatures to anyone. This is, however, in the signer's interest as the signer is the one being protected by the untransferability properties.

Our Results. We give a secure and efficient scheme similar to a designated confirmer signature scheme under general assumptions, without random oracles or general zero-knowledge proofs for secure designated confirmer signatures. If we assume the recipient and the third party (the transferee) were not conspiring at the time the recipient registers his or her public key, even online transfer cannot occur in our scheme. However this assumption is not critical in any other way; all other properties can be proven without it, including the impossibility of offline transfer.

2   Definitions

2.1   Intuitive Description

There are three players, the signer S, the confirmer C, and the recipient R. Before any signatures are issued, there is a setup phase in which all three parties generate public keys, PK_S, PK_C and PK_R respectively, that are assumed to be known to all parties (or are certified by a PKI). Each party also generates a secret key: $SK_S, SK_C,$ and SK_R, respectively.

It is assumed that in any algorithm or protocol, each party has their own secret key and all public keys as inputs. It is further assumed that 1^k is an input to all parties in all algorithms or protocols, where k is a system-wide security parameter.

An *online-untransferable signature scheme with confirmer* consists of the following protocols:

- KeyGen$_S$, KeyGen$_C$, KeyGen$_R$ are algorithms for generating the public and private keys of each party.
- Setup. This is an algorithm run by the confirmer, once per signer, in which the confirmer produces an additional public key $PK_{C,S}$ which is to be used by the signer S in creating designated confirmer signatures for confirmer C, and a secret key $SK_{C,S}$ which the confirmer remembers for use later.[2]
- Sign. This is an interactive protocol between the signer and the recipient on common input a message m. At the end of the protocol, the recipient outputs an online-untransferable signature σ and either accepts or rejects, while the signer outputs an online-untransferable signature σ'.
- Disavow. This in an interactive protocol between the confirmer and the recipient, in which the confirmer proves that the given signature σ is not a valid one.
- Extract$_C$, Extract$_S$. This is a non-interactive algorithm in which the confirmer or signer, respectively, on input an online-untransferable signature σ, outputs an extracted signature σ^*.
- ExVerify. This is a non-interactive algorithm that can be performed by any party, given the public keys, on input an extracted signature σ^* that either accepts or rejects that signature.
- FakeSign. In order to prove the impossibility of online transfer, the simulator will need an invalid but valid-looking signature from the signer; that created and given to the simulator in this protocol.[3] At the end of the protocol, the signer outputs an online untransferable signature σ, and the simulator outputs an online-untransferable signature σ'.

The security requirements, informally, are the following:

Completeness: When all players are honest, the online untransferable signature produced by the recipient in Sign will be valid (that is, a valid extracted signature

---

[2] This algorithm is not one included traditionally, but its addition is reasonable: we expect that it will be performed offline, just after key generation. We can avoid having this additional setup step if we make the stronger assumption that identity-based encryption [3] exists.

[3] It may seem strange to describe this algorithm as part of the scheme: it is only to be used in the proofs of non-transferability, and need never be run in practice. However, it is important that the signer be willing to engage in it, because the third party *must believe* that the signer would. Because of this, it is important to include it in the description of the scheme, because the signer's willingness to engage in this protocol should not affect any other security properties of the scheme.

can be extracted from it). Also, the signatures produced by the signer in FakeSign will not be valid, and the recipient will accept in Disavow on such a signature.

Soundness: No dishonest signer can succeed in making the honest recipient accept in Sign unless the resulting designated confirmer signature is valid (that is, can be successfully extracted by the designated confirmer.)

Non-repudiation: No dishonest confirmer can succeed in making the honest recipient accept in Disavow on a valid (extractable) signature.

Unforgeability: No adversary with the ability to engage in any of the above protocols with the honest confirmer and the honest signer (including FakeSign) in any role and on any common input, can produce either a valid online-untransferable signature σ' on a message the adversary never requested a signature of, nor a valid extracted signature $\sigma^{*\prime}$, on a message the adversary didn't first request a signature, and later request extraction.

Online untransferability: Sign can be simulated in such a way that is indistinguishable from a real interaction to any distinguisher, so long as the adversary does not request an extraction of that signature. The simulator is assumed to have access to the secret key of the recipient, and may engage in FakeSign with the signer, but must engage in the Sign protocol interactively with the distinguisher.

Offline untransferability: There is a simulator that can produce a view indistinguishable from that of the dishonest recipient in the Sign protocol with the real signer, so long as the adversary never requests an extraction of the result of that protocol. The simulator is assumed to be able to engage in the FakeSign protocol with the signer.

2.2   Notation

When S is a finite set, the notation $x \leftarrow S$ refers to x being chosen uniformly at random from S. When M denotes a randomized algorithm, $x \leftarrow M(i)$ refers to x being determined by a random execution of M on input i. When we write $x_1 \leftarrow D_1; x_2 \leftarrow D_2(x_1); \ldots, x_r \leftarrow D_r(x_1, \ldots, x_{r-1})$ we refer to the probability distribution on $\{x_1, \ldots, x_r\}$ determined by first assigning x_1 according to D_1, then assigning x_2 according to D_2 on input x_1, et cetera.

When M is a two-party protocol, $(x_A, x_B) \leftarrow M^{A,B}(i_A; i_B; i)$ refers to an assignment where M is executed between parties A and B, where A's private input is i_A, B's private input is i_B, and i is the common input, and where x_A becomes the output of A, and x_B becomes the output of B. We omit the inclusion of A's secret key in i_A, B's secret key in i_B, and all public keys in i; we write only $M^{A,B}(i)$ to indicate that no unusual secret inputs are required. We use $x \leftarrow_b M^{A,B}(i_A; i_B; i)$ to refer to an assignment where x becomes x_A if $b = 1$ and x becomes x_B if $b = 2$; that is, b specifies which party's output is to be denoted by x.

When M is a two-party protocol, and P is one of the parties that participates in M, the notation $M^{P,\cdot}$ or $M^{\cdot,P}$ refers to the set of interactive Turing machines run by the honest party P in their execution of M. Thus, when an adversary is said to have oracle access to $M^{\cdot,P}$, this means the adversary has oracle access to all the Turing machines used by P during honest execution of M, where P has all ordinary inputs (the public keys of all parties, the security parameter 1^k, and P's own private keys), however, the adversary has control of all other inputs.

Similarly, when M is an algorithm, M^P (where P is the party that runs algorithm M) is that algorithm with the standard inputs of P specified, that is, all public keys, the security parameter, and P's own secret key. When M is an algorithm, we denote by $M(i;r)$ that we run M on input i with randomness r. When r is not previously specified, it is assumed to be chosen at random and remembered.

Honest parties are assumed to be state-preserving interactive Turing machines. Adversaries are assumed to be state-preserving oracle Turing machines. We write $\mathcal{O} = \{\mathcal{O}_1, \ldots, \mathcal{O}_r\}$ to indicate a single oracle that can be used to query any of the sub-oracles $\mathcal{O}_1, \ldots, \mathcal{O}_r$.

We use the symbol ν to designate a *negligible function*. A function is negligible if, for any $c > 0$, $\nu(k) < k^{-c}$ for all sufficiently large k.

2.3   Formal Definitions

Online-untransferable signatures. An online untransferable signature scheme is a tuple of several algorithms and two-party protocols:

1. $\mathsf{KeyGen}_S, \mathsf{KeyGen}_R, \mathsf{KeyGen}_C, \mathsf{Setup}, \mathsf{ExVerify}, \mathsf{Extract}_S$, and $\mathsf{Extract}_C$ are algorithms,
2. Sign and $\mathsf{FakeSign}$ are two-party protocols run between the signer (the first party) and a recipient (second party).
3. $\mathsf{Disavow}$ is a two-party protocol run between the confirmer (first party) and a recipient (second party).

Such algorithms and two-party protocols constitute a secure online-untransferable signature scheme if the following properties hold:

Efficiency: All algorithms, and all defined behavior for honest parties in two-party protocols, are probabilistic polynomial-time.

Completeness: If keys are generated honestly and setup is performed honestly, and the signing protocol is performed between honest parties, the result will be an online-untransferable signature that produces a valid extracted signature under both $\mathsf{Extract}^C$ and $\mathsf{Extract}^S$. If the FakeSign protocol is performed between an honest S and an honest R, the result is an online-untransferable signature that will be disavowed by $\mathsf{Disavow}$. Formally,

$\forall m,$
$\Pr[\ (PK_S, SK_S) \leftarrow \mathsf{KeyGen}_S(1^k); (PK_R, SK_R) \leftarrow \mathsf{KeyGen}_R(1^k);$
$\quad (PK_C, SK_C) \leftarrow \mathsf{KeyGen}_C(1^k); (PK_{S,C}, SK_{S,C}) \leftarrow \mathsf{Setup}^C(PK_S);$
$\quad (\sigma, x) \leftarrow_2 \mathsf{Sign}^{S,R}(m);$
$\quad \sigma' \leftarrow_2 \mathsf{FakeSign}^{S,R}(m);$

$y \leftarrow \mathsf{ExVerify}(\mathsf{Extract}_S(\sigma)); z \leftarrow \mathsf{ExVerify}(\mathsf{Extract}_C(\sigma));$
$w \leftarrow_2 \mathsf{Disavow}^{C,R}(\sigma') :$
$x = y = z = w = \mathrm{accept}] = 1$

Soundness: For all S' with oracle access to all of the algorithms and two party protocols run by parties C and R, and for all σ, if PK_C and PK_R are generated according to KeyGen_C and KeyGen_R, the probability that σ is not a valid signature, but S' succeeds in making the recipient accept and output σ in Sign is negligible. Formally, let $\mathcal{O} = \{\mathsf{Sign}^{\cdot,R}, \mathsf{Setup}^C, \mathsf{Disavow}^{\cdot,R}, \mathsf{FakeSign}^{\cdot,R}, \mathsf{Disavow}^{C,\cdot}, \mathsf{Extract}_C^C\}$. Then,

$\forall A$ oracle PPT, $\exists \nu\ \forall k$
$\Pr[\ (PK_R, SK_R) \leftarrow \mathsf{KeyGen}_R(1^k); (PK_C, SK_C) \leftarrow \mathsf{KeyGen}_C(1^k);$
$\quad PK_S \leftarrow A^{\mathcal{O}}(PK_R, PK_C, 1^k); (PK_{S,C}, SK_{S,C}) \leftarrow \mathsf{Setup}^C(PK_S);$
$\quad m \leftarrow A^{\mathcal{O}}; (\sigma, x) \leftarrow_2 \mathsf{Sign}^{A^{\mathcal{O}},R}(m);$
$\quad z \leftarrow \mathsf{ExVerify}(\mathsf{Extract}_C^C(\sigma), m) :$
$\quad x = \mathrm{accept} \wedge z \neq \mathrm{accept}\ ] < \nu(k)$

Non-Repudiation: The weakest possible notion here is that it should be hard for a dishonest signer and a dishonest confirmer to conspire to create a valid online-untransferable signature that could be successfully disavowed. We will use a stronger formulation, namely, that no such signatures exist for validly generated keys.

$\forall C'$ PPT adversary, $\forall (PK_C, SK_C) \in \mathsf{KeyGen}_C, (PK_S, SK_S) \in \mathsf{KeyGen}_S,$
$\qquad (PK_{C,S}, SK_{C,S}) \in \mathsf{Setup}, m, \sigma,$
$\Pr[\ x \leftarrow \mathsf{ExVerify}(\mathsf{Extract}_C^C(\sigma), m); y \leftarrow_2 \mathsf{Disavow}^{C',R}(SK_C, SK_S, SK_{C,S}; ; \sigma) :$
$\quad x = y = \mathrm{accept}] = 0$

Unforgeability: For all adversaries with oracle access to all algorithms run by all honest parties, if keys are generated honestly, cannot succeed in either (1) producing a valid signature σ on a message he never requested a signature of, or (2) producing a valid extracted signature σ^* on a message he never requested a signature of and then later requested extraction of. Formally, let $\mathcal{O} = \{\mathsf{Sign}^{\cdot,R}, \mathsf{FakeSign}^{\cdot,R}, \mathsf{FakeSign}^{S,\cdot}, \mathsf{Disavow}^{\cdot,R}, \mathsf{Extract}_S, \mathsf{Extract}_C, \mathsf{Setup}^C\}$. Then

$\forall A$ oracle PPT, $\forall p\ \exists \nu\ \forall k$
$\Pr[\ (PK_S, SK_S) \leftarrow \mathsf{KeyGen}_S(1^k); (PK_R, SK_R) \leftarrow \mathsf{KeyGen}_R(1^k);$
$\quad (PK_C, SK_C) \leftarrow \mathsf{KeyGen}_C(1^k); (PK_{S,C}, SK_{S,C}) \leftarrow \mathsf{Setup}^C(PK_S);$
$\quad m_1 \leftarrow A^{\mathcal{O}}(PK_S, PK_C, PK_R, PK_{S,C}); (\sigma_1, \omega_1) \leftarrow \mathsf{Sign}^{S,A^{\mathcal{O}}}(m_1); \ldots;$
$\quad m_{p(k)} \leftarrow A^{\mathcal{O}}(\sigma_{p(k)-1}); (\sigma_{p(k)}, \omega_{p(k)}) \leftarrow \mathsf{Sign}^{S,A^{\mathcal{O}}}(m_{p(k)});$
$\quad (m, \sigma) \leftarrow A^{\mathcal{O}}(\sigma_{p(k)}); y \leftarrow \mathsf{ExVerify}(\mathsf{Extract}_C^C(\sigma), m); z \leftarrow \mathsf{ExVerify}(\sigma, m) :$
$\quad z = \mathrm{accept}, \text{ and if } m = m_i \text{ then } A \text{ did not query } \mathsf{Extract} \text{ on } \sigma_i, \text{ or}$
$\quad y = \mathrm{accept}, \text{ but } m \notin \{m_1, \ldots, m_{p(k)}\}] < \nu(k)$

Online Untransferability: For all adversaries with oracle access to all algorithms run by all honest parties, if keys for $C, S,$ and R are generated honestly, then the adversary cannot distinguish between interacting with the real signer in Sign about a chosen message m and interacting with a simulator with access only to FakeSign on m, so long as the adversary never requests Extract or Disavow be run on the resulting signature. Let $\mathcal{O} = \{\text{Sign}^{\cdot,R}, \text{Sign}^{S,\cdot}, \text{FakeSign}^{\cdot,R}, \text{FakeSign}^{S,\cdot}, \text{Extract}_S^C, \text{Disavow}^{\cdot,R}, \text{Disavow}^{C,\cdot}, \text{Extract}_C^C, \text{Setup}^C\}$, and let $\mathcal{O}_\sigma$ be $\mathcal{O}$ except where the Disavow, Extract_C, Extract_S oracles will not operate if given σ as input. Then:

$\forall A$ oracle PPT, $\exists \text{Sim}\ \exists \nu\ \forall k$
$|\Pr[\ (PK_S, SK_S) \leftarrow \text{KeyGen}_S(1^k); (PK_R, SK_R) \leftarrow \text{KeyGen}_R(1^k);$
$\quad (PK_C, SK_C) \leftarrow \text{KeyGen}_C(1^k); (PK_{S,C}, SK_{S,C}) \leftarrow \text{Setup}^C(PK_S);$
$\quad m \leftarrow A^{\mathcal{O}}(PK_S, PK_R, PK_C, PK_{S,C}, SK_R); (\sigma, \omega) \leftarrow \text{Sign}^{S,A}(m);$
$\quad b \leftarrow A^{\mathcal{O}_\sigma} : b = 1] -$
$\Pr[\ (PK_S, SK_S) \leftarrow \text{KeyGen}_S(1^k); (PK_R, SK_R) \leftarrow \text{KeyGen}_R(1^k);$
$\quad (PK_C, SK_C) \leftarrow \text{KeyGen}_C(1^k); (PK_{S,C}, SK_{S,C}) \leftarrow \text{Setup}^C(PK_S);$
$\quad m \leftarrow A^{\mathcal{O}}(PK_S, PK_R, PK_C, PK_{S,C}, SK_R);$
$\quad (\sigma, \omega) \leftarrow \text{Sign}^{\text{Sim}^{\text{FakeSign}^S}, A}(SK_R; -; m); b \leftarrow A^{\mathcal{O}_\sigma} : b = 1]| < \nu(k)$

Offline Untransferability: For all dishonest recipients R' and for all adversaries with oracle access to all algorithms run by all honest parties, there is a simulator Sim such that if keys for C and S are generated honestly, the adversary cannot distinguish between R' after interacting with the signer in Sign and Sim after interacting only with the signer in FakeSign. Let $\mathcal{O}$ and $\mathcal{O}_\sigma$ be as in the online untransferability definition. Then:

$\forall A$ oracle PPT, $\forall R'$ PPT $\exists \text{Sim}$ oracle PPT $\exists \nu\ \forall k$
$\Pr[\ (PK_S, SK_S) \leftarrow \text{KeyGen}_S(1^k); (PK_C, SK_C) \leftarrow \text{KeyGen}_C(1^k);$
$\quad (PK_{S,C}, SK_{S,C}) \leftarrow \text{Setup}^C(PK_S);$
$\quad (m, PK_R, \alpha) \leftarrow A^{\mathcal{O}}; x_0 \leftarrow_2 \text{Sign}^{S,R'}(SK_S; \alpha; m);$
$\quad x_1 \leftarrow \text{Sim}^{\{R', \text{FakeSign}^S\}}(\alpha, m); b \leftarrow \{0, 1\}$
$\quad b' \leftarrow A^{\mathcal{O}_{\sigma_b}}(\sigma_b, \omega_b) : b' = b] < 1/2 + \nu(k)$

There are two main differences between the online and offline definitions for untransferability. First, in the online untransferability definition, there is only the simulator Sim and the adversary A; the adversary in this case is meant to model both the recipient and the third party. In the offline untransferability definition, there are two adversaries: the dishonest recipient R' and the third party, represented by A. A receives output either from the real signing protocol or from the simulator, but cannot interact in those protocols directly. The second difference is that in the online untransferability definition, the simulator knows the receiver's secret key SK_R (this models the notion that the recipient is aware of his own key), whereas the simulator is not given this information in the offline definition. Naturally, if the recipient is required to perform a proof of knowledge of SK_R during key registration, then online untransferability implies offline untransferability.

3 Our Construction

Our construction is fairly complex, so to help the reader understand it, we present our ideas incrementally.

As a first idea, we imagine that to make a designated confirmer signature on message m, the signer will create k random pairs of strings α_i, β_i such that $\alpha_i \oplus \beta_i = m$, and encrypt these values in the confirmer's encryption key to obtain $a_i = E_{PK_C}(\alpha_i)$ and $b_i = E_{PK_C}(\beta_i)$. The signer will then sign m along with $a_1, b_1, \ldots, a_k, b_k$; the signature is considered valid so long as σ is valid, and some pair a_i, b_i decrypt to values that XOR to m.

The recipient can verify on his own that σ is valid, but the signer and recipient must engage in a protocol for the recipient to be convinced that some pair decrypts to values that XOR to m. In order to accomplish this, the recipient first sends a commitment to a challenge string CH. The signer responds with $(\sigma, a_1, \ldots, b_k)$. The recipient checks σ and responds by opening CH. The signer then "opens" the encryption of a_i or b_i, depending on the ith bit of CH. Note that if none of the pairs actually decrypt to a pair that XOR to m, the probability that the signer will be able to succeed is 2^{-k}.

To extract a (valid) signature, the signer can simply decommit some pair of encryptions; this, along with the signature and the α_i value, is proof to anyone that the signature is valid.

Offline untransferability. In order to provide deniability, the signer must be willing to freely give out signatures that are valid *in format* but not valid *in content*. That is, the signer should provide a signature to any recipient on any m and any sequence of pairs $a_1, b_1, \ldots, a_k, b_k$ so long as (1) the signer obtains the decommitments of each a_i and b_i, and (2) the decryptions of each pair actually do not XOR to m. Thus, the mere signature of the signer proves nothing. Given this, a simulator can be constructed for the proof system: this fake signature service can be used to make the recipient reveal CH; once it is revealed, the simulator can rewind and use the fake signature service again to obtain an invalid signature for which the challenge CH can be answered.

Confirmer extractability. Another issue we must resolve is how the confirmer will actually extract plain signatures. In the current scheme, the confirmer will be able to decrypt all the pairs, but this does not necessarily imply that the confirmer will be able to *decommit* them.

In order to handle this, we modify our scheme. We ask that the signer assist the confirmer by encrypting the randomness used in producing a_i, b_i and including this in the signature. Now, if the signer is honest, the confirmer will be able to give the same decommitment information the signer would. If the signer is not honest, and does not properly include the decommitment information, the confirmer can always reveal his decryption secret key as an alternative form of decommitment. However, this is obviously not an ideal solution since it ruins the confirmer's keys. To fix this problem, we modify the setting so that the confirmer's true public key is a signing key, and the confirmer creates a different encryption key pair for each signer, and signs the public encryption key along with the signer's public key. The signature assures the recipient that the signer is using the correct key. Now, if the signer doesn't help the confirmer extract signatures in the normal way, C can reveal this secret encryption key: in effect, C is still able to extract signatures, but S's assurance that signatures cannot be transferred is lost. Of course, S has no one else to blame, since S was the one who was dishonest.

This mechanism allows the confirmer not only to extract, but also to disavow signatures (disavowal is necessary because of the FakeSign protocol the signer provides) by decrypting all the pairs, or by revealing the secret key.

Reconfirmation. In designated confirmer signature schemes, a Verify protocol and a Disavow is typically provided both for the signer and for the confirmer, in order to prove the validity or invalidity of a designated confirmer signature to the recipient. Verify is often given as a separate protocol from Sign, in order to establish, initially, the validity of a signature. Here, though, the proof of validity is part of the Sign protocol, so Verify would be unneeded initially, and later, there would be no need for the recipient to reconfirm the validity of a signature already established as valid. We insist that the recipient sign the messages they send during the initial proof of validity, so that it will be clear that a given online-untransferable signature was produced after a proof was provided to the recipient.

Online untransferability. The difference between online untransferability and offline is that in an attempt at online transfer, the dishonest recipient interacts concurrently with both the signer and some third party. To prevent online transfer, we will need to assume that the recipient knows their secret key. As part of key generation for a recipient, the recipient generates an encryption key pair, that will be used for the initial commitment to CH. If we assume that the simulator knows the corresponding secret key, the simulator can determine CH *without rewinding*, which is what allows us to simulate signing in the presence of an actively interacting adversary.

3.1   The Scheme

Now, we will give the full specification of our scheme. We assume the existence of a secure (IND-CPA), perfectly-faithful[4], checkable[5] public-key cryptosystem (G, E, D) and a secure (CMA) signature scheme $(\mathsf{KeyGen}, \mathsf{Sig}, \mathsf{Ver})$.

---

[4] That is, decryption inverts encryption with probability 1.

[5] That is, there is a simple check given PK and SK to determine whether SK could be generated along with PK. It is easy to make any cryptosystem checkable, by simply including the randomness used in key generation in the secret key.

The specification of the algorithms and protocols for our scheme are as follows:

- KeyGen$_S$: Generate a signature key pair (PK_S, SK_S) using KeyGen.
- KeyGen$_C$: Generate a signature key pair (PK_C, SK_C) using KeyGen.
- KeyGen$_R$: The recipient uses G to generate a key pair (PK_R^E, SK_R^E), and uses KeyGen to generate a signature pair PK_R^{sig}, SK_R^{sig}. The recipient's public key $PK_R = (PK_R^E, PK_R^{sig})$ and the recipient's secret key is $SK_R = (SK_R^E, SK_R^{sig})$.
- Setup: The confirmer generates an encryption key pair $(PK_{C,S}^E, SK_{C,S}^E)$ from G, and creates a signature σ_0 on the pair $(PK_S, PK_{C,S}^E)$ using SK_C. The key $PK_{C,S}$ consists of the triple $(\sigma_0, PK_S, PK_{C,S}^E)$, while $SK_{C,S} = SK_{C,S}^E$.
  Sign: The protocol runs in the following steps:
  1. The recipient generates a uniform random string CH of length k and sends $e = E_{PK_R^E}(CH; r)$ to the signer and remembers r for later use.
  2. The signer generates k uniform random strings $\alpha_1, \dots, \alpha_k$ each of the same length as the message m. The signer produces $3k$ encryptions under the encryption key of $PK_{C,S}$: $a_i = E_{PK_{C,S}^E}(\alpha_i; r_i^0)$, $b_i = E_{PK_{C,S}^E}(\alpha_i \oplus m; r_i^1)$, and $c_i = E_{PK_{C,S}^E}(r_i^0 \| r_i^1)$. The signer then sends the public key $PK_{C,S}$, and for each i, α_i, a_i, b_i, c_i to the recipient. The signer remembers r_i^0, r_i^1 for later use.
  3. The recipient checks that $PK_{C,S}$ contains a valid signature σ_0; if not, the recipient rejects. Otherwise, the recipient sends CH and r, as well as a signature σ_R on the tuple $(m, CH, PK_{C,S}, \alpha_1, \dots, c_k)$ under SK_R^{sig}.
  4. The signer checks validity of the signature σ_R, and checks that $e = E_{PK_R^E}(CH; r)$; if either check fails, the signer aborts. The signer then sends $r_i^{CH_i}$ for each bit CH_i of the challenge string, to the recipient, along with a signature σ on $(m, CH, PK_{C,S}, PK_R, \alpha_1, \dots, c_k, \sigma_R)$.
  5. The recipient checks, for each i such that $CH_i = 0$, that r_i^0 provided by S, used to encrypt α_i under $PK_{C,S}$, gives a_i. The recipient then checks, for each i such that $CH_i = 1$, that r_i^1 provided by S, used to encrypt $\alpha_i \oplus m$ under $PK_{C,S}$, gives b_i. The recipient then checks that the signature σ is a valid one. If all these checks are successful, the recipient accepts and outputs σ along with $(m, CH, PK_{C,S}, PK_R, \alpha_1, \dots, c_k, \sigma_R)$, otherwise the recipient rejects.

At this point we pause to make a couple of remarks, which simplify the task of describing the remaining parts of the scheme. In our scheme, an online-untransferable signature is a signature σ on $m_\sigma = (m, CH, PK_{C,S}, PK_R, \alpha_1, \dots, c_k, \sigma_R)$. Three things can be checked about σ and m_σ based only on public information, namely:

1. σ should be a valid signature under PK_S, and PK_S should be specified as part of the signature σ_0 in $PK_{C,S}$.
2. The signature σ_0 in $PK_{C,S}$ should be valid.
3. The signature σ_R should be a valid on $(m, CH, PK_{C,S}, \alpha_1, \dots, c_k)$, checked with the verifying key PK_R^{sig} of PK_R.

For simplicity, we say that an online-untransferable signature σ is *format-valid* if all these checks are passed, and we assume that any of the below methods halt with an error if given a format-invalid online-untransferable signature.

- Extract$_S$: On input a valid online-untransferable signature σ, m_σ the signer reveals $\sigma^* = (\sigma, i, r_i^0, r_i^1, \epsilon)$ for an arbitrary i.[6] Given an invalid online-untransferable signature, the signer rejects.
- Extract$_C$: On input a format-valid online-untransferable signature σ, m_σ, the confirmer decrypts $a_1, b_1, \ldots, a_k, b_k$ under $SK_{C,S}$, and finds some i such that $D_{SK_{C,S}^E}(a_i) \oplus D_{SK_{C,S}^E}(b_i) = m$, and rejects if there is no such i. The confirmer then finds r_i^0 and r_i^1 by computing $D_{SK_{C,S}^E}(c_i)$, and checks to see if $E_{PK_{C,S}^E}(\alpha_i; r_i^0) = a_i$ and $E_{PK_{C,S}^E}(\alpha_i \oplus m; r_i^1) = b_i$. If so, the confirmer publishes $\sigma^* = (\sigma, m_\sigma, i, r_i^0, r_i^1, \epsilon)$. If not, the confirmer publishes $\sigma^* = (\sigma, m_\sigma, i, \epsilon, \epsilon, SK_{C,S})$.
- ExVerify: On input a quadruple $(\sigma, i, r^0, r^1, SK)$, we first check that σ is format-valid, and then check that either $E_{PK_{C,S}}(\alpha_i; r^0) = a_i$ and $E_{PK_{C,S}}(\alpha_i \oplus m; r^1) = b_i$ or that if this is not the case, that SK is the secret key associated with $PK_{C,S}$ and that $D_{SK}(a_i) \oplus D_{SK}(b_i) = m$.[7]
- Disavow: On input σ an invalid but format-valid untransferable signature, the confirmer decrypts each c_i to obtain r_i^0, r_i^1, and checks that for all i, $E_{PK_{C,S}^E}(D_{SK_{C,S}^E}(a_i)); r_i^0) = a_i$ and $E_{PK_{C,S}^E}(D_{SK_{C,S}^E}(b_i)); r_i^1) = b_i$. If so, the confirmer reveals $D_{SK_{C,S}^E}(a_i), D_{SK_{C,S}^E}(b_i), r_i^0$, and r_i^1 for each i. If not, but $D_{SK_{C,S}^E}(a_i) \oplus D_{SK_{C,S}^E}(b_i) \neq m$ for any i, the confirmer reveals $SK_{C,S}^E$. The recipient checks that no pair XORs to make m. Then, in the former case, the recipient checks that the r values properly decommit all of the a_i and b_is; in the latter case, the recipient checks that $SK_{C,S}^E$ is the secret key relating to $PK_{C,S}^E$.
- FakeSign: The recipient first asks the signer to provide $PK_{C,S}$, and then
  1. Chooses any $\alpha_1, \beta_1, \ldots, \alpha_k, \beta_k$,
  2. Chooses random strings r_i^0, r_i^1, r_i^2 for each $1 \leq i \leq k$,
  3. Computes $a_i = E_{PK_{C,S}}(\alpha_i; r_i^0)$, $b_i = E_{PK_{C,S}}(\beta_i; r_i^1)$, and $c_i = E_{PK_{C,S}}(r_i^0 || r_i^1; r_i^2)$ for each i,
  4. Computes $\sigma_R = \text{Sig}_{SK_R}(m, CH, PK_{C,S}, \alpha_1, a_1, b_1, c_1, \ldots, \alpha_k, a_k, b_k, c_k)$,
  and sends $m, CH, PK_{C,S}, PK_R, \sigma_R$ and for each i, $\alpha_i, \beta_i, a_i, b_i, c_i, r_i^0, r_i^1$, and r_i^2 to the signer. The signer then checks that r_i^0, r_i^1 and r_i^2 properly decommit a_i, b_i, c_i to α_i, β_i, and $r_i^0 || r_i^1$, respectively, and that for each i, $\alpha_i \oplus \beta_i \neq m$. If so, the signer produces a signature of $(m, CH, PK_{C,S}, PK_R, \alpha_1, \ldots, c_k, \sigma_R)$ and if it is format-valid, sends it to the recipient.

---

[6] In order to perform this function, the signer will need to be able to remember, for each online untransferable signature it issues, what the random strings r_i^0 and r_i^1 are that it used. This can be simplified by generating r_i^b according to a pseudorandom function with fixed seed and input, say, c.

[7] For simplicity, we imagine that the decryption key $SK_{C,S}$ includes the randomness used to generate the key pair $(PK_{C,S}, SK_{C,S})$, so checking that SK is the secret key associated with $PK_{C,S}$ involves regenerating the key pair from the same randomness.

We can now state our main result.

Theorem 1. (KeyGen_S, KeyGen_R, KeyGen_C, Setup, $\mathsf{ExVerify}$, $\mathsf{Extract}_S$, $\mathsf{Extract}_C$, Sign, $\mathsf{FakeSign}$, $\mathsf{Disavow}$) *is an online-untransferable signature scheme.*

Proof. It should be clear that all the algorithms involved in our construction are efficient, and that our scheme satisfies completeness and non-repudiation.

Soundness: In order for adversary to succeed, the adversary must be able, with non-negligible probability, make the recipient accept in Sign but output a result that is not confirmed as valid by the confirmer. Such an adversary must either make the recipient accept with a σ_0 not produced by the confirmer, or make the recipient accept with a σ_0 produced by the confirmer, for an invalid signature. If the former occurs with non-negligible probability, the adversary can be used in a simple reduction to forge signatures relative to PK_C.

Otherwise, the adversary can make the recipient accept an invalid signature but with a σ_0 produced by the confirmer, with non-negligible probability.[8] If this is the case, note that if the signer sends encrypted pairs for an invalid signature, there is at most one string CH for which the adversary can send a satisfactory response in step 4. When the adversary sends its step 2 message, however, CH has not yet been revealed. We can therefore use the adversary's choice of encrypted pairs to break the security of encryption under PK_R^E.

The reduction is simple: we choose two random messages to distinguish, CH and CH', and obtain the encryption of one or the other under the key we are to break. We run the adversary in its attack, using this key as PK_R^E, and generating all other keys normally. In the sign protocol, we send the challenge ciphertext in step 1. In step 2, if the adversary responds with $PK_{C,S}$ that was produced by the confirmer (so we are aware of $SK_{C,S}^E$), we decrypt all the pairs and determine if the ultimate signature would be invalid. If the adversary uses an unexpected $PK_{C,S}$, or if the ultimate signature would be valid, we flip a coin. Otherwise, we determine if there exists a challenge string CH'' for which the adversary could give an answer in step 4; if so, and $CH'' = CH$, we output 0, otherwise, we output a random bit. It can be readily verified that a successful adversary results in a successful attack against PK_R^E.

Unforgeability: Note that any valid untransferable signature or extracted signature must first be a format-valid signature, and thus, a signature under the signer's key. The adversary cannot produce a forgery with an original signature (i.e. not issued by the signer) except with negligible probability, by the existential unforgeability of the signature scheme. Similarly, the adversary cannot reuse a signature issued in $\mathsf{FakeSign}$ because such a signature will never be valid. The remaining case is where the adversary is able to extract a signature obtained via Sign.

There are two ways this can happen: either the adversary produces and reveals $SK_{C,S}^E$ or it can demonstrate the decryption for both parts of one of the pairs. If

---

[8] Note that in this case the pairs must *be* invalid: otherwise, the confirmer would succeed in extracting a signature, since the confirmer knows $SK_{C,S}^E$.

the former happens with non-negligible probability, there are two sub-cases: either the adversary manages to query $\mathsf{Extract}_C$ on an input that will cause $SK_{C,S}^E$ to be revealed, or the adversary produces $SK_{C,S}^E$ without that information.

Note that any signature produced by the signer in Sign will not result in the key being revealed by $\mathsf{Extract}_C$. Similarly, a signature produced in $\mathsf{FakeSign}$ will not result in any answer from $\mathsf{Extract}_C$ since the signature will be invalid. Thus, if the adversary obtains $SK_{C,S}^E$ from $\mathsf{Extract}_C$, the adversary must have produced a signature never created by the signer. If this happens with non-negligible probability, a simple reduction shows that the existential unforgeability of the signature scheme is violated.

If the adversary outputs $SK_{C,S}^E$ but not via $\mathsf{Extract}_C$, we can attack the encryption scheme under key $PK_{C,S}^E$. We can run the adversary in its attack without knowing $SK_{C,S}^E$ ourselves (and, without ever needing to decrypt with it); if the adversary can determine the correct $SK_{C,S}^E$ in such a circumstance, we can easily decipher messages.

If the adversary reveals both parts of one of the pairs, we can make a reduction to break the security of the encryption scheme. The proof is a hybrid argument. First we argue that the adversary cannot distinguish between a normal setting in which for one random instance of the Sign protocol, the adversary never requests extraction of that signature, and one in which for one random instance of the Sign protocol, all the c_i values are encryptions of random values unrelated to the randomness used in encrypting a_i and b_i, and the adversary never requests extraction of that signature. If not, we can distinguish between the encryption of two random messages.

Given that the adversary cannot distinguish between these two scenarios, we can make a reduction directly. The reduction works by choosing one instance of Sign at random, giving encryptions of unrelated random values for all the c_i, and choosing one element of one pair at random and substituting an unknown challenge ciphertext there: either the proper encryption of α_i or β_i, or a distinct random value. If the unknown ciphertext encrypts the correct value, the adversary has a non-negligible chance of revealing it, in which case we discover the value. If the adversary does not reveal the ciphertext we hope for, we simply output a random guess. The adversary cannot reveal the ciphertext to be other than it is, so the non-negligible advantage we obtain is not offset at all.

Thus, if the adversary can break unforgeability, he can either break encryption under $PK_{C,S}^E$ or he can forge signatures under PK_S.

Online untransferability: We show how a simulator, with the secret information of the recipient (including the secret decryption key SK_R^E, which is part of the recipient's secret key), and working with the signer, can make a transcript computationally indistinguishable from one obtained in Sign on message m, but for which the signature is invalid. The simulator works as follows:

1. The simulator initiates $\mathsf{FakeSign}$ with the signer and obtains $PK_{C,S}$.
2. On input m and e, the simulator decrypts e to obtain CH. The simulator then generates $2k$ random strings $\alpha_1, \ldots, \alpha_k, \beta_1, \ldots, \beta_k$ such that for

all i, $\alpha_i \oplus \beta_i \neq m$. The simulator then computes a_i and b_i as follows: If $CH_i = 0$ then $a_i = E_{PKE_{C,S}}(\alpha_i; r_i^0)$ and $b_i = E_{PKE_{C,S}}(\beta_i; r_i^1)$. If $CH_i = 1$ then $a_i = E_{PKE_{C,S}}(\beta_i \oplus m; r_i^0)$ and $b_i = E_{PKE_{C,S}}(\alpha_i \oplus m; r_i^1)$. The simulator then generates $c_i = E_{PKE_{C,S}}(r_i^0 || r_i^1; r_i^2)$ and sends $PK_{C,S}^E$, and for each i, α_i, a_i, b_i, c_i to the dishonest recipient.

3. If the recipient responds with a decommitment of e to the string CH and a signature σ_R, the simulator checks the decommitment and σ_R, and if they are both valid, sends $m, CH, PK_{C,S}, PK_R, \sigma_R$, and for each i the values $\alpha_i', \beta_i', a_i, b_i, c_i, r_i^0, r_i^1, r_i^2$ to the signer in FakeSign, where if $CH_i = 0$, $\alpha_i' = \alpha_i$ and $\beta_i' = \beta_i$, and where $\alpha_i' = \beta_i \oplus m$ and $\beta_i' = \alpha_i \oplus m$ if $CH_i = 1$. When the signer responds with σ, the simulator sends the recipient with $r_i^{CH_i}$ for each i along with σ.

The only distinction between the messages generated by the simulator and the messages generated in the real signing protocol is that in the simulated messages, each pair (a_i, b_i) do not represent encryptions of two plaintexts that XOR to m, whereas in the real protocol, they do. A simple reduction proves that distinguishing these transcripts implies the ability to break encryption under $PK_{C,S}^E$. It should be clear this simulator is efficient.

Offline untransferability: We show how a simulator, with the ability to rewind the dishonest recipient, can produce a view indistinguishable from the one the dishonest recipient produces with the signer in Sign. The simulator works as follows:

1. Initiate FakeSign with the signer and obtain $PK_{C,S}$.
2. Run the Sign protocol honestly until the beginning of step 4. If the recipient sends an invalid decommitment CH, r, abort to the recipient, and output what it outputs.
3. Rewind to step 2 of Sign. Pick new random strings α_i for each i, and if $CH_i = 0$ we let $\beta_i \neq \alpha_i \oplus m$ be random and let $a_i = E_{PKE_{C,S}}(\alpha_i; r_i^0)$ and $b_i = E_{PKE_{C,S}}(\beta_i; r_i^1)$ and compute c_i normally. If $CH_i = 1$ we let $\alpha_i' \neq \alpha_i$ be random and let $a_i = E_{PKE_{C,S}}(\alpha_i'; r_i^0)$ and $b_i = E_{PKE_{C,S}}(\alpha_i \oplus m; r_i^1)$ and compute c_i normally. Send $PK_{C,S}$ and for each i, α_i, a_i, b_i, c_i to the recipient; remember r_i^0, r_i^1, r_i^2 for use later.
4. If the recipient sends back an invalid decommitment, go back to (simulator) step 3 and try again with new random values. Otherwise, if the recipient sends a valid decommitment but an invalid signature, abort to the recipient and output what it outputs. If the recipient sends a valid decommitment and a valid signature, send $m, CH, PK_{C,S}, PK_R, \sigma_R$, and for each i, send $\alpha_i, \beta_i, a_i, b_i, c_i, r_i^0, r_i^1$, and r_i^2 to the signer in FakeSign and obtain σ. Send σ to the recipient and output what it outputs.

The main point, again, is that the adversary should not be able to distinguish between being given pairs that decrypt to values that XOR to m from being given pairs that do not, so long as all the decrypted responses are as expected. This is important for two reasons: first of all, it makes the views computationally indistinguishable, and second, it guarantees that the simulator runs in expected polynomial time.

Let p be the probability that the dishonest recipient reveals a proper decommitment in step 3 of Sign with the real signer. Since the Simulator does exactly as the signer does until that decommitment is given, the simulator has a probability p of producing a recipient output in which a proper decommitment is given. (Note that if one is given, the simulator will continue to try its steps 3 and 4 until the recipient decommits properly in one of them. Given this as a precondition, the outputs are computationally indistinguishable, since the only difference is whether the pairs decrypt properly or not.

With probability $1 - p$, the signer (or the simulator) encounters an invalid decommitment from the recipient. Given this as a precondition, the outputs are identical, since the simulator and signer act exactly the same.

It only remains to prove that the simulator runs in expected polynomial time. We can consider the probability p^0 that the recipient decommits properly when interacting with the signer, and the probability p^1 that the recipient decommits properly when interacting with the simulator's further attempts. If it is likely that an e is chosen such that p^0 is significantly larger than p^1, this leads directly to an attack on the encryption system. If not, then for all e without this property, the expected number of attempts taken by the simulator is $1 + \frac{p^0|_e}{p^1|_e} = 1 + \frac{p^0|_e}{p^0|_e + \nu} \le 2$. The probability that an e is chosen without this property is negligible; therefore, with all but negligible probability, the simulator runs in expected polynomial time.

4 Analysis

4.1 Efficiency and Assumptions

In our Sign protocol, the signer must compute $3k$ encryptions and a signature, and must check a signature and an encryption. The recipient must check k encryptions and a signature, and produce one encryption and two signatures. Thus, each party computes $O(k)$ cryptographic operations. The signing protocol is four rounds. In our Disavow protocol, each party must compute a similar amount but the protocol is non-interactive, and we have no need for Verify protocols. The remaining protocols are similarly efficient but less important.

Only the schemes of Camenisch and Shoup [6] and Gentry, Molnar, and Ramzan [15] attain a confirmation protocol with $O(1)$ operations but both of those results were based on specific computational assumptions, and all prior schemes require at least $O(k)$ operations for disavowal.

The security of our scheme is based on the security of (1) the underlying signature scheme, and (2) the underlying encryption scheme. These assumptions are minimal, as such a scheme obviously implies signatures, and it is known the designated confirmer signatures imply public-key encryption [22].

4.2 Model and Variants

In addition, we make an assumption for the online security case that the recipient knows SK_R. The most natural way to ensure this assumption is to force the recipient to prove knowledge of SK_R when key registration takes place. This simplifies things significantly, because then the simulator for *offline* untransferability can extract the secret key, so online untransferability implies offline untransferability. However, requiring proofs of knowledge at key registration is burdensome.

The other way to deal with this assumption is to not require a proof of knowledge but simply to assume the recipient knows their own key. This is fairly reasonable, since we imagine "piggybacking" on an already existing PKI, in which the recipient probably already needs to know his or her key. In this scenario, we still guarantee online untransferability for any recipient that is honest during key registration (this reflects the likely case in the job offer scenario: Berkeley may believe that Alice was honest initially, although she might have become tempted later on.) Recipients that are dishonest during key registration may circumvent this, but as we show, this still does not allow them to perform offline transfer attacks.

The recipient's *signature* key does not serve the most important function. It is used to sign σ_R, which exists to satisfy the recipient should they ever want to reconfirm an online-untransferable signature without extracting it, a property that prior schemes have. If this requirement is unnecessary, the recipient's signature key can be dropped entirely.

For simplicity of presentation, we assume that the confirmer generates a separate encryption key for each signer. This may be objectionable, as it increases the interaction necessary for the scheme to proceed. However, if we are willing to assume the existence of identity-based encryption schemes, we can do away with the extra step. Instead, then, PK_C will be a master key for an IBE scheme, and $PK_{C,S}^E$ will be defined as the public key associated with identity S. By the security properties of IBE schemes, the encryption remains secure for other identities, even when the secret keys for certain identities are revealed (thus, one dishonest signer will not "ruin" the security for any honest signer).

Finally, it may seem to be a drawback of our scheme that the signer must be willing to engage in the FakeSign protocol on request. This does put a potential burden on the signer, but the ability of others to engage in the FakeSign protocol with the signer is only useful in the proofs of security: thus, offering this service will have little drawback, and will ensure untransferability.

5 Conclusion

Designated confirmer signatures were designed to be a solution that balances untransferability of signatures with accountability of the signer. Much of the work done on designated confirmer signatures was concerned with enhancing its efficiency and reducing the assumptions involved. However, even the original definitions were somewhat lacking in terms of online transferability. Fortunately, the notion of public keys comes to our rescue: by assuming the existence of an established public key, we can push the window of opportunity for collusion between the recipient and the third party back in time: now, instead of colluding only during the actual signature protocol, they must have been colluding ever since the recipient's key was registered.

We have shown how to attain this level of online untransferability, while at the same time giving a protocol that is efficient, does not rely on the random oracle assumption, and uses general cryptographic assumptions.

We wish to thank Jens Groth, David Molnar, and the anonymous reviewers for their valuable input.

References

1. Baek, J., Safavi-Naini, R., Susilo, W.: Universal Designated Verifier Signature Proof. In: Roy [25], pp. 644–661
2. Barak, B., Canetti, R., Nielsen, J., Pass, R.: Universally Composable Protocols with Relaxed Set-up Assumptions. In: 45th Annual IEEE Symposium on Foundations of Computer Science (FOCS 2004), pp. 186–195 (2004)
3. Boneh, D., Franklin, M.: Identity-Based Encryption from the Weil Pairing. SIAM Journal on Computing 32(3), 586–615 (2003)
4. Boneh, D. (ed.): CRYPTO 2003. LNCS, vol. 2729. Springer, Heidelberg (2003)
5. Camenisch, J., Michels, M.: Confirmer Signature Schemes Secure Against Adaptive Adversaries. In: Preneel, B. (ed.) EUROCRYPT 2000. LNCS, vol. 1807, pp. 14–18. Springer, Heidelberg (2000)
6. Camenisch, J., Shoup, V.: Practical Verifiable Encryption and Decryption of Discrete Logarithms. In: Boneh [4], pp. 126–144
7. Camenisch, J., Lysyanskaya, A.: An Identity Escrow Scheme with Appointed Verifiers. In: Kilian, J. (ed.) CRYPTO 2001. LNCS, vol. 2139, pp. 388–407. Springer, Heidelberg (2001)
8. Canetti, R., Goldreich, O., Goldwasser, S., Micali, S.: Resettable Zero-Knowledge. In: Proceedings of the Thirty-Second Annual ACM Symposium on Theory of Computing (May 21–23, 2000)
9. Chaum, D.: Designated Confirmer Signatures. In: De Santis [12], pp. 86–91
10. Chaum, D., Van Antwerpen, H.: Undeniable Signatures. In: Brassard, G. (ed.) CRYPTO 1989. LNCS, vol. 435, pp. 20–24. Springer, Heidelberg (1990)
11. Davies, D.W. (ed.): EUROCRYPT 1991. LNCS, vol. 547, pp. 8–11. Springer, Heidelberg (1991)
12. De Santis, A. (ed.): EUROCRYPT 1994. LNCS, vol. 950, pp. 9–12. Springer, Heidelberg (1995)
13. Desmedt, Y., Yung, M.: Weaknesses of Undeniable Signature Schemes (Extended Abstract). In: Davies [11], pp. 205–220
14. Dolev, D., Dwork, C., Naor, M.: Nonmalleable Cryptography. SIAM Journal on Computing 30(2), 391–437 (2000)
15. Gentry, C., Molnar, D., Ramzan, Z.: Efficient Designated Confirmer Signatures Without Random Oracles or General Zero-Knowledge Proofs. In: Roy [25], pp. 662–681.
16. Goldwasser, S., Waisbard, E.: Transformation of Digital Signature Schemes into Designated Confirmer Signature Schemes. In: Naor, M. (ed.) TCC 2004. LNCS, vol. 2951, pp. 77–100. Springer, Heidelberg (2004)

17. Herzog, J., Liskov, M., Micali, S.: Plaintext Awareness via Key Registration. In: Boneh [4], pp. 548–564
18. Jakobsson, M.: Blackmailing Using Undeniable Signatures. In: De Santis [12], pp. 425–427
19. Jakobsson, M., Sako, K., Impagliazzo, R.: Designated Verifier Proofs and their Applications. In: Maurer, U.M. (ed.) EUROCRYPT 1996. LNCS, vol. 1070, pp. 12–16. Springer, Heidelberg (1996)
20. Michels, M., Stadler, M.: Generic Constructions for Secure and Efficient Confirmer Signature Schemes. In: Nyberg, K. (ed.) EUROCRYPT 1998. LNCS, vol. 1403, pp. 406–421. Springer, Heidelberg (1998)
21. Monnerat, J., Vaudenay, S.: Chaum's Designated Confirmer Signature Revisited. In: Zhou, J., López, J., Deng, R.H., Bao, F. (eds.) ISC 2005. LNCS, vol. 3650, pp. 20–23. Springer, Heidelberg (2005)
22. Okamoto, T.: Designated Confirmer Signatures and Public-Key Encryption are Equivalent. In: Desmedt, Y.G. (ed.) CRYPTO 1994. LNCS, vol. 839, pp. 21–25. Springer, Heidelberg (1994)
23. Paillier, P.: Public-Key Cryptosystems Based on Composite Degree Residue Classes. In: Stern, J. (ed.) EUROCRYPT 1999. LNCS, vol. 1592, pp. 2–6. Springer, Heidelberg (1999)
24. Pedersen, T.P.: A Threshold Cryptosystem without a Trusted Party (Extended Abstract). In: Davies [11], pp. 522–526
25. Roy, B. (ed.): ASIACRYPT 2005. LNCS, vol. 3788, pp. 4–8. Springer, Heidelberg (2005)
26. Steinfeld, R., Bull, L., Wang, H., Pieprzyk, J.: Universal Designated-Verifier Signatures. In: Laih, C.-S. (ed.) ASIACRYPT 2003. LNCS, vol. 2894, pp. 523–542. Springer, Heidelberg (2003)

Security of Digital Signature Schemes in Weakened Random Oracle Models

Akira Numayama[1], Toshiyuki Isshiki[1,2], and Keisuke Tanaka[1]

[1] Department of Mathematical and Computing Sciences, Tokyo Institute of Technology,
W8-55, 2-12-1 Ookayama Meguro-ku, Tokyo 152-8552, Japan
{numayama.a.aa@m,keisuke@is}.titech.ac.jp
[2] NEC Corporation, 1753 Shimonumabe Nakahara-ku Kawasaki, Kanagawa 211-8666, Japan
t-issiki@bx.jp.nec.com

Abstract. We formalize the notion of several weakened random oracle models in order to capture which property of a hash function is crucial to prove the security of a cryptographic scheme. In particular, we focus on augmenting the random oracle with additional oracles that respectively return collisions, second-preimages, and first-preimages. We study the security of the full domain hash signature scheme, as well as three variants thereof in the weakened random oracle models, leading to a separation result.

Keywords: random oracle model, digital signature, collision, preimage.

1 Introduction

BACKGROUND. When analyzing the security of cryptographic schemes, we often idealize hash functions as truly random functions called random oracles. A number of schemes were proposed and proved secure in the random oracle model (ROM) [1,2,3,4,5].

When it comes to implementations of the cryptographic schemes, we have to replace the random oracles by cryptographic hash functions. This replacement might make the cryptographic schemes insecure.

An important thing is that one should carefully observe the properties of the ROM, which are necessary for proving the security of the schemes, and replace the random oracles with some *suitable* hash functions. For example the security of the *hash-and-sign* type signature schemes, which are secure in the ROM, relies on the collision resistance property of the ROM. If one can obtain two distinct m, m' such that $h(m) = h(m')$ and the signature $\sigma = \mathsf{Sig}(h(m))$, then (m', σ) is a valid forgery. Therefore, this case requires that a hash function is collision resistant.

Recent progress [6,7] on the attacks against cryptographic hash functions such as SHA-1 and MD5, raises the question on the assumption that hash functions are collision resistant. Therefore, it is interesting to know whether the collision resistance property of the ROM is necessary for proving the security of the schemes. More generally, it is worth classifying the schemes by the properties of the ROM that their security essentially rely on.

R. Cramer (Ed.): PKC 2008, LNCS 4939, pp. 268–287, 2008.

PREVIOUS WORKS. Recent works [8,9,10,11] introduced variants of the random oracle model, where some properties of the ROM are weakened. If one can prove that a cryptographic scheme is secure in the ROM but not in a weakened random oracle model, then the security of the scheme essentially relies on the difference between these models.

Unruh [8] proposed a random oracle model where *oracle-dependent* auxiliary inputs are allowed. In this setting, the adversary of some cryptographic protocol obtains an auxiliary input that can contain information about the random oracle (e.g. collisions). He showed that the RSA-OAEP encryption scheme [2] is secure in the random oracle model even in the presence of *oracle-dependent* auxiliary inputs.

Nielsen [9] proposed the *non-programmable* random oracle model where the random oracle is not *programmable*. In this model, one cannot set the value that the random oracle answers to some appropriate value. The author showed that a non-interactive non-committing encryption scheme exists in the ROM (assuming trapdoor permutations exists), but not in the *non-programmable* random oracle model.

Liskov [10] proposed the models of weak hash functions where there exist the random oracle and the additional oracles that break some properties of the ROM. He listed several such oracles that provide, for example, collisions. He also proposed a general construction of a hash function from weak hash functions. Pasini and Vaudenay [11] applied Liskov's idea to the security analysis of digital signature schemes. They considered the security of *hash-then-sign* type signature schemes in the random oracle model with an additional oracle that returns first-preimages. In the security analysis of signature schemes in their model, the reduction algorithm simulates both the random oracle and the additional oracle.

OUR CONTRIBUTIONS. By using Liskov's idea, we propose the following three models: the *collision tractable* random oracle model (CT-ROM), the *second-preimage tractable* random oracle model (SPT-ROM), and the *first-preimage tractable* random oracle model (FPT-ROM). The CT-ROM (resp. SPT-ROM, FPT-ROM) consists of the random oracle and the collision (resp. second-preimage, first-preimage) oracle that returns collisions (resp. second-preimages, first-preimages).

Our models are a bit different from those of Liskov with respect to: first, in our model, the collision oracle may not provide a collision even if there are collisions, while in the Liskov model it always provides a collision; second, in our model, the second-preimage (resp. first-preimage) oracle provides $\perp$ if there is no second-preimage (resp. first-preimage). Liskov only considered compression functions, where there are some collisions and preimages with high probability. When taking into account expanding functions, the Liskov model turns out to be too strong.

Notice here that it can be shown that the security with respect to the random oracle model with *oracle-dependent* auxiliary input implies the security with respect to the CT-ROM, since the *oracle-dependent* auxiliary input can contain a sufficiently long list of collisions. For the security with respect to the SPT-ROM and the FPT-ROM, the proof technique employed in [8] cannot be applied to our models. This is because the random oracle model with *oracle-dependent* auxiliary input does not capture the attack models with adaptive queries.

In almost all the proofs employing the random oracles, the reduction algorithms simulate the random oracles with embedding the target problem instances. We give new oracle simulation methods that are applicable for our models. These methods are useful to simulate both the random oracle and the additional oracles when analyzing the security of cryptographic schemes.

In our models, we consider the security of two RSA-based signature schemes: RSA-FDH [3] and RSA-PFDH [12], which are simple and popular. In particular, we focus on the existential unforgeability under the adaptive chosen message attack [13], and show the following statements.

1. RSA-FDH is *not* secure in the CT-ROM.
2. RSA-PFDH is secure in the CT-ROM, but *not* secure in the SPT-ROM.

Moreover, we slightly modify RSA-PFDH to obtain two variants which we call RSA-PFDH⁺ and RSA-PFDH⊕. We consider their security and show the following statements.

3. RSA-PFDH⁺ is secure in the SPT-ROM, but *not* secure in the FPT-ROM.
4. RSA-PFDH⊕ is secure in the FPT-ROM.

We summarize the security of the four schemes in Table 1.

Table 1. Security of four schemes

scheme\model	ROM	CT-ROM	SPT-ROM	FPT-ROM
RSA-FDH	secure	insecure		
RSA-PFDH	secure		insecure	
RSA-PFDH⁺	secure			insecure
RSA-PFDH⊕	secure			

In conclusion, we show the relations among our models. Let S be a security notion and M_1, M_2 models. Let $S/M_1 \Rightarrow S/M_2$ and $S/M_1 \nRightarrow S/M_2$ be as follows.

- $S/M_1 \Rightarrow S/M_2$: for any signature scheme Σ if Σ meets a security notion S in the model M_1, then Σ also meets S in the model M_2.
- $S/M_1 \nRightarrow S/M_2$: there exists a signature scheme Σ such that Σ meets a security notion S in the model M_1 while Σ doesn't meet S in the model M_2.

It is clear from the definitions of the models that the following relations hold for any security notion S (see Section 3).

$$S/\text{ROM} \Leftarrow S/\text{CT-ROM} \Leftarrow S/\text{SPT-ROM} \Leftarrow S/\text{FPT-ROM}$$

From Table 1, under the RSA assumption we can show the separations for the security notion S': the existential unforgeability under the adaptive chosen message attack, that is, the following relations hold.

$$S'/\text{ROM} \nRightarrow S'/\text{CT-ROM} \nRightarrow S'/\text{SPT-ROM} \nRightarrow S'/\text{FPT-ROM}$$

ORGANIZATION. In Section 2, we give some notation. Our models are presented in Section 3. We discuss the security of the schemes in Section 4. Finally, in Section 5, we make a few remarks on our models and schemes.

2   Preliminaries

2.1   Notation

If $\mathcal{D}$ is a distribution, $x \leftarrow \mathcal{D}$ denote that x is sampled according to $\mathcal{D}$, and let $f_{\mathcal{D}}(x)$ be the probability mass function of distribution $\mathcal{D}$. Let $B(N, p)$ be the binomial distribution with N trials and success probability p.

Let S be a finite set. Let $s \leftarrow S$ denote that s is sampled from the uniform distribution on S. $\#S$ denotes the number of elements in S.

If $\mathcal{A}$ is a probabilistic machine and x is an input, let $\mathcal{A}(x)$ denote the output distribution of $\mathcal{A}$ on input x.

Let ϕ be a boolean function. Let $\Pr_s[d \leftarrow \mathcal{D} : \phi(s, d)]$ be the probability that $\phi(s, d)$ is true after sampling $s \leftarrow S$ and $d \leftarrow \mathcal{D}$.

Let "$\|$" denote concatenation, and $w_1 \| w_2 \xleftarrow{p} w$ that string w is parsed as w_1 and w_2. Finally, for a table $\mathbb{T} = \{(x, y)\}$, we define $\mathbb{T}(y) = \{(\tilde{x}, \tilde{y}) \in T \mid y = \tilde{y}\}$.

2.2   Digital Signature Schemes

We review a model of digital signature schemes.

SYNTAX. A digital signature scheme over message space $\mathcal{M}$ is defined by the following three algorithms.

– The key generation algorithm Gen. On input 1^k, where k is the security parameter, the algorithm produces a public/secret key pair (pk, sk).
– The signing algorithm Sig. Given a secret key sk and a message $m \in \mathcal{M}$, the algorithm produces a signature σ on the message m.
– The verification algorithm Ver. Given a public key pk, a message m, and a signature σ, the algorithm outputs a bit τ. If $\tau = 1$ the signature is accepted with respect to pk and rejected otherwise.

We require that for all (pk, sk) output by $\mathsf{Gen}(1^k)$ and for all message $m \in \mathcal{M}$, $\mathsf{Ver}(\mathsf{pk}, m, \mathsf{Sig}(\mathsf{sk}, m)) = 1$ should be satisfied.

In the rest of the paper we omit pk, sk and write $\mathsf{Ver}(m, \sigma)$ as $\mathsf{Ver}(\mathsf{pk}, m, \sigma)$, and $\mathsf{Sig}(m)$ as $\mathsf{Sig}(\mathsf{sk}, m)$ for short.

SECURITY NOTIONS. A widely accepted standard security notion was defined by Goldwasser, Micali and Rivest [13], as the existential unforgeability under the adaptive chosen message attack (EUF-CMA).

Definition 1. *A polynomial-time oracle query machine $\mathcal{A}$ is said to break the signature scheme (Gen, Sig, Ver) if after making signing queries adaptively, it outputs, with non-negligible probability, a valid forgery that was never queried.*

Definition 2 (EUF-CMA). *A signature scheme (Gen, Sig, Ver) is said to be secure if there is no polynomial-time oracle query machine that breaks the scheme.*

3   Our Models

We formalize the notion of weakened random oracle models that were mentioned by Liskov [10]. Each of our models provides a random oracle together with another oracle that breaks some property of the random oracle model. First we review the random oracle model, and then propose three models.

3.1   The Random Oracle Model (ROM)

Let X, Y be finite sets. The random oracle model has a hash function h chosen randomly from all of the functions from X to Y and the random oracle associated with h. A hash function h can be considered as a hash table $\mathbb{T}_h$ which defines the correspondence of the elements in X with the elements in Y. In this model, all of the parties (including the adversary) have access to the random oracle. When the hash value of x is queried, the random oracle answers the corresponding value y in $\mathbb{T}_h$.

In almost all the proofs employing the random oracles, the reduction algorithms simulate the random oracles with embedding the target problem instances. We consider how to simulate the random oracle except for the embedding. In a standard way, we simulate the random oracle maintaining a table $\mathbb{T}$ that is initially empty as follows. When the hash value of x is queried, if there is an entry $(\tilde{x}, \tilde{y}) \in \mathbb{T}$ such that $x = \tilde{x}$, then return $\tilde{y}$; otherwise pick uniformly $y \leftarrow Y$, insert (x, y) in the hash table $\mathbb{T}$, and return y.

Alternatively, we propose a different algorithm RO to simulate the random oracle. We manage a hash table $\mathbb{T}$ and a table $\mathbb{L}$ that are initially empty. The table $\mathbb{T}$ does the same role as above, whereas the table $\mathbb{L}$ manages the number of elements in X that map to $y \in Y$. For example, if there is $(y, n) \in \mathbb{L}$ then it is expected that there are exactly n elements in X that map to $y \in Y$. When we insert (x, y) in the hash table $\mathbb{T}$ such that y is not yet in $\mathbb{T}$, we also determine the number n of preimages of y and add (y, n) to the table $\mathbb{L}$.

Algorithm RO(x):

1. If there is an entry $(\tilde{x}, \tilde{y}) \in \mathbb{T}$ such that $x = \tilde{x}$, then return $\tilde{y}$.
2. Compute the following value:

$$p = \frac{\sum_{(\tilde{y}, \tilde{n}) \in \mathbb{L}} (\tilde{n} - \#\mathbb{T}(\tilde{y}))}{\#X - \#\mathbb{T}}.$$

   (p is the probability to answer $\tilde{y} \in Y$ that is not new, i.e. $(\tilde{x}, \tilde{y}) \in \mathbb{T}$ for some $\tilde{x}$.)
3. Flip a biased coin with probability $\Pr[\alpha = 0] = p$.
   (Decide whether the simulation returns a new value or not. "$\alpha = 0$" indicates "not new", and "$\alpha = 1$" indicates "new".)
4. If $\alpha = 0$,
      then pick y according to the following distribution, and go to Step 8.

$$y \leftarrow \mathcal{D},$$

$$\text{where } f_{\mathcal{D}}(y) = \frac{n - \#\mathbb{T}(y)}{\sum_{(\tilde{y}, \tilde{n}) \in \mathbb{L}} (\tilde{n} - \#\mathbb{T}(\tilde{y}))} \text{ for } (y, n) \in \mathbb{L}.$$

5. If $\alpha \neq 0$,

   then pick uniformly $y \leftarrow Y \setminus \bigcup_{(\tilde{y},\tilde{n})\in\mathbb{L}}\{\tilde{y}\}$.

6.   Pick n' according to the following binomial distribution:

$$n' \leftarrow B(\#X - \sum_{(\tilde{y},\tilde{n})\in\mathbb{L}} \tilde{n} - 1, \frac{1}{\#Y - \#\mathbb{L}}).$$

   (n' is the number of preimages of y excluding (x, y).)

7.   Set $n = n' + 1$ and insert (y, n) in $\mathbb{L}$.

8. Insert (x, y) in $\mathbb{T}$, and return y.

Remark 1. In the rest of the paper, we denote by $\mathbb{T}_h$ the table in the ROM (CT-ROM, SPT-ROM, FPT-ROM), and denote by $\mathbb{T}$ and $\mathbb{L}$ the tables in the simulation.

In order to analyze this algorithm, we assume that we can efficiently sample from the binomial distribution $B(N, p)$ perfectly. There are quite many papers on the efficient sampling from the binomial distribution [14]. However, we could neither find precise analysis of their methods nor analyze precisely by ourselves. Therefore, we have to employ the following assumption in the analyses of all of our simulations.

Assumption 1. *There is a polynomial-time machine $\mathcal{A}$ such that the distribution $\mathcal{A}(N, p)$ output by the algorithm $\mathcal{A}$ is equal to the binomial distribution $B(N, p)$, where N is a positive integer and $0 \leq p \leq 1$.*

Lemma 1. *The simulation of the random oracle is perfect. That is, the distribution on the outputs of the random oracle is equal to the distribution on the outputs of Algorithm* RO.

Proof. We consider the probability that Algorithm RO replies y^* as the hash value of x^*. Fix the tables $\mathbb{T}$ and $\mathbb{L}$ at an arbitrary point according to Algorithm RO . Let $\mathbb{T}^*$ and $\mathbb{L}^*$ be the tables after replying y^* for the hash value of x^*.

First, we consider the case where y^* is not new (i.e. $(y^*, n^*) \in \mathbb{L}$). Note that in this case $\mathbb{L}^* = \mathbb{L}$. Let $\mathsf{old}(x^*, y^*)$ be the event $\mathbb{T}^* = \mathbb{T} \cup (x^*, y^*) \wedge \mathbb{L}^* = \mathbb{L}$.

According to our method, for any y^* that is not new, we have

$$\Pr[\mathsf{old}(x^*, y^*)] = p \times \frac{n^* - \#\mathbb{T}(y^*)}{\sum_{(\tilde{y},\tilde{n})\in\mathbb{L}}(\tilde{n} - \#\mathbb{T}(\tilde{y}))}$$

$$= \frac{n^* - \#\mathbb{T}(y^*)}{\#X - \#\mathbb{T}}. \tag{1}$$

Second, we consider the case where y^* is new (i.e. $(y^*, n^*) \notin \mathbb{L}$). Let $N_X = \#X - \sum_{(\tilde{y},\tilde{n})\in\mathbb{L}} \tilde{n}$ and $N_Y = \#Y - \#\mathbb{L}$. The former represents the number of elements in X that are not to be assigned to some $\tilde{y}$ such that there is $(\tilde{y}, \tilde{n}) \in \mathbb{L}$, and the latter represents the number of elements in Y that are not defined in $\mathbb{L}$. Let $\mathsf{new}(x^*, y^*, n^*)$ be the event $\mathbb{T}^* = \mathbb{T} \cup (x^*, y^*) \wedge \mathbb{L}^* = \mathbb{L} \cup (y^*, n^*)$.

According to our method, for any y^* that is new and for any $n^* = n' + 1$ such that $0 \le n' \le N_X - 1$, we have

$$\Pr[\text{new}(x^*, y^*, n^*)] = (1 - p) \times \frac{1}{N_Y} \times \binom{N_X - 1}{n'} (\frac{1}{N_Y})^{n'} (1 - \frac{1}{N_Y})^{N_X - 1 - n'}$$

$$= (1 - p) \frac{n' + 1}{N_X} \binom{N_X}{n' + 1} (\frac{1}{N_Y})^{n' + 1} (1 - \frac{1}{N_Y})^{N_X - 1 - n'}.$$

Notice here that $\#\mathbb{T} = \sum_{(\tilde{y}, \tilde{n}) \in \mathbb{L}} \#\mathbb{T}(\tilde{y})$, and we have

$$1 - p = 1 - \frac{\sum_{(\tilde{y}, \tilde{n}) \in \mathbb{L}} (\tilde{n} - \#\mathbb{T}(\tilde{y}))}{\#X - \#\mathbb{T}}$$

$$= \frac{N_X}{\#X - \#\mathbb{T}}.$$

Therefore we have

$$\Pr[\text{new}(x^*, y^*, n^*)] = \frac{n^*}{\#X - \#\mathbb{T}} \binom{N_X}{n^*} (\frac{1}{N_Y})^{n^*} (1 - \frac{1}{N_Y})^{N_X - n^*}. \tag{2}$$

Now let us consider what the probabilities given by Equations (1) and (2) imply. Both of the probabilities are equivalent to the probability that a hash function h chosen in the ROM satisfies $(x^*, y^*) \in \mathbb{T}_h$ and $\#\mathbb{T}_h(y^*) = n^*$ under the condition where $(x, y) \in \mathbb{T}_h$ for any $(x, y) \in \mathbb{T}$ and $\#\mathbb{T}_h(y) = n$ for any $(y, n) \in \mathbb{L}$.

Therefore the distribution on the outputs of the random oracle is equal to the distribution on the outputs of Algorithm RO. □

3.2   The Collision Tractable Random Oracle Model (CT-ROM)

Let X, Y be finite sets. The *collision tractable* random oracle model has the collision oracle that is used to find collisions, in addition to a hash function h chosen randomly from all of the functions from X to Y and the random oracle associated with h. In this model the adversary has access to the collision oracle.

When the hash value of x is queried, the random oracle answers the corresponding value y in $\mathbb{T}_h$. When a collision is queried, the collision oracle answers as follows. The collision oracle picks uniformly one entry $(x, y) \in \mathbb{T}_h$. If there is no other entry $(x', y) \in \mathbb{T}_h$, then answers $\bot$. Otherwise, it picks uniformly one entry $(x', y) \in \mathbb{T}_h$ satisfying $x \ne x'$ and answers (x, x').

For this model, in addition to Algorithm RO, we construct an algorithm CO. Algorithms RO and CO are used to simulate the random oracle and the collision oracle, respectively. Algorithm CO uses the tables $\mathbb{T}$ and $\mathbb{L}$ that are commonly used in Algorithm RO.

Algorithm CO():

1. Pick uniformly $x \leftarrow X$.
2. In order to obtain the hash value $y = h(x)$, run Algorithm RO(x).

3. If $n = 1$ for $(y, n) \in \mathbb{L}$, then return $\perp$.
4. If $n \neq 1$ for $(y, n) \in \mathbb{L}$, then compute the following value:

$$q_{(y,n)} = \frac{\#\mathbb{T}(y) - 1}{n - 1}.$$

($q_{(y,n)}$ is the probability to answer $\tilde{x} \in X$ that is not new.)

5. Flip a biased coin with probability $\Pr[\beta = 0] = q_{(y,n)}$.
6. If $\beta = 0$, then pick uniformly one entry $(\tilde{x}, y) \in \mathbb{T}$ satisfying $x \neq \tilde{x}$ and return $(x, \tilde{x})$.
7. If $\beta \neq 0$, then pick uniformly $x' \leftarrow X$ such that there is no entry $(x', \tilde{y}) \in \mathbb{T}$ for any $\tilde{y} \in Y$.
8. Insert (x', y) in $\mathbb{T}$, and return (x, x').

Corollary 1. *The simulations of the random oracle and the collision oracle are perfect. That is, the distribution on the outputs of the random oracle and the collision oracle is equal to the distribution on the outputs of Algorithms* RO *and* CO.

Proof. From Lemma 1, the simulation of the random oracle is perfect. In this simulation, the table $\mathbb{L}$ indicates that the number of preimages of y. This implies that the simulation of the collision oracle are perfect. $\square$

3.3   The Second-Preimage Tractable Random Oracle Model (SPT-ROM)

Let X, Y be finite sets. The *second-preimage tractable* random oracle model has the second-preimage oracle that is used to find second-preimages, in addition to a hash function h chosen randomly from all of the functions from X to Y and the random oracle associated with h. In this model the adversary has access to the second-preimage oracle.

When the hash value of x is queried, the random oracle answers the corresponding value y in $\mathbb{T}_h$. When a second-preimage of (x, y) is queried, the second-preimage oracle answers as follows. If it has not answered that h maps x to y, it answers $\perp$. If there is only one entry $(\tilde{x}, \tilde{y}) \in \mathbb{T}_h$ such that $y = \tilde{y}$, then it answers $\perp$. Otherwise, it answers uniformly one x' such that $(x', y) \in \mathbb{T}_h$ satisfying $x' \neq x$.

For this model, in addition to Algorithm RO, we construct an algorithm SPO. Algorithms RO and SPO are used to simulate the random oracle and the second-preimage oracle, respectively. Algorithm SPO uses the tables $\mathbb{T}$ and $\mathbb{L}$ that are commonly used in Algorithm RO.

Algorithm SPO(x, y):

1. If $(x, y) \notin \mathbb{T}$, then return $\perp$.
2. If $n = 1$ for $(y, n) \in \mathbb{L}$, then return $\perp$.
3. If $n \neq 1$ for $(y, n) \in \mathbb{L}$, then compute the following value:

$$q_{(y,n)} = \frac{\#\mathbb{T}(y) - 1}{n - 1}.$$

4. Flip a biased coin with probability $\Pr[\beta = 0] = q_{(y,n)}$.

5. If $\beta = 0$, then pick uniformly one entry $(\tilde{x}, y) \in \mathbb{T}$ satisfying $x \neq \tilde{x}$ and return $\tilde{x}$.
6. If $\beta \neq 0$, then pick uniformly $x' \leftarrow X$ such that there is no entry $(x', \tilde{y}) \in \mathbb{T}$ for any $\tilde{y} \in Y$.
7. Insert (x', y) in $\mathbb{T}$, and return x'.

Corollary 2. *The simulations of the random oracle and the second-preimage oracle are perfect. That is, the distribution on the outputs of the random oracle and the second-preimage oracle is equal to the distribution on the outputs of Algorithms RO and SPO.*

3.4   The First-Preimage Tractable Random Oracle Model (FPT-ROM)

Let X, Y be finite sets. The *first-preimage tractable* random oracle model has the first-preimage oracle that is used to find first-preimages, in addition to a hash function h chosen randomly from all of the functions from X to Y and the random oracle associated with h. In this model the adversary has access to the first-preimage oracle.

When the hash value of x is queried, the random oracle answers the corresponding value y in $\mathbb{T}_h$. When a first-preimage of y is queried, the first-preimage oracle answers as follows. If there is no $(\tilde{x}, \tilde{y}) \in \mathbb{T}_h$ such that $y = \tilde{y}$, then answers $\perp$. Otherwise it answers uniformly one $\tilde{x}$ such that $(\tilde{x}, \tilde{y}) \in \mathbb{T}_h$ satisfying $y = \tilde{y}$.

For this model, in addition to Algorithm RO, we construct an algorithm FPO. Algorithms RO and FPO are used to simulate the random oracle and the first-preimage oracle, respectively. Algorithm FPO uses the tables $\mathbb{T}$ and $\mathbb{L}$ that are commonly used in Algorithm RO.

Algorithm FPO(y)*:*

1. If there is no entry $(y, \tilde{n}) \in \mathbb{L}$ then pick n according to the binomial distribution:

$$n \leftarrow B(\#X - \sum_{(\tilde{y}, \tilde{n}) \in \mathbb{L}} \tilde{n}, \frac{1}{\#Y - \#\mathbb{L}}).$$

2. Insert (y, n) in $\mathbb{L}$.
3. If $n = 0$ for $(y, n) \in \mathbb{L}$, then return $\perp$.
4. If $n \neq 0$ for $(y, n) \in \mathbb{L}$, then compute the following value:

$$q_{(y,n)} = \frac{\#\mathbb{T}(y)}{n}.$$

5. Flip a biased coin with probability $\Pr[\beta = 0] = q_{(y,n)}$.
6. If $\beta = 0$, then pick uniformly one entry $(\tilde{x}, y) \in \mathbb{T}$ and return $\tilde{x}$.
7. If $\beta \neq 0$, then pick uniformly $x \leftarrow X$ such that there is no entry $(x, \tilde{y}) \in \mathbb{T}$ for any $\tilde{y} \in Y$.
8. Insert (x, y) in $\mathbb{T}$, and return x.

Corollary 3. *The simulations of the random oracle and the first-preimage oracle are perfect. That is, the distribution on the outputs of the random oracle and the first-preimage oracle is equal to the distribution on the outputs of Algorithms RO and FPO.*

Proof. From Lemma 1 the simulation of the random oracle is perfect. Now let us consider the case where the table $\mathbb{L}$ is updated in Algorithm FPO. In the following, we use the same notation as in Lemma 1. The number n^* is defined according to the binomial distribution described in Steps 1 and 2. The probability that the table $\mathbb{L}$ is updated to be $\mathbb{L}^*$ such that $\mathbb{L}^* = \mathbb{L} \cup (y^*, n^*)$ in Steps 1 and 2 is equal to the probability that a hash function h chosen in the FPT-ROM satisfies $\#\mathbb{T}_h(y^*) = n^*$ under the condition that $(x, y) \in \mathbb{T}_h$ for any $(x, y) \in \mathbb{T}$ and $\#\mathbb{T}_h(y) = n$ for any $(y, n) \in \mathbb{L}$. In Algorithm FPO, the table $\mathbb{L}$ correctly indicates the number of the preimages of y. This implies that the simulations of the random oracle and the first-preimage oracle are perfect.   □

4   Security of Signature Schemes

In this section, we consider the security of RSA-FDH [3] and RSA-PFDH [12] in four variants of the random oracle models. We also propose new signature schemes called RSA-PFDH$^+$ and RSA-PFDH$^\oplus$, and consider the security in four variants of the random oracle models.

We review the RSA assumption on which the security of four schemes are based.

Definition 3 (The RSA Generator). *The RSA generator* RSA, *which on input* 1^k, *randomly choose distinct* $k/2$-*bit primes* p, q *and computes the RSA modulus* $N = pq$. *It randomly picks* $e \leftarrow \mathbb{Z}_{\phi(N)}$ *and computes* d *such that* $ed = 1 \bmod \phi(N)$, *where* $\phi(\cdot)$ *is Euler's totient function. Finally the RSA generator* RSA *outputs* (N, e, d).

Assumption 2 (The RSA Assumption). *A polynomial-time machine* $\mathcal{A}$ *is said to solve the RSA problem if given an RSA challenge* (N, e, z) *where* N, e *is generated by* RSA(1^k) *and* $z \leftarrow \mathbb{Z}_N^*$, *it outputs* $z^{1/e} \bmod N$ *with non-negligible probability.*

The RSA assumption is that there is no polynomial-time machine that solves the RSA problem.

4.1   RSA-FDH

In this section, we show that RSA-FDH [3] is secure in the ROM, but not secure in the CT-ROM.

THE SCHEME. We review RSA-FDH [3] .
Let $\mathcal{M} = \{0, 1\}^l$ be the message space and h a hash function such as

$$h : \{0, 1\}^l \rightarrow \{0, 1\}^k.$$

Then RSA-FDH is described as follows.

Gen(1^k)	Sig(m)	Ver(m, σ)
$(N, e, d) \leftarrow$ RSA(1^k)	$y \leftarrow h(m)$	$y \leftarrow \sigma^e \bmod N$
pk $\leftarrow (N, e)$	$\sigma \leftarrow y^d \bmod N$	if $h(m) = y$
sk $\leftarrow (N, d)$	return σ	return 1
return (pk, sk)		else
		return 0

THE SECURITY. RSA-FDH is secure in the ROM. More precisely the following proposition was proved [3,15]. We omit the proof, see [3,15] for details.

Proposition 1. *In the* ROM, *if the RSA assumption holds, there is no polynomial-time oracle query machine that breaks* RSA-FDH *by making queries to the signing oracle and the random oracle for h.*

We show that RSA-FDH is insecure in the CT-ROM.

Theorem 1. *In the* CT-ROM, *there exists a polynomial-time oracle query machine $\mathcal{A}$ that breaks* RSA-FDH *by making queries to the signing oracle and the collision oracle for h with probability at least $1 - e^{-(2^l-1)/2^k}$.*

Proof. We construct an algorithm $\mathcal{A}$ as follows.

1. Query to the collision oracle, and obtain ξ.
2. If $\xi = \perp$ then abort, otherwise $(m_1, m_2) \xleftarrow{p} \xi$, where $h(m_1) = h(m_2)$.
3. Query the signature of m_1 to the signing oracle, and obtain a signature σ.
4. Output (m_2, σ) as a valid forgery.

If $\mathcal{A}$ does not abort, then $\mathcal{A}$ can output a valid forgery. Therefore it is sufficient to bound the probability that $\mathcal{A}$ aborts (abort). In the following we use the same notation as in Section 3. Let $X = \{0, 1\}^l$, $Y = \{0, 1\}^k$, and $N = \#X$, $p = \frac{1}{\#Y}$. Then we have

$$
\begin{aligned}
\Pr[\text{abort}] &= \Pr[\xi = \perp] \\
&= \Pr_{x,h}[\#\mathbb{T}_h(y) \le 1 \text{ for } (x, y) \in \mathbb{T}_h] \\
&= \Pr[n' \leftarrow B(N - 1, p) : n' = 0] \\
&= (1 - p)^{N-1} \\
&\le e^{-p(N-1)}.
\end{aligned}
$$

For example, in the case of $\#X = \#Y \ge 2$, we can bound this value as

$$
\Pr[\text{abort}] \le e^{-(1-p)} \le e^{-1/2}.
$$

Therefore $\mathcal{A}$ can output a valid forgery with probability at least $1 - e^{-1/2}$.   □

4.2   RSA-PFDH

In this section, we show that RSA-PFDH [12] is secure in the CT-ROM, but not secure in the SPT-ROM.

THE SCHEME. We review RSA-PFDH [12].
Let $\mathcal{M} = \{0, 1\}^l$ be the message space and h hash function such as

$$
h : \{0, 1\}^{l+k_1} \rightarrow \{0, 1\}^k.
$$

Then RSA-PFDH is described as follows.

Gen(1^k)	Sig(m)	Ver(m, σ)
$(N, e, d) \leftarrow$ RSA(1^k)	$r \leftarrow \{0, 1\}^{k_1}$	$(r, x) \overset{p}{\leftarrow} \sigma$
pk $\leftarrow (N, e)$	$y \leftarrow h(\mathsf{m} \parallel r)$	$y \leftarrow x^e \bmod N$
sk $\leftarrow (N, d)$	$x \leftarrow y^d \bmod N$	if $h(\mathsf{m} \parallel r) = y$
return (pk, sk)	$\sigma \leftarrow (r, x)$	return 1
	return σ	else
		return 0

THE SECURITY. We show RSA-PFDH is secure in the CT-ROM. Intuitively, in order to break RSA-PFDH in a straightforward way, it would be necessary to obtain a collision m $\parallel$ r, m' $\parallel$ r' such that $h(\mathsf{m} \parallel r) = h(\mathsf{m}' \parallel r')$ and the signature of m. However the randomness in the signature makes it difficult to make use of collisions, which are also randomly provided by the collision oracle.

Theorem 2. *In the* CT-ROM, *for all polynomial-time oracle query machines that break* RSA-PFDH *with probability* ϵ_{euf} *by making* $q_s, q_h,$ *and* q_h^c *queries to the signing oracle, the random oracle for h, and the collision oracle for h, respectively, there exists a probabilistic machine that solves the RSA problem with probability* ϵ_{rsa} *such that*

$$\epsilon_{\mathrm{euf}} \leq \epsilon_{\mathrm{rsa}} + \frac{1}{2^k - Q_1} + \frac{(Q_1)^2}{2^k} + \frac{q_s Q_2}{2^{k_1}} + (1 - \frac{Q_2}{2^{l+k_1}})^{-1} \frac{(Q_1)^2}{2^k - Q_1},$$

where $Q_1 = q_s + q_h + q_h^c + 1$ *and* $Q_2 = q_s + q_h + 2q_h^c + 1$.

Proof. (*Sketch*) We start with the original attack game with respect to EUF-CMA in the CT-ROM, and modify it step by step in order to obtain a game directly related to the adversary which solves the RSA problem. Let (N, e, y) be the RSA challenge. Let dist(i, j) be the difference between the probability that the adversary outputs a valid forgery in the **Game**$_i$ and that in the **Game**$_j$.

- **Game$_0$**: The original attack game with respect to EUF-CMA in the CT-ROM.
- **Game$_1$**: We replace the random oracle and the collision oracle with Algorithms RO and CO in Section 3, respectively. Let us denote by $\mathbb{T}$ and $\mathbb{L}$ the tables commonly used in Algorithms RO and CO. Then, we have

$$\mathrm{dist}(0, 1) = 0.$$

- **Game$_2$**: We remove Steps 2–4 in Algorithm RO, and set $\alpha = 1$ (i.e. Algorithm RO always answers a new value). Then, we have

$$\mathrm{dist}(1, 2) \leq (1 - \frac{Q_2}{2^{l+k_1}})^{-1} \frac{(Q_1)^2}{2^k - Q_1}.$$

- **Game$_3$**: When the signing algorithm runs Algorithm RO on input m $\parallel$ r, if (m $\parallel$ $r, \tilde{y}$) is already in the table $\mathbb{T}$ for some $\tilde{y}$, then Algorithm RO aborts. Then, we have

$$\mathrm{dist}(2, 3) \leq \frac{q_s Q_2}{2^{k_1}}.$$

- **Game$_4$:** Instead of randomly choosing $y \in \mathbb{Z}_N$ and setting $h(m \| r) = y$, Algorithm RO chooses y as follows.
  - If the hash value is queried by the signing algorithm,
    1. then, Algorithm RO randomly chooses $x \in \mathbb{Z}_N$ and $y \leftarrow x^e \bmod N$.
    2. If $(\tilde{m} \| \tilde{r}, y)$ is already in the table $\mathbb{T}$ for some $\tilde{m}, \tilde{r}$, then Algorithm RO aborts.
  - If the hash value is queried by the adversary,
    1. then, Algorithm RO randomly chooses $x \in \mathbb{Z}_N$ and $y \leftarrow zx^e \bmod N$.
    2. If $(\tilde{m} \| \tilde{r}, y)$ is already in the table $\mathbb{T}$ for some $\tilde{m}, \tilde{r}$, then Algorithm RO aborts.

  Then, we have

  $$\text{dist}(3, 4) \leq \frac{(Q_1)^2}{2^k}.$$

- **Game$_5$:** We modify the signing algorithm in the computation y^d to search (x, y) such that $x^e = y$, instead of using the secret key d. Then, we have

  $$\text{dist}(4, 5) = 0.$$

If the adversary outputs a valid forgery (m^*, σ^*) in the last game, it satisfies the equation $h(m^* \| r^*) = y = (x^*)^e \bmod N$ where $(r^*, x^*) \overset{p}{\leftarrow} \sigma^*$. In order to satisfy the equation, the adversary must have queried the hash value of $m^* \| r^*$ with probability at least $1 - \frac{1}{2^k - Q_1}$, and then we know the value x such that $y = zx^e \bmod N$. We can invert the RSA challenge z by computing $z^{1/e} = x^*/x^{-1} \bmod N$. $\qquad\qquad\square$

Next, we show that RSA-PFDH is insecure in the SPT-ROM.

Theorem 3. *In the* SPT-ROM, *there exists a polynomial-time oracle query machine $\mathcal{A}$ that breaks* RSA-PFDH *by making queries to the signing oracle, the random oracle for h, and the second-preimage oracle for h, with probability at least $1 - e^{-(2^{l+k_1} - 1)/2^k} - \frac{1}{2^l}$.*

Proof. We construct an algorithm $\mathcal{A}$ as follows.

1. Query the signature of m to the signing oracle, and obtain a signature σ.
2. $(r, x) \overset{p}{\leftarrow} \sigma$.
3. Query the hash value of $m \| r$ to the random oracle for h, and obtain $y = h(m \| r)$.
4. Query the second-preimage of $(m \| r, y)$ to the second-preimage oracle, and obtain ξ.
5. If $\xi = \perp$ then abort$_1$, otherwise $m' \| r' \overset{p}{\leftarrow} \xi$, where $h(m \| r) = h(m' \| r')$.
6. If $m' = m$ then abort$_2$, otherwise $\sigma' \leftarrow (r', x)$.
7. Output (m', σ') as a valid forgery.

If $\mathcal{A}$ does not abort, then $\mathcal{A}$ can output a valid forgery. Therefore it is sufficient to bound the probability that $\mathcal{A}$ aborts. In the following we use the same notation as in Section 3. Let $X = \{0, 1\}^{l+k_1}$, $Y = \{0, 1\}^k$, and $N = \#X$, $p = \frac{1}{\#Y}$. Then, we have

$$\Pr[\text{abort}] \leq \Pr[\text{abort}_1] + \Pr[\text{abort}_2].$$

The first probability is evaluated in a similar way as in Theorem 1. We have

$$\Pr[\text{abort}_1] = (1 - p)^{N-1} \leq e^{-p(N-1)}.$$

The second probability is bounded as

$$\Pr[\text{abort}_2] = \Pr[m = m'] \leq \frac{1}{2^l}.$$

Thus, we have

$$\Pr[\text{abort}] \leq e^{-p(N-1)} + \frac{1}{2^l}.$$

For example, in the case of $\#X = \#Y \geq 2$, we can bound this value as

$$\Pr[\text{abort}] = e^{-(1-p)} + \frac{1}{2^l} \leq e^{-1/2} + \frac{1}{2^l}.$$

Therefore, $\mathcal{A}$ can output a valid forgery with probability at least $1 - e^{-1/2} - \frac{1}{2^l}$. □

4.3 RSA-PFDH$^+$

In this section, we propose RSA-PFDH$^+$, and show that RSA-PFDH$^+$ is secure in the SPT-ROM, but not secure in the FPT-ROM.

THE SCHEME. We construct RSA-PFDH$^+$.
Let $\mathcal{M} = \{0, 1\}^l$ be the message space and g, h hash functions such that

$$g : \{0, 1\}^{k_1} \rightarrow \{0, 1\}^{k_1}, \ h : \{0, 1\}^{l+k_1} \rightarrow \{0, 1\}^k.$$

Then RSA-PFDH$^+$ is described as follows.

Gen(1^k)	Sig(m)	Ver(m, σ)
$(N, e, d) \leftarrow$ RSA(1^k)	$r \leftarrow \{0, 1\}^{k_1}$	$(r, x) \xleftarrow{p} \sigma$
pk $\leftarrow (N, e)$	$s \leftarrow g(r)$	$y \leftarrow x^e \bmod N$
sk $\leftarrow (N, d)$	$y \leftarrow h(m \parallel s)$	$s \leftarrow g(r)$
return (pk, sk)	$x \leftarrow y^d \bmod N$	if $h(m \parallel s) = y$
	$\sigma \leftarrow (r, x)$	return 1
	return σ	else
		return 0

THE SECURITY. We show RSA-PFDH$^+$ is secure in the SPT-ROM. Intuitively, the adversary similar to that described in Theorem 3 does not work well. The reason is as follows. The adversary queries the signature of m, and obtain $\sigma = (r, x)$. For $s = g(r), y = h(m \parallel s)$, the adversary then queries the second-preimage of y to the second-preimage oracle for h, and obtain m' $\parallel$ s'. However the adversary would not know a preimage of s', and would not obtain r' such that $s' = g(r')$. Therefore this straightforward way does not work.

Theorem 4. In the SPT-ROM, for all polynomial-time oracle query machines that break RSA-PFDH$^+$ with probability ϵ_{euf} by making q_s, q_g, q_h, and q_g^{sp}, q_h^{sp} queries to *the signing oracle, the random oracles for g, h, and the second-preimage oracles for g, h, respectively, there exists a probabilistic machine that solves the RSA problem with probability ϵ_{rsa} such that*

$$\epsilon_{euf} \leq \epsilon_{rsa} + \frac{1}{2^k - (q_s + q_h)} + \frac{(q_s + q_h)^2}{2^k} + \frac{q_s Q_h}{2^{k_1}} + \frac{q_g^{sp}(q_s + q_g)}{2^{l+k_1} - Q_h}$$

$$+ \frac{(q_s + q_g)Q_h}{2^{k_1} - (q_s + q_g)} + (1 - \frac{Q_h}{2^{l+k_1}})^{-1} \frac{(Q_h)^2}{2^k - (q_s + q_h)} + (1 - \frac{Q_g}{2^{k_1}})^{-1} \frac{(Q_g)^2}{2^{k_1} - (q_s + q_g)},$$

where $Q_h = q_s + q_h + q_h^{sp} + 1, Q_g = q_s + q_g + q_g^{sp} + 1$.

Proof. (Sketch) We start with the original attack game with respect to **EUF-CMA** in the SPT-ROM, and modify it step by step in order to obtain a game directly related to the adversary which solves RSA problem. Let (N, e, y) be the RSA challenge.

- **Game$_0$**: The original attack game with respect to **EUF-CMA** in the SPT-ROM.
- **Game$_1$**: We replace the random oracles for g and h with Algorithms RO$_g$ and RO$_h$, and also replace the second-preimage oracles for g and h with Algorithms SPO$_g$ and SPO$_h$ in Section 3, respectively. Let us denote by $\mathbb{T}_1$ and $\mathbb{L}_1$ the tables commonly used in Algorithms RO$_g$ and SPO$_g$, and also denote by $\mathbb{T}_2$ and $\mathbb{L}_2$ the tables commonly used in Algorithms RO$_h$ and SPO$_h$.
- **Game$_2$**: We remove Steps 2–4 in Algorithms RO$_g$ and RO$_h$, and set $\alpha = 1$ (i.e. Algorithms RO$_g$ and RO$_h$ always answer a new value).
- **Game$_3$**: In Algorithm RO$_g$ at Step 5 (i.e. $s \leftarrow \{0, 1\}^{k_1} \setminus \bigcup_{(\tilde{s},\tilde{n}) \in \mathbb{L}_1} \{\tilde{s}\}$), if $(\tilde{m} \| s, \tilde{y})$ is already in the table $\mathbb{T}_2$ for some $\tilde{r}$, then Algorithm RO$_g$ aborts.
- **Game$_4$**: In Algorithm SPO$_h$ at Step 6 (i.e. m$' \| s' \leftarrow \{0, 1\}^{l+k_1} \setminus \bigcup_{(\tilde{m}\|\tilde{s},\tilde{y}) \in \mathbb{T}_2} \{\tilde{m} \| \tilde{s}\}$), if $(\tilde{r}, s')$ is already in the table $\mathbb{T}_1$ for some $\tilde{r}$, then Algorithm SPO$_h$ aborts.
- **Game$_5$**: When the signing algorithm runs Algorithm RO$_h$ on input m $\| s$, if (m $\| s, \tilde{y}$) is already in the table $\mathbb{T}_2$, then Algorithm RO$_h$ aborts.
- **Game$_6$**: Instead of randomly choosing $y \in \mathbb{Z}_N$ and setting $h(\text{m} \| s) = y$, Algorithm RO$_h$ chooses y as follows.
  - If the hash value is queried by the signing algorithm,
    1. then, Algorithm RO$_h$ randomly chooses $x \in \mathbb{Z}_N$ and $y \leftarrow x^e \mod N$.
    2. If $(\tilde{m} \| \tilde{s}, y)$ is already in the table $\mathbb{T}_2$ for some $\tilde{m}, \tilde{s}$, then Algorithm RO$_h$ aborts.
  - If the hash value is queried by the adversary,
    1. then, Algorithm RO$_h$ randomly chooses $x \in \mathbb{Z}_N$ and $y \leftarrow zx^e \mod N$.
    2. If $(\tilde{m} \| \tilde{s}, y)$ is already in the table $\mathbb{T}_2$ for some $\tilde{m}, \tilde{s}$, then Algorithm RO$_h$ aborts.
- **Game$_7$**: We modify the signing algorithm in the computation y^d to search (x, y) such that $x^e = y$, instead of using the secret key d. Then, we have

If the adversary outputs a valid forgery (m^*, σ^*) in the last game, it satisfies the equation $h(\text{m}^* \| s^*) = y = (x^*)^e \mod N$ where $(r^*, x^*) \xleftarrow{p} \sigma^*, s^* = g(r^*)$. In order to satisfy the equation, the adversary must have queried the hash value of m$^* \| s^*$, and then we know the value x such that $y = zx^e \mod N$. We can invert the RSA challenge z by computing $z^{1/e} = x^*/x^{-1} \mod N$. □

Next, we show that **RSA-PFDH$^+$** is insecure in the **FPT-ROM**.

Theorem 5. *In the FPT-ROM, there exists a polynomial-time oracle query machine $\mathcal{A}$ that breaks RSA-PFDH$^+$ by making queries to the signing oracle, the random oracles for g, h, and the first-preimage oracles for g, h, with probability at least $1 - e^{-(2^{l+k_1}-1)/2^k} - e^{-(1-\frac{1}{2^{k_1}})} - \frac{1}{2^l} - \frac{1}{2^{k_1}}$.*

Proof. We construct an algorithm $\mathcal{A}$ as follows.

1. Query the signature of m to the signing oracle, and obtain a signature σ.
2. $(r, x) \overset{p}{\leftarrow} \sigma$.
3. Query the hash value of r to the random oracle for g, and obtain $s = g(r)$.
4. Query the hash value of m $\|$ s to the random oracle for h, and obtain $y = h($m $\|$ $s)$.
5. Query the first-preimage of y to the first-preimage oracle for h, and obtain ξ.
6. m$'$ $\|$ s' $\overset{p}{\leftarrow} \xi$, where $h($m$'$ $\|$ $s') = h($m $\|$ $s)$.
7. If m$'$ $\|$ s' = m $\|$ s then abort$_1$.
8. If m = m$'$ then abort$_2$.
9. Query the first-preimage of s' to the first-preimage oracle for g, and obtain η.
10. If $\eta = \bot$ then abort$_3$, otherwise $r' \overset{p}{\leftarrow} \eta$.
11. $\sigma' \leftarrow (r', x)$.
12. Output $($m$', \sigma')$ as a valid forgery.

If $\mathcal{A}$ does not abort, then $\mathcal{A}$ can output a valid forgery. Therefore it is sufficient to bound the probability that $\mathcal{A}$ aborts. In the following we use the same notation as in Section 3. Let $X = \{0,1\}^{l+k_1}, Y = \{0,1\}^k, R = \{0,1\}^{k_1}, S = \{0,1\}^{k_1}, g : R \to S$, and $N_1 = \#X, p_1 = \frac{1}{\#Y} N_2 = \#R, p_2 = \frac{1}{\#S}$. Then, we have

$$\Pr[\text{abort}] \le \Pr[\text{abort}_1] + \Pr[\text{abort}_2] + \Pr[\text{abort}_3].$$

The first probability is evaluated in the a similar way as in Theorem 1. We have

$$\Pr[\text{abort}_1] = (1 - p_1)^{N_1-1} \le e^{-p_1(N_1-1)}.$$

The second probability is bounded as

$$\Pr[\text{abort}_2] = \Pr[\text{m} = \text{m}'] \le \frac{1}{2^l}.$$

Next, we evaluate the third probability as

$$\begin{aligned}
\Pr[\text{abort}_3] &= \Pr[\eta = \bot] \\
&= \Pr_{g,r,s'}[(r, s) \in \mathbb{T}_g \land \#\mathbb{T}_g(s') = 0] \\
&= \Pr_{g,r,s'}[(r, s) \in \mathbb{T}_g \land \#\mathbb{T}_g(s') = 0 \land s = s'] \\
&\quad + \Pr_{g,r,s'}[(r, s) \in \mathbb{T}_g \land \#\mathbb{T}_g(s') = 0 \land s \ne s'].
\end{aligned}$$

The first probability is bounded as

$$\Pr[s = s'] \le \frac{1}{2^{k_1}}.$$

The second probability is bounded as

$$\Pr_{g,r,s'}[(r,s) \in \mathbb{T}_g \wedge \#\mathbb{T}_g(s') = 0 \mid s \ne s'] = \Pr[n \leftarrow B(N_2 - 1, p_2) : n = 0]$$

$$= (1 - p_2)^{N_2 - 1}$$

$$< e^{-p_2(N_2 - 1)}$$

$$= e^{-(1 - \frac{1}{2^{k_1}})}.$$

Thus, we have

$$\Pr[\text{abort}] < e^{-p_1(N_1 - 1)} + \frac{1}{2^l} + \frac{1}{2^{k_1}} + e^{-(1 - \frac{1}{2^{k_1}})}.$$

For example, in the case of $\#X = \#Y \ge 2$, we can bound this value as

$$\Pr[\text{abort}] < e^{-(1 - p_1)} + \frac{1}{2^l} + \frac{1}{2^{k_1}} + e^{-(1 - \frac{1}{2^{k_1}})}$$

$$< e^{-1/2} + e^{-(1 - \frac{1}{2^{k_1}})} + \frac{1}{2^l} + \frac{1}{2^{k_1}}.$$

Therefore, $\mathcal{A}$ can output a valid forgery with probability at least $1 - e^{-1/2} - e^{-(1 - \frac{1}{2^{k_1}})} - \frac{1}{2^l} - \frac{1}{2^{k_1}}$.   □

4.4   RSA-PFDH⊕

In this section, we propose RSA-PFDH⊕, and show that RSA-PFDH⊕ is secure in the FPT-ROM.

THE SCHEME.   We construct RSA-PFDH⊕.
Let $\mathcal{M} = \{0, 1\}^l$ be the message space and h a hash function such that

$$h : \{0, 1\}^{l+k} \to \{0, 1\}^k.$$

Then RSA-PFDH⊕ is described as follows.

Gen(1^k)	Sig(m)	Ver(m, σ)
$(N, e, d) \leftarrow \text{RSA}(1^k)$	$r \leftarrow \{0, 1\}^{k_1}$	$(r, x) \overset{p}{\leftarrow} \sigma$
pk $\leftarrow (N, e)$	$w \leftarrow h(m \parallel r)$	$y \leftarrow x^e \bmod N$
sk $\leftarrow (N, d)$	$y \leftarrow w \oplus r$	$w \leftarrow h(m \parallel r)$
return (pk, sk)	$x \leftarrow y^d \bmod N$	if $w \oplus r = y$
	$\sigma \leftarrow (r, x)$	return 1
	return σ	else
		return 0

THE SECURITY.   We show RSA-PFDH⊕ is secure in the FPT-ROM. Intuitively, the adversary similar to that described in Theorem 5 does not work well. The reason is as follows.

The adversary queries the signature of m, and obtain $\sigma = (r, x)$. For $w = h(m \parallel r)$, the adversary queries the first-preimage of w to the first-preimage oracle, and obtain m' $\parallel$ r'. However, r' would not equal to r. Therefore this straightforward way does not work.

Theorem 6. *In the* FPT-ROM, *for all polynomial-time oracle query machines that break* RSA-PFDH$^+$ *with probability* ϵ_{euf} *by making* $q_s, q_h,$ *and* q_h^{fp} *queries to the signing oracle, the random oracle for h, and the first-preimage oracle for h, respectively, there exists a probabilistic machine that solves the RSA problem with probability* ϵ_{rsa} *such that*

$$\epsilon_{\text{euf}} \leq \epsilon_{\text{rsa}} + \frac{1}{2^k - Q} + \frac{Q^2}{2^{k-1}} + \frac{q_s Q}{2^k} + (1 - \frac{Q}{2^{l+k}})^{-1} \frac{Q^2}{2^k - Q},$$

where $Q = q_s + q_h + q_h^{fp} + 1$.

Proof. (Sketch) We start with the original attack game with respect to EUF-CMA in the FPT-ROM, and modify it step by step in order to obtain a game directly related to the adversary which solves RSA problem. Let (N, e, y) be the RSA challenge.

- **Game$_0$:** The original attack game with respect to EUF-CMA in the FPT-ROM.
- **Game$_1$:** We replace the random oracle and the first-preimage oracle with Algorithms RO and FPO in Section 3, respectively. Let us denote by $\mathbb{T}$ and $\mathbb{L}$ the tables commonly used in Algorithms RO and FPO.
- **Game$_2$:** We remove Steps 2–4 in Algorithm RO, and set $\alpha = 1$ (i.e. Algorithm RO always answers a new value).
- **Game$_3$:** When the signing algorithm runs Algorithm RO on input m $\parallel$ r, if (m $\parallel$ $r, \tilde{w}$) is already in the table $\mathbb{T}$ for some $\tilde{w}$, then Algorithm RO aborts.
- **Game$_4$:** Instead of randomly choosing $w \in \mathbb{Z}_N$ and setting $h(m \parallel r) = w$, Algorithm RO chooses w as follows.
  - If the hash value of is queried by the signing algorithm,
    1. then, Algorithm RO randomly chooses $x \in \mathbb{Z}_N$ and $y \leftarrow x^e \bmod N$. Then Algorithm RO sets $w = y \oplus r$.
    2. If ($\tilde{m} \parallel \tilde{r}, w$) is already in the table $\mathbb{T}$ for some $\tilde{m}, \tilde{r}$, then Algorithm RO aborts.
  - If the hash value is queried by the adversary,
    1. then, Algorithm RO randomly chooses $x \in \mathbb{Z}_N$ and $y \leftarrow zx^e \bmod N$. Then Algorithm RO sets $w = y \oplus r$.
    2. If ($\tilde{m} \parallel \tilde{r}, w$) is already in the table $\mathbb{T}$ for some $\tilde{m}, \tilde{r}$, then Algorithm RO aborts.
- **Game$_5$:** Instead of randomly choosing m $\parallel$ $r \in X$ and setting $h(m \parallel r) = w$, Algorithm FPO chooses m $\parallel$ r as follows.
  - If a first-preimage is queried by the adversary,
    1. then, Algorithm FPO randomly chooses $x \in \mathbb{Z}_N$ and $y \leftarrow zx^e \bmod N$. Then Algorithm FPO sets $r = y \oplus w$ and randomly chooses m.
    2. If ($\tilde{m} \parallel r, \tilde{w}$) is already in the table $\mathbb{T}$ for some $\tilde{m}, \tilde{w}$, then Algorithm FPO aborts.
- **Game$_6$:** We modify the signing algorithm in the computation y^d to search (x, y) such that $x^e = y$, instead of using the secret key d.

If the adversary outputs a valid forgery (m^*, σ^*), then it satisfies the equation $h(m^* \parallel r^*) \oplus r^* = y = (x^*)^e \bmod N$ where $(r^*, x^*) \xleftarrow{p} \sigma^*$. In order to satisfy the equation, the adversary must have queried the hash value of $m^* \parallel r^*$, and then we know the value x such that $y = zx^e \bmod N$. We can invert the RSA challenge z by computing $z^{1/e} = x^*/x^{-1} \bmod N$.   □

5   Concluding Remarks

In this paper, by applying Liskov's idea, we have proposed the weakened random oracle models, i.e. the CT-ROM, the SPT-ROM, and the FPT-ROM.

The main purpose of this paper is to focus on the random oracle model and to capture its crucial properties which make the cryptosystems secure. Note that Halevi and Krawczyk [16] posed a question of exhibiting variants of the random oracle model where one can argue about functions that "behave randomly but are not collision resistant". Our formalization of the CT-ROM gives a partial answer to their question.

We do not intend to model the attacks recently presented by Wang et al. against MD5, SHA-1, etc [6,7]. One important extension/generalization of our research would be to study the weakness of cryptosystems by taking into consideration the recently presented attacks. This direction is out of our scope in this paper.

Another direction of research would be to replace the basic property of the ROM that each entry is chosen uniformly at random and independent of the other entries. For example, we can extend our result concerning the FPT-ROM to the random permutation model. In this case, we would consider the oracles for both directions of the permutation, that is, the ideal cipher with a fixed key.

In order to show the differences of our models, we have focused on the RSA-based signature schemes. By replacing the RSA function with a trapdoor one-way permutation with the multiplicatively homomorphic property (i.e. $f(x \cdot y) = f(x) \cdot f(y)$), we can generalize our results. The efficiency of the reduction would be the same as that of the RSA-based schemes. If a trapdoor one-way permutation does not have the multiplicatively homomorphic property, we can still generalize our results, but the reductions are not tight. When f has the multiplicatively homomorphic property, then we can embed the information of y (the challenge instance of one-wayness) into all of the hash values queried by the adversary. When f does not have the multiplicatively homomorphic property, we cannot embed in a similar way as in the case with the multiplicatively homomorphic property. Therefore we have to choose one hash value to embed the information of y.

In order to analyze the security of schemes, we have assumed that we can efficiently sample from the binomial distribution $B(N, p)$ perfectly. We could relax this perfectness to statistically closeness by modifying the security proofs. Making polynomial-time algorithms or analyzing precisely the algorithms proposed before are also interesting problems found in this paper.

It is also interesting to analyze the security of other cryptosystems, e.g., encryption, identification, in our models.

Acknowledgements

We are grateful to Martijn Stam for giving us many valuable comments on both technical and editorial problems in the initial version of this paper. His suggestions also helps us to improve the representation of this paper. We would also like to thank anonymous referees for their constructive comments including possible future works. We mention some of these in the concluding remarks.

References

1. Bellare, M., Rogaway, P.: Random oracles are practical: A paradigm for designing efficient protocols. In: ACM Conference on Computer and Communications Security, pp. 62–73 (1993)
2. Bellare, M., Rogaway, P.: Optimal asymmetric encryption. In: De Santis, A. (ed.) EUROCRYPT 1994. LNCS, vol. 950, pp. 92–111. Springer, Heidelberg (1995)
3. Bellare, M., Rogaway, P.: The exact security of digital signatures - how to sign with RSA and Rabin. In: Maurer, U.M. (ed.) EUROCRYPT 1996. LNCS, vol. 1070, pp. 399–416. Springer, Heidelberg (1996)
4. Pointcheval, D., Stern, J.: Security arguments for digital signatures and blind signatures. J. Cryptology 13(3), 361–396 (2000)
5. Fujisaki, E., Okamoto, T., Pointcheval, D., Stern, J.: RSA-OAEP is secure under the RSA assumption. J. Cryptology 17(2), 81–104 (2004)
6. Wang, X., Yu, H.: How to break MD5 and other hash functions. In: Cramer, R.J.F. (ed.) EUROCRYPT 2005. LNCS, vol. 3494, pp. 19–35. Springer, Heidelberg (2005)
7. Wang, X., Yin, Y.L., Yu, H.: Finding collisions in the full SHA-1. In: Shoup, V. (ed.) CRYPTO 2005. LNCS, vol. 3621, pp. 17–36. Springer, Heidelberg (2005)
8. Unruh, D.: Random oracles and auxiliary input. In: Menezes, A. (ed.) CRYPTO 2007. LNCS, vol. 4622, pp. 205–223. Springer, Heidelberg (2007)
9. Nielsen, J.B.: Separating random oracle proofs from complexity theoretic proofs: The non-committing encryption case. In: Yung, M. (ed.) CRYPTO 2002. LNCS, vol. 2442, pp. 111–126. Springer, Heidelberg (2002)
10. Liskov, M.: Constructing an ideal hash function from weak ideal compression functions. In: Biham, E., Youssef, A.M. (eds.) SAC 2006. LNCS, vol. 4356, pp. 358–375. Springer, Heidelberg (2007)
11. Pasini, S., Vaudenay, S.: Hash-and-sign with weak hashing made secure. In: Pieprzyk, J., Ghodosi, H., Dawson, E. (eds.) ACISP 2007. LNCS, vol. 4586, pp. 338–354. Springer, Heidelberg (2007)
12. Coron, J.S.: Optimal security proofs for PSS and other signature schemes. In: Knudsen, L.R. (ed.) EUROCRYPT 2002. LNCS, vol. 2332, pp. 272–287. Springer, Heidelberg (2002)
13. Goldwasser, S., Micali, S., Rivest, R.L.: A digital signature scheme secure against adaptive chosen-message attacks. SIAM Journal on Computing 17(2), 281–308 (1988)
14. Ahrens, J.H., Dieter, U.: Computer methods for sampling from Gamma, Beta, Poisson and Binomial distributions. Computing 12, 223–246 (1974)
15. Coron, J.S.: On the exact security of full domain hash. In: Bellare, M. (ed.) CRYPTO 2000. LNCS, vol. 1880, pp. 229–235. Springer, Heidelberg (2000)
16. Halevi, S., Krawczyk, H.: Strengthening digital signatures via randomized hashing. In: Dwork, C. (ed.) CRYPTO 2006. LNCS, vol. 4117, pp. 41–59. Springer, Heidelberg (2006)

A Digital Signature Scheme Based on $CVP_\infty{}^\star$

Thomas Plantard, Willy Susilo, and Khin Than Win

Centre for Computer and Information Security Research
School of Computer Science and Software Engineering
University of Wollongong
Wollongong NSW 2522, Australia
{thomaspl,wsusilo,win}@uow.edu.au

Abstract. In Crypto 1997, Goldreich, Goldwasser and Halevi (GGH) proposed a lattice analogue of McEliece public key cryptosystem, which security is related to the hardness of approximating the closest vector problem (CVP) in a lattice. Furthermore, they also described how to use the same principle of their encryption scheme to provide a signature scheme. Practically, this cryptosystem uses the euclidean norm, l_2-norm, which has been used in many algorithms based on lattice theory. Nonetheless, many drawbacks have been studied and these could lead to cryptanalysis of the scheme. In this paper, we present a novel method of reducing a vector under the l_∞-norm and propose a digital signature scheme based on it. Our scheme takes advantage of the l_∞-norm to increase the resistance of the GGH scheme and to decrease the signature length. Furthermore, after some other improvements, we obtain a very efficient signature scheme, that trades the security level, speed and space.

1 Introduction

After the seminal work by Ajtai and Dwork [3] and the first lattice-based cryptosystem from Goldreich, Goldwasser and Halevi [21], many cryptosystems based on lattice theory have been proposed. These systems use the Shortest Vector Problem (SVP) or the Closest Vector Problem (CVP) as their underlying hard problem to construct the trapdoor functions. For a recent survey on the SVP-based cryptosystem, we refer the readers to [47].

In Crypto 1997, Goldreich, Goldwasser and Halevi (GGH) proposed a cryptosystem based on the lattice theory [21], which is a lattice analogue of the McEliece cryptosystem [37]. The security of GGH is related to the hardness of approximating the CVP in a lattice. Furthermore, they also noted that using the underlying principle of their encryption scheme, a signature scheme can be constructed. Nonetheless, the resulting signature scheme did not attract much interest in the research community until a relatively efficient signature scheme called the NTRUSign was proposed [28]. The GGH signature system can be described using three algorithms:

Setup: Compute a "good basis" and a "bad basis" of a lattice $\mathcal{L}$. $\mathcal{L}(G) = \mathcal{L}(B)$. Provide B as public and keep G secret.

---

* This work is supported by ARC Discovery Grant DP0663306.

R. Cramer (Ed.): PKC 2008, LNCS 4939, pp. 288–307, 2008.

Sign: Use the good basis to have an efficient approximation of the closest vector of a vector. The initial vector is the *message* and the approximation is the *signature*. GGH uses the first Babai's method [6] to approximate CVP: $s = \lceil mG^{-1} \rfloor G$ where $\lceil x \rfloor$ represent the closest integer of x if x is a real and the vector $[\lceil x_0 \rfloor, \lceil x_1 \rfloor, \ldots, \lceil x_{n-1} \rfloor]$ if x is a vector of $\mathbb{R}^n$.

Verify: Check if the approximation is in the lattice of basis $\mathcal{L}(B)$: $\exists x \overset{?}{\in} \mathbb{Z}^n, s = xB$. The vector-signature should be also a good approximation of the vector-message.

The important points for the security and efficiency of this cryptosystem are defined as follows.

  i) It is easy to compute a "bad basis" from a "good basis", but it is difficult to compute a "good basis" from a "bad basis".
 ii) It is easy to compute a good approximation of CVP with a "good basis" but difficult to do so with a "bad basis".
iii) It is easy to check the inclusion of a vector in a lattice even with a "bad basis".

In 1999, Nguyen [41] proposed the first attack against the GGH cryptosystem. This attack is based on the utilization by GGH of a non singular matrix with a small norm for a good basis to use Babai's method. Due to this attack, the utilization of GGH requires a lattice with big dimension (> 500), to ensure its security. Nonetheless, the computation of the Babai's approximation becomes very expensive. In 2001, Micciancio [38] proposed some major improvements of the speed and the security of GGH. In this scheme, the public key uses the Hermite Normal Form (HNF) basis for the "bad basis". The HNF basis is better to answer the inclusion question and it also seems to be more difficult to transform to a "good basis" compared to another basis. For the signature scheme, Micciancio used the reduced-vector instead of a closest vector. The reduced vector is in fact the difference between a vector and its closest vector. Using this method, the length of the signature is shorter. In 2002, Gentry and Szydlo [19] found a problem in GGH signature scheme which seems to be not zero-knowledge. Szydlo gave an algorithm [53] to elaborate this problem further. This method uses several vector-signatures given by the Babai's method to attack GGH. However, this method seems to be not very efficient. In 2003, NTRUSign [28] was created based on a very similar method to GGH but with most improvements on the utilization of NTRU basis [29] for the "good basis". Those basis seem to be more resistant against the previously known attacks. Nevertheless, in 2006, Nguyen and Regev [42] proposed a general attack against both GGH signature scheme and NTRUSign. This clever attack used the large CVP approximations naturally given by the signature of messages to design the fundamental parallelepiped of the "good basis".

Our Results
In this paper, we intend to use the l_∞-norm instead of the l_2-norm to construct a digital signature scheme which is similar to GGH signature scheme. By using

the l_∞-norm, we aim to increase the security of the resulting cryptosystems, together with its efficiency in terms of signature length and time computation.

Paper Organization

This paper is organized as follows. We start the paper by providing some preliminary work and knowledge on lattice theory for cryptography. Then, we proceed with the eigenvalue theory and other useful definitions used throughout this paper. Then, we present the main part of the work, which is the reduction vector in l_∞-norm and the related theorems, followed by a signature scheme and its further improvements. Finally, we conclude the paper by comparing our scheme with the GGH signature scheme.

2   Lattice Theory for Cryptography

In this section, we will review some basic concepts of the lattice theory, and in particular addressing the NP-hardness of the trapdoor problems used. For a more complex account, we refer the readers to [45].

The lattice theory, also known as the geometry of numbers, has been introduced by Minkowski in 1896 [40]. The complete discussion on the basic of lattice theory can be found from [11,36,15].

Definition 1 (Lattice). *A lattice $\mathcal{L}$ is a discrete sub-group of $\mathbb{R}^n$, or equivalently the set of all the integral combinations of $d \leq n$ linearly independent vectors over $\mathbb{R}$.*

$$\mathcal{L} = \mathbb{Z}\,b_1 + \cdots + \mathbb{Z}\,b_d, \quad b_i \in \mathbb{R}^n.$$

$B = (b_1, ..., b_d)$ *is called a basis of $\mathcal{L}$, d, the dimension of $\mathcal{L}$.*

Definition 2 (Full-rank Lattice). *Let $\mathcal{L} \subset \mathbb{R}^n$ be a lattice. If its dimension d is equal to n then the lattice $\mathcal{L}$ is called full-rank.*

Definition 3 (Fundamental Parallelepiped). *Let be $B = (b_1, ..., b_n)$ a basis of a full-rank lattice $\mathcal{L} \subset \mathbb{R}^n$ then the set*

$$\mathcal{H} = \left\{ \sum_{i=1}^n x_i b_i, (x_1, \ldots, x_n) \in [0, 1[^n \right\}$$

is called a fundamental parallelepiped.

The volume of a fundamental parallelepiped is invariant regardless of the chosen basis. This invariant is called the *determinant* of $\mathcal{L}$ and can be computed as $\det \mathcal{L} = |\det B|$.

Remark 1. There also exists a definition of the determinant for a non full-rank lattice. However, in this paper, we only focus on the basic of lattice theory that is required throughout the paper. Since we only deal with full-rank integer lattice, consequently with a basis $B \in \mathbb{Z}^{n,n}$, therefore we simplify the definition as above.

For a given lattice $\mathcal{L}$, there exists an infinity of basis. However, the Hermite Normal Form basis (Definition 4) is unique [13].

Definition 4 (HNF). *Let $\mathcal{L}$ be a full-rank lattice and H a basis of $\mathcal{L}$. H is a Hermite Normal Form basis of $\mathcal{L}$ if and only if*

$$\forall i, j, \quad H_{i,j} \begin{cases} = 0 & \text{if } i < j \\ \geq 0 & \text{if } i \geq j \\ < H_{j,j} & \text{if } i > j \end{cases}$$

The HNF basis can be computed from a given basis in a polynomial time [32]. For efficient solutions, we refer the readers to [39].

Remark 2. The HNF basis is a "good basis" for solving the problem of inclusion of a vector in a lattice [13]. As it was successfully used by [38], we will also incorporate it in this paper with some further improvements.

Many algorithmic problems of the lattice theory are built upon two other problems which are clearly more difficult, namely the Shortest Vector Problem (SVP) and the Closest Vector Problem (CVP).

Definition 5 (SVP). *Let B be a given basis of a lattice $\mathcal{L}$. The Shortest Vector Problem is to find a vector $u \neq 0$ such that $\forall v \in \mathcal{L}, \|u\| \leq \|v\|$ for a given norm $\|.\|$.*

Definition 6 (CVP). *Let B be a given basis of a lattice $\mathcal{L}$ and w a vector. The Closest Vector Problem is to find a vector u such that $\forall v \in \mathcal{L}, \|w - u\| \leq \|w - v\|$ for a given norm $\|.\|$.*

CVP is NP-hard for all norms l_p (Definition 7) including l_∞-norm [9].

Definition 7 (l_p-norm). *Let w be a vector of $\mathbb{R}^n$. The l_p-norm is the function $\|.\|_p$ such that $\|w\|_p = \left(\sum_{i=0}^{n-1} |w_i|^p \right)^{1/p}$.*
   The l_2-norm is also known as the euclidean norm. The l_∞-norm, also known as the infinity norm, is computed as $\|w\|_\infty = \max \{|w_i|, 0 \leq i < n\}$.

The l_2 and l_∞ norms have been studied and used in the lattice theory. The NP-hardness of the two problems for these two norms has been proven. In 1981, Emde Boas proved the NP-hardness of CVP_∞, SVP_∞ and CVP_2 in [9]. Subsequently, in 1998, Ajtai proved the NP-hardness of SVP_2 in [2]. Consequently, there exists only some exponential algorithms to completely solve those problems. We summarize this result in the table 1.

However, some approximation versions of these two problems exist in the literature.

Definition 8 (AppSVP, resp. AppCVP). *Let B be a given basis of a lattice $\mathcal{L}$, w a vector and a real $\gamma \geq 1$. The AppSVP, resp. AppCVP, is to find a vector u such that $\forall v \in \mathcal{L}, \|u\| \leq \gamma \|v\|$, resp. $\|w - u\| \leq \gamma \|w - v\|$ for a given norm $\|.\|$.*

Table 1. Exponential algorithms for SVP and CVP

	Deterministic	Probabilistic
SVP	$d^{\frac{d}{2e}}$ [31,26,24]	$(2+\frac{1}{\epsilon})^d$ [4,8]
CVP	$d^{\frac{d}{2}}$ [31,26,24]	$(2+\frac{1}{\epsilon})^d$ [5,8]

The NP-hardness of these two approximation problems has also been well studied (for more detail, see [10] or more recently [46]). Table 2 summarizes some main results on the NP-hardness of these two approximation problems for the euclidean and the infinity norms for the approximation factor γ in function of the dimension d of the studied lattice.

[22] proved that SVP is not harder than CVP.

Table 2. The approximation factor γ for the NP-hardness of AppSVP and AppCVP with l_2 and l_∞ norms

Problems	Euclidean Norm		Infinity Norm	
	$AppSVP_2$	$AppCVP_2$	$AppSVP_\infty$	$AppCVP_\infty$
NP-hard	$2^{\log^{1-\epsilon} d}$ [25]	$2^{\log^{1-\epsilon} d}$ [17]	$d^{1/\log\log d}$ [16]	$d^{1/\log\log d}$ [16]
not NP-hard [1]	$\sqrt{d/\log d}$ [20]	$\sqrt{d/\log d}$ [20]	$d/\log d$ [20]	$d/\log d$ [20]

Remark 3. Table 2 seems to show that the approximation problems seem to be more difficult for the l_∞-norm compared to the l_2-norm. This impression is supported by a recent paper by Khot [33] which presented a result that proved that SVP will be more and more difficult in l_p if p grows. A more recent paper of Regev and Rosen [48] proved that a lot of classic problems, including SVP and CVP, are easier under the l_2-norm than under every other l_p-norm, including l_∞-norm.

Remark 3 is supported by the fact that most of the polynomial and efficient algorithm to approximate SVP and CVP are for the l_2-norm.

- For SVP, in 1982 Lenstra, Lenstra and Lovasz [35] proposed a powerful polynomial algorithm, known as the LLL algorithm, to efficiently approximate SVP and more generally the length of the basis itself. This algorithm approximate SVP for the l_2-norm within an approximation factor $\gamma = 2^{(d-1)/2}$ in theory but seems to be much more efficient in practice [44]. In addition, a lot of improvements have been proposed on LLL to obtain a better approximation factor and/or a better time complexity. For the recent result on LLL, refer to [43,52]. Combining this approach with the BKZ method [49,50], which can be seen as a generalization of LLL, is a very powerful way to attack a cryptosystem based or linked to SVP_2.

---

[1] Unless the polynomial hierarchy collapses.

- For CVP, in 1986 Babai [6] proposed two polynomial methods. Those algorithms approximate CVP for the l_2-norm within a factor $\gamma = 1 + 2d(9/2)^{d/2}$ and $\gamma = 2^{d/2}$, respectively. Babai's algorithms use an LLL-reduced basis. Consequently all the variants of LLL, including BKZ utilization [51] proposed by Schnorr, are naturally the improvement of Babai's methods. Moreover, there exists an heuristic way to directly approximate CVP using an approximate algorithm for SVP [41]. See [1] for a general survey of AppCVP.

All the existing algorithms have been created for the euclidean norm. Nevertheless, the l_2-norm algorithm can be used to approximate SVP and CVP for the l_∞-norm using the equivalence of norms, $\forall v \in \mathbb{R}^n, \|v\|_\infty \leq \|v\|_2 \leq n^{1/2}\|v\|_\infty$ [23].

The final approximation for l_∞ will be clearly worst than for l_2 and this method cannot be used to solve exactly the SVP and CVP under l_∞.

Remark 4. In this paper, we aim to construct a lattice-based cryptosystem which is more resistant than the existing ones in the literature using the l_∞-norm. A recent work by Chen and Meng [12] clearly went this way. They proved the NP-hardness of the closest vector problem with preprocessing over l_∞-norm. Regev and Rosen [48] gave the factor of $\log d^{1/2-\epsilon}$ for the NP-hardness of CVP with preprocessing under l_p-norm, $2 \leq p \leq \infty$.

3   Matrix Norm, Eigenvalues, Spectral Radius and Condition Number

In this section, we briefly review some definitions of the eigenvalue theory that will be required throughout this paper. Most of the following definitions and properties can been found in [14,55,30]. In the following definitions, let $n \in \mathbb{N}$.

Definition 9 (Matrix Norm). *Let A be a square matrix in $\mathbb{C}^{n,n}$. A matrix norm denoted as $\|A\|$ is said to be* consistent *to a vector norm $\|.\|$, if we have $\|A\| = \sup\{\|xA\|, \quad x \in \mathbb{C}^n, \quad \|x\| = 1\}$.*

The matrix norm $\|.\|_p$, consistent to the vector norm defined in Definition 7, can be easily computed for $p = 1, 2, \infty$. For other values of p, see [27] for estimating methods of $\|.\|_p$.

Definition 10 (Polytope Norm). *We denote $\|.\|_P$ as the matrix norm consistent to the vector norm $\|.\|_P$ defined as $\forall v \in \mathbb{C}^n, \quad \|v\|_P = \|vP^{-1}\|_\infty$ where P is a non singular matrix.*

To compute the polytope norm $\|.\|_P$ of a matrix, we have $\forall A \in \mathbb{C}^{n,n}, \quad \|A\|_P = \|PAP^{-1}\|_\infty$.

Definition 11 (Eigenvalue). *Let A be a square matrix in $\mathbb{C}^{n,n}$, a complex number λ is called a eigenvalue of A if there exists a column-vector $h \neq 0$ such that $Ah = \lambda h$. The column-vector h is called an eigenvector of A.*

If h is an eigenvector then for any real number $\alpha \neq 0$, αh is also an eigenvector. A matrix composed by n eigenvectors of n eigenvalues is an eigenmatrix. There is an infinity of eigenmatrix. We specially focus on the eigenmatrix H which minimizes the *condition number* (Definition 12) of the infinity norm.

Definition 12 (Condition Number). *Let $\|.\|$ be a matrix norm and A a non singular matrix. The condition number of A, denoted as $\kappa(A)$, is such that $\kappa(A) = \|A\|\|A^{-1}\|$.*

In this paper, $\kappa(A)$ use the l_∞-norm: $\kappa(A) = \|A\|_\infty \|A^{-1}\|_\infty$.

Definition 13 (Spectral Radius). *Let A be a square matrix in $\mathbb{C}^{n,n}$. We denote $\rho(A)$ as the spectral radius of A defined as the maximum of the absolute value of the eigenvalues of A: $\rho(A) = max\{|\lambda|, Ax = x\lambda\}$.*

Theorem 1. *For any matrix norm $\|.\|$, $\forall A \in \mathbb{C}^{n,n}$, $\quad \rho(A) \leq \|A\|$.*

In fact, the spectral radius can be seen as the lower bound of all the matrix norm of a matrix: $\rho(A) = inf\{\|A\|\}$.

The spectral radius has some useful properties as follows.

Theorem 2. *For any matrix norm $\|.\|$ and any square matrix A, $\lim_{k\to\infty}\|A^k\| = \rho(A)^k$.*

Using this property, we can obtain the following property.

Theorem 3. *Let $A \in \mathbb{C}^{n,n}$ be a square matrix, the series $I + A + A^2 + A^3 + \ldots$ converge to $\frac{1}{1-A}$ if and only if $\rho(A) < 1$ where $\rho(A)$ is the spectral radius of A.*

See [55] for the proofs of Theorems 1, 2 and 3.
The last property of the spectral radius that will be used in this paper is provided in the Theorem 4.

Theorem 4. *For any square matrix A and any real number $\epsilon > 0$, there exists a polytope norm $\|.\|_P$ such that $\|A\|_P \leq \rho(A) + \epsilon$.*

The proof of Theorem 4 is given in [30] by providing a way to compute the matrix P. In fact, there exists an infinity of such matrix P connected by a multiplication by a non singular diagonal matrix. If the eigenvalues are distinct, we can use an eigenmatrix for P. Here, we focus on the matrix P that minimizes $\kappa(P)$.

4   Vector Reduction in l_∞-Norm

In this section, we propose a new method of vector reduction using a modification of the Babai's method. This new algorithm uses another definition of a "good basis" to obtain an approximation of CVP_∞. To approximate the closest vector w of a vector v, Babai used the approximation given by the equation

$u = \lceil vG^{-1} \rceil G$. As explained previously, this approximation has two major problems when it is used in cryptography, namely an expensive computation and a mark of the "good basis" on the approximate vector. To solve these two problems, we propose a new approximation of the vector v. This approximation is inspired by the work of Bajard, Imbert and Plantard [7] which proposed a method to reduce some number representation for modular arithmetic. The method used in this paper can be seen as a generalization of their technique. An important point is the conservation of the efficiency which is main feature in modular arithmetic operations.

Our focus is on the reduced vector, $v \bmod \mathcal{L}$, and *not* on the closest vector. We note that these two problems are completely equivalent. The reduced vector w is equal to the difference between a vector v and its closest vector u. So to reduce a vector, the Babai method becomes $w = v - \lceil vG^{-1} \rceil G$. We decompose G into two matrices: $G = D - M$. We will see that the choice of D and M determine if G is a "good basis" or not. We use this decomposition to approximate v.

$$w = v - \lceil v(D - M)^{-1} \rceil G.$$

We assume that D is non singular, so we are able to compute D^{-1}.

$$w = v - \lceil v((1 - MD^{-1})D)^{-1} \rceil G$$
$$w = v - \lceil vD^{-1}(1 - MD^{-1})^{-1} \rceil G.$$

We modify the Babai's approximation to a new approximation.

$$w' = v - \lceil vD^{-1} \rceil \lceil (1 - MD^{-1})^{-1} \rceil G.$$

Let's analyze more precisely the second part of this approximation. If we have the spectral radius $\rho(MD^{-1}) < 1$, we can use the Theorem 3 to obtain

$$\lceil (1 - MD^{-1})^{-1} \rceil = \lceil 1 + MD^{-1} + (MD^{-1})^2 + (MD^{-1})^3 + \dots \rceil$$

Since $\rho(MD^{-1}) < 1$, this series on the right term converges. Here, we make a very quick approximation of $\lceil (1 - MD^{-1})^{-1} \rceil$ to 1. At the end of this analysis, we propose a new approximation w of the closest vector of v.

$$w = v - \lceil vD^{-1} \rceil (D - M).$$

We will consider this approximation to be *precise enough* if $\rho(MD^{-1}) < 1$. Hence, we propose a new definition of a "good basis" as follows.

Definition 14 (Good Basis). *Let D, M be two square matrices and $\mathcal{L}$ be the lattice which has $D - M$ for the basis. $D - M$ is called a "good basis" of $\mathcal{L}$ if $\rho(MD^{-1}) < 1$.*

Now, we can propose an algorithm to reduce a vector v with a "good basis".

Algorithm 1. Vector Reduction

Input : A vector $v \in \mathbb{Z}^n$.
Data   : A non-singular diagonal matrix $D \in \mathbb{Z}^{n,n}$ and a square matrix
$M \in \mathbb{Z}^{n,n}$. A lattice $\mathcal{L}$ of basis $D - M$.
Output: A vector $w \in \mathbb{Z}^n$ such that $w \equiv v \pmod{\mathcal{L}}$ and $\|w\|_D < 1$.
begin
$\quad w \leftarrow v$;
$\quad$**repeat**
$\qquad q \leftarrow \lceil wD^{-1} \rfloor$;
$\qquad w \leftarrow w - q(D - M)$;
$\quad$**until** $\|w\|_D < 1$;
end

Algorithm 1 has a loop and hence, it repeats its approximation several times. This is different from the Babai's algorithm which does not have any loop. In our case, the loop is required to replace the approximation of $\lceil (1 - MD^{-1})^{-1} \rfloor$ by 1. The loop corresponds to the different power of MD^{-1} that we have omitted.

Remark 5. The Algorithm 1 returns a vector with $\|w\|_D = \|wD^{-1}\|_\infty < 1$, which is the reason why we consider it like an approximation of CVP_∞. However, it is only true when $D = \beta Id$ that we have a classic definition of l_∞ reduction. The important point is that the coefficients $|w_i| < D_{i,i}$ do not depend on any average or any direct influence from the other coefficients of w. This property comes from the polytope norm which includes the l_∞-norm. That is the intrinsic difference between the l_∞-norm, a polytope norm, and the l_2-norm, a ellipsoidal norm.

It is trivial to prove that Algorithm 1 is exact.

a) $w = w - q(D - M)$ with $q \in \mathbb{Z}^n$. The loop does not change the congruence of $w \bmod \mathcal{L}$. So at the end, $w \equiv v \bmod \mathcal{L}$ holds.
b) If Algorithm 1 ends then $\|w\|_D < 1$.

However, condition for Algorithm 1 termination has to be defined. There exists a very similar problem of successive approximation convergence in the literature. To compute a vector x with $xA = y$ for some problematic matrix A, a complete theory has been developed with some equivalent decomposition, $A = D - M$ where A is called M-matrix. Some equivalent result for convergence, $\rho(MD^{-1}) < 1$ has been found. See [54,34] for more detail on this theory.

However, even if this theory is very similar, it does not solve the question of Algorithm 1 termination. Therefore, we propose Theorem 5 which is inspired by such a theory to answer this question.

Theorem 5. *Let $n \in \mathbb{N}$, $D, M \in \mathbb{Z}^{n,n}$ be two square matrices with D non singular and diagonal. The successive approximation w_i of a vector w given by $w_0 = w$ and $w_i = w_{i-1} - \lceil w_{i-1}D^{-1} \rfloor (D - M)$ for $i > 0$.*

i) *For any l_p-norm with $\|MD^{-1}\|_p < 1$, we have $\lim_{i \to \infty} \|w_i\|_D \le \frac{\|1 - MD^{-1}\|_p}{1 - \|MD^{-1}\|_p} \frac{n^{1/p}}{2}$.*

ii) *For any polytope norm with $\|MD^{-1}\|_P < 1$, we have $\lim_{i \to \infty} \|w_i\|_D \le \frac{\|1 - MD^{-1}\|_P}{1 - \|MD^{-1}\|_P} \frac{\kappa(P)}{2}$.*

iii) *For any non singular eigenmatrix P of MD^{-1}, we have $\lim_{i \to \infty} \|w_i\|_D \le \frac{\rho(1 - MD^{-1})}{1 - \rho(MD^{-1})} \frac{\kappa(P)}{2}$.*

Proof. First, we decompose the successive approximation

$$w_i = w_{i-1} - \lceil w_{i-1}D^{-1}\rfloor (D - M)$$
$$w_i = w_{i-1} - (w_{i-1}D^{-1} + \epsilon_i)(D - M) \text{ where } \epsilon_i \in [-1/2, 1/2]^n$$
$$w_i = w_{i-1} - w_{i-1} + w_{i-1}D^{-1}M - \epsilon_i(D - M)$$
$$w_i = w_{i-1}D^{-1}M - \epsilon_i(D - M)$$

We want to evaluate $w_i D^{-1} = w_{i-1}D^{-1}MD^{-1} - \epsilon_i(1 - MD^{-1})$. Now, for any norm $\|.\|$, we have

$$\|w_i D^{-1}\| = \|w_{i-1}D^{-1}MD^{-1} - \epsilon_i(1 - MD^{-1})\|$$
$$\|w_i D^{-1}\| \le \|w_{i-1}D^{-1}\|\|MD^{-1}\| + \|\epsilon_i\|\|(1 - MD^{-1})\|$$

Let be Δ the max of $\|\epsilon_i\|$, we obtain $\|w_i D^{-1}\| = \|w_{i-1}D^{-1}\|\|MD^{-1}\| + \Delta\|(1 - MD^{-1})\|$. So, if $\|MD^{-1}\| < 1$ this sequence converge to $\lim_{i \leftarrow \infty} \|w_i D^{-1}\| \le \Delta\|(1 - MD^{-1})\| \sum_{i=0}^{\infty} \|MD^{-1}\|$. Because we have $\|MD^{-1}\| < 1$, we obtain

$$\lim_{i \leftarrow \infty} \|w_i D^{-1}\| \le \Delta \frac{\|(1 - MD^{-1})\|}{1 - \|MD^{-1}\|}.$$

To finish this proof, we have to adapt this result to different norm.

i) If $\|.\|$ is a l_p-norm, we obtain $\lim_{i \leftarrow \infty} \|w_i D^{-1}\|_p \le \Delta \frac{\|(1 - MD^{-1})\|_p}{1 - \|MD^{-1}\|_p}$. We can evaluate $\Delta = \frac{n^{1/p}}{2}$.

$$\lim_{i \leftarrow \infty} \|w_i D^{-1}\|_p \le \frac{\|(1 - MD^{-1})\|_p}{1 - \|MD^{-1}\|_p} \frac{n^{1/p}}{2}$$

We know also that for any vector v, $\|v\|_\infty \le \|v\|_p$.

$$\lim_{i \leftarrow \infty} \|w_i D^{-1}\|_\infty \le \frac{\|(1 - MD^{-1})\|_p}{1 - \|MD^{-1}\|_p} \frac{n^{1/p}}{2}$$

With the definition of the $\|.\|_D$ norm, we obtain

$$\lim_{i \leftarrow \infty} \|w_i\|_D \le \frac{\|(1 - MD^{-1})\|_p}{1 - \|MD^{-1}\|_p} \frac{n^{1/p}}{2}$$

ii) If $\|.\|$ is a polytope norm $\|.\|_P$, we obtain $\lim_{i \leftarrow \infty} \|w_i D^{-1}\|_P \leq \Delta \frac{\|(1-MD^{-1})\|_P}{1-\|MD^{-1}\|_P}$.
   We can evaluate $\Delta = \frac{1}{2}\|P^{-1}\|_\infty$.

$$\lim_{i \leftarrow \infty} \|w_i D^{-1}\|_P \leq \frac{\|(1-MD^{-1})\|_P}{1-\|MD^{-1}\|_P} \frac{\|P^{-1}\|_\infty}{2}$$

By definition, we have $\|wD^{-1}\|_P = \|wD^{-1}P^{-1}\|_\infty$. To evaluate $\|w\|_D$, we have $\|w\|_D = \|wD^{-1}\|_\infty = \|wD^{-1}P^{-1}P\|_\infty \leq \|wD^{-1}P^{-1}\|_\infty \|P\|_\infty$.
Now, we can evaluate the limit of $\|w_i\|_D$.

$$\lim_{i \leftarrow \infty} \|w_i\|_D \leq \frac{\|(1-MD^{-1})\|_P}{1-\|MD^{-1}\|_P} \frac{\|P^{-1}\|_\infty}{2} \|P\|_\infty$$
$$\lim_{i \leftarrow \infty} \|w_i\|_D \leq \frac{\|(1-MD^{-1})\|_P}{1-\|MD^{-1}\|_P} \frac{\kappa(P)}{2}$$

iii) If $\|.\|$ is a polytope norm $\|.\|_P$ where P is an non singular eigenmatrix of MD^{-1}, we obtain the same result with $\|MD^{-1}\|_P = \rho(MD^{-1})$. We have also $\|1 - MD^{-1}\|_P = \rho(1 - MD^{-1})$ because an eigenmatrix of A is also a eigenmatrix of any polynomial composition of A.

$$\lim_{i \leftarrow \infty} \|w_i\|_D \leq \frac{\rho(1 - MD^{-1})}{1 - \rho(MD^{-1})} \frac{\kappa(P)}{2} \qquad \square$$

We note that this proof is very similar and inspired by some proofs found in [34] to solve close problem of successive approximation convergence.

Remark 6. Theorem 5 clearly provides some conditions to terminate Algorithm 1. These three conditions are complementary.

i) The l_p-norm can be used to have a fast approximation. See [27] for some methods to compute l_p norm for a matrix if p is not simple $p = 1, 2, \infty$.
ii) The polytope norm provides a way to be closer to $\|MD^{-1}\|_P \sim \rho(MD^{-1})$ which is the lower bound. But its computation can be long to minimize $\kappa(P)$.
iii) The non singular eigenmatrix are the best evaluation but it requires us to have distinct eigenvalues, which we do not always have.

In fact, after several practical tests and theoretical analysis, we are able to make a conjecture.

Conjecture 1. Let $n \in \mathbb{N}$, $D, M \in \mathbb{Z}^{n,n}$ be two square matrices with D non singular and diagonal. The successive approximation w_i of a vector w given by $w_0 = w$ and $w_i = w_{i-1} - \lfloor w_{i-1}D^{-1} \rfloor (D-M)$ for $i > 0$ converge if $\rho(MD^{-1}) < \frac{1}{2}$.

This conjecture will be used for the practical implementation of Algorithm 1. For the rest of this paper, sometimes we refer to $\rho(MD^{-1})$ only with ρ, when the context is clear.

5 Signature Scheme

In this section, we describe our new signature scheme, which comprises of the three algorithms: *Setup*, *Sign* and *Verify*.

Setup
a) Choose an integer n.
b) Compute a randomly integer matrix $M \in \{-1, 0, 1\}^{n,n}$.
c) Compute $D = \lfloor 2\rho(M) + 1 \rfloor Id$.
d) Compute the Hermite Normal Form H of the basis $D - M$.
e) The public key is (D, H), and the secret key is M.

Sign To sign a message $m \in \{0, 1\}^*$, one does the following.
a) Compute the vector $v = h(m) \in \mathbb{Z}^n$ where h is a hash function such that

$$h : \quad m \quad \to v$$
$$: \{0, 1\}^* \to \{x \in \mathbb{Z}^n, \quad \|x\|_{D^2} < 1\}$$

b) Using Algorithm 1, compute w, which is a reduced vector of v.
c) The signature on m is w.

Remark 7. The three choices of $M \in \{-1, 0, 1\}^{n,n}$, $\rho < 1/2$ and $\|x\|_{D^2} < 1$ are arbitrary and they can be changed. However these choices seem to be practically reasonable.

Verify To verify a message-signature pair, (m, w), one does the following.
a) Check if $\|w\|_D < 1$.
b) Compute the vector $h(m) \in \mathbb{Z}^n$.
c) Check if the vector $h(m) - w$ is in the lattice of basis H.

6 Improvements

In this section, we present some improvements to our scheme to make it practical. These improvements provide some choices to the main algorithm, in order to optimize it during the implementation of the algorithm.

6.1 Signature

The main part of the signing algorithm is in the reduction part as defined in (Algorithm 1). The fact that D is a diagonal matrix will simplify a lot of computations of wD^{-1}. This computation corresponds to the computation of the quotient of $\frac{w_i}{D_{i,i}}$. In fact the reduction algorithm needs the rest of this division as well. Based on this observation, we can rewrite Algorithm 1 as shown in Algorithm 2.

Remark 8. Algorithm 2 could be completely optimized by the utilization of $D = \beta Id$ with β be a power of two. This choice transforms the division corresponding to the two first lines of the loop to a shift operation. Hence, the reduction of a vector can be summarized to shift and addition operations, assuming that the matrix has low coefficients.

Algorithm 2. Sign

Input   : A vector $v \in \mathbb{Z}^n$
Data   : Two square matrices D, M
Output: A vector $w \in \mathbb{Z}^n$
begin
$\quad\vert\quad w \leftarrow v;$
$\quad\vert\quad i \leftarrow 0;$
$\quad\vert\quad$ **repeat**
$\quad\vert\quad\quad\vert\quad k \leftarrow 0;$
$\quad\vert\quad\quad\vert\quad q \leftarrow \left\lfloor \frac{w_i}{D_{i,i}} \right\rfloor;$
$\quad\vert\quad\quad\vert\quad w_i \leftarrow w_i - qD_{i,i};$
$\quad\vert\quad\quad\vert\quad$ **for** $j = 0$ **to** $n - 1$ **do**
$\quad\vert\quad\quad\vert\quad\quad\vert\quad w_{i+j \bmod n} \leftarrow w_{i+j \bmod n} + q \times M_{i,j};$
$\quad\vert\quad\quad\vert\quad\quad\vert\quad$ **if** $|w_{i+j \bmod n}| < D_{i+j \bmod n, i+j \bmod n}$ **then** $k = k + 1;$
$\quad\vert\quad\quad\vert\quad$ **end**
$\quad\vert\quad\quad\vert\quad i \leftarrow i + 1 \bmod n;$
$\quad\vert\quad$ **until** $k = n;$
end

6.2   Verification

The main part of the verification algorithm is the time to verify the inclusion of w in the lattice $\mathcal{L}$. As we described in Remark 2, the utilization of the HNF accelerates this computation and it was successfully used in [38]. If we choose to keep only some special lattices, then we can also do some further improvements.

Definition 15. *Let be H the HNF basis of a full-rank lattice $\mathcal{L}$, we will called H optimal if $\forall i > 1 \quad H_{i,i} = 1$.*

With an optimal HNF basis H, a vector w is in the lattice of basis H if and only if $\sum_{i=1}^{n-1} w_i \times H_{i,0} \equiv w_0 \pmod{H_{0,0}}$.
     With this setting, we can propose a very simple algorithm to verify the signature as follows.

Algorithm 3. Verify

Data   : Two square matrices D, H
Input : Two vectors $v, w \in \mathbb{Z}^n$
Output: A boolean
begin
$\quad\vert\quad$ **for** $i = 0$ **to** $n - 1$ **do** **if** $|w_i| \geq D_{i,i}$ **then return** *False;*
$\quad\vert\quad s \leftarrow 0;$
$\quad\vert\quad$ **for** $i = 1$ **to** $n - 1$ **do** $s \leftarrow s + (v_i - w_i) \times H_{i,0};$
$\quad\vert\quad$ **if** $s = v_0 - w_0 \bmod H_{0,0}$ **then return** *True* **else return** *False*
end

Remark 9. Optimal HNF simplifies the verification method and also minimizes the size of the public key. We note that in this case, we only need to send the first column of the matrix H. Consequently, we will use the optimal HNF for a "bad basis".

7 Comparison with GGH Signature Scheme

The advantage that our system has compared to the GGH signature scheme is the use of the l_∞-norm, which will make the scheme more resistant and difficult to attack. Furthermore, a shorter signature length and an efficient computation to compute with Algorithm 1 can be achieved with the help of fast arithmetic operations. The details of these advantages are provided in this section.

7.1 Resistance

An approximation of CVP_∞ also provides an approximation of CVP_2 by the equivalence of norm. Theoretically, the complexity of our cryptosystem cannot be less than the initial GGH signature scheme and Micciancio's improvements. However, parameter choices are essential to achieve a practical high resistance scheme.

The best basic way to attack our scheme is by finding M using D on $\mathcal{L}(H)$: $D \equiv M \pmod{\mathcal{L}(H)}$. In other words, $\forall i, \quad (0, \ldots, 0, D_{i,i}, 0, \ldots, 0) \equiv (M_{i,1}, \ldots, M_{i,n}) \pmod{\mathcal{L}(H)}$. The attacker has to find some very good approximations (most of the time the exact result) of the CVP for the l_∞-norm. This attack seems to be the easiest way compared to solving CVP_∞ for a given vector-message. If the attacker can solve CVP_∞ for every vector of D, he can use Algorithm 1 to create a false signature. Therefore, we consider an attack to be successful if the attacker can find a matrix M' such that $D \equiv M' \pmod{\mathcal{L}(H)}$ with $\rho(M'D^{-1}) < 1$ and not only if $M' = M$.

As remarked in Remark 3 the l_∞-norm seems to be more resistant. A powerful advantage of its system clearly comes from the intrinsic difference between the l_2 and the l_∞ norms. Effectively, the utilization of approximation algorithms for the l_2-norm to solve approximation problem for l_∞-norm will be worst. Moreover, some special matrices M could be used to take advantage of the intrinsic difference between those two norms to make those algorithms completely inefficient: the row vector M_i of M are such that $\|M_i\|_\infty < D_{i,i}$. If we take $\|M_i\|_2 > D_{i,i}$ or at least $\|M_i\|_2 \sim D_{i,i}$, it will raise some problems to use l_2 algorithm.

A brute force attack to find a row vector of M, where $M_{i,j} \in \{-1, 0, 1\}$, is $O(3^n)$. This brute force attack is faster than solving exactly a CVP using Kannan's method [31], which has the complexity of $n^{O(n)}$. Note that these two possible attacks are in the exponential order. When n is chosen to be large, then these techniques cannot be employed. Therefore, in order to attack it, only an approximation of CVP that can be computed, rather than solving it. Although the approximation of CVP is polynomial, the attack is a heuristic attack and therefore there is no assurance that the result is precise enough.

A theoretical timing attack is also possible as the time of the signature depends on the message-vector. However, such an attack seems very unlikely: to obtain information on the form of message vector if its reduction took 4 or 5 loops instead of

6 seems very hard. There exists a simple way to completely prevent this hypothetical attack. A simple improvement of Algorithm 2 is the utilization of a random initialization of i: $i \leftarrow rand(0 \ldots n-1)$ instead of a classic $i \leftarrow 0$. Besides the fact that there is no real reason to begin with 0, this improvement will provide two advantages. Firstly, temporary approximation vectors are not the same between two reductions of the same vector: that will change the number of loops to reduce to the same vector. This property gives an advantage against side-channel attacks, like timing attack. The most important advantage is that this method grows the length of the set of vectors of $\{v, \|v\|_D\}$ that can be returned. This property provides a strong resistance against the attack described in [42].

Another remark is on the fact that D is public. However, GGH basis where taken as $\sqrt{n}Id - M$ with $M_{i,j} \in [-4, 4]$. So D can be easily guessed as well for GGH and attacks on GGH do not use this fact.

To finalize the comments on the security, we need to comment our scheme against the most successful attack against GGH signature scheme and NTRUSign. In 2006, Nguyen and Regev [42] proposed a clever way to design the fundamental parallelepiped using some signature-message which represent a CVP approximation. We also note that this attack will be ineffective against our system. All the signature-message are in $\{xD, x \in]-1, 1[^n\}$. Finding the design of this volume is not particularly useful since D is already given as a public parameter. In Figure 1, we present an example of some signature-message on $\mathbb{R}^2$ after reduction with Babai's method or with our method. Even if the dimension 2 is far away of cryptographic dimension, we can still see the mark used by [42]. In fact, we see that the vectors of the basis can be designed after enough Babai reductions, but that we can only design D after reduction by Algorithm 2.

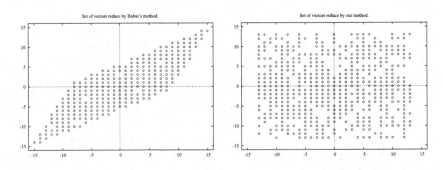

Fig. 1. Signature-message on $\mathbb{R}^2$ for Babai's reduction and our reduction

7.2   Speed

For an optimized version of the signature scheme (Algorithm 2), Algorithm 1 uses only shift and addition operations. However, we need to know the average number of loops to reduce a signature vector. Even if the proof of Theorem 5 gives us a bound on the worst case, the average case seems to be difficult to evaluate. In Figure 2, we present an average number of iterations from Algorithm 2. On every dimension $n \in [50, 350]$, we have compute a 100 random couples D, M following the methods used in the Setup algorithm: $M \in \{-1, 0, 1\}^{n,n}$ and $D = \lfloor 2\rho(M) + 1 \rfloor Id$. With each of this basis $D - M$, we have reduced 100 random message vector chosen in $[0, \lfloor 2\rho(M) + 1 \rfloor]^2[^n$. Figure 2 shows the average of the number of loops required to reduce a message vector to a signature vector.

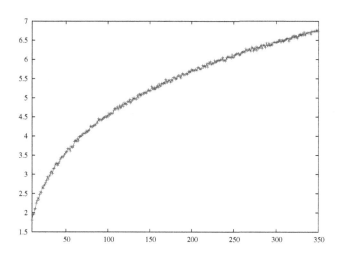

Fig. 2. Average number of loops used to reduce a message vector to a signature vector

From Figure 2, one can conclude that on average, the number of loops required for signing is between 5 and 7 to achieve a good security level, which is approximately began from 200. Furthermore, Figure 2 also shows that the average number of loops are logarithmic on n, $O(\log n)$. We note that our reduction is applicable only for some special lattices. Nevertheless, the resulting efficiency obtained from these lattices are very interesting to develop efficient and fast digital signature schemes. As explained earlier, a loop can be minimized to only shift and addition operations. It provides us with a very competitive way to reduce a vector when the first Babai's reduction uses two matrix multiplications. The first matrix multiplication in Babai's reduction is the most expensive operation, since it requires a high precision on a floating point matrix multiplication. In contrast to Babai's method, our method can be used in a huge dimension that will provide higher level of security without any time constraint.

7.3 Space

In this section, we provide some evaluation on the signature space. l_∞-norm is naturally the norm used to evaluate the space complexity of a signature. The fact that Algorithm 1 deals directly with this norm makes an important difference with Babai's method.

Figure 3 shows result of test on the l_∞-norm of reduce vector. We present three curves corresponding to three parameters. For every dimension n ($n \in [50, 350]$), we compute on 100 random matrices chosen in $M \in \{-1, 0, 1\}^{n,n}$,

i) the average spectral radius of M,
ii) the average $\|D\|_\infty$ that we can pick to have $\rho(MD^{-1}) < \frac{1}{2}$. This result correspond also on the max l_∞-norm of any vector reduced by our method,
iii) the average max l_∞-norm of any vector reduced by Babai's method with the same basis $D - M$.

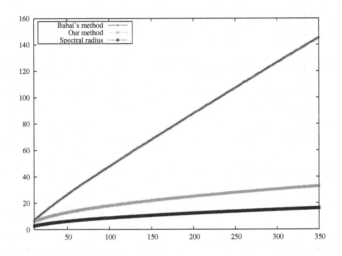

Fig. 3. Average l_∞-norm of signature-vector using different reduction method

Figure 3 has been obtained from the same data set used to generate Figure 2.

The important point of this result is that we can observe that the l_∞ norm of a reduced vector with this type of basis is in $O(n)$ after Babai's reduction and in $O(\sqrt{n})$ after our reduction. This difference clearly comes from the difference between l_2 and l_∞-norm.

To obtain a theoretical limit of this result, we use the result of German [18] which evaluates the limit when the dimension n grow of the spectral radius of a random matrix $A \in \mathbb{C}^{n,n}$ as $\rho(A) = \omega\sqrt{n}$ with $\omega^2 = \frac{1}{n^2} \sum_{i,j=0}^{i,j<n} A_{i,j}^2$.

This limit provides a good approximation of the spectral radius of a random matrix. Using this limit, we obtain the following result for a random matrix M taken in $\{-1, 0, 1\}^{n,n}$ an average approximation about $\rho(M) \sim \sqrt{\frac{2n}{3}}$. Finally, if we want $\rho(MD^{-1}) < \frac{1}{2}$ we need $\|D\|_\infty \sim 2\sqrt{\frac{2n}{3}} \sim 1.63\sqrt{n} = O(\sqrt{n})$. The theoretical approximation of $\rho(M)$ and $\|D\|_\infty$ obtained using German's theorem is very close to our own practical test given in Figure 3.

8   Conclusion and Open Problems

In this paper, we presented a new method of vector reduction under the l_∞-norm. Then, we constructed a signature scheme based on this norm. The resulting scheme seems very interesting, in terms of security, length and speed. We conclude this paper by providing two open research problems. Firstly, how to prove Conjecture 1 of $\rho < \frac{1}{2}$ and secondly, how to derive a formula to compute the average number of iterations in Algorithm 1 which is logarithmic in n as the test has demonstrated.

References

1. Agrell, E., Eriksson, T., Vardy, A., Zeger, K.: Closest point search in lattices. IEEE Transactions on Information Theory 48(8), 2201–2214 (2002)
2. Ajtai, M.: The shortest vector problem in l_2 is NP-hard for randomized reductions. In: 13th Annual ACM Symp. on the Theory of Computing, pp. 10–19 (1998)
3. Ajtai, M., Dwork, C.: A public-key cryptosystem with worst-case/average-case equivalence. In: 29th Annual ACM Symp. on the Th. of Comp., pp. 284–293 (1997)
4. Ajtai, M., Kumar, R., Sivakumar, D.: A sieve algorithm for the shortest lattice vector problem. In: 33rd Annual ACM Symp. on Th. of Comp., pp. 601–610 (2001)
5. Ajtai, M., Kumar, R., Sivakumar, D.: Sampling short lattice vectors and the closest lattice vector problem. In: IEEE CCC, pp. 53–57 (2002)
6. Babai, L.: On Lovász' lattice reduction and the nearest lattice point problem. Combinatorica 6(1), 1–13 (1986)
7. Bajard, J.-C., Imbert, L., Plantard, T.: Modular number systems: Beyond the Mersenne family. In: Handschuh, H., Hasan, M.A. (eds.) SAC 2004. LNCS, vol. 3357, pp. 159–169. Springer, Heidelberg (2004)
8. Blömer, J., Naewe, S.: Sampling Methods for Shortest Vectors, Closest Vectors and Successive Minima. In: Arge, L., Cachin, C., Jurdziński, T., Tarlecki, A. (eds.) ICALP 2007. LNCS, vol. 4596, pp. 65–77. Springer, Heidelberg (2007)
9. Boas, P.V.E.: Another NP-complete problem and the complexity of computing short vectors in lattices. TR 81-04, Math. Dept., Univ. of Amsterdam (1981)
10. Cai, J.-Y.: Some recent progress on the complexity of lattice problems. In: 14th Annual IEEE Conference on Computational Complexity, pp. 158–178 (1999)
11. Cassels, J.W.S.: An Introduction to The Geometry of Numbers. Springer, Heidelberg (1959)
12. Chen, W., Meng, J.: The hardness of the closest vector problem with preprocessing over ℓ_∞ norm. IEEE Trans on Inf Theory 52(10), 4603–4606 (2006)
13. Cohen, H.: A course in computational algebraic number theory. Graduate Texts in Mathematics, vol. 138. Springer, Heidelberg (1993)
14. Collatz, L.: Functional Analysis and Numerical Mathematics. Academic Press Inc., U.S. (1966)
15. Conway, J.H., Sloane, N.J.A.: Sphere Packings, Lattices and Groups. Springer, Heidelberg (1988)
16. Dinur, I.: Approximating SVP_∞ to within almost-polynomial factors is NP-Hard. In: Bongiovanni, G., Petreschi, R., Gambosi, G. (eds.) CIAC 2000. LNCS, vol. 1767, pp. 263–276. Springer, Heidelberg (2000)
17. Dinur, I., Kindler, G., Safra, S.: Approximating CVP to within almost polynomial factor is NP-hard. In: FOCS 1998, pp. 99–111 (1998)

18. Geman, S.: The spectral radius of large random matrices. The Annals of Probability 14(4), 1318–1328 (1986)
19. Gentry, C., Szydlo, M.: Cryptanalysis of the revised NTRU signature scheme. In: Knudsen, L.R. (ed.) EUROCRYPT 2002. LNCS, vol. 2332, pp. 299–320. Springer, Heidelberg (2002)
20. Goldreich, O., Goldwasser, S.: On the limits of non-approximability of lattice problems. In: the 30th Annual ACM Symp on Th of Computing, pp. 1–9 (1998)
21. Goldreich, O., Goldwasser, S., Halevi, S.: Public-key cryptosystems from lattice reductions problems. In: Kaliski Jr., B.S. (ed.) CRYPTO 1997. LNCS, vol. 1294, pp. 112–131. Springer, Heidelberg (1997)
22. Goldreich, O., Micciancio, D., Safra, S., Seifert, J.-P.: Approximating shortest lattice vectors is not harder than approximating closest lattice vectors. Information Processing Letters 71(2), 55–61 (1999)
23. Golub, G.H., Loan, C.F.V.: Matrix Computations. The Johns Hopkins University Press (1983)
24. Hanrot, G., Stehle, D.: Improved analysis of Kannan's shortest lattice vector algorithm. In: Menezes, A. (ed.) CRYPTO 2007. LNCS, vol. 4622, Springer, Heidelberg (2007)
25. Haviv, I., Regev, O.: Tensor-based hardness of the shortest vector problem to within almost polynomial factors. In: Thirty-nineth annual ACM symposium on Theory of computing, pp. 469–477 (2007)
26. Helfrich, B.: Algorithms to construct Minkowski reduced an Hermite reduced lattice bases. Theoretical Computer Science 41, 125–139 (1985)
27. Higham, N.J.: Estimating the matrix p-norm. Numerische Mathematik 62, 539–556 (1992)
28. Hoffstein, J., Howgrave-Graham, N., Pipher, J., Silverman, J.H., Whyte, W.: NTRUSign: Digital signatures using the NTRU lattice. In: Joye, M. (ed.) CT-RSA 2003. LNCS, vol. 2612, pp. 122–140. Springer, Heidelberg (2003)
29. Hoffstein, J., Pipher, J., Silverman, J.H.: NTRU: A ring-based public key cryptosystem. In: Buhler, J.P. (ed.) ANTS 1998. LNCS, vol. 1423, pp. 267–288. Springer, Heidelberg (1998)
30. Householder, A.S.: The theory of matrices in numerical analysis. Blaisdell Pub. Co., New York (1964)
31. Kannan, R.: Improved algorithms for integer programming and related lattice problems. In: Proceedings of the Fifteenth Annual ACM Symposium on Theory of Computing, Boston, Massachusetts, April 1983, pp. 193–206 (1983)
32. Kannan, R., Bachem, A.: Polynomial algorithms for computing the Smith and Hermite normal forms of an integer matrix. SIAM J. of Comp 8(4), 499–507 (1979)
33. Khot, S.: Hardness of approximating the shortest vector problem in high l_p norms. In: The 44th Annual IEEE Symposium on FOCS, pp. 290–297 (2003)
34. Krasnosel'Skii, M.A., Vainikkov, G.M., Zabreiko, P.P., Rutitskii, Y.B., Stetsenko, V.Y.: Approximate solution of operator equations (1972)
35. Lenstra, A.K., Lenstra, H.W., Lovász, L.: Factoring polynomials with rational coefficients. Mathematische Annalen 261, 513–534 (1982)
36. Lovász, L.: An Algorithmic Theory of Numbers, Graphs and Convexity. In: CBMS-NSF Regional Conference Series in Applied Mathematics, vol. 50, SIAM Publications, Philadelphia (1986)
37. McEliece, R.J.: A public-key cryptosystem based on algebraic coding theory. Deep Space Network Progress Report 44, 114–116 (1978)

38. Micciancio, D.: Improving lattice based cryptosystems using the Hermite normal form. In: Silverman, J.H. (ed.) CaLC 2001. LNCS, vol. 2146, pp. 126–145. Springer, Heidelberg (2001)

39. Micciancio, D., Warinschi, B.: A linear space algorithm for computing the Hermite normal form. In: Intl. Symp. on Symb. Alg. Comp., pp. 231–236 (2001)

40. Minkowski, H.: Geometrie der Zahlen. B.G. Teubner, Leipzig (1896)

41. Nguyen, P.Q.: Cryptanalysis of the Goldreich-Goldwasser-Halevi cryptosystem from crypto 1997. In: Wiener, M.J. (ed.) CRYPTO 1999. LNCS, vol. 1666, pp. 288–304. Springer, Heidelberg (1999)

42. Nguyen, P.Q., Regev, O.: Learning a parallelepiped: Cryptanalysis of GGH and NTRU signatures. In: Vaudenay, S. (ed.) EUROCRYPT 2006. LNCS, vol. 4004, pp. 271–288. Springer, Heidelberg (2006)

43. Nguyen, P.Q., Stehlé, D.: Floating-point LLL revisited. In: Cramer, R.J.F. (ed.) EUROCRYPT 2005. LNCS, vol. 3494, pp. 215–233. Springer, Heidelberg (2005)

44. Nguyen, P.Q., Stehlé, D.: LLL on the average. In: Hess, F., Pauli, S., Pohst, M. (eds.) ANTS 2006. LNCS, vol. 4076, pp. 238–256. Springer, Heidelberg (2006)

45. Nguyen, P.Q., Stern, J.: The two faces of lattices in cryptology. In: Silverman, J.H. (ed.) CaLC 2001. LNCS, vol. 2146, pp. 146–180. Springer, Heidelberg (2001)

46. Peikert, C.: Limits on the hardness of lattice problems in ℓ_p norms. In: Twenty-Second Annual IEEE Conference on Computational Complexity, pp. 333–346 (2007)

47. Regev, O.: Lattice-based cryptography. In: Dwork, C. (ed.) CRYPTO 2006. LNCS, vol. 4117, pp. 131–141. Springer, Heidelberg (2006)

48. Regev, O., Rosen, R.: Lattice problems and norm embeddings. In: Thirty-eighth annual ACM symposium on Theory of computing, pp. 447–456 (2006)

49. Schnorr, C.-P.: A hierarchy of polynomial time lattice basis reduction algorithms. Theoretical Computer Science 53(2–3), 201–224 (1987)

50. Schnorr, C.-P.: A more efficient algorithm for lattice basis reduction. Journal of Algorithms 9(1), 47–62 (1988)

51. Schnorr, C.-P.: Block Korkin-Zolotarev bases and successive minima (1996)

52. Schnorr, C.-P.: Fast LLL-type lattice reduction. Information and Computation 204(1), 1–25 (2006)

53. Szydlo, M.: Hypercubic lattice reduction and analysis of GGH and NTRU signatures. In: Biham, E. (ed.) EUROCRYPT 2003. LNCS, vol. 2656, pp. 433–448. Springer, Heidelberg (2003)

54. Varga, R.S.: Matrix Iterative Analysis. Prentice-Hall, Englewood Cliffs (1962)

55. Wilkinson, J.H.: The algebraic eigenvalue problem. Oxford University Press, Inc., New York (1965)

An Analysis of the Vector Decomposition Problem

Steven D. Galbraith[1] and Eric R. Verheul[2]

[1] Mathematics Department,
Royal Holloway, University of London,
Egham, Surrey, TW20 0EX,
United Kingdom
steven.galbraith@rhul.ac.uk
[2] PricewaterhouseCoopers Advisory, Radboud University Nijmegen,
P.O. Box 22735, 1100 DE, Amsterdam, The Netherlands
eric.verheul@{nl.pwc.com, cs.ru.nl}

Abstract. The vector decomposition problem (VDP) has been proposed as a computational problem on which to base the security of public key cryptosystems. We give a generalisation and simplification of the results of Yoshida on the VDP. We then show that, for the supersingular elliptic curves which can be used in practice, the VDP is equivalent to the computational Diffie-Hellman problem (CDH) in a cyclic group. For the broader class of pairing-friendly elliptic curves we relate VDP to various co-CDH problems and also to a generalised discrete logarithm problem 2-DL which in turn is often related to discrete logarithm problems in cyclic groups.

Keywords: Vector decomposition problem, elliptic curves, Diffie-Hellman problem, generalised discrete logarithm problem.

1 Introduction

The vector decomposition problem (VDP) is a computational problem in non-cyclic groups G (see Section 2 for the definition of this problem). It was introduced by Yoshida [22,23] as an alternative to the discrete logarithm or Diffie-Hellman problems for the design of cryptographic systems. Yoshida proved that if certain conditions hold then the VDP is at least as hard as the computational Diffie-Hellman problem (CDH) in a certain cyclic subgroup G_1 of G. Since the CDH in G_1 may be hard, it follows that VDP may be hard, and so it is a potentially useful problem on which to base public key cryptography. Indeed, cryptosystems based on the VDP have been proposed in [22,23,10].

As with any new computational problem in cryptography, it is important to understand the hardness of VDP if one is to use it in practice. Apart from the result of Yoshida, there is no discussion in the literature of the difficulty of the VDP. Hence, it is an open problem to determine the precise security level of the VDP and thus to evaluate the security/performance of cryptosystems based on it. That is the primary motivation of this paper.

R. Cramer (Ed.): PKC 2008, LNCS 4939, pp. 308–327, 2008.

We prove that the VDP in G is equivalent with certain co-CDH problems in G if a mild condition holds. A corollary is that CDH $\leq$ VDP for a much larger class of groups than considered by Yoshida. We then prove that VDP $\leq$ CDH for groups satisfying a condition similar to that considered by Yoshida (namely, existence of what we call a "distortion eigenvector base"). We show that all the supersingular elliptic curves which can be used in practice satisfy this condition. It follows that CDH and VDP are equivalent in practice for supersingular curves. We also prove this equivalence for the non-supersingular genus 2 curves proposed by Duursma and Kiyavasch [9]. Our results therefore completely resolve the issue of the difficulty of the VDP in the groups considered by [22,23,9,10].

Duursma and Park [10] proposed a signature scheme based on VDP. Our results imply that their signature scheme has no security advantages over systems based on CDH or DLP. One can therefore compare the performance of the scheme in [10] with, say, Schnorr signatures and deduce that their scheme has no advantages in practice.

To summarise the paper: the main definitions and results are in Section 2. Section 3 proves that distortion eigenvector bases exist for the supersingular elliptic curves which can be used in practice. Section 4 explains how our conditions relate to the definitions given by Yoshida. In Section 5 we review possible constructions of non-cyclic groups for cryptography. Finally, Section 6 gives some methods to reduce the VDP to various generalised discrete logarithm problems.

2   The Vector Decomposition Problem and Relations with CDH

Let $r > 3$ be a prime. The vector decomposition problem is usually expressed in terms of a 2-dimensional vector space over $\mathbb{F}_r$. However, it has currently only been instantiated on subgroups of exponent r of the divisor class group of a curve over a finite field. Hence, in this paper we use a group-theoretic formulation.

Throughout the paper G will be an abelian group of exponent r and order r^2 (i.e., G is isomorphic to $(\mathbb{Z}/r\mathbb{Z}) \times (\mathbb{Z}/r\mathbb{Z})$). We assume implicitly that G can be represented compactly and that the group operation can be computed in polynomial time. For examples of such groups see Section 5. We write such groups additively and use capital letters P, Q, R for elements of G. We use the notation $\langle P_1, \ldots, P_n \rangle$ for the subgroup of G generated by $\{P_1, \ldots, P_n\}$. We call a pair (P_1, P_2) a *base* for G if it generates G, i.e. each element in $Q \in G$ can be uniquely written as a linear combination in P_1 and P_2.

If A and B are computational problems then we denote Turing reduction of A to B by A $\leq$ B. This means that there is a polynomial time algorithm for solving problem A given access to an oracle to solve problem B. We call such a reduction tight if the probability of success of algorithm A is at least the probability of success of oracle B.

Definition 1. *The **vector decomposition problem (VDP)**: given a base (P_1, P_2) for G and an element $Q \in G$, compute an element $R \in G$ such that $R \in \langle P_1 \rangle$ and $Q - R \in \langle P_2 \rangle$.*

For a fixed base (P_1, P_2) we define $VDP_{(P_1, P_2)}$ as: given $Q \in G$ find R as above.

Clearly, such an element R is unique and if we write $Q = aP_1 + bP_2$ for unique $a, b \in \mathbb{Z}/r\mathbb{Z}$ then $R = aP_1$. We stress that an algorithm to solve the vector decomposition problem should take as input a triple (P_1, P_2, Q) and output a point R such that $R \in \langle P_1 \rangle$ and $Q - R \in \langle P_2 \rangle$. The **VDP conjecture** is that there exist families of groups for which the VDP is hard in the sense that there is no polynomial time algorithm which succeeds in solving the VDP on groups in the family with non-negligible probability over all possible input triples.

Yoshida proved that CDH ≤ VDP under certain conditions (see below). This suggests that VDP can be a hard problem. Our main goal in this paper is to give results in the other direction. As pointed out by an anonymous referee, an easy example of such a result can be obtained in the direct product of a cyclic group.

Definition 2. *Let G_1 be a cyclic group of order r. The* **computational Diffie-Hellman problem** *$CDH(G_1)$ is: given $P, aP, bP \in G_1$, compute abP.*

Lemma 1. *Let G_1 be a cyclic group of prime order r and let $G = G_1 \times G_1$. If one can solve the VDP in G then one can solve CDH in G_1.*

Proof. Let P, aP, bP be the input CDH problem. Let $P_1 = (P, aP)$, $P_2 = (0, P)$ and $Q = (bP, rP)$ for a random integer r. Note that $Q = bP_1 + (r - ab)P_2$ so solving the VDP instance (P_1, P_2, Q) gives $R = bP_1 = (bP, abP)$ and extracting the second component solves CDH.   □

The literature on the VDP seems to contain only three examples of suitable groups. Precisely, Yoshida [23] suggests the supersingular elliptic curve $y^2 = x^3 + 1$ (see Example 1 below) and Duursma-Kiyavash [9] suggest two non-supersingular genus 2 curves. However, it is obvious that one could use any pairing-friendly elliptic curve for applications based on the VDP.

We remark that VDP does not seem to trivially be random self-reducible. In other words, if we have an algorithm $\mathcal{A}$ which solves VDP for some non-negligible proportion of instances then it is not trivial to convert $\mathcal{A}$ into an algorithm which solves VDP with overwhelming probability over all instances. However, we show in Corollary 2 that one can obtain random self-reducibility for the VDP.

The following definition is the key concept which underlies most of the results in the paper.

Definition 3. *Let G be a group of exponent r and order r^2. Let $F : G \to G$ be a group isomorphism computable in polynomial time. A pair of elements $S, T \in G$ is an* **eigenvector base** *with respect to F if $G = \langle S, T \rangle$ and if $F(S) = \lambda_1 S$ and $F(T) = \lambda_2 T$ for some distinct, non-zero $\lambda_1, \lambda_2 \in \mathbb{Z}/r\mathbb{Z}$.*

In practice F will usually be the Frobenius map (more details are given later). Hence we often abbreviate 'eigenvector base with respect to F' by 'eigenvector base'.

Example 1. A standard example of such a group is as follows: Let $p \equiv 3 \pmod 4$ be prime and let $E : y^2 = x^3 + x$ over $\mathbb{F}_p$. Then E is a supersingular elliptic curve and $\#E(\mathbb{F}_p) = p + 1$. Let $r > 3$ be a prime such that $r \mid (p + 1)$. Then we can let $G = E[r] \subseteq E(\mathbb{F}_{p^2})$ be the group of all points on E of order r. Let S be a generator for $E(\mathbb{F}_p)[r]$. Denote by F the p-power Frobenius map $F(x, y) = (x^p, y^p)$. Note that $F(S) = S$ so $\lambda_1 = 1$. Consider the isomorphism ϕ defined by $\phi(x, y) = (x, iy)$ where $i \in \mathbb{F}_{p^2}$ satisfies $i^2 = -1$. Setting $T = \phi(S)$ we have $G = \langle S, T \rangle$ and $F(T) = -T$. Hence (S, T) is an eigenvector base with respect to F. (Indeed, this is also a distortion eigenvector base, which will be defined later.)

Proposition 1. *The* $VDP_{(P_1, P_2)}$ *with respect to a fixed base* (P_1, P_2) *is solvable in polynomial time iff* (P_1, P_2) *is an eigenvector base.*

Proof. For the proof of the "if" part of the result: let $F : G \to G$ be the group isomorphism as in the definition of eigenvector base. Let $\alpha = (\lambda_2 - \lambda_1)^{-1}$ $(\mod r)$. For $i = 1, 2$ define the projection map $\psi_i : G \to \langle P_i \rangle$ by

$$\psi_1(R) = \alpha(\lambda_2 R - F(R)) \ ; \ \psi_2(R) = \alpha(F(R) - \lambda_1 R).$$

These are efficiently computable group homomorphisms. Note that $\psi_1(P_1) = P_1$ and $\psi_1(P_2) = 0$ and so ψ_1 maps to $\langle P_1 \rangle$. Similarly, ψ_2 maps to $\langle P_2 \rangle$. Since $Q = \psi_1(Q) + \psi_2(Q)$ for all $Q \in G$ and the maps ψ_1, ψ_2 are easily computable, it follows that VDP with respect to (P_1, P_2) is easily solvable.

For the proof of the "only if" part of the result: suppose $\mathcal{A}$ is a polynomial time algorithm to solve $VDP_{(P_1, P_2)}$. Define

$$\psi_1(Q) = \mathcal{A}(Q) \text{ and } \psi_2(Q) = Q - \psi_1(Q).$$

Then ψ_i $(i = 1, 2)$ are group homomorphisms to $\langle P_i \rangle$ which can be computed in polynomial time. Any linear combination $F = \lambda_1 \psi_1 + \lambda_2 \psi_2$ with distinct, non-zero $\lambda_1, \lambda_2 \in \mathbb{Z}/r\mathbb{Z}$ has the desired properties so that (P_1, P_2) is an eigenvector base. $\qquad\square$

The fact that there are easy instances of $VDP_{(P_1, P_2)}$ does not affect the VDP conjecture for such curves. The conjecture is that the VDP should be hard for a randomly chosen input triple from the set G^3. In other words, it is permitted that the VDP be easy for a negligible proportion of triples in G^3.

2.1 Diffie-Hellman Problems and Relation with VDP

We recall the co-CDH problem as defined by Boneh, Lynn and Shacham [5].

Definition 4. *Let* G_1 *and* G_2 *be cyclic groups of order* r. *The* **co-Computational Diffie-Hellman problem** *co-CDH*(G_1, G_2) *is: Given* $P, aP \in G_1$ *and* $Q \in G_2$, *compute* aQ.

Note that having a perfect algorithm to solve co-CDH is equivalent to being able to compute a group homomorphism $\psi : G_1 \to G_2$ such that $\psi(P) = Q$.

Lemma 2. *Let G_1, G_2 be cyclic groups of order r. Then $CDH(G_1) \leq$ (co-CDH(G_1, G_2) and co-CDH(G_2, G_1)).*

Proof. Suppose we have oracles to solve both co-CDH problems which succeed with probability at least ϵ. Let P, aP, bP be given. Choose a random $Q \in G_2$ and a random $x \in (\mathbb{Z}/r\mathbb{Z})^*$ and call the co-CDH(G_1, G_2) oracle on (xP, xaP, Q) to get aQ with probability at least ϵ.

Now, choose random $x_1, x_2 \in (\mathbb{Z}/r\mathbb{Z})^*$ and call the co-CDH(G_2, G_1) oracle on $(x_1 Q, x_1 aQ, x_2 bP)$ to get $x_2 abP$ with probability at least ϵ. Exponentiating by x_2^{-1} gives abP as desired. The probability of success is at least ϵ^2. □

In Lemma 4 we give a converse to the above result if additional conditions hold (e.g., for supersingular elliptic curves). Note that if one can solve CDH(G_1) and one has a suitable auxiliary elliptic curve for the Maurer reduction [15,16] then one can solve the DLP in G_1 and hence solve co-CDH(G_1, G_2). Hence it is natural to conjecture that CDH(G_1) and co-CDH(G_1, G_2) are equivalent. However, it could conceivably be the case that there exist groups such that (co-CDH(G_1, G_2) and co-CDH(G_2, G_1)) is strictly harder than CDH(G_1). It would follow from Theorem 1 below that VDP is a strictly harder problem than CDH(G_1) for these groups.

The following computational problem is similar to the problem DCDH defined by Bao et al [2], who also proved equivalence with CDH. For completeness we give a trivial Lemma which is needed later.

Definition 5. *The **co-Divisional Computational Diffie-Hellman problem** co-DCDH(G_1, G_2) is, given (S, aS, T) for $S \in G_1, T \in G_2$, to compute $a^{-1}T$.*

Lemma 3. *co-DCDH$(G_1, G_2) \leq$ co-CDH(G_1, G_2).*

Proof. Given a co-DCDH instance (S, aS, T) choose uniformly at random $x_1, x_2, x_3 \in (\mathbb{Z}/r\mathbb{Z})^*$ and return $(x_2 x_3)^{-1}$co-CDH$(x_1 aS, x_1 x_2 S, x_3 T)$. Hence, if we can solve co-CDH with probability at least ϵ then one can solve co-DCDH with probability at least ϵ. □

Yoshida [22,23] showed that CDH $\leq$ VDP for supersingular elliptic curves having endomorphisms satisfying certain conditions. Theorem 1 below gives a major extension of Yoshida's result, since it has much weaker conditions and can be applied to ordinary curves (we give more discussion of this later). Also note that Yoshida's result requires a perfect oracle to solve VDP (i.e., one which always succeeds) whereas our proof allows an oracle with only some non-negligible probability of success (this is a non-trivial improvement since VDP does not seem to trivially have random self-reducibility).

Theorem 1. *Let G have an eigenvector base (S, T) and define $G_1 = \langle S \rangle$, $G_2 = \langle T \rangle$. Then VDP is equivalent to (co-CDH(G_1, G_2) and co-CDH(G_2, G_1)).*

More precisely, if one can solve VDP with probability at least ϵ then one can solve (co-CDH(G_1, G_2) and co-CDH(G_2, G_1)) with probability at least ϵ. If one can solve (co-CDH(G_1, G_2) and co-CDH(G_2, G_1)) with probability at least ϵ then one can solve VDP with probability at least ϵ^9.

Proof. First we show that co-CDH$(G_1, G_2) \leq$ VDP (the full statement follows by symmetry). We assume that we have a VDP oracle which succeeds with probability ϵ and show that one can solve co-CDH(G_1, G_2) with probability ϵ.

Let S, aS, T be given. Choose uniformly at random $x_1, x_2, y_1, y_2 \in (\mathbb{Z}/r\mathbb{Z})$ such that $x_1 x_2 - y_1 y_2 \not\equiv 0 \pmod{r}$. Then $(P_1 = x_1 S + y_1 T, P_2 = y_2 S + x_2 T)$ is a uniformly random base for G. There exist $\lambda, \mu \in (\mathbb{Z}/r\mathbb{Z})$ such that $aS = \lambda P_1 + \mu P_2$. One has

$$aS = \lambda(x_1 S + y_1 T) + \mu(y_2 S + x_2 T) = (\lambda x_1 + \mu y_2)S + (\lambda y_1 + \mu x_2)T$$

and so

$$\begin{pmatrix} x_1 & y_2 \\ y_1 & x_2 \end{pmatrix} \begin{pmatrix} \lambda \\ \mu \end{pmatrix} = \begin{pmatrix} a \\ 0 \end{pmatrix}. \tag{1}$$

Calling a VDP oracle on $(P_1, P_2, aS + u_1 P_1 + u_2 P_2)$ for uniformly random $u_1, u_2 \in (\mathbb{Z}/r\mathbb{Z})$ and subtracting $u_1 P_1$ from the output gives $\lambda P_1 = \lambda x_1 S + \lambda y_1 T$ with probability ϵ. Using Proposition 1 one can compute $R = \lambda y_1 T$.

Equation (1) implies that $\lambda \equiv (x_1 x_2 - y_1 y_2)^{-1} x_2 a \pmod{r}$. It follows that one can compute aT as

$$aT = (x_1 x_2 - y_1 y_2)(y_1 x_2)^{-1} R.$$

This completes the first part of the proof.

For the second part, we assume oracles to solve co-CDH(G_1, G_2) and co-CDH(G_2, G_1) which work with probability at least ϵ. By Lemma 2 we can also solve ordinary CDH in $\langle S \rangle$ and $\langle T \rangle$ with probability at least ϵ^2. We will show how to solve VDP with probability at least ϵ^9.

Let (P_1, P_2, Q) be the input instance of the VDP. Then

$$Q = aP_1 + bP_2$$

for unknown integers (a, b). Our goal is to compute aP_1.

There exist (unknown) integers $u_{i,j}$ for $1 \leq i, j \leq 2$ such that

$$P_i = u_{1,i} S + u_{2,i} T \tag{2}$$

and integers (v_1, v_2) such that $Q = v_1 S + v_2 T$. By Proposition 1, we can compute $u_{1,i}S, u_{2,i}T, v_1 S$ and $v_2 T$.

Write

$$U = \begin{pmatrix} u_{1,1} & u_{1,2} \\ u_{2,1} & u_{2,2} \end{pmatrix}.$$

Since $\{S, T\}$ and $\{P_1, P_2\}$ both generate G, it follows that U is invertible. Clearly,

$$v_1 S + v_2 T = Q = aP_1 + bP_2 = (au_{1,1} + bu_{1,2})S + (au_{2,1} + bu_{2,2})T \tag{3}$$

and so

$$U \begin{pmatrix} a \\ b \end{pmatrix} = \begin{pmatrix} v_1 \\ v_2 \end{pmatrix}.$$

Hence,

$$\begin{pmatrix} a \\ b \end{pmatrix} = (u_{1,1}u_{2,2} - u_{1,2}u_{2,1})^{-1} \begin{pmatrix} u_{2,2} & -u_{1,2} \\ -u_{2,1} & u_{1,1} \end{pmatrix} \begin{pmatrix} v_1 \\ v_2 \end{pmatrix}$$

and so

$$aP_1 = (u_{1,1}u_{2,2} - u_{1,2}u_{2,1})^{-1}(u_{2,2}v_1 - u_{1,2}v_2)(u_{1,1}S + u_{2,1}T).$$

Compute $u_{2,2}v_1T, u_{1,1}u_{2,2}S$ and $u_{1,2}u_{2,1}S$ using 3 calls to co-CDH oracles and $u_{1,2}v_2T$ using one call to a CDH oracle for $\langle T \rangle$ (which is achieved using 2 calls to co-CDH oracles). Then solve co-DCDH$(S, (u_{1,1}u_{2,2}-u_{1,2}u_{2,1})S, (u_{2,2}v_1 - u_{1,2}v_2)T)$ using Lemma 3 to get aT.

Given $S, u_{1,1}S, aT$ and $u_{2,1}T$ one can compute aP_1 with one call to a CDH oracle for $\langle T \rangle$ and one call to a co-CDH oracle. It follows that we require 5 co-CDH queries and 2 CDH queries, which means that the algorithm succeeds with probability at least ϵ^9.   □

Corollary 1. *Let G be as above and suppose G has an eigenvector base (S,T). Let $G_1 = \langle S \rangle$. Then CDH(G_1) $\leq$ VDP.*

More precisely, if one has an oracle to solve VDP with probability at least ϵ then one can solve CDH(G_1) with probability at least ϵ^2.

Proof. This is immediate from Theorem 1 and Lemma 2.   □

Corollary 2. *Suppose G has an eigenvector base. Then the VDP has random self-reducibility.*

Proof. The second part of the proof of Theorem 1 shows how to convert a VDP instance into a number of co-CDH instances. The first part of the proof of Theorem 1 shows how to convert a co-CDH instance into a uniformly random instance of the VDP in G. Hence, a specific VDP instance in G is reduced to a number of uniformly random VDP instances in G.   □

2.2   Distortion Eigenvector Bases and Equivalence of VDP and CDH

Definition 6. *An eigenvector base (S,T) is said to be a **distortion eigenvector base** if there are group homomorphisms $\phi_1 : \langle S \rangle \to \langle T \rangle$ and $\phi_2 : \langle T \rangle \to \langle S \rangle$ computable in polynomial time and if an integer $d \not\equiv 0 \pmod{r}$ is given such that $\phi_2(\phi_1(S)) = dS$.*

In Section 3 we will show that the commonly used pairing-friendly supersingular elliptic curves all have a distortion eigenvector base.

Lemma 4. *Let G be as above and suppose G has a distortion eigenvector base (S,T). Let $G_1 = \langle S \rangle$ and $G_2 = \langle T \rangle$. Then CDH(G_1) is equivalent to co-CDH(G_1, G_2) and co-CDH(G_2, G_1). Moreover, the reductions in both directions are tight.*

Proof. Suppose we have an oracle to solve CDH with probability at least ϵ. Given a co-CDH instance (S, aS, T) we want to compute aT. Note that $\phi_2(T) = cS$ for some (not necessarily explicitly known) integer c and that $\phi_1(cS) = dT$ for known d. Since $CDH(S, aS, cS) = acS$ it follows that the solution to the co-CDH problem is given by

$$(d^{-1} \pmod r)\phi_1(CDH(S, aS, \phi_2(T))).$$

Hence, we can solve co-CDH with probability at least ϵ (note that CDH and co-CDH are clearly random self-reducible).

For the converse, suppose S, aS, bS is an instance of $CDH(G_1)$. Then one obtains the co-CDH instance $(S, aS, \phi_1(bS))$ and the solution to the CDH is $(d^{-1} \pmod r)\phi_2(\text{co-}CDH(S, aS, \phi_1(bS)))$. □

This allows a refinement of Corollary 1.

Corollary 3. *Suppose G has a distortion eigenvector base (S, T) and let $G_1 = \langle S \rangle$. Suppose one has an oracle to solve VDP with probability at least ϵ. Then one can solve $CDH(G_1)$ with probability at least ϵ.*

We then obtain one of the main results in the paper, that VDP is equivalent to CDH in many cases. This is a significant sharpening of Yoshida's result, and gives a complete understanding of VDP for supersingular curves.

Corollary 4. *Let (S, T) be a distortion eigenvector base for G. Then VDP is equivalent to $CDH(\langle S \rangle)$.*

Proof. Let $G_1 = \langle S \rangle$ and $G_2 = \langle T \rangle$. Theorem 1 showed VDP equivalent to co-CDH(G_1, G_2) and co-CDH(G_2, G_1) and so the result follows by Lemma 4. □

Note that when given a CDH oracle then the probability of success in Theorem 1 is ϵ^7 instead of ϵ^9.

2.3   An Application of Trapdoor VDP

Proposition 1 shows that VDP is easy for certain bases while Theorem 1 indicates that VDP is hard in general. Hence it is natural to ask if there is a way to set up a trapdoor VDP system. We now explain how to do this.

Proposition 2. *Let (S, T) be a distortion eigenvector base for G normalised such that $T = \phi_1(S)$. Let $u_{1,1}, u_{1,2}, u_{2,1}, u_{2,2} \in \mathbb{Z}/r\mathbb{Z}$ be such that $u_{1,1}u_{2,2} - u_{1,2}u_{2,1} \not\equiv 0 \pmod r$. Let $P_1 = u_{1,1}S + u_{2,1}T$ and $P_2 = u_{1,2}S + u_{2,2}T$. Given any $Q \in G$, if one knows the $u_{i,j}$ then one can solve the VDP of Q to the base (P_1, P_2).*

Proof. We have $T = \phi_1(S)$ and replacing ϕ_2 by $(d^{-1} \pmod r)\phi_2$ we have $\phi_2(T) = S$.

Write $Q = aP_1 + bP_2$. We are required to compute aP_1. Since (S, T) is an eigenvector base we can compute $v_1 S$ and $v_2 T$ such that $Q = v_1 S + v_2 T$. Using ϕ_1

and ϕ_2 we can compute v_1T and v_2S. By the same arguments as in Theorem 1, writing $w = (u_{1,1}u_{2,2} - u_{1,2}u_{2,1})^{-1} \pmod{r}$, it follows that

$$aP_1 = w(u_{2,2}v_1 - u_{1,2}v_2)(u_{1,1}S + u_{2,1}T)$$
$$= w(u_{2,2}u_{1,1}v_1S + u_{2,2}u_{2,1}v_1T - u_{1,1}u_{1,2}v_2S - u_{1,2}u_{2,1}v_2T)$$

which is easily computed. $\square$

Note that we do not have a full trapdoor which allows solving any instance (P_1, P_2, Q) of the VDP. Instead, we construct an easy base (P_1, P_2) for the VDP from an existing easy base (S, T).

This idea has several cryptographic applications. For example, one can obtain a public key encryption scheme (having OW-CPA security depending on VDP) with public key $(S, Q = u_{1,2}S + u_{2,2}T)$ and where the private key consists of the $u_{i,j}$. A message $M \in \langle S \rangle$ is encrypted as $C = M + bQ$ for random $1 \le b < r$.

2.4   The Decision Vector Decomposition Problem

As suggested by an anonymous referee, one can consider a decision variant of the VDP.

Definition 7. *The **decision vector decomposition problem (DVDP)** is: given (P_1, P_2, Q, R) to test whether $R \in \langle P_1 \rangle$ and $(Q - R) \in \langle P_2 \rangle$.*

Hence the DVDP is just testing subgroup membership, which is a computational problem in cyclic groups rather than in G and which may or may not be easy depending on the groups in question. For example, if $G = E[r]$ for an elliptic curve then one can test subgroup membership using the Weil pairing (namely, $R \in \langle P_1 \rangle$ if and only if $e_r(P_1, R) = 1$). Also, if (S, T) is an eigenvector base with respect to F then testing subgroup membership is easy ($P \in \langle S \rangle$ if and only if $F(P) = \lambda_1 P$ where λ_1 is the eigenvalue of F on S).

The decision version of the co-CDH problem is defined as follows [5].

Definition 8. *Let G_1 and G_2 be distinct cyclic groups of order r. The **co-decision Diffie-Hellman problem** co-DDH(G_1, G_2) is: Given $S, aS \in G_1$ and $T, T' \in G_2$ to determine whether or not $T' = aT$.*

Note that co-DDH(G_1, G_2) is trivially equivalent to co-DDH(G_2, G_1).

Lemma 5. *If G_1 and G_2 are distinct cyclic subgroups of G then co-DDH(G_1, G_2) $\le$ DVDP in G.*

Proof. Suppose we have an oracle to solve DVDP and let (S, aS, T, T') be the input co-DDH instance. We assume that $\langle S \rangle \cap \langle T \rangle = \{0\}$ and that $T' \in \langle T \rangle$. Let $b \in (\mathbb{Z}/r\mathbb{Z})$ be such that $T' = bT$.

Choose random $x_{1,1}, x_{1,2}, x_{2,1}, x_{2,2}, z \in (\mathbb{Z}/r\mathbb{Z})^*$ such that $x_{1,1}x_{2,2} - x_{1,1}x_{2,1} \not\equiv 0 \pmod{r}$. Let $P_1 = x_{1,1}S + x_{2,1}T$, $P_2 = x_{1,2}S + x_{2,2}T$, $Q = x_{1,1}aS + x_{2,1}T' + zP_2$ and $R = x_{1,1}aS + x_{2,1}T'$ and call the DVDP oracle on (P_1, P_2, Q, R). If $b \equiv a \pmod{r}$ then $R \in \langle P_1 \rangle$ and the oracle should answer 'true'. If $b \not\equiv a \pmod{r}$ then $R \notin \langle P_1 \rangle$ and the oracle should answer 'false'. $\square$

One can verify that for the case $G = E[r]$, where DVDP is easily solved using the Weil pairing, the proof of Lemma 5 leads to the standard method for solving co-DDH using pairings (note that if G_1 and G_2 are distinct in $E[r]$ then $e_r(S,T) \neq 1$).

Theorem 2. *Let G have an eigenvector base (S,T) and define $G_1 = \langle S \rangle$, $G_2 = \langle T \rangle$. Then DVDP is equivalent to co-DDH(G_1, G_2).*

Proof. Lemma 5 gives co-DDH$(G_1, G_2) \leq$ DVDP. To prove the converse we show how to solve the subgroup membership problem for any subgroup $H = \langle R \rangle \subset G$. If $H = \langle S \rangle$ or $H = \langle T \rangle$ then, as mentioned, we can efficiently solve membership. Hence, we may assume that the projections $\psi_1(R)$ and $\psi_2(R)$ in the proof of Proposition 1 are non-trivial. Let $P \in G$. Then $P \in \langle R \rangle$ if and only if $(\psi_1(R), \psi_1(P), \psi_2(R), \psi_2(P))$ is a valid co-DDH(G_1, G_2) instance. The result follows. □

One might expect a version of the Theorem 2 without the requirement to have an eigenvector base. In fact, the ability to test subgroup membership (and hence solve DVDP) is essentially implicit in the statement of co-DDH: How does one know that $S, aS \in G_1$ and $T, T' \in G_2$? What is the behaviour of a co-DDH oracle if any of these conditions does not hold?

3 Existence of Distortion Eigenvector Bases

We have shown that VDP is equivalent to CDH when G has an distortion eigenvector base. The goal of this section is to show that all the supersingular elliptic curves used in practice have a distortion eigenvector basis. The restriction to "curves used in practice" is because for the case of elliptic curves over $\mathbb{F}_p$ we use an algorithm from [14] whose complexity is exponential in the class number h of the CM field $\mathbb{Q}(\sqrt{t^2 - 4p})$. Although this algorithm has exponential complexity in general, it has polynomial complexity if the class number is bounded by a polynomial in $\log(p)$ (for the purposes of this paper let's insist that $h \leq \log(p)^2$). Hence the algorithm runs in polynomial time for all curves which can be constructed in polynomial time using the CM method (which is all supersingular curves used in practice).[1] See [14] for more discussion of this issue.

We summarise some standard examples of supersingular elliptic curves and distortion maps ϕ in Table 1. The triple $(\alpha_1, \alpha_2, \alpha_3)$ in the table means that for $S \in E(\mathbb{F}_q)$ and π the q-power Frobenius map we have $\pi(S) = \alpha_1 S$ and $\pi(\phi(S)) = \alpha_2 S + \alpha_3 \phi(S)$ (this is the notation of Yoshida [23]). Using Proposition 3 below we can obtain from the table the maps ϕ_1 and ϕ_2 required in Definition 6. Specifically, for the first row of Table 1 one can take (see Theorem 4 for details) $\phi_1 = m + \phi$ and $\phi_2 = m + \phi^2$ where $m \equiv 2^{-1} \pmod{r}$ (giving $d \equiv m^2 - m + 1 \pmod{r}$, where d is such that $\phi_2(\phi_1(S)) = dS$), for the last row take $\phi_1 = \phi$ and

---

[1] One can construct E such that $\text{End}(E)$ is not the maximal order in $\mathbb{Q}(\sqrt{t^2 - 4p})$. However, one can use isogenies to reduce to the case where $\text{End}(E)$ is maximal, so throughout the paper we assume this is the case.

Table 1. Suitable elliptic curves for the Yoshida conditions

E	q	k	$\phi(x,y)$	$(\alpha_1,\alpha_2,\alpha_3)$
$y^2 = x^3 + 1$	p $p \equiv 2 \pmod 3$	2	$(\zeta_3 x, y)$ where $\zeta_3^2 + \zeta_3 + 1 = 0$	$(1,-1,-1)$
$y^2 = x^3 + x$	p $p \equiv 3 \pmod 4$	2	$(-x, iy)$ where $i^2 = -1$	$(1,0,-1)$
$y^2 + y = x^3 + x + b$	2^m $\gcd(m,2) = 1$	4	$(x + \zeta_3^2, y + \zeta_3 x + t)$ $\zeta_3^2 + \zeta_3 + 1 = 0, t^2 + t = \zeta_3$	$(1,0,-1)$
$y^2 = x^3 - x + b$	3^m $\gcd(m,6) = 1$	6	$(\rho - x, iy)$ where $\rho^3 - \rho = b, i^2 = -1$	$(1,0,-1)$
$y^2 = x^3 + A$ where $A \in \mathbb{F}_{p^2}$ is a square but not a cube	p^2 $p \equiv 2 \pmod 3$	3	$(\gamma^2 x^p, uy^p)$ where $u^2 = A/A^q, u \in \mathbb{F}_{p^2}$ $\gamma^3 = u, \gamma \in \mathbb{F}_{p^6}$	$(1,0,\lambda)$ where $\lambda^2 + \lambda + 1 \equiv 0$ $\pmod r$

$\phi_2(x,y) = ((x/\gamma^2)^p, (y/u)^p)$ (so $d = 1$) and for the other three entries one can take $\phi_1 = \phi_2 = \phi$ (so $d = -1$). This shows that all the elliptic curves in Table 1 have a distortion eigenvector base.

A corollary of Theorem 3 below is that for every supersingular elliptic curve used in practice there are (P, ϕ, F) satisfying the Yoshida conditions. Recall that Duursma and Kiyavash showed that if E is an elliptic curve over a finite field with a point P and maps ϕ, F which satisfy the Yoshida conditions (see Section 4 below) then E is supersingular. Hence our corollary gives a complete classification of elliptic curves used in practice satisfying the Yoshida conditions.

The restriction to supersingular curves is not surprising: If E is an elliptic curve with a distortion eigenvector base and if F and the group homomorphisms ϕ_1, ϕ_2 are endomorphisms of the elliptic curve, then E must be supersingular (F and ϕ_1 do not commute, so the endomorphism ring is non-commutative).

The case of embedding degree 1 is more subtle. Frobenius acts as the identity, so for an eigenvector base one must take F to be an endomorphism which is not in $\mathbb{Z}[\pi]$ (where π is the q-power Frobenius) but which has (at least) two eigenspaces. Such endomorphisms may or may not exist (see Charles [7]). Distortion eigenvector bases do not exist when $k = 1$ since a further endomorphism is required which does not commute with F or π, and for elliptic curves there can be no such maps.

We begin with three lemmas to deal with the case of embedding degree 3 (i.e., $r \mid \#E(\mathbb{F}_q)$ has $r \mid (q^3 - 1)$). For background in this section see [4,8,19]

Lemma 6. Let E be an elliptic curve over $\mathbb{F}_{q^2}$ with $\#E(\mathbb{F}_{q^2}) = q^2 \pm q + 1$. Then $j(E) = 0$.

Proof. Let π be the q^2-power Frobenius map, which has degree q^2 and is purely inseparable. Since E is supersingular (q divides the trace of Frobenius) it follows that $[q]$ is also purely inseparable of degree q^2. Therefore (see Silverman [19] Corollary II.2.12), $[q] = \phi\pi$ where $\phi \in \mathrm{End}(E)$. Taking degrees implies that $\deg(\phi) = 1$ and, since π and $[q]$ are defined over $\mathbb{F}_{q^2}$, it follows that ϕ is also defined over $\mathbb{F}_{q^2}$ and so $\pi\phi = \phi\pi$.

Substituting $q = \phi\pi$ into the characteristic polynomial of Frobenius gives

$$0 = \pi^2 \pm q\pi + q^2 = (\phi^2 \pm \phi + 1)\pi^2$$

and hence the automorphism ϕ satisfies $\phi^2 \pm \phi + 1 = 0$. It follows that $\pm\phi \in$ End(E) is an automorphism of order 3. This implies (see [19] Theorem III.10.1) that $j(E) = 0$. $\qquad\square$

Lemma 7. *Let $E_A : y^2 = x^3 + A$ be an elliptic curve over $\mathbb{F}_{q^2}$ with $q = p^m$ such that $p > 3$. Then $\#E_A(\mathbb{F}_{q^2}) = q^2 \pm q + 1$ if and only if $p \equiv 2 \pmod 3$ and A is not a cube.*

Proof. We sketch the proof; see the full version of the paper for all the details.

It is a standard fact [19] that E is supersingular if and only if $p \equiv 2 \pmod 3$. Let g be a primitive element of $\mathbb{F}_{q^2}$. Then E_A is isomorphic over $\mathbb{F}_{p^2}$ to one of the curves $E_{g^i} : y^2 = x^3 + g^i$ for $0 \le i < 6$. We will determine which of these curves has $q^2 \pm q + 1$ points.

It is easy to check that $E_1 : y^2 = x^3 + 1$ over $\mathbb{F}_q$ has $q + 1 = p^m + 1$ points if m is odd, $(p^d + 1)^2$ points if $m = 2d$ where d is odd, and $(p^d - 1)^2$ points if $m = 2d$ where d is even. Hence the characteristic polynomial of Frobenius over $\mathbb{F}_{q^2}$ is $(T \pm q)^2$ and $\#E_1(\mathbb{F}_{q^2}) = (q \pm 1)^2$. The quadratic twist $E_{g^3} : y^2 = x^3 + g^3$ has $(q \mp 1)^2$ points over $\mathbb{F}_{q^2}$.

We consider $E_g : y^2 = x^3 + g$ over $\mathbb{F}_{q^2}$. Let $\phi : E_g \to E_1$ be the isomorphism $\phi(x, y) = (\alpha x, \beta y)$ where $\alpha \in \mathbb{F}_{q^6}$ and $\beta \in \mathbb{F}_{q^4}$ satisfy $\alpha^3 = g$ and $\beta^2 = g$. Let π be the q^2-power Frobenius on E_g and π' be the q^2-power Frobenius on E_1. Then $\pi' = \mp[q]$ and so $\phi^{-1}\pi'\phi = \mp[q]$. One can show that π satisfies $T^2 \pm qT + q^2 = 0$ and so $\#E_g(\mathbb{F}_{q^2}) = q^2 \pm q + 1$. It then follows that E_{g^2}, E_{g^4} and E_{g^5} also have $q^2 \pm q + 1$ points. $\qquad\square$

Lemma 8. *Let E be a supersingular elliptic curve over $\mathbb{F}_q$ (characteristic > 3). Let $r \mid \#E(\mathbb{F}_q)$ with $r > 3$ have security parameter $3/2$ or 3. Then there is a distortion map ϕ on E, with easily computed inverse, such that if $P \in E(\mathbb{F}_q)[r]$ then $\phi(P) \in E(\mathbb{F}_{q^3})[r]$ is a q-power Frobenius eigenvector with eigenvalue q.*

Proof. Let π be the q-power Frobenius. Then security parameter $3/2$ or 3 implies that π satisfies $\pi^2 \pm q\pi + q = 0$. Waterhouse [21] implies $q = p^{2m}$ where $p \equiv 2 \pmod 3$. Hence, by Lemma 6, E is of the form $y^2 = x^3 + A$. Further, by Lemma 7, E is of the form $y^2 = x^3 + A$ where $A \in \mathbb{F}_{q^2}$ is not a cube.

We now define a distortion map on E. Note that A may or may not be a square, but in either case A/A^q is a square. Denote by u a square root of A/A^q, and note that u is not a cube. Let $\gamma \in \mathbb{F}_{q^6}$ satisfy $\gamma^3 = u$ and note that $\gamma^{q^2} = \zeta_3\gamma$ for $\zeta_3 \in \mathbb{F}_{q^2}$ such that $\zeta_3^2 + \zeta_3 + 1 = 0$.

Define

$$\phi(x, y) = (\gamma^2 x^q, uy^q).$$

One can check that if $P \in E(\mathbb{F}_{q^2})$ then $\phi(P) \in E(\mathbb{F}_{q^6})$. Clearly ϕ and ϕ^{-1} are easily computed.

It remains to prove that $\phi(P)$ is a Frobenius eigenvector, which we do in two stages. Let $P \in E(\mathbb{F}_{q^2})[r]$, let $Q \in E(\mathbb{F}_{q^6})[r]$ be a non-trivial point in the q-eigenspace of Frobenius, and let π be the q^2-power Frobenius on E. One can show (see the full version of the paper for details) that

$$\pi\phi(P) = \zeta_3^2\phi(P) \tag{4}$$

where $\zeta_3(x,y) = (\zeta_3 x, y)$ and $\zeta_3^2(x,y) = \zeta_3 \circ \zeta_3(x,y) = (\zeta_3^2 x, y)$. One can then show that

$$(\pi^2 + \pi + 1)(\phi(P)) = (\zeta_3^2 + \zeta_3 + 1)(\phi(P)) = 0$$

and so $\phi(P), \zeta_3\phi(P) \in \langle Q \rangle$ and $\phi(P)$ is a Frobenius eigenvector. □

Theorem 3. *Let E be a supersingular elliptic curve over a finite field $\mathbb{F}_q$ suitable for pairing-based cryptography (i.e., with embedding degree $2 \leq k \leq 6$ and such that the class number of the field $\mathbb{Q}(\sqrt{t^2 - 4q})$ is at most $\log(q)^2$). Let $r > 3$ be prime and coprime to q. Suppose that $r \mid \#E(\mathbb{F}_q)$ and that not all points in $E[r]$ are defined over $\mathbb{F}_q$. Let k be the smallest positive integer such that $r \mid (q^k - 1)$. Let π be the q-power Frobenius map. Then $E[r]$ has a distortion eigenvector basis with respect to $F = \pi$.*

Proof. Let π be the q-power Frobenius. Since $r \mid \#E(\mathbb{F}_q)$ and $E[r] \not\subseteq E(\mathbb{F}_q)$ it follows from Balasubramanian and Koblitz [1] that $k > 1$. Hence $q \not\equiv 1 \pmod{r}$. Furthermore, $E[r]$ has a basis $\{P, Q\}$ such that $\pi(P) = P$ (i.e., $P \in E(\mathbb{F}_q)$) and $\pi(Q) = qQ$. It remains to prove the existence of a homomorphism $\phi : \langle P \rangle \to \langle Q \rangle$ for which ϕ and ϕ^{-1} can be computed in polynomial time.

In characteristic 2, there are only finitely many $\mathbb{F}_q$-isomorphism classes of supersingular elliptic curves and we have $k \leq 4$ (see Menezes [18]). For applications we take $k = 4$, in which case we may assume that E is the elliptic curve

$$E : y^2 + y = x^3 + x + b$$

over $\mathbb{F}_{2^m}$ where $b = 0$ or 1 and m is odd. The field $\mathbb{F}_{2^{4m}}$ has elements s, t such that $s^2 = s + 1$ and $t^2 = t + s$. Following [3] we consider the distortion map $\phi(x,y) = (x + s^2, y + sx + t)$. Note that ϕ and ϕ^{-1} are easily computed. It is immediate that if $P \in E(\mathbb{F}_{2^m})$ then $\pi^2(\phi(P)) = -\phi(P)$. Hence, $(P, \phi(P))$ is a distortion eigenvector base with respect to $F = \pi^2$.

To prove the result for $F = \pi$ suppose $\pi(\phi(P)) = aP + b\phi(P)$ for some $0 \leq a, b < r$. Then $-\phi(P) = \pi(\pi(\phi(P))) = a(b+1)P + b^2\phi(P)$ and so $a(b+1) \equiv 0 \pmod{r}$ and $b^2 \equiv -1 \pmod{r}$. It follows that $a = 0$ and $\phi(P)$ is an eigenvector for Frobenius (with eigenvalue $\pm q \pmod{r}$).

In characteristic 3, there are also only finitely many $\mathbb{F}_q$-isomorphism classes of supersingular elliptic curves and we have $k \leq 6$. For cryptographic applications we take $k = 6$ and so we may assume that

$$E : y^2 = x^3 - x + b$$

over $\mathbb{F}_{3^m}$ where $b = \pm 1$ and $\gcd(m, 6) = 1$. We consider the distortion map $\phi(x,y) = (\rho - x, \sigma y)$ where $\sigma, \rho \in \mathbb{F}_{3^6}$ satisfy $\sigma^2 = -1$ and $\rho^3 = \rho + b$. It is easy to check that if $P \in E(\mathbb{F}_{3^m})$ and if π is the 3^m-power Frobenius then $\pi^3(\phi(P)) = -\phi(P)$ so $(P, \phi(P))$ is a distortion eigenvector base with respect to $F = \pi^3$. The result also follows for $F = \pi$ using the same method as used in the case of characteristic 2: write $\pi(\phi(P)) = aP + b\phi(P)$, then $-\phi(P) = \pi^3(\phi(P)) = a(b^2 + b + 1)P + b^3\phi(P)$ and so $a = 0$ and $b \equiv q \pmod{r}$.

The case $k = 3$ is of interest when $p > 3$ satisfies $p \equiv 2 \pmod{3}$. The result is proved in Lemma 8.

Finally, we consider the case $k = 2$. Galbraith and Rotger [14] have given an algorithm to construct a distortion map ϕ for any supersingular elliptic curve E over $\mathbb{F}_q$ where $q = p^m$ with $k = 2$. The running time of the algorithm is polynomial in the running time of the CM method for constructing such an elliptic curve (and all known constructions of elliptic curves for pairing applications have small class number CM). Proposition 6.1 of [14] constructs the distortion map $\phi = \sqrt{-d}$ in $\text{End}(E)$ where d may be taken to be square-free. Then ϕ is an isogeny of degree d which may be computed using Algorithm 1 of [14]. If E has been constructed in polynomial time then we may assume that d is bounded by a polynomial in $\log(p)$ and so this algorithm is polynomial time and it follows that ϕ may be computed in polynomial time.

Similarly, the dual isogeny $\hat{\phi}$ (see [19]) can be computed in polynomial time using an analogous algorithm. Recall that $\hat{\phi}\phi = [d]$.

Finally, the statement that $\phi(P)$ is a Frobenius eigenvector follows from the proof of Proposition 6.1 of [14]. The q-power Frobenius lifts to the Galois element σ in the proof, and ϕ lifts to an endomorphism Φ satisfying $\Phi^\sigma = -\Phi$. This implies $\pi\phi(P) = -\phi(P) = q\phi(P)$ as required.   □

A significant case not covered by the above theorem is the non-supersingular genus 2 curves proposed by Duursma and Kiyavash [9]. They consider the curves $y^2 = x^6 - ax^3 + 1$ and $y^2 = x^6 - ax^3 - 3$ over $\mathbb{F}_p$ (where $p \equiv 2 \pmod{3}$). Define the isomorphism $\phi(x, y) = (\zeta_3 x, y)$ where $\zeta_3 \in \mathbb{F}_{p^2}$ is a primitive cube root of 1. Note that $\phi^2 + \phi + 1 = 0$ in $\text{End}(\text{Jac}(C))$. Duursma and Kiyavash show that these curves satisfy the Yoshida conditions (see below). In particular, if $S \in \text{Jac}(C)(\mathbb{F}_p)$ is a divisor class of order r and if F is the p-power Frobenius then $F(S) = S$ and $F(\phi(S)) = -S - \phi(S)$.

Theorem 4. *Let C be one of the Duursma-Kiyavash curves and let notation be as above. Let $m = 2^{-1} \pmod{r}$ and define $\phi' = m + \phi$. Then $(S, \phi'(S))$ is a distortion eigenvector base.*

Proof. It is easy to check (see Proposition 3 below) that $F\phi'(S) = -\phi'(S)$. Hence $(S, \phi'(S))$ is an eigenvector base. Note also that ϕ' is an efficiently computable group homomorphism.

To show that $(S, \phi'(S))$ is a distortion eigenvector base it remains to prove that there is an efficiently computable homomorphism ϕ'' such that $\phi''\phi = d$ on $\langle S \rangle$. Consider the dual isogeny

$$\widehat{m + \phi} = m + \hat{\phi}.$$

Since $\widehat{\phi} = \phi^2$ we have

$$(m + \widehat{\phi})(m + \phi) = m^2 + m(\phi + \widehat{\phi}) + \widehat{\phi}\phi = m^2 - m + 1.$$

Hence, define $d = (m^2 - m + 1) \pmod{r}$ and $\phi'' = m + \phi^2$ so that ϕ'' is efficiently computable and $\phi''\phi' = d$ on $\langle S \rangle$. $\qquad\square$

Corollary 4 can therefore be applied to deduce that VDP is equivalent to CDH for the Duursma-Kiyavash curves.

4 Relation with the Yoshida Conditions

Yoshida showed that CDH $\leq$ VDP when certain conditions on G are satisfied. We have shown that CDH $\leq$ VDP when the group G has an eigenvector base. In this section we show that Yoshida's result is a subcase of ours, by showing that if G satisfies the Yoshida conditions then it has an eigenvector base. First we recall the conditions introduced by Yoshida in [23].

Definition 9. *We say that G satisfies the **Yoshida conditions for** $S \in G$ if there exist group isomorphisms $\phi, F : G \to G$ such that:*

1. *ϕ and F can be computed in polynomial time;*
2. *$(S, \phi(S))$ is a base for G*
3. *Constants $\alpha_1, \alpha_2, \alpha_3 \in \mathbb{Z}/r\mathbb{Z}$ are given, such that $\alpha_1\alpha_2\alpha_3 \neq 0$ and*

$$F(S) = \alpha_1 S, \qquad F(\phi(S)) = \alpha_2 S + \alpha_3 \phi(S).$$

We remark that we have been unable to find any groups satisfying the Yoshida conditions with $\alpha_1 = \alpha_3$. Indeed, all known examples of groups satisfying the Yoshida conditions are when G is a subgroup of a divisor class group of a curve over $\mathbb{F}_q$, P is an element of prime order r defined over the ground field $\mathbb{F}_q$, F is a Frobenius map and ϕ is a non-$\mathbb{F}_q$-rational endomorphism of the curve. It follows that $\alpha_1 = 1$.

Proposition 3. *If G satisfies the Yoshida conditions for S then one can calculate $T \in G$ such that (S, T) is an eigenvector base.*

Proof. Suppose S, F, ϕ satisfy the Yoshida conditions.

First suppose that $\alpha_1 \neq \alpha_3$. Let $m = (\alpha_3 - \alpha_1)^{-1}\alpha_2 \pmod{r}$ and let $\phi' = m + \phi$. Then

$$\begin{aligned}
F(\phi'(S)) = F(mS + \phi(S)) &= \alpha_1 mS + \alpha_2 S + \alpha_3 \phi(S) \\
&= (\alpha_1 m + \alpha_2 - \alpha_3 m)S + \alpha_3 \phi'(S) \\
&= \alpha_3 \phi'(S).
\end{aligned}$$

It follows that $(S, \phi'(S))$ is an eigenvector base.

Now we deal with the case $\alpha_1 = \alpha_3$ (which possibly never occurs in practice). Set $\theta = \alpha_2^{-1}$ (mod r), $\gamma = \alpha_2^{-1}\alpha_1$ (mod r) and define

$$\psi(R) = \theta F(R) - \gamma R$$

for $R \in G$. It follows that

$$\psi(S) = (\theta\alpha_1 - \gamma)S = 0$$

and

$$\psi(\phi(S)) = \theta\alpha_2 S + (\theta\alpha_3 - \gamma)\phi(S) = S.$$

Consequently, if we take $\psi' = \phi \circ \psi$ we get that $\psi'(S) = 0$ and $\psi'(\phi(S)) = \phi(S)$. That is, ψ' is the projection on $\langle\phi(S)\rangle$ w.r.t. the base $(S, \phi(S))$. So $R - \psi'(R)$ is the projection of R on $\langle S \rangle$ w.r.t. the base $(S, \phi(S))$. Consequently if we take $F'(R) = \lambda_2\psi'(R) + \lambda_1(R - \psi'(R))$ for any distinct non-zero $\lambda_1, \lambda_2 \in \mathbb{Z}/r\mathbb{Z}$ it easily follows that $(S, \phi(S))$ is an eigenvector base for F' and ϕ. □

Note that in many cases the above proof yields a distortion eigenvector base. However, we cannot prove this in all cases since the Yoshida conditions contain no requirement that the dual isogeny of ϕ be efficiently computable.

For completeness we show how to transfrom a distortion eigenvector base to satisfy the Yoshida conditions.

Lemma 9. *Let G be a group with homomorphisms ϕ, F and an eigenvector base $(S, \phi(S))$. Let $\phi' = 1 + \phi$. Then G together with ϕ', F satisfies the Yoshida conditions.*

Proof. Clearly the first two Yoshida conditions hold. For the third, one checks that

$$F(\phi'(S)) = F(S + \phi(S)) = \lambda_1 S + \lambda_2\phi(S) = (\lambda_1 - \lambda_2)P + \lambda_2\phi'(P)$$

which completes the proof □

Corollary 5. *Let E be any supersingular elliptic curve used in practice as above. Then one can construct a triple (P, F, ϕ) satisfying the Yoshida conditions.*

5   Non-cyclic Groups

The VDP is defined for any group G of exponent r and order r^2. In this section we very briefly recall some non-cyclic groups which might be suitable for cryptography. Recall that the main groups of interest in discrete-logarithm based cryptography are the multiplicative group of a finite field (which is always cyclic) and elliptic curves or divisor class groups of curves (which can be non-cyclic). For background on elliptic curves in cryptography (and pairings) see [4,8].

1. Direct products $G = G_1 \times G_2$ where G_1, G_2 are cyclic subgroups of finite fields, elliptic curves or divisor class groups.

2. Elliptic curves E over $\mathbb{F}_q$ such that the group of points of order r (called the r-torsion subgroup) is defined over a small degree extension $\mathbb{F}_{q^k}$. Such curves are automatically 'pairing-friendly'. There are two cases:
   (a) Supersingular curves.
   (b) Ordinary curves. There are many methods to generate pairing-friendly ordinary curves (see [11] for a survey).
3. Subgroups of exponent r and order r^2 of the divisor class group of a curve of genus $g \geq 2$ over $\mathbb{F}_{q^k}$. In this case, the full r-torsion is not necessarily defined over $\mathbb{F}_{q^k}$ and so the divisor class group is not necessarily pairing-friendly. Again, there are two cases.
   (a) Supersingular. These curves are necessarily pairing-friendly. There are many examples of supersingular hyperelliptic curves given in the literature (see [13]).
   (b) Non-supersingular. For example the curves with complex multiplication presented by Duursma and Kiyavash [9].
4. The subgroup of order r^2 in $(\mathbb{Z}/n\mathbb{Z})^*$ where $n = pq$ is a product of two primes such that $r \mid (p-1)$ and $r \mid (q-1)$. Care must be taken that r is not too large, or else it is easy to factor n (see McKee and Pinch [17]).
   This case has a very different flavour to the other groups described above, and the methods of the paper do not seem to apply in this case.

Note that not all of the above groups will necessarily have an eigenvector base.

6   Generalised Discrete Logarithm Problems

We have proved that VDP is equivalent to CDH in a cyclic group for all examples proposed in the literature. But one might consider VDP in a more general context where distortion maps ϕ are not available. Hence we give some results relating VDP to generalisations of the discrete logarithm problem. As always, G denotes a group of order r^2 and exponent r where r is prime. Due to lack of space, many of the proofs in this section have removed; they can be found in the full version of the paper.

We recall the discrete logarithm problem (DLP_{G_1}) for a cyclic group G_1: Given $P, Q \in G_1$, compute an integer a (if it exists) such that $Q = aP$. The discrete logarithm problem has been generalized by many authors in different ways. For example, if G_1 is a cyclic group of prime order and $P_1, P_2 \in G_1$ then Brands [6] defined the **representation problem**: Given $Q \in G_1$ find (a, b) such that $Q = aP_1 + bP_2$. It is easy to show that the the representation problem in the cyclic group G_1 is equivalent to the DLP in G_1.

For groups G of exponent r and order r^2 we define the following generalisation of the discrete logarithm problem.

Definition 10. *The computational problem* **2-DL** *is: Given* $P_1, P_2, Q \in G$ *such that* $G = \langle P_1, P_2 \rangle$ *compute a pair of integers* (a, b) *such that* $Q = aP_1 + bP_2$.

The following three results are straightforward.

Lemma 10. *The computational problem 2-DL is random self-reducible.*

Lemma 11. *Let G_1 be a cyclic subgroup of G. Then $DLP_{G_1} \leq$ 2-DL.*

Theorem 5. *Let G be as above. Then $VDP \leq$ 2-DL.*

The computational problems VDP and 2-DL are both defined for non-cyclic groups. Computational problems in non-cyclic groups have not been studied as closely as those in cyclic groups. The remainder of this section relates the 2-DL problem in non-cyclic groups to discrete logarithm problems in one or more cyclic groups.

Let G_1, G_2 be cyclic groups of order r. We say that two group homomorphisms $\psi_i : G \to G_i$, for $i = 1, 2$, are **independent** if $\ker \psi_1 \cap \ker \psi_2 = \{0\}$. An example of independent group homomorphisms are the projection maps in the proof of Proposition 1.

Theorem 6. *Let G and G_1 be as above and suppose there are two independent group homomorphisms $\psi_1, \psi_2 : G \to G_1$ which can be computed in polynomial time. Then 2-DL is equivalent to DLP_{G_1}.*

This result is a special case of the following.

Theorem 7. *Let G be as above and let G_1, G_2 be cyclic groups of order r. Suppose there are two independent group homomorphisms $\psi_i : G \to G_i$ for $i = 1, 2$ which can be computed in polynomial time. Then 2-DL is equivalent to $(DLP_{G_1}$ and $DLP_{G_2})$.*

Proof. It is trivial from Lemma 11 that $(DLP_{G_1}$ and $DLP_{G_2}) \leq$ 2-DL. One can prove the opposite using essentially the same ideas as those used in the proof of Theorem 1. ∎

Corollary 6. *If G has an eigenvector base (S, T) then 2-DL is equivalent to $(DLP_{\langle S \rangle}$ and $DLP_{\langle T \rangle})$.*

Corollary 7. *Let G be a group which has a distortion eigenvector base (S, T). Let $G_1 = \langle S \rangle$. Then 2-DL is equivalent to DLP_{G_1}.*

Proof. We let ψ_1 be as in the proof of Proposition 1 and let $\psi_2(Q) = \psi_1(\phi(Q))$. One can check that these are independent homomorphisms to $\langle S \rangle$, and so the result follows from Theorem 6. ∎

Direct products (case 1 of Section 5) are easy to handle.

Corollary 8. *Let G be a direct product of two cyclic groups G_1, G_2 of prime order r. Then 2-DL $\leq (DLP_{G_1}$ and $DLP_{G_2})$.*

On ordinary pairing-friendly elliptic curves (i.e., case 2(b) of Section 5) we do not have distortion maps and so it is not possible to have a distortion eigenvector base. We now state the obvious fact that the 2-DL can be reduced to the DLP in a finite field using pairings.

Theorem 8. *Let G be a subgroup of $E(\mathbb{F}_{q^k})$ of exponent r and order r^2. Then $r \mid (q^k - 1)$. Let G_1 be the subgroup of r-th roots of unity in $\mathbb{F}_{q^k}^*$. Then 2-DL $\leq DLP_{G_1}$.*

In the ordinary genus 2 case (again, case 3(b) of Section 5) there is another way to potentially attack the 2-DL. One natural approach to constructing a curve C over $\mathbb{F}_q$ whose Jacobian has non-cyclic group order is to choose C such that there are rational maps $\psi_i : C \to E_i$ (for $i = 1, 2$) over $\mathbb{F}_q$ where E_i are elliptic curves over $\mathbb{F}_q$. Then the Jacobian of C is isogenous over $\mathbb{F}_q$ to $E_1 \times E_2$ and if $r \mid \#E_i(\mathbb{F}_q)$ for $i = 1, 2$ then r^2 divides the order of $\mathrm{Jac}(C)(\mathbb{F}_q)$. This approach was used by Duursma and Kiyavash [9]. Since the rational maps ψ_i induce explicit isogenies

$$\psi_i : \mathrm{Jac}(C)(\mathbb{F}_q) \to E_i(\mathbb{F}_q)$$

for $i = 1, 2$ one can apply Theorem 7 to reduce the 2-DL to two DLPs in cyclic groups.

7 Conclusion

We present a thorough analysis of the vector decomposition problem (VDP). We have shown that, for all the supersingular elliptic curves which could be used in practice, VDP is equivalent to CDH in a cyclic group. We have also related VDP to various co-CDH problems and a generalised discrete logarithm problem 2-DL which in turn is often related to discrete logarithm problems in cyclic groups.

Acknowledgements

We thank Iwan Duursma, Seung-Kook Park, Maura Paterson and a number of anonymous referees for helpful comments on a much earlier draft of the paper. Takakazu Satoh is thanked for proof reading. Galbraith also thanks the Fields Institute in Toronto for providing a stimulating research environment during some of this research and EPSRC Research Grant EP/D069904/1 for financial support.

References

1. Balasubramanian, R., Koblitz, N.: The improbability that an elliptic curve has subexponential discrete log problem under the Menezes-Okamoto-Vanstone algorithm. J. Cryptology 11(2), 141–145 (1998)
2. Bao, F., Deng, R.H., Zhu, H.: Variations of Diffie-Hellman Problem. In: Qing, S., Gollmann, D., Zhou, J. (eds.) ICICS 2003. LNCS, vol. 2836, pp. 301–312. Springer, Heidelberg (2003)
3. Barreto, P.S.L.M., Kim, H.Y., Lynn, B., Scott, M.: Efficient algorithms for pairing-based cryptosystems. In: Yung, M. (ed.) CRYPTO 2002. LNCS, vol. 2442, pp. 354–368. Springer, Heidelberg (2002)

4. Blake, I., Seroussi, G., Smart, N.P. (eds.): Advances in elliptic curve cryptography. Cambridge University Press, Cambridge (2005)
5. Boneh, D., Lynn, B., Shacham, H.: Short signatures from the Weil pairing. Journal of Cryptology 7, 297–319 (2004)
6. Brands, S.: An efficient off-line electronic cash system based on the representation problem, CWI Technical Report CS-R9323 (1993)
7. Charles, D.: On the existence of distortion maps on ordinary elliptic curves, arXiv:math/0603724 (2006)
8. Cohen, H., Frey, G. (eds.): Handbook of elliptic and hyperelliptic curve cryptography. CRC Press, Boca Raton (2006)
9. Duursma, I., Kiyavash, N.: The vector decomposition problem for elliptic and hyperelliptic curves. J. Ramanujan Math. Soc. 20(1), 59–76 (2005)
10. Duursma, I.M., Park, S.K.: ElGamal type signature schemes for n-dimensional vector spaces, eprint 2006/311
11. Freeman, D., Scott, M., Teske, E.: A taxonomy of pairing-friendly elliptic curves (2006)
12. Frey, G., Rück, H.-G.: A remark concerning m-divisibility and the discrete logarithm in the divisor class group of curves. Math. Comp. 62, 865–874 (1994)
13. Galbraith, S.D.: Supersingular curves in cryptography. In: Boyd, C. (ed.) ASIACRYPT 2001. LNCS, vol. 2248, pp. 495–513. Springer, Heidelberg (2001)
14. Galbraith, S.D., Rotger, V.: Easy decision Diffie-Hellman groups. LMS J. Comput. Math. 7, 201–218 (2004)
15. Maurer, U.: Towards the equivalence of breaking the Diffie-Hellman protocol and computing discrete logarithms. In: Desmedt, Y.G. (ed.) CRYPTO 1994. LNCS, vol. 839, pp. 271–281. Springer, Heidelberg (1994)
16. Maurer, U., Wolf, S.: The relationship between breaking the Diffie-Hellman protocol and computing discrete logarithms. SIAM Journal on Computing 28(5), 1689–1721 (1999)
17. McKee, J.F., Pinch, R.G.E.: Further attacks on server-aided RSA cryptosystems, unpublished manuscript (1998)
18. Menezes, A.J.: Elliptic curve public key cryptosystems. Springer, Heidelberg (1993)
19. Silverman, J.H.: The arithmetic of elliptic curves. Springer, Heidelberg (1986)
20. Verheul, E.R.: Evidence that XTR Is More Secure than Supersingular Elliptic Curve Cryptosystems. J. Cryptology 17(4), 277–296 (2004)
21. Waterhouse, W.C.: Abelian varieties over finite fields. Annales Scientifiques de l'École Normale Supérieure 4 (1969)
22. Yoshida, M., Mitsunari, S., Fujiwara, T.: Vector decomposition problem and the trapdoor inseparable multiplex transmission scheme based the problem. In: Proceedings of the 2003 Symposium on Cryptography and Information Security (SCIS), pp. 491–496 (2003)
23. Yoshida, M.: Inseparable multiplex transmission using the pairing on elliptic curves and its application to watermarking. In: Proc. Fifth Conference on Algebraic Geometry, Number Theory, Coding Theory and Cryptography, University of Tokyo (2003), http://www.math.uiuc.edu/~duursma/pub/yoshida_paper.pdf

A Parameterized Splitting System and Its Application to the Discrete Logarithm Problem with Low Hamming Weight Product Exponents

Sungwook Kim and Jung Hee Cheon

Department of Mathematical Sciences and ISaC-RIM,
Seoul National University, Seoul, 151-747, Korea
{avel17,jhcheon}@snu.ac.kr

Abstract. A low Hamming weight product (LHWP) exponent is used to increase the efficiency of cryptosystems based on the discrete logarithm problem (DLP). In this paper, we introduce a new tool, called a *Parameterized Splitting System*, to analyze the security of the DLP with LHWP exponents.

We apply a parameterized splitting system to attack the GPS identification scheme modified by Coron, Lefranc and Poupard in CHES'05 and obtain an algorithm of $2^{61.6}$ time complexity which was expected to be 2^{78}. Also a parameterized splitting system can be used to solve the DLP with a LHWP exponent proposed by Hoffstein and Silverman in $2^{54.51}$ time complexity, that is smaller than 2^{59} in the recent Cheon-Kim attack.

Keywords: Discrete Logarithm Problem with Low Hamming Weight Product (LHWP) Exponents, Parameterized Splitting Systems.

1 Introduction

It is important to compute exponentiations efficiently in cryptosystems based on the DLP. One approach to achieve this is to choose an exponent of low Hamming weight. For example, the GPS identification scheme proposed by Girault [4,5,7] uses as a secret key a product of two integers having low Hamming weight [4,5,7]. Hoffstein and Silverman suggested a use of exponent $x = x_1x_2x_3$, where each integer x_i has very low Hamming weight [9]. But a use of low Hamming weight exponents may weaken the security.

The Heiman-Odlyzko algorithm [8] and the Coppersmith's splitting system [3,10,16] have been used to analyze the DLP with low Hamming weight exponents. The complexity of solving the DLP with the Coppersmith's splitting system is about the square root of the size of the key space when the exponent is a single integer. It can be regarded to be almost optimal since the DLP has the square root complexity in the generic model [14].

In [9], Hoffstein and Silverman proposed an attack against low Hamming weight product (LHWP) exponents. In [4], Coron, Lefranc and Poupard combined the above attack with the Coppersmith's splitting system and described an algorithm that can be applied when the order of a group is unknown. But the complexity of the attack is far from the square root of the size of the key space.

R. Cramer (Ed.): PKC 2008, LNCS 4939, pp. 328–343, 2008.

Our Results: In this paper, we generalize the Coppersmith's splitting system into a parameterized splitting system and propose its construction. It can be used to show that given a bit string of length n, weight t and a positive integer $t_1 < t$, there exists a part of the string of length n_1 and weight t_1 where $\frac{n_1}{t_1} \approx \frac{n}{t}$.

We apply a parameterized splitting system to the private key of the GPS identification scheme [4,7] and the Hoffstein and Silverman's exponent [9] (originally designated for 2^{80} bit security). In [4], Coron, Lefranc and Poupard proposed an attack with 2^{52} complexity to recover the private key of the GPS identification scheme from CHES'04 and suggested a new private key which is claimed to have the security level of 2^{78}. But our parameterized splitting system reduces them to $2^{47.7}$ and $2^{65.5}$, respectively, and its randomized version reduces them to $2^{43.5}$ and $2^{61.6}$, respectively. In [1], Cheon and Kim introduced the notion of rotation-free elements and proposed an attack of $2^{55.9}$ complexity to the Hoffstein and Silverman's exponent. By combining the parameterized splitting system and the concept of rotation-freeness, we reduce it further to $2^{54.51}$.

Organization of the Paper: In Section 2, we briefly introduce the Heiman-Odlyzko algorithm, the Coppersmith's splitting system and the rotation-free elements. In Section 3, we propose a parameterized splitting system and its application to the DLP of LHWP exponents. In Section 4, we analyze the complexity of the GPS identification scheme and the DLP with the Hoffstein and Silverman's exponent. Finally, we conclude in Section 5.

2 Preliminaries

Let g be a generator of a group G and x is an integer. From now on, *ord* g and $wt(x)$ denote the order of g and the Hamming weight of x, respectively.

Shanks' Baby-Step Giant-Step [13] and Pollard's Rho algorithm [11] are representative algorithms for the DLP. Algorithms for the DLP with low Hamming weight exponents are variants of Shanks' Baby-Step Giant-Step. In this section, we introduce the Heiman-Odlyzko algorithm, the Coppersmith's splitting system and the rotation-free elements. In this section, we assume *ord* g is known.

2.1 The Heiman-Odlyzko Algorithm

The Heiman-Odlyzko algorithm [8] was introduced by Heiman and Odlyzko independently. (In [8], Heiman remarked this algorithm was independently noticed by Odlyzko.) In this section, we sketch the Heiman-Odlyzko algorithm.

We use the notations from [16]. We regard the binary representation of

$$x = \sum_{i=0}^{n-1} x_i 2^i$$

as the vector

$$x = (x_0, \ldots, x_{n-1}).$$

Then this set of vectors corresponds to

$$\{i : x_i = 1\} \subset \mathbb{Z}_n.$$

The following two mappings, which are inverse to each other, express the above correspondence.

$$set : \{0, 1, \ldots, 2^n - 1\} \rightarrow 2^{\mathbb{Z}_n}, \ set(x = (x_0, \ldots, x_{n-1})) = \{i : x_i = 1\}$$
$$val : 2^{\mathbb{Z}_n} \rightarrow \{0, 1, \ldots, 2^n - 1\}, \ val(Y) = \sum_{i \in Y} 2^i$$

Consider the following equation

$$y = g^x = g^{x_1 + x_2},$$

where $t = wt(x) = wt(x_1) + wt(x_2)$, $wt(x_1) = t_s$ and $set(x_1) \cap set(x_2) = \emptyset$.

From the above equation, we get

$$yg^{-x_1} = g^{x_2}. \tag{1}$$

Now we compute yg^{-x_1} for all $x_1 \in \mathbb{Z}_n$ such that $wt(x_1) = t_s$ and build a lookup table that contains all the pairs (yg^{-x_1}, x_1) and support an efficient search on the first component. Then we compute g^{x_2} for each x_2 such that $wt(x_2) = t - t_s$ and look up the table until a collision is found.

Neglecting logarithmic factors, the time complexity of the Heiman-Odlyzko Algorithm is $O\left(\binom{n}{t_s} + \binom{n}{t-t_s}\right)$. Since we need store only either the left or the right hand side, the space complexity of the Heiman-Odlyzko Algorithm is $O\left(\min\{\binom{n}{t_s}, \binom{n}{t-t_s}\}\right)$.

2.2   The Coppersmith's Splitting System

The Coppersmith's splitting system was introduced in [10], based on the idea from [2]. Later, Stinson gave a good description of it in [16]. We follow this description.

Definition 1. *(The Splitting System)*
Suppose n and t are even integers, $0 < t < n$.[1] A (n, t)-splitting system is a pair $(X, \mathcal{B})$ that satisfies the following properties.
1. $|X| = n$ and $\mathcal{B}$ is a set of $\frac{n}{2}$-subsets of X called blocks.
2. For every $Y \subseteq X$ such that $|Y| = t$, there exists a block $B \in \mathcal{B}$ such that $|Y \cap B| = \frac{t}{2}$.

Remark. An (n, t)-splitting system is denoted by an $(N; n, t)$-splitting system if it has N blocks.

The existence of a splitting system follows from this construction: Suppose $X = \mathbb{Z}_n = \{0, 1, \ldots, n-1\}$, $B_i = \{i + j \bmod n : 0 \leq j \leq \frac{n}{2} - 1\}$, $\mathcal{B} = \{B_i : 0 \leq i \leq \frac{n}{2} - 1\}$. Then, $(X, \mathcal{B})$ is an $(\frac{n}{2}; n, t)$-splitting system.

The Coppersmith's splitting system enables us to restrict to $\mathcal{B}$ the search space of x_1 and x_2 in Equation (1). Hence This algorithm requires $N\binom{n/2}{t/2}$ time complexity and $\binom{n/2}{t/2}$ space complexity.

---

[1] Stinson constructed the splitting system even for odd n and t in [16].

A Randomized Algorithm. The randomized version of the above algorithm is summarized in [16], which is also due to [3]. The time complexity of the randomized version is $O\left(\sqrt{t}\binom{\frac{n}{2}}{\frac{t}{2}}\right)$ and the space complexity of the randomized version is $O\left(\binom{\frac{n}{2}}{\frac{t}{2}}\right)$.

2.3   Rotation-Free Elements

In [1], Cheon and Kim defined an equivalent relation $\sim$ on $\mathbb{Z}_{2^n-1}$ as follows:

$a \sim b$ if and only if there exists a non-negative integer i such that $a = 2^i b$.

The idea of Cheon and Kim's attack on LHWPs is to reduce the key search space by considering only one element from each equivalent class.

Since there is no known algorithm to generate such representatives efficiently, they suggested a use of the set of *rotation-free elements* which contains at least one representative for each equivalent class. The set is only little bit larger than the number of equivalent classes and easily generated.

The definition of rotation-free elements is as follows:

Definition 2. *(Rotation-Free Elements [1])*
An element $z \in \mathbb{Z}_{2^n-1}$ is called a rotation-free element if there is a k-tuple $(a_1, a_2, \ldots, a_k)$ for a positive integer k satisfying

1. $a_i \geq a_1$ for $1 \leq i \leq k$.
2. $\displaystyle\sum_{i=1}^{k} a_i = n$.
3. $z = 2^{n-1} + 2^{n-1-a_1} + \cdots + 2^{n-1-(a_1+a_2+\cdots+a_{k-1})}$.

Let n, k be positive integers with $k < n$ and $RF(n, k)$ be the number of rotation-free elements of weight k in $\mathbb{Z}_{2^n-1}$. Then $RF(n, k)$ is given in [1] by

$$RF(n,k) = \sum_{i=0}^{\lfloor \frac{n}{k} \rfloor - 1} \binom{n-2-ki}{k-2}.$$

3   Parameterized Splitting Systems

In this section, we construct a *Parameterized Splitting System*, that is a generalization of the Coppersmith's splitting system. In the Coppersmith's splitting system, given $Y \subset \mathbb{Z}_n$, the size of a block B such that $|Y \cap B| = \frac{t}{2}$ is fixed to $\frac{n}{2}$. We show that the size of a block B can be flexible so that $|Y \cap B| = t_s$ and $|B| = \lfloor \frac{t_s n}{t} \rfloor$ for any $0 \leq t_s \leq t$. This flexibility yields an efficient algorithm for the DLP with LHWP exponents.

3.1   Parameterized Splitting Systems

We start with the definition of parameterized splitting systems.

Definition 3. *(Parameterized Splitting Systems)*
Suppose n and t are integers such that $0 < t < n$. For any t_s such that $0 \le t_s \le t$, a $(N; n, t, t_s)$-parameterized splitting system is a pair $(X, \mathcal{B})$ that satisfies the following properties.
1. *$|X| = n$ and $\mathcal{B} = \{B \subset X : |B| = \lfloor \frac{t_s n}{t} \rfloor\}$.*
2. *$|\mathcal{B}| = N$.*
3. *For every $Y \subseteq X$ such that $|Y| = t$, there exists a block $B \in \mathcal{B}$ such that $|Y \cap B| = t_s$.*

Remark. We may assume $0 < t < \frac{n}{2}, 1 \le t_s \le \frac{t}{2}$.

The following Lemma 1 constructs an efficient parameterized splitting system.

Lemma 1. $X = \{0, 1, \ldots, n-1\}$, $Y = \{y_1, y_2, \ldots, y_t\} \subset X$ *such that* $|Y| = t$. *Suppose t_s is an integer such that $0 \le t_s \le t$. Let $B_i = \{i \bmod n, i + 1 \bmod n, \ldots, i + \lfloor \frac{t_s n}{t} \rfloor - 1 \bmod n\}$, $i = 0, 1, \ldots, n-1$. Then, there exists i such that $|Y \cap B_i| = t_s$.*

Proof. For each $y \in Y$, let $\nu(y) = \{i : y \in B_i, \ i = 0, 1, \ldots, n-1\}$. Then, $|\nu(y)| = \lfloor \frac{t_s n}{t} \rfloor$.

Let M be $\frac{1}{n} \sum_{i=0}^{n-1} |Y \cap B_i|$. Since $Y \cap B_i = \bigcup_{y \in Y}(\{y\} \cap B_i)$ and if $y_i \ne y_j$, then $(y_i \cap B_i) \cap (y_j \cap B_i) = \emptyset$,

$$M = \frac{1}{n} \sum_{I=0}^{n-1} |Y \cap B_i| = \frac{1}{n} \sum_{i=0}^{n-1} |\bigcup_{y \in Y}(\{y\} \cap B_i)| = \frac{1}{n} \sum_{i=0}^{n-1} \sum_{y \in Y} |\{y\} \cap B_i|$$

$$= \frac{1}{n} \sum_{y \in Y} \sum_{i=0}^{n-1} |\{y\} \cap B_i| = \frac{1}{n} \sum_{y \in Y} |\nu(y)| = \frac{t}{n} \left\lfloor \frac{t_s n}{t} \right\rfloor.$$

From $\frac{t_s n}{t} - 1 < \lfloor \frac{t_s n}{t} \rfloor \le \frac{t_s n}{t}$,

$$t_s - 1 < t_s - \frac{t}{n} = \frac{t}{n} \cdot \left(\frac{t_s n}{t} - 1\right) < \frac{t}{n} \left\lfloor \frac{t_s n}{t} \right\rfloor = M \le \frac{t}{n} \cdot \frac{t_s n}{t} = t_s. \qquad (2)$$

Suppose there doesn't exist B_i such that $|Y \cap B_i| = t_s$. If $|Y \cap B_i| < t_s$ for all i, then $M \le t_s - 1$, which contradicts with Equation (2). If $|Y \cap B_i| > t_s$ for all i, then $t_s + 1 \le M$, which contradicts with Equation (2).

By the above discussions, there exists B_i and B_j such that $|Y \cap B_i| \le t_s$ and $|Y \cap B_j| \ge t_s$. However, from the fact $|Y \cap B_i| - |Y \cap B_{i+1}| \in \{-1, 0, 1\}$, $|Y \cap B_k|$ should be t_s for some $k \in \{i \bmod n, i+1 \bmod n, \ldots, j-1 \bmod n, j \bmod n\}$, which contradicts with the assumption.

Therefore, there exists B_i such that $|Y \cap B_i| = t_s$. $\qquad \square$

Theorem 1. *Let $X = \{0, 1, \ldots, n-1\}$, $B_i = \{i \bmod n, i+1 \bmod n, \ldots, i + \lfloor \frac{t_s n}{t} \rfloor - 1 \bmod n\}$, $\mathcal{B} = \{B_i : 0 \le i \le n-1\}$. Then, $(X, \mathcal{B})$ is a $(n; n, t, t_s)$-parameterized splitting system.*

A Randomized Version. For given Y and t_s, Theorem 1 implies that if we try at most n blocks, we can find some block B such that $|Y \cap B| = t_s$. In a randomized version, we randomly choose $B \subset \mathbb{Z}_n$ such that $|B| = \lfloor \frac{t_s n}{t} \rfloor$ and check whether $|Y \cap B| = t_s$. Then the probability of success is

$$p = \frac{\binom{t}{t_s}\binom{n-t}{\lfloor \frac{t_s n}{t} \rfloor - t_s}}{\binom{n}{\lfloor \frac{t_s n}{t} \rfloor}}.$$

Lemma 3 shows that the expected number of trials to find a good block B such that $|Y \cap B| = t_s$ is $O(\sqrt{t})$. We require Lemma 2 from [16] to get Lemma 3.

Lemma 2. *Suppose that n and λn are positive integers, where $0 < \lambda < 1$. Define*

$$H(\lambda) = \lambda \log_2 \lambda - (1 - \lambda) \log_2(1 - \lambda).$$

Then

$$\frac{2^{nH(\lambda)}}{\sqrt{8n\lambda(1 - \lambda)}} \leq \binom{n}{\lambda n} \leq \frac{2^{nH(\lambda)}}{\sqrt{2\pi n\lambda(1 - \lambda)}}.$$

Lemma 3. $p > \sqrt{\frac{\pi}{2}} \cdot \sqrt{\left(\frac{t_s}{t} - \frac{1}{n}\right)\left(1 - \frac{t_s}{t}\right)} \cdot t^{-1/2} \geq \frac{\sqrt{\pi}}{4} t^{-1/2}$.

Proof.

$$p = \binom{t}{t_s} \frac{\binom{n-t}{\lfloor \frac{t_s n}{t} \rfloor - t_s}}{\binom{n}{\lfloor \frac{t_s n}{t} \rfloor}} = \binom{t}{\lambda_1 t} \frac{\binom{n-t}{\lambda_2(n-t)}}{\binom{n}{\lambda n}},$$

where $\lambda_1 = \frac{t_s}{t}$, $\lambda_2 = \frac{\lfloor \frac{t_s n}{t} \rfloor - t_s}{n - t}$ and $\lambda = \frac{\lfloor \frac{t_s n}{t} \rfloor}{n}$.

From Lemma 2,

$$p \geq \frac{2^{tH(\lambda_1)}}{\sqrt{8t\lambda_1(1 - \lambda_1)}} \cdot \frac{2^{(n-t)H(\lambda_2)}}{\sqrt{8(n-t)\lambda_2(1 - \lambda_2)}} \cdot \frac{\sqrt{2\pi n\lambda(1 - \lambda)}}{2^{nH(\lambda)}}$$

$$= \frac{2^{tH(\lambda_1)+(n-t)H(\lambda_2)}}{2^{nH(\lambda)}} \cdot \frac{\sqrt{2\pi n\lambda(1 - \lambda)}}{8\sqrt{t(n-t)\lambda_1(1 - \lambda_1)\lambda_2(1 - \lambda_2)}}.$$

Since $H(\lambda)$ is convex,

$$tH(\lambda_1) + (n - t)H(\lambda_2) \geq nH(\lambda),$$

hence,

$$p \geq \frac{\sqrt{2\pi n\lambda(1 - \lambda)}}{8\sqrt{t(n-t)\lambda_1(1 - \lambda_1)\lambda_2(1 - \lambda_2)}}.$$

Since $0 < \lambda_i < 1$,

$$\frac{1}{\sqrt{\lambda_i(1 - \lambda_i)}} \geq 2$$

for $i = 1, 2$, hence,

$$p \geq \sqrt{\frac{\pi}{2}} \cdot \sqrt{\lambda(1 - \lambda)} \cdot t^{-1/2}.$$

We may assume $1 \leq t_s \leq \frac{t}{2}$ and $2 \leq t \leq \frac{n}{2}$. From $\lambda = \lfloor \frac{t_s n}{t} \rfloor / n$, we have

$$\lambda(1 - \lambda) > (\frac{t_s}{t} - \frac{1}{n})(1 - \frac{t_s}{t}) \geq \frac{1}{8}.$$ □

3.2   The DLP with LHWP Exponents When the Order of g Is Known

Before detailing how parameterized splitting systems can be used, we review some known methods.

For an integer x, we denote by $|x|$ the bit-length of x. Let $X_1 = \{x_1 : |x_1| = n_1,\ wt(x_1) = t_1\}$ and $X_2 = \{x_2 : |x_2| = n_2,\ wt(x_2) = t_2\}$. Consider $x = x_1 x_2$, where $x_1 \in X_1$ and $x_2 \in X_2$.

As in [4,9], from the following equation

$$y = (g^{x_1})^{x_2} = h^{x_2},$$

x can be computed by repeating an algorithm for the DLP by $|X_1|$. So, the time complexity and the space complexity of the Heiman-Odlyzko algorithm are

$$O\left(|X_1|\left(\binom{n_2}{t_s} + \binom{n_2}{t - t_s}\right)\right) \text{ and } O\left(\min\left\{\binom{n_2}{t_s}, \binom{n_2}{t - t_s}\right\}\right),$$

respectively. To minimize the time complexity, t_s should be $\lceil \frac{t}{2} \rceil$ or $\lfloor \frac{t}{2} \rfloor$. The time complexity and the space complexity of the parameterized splitting system are

$$O\left(|X_1| \cdot n_2 \binom{\frac{n_2}{2}}{\frac{t_2}{2}}\right) \text{ and } O\left(\binom{\frac{n_2}{2}}{\frac{t_2}{2}}\right),$$

respectively.

Another attack, which is also followed from [4,9], takes the trade-off between time and space. $y = g^{x_1 x_2}$ can be converted into

$$y^{x_1^{-1}} g^{-x_3} = g^{x_4},$$

where $x_2 = x_3 + x_4$ and $set(x_3) \cap set(x_4) = \emptyset$. Note that x_1^{-1} denotes the multiplicative inverse of x_1 modulo the order of g.

Put $wt(x_3) = t_s$. From the above equation, we find x_1 and x_2 by computing both sides and comparing them.

Therefore the time complexity and the space complexity of the Heiman-Odlyzko algorithm are

$$O\left(|X_1|\binom{n_2}{t_s} + \binom{n_2}{t - t_s}\right) \text{ and } O\left(\min\left\{|X_1|\binom{n_2}{t_s}, \binom{n_2}{t - t_s}\right\}\right),$$

respectively. t_s is an integer such that $0 \leq t_s \leq \lceil \frac{t_2}{2} \rceil$. Comparing to the first application, the time complexity is lower.

The time complexity and the space complexity of the splitting system are

$$
O\left(|X_1| \cdot \frac{n_2}{2}\binom{\frac{n_2}{2}}{\frac{t_2}{2}} + \frac{n_2}{2}\binom{\frac{n_2}{2}}{\frac{t_2}{2}}\right) = O\left(|X_1| \cdot \frac{n_2}{2}\binom{\frac{n_2}{2}}{\frac{t_2}{2}}\right) \text{ and } O\left(\frac{n_2}{2}\binom{\frac{n_2}{2}}{\frac{t_2}{2}}\right),
$$

respectively. Comparing to the first application, the efficiency of the time complexity is hardly improved.

In the case of the DLP with a single integer exponent of low Hamming weight, the splitting system appears to be more efficient than the Heiman-Odlyzko algorithm since one of the factors of the time complexity, n_2, is reduced to $\frac{n_2}{2}$ in the splitting system. But the splitting system fixes $t_s = \frac{t_2}{2}$ while the Heiman-Odlyzko algorithm is able to choose t_s arbitrary. This difference yields the Heiman-Odlyzko algorithm carries out trade-off efficiently while the splitting system does not.

Now we propose a new algorithm using parameterized splitting systems, which takes the advantages from both of previous algorithms. From Section 3.1, for $t_s \in [0, \lceil\frac{t_2}{2}\rceil]$, there exists a $(n_2; n_2, t_2, t_s)$-parameterized splitting system $(\mathbb{Z}_{n_2}, \mathcal{B})$. So, there is a block $B_i \in \mathcal{B}$ such that $|set(x_2) \cap B_i| = t_s$. Let

$$
set(x_3) = set(x_2) \cap B_i \text{ and } set(x_4) = set(x_2) \cap (\mathbb{Z}_{n_2} - B_i).
$$

Then, we get the following equation

$$
y^{x_1^{-1}} g^{-val(set(x_2) \cap B_I)} = g^{val(set(x_2) \cap (\mathbb{Z}_{n_2} - B_i))}.
$$

From the above equation, we get Algorithm 1. The first part of Algorithm 1 is to compute and store all the values of the left-hand side. The second part of Algorithm 1 is to compute each value of the right-hand side and check if it is in the list from the first part.

Now we present Algorithm 1 and its randomized version.

Analysis: Algorithm 1 needs $|X_1| \cdot n_2\binom{\lfloor\frac{t_s n_2}{t_2}\rfloor}{t_s}$ exponentiations in the first part and $n_2\binom{n_2 - \lfloor\frac{t_s n_2}{t_2}\rfloor}{t_2 - t_s}$ exponentiations in the second part. In Algorithm 1, we can store $(val(Y_{2,i}), g^{val(Y_{2,i})})$'s instead of $(x_1, val(Y_{1,i}), y^{x_1^{-1}} g^{-val(Y_{1,i})})$'s. In this case, we compute $y^{x_1^{-1}} g^{-val(Y_{1,i})}$ and find a collision. So, we store one of two sets which has smaller cardinality. Thus, the time complexity and the space complexity (neglecting logarithmic factors) are

$$
O\left(|X_1| \cdot n_2\binom{\lfloor\frac{t_s n_2}{t_2}\rfloor}{t_s} + n_2\binom{n_2 - \lfloor\frac{t_s n_2}{t_2}\rfloor}{t_2 - t_s}\right) \text{ and}
$$

$$
O\left(\min\left\{|X_1| \cdot n_2\binom{\lfloor\frac{t_s n_2}{t_2}\rfloor}{t_s}, n_2\binom{n_2 - \lfloor\frac{t_s n_2}{t_2}\rfloor}{t_2 - t_s}\right\}\right),
$$

respectively.

Algorithm 1

Finding discrete logarithm when the order of g is known (deterministic)

Input: g, $y \in G$, X_1, $(n_2; n_2, t_2, t_s)$-parameterized splitting system $(\mathbb{Z}_{n_2}, \mathcal{B})$
Output: $\log_g y$

1: **for all** $x_1 \in X_1$ **do**
2:     **for all** B_i **do**
3:         **for all** $Y_{1,i} \subset B_i$ such that $|Y_{1,i}| = t_s$ **do**
4:             Compute $y^{x_1^{-1}} g^{-val(Y_{1,i})}$
5:             Add $(x_1, val(Y_{1,i}), y^{x_1^{-1}} g^{-val(Y_{1,i})})$ to the list L
6:             Sort L by third coordinate
7:         **end for**
8:     **end for**
9: **end for**
10: **for all** $\mathbb{Z}_{n_2} - B_i$ **do**
11:     **for all** $Y_{2,i} \subset \mathbb{Z}_{n_2} - B_I$ such that $|Y_{2,i}| = t_2 - t_s$ **do**
12:         Compute $g^{val(Y_{2,i})}$
13:         **if** $g^{val(Y_{2,i})}$ is the third coordinate of some entry in the list L **then**
14:             **return** $x_1(val(Y_{1,i}) + val(Y_{2,i}))$
15:         **end if**
16:     **end for**
17: **end for**

Algorithm 2

Finding discrete logarithm when the order of g is known (randomized)

Input: g, $y \in G$, X_1, t_s
Output: $\log_g y$

1: **loop**
2:     Choose randomly $B \subset \mathbb{Z}_{n_2}$ such that $|B| = \lfloor \frac{t_s n_2}{t_2} \rfloor$
3:     **for all** $x_1 \in X_1$ **do**
4:         **for all** $Y_1 \subset B$ such that $|Y_1| = t_s$ **do**
5:             Compute $y^{x_1^{-1}} g^{-val(Y_1)}$
6:             Add $(x_1, val(Y_1), y^{x_1^{-1}} g^{-val(Y_1)})$ to the list L
7:             Sort L by third coordinate
8:         **end for**
9:     **end for**
10:     **for all** $Y_2 \subset \mathbb{Z}_{n_2} - B$ such that $|Y_2| = t_2 - t_s$ **do**
11:         Compute $g^{val(Y_2)}$
12:         **if** $g^{val(Y_2)}$ is the third coordinate of some entry in the list L **then**
13:             **return** $x_1(val(Y_1) + val(Y_2))$
14:         **end if**
15:     **end for**
16: **end loop**

Lemma 3 implies that in about $\frac{4}{\sqrt{\pi}}t_2^{1/2}$ iterations Algorithm 2 outputs $\log_g y$. And we only make L for each B. Thus, if we count the number of group exponentiations, the time complexity and the space complexity are

$$O\left(|X_1| \cdot \sqrt{t_2}\left(\frac{\lfloor \frac{t_s n_2}{t_2} \rfloor}{t_s}\right) + \sqrt{t_2}\left(\frac{n_2 - \lfloor \frac{t_s n_2}{t_2} \rfloor}{t_2 - t_s}\right)\right) \text{ and}$$

$$O\left(\min\left\{|X_1| \cdot \left(\frac{\lfloor \frac{t_s n_2}{t_2} \rfloor}{t_s}\right), \left(\frac{n_2 - \lfloor \frac{t_s n_2}{t_2} \rfloor}{t_2 - t_s}\right)\right\}\right),$$

respectively.

3.3 The DLP with LHWP Exponents When the Order of g Is Unknown

Recall the following equation in Section 3.2,

$$y^{x_1^{-1}} g^{-x_3} = g^{x_4}, \tag{3}$$

If *ord* g is unknown, x_1^{-1} is not easy to compute from x_1 and so Equation (3) cannot be checked directly.

However, we can use Algorithm 1 or 2 from following trick from [4] and, earlier, proposed by Shoup [15]. Let

$$\chi = \prod_{x \in X_1} x \text{ and } \hat{g} = g^\chi.$$

From

$$(y^{x_1^{-1}} g^{-x_3})^\chi = (g^{x_4})^\chi,$$

we get

$$y^{\prod_{x \in X_1 - \{x_1\}} x} \cdot \hat{g}^{-x_3} = \hat{g}^{x_4}, \tag{4}$$

where $x_2 = x_3 + x_4$ and $set(x_3) \cap set(x_4) = \emptyset$.

To solving the DLP, we should perform the precomputation of $y^{\prod_{x \in X_1 - \{x_1\}} x}$, $\hat{g}$ and $\hat{g}^{-1}$ and store them.

$\{y^{\prod_{x \in X_1 - \{x_1\}} x} : x_i \in X_1\}$ can be computed by the algorithm proposed by Coron, Lefranc and Poupard in [4]. According to the algorithm, $|X_1| \cdot \log_2 |X_1|$ group exponentiations are necessary.

Therefore if we are able to learn $\hat{g}^{-1}$, we have Algorithm 3 and Algorithm 4.

Analysis: First, we analyze Algorithm 3. In Step 1, we perform $|X_1| \cdot \log_2 |X_1|$ group exponentiations and store the results. There is no change of the time complexity and space complexity in Step 2. Therefore, the time complexity is

$$O\left(|X_1| \cdot \log_2 |X_1| + |X_1| \cdot n_2\left(\frac{\lfloor \frac{t_s n_2}{t_2} \rfloor}{t_s}\right) + n_2\left(\frac{n_2 - \lfloor \frac{t_s n_2}{t_2} \rfloor}{t_2 - t_s}\right)\right)$$

Algorithm 3

Finding discrete logarithm when the order of g is unknown (deterministic)

Input: g, $y \in G$, X_1, $(n_2; n_2, t_2, t_s)$-parameterized splitting system $(\mathbb{Z}_{n_2}, \mathcal{B})$
Output: $\log_g y$
1: Compute $y^{\prod_{x \in X_1 - \{x_1\}} x}$, $\hat{g}$ and $\hat{g}^{-1}$ and store them
2: Substituting $\hat{g}$ for g, $\hat{g}^{-1}$ for g^{-1} and $\{y^{\prod_{x \in X_1 - \{x_1\}} x} : x_i \in X_1\}$ for X_1, carry out Algorithm 1

Algorithm 4

Finding discrete logarithm when the order of g is unknown (randomized)

Input: g, $y \in G$, X_1
Output: $\log_g y$
1: Compute $y^{\prod_{x \in X_1 - \{x_1\}} x}$, $\hat{g}$ and $\hat{g}^{-1}$ and store them
2: Substituting $\hat{g}$ for g, $\hat{g}^{-1}$ for g^{-1} and $\{y^{\prod_{x \in X_1 - \{x_1\}} x} : x_i \in X_1\}$ for X_1, carry out Algorithm 2

---

and the space complexity is

$$O\left(|X_1| \cdot \log_2 |X_1| + \min\left\{|X_1| \cdot n_2 \binom{\lfloor \frac{t_s n_2}{t_2} \rfloor}{t_s}, \; n_2 \binom{n_2 - \lfloor \frac{t_s n_2}{t_2} \rfloor}{t_2 - t_s}\right\}\right).$$

The best efficiency of the time complexity can be achieved when $|X_1|\binom{\lfloor \frac{t_s n_2}{t_2} \rfloor}{t_s}\approx\binom{n_2 - \lfloor \frac{t_s n_2}{t} \rfloor}{t_2 - t_s}$. At this t_s, $|X_1| \cdot \log_2 |X_1|$ is negligible.

The only difference with Algorithm 3 is Step 2. Therefore, the time complexity is

$$O\left(|X_1| \cdot \log_2 |X_1| + |X_1| \cdot \sqrt{t_2}\binom{\lfloor \frac{t_s n_2}{t_2} \rfloor}{t_s} + \sqrt{t_2}\binom{n_2 - \lfloor \frac{t_s n_2}{t_2} \rfloor}{t_2 - t_s}\right)$$

and the space complexity is

$$O\left(|X_1| \cdot \log_2 |X_1| + \min\left\{|X_1| \cdot \binom{\lfloor \frac{t_s n_2}{t_2} \rfloor}{t_s}, \; \binom{n_2 - \lfloor \frac{t_s n_2}{t_2} \rfloor}{t_2 - t_s}\right\}\right).$$

Remark. We note that Algorithm 3 and 4 might output false answers. These errors come from the fact that the order of $\hat{g}$ of Equation (4) might be smaller than that of g. The worst case is that the order of g is a divisor of that of $\hat{g}$. In this case, Equation (4) is an identical equation.

4   Applications

In this section, we attack the private keys of the GPS identification scheme [5,6,12] and the exponent proposed by Hoffstein and Silverman [9].

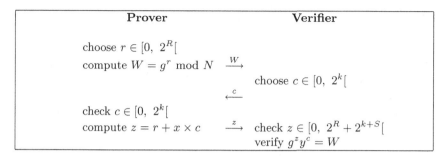

Fig. 1. The GPS Identification Scheme

4.1 Attacks on Private Keys of the GPS Identification Scheme

We briefly introduce the GPS identification scheme.

GPS Identification Scheme. The GPS identification scheme, such as labelled by the NESSIE project, is an interactive protocol between a prover and a verifier which contains one or several rounds of three passes [7]. The GPS identification scheme is based on the DLP over $\mathbb{Z}_N^*$. Precisely, when g is an element of $\mathbb{Z}_N^*$ of maximal order m, the GPS identification scheme is based on the DLP over $G = \langle g \rangle$, where $ord\ g$ is secret. When $y = g^{-x} \bmod N$, a private key of a prover is x and public keys are $(N,\ g,\ y)$. N is the product of two primes and the factorization of N should be difficult.

There are four security parameters as follows:

I. S is the binary size of x. Typically, $S=160$.
ii. k is the binary size of the challenges sent to the prover and determines the level of security of the scheme.
iii. R is the binary size of the exponents used in the commitment computation. It typically verifies $R = S + k + 80$.
iv. m is the number of rounds the scheme is iterated. Theoretically, m is polynomial in the size of the security parameter. But, in practice, m is often chosen equal to 1.

Private Keys of the GPS Identification Scheme. For the efficiency of the protocol, Girault and Lefranc proposed a private key x as $x = x_1 x_2$ in [7], where x_1 is a 19-bit number with 5 random bits equal to 1 chosen among the 16 least significant ones, x_2 is a 142-bit number with 16 random bits equal to 1 chosen among the 138 least significant ones in CHES'04.

Later in CHES'05, to strengthen the security, Coron, Lefranc and Poupard suggest the modified x_1 and x_2 in [4], where x_1 is a 30-bit number with 12 nonzero bits and x_2 is a 130-bit number with 26 nonzero bits.

Attacks on Private Keys. We put $|X_1| = \binom{16}{5}$, $n_2 = 138$, $t_2 = 16$ for private keys from [7] and $|X_1| = \binom{30}{12}$, $n_2 = 130$, $t_2 = 26$ for private keys from [4]. Since N is public we can easily compute $\hat{g}^{-1}$ of Algorithm 2, using the extended

Euclidean algorithm. Before applying these private keys to Algorithm 3 and Algorithm 4, we note that when t_s is chosen to guarantee the most efficient time complexity, the cost of precomputation is negligible.

Table 1 compares the complexities of recovering private keys from [7] and Table 2 for [4]. The private key from [7] was broken in [4], which needs 2^{52} group exponentiations. But the parameterized splitting system and its randomized version reduce it further to $2^{47.7}$ and $2^{43.5}$, respectively.

Table 1. Private Keys from [7]

Method	Exponentiations	Storage
[7]	2^{52}	2^{33}
Ours (Algorithm 3), $t_s = 7$	$2^{47.7}$	$2^{44.5}$
Ours (Algorithm 4), $t_s = 7$	$2^{43.5}$	2^{41}

Table 2 shows that the parameterized splitting system and its randomized version reduce the complexity of the DLP with the private key proposed in [4] from 2^{78} to $2^{65.5}$ and $2^{62.1}$, respectively.

Table 2. Private Keys from [4]

Method	Exponentiations	Storage
[4]	2^{78}	$2^{43.9}$
Ours (Algorithm 3), $t_s = 9$	$2^{65.5}$	$2^{63.1}$
Ours (Algorithm 4), $t_s = 9$	$2^{61.6}$	$2^{59.2}$

4.2   Attacks on the Hoffstein and Silverman's Exponent

The Hoffstein and Silverman's Exponent. Hoffstein and Silverman proposed a use of exponent $x = x_1 x_2 x_3 \in \mathbb{Z}_{2^{1000}-1}$, where x_1, x_2 and x_3 are integers of $wt(x_1) = 6$, $wt(x_2) = 7$ and $wt(x_3) = 7$ or $wt(x_1) = 2$, $wt(x_2) = 2$ and $wt(x_3) = 11$ [9]. In the case of $wt(x_1) = 6$, $wt(x_2) = 7$ and $wt(x_3) = 7$, all values of the Hamming weight are similar, hence, splitting of one's Hamming weight doesn't give advantages. So we focus on the case of $wt(x_1) = 2$, $wt(x_2) = 2$ and $wt(x_3) = 11$.

Let $y = g^x$ for $x = x_1 x_2 x_3$ where x_i's are of weight $(2,2,11)$. Following the trick in [1], we rewrite x as $x = 2^k \bar{x}_1 \bar{x}_2 x_3$ where $0 \le k < n$ and each of $\bar{x}_i$ are rotation-free elements in the same equivalent class with x_i for each i. We further split x_3 by $x_3 = x_3' + x_3''$ where x_3' and x_3'' have weight 3 and 8, respectively. Then we can find x by checking the following equations:

$$y^{2^{-k} \bar{x}_1^{-1} \bar{x}_2 - 1} g^{-x_3'} = g^{x_3''}.$$

In [1], Cheon and Kim modify k so that x_3'' becomes rotation-free. Then the complexity for $n = 1000$ is

$$n \cdot RF(n,2)^2 \binom{n-1}{3} + RF(n,8) \approx 2^{55.2} + 2^{54.5} \approx 2^{55.9}.$$

On the other hand, if we combine the existence of a parameterized splitting system and the notion of the rotation-free, we get a little bit smaller complexity. When we split x_3, we apply the Theorem 1 to find a block B such that $|B| = \lfloor \frac{3n}{11} \rfloor$ and $|set(x_3) \cap B| = 3$. We write $set(x_3) \cap (\mathbb{Z}_n - B) = \{s_0, s_1, \ldots, s_7\}$ and let l_i be the number of elements of $\mathbb{Z}_n$ in $[s_i, s_{i+1}]$ for $i = 0, 1, \ldots, 7$, where we set $s_8 = s_1$ and $[s_7, s_1] = \{s_7, \ldots, n-1, 0, \ldots, s_1\}$. Suppose l_j is the maximum of l_i's. Then, l_j should be larger than $\lfloor \frac{3n}{11} \rfloor$. We shift x_3 so that s_j is placed at 0.

From the above discussions, there exists an integer k' such that $2^{k'} x_3 = x_3' + x_3''$, where x_3' and x_3'' satisfy

1. x_3' is a string of length n and weight 3. If we write $set(x_3') = \{a_0, a_1, a_2\}$ for $0 < a_0 < a_1 < a_2 \le n-1$, then $a_2 - a_0 + 1 \le \lfloor \frac{3n}{11} \rfloor$.
2. x_3'' is a string of length n and weight 8. If we write $set(x_3'') = \{b_0, b_1, \ldots, b_7\}$ for $0 = b_0 < b_1 < \cdots < b_7 \le n-1$, then $b_i - b_{i-1} \le b_1$ and $\lfloor \frac{3n}{11} \rfloor \le b_1$.

To enumerate the number N_1 of x_3', we first fix $a_0 \in [1, n-3]$ and then choose distinct $a_1, a_2 \in [a_0 + 1, \min\{a_0 - 1 + \lfloor \frac{3n}{11} \rfloor, n-1\}]$. Hence

$$N_1 = \sum_{a_0=1}^{\lceil \frac{8n}{11} \rceil} \binom{\lfloor \frac{3n}{11} \rfloor - 1}{2} + \sum_{a_0=\lceil \frac{8n}{11} \rceil + 1}^{n-3} \binom{n-1-a_0}{2}.$$

To enumerate the number N_2 of x_3'', we let $l_0 = b_1$, $l_i = b_{i+1} - b_i$ for $i = 1, \ldots, 6$ and $l_7 = n - 1 - b_7$. Then, N_2 is the number of 8-tuple $(l_0, \ldots, l_7)$ satisfying

1. $\sum_{i=0}^{7} l_i = n - 1$.
2. $\lfloor \frac{3n}{11} \rfloor \le l_0 \le n - 7$.
3. $1 \le l_i \le l_0$ for $i = 1, \ldots, 6$ and $0 \le l_7 \le l_0$.

First, we enumerate the number of solutions satisfying the above conditions when $l_7 \ne 0$. Consider the following equation.

$$\sum_{i=1}^{7} l_i = n - 1 - l_0. \tag{5}$$

This is the problem that how many solutions of positive integers the linear Diophantine equation (5) has when $1 \le l_i \le 0$ for $i = 1, \cdots, 6$.

Given l_0, Let $A(l_0)$ be the set of solutions of Equation (5), $A_i(l_0)$ be the set of solutions when $l_i > l_0$ and $A_{i,j}(l_0)$ be the set of solutions when $l_i > l_0$ and $l_j > l_0$. Note that when $\lfloor \frac{3n}{11} \rfloor \le l_0 \le \lfloor \frac{n-2}{3} \rfloor$, only up to two values of l_i, $i = 1, \cdots, 7$ can be larger than l_0, because otherwise, the sum of the others should be less than 0. Similarly, when $\lfloor \frac{n-2}{3} \rfloor + 1 \le l_0 \le \lfloor \frac{n-2}{2} \rfloor$, only one value can be larger than l_0

and when $\lfloor \frac{n-2}{2} \rfloor + 1 \le l_0 \le n - 7$, any value cannot be larger than l_0. Thus for given l_0, the number of solutions in the case of $l_7 \ne 0$ is

$$N_{2,1}(l_0)' = |A(l_0)| - |\bigcup_{i=0}^{7} A_i(l_0)^c| = |A(l_0)| - \{\sum_{i=0}^{7} |A_i(l_0)| - \sum_{i \ne j} |A_{i,j}(l_0)|\}$$

$$= \binom{n-2-l_0}{6} - \{7\binom{n-2-2l_0}{6} - \binom{7}{2}\binom{n-2-3l_0}{6}\}$$

when $\lfloor \frac{3n}{11} \rfloor \le l_0 \le \lfloor \frac{n-2}{3} \rfloor$. When $\lfloor \frac{n-2}{3} \rfloor + 1 \le l_0 \le \lfloor \frac{n-2}{2} \rfloor$,

$$N_{2,2}(l_0)' = |A(l_0)| - |\bigcup_{i=0}^{7} A_i(l_0)^c| = |A(l_0)| - \sum_{i=0}^{7} |A_i(l_0)|$$

$$= \binom{n-2-l_0}{6} - 7\binom{n-2-2l_0}{6}.$$

When $\lfloor \frac{n-2}{2} \rfloor + 1 \le l_0 \le n - 7$,

$$N_{2,3}(l_0)' = |A(l_0)| = \binom{n-2-l_0}{6}.$$

When $l_7 = 0$, the number of solutions $N_{2,i}(l_0)''$, $i = 1, 2, 3$, can be computed in a similar way, i.e., 6 in each binomial is replaced to 5.

Thus,

$$N_2 = \sum_{l_0=\lfloor \frac{3n}{11} \rfloor}^{\lfloor \frac{n-2}{3} \rfloor} (N_{2,1}(l_0)' + N_{2,1}(l_0)'') + \sum_{l_0=\lfloor \frac{n-2}{3} \rfloor+1}^{\lfloor \frac{n-2}{2} \rfloor} (N_{2,3}(l_0)' + N_{2,3}(l_0)'')$$

$$+ \sum_{\lfloor \frac{n-2}{2} \rfloor+1}^{n-7} (N_{2_3}(l_0)' + N_{2,3}(l_0)'').$$

Therefore, the total time complexity of the combined algorithm is

$$n \cdot RF(n, 2)^2 N_1 + N_2 \approx 2^{52.75} + 2^{54.01} \approx 2^{54.51}.$$

And the space complexity of the combined algorithm is about $2^{52.75}$.

5   Conclusion

In this paper, we have proposed a *Parameterized Splitting System* and its randomized version. Since a parameterized splitting system takes the advatages from both of the splitting system and the Heiman-Odlyzko algorithm, it gives an efficient algorithm for the DLP with LHWP exponents.

Acknowledgements. The authors would like to thank Martijn Stam and the anonymous referees for valuable comments. The first author also would like to thank Namsu Jho for helpful discussions. This work was supported by the Korea Science and Engineering Foundation (KOSEF) grant funded by the Korea government (MOST) (No. R11-2007-035-01002-0).

References

1. Cheon, J., Kim, H.: Analysis of Low Hamming Weight Products; Discrete Applied Mathematics (to appear)
2. Coppersmith, D., Seroussi, G.: On the Minimum Distance of Some Quadratic Residue Codes. IEEE Trans. Inform. Theory 30, 407–411 (1984), MR 86c:94025
3. Coppersmith, D.: Private communication to Scott Vanstone (December 1997)
4. Coron, J., Lefranc, D., Poupard, G.: A New Baby-Step Giant-Step Algorithm and Some Application to Cryptanalysis. In: Rao, J.R., Sunar, B. (eds.) CHES 2005. LNCS, vol. 3659, pp. 47–60. Springer, Heidelberg (2005)
5. Girault, M.: Self-Certified Public Keys. In: Davies, D.W. (ed.) EUROCRYPT 1991. LNCS, vol. 547, pp. 490–497. Springer, Heidelberg (1991)
6. Girault, M., Poupard, G., Stern, J.: Some Modes of Use of the GPS Identification Scheme. In: 3rd Nessie Conference, Springer, Heidelberg (November 2002)
7. Girault, M., Lefranc, D.: Public Key Authentication with One Single (on-line) Addition. In: Joye, M., Quisquater, J.-J. (eds.) CHES 2004. LNCS, vol. 3156, pp. 413–427. Springer, Heidelberg (2004)
8. Heiman, R.: A Note on Discrete Logarithms with Special Structure. In: Rueppel, R.A. (ed.) EUROCRYPT 1992. LNCS, vol. 658, pp. 454–457. Springer, Heidelberg (1993)
9. Hoffstein, J., Silverman, J.: Random Small Hamming Weight Products with Application to Cryptography. Discrete Appl. Math. 130(1), 37–49 (2003)
10. Menezes, A., van Oorschot, P., Vanstone, S.: Handbook of Applied Cryptography, p. 128. CRC Press, Boca Raton (1997)
11. Pollard, J.: Monte Carlo Methods for Index Computation (mod p). Mathematics of Computation 32(143), 918–924 (1978)
12. Poupard, G., Stern, J.: Security Analysis of a Practical "On the Fly" Authentication and Signature Generation. In: Nyberg, K. (ed.) EUROCRYPT 1998. LNCS, vol. 1403, pp. 422–436. Springer, Heidelberg (1998)
13. Shanks, D.: Class Number, a Theory of Factorization and Genera. Proc. Symp. Pure Math. 20, 415–440 (1971)
14. Shoup, V.: Lower Bounds for discrete Logarithms and Related Problems. In: Fumy, W. (ed.) EUROCRYPT 1997. LNCS, vol. 1233, pp. 256–266. Springer, Heidelberg (1997)
15. Shoup, V.: Practical Threshold Signatures. In: Preneel, B. (ed.) EUROCRYPT 2000. LNCS, vol. 1807, pp. 207–220. Springer, Heidelberg (2000)
16. Stinson, D.: Some Baby-Step Giant-Step Algorithms for the Low Hamming Weight Discrete Logarithm Problem. Mathematics of Computation 71(237), 379–391 (2002)

Certificateless Encryption Schemes Strongly Secure in the Standard Model

Alexander W. Dent[1], Benoît Libert[2], and Kenneth G. Paterson[1]

[1] Information Security Group,
Royal Holloway, University of London (United Kingdom)
[2] UCL, Microelectronics Laboratory, Crypto Group (Belgium)

Abstract. This paper presents the first constructions for certificateless encryption (CLE) schemes that are provably secure against strong adversaries in the standard model. It includes both a generic construction for a strongly secure CLE scheme from any passively secure scheme as well as a concrete construction based on the Waters identity-based encryption scheme.

Keywords: certificateless encryption, standard model, strong security.

1 Introduction

Certificateless public key cryptography (CL-PKC), as proposed by Al-Riyami and Paterson [1], represents an interesting and potentially useful balance between identity-based cryptography and public key cryptography based on certificates. It eliminates the key escrow associated with identity-based cryptography without requiring the introduction of certificates, which pose many operational difficulties in PKIs. The main idea of CL-PKC is that a user Alice combines two key components to form her private key: one component (the partial private key, PPK) is generated by a Key Generation Centre (KGC) using a master secret, and another component (the secret value) is generated by the user herself. The user also publishes a public key derived from her secret value; a party who wishes to encrypt to Alice only needs to have Alice's identity and public key along with the KGC's public parameters. One novel aspect of CL-PKC is the modelling of adversaries who are capable of replacing the public keys of users with keys of their choice. This is necessary because there are no certificates to authenticate users' public keys in CL-PKC.

The topic of certificateless cryptography has undergone quite rapid development, with many schemes being proposed for encryption (CLE) [1,3,6,12,25] and signatures (CLS) [1,20,22,32,35]. One notable feature has been the development of a number of alternative security models for CLE that are substantially weaker than the original model of [1]. These different models are summarised by Dent [13]. In the model of [1], the attacker is of one of two types. The Type I attacker models an "outsider" adversary, who can replace the public keys of users, obtain PPKs and private keys, and make decryption queries. The Type II attacker models an "honest-but-curious" KGC who is given the master secret (and can therefore

R. Cramer (Ed.): PKC 2008, LNCS 4939, pp. 344–359, 2008.

generate any PPK), can obtain private keys and make decryption queries, but is trusted not to replace any public keys. (We actually use a slightly stronger model of security for Type II attackers, in which the attacker can replace public keys providing that they do not allow the attacker to trivially break the scheme.)

In their original security model, Al-Riyami and Paterson chose to make the Type I adversary as strong as possible, insisting in their model that a challenger should correctly respond to decryption queries even if the public key of a user had been replaced. This is called a Strong Type I attacker in [13]. Currently, the only published CLE schemes that have been proven secure against strong Type I adversaries [1,25] make use of the random oracle model [4]. Notably, Libert and Quisquater [25] provide a generic construction which converts a CLE scheme secure against passive adversaries (who do not have access to a decryption oracle) into a scheme secure against strong adversaries, using a Fujisaki-Okamoto-style conversion [17]. This conversion allows decryption queries to be handled using a form of knowledge extraction, but does require the use of random oracles.

Related Work

In 2003, Gentry [19] introduced a different but related concept named certificate based encryption (CBE). This approach is closer to the context of a traditional PKI model as it involves a certification authority (CA) providing an efficient implicit certification service for clients' public keys.

Subsequent works [33,31] considered the relations between identity-based (IBE), certificate based (CBE) and certificateless encryption schemes (CLE) and established a result of essential equivalence [33] between the three primitives. The generic transformations of [33,31] do not use random oracles but those results do not hold in the full security model developed in [1] for CLE schemes; indeed, they were even shown not to hold in relaxed CLE models [18].

In [15], Dodis and Katz described generic methods to construct IND-CCA secure multiple-encryption schemes from public key encryption schemes which are individually IND-CCA. They proved that their methods apply to the design of certificate-based encryption schemes [19] and yield CBE schemes without random oracles. Because of the strong properties required of decryption oracles in [1], these techniques do not directly apply in the present context. In security proofs, the technical difficulty is that the simulator does not know the secret value of entities whose public key was replaced. In other words, the constructions of [15] are not designed to handle decryption queries for arbitrary public keys chosen "on-the-fly" by adversaries who may not even know the matching secret as in the present context.

Other authors [26] have also recently attempted to address the problem of designing certificateless cryptosystems (or related primitives) in the standard model. However their results are not presented in the full model of [1]. In particular, the recent work of Huang and Wong [21] constructs a certificateless encryption scheme that is secure in the standard model but does not permit a Strong Type I adversary.

Finally, a recently initiated research direction considers authorities that maliciously generate system-wide parameters [2]. As we shall see, the model of [2] makes it even more difficult to devise schemes that are provably secure in the standard model. Neither of the schemes we present are secure against adversaries that maliciously generate the system-wide parameters.

Our Contributions

We make two contributions which resolve questions raised by the above debate concerning CLE security models.

Firstly, we present a generic construction for strongly secure CLE. Our construction uses any CLE scheme and any normal public key encryption (PKE) scheme as components, but these only need to be secure against passive adversaries. In contrast to [25], our construction does not intrinsically require the use of random oracles. Instead, we use an extension of the techniques of Naor-Yung [27] and Sahai [29]; however, some additional ideas are needed to handle decryption queries for adversarially-selected public keys. As it makes use of non-interactive zero-knowledge (NIZK) proofs for general statements in NP, our generic construction cannot be regarded as being practical.

Secondly, we provide the first concrete and efficient construction for a CLE scheme that is secure in the standard model against strong adversaries. In fact, our scheme is secure against both Strong Type I attackers and Strong Type II adversaries. The latter represents a natural strengthening of the original Type II adversary introduced in [1]. The construction is based upon the Waters identity-based encryption (IBE) scheme, modifying this scheme using ideas from [1]. The scheme enjoys relatively short public keys and ciphertexts; its security is based on the hardness of a slight and natural generalisation of the DBDH problem.

Why Consider Strong Decryption Oracles?

There has been some debate on whether the Strong Type I and Strong Type II security models correctly model the security capabilities of an attacker against a certificateless encryption scheme [1,6,12,21]. A full discussion of this issue is given in the survey by Dent [13]. It can be argued that an attacker should be given access to an oracle if it supplies information that an attacker might be able to obtain in real life. For example, a decryption oracle provides information about a message that an attacker might be able to obtain by observing how a system behaves after receiving and decrypting a ciphertext or by bribing/threatening the user who received a ciphertext. In certificateless encryption, it is necessary to model the adversary's ability to fool a sender into using the wrong public key when encrypting a message, because public keys are not supported by certificates. This is done by allowing the adversary to replace public keys at will in the model. But there is no reason to suppose that a recipient would use anything other than its own, original private key when decrypting. So there is no practical reason to require that a decryption oracle for a replaced public key should be available to the attacker.

However, we still believe that the results of this paper are of theoretical interest to the research community, even if they are not practically relevant. There are several reasons for this:

- The strong models have been widely used in the previous papers and the question of whether it is possible to construct a scheme that is secure in the

Strong Type I and Strong Type II models without using the random oracle methodology has been widely discussed. Indeed, it has even been conjectured that it was impossible to construct schemes that are both Strong Type I and Strong Type II secure in the standard model. In this paper, we show this conjecture to be false.

- Even if the strong model is not of practical interest, security in this model does guarantee security in the weaker, but more practically relevant, security models. Hence, at a basic level, this paper can be seen to be proving the security of several certificateless encryption schemes in the standard model (assuming honest-but-curious KGCs). Of particular interest is the generic construction presented in Section 3, which demonstrates that certificateless encryption schemes can be constructed from generic assumptions.
- Lastly, our work demonstrates that it is possible for a polynomial-time scheme to be secure in a model that allows the attacker access to oracles that compute non-polynomial-time functions (in this case computing the decryptions of ciphertexts created using arbitrary public keys). We believe that the idea of considering the security of schemes in non-polynomial-time models to be theoretically interesting.

2 Preliminaries

2.1 Notation

We use the following notation. Let $\emptyset$ denote the empty bitstring. If $\mathcal{A}$ is a deterministic algorithm, then $y \leftarrow \mathcal{A}(x)$ denotes the assignment to y of the output of $\mathcal{A}$ when run on the input x. If $\mathcal{A}$ is a randomised algorithm, then $y \xleftarrow{\$} \mathcal{A}(x)$ the assignment to y of the output of $\mathcal{A}$ when run on the input x with a fresh random tape. We let $y \leftarrow A(x; r)$ denote the assignment to y of the output of $\mathcal{A}$ when run on the input x with the random tape r. If $\mathcal{A}$ is a probabilistic polynomial-time (PPT) algorithm, then we may assume that r is of polynomial length. If S is a finite set, then $y \xleftarrow{\$} S$ denotes the random generation of an element $x \in S$ using the uniform distribution. A function $\nu : \mathbb{N} \to [0, 1]$ is said to be *negligible* if for all $c \in \mathbb{N}$ there exists a $k_c \in \mathbb{N}$ such that $\nu(k) < k^{-c}$ for all $k > k_c$.

2.2 Certificateless Encryption Schemes

The notion of a certificateless encryption scheme was introduced by Al-Riyami and Paterson [1]. A certificateless public-key encryption scheme is defined by seven probabilistic, polynomial-time algorithms:

- **Setup**: takes as input a security parameter 1^k and returns the master private key msk and the master public key mpk. This algorithm is run by a KGC to initially set up a certificateless system.
- **Extract**: takes as input the master public key mpk, the master private key msk, and an identifier $\mathsf{ID} \in \{0, 1\}^*$. It outputs a partial private key d_{ID}. This

algorithm is run by a KGC once for each user, and the corresponding partial private key is distributed to that user in a suitably secure manner.

- SetSec: given the master public key mpk and an entity's identifier ID as input, and outputs a secret value x_{ID} for that identity. This algorithm is run once by the user.
- SetPriv: takes as input the master public key mpk, an entity's partial private key d_{ID} and an entity's secret value x_{ID}. It outputs the full private key sk_{ID} for that user. This algorithm is run once by the user.
- SetPub: given the master public key mpk and an entity's secret value x_{ID}, this algorithm outputs a public key $pk_{ID} \in \mathcal{PK}$ for that user. This algorithm is run once by the user and the resulting public key is widely and freely distributed. The public-key space $\mathcal{PK}$ is defined using mpk and is assumed to be publicly recognisable: given mpk, public keys having a matching private key should be easily distinguishable from ill-formed public keys.
- Encrypt: this algorithm takes as input the master public key mpk, a user's identity ID, a user's public key $pk_{ID} \in \mathcal{PK}$ and a message $m \in \mathcal{M}$. It outputs either a ciphertext $C \in \mathcal{C}$ or the error symbol $\perp$.
- Decrypt: this algorithm takes as input the master public key mpk, a user's private key sk_{ID} and a ciphertext $C \in \mathcal{C}$. It returns either a message $m \in \mathcal{M}$ or the error symbol $\perp$.

We insist that all certificateless encryption schemes satisfy the obvious correctness conditions (that decryption "undoes" encryption).

Dent [13] has surveyed the numerous different security models proposed for certificateless encryption. In this paper, we will only be concerned with the Strong Type I and Strong Type II security definitions. Both of these security models consider attack games that extend the standard IND-CCA attack game for public-key encryption. In both games, we are concerned with the difference in probability

$$Adv_{\mathcal{A}}^{\text{CL-CCA-X}}(k) = |Pr[Expt_{\mathcal{A}}^{\text{CL-CCA-X}}(0,k) = 1] - Pr[Expt_{\mathcal{A}}^{\text{CL-CCA-X}}(1,k) = 1]|$$

for $\text{X} \in \{\text{I}, \text{II}\}$ where $\mathcal{A}$ is any PPT adversary $\mathcal{A} = (\mathcal{A}_1, \mathcal{A}_2)$ and the experiment $Expt_{\mathcal{A}}^{\text{CL-CCA-X}}(b,k)$ is defined as:

$$Expt_{\mathcal{A}}^{\text{CL-CCA-X}}(b,k):$$
$$(mpk, msk) \xleftarrow{\$} \text{Setup}(1^k)$$
$$(m_0, m_1, \text{ID}^*, state) \xleftarrow{\$} \mathcal{A}_1(1^k, mpk, aux)$$
$$C^* \xleftarrow{\$} \text{Encrypt}(m_b, pk_{\text{ID}^*}, \text{ID}^*, mpk)$$
$$b' \xleftarrow{\$} \mathcal{A}_2(C^*, state)$$
$$\text{Output } b'$$

We insist that $\mathcal{A}_1$ outputs messages (m_0, m_1) such that $|m_0| = |m_1|$. The Type I security model ($\text{X} = \text{I}$) and the Type II security model ($\text{X} = \text{II}$) are distinguished by the value aux and the oracles to which the attacker has access. The Type I model is meant to represent an outside attacker and so $aux = \emptyset$. The Type II model captures the actions of an honest-but-curious KGC and so $aux = msk$. We consider the following oracles:

- **Request public key:** the attacker supplies an identity ID and the oracle returns the public key pk_{ID} for that identity. If pk_{ID} has not previously been defined, the oracle generates it.
- **Replace public key:** the attacker supplies an identity ID and a public key $pk_{ID} \in \mathcal{PK}$, and the oracle replaces any previously generated public key for ID with pk_{ID}. Such a query is only allowed for correctly shaped new keys. Recall that the model of [1] requires the well-formedness of pk_{ID} (and the existence of a secret value) to be publicly checkable.
- **Extract partial private key:** the attacker supplies an identity ID and the oracle returns the partial private key d_{ID} for that identity.
- **Extract private key:** the attacker supplies an identity ID and the oracle responds with the full private key sk_{ID} for that identity.
- **Strong decrypt (or decrypt):** the attacker supplies an identity ID and a ciphertext C, and the oracle responds by constructing a private key sk_{ID} that corresponds to the identity ID and its associated public key. The oracle returns the decryption of C under this private key. Note that the oracle has to respond to decryption oracle queries even if the public key for the identity has been replaced.

Definition 1. *A CLE scheme is Strong Type I secure if, for every PPT adversary $\mathcal{A}$ that respects the following oracle constraints*

- *$\mathcal{A}$ cannot extract the private key for the identity ID^* at any time,*
- *$\mathcal{A}$ cannot extract the private key of any identity for which it has replaced the public key,*
- *$\mathcal{A}$ cannot extract the partial private key of ID^* if $\mathcal{A}$ replaced the public key pk_{ID^*} before the challenge was issued,*
- *$\mathcal{A}_2$ cannot query the strong decrypt oracle on the challenge ciphertext C^* for the identity ID^* unless the public key pk_{ID^*} used to create the challenge ciphertext has been replaced,*

we have that $Adv_{\mathcal{A}}^{CL-CCA-I}(k)$ is negligible. In this model, $aux = \emptyset$.

Definition 2. *A CLE scheme is Strong Type II secure if, for every PPT adversary $\mathcal{A}$ that respects the following oracle constraints*

- *$\mathcal{A}$ cannot extract the private key for the identity ID^* at any time,*
- *$\mathcal{A}$ cannot extract the private key of any identity for which it has replaced the public key,*
- *$\mathcal{A}$ does not query the partial private key oracle (since it can compute them itself given msk),*
- *$\mathcal{A}_1$ cannot output a challenge identity ID^* for which it has replaced the public key,*
- *$\mathcal{A}_2$ cannot query the strong decrypt oracle on the challenge ciphertext C^* for the identity ID^* unless the public key pk_{ID^*} used to create the challenge ciphertext has been replaced.*

we have that $Adv_{\mathcal{A}}^{CL-CCA-II}(k)$ is negligible. In the Type II model, we have aux = msk, i.e. $\mathcal{A}_1$ takes the master private key as an additional input.

We note that the definition of Type II security only covers honest-but-curious KGCs, as originally defined by Al-Riyami and Paterson [1]. An alternative definition, proposed by Au et al. [2], attempts to model security against a KGC that can maliciously generate its master public and private keys. We note that our schemes are not secure in this model. Nevertheless, we claim that the original security model still captures a significant level of security and that the design of secure standard model schemes fitting the original definitions represents a significant step forward in the theory of certificateless encryption. We do not find it unrealistic to assume that KGCs are honest at key generation time and erase relevant crucial information in case they are later broken into. Furthermore, it is difficult to see how a scheme can be proven secure against malicious key generation centres and outside attackers in the standard model and with strong decryption oracles using known proof techniques. The recent work of Huang and Wong [21] proves the security of a scheme against malicious KGCs in the standard model but does not permit a Strong Type I adversary, so the construction of such a scheme should still be considered an open problem.

A certificateless encryption scheme is said to be strongly secure if it is both Strong Type I and Strong Type II secure. A certificateless encryption scheme is said to be passively secure if it is Strong Type I and Strong Type II secure against adversaries who make no decryption oracle queries.

3   Generic Construction

In this section we develop a generic construction of a strongly secure certificateless encryption scheme from a passively secure certificateless encryption scheme, a passively secure public key encryption scheme, and a non-interactive zero-knowledge proof system. We do this by adapting the ideas of Naor-Yung [27] and Sahai [29] to the certificateless setting. The requirement that the simulator be able to decrypt ciphertexts encrypted using arbitrary public keys makes the construction slightly more complicated than in the public-key encryption case.

We first recall the notion of an NP language and that of a simulation-sound non-interactive zero-knowledge proof system. Our requirements are similar to those of Sahai [29], but slightly more demanding.

Definition 3. *A language* $L \in \{0,1\}^*$ *is an NP language* ($L \in$ NP) *if there exists a (deterministic) Turing machine* R *that is polynomial-time with respect to its first input and satisfies:*

$$x \in L \iff \exists w \in \{0,1\}^* \text{ such that } R(x, w) = 1$$

We require a NIZK proof system that is statistically sound, computationally simulation-sound and computationally zero-knowledge. We require statistical soundness because (at one point in the proof) we will be forced to simulate a decryption oracle that can provide functionality that cannot be computed in polynomial-time, i.e. decrypting ciphertexts that are encrypted under adversarially chosen public keys.

Definition 4. *A statistically sound, computationally simulation-sound, and computationally zero knowledge non-interactive zero-knowledge proof system (NIZK) for a language $L \in NP$ is a tuple $\Pi = (f, P, V, S_1, S_2)$ where f is a polynomial and P, V, S_1 and S_2 are probabilistic, polynomial-time Turing machines that satisfy the following conditions:*

- **Complete:** *For all $x \in L$ and all w such that $R(x, w) = 1$, and for all strings $\sigma \in \{0, 1\}^{f(k)}$, we have that $V(x, \pi, \sigma) = 1$ for all $\pi \xleftarrow{\$} P(x, w, \sigma)$.*
- **Simulation complete:** *For all $x \in \{0, 1\}^*$ and all strings $(\sigma, \kappa) \xleftarrow{\$} S_1(1^k)$, we have that $V(x, \pi, \sigma) = 1$ for all $\pi \xleftarrow{\$} S_2(x, \kappa)$. κ can be thought of as a secret key that allows S_2 to produce false proofs.*
- **Statistically sound:** *Almost all common random strings σ should not allow any false theorem to be proven. In other words,*

$$Pr[\exists x \in \{0, 1\}^* \setminus L \, \exists \pi \in \{0, 1\}^* \text{ such that } V(x, \pi, \sigma) = 1]$$

is negligible as a function of the security parameter k where the probability is taken over the choice of $\sigma \xleftarrow{\$} \{0, 1\}^{f(k)}$.
- **Simulation sound:** *For all non-uniform PPT adversaries $\mathcal{A} = (\mathcal{A}_1, \mathcal{A}_2)$ we have that $Adv_{\mathcal{A}}^{NZIK\text{-}SS}(k) = Pr[Expt_{\mathcal{A}}^{SS}(k) = 1]$ is negligible as a function of k, where*

$Expt_{\mathcal{A}}^{SS}(k)$:
$(\sigma, \kappa) \xleftarrow{\$} S_1(1^k)$
$(x, state) \xleftarrow{\$} \mathcal{A}_1(1^k, \sigma)$
$\pi \xleftarrow{\$} S_2(x, \kappa)$
$(x', \pi') \xleftarrow{\$} \mathcal{A}_2(\pi, state)$

Output 1 if and only if:
- $(x', \pi') \neq (x, \pi)$
- $x' \notin L$
- $V(x', \pi', \sigma) = 1$

- **Zero knowledge:** *For all non-uniform PPT adversaries $\mathcal{A} = (\mathcal{A}_1, \mathcal{A}_2)$ we have that*

$$Adv_{\mathcal{B}}^{NIZK\text{-}ZK}(k) = |Pr[Expt_{\mathcal{A}}(k) = 1] - Pr[Expt_{\mathcal{A}}^{S}(k) = 1]|$$

is negligible as a function of k, where

$Expt_{\mathcal{A}}(k)$:
$\sigma \xleftarrow{\$} \{0, 1\}^{f(k)}$
$(x, w, state) \xleftarrow{\$} \mathcal{A}_1(1^k, \sigma)$
If $R(x, w) = 0$, then $\pi \leftarrow \emptyset$
Otherwise $\pi \xleftarrow{\$} P(x, w, \sigma)$
Return $\mathcal{A}_2(\pi, state)$

$Expt_{\mathcal{A}}^{S}(k)$:
$(\sigma, \kappa) \xleftarrow{\$} S_1(1^k)$
$(x, w, state) \xleftarrow{\$} \mathcal{A}_1(1^k, \sigma)$
If $R(x, w) = 0$, then $\pi \leftarrow \emptyset$
Otherwise $\pi \xleftarrow{\$} S_2(x, \kappa)$
Return $\mathcal{A}_2(\pi, state)$

Sahai [29] uses a (single theorem) computationally sound and computationally zero-knowledge NIZK proof system to construct a (multiple theorem) computationally sound, computationally simulation-sound and computationally zero-knowledge NIZK proof system. This construction assumes that one-way permutations exist. A brief examination of the proof verifies that we can construct a statistically sound, computationally simulation-sound NIZK proof system from a statistically sound NIZK proof system. Furthermore, it is not difficult to verify that statistically sound NIZK proof systems can be constructed for any NP language using the techniques of Feige, Lapidot and Shamir [16] under the assumption that certified trapdoor permutations exist. This condition is relaxed by Bellare and Yung [5] to require only that trapdoor permutations exist. Therefore we can construct suitably secure NIZK proof systems under the assumption that trapdoor permutations exist. Our construction will also make use of a passively-secure encryption scheme.

Definition 5. *A triple of PPT algorithms* $(\mathcal{G}, \mathcal{E}, \mathcal{D})$ *is an encryption scheme if (1)* $\mathcal{G}$ *takes as input a security parameter* 1^k *and outputs a public key pk and a private key sk; (2)* $\mathcal{E}$ *takes as input a message* $m \in \mathcal{M}$ *and a public key pk, and outputs a ciphertext* $C \in \mathcal{C}$; *and (3)* $\mathcal{D}$ *takes as input a ciphertext* $C \in C$ *and a private key sk, and outputs either a message* $m \in \mathcal{M}$ *or the error symbol* $\perp$. *This encryption scheme is said to be passively secure if the difference in probabilities*

$$Adv_{\mathcal{A}}^{PKE\text{-}CPA}(k) = |Pr[Expt_{\mathcal{A}}^{PKE\text{-}CPA}(0,k)=1] - Pr[Expt_{\mathcal{A}}^{PKE\text{-}CPA}(1,k)=1]|$$

is negligible for every probabilistic, polynomial-time attacker $\mathcal{A} = (\mathcal{A}_1, \mathcal{A}_2)$. *The experiment* $Expt_{\mathcal{A}}^{PKE\text{-}CPA}(b,k)$ *is defined as*

$$Expt_{\mathcal{A}}^{PKE\text{-}CPA}(b,k):$$
$$(pk, sk) \xleftarrow{\$} \mathcal{G}(1^k)$$
$$(m_0, m_1, state) \xleftarrow{\$} \mathcal{A}_1(1^k, pk)$$
$$C^* \xleftarrow{\$} \mathcal{E}(m_b, pk)$$
$$Return\ \mathcal{A}_2(C^*, state)$$

where we insist that $|m_0| = |m_1|$.

We construct a strongly secure CLE scheme from a passively secure one and *two* distinct instances of a public-key encryption scheme. We use the NIZK proof system to prove that these independently generated ciphertexts all encrypt the same message. Let (Setup, Extract, SetSec, SetPriv, SetPub, Encrypt, Decrypt) be a passively secure CLE scheme and $(\mathcal{G}, \mathcal{E}, \mathcal{D})$ be a passively secure public-key encryption scheme. Furthermore, let (f, P, V, S_1, S_2) be a statistically sound and computationally simulation-sound NIZK proof system for the language

$$L = \{(C_1, pk, \mathsf{ID}, mpk_1, C_2, mpk_2, C_3, mpk_3) \mid \exists\, (m, r_1, r_2, r_3)$$
$$\text{such that } C_1 = \mathtt{Encrypt}(m, pk, \mathsf{ID}, mpk_1; r_1)$$
$$\wedge\, C_2 = \mathcal{E}(m, mpk_2; r_2) \wedge C_3 = \mathcal{E}(m, mpk_3; r_3)\}$$

Let (Setup', Extract, SetSec, SetPriv, SetPub, Encrypt', Decrypt') be the certificateless encryption scheme derived from the passively secure scheme and the algorithms given in Figure 1. We assume that users' public key pk and identity

Setup$'(1^k)$:
$(mpk_1, msk_1) \xleftarrow{\$} $ Setup(1^k)
$(mpk_2, msk_2) \xleftarrow{\$} \mathcal{G}(1^k)$
$(mpk_3, msk_3) \xleftarrow{\$} \mathcal{G}(1^k)$
$\sigma \xleftarrow{\$} \{0,1\}^{f(k)}$
$mpk' \leftarrow (mpk_1, mpk_2, mpk_3, \sigma)$
$msk' \leftarrow msk_1$
Output (mpk', msk')

Encrypt$'(m, pk, \mathsf{ID}, mpk')$:
$r_1, r_2, r_3 \xleftarrow{\$} \{0,1\}^{poly(k)}$
$C_1 \xleftarrow{\$} $ Encrypt$(m, pk, \mathsf{ID}, mpk_1; r_1)$
$C_2 \xleftarrow{\$} \mathcal{E}(m, mpk_2; r_2)$
$C_3 \xleftarrow{\$} \mathcal{E}(m, mpk_3; r_3)$
$x \leftarrow (C_1, pk, \mathsf{ID}, mpk_1, C_2, mpk_2, C_3, mpk_3)$
$\pi \xleftarrow{\$} P(x, (m, r_1, r_2, r_3), \sigma)$
$C \leftarrow (C_1, C_2, C_3, \pi)$
Output C

Decrypt$'(C, sk, mpk')$:
$x \leftarrow (C_1, pk, \mathsf{ID}, mpk_1, C_2, mpk_2, C_3, mpk_3)$
If $V(x, \pi, \sigma) \neq 1$ then output $\perp$
Otherwise set $m \xleftarrow{\$} $ Decrypt(C_1, sk, mpk)
Output m

Fig. 1. A construction for a strongly secure certificateless encryption scheme

ID are included in their full private key sk. We also assume (for simplicity and without loss of generality) that the random tapes used by each of the algorithms is of length $poly(k)$.

Theorem 1. *If*

- *($\mathsf{Setup}, \mathsf{Extract}, \mathsf{SetSec}, \mathsf{SetPriv}, \mathsf{SetPub}, \mathsf{Encrypt}, \mathsf{Decrypt}$) is a passively secure certificateless encryption scheme,*
- *($\mathcal{G}, \mathcal{E}, \mathcal{D}$) is a passively secure public-key encryption scheme,*
- *(f, P, V, S_1, S_2) is a statistically sound, computationally simulation-sound and computationally zero-knowledge NIZK proof system for the NP language*

$$L = \{(C_1, pk, \mathsf{ID}, mpk_1, C_2, mpk_2, C_3, mpk_3) \mid \exists\, (m, r_1, r_2, r_3)$$
$$\text{such that } C_1 = \mathsf{Encrypt}(m, pk, \mathsf{ID}, mpk_1; r_1)$$
$$\wedge\, C_2 = \mathcal{E}(m, mpk_2; r_2) \wedge C_3 = \mathcal{E}(m, mpk_3; r_3)\}$$

then the certificateless encryption scheme given in Figure 1 is secure in the Strong Type I and Strong Type II models.

The proof is given in the full version of the paper [14]. It depends upon the fact that the master private key msk' does not contain the decryption keys for the public-key encryption schemes (msk_2, msk_3) or the simulation key κ for the NIZK proof system. We stress that this proof only works against Strong Type II adversaries who follow the setup procedure precisely, including the secure deletion of (msk_2, msk_3) and κ. The scheme can be trivially broken by a KGC that can generate the master public key in an adversarial way. In the standard model, it remains an open problem to construct a scheme that is strongly secure against adversaries who can generate the master public key.

Remark 1. This construction can also be thought of as using a NIZK proof to bind the encryption of a message under a passively secure certificateless encryption scheme to the encryption of the same message under an IND-CCA2 secure encryption scheme. In the specific case of the construction that we have proposed, the IND-CCA2 encryption scheme is the Sahai [29] construction of an IND-CCA2 encryption scheme from two passively secure encryption schemes and a (separate) NIZK proof system. The proofs of security can easily be adapted to the case where an arbitrary IND-CCA2 secure encryption scheme is used.

Remark 2. We note that we may construct passively secure encryption schemes and suitably secure NIZK proof systems for any NP language from trapdoor one-way permutations [29]. Furthermore, we may construct passively secure CLE schemes from passively secure public-key encryption schemes and passively secure identity-based encryption schemes [25]. Hence, we can conclude that strongly secure certificateless encryption schemes exist provided that NIZK proof systems and passively secure identity-based encryption schemes exist. It is an open problem to show that a passively secure identity-based encryption scheme can be constructed from any recognised minimal assumption. Since it is possible to construct NIZK proof systems [10] and passively secure identity-based encryption schemes [30] under the DBDH assumption, we can conclude that there exists a strongly secure certificateless encryption schemes under the DBDH assumption alone.

Remark 3. Two public-key encryption scheme are required in order to provide security against attackers with access to a strong decryption oracle. In weaker security models, where the attacker does not have access to a strong decryption oracle, a single public-key encryption scheme suffices.

4   Concrete Construction

Our concrete construction for CLE uses *bilinear map groups*, i.e. groups $(\mathbb{G}, \mathbb{G}_T)$ of prime order p for which there is an efficiently computable mapping $e : \mathbb{G} \times \mathbb{G} \to \mathbb{G}_T$ with the following properties:

1. bilinearity: $e(g^a, h^b) = e(g, h)^{ab}$ for any $(g, h) \in \mathbb{G} \times \mathbb{G}$ and $a, b \in \mathbb{Z}$;
2. non-degeneracy: $e(g, h) \neq 1_{\mathbb{G}_T}$ whenever $g, h \neq 1_{\mathbb{G}}$.

In such groups, we require the intractability of the following decisional problem that was suggested for the first time in [7] as a natural variant of the DBDH and DDH problems.

Definition 6. *The* Decision 3-Party Diffie-Hellman Problem *(3-DDH) is to decide if $T = g^{abc}$ given $(g^a, g^b, g^c, T) \in \mathbb{G}^4$. Formally, we define the advantage of a PPT algorithm $\mathcal{A}$ as*

$$Adv_{\mathcal{A}}^{3\text{-}DDH}(k) = \begin{vmatrix} Pr[1 \xleftarrow{\$} \mathcal{A}(g^a, g^b, g^c, T) \mid T \xleftarrow{\$} g^{abc} \wedge a, b, c \xleftarrow{\$} \mathbb{Z}_p^*] \\ -Pr[1 \xleftarrow{\$} \mathcal{A}(g^a, g^b, g^c, T) \mid T \xleftarrow{\$} \mathbb{G} \wedge a, b, c \xleftarrow{\$} \mathbb{Z}_p^*] \end{vmatrix}$$

We will assume that $Adv_{\mathcal{A}}^{3\text{-}DDH}(k)$ is negligible for all PPT algorithms $\mathcal{A}$.

Our scheme is easily adapted to work in the more general setting of prime-order groups $(\mathbb{G}_1, \mathbb{G}_2, \mathbb{G}_T)$ with a pairing $e : \mathbb{G}_1 \times \mathbb{G}_2 \to \mathbb{G}_T$ (instantiable from ordinary elliptic curve unlike the symmetric configuration that requires supersingular curves), in which case we need to use the obvious variant of the above hardness assumption. We also require a hash function H drawn from a family of collision resistant hash functions.

Definition 7. *A hash function $H \xleftarrow{\$} \mathcal{H}(k)$ is* collision resistant *if for all PPT algorithms $\mathcal{A}$ the advantage*

$$Adv_{\mathcal{A}}^{CR}(k) = Pr[H(x) = H(y) \wedge x \neq y \mid (x,y) \xleftarrow{\$} \mathcal{A}(1^k, H) \wedge H \xleftarrow{\$} \mathcal{H}(k)]$$

is negligible as a function of the security parameter.

Our scheme is an extension of the chosen-ciphertext secure IBE obtained by applying ideas from Boyen, Mei and Waters [9] to the 2-level hierarchical extension of the Waters IBE.

Setup($1^k, n$): Let $(\mathbb{G}, \mathbb{G}_T)$ be bilinear map groups of order $p > 2^k$ and let g be a generator for $\mathbb{G}$. Set $g_1 = g^\gamma$, for a random $\gamma \xleftarrow{\$} \mathbb{Z}_p^*$, and pick a group element $g_2 \xleftarrow{\$} \mathbb{G}$ and vectors $(u', u_1, \ldots, u_n), (v', v_1, \ldots, v_n) \xleftarrow{\$} \mathbb{G}^{n+1}$. We note that these vectors define the hash functions

$$F_u(\mathsf{ID}) = u' \prod_{i=1}^{n} u_j^{i_j} \qquad \text{and} \qquad F_v(w) = v' \prod_{i=1}^{n} v_j^{w_j}$$

where $\mathsf{ID} = i_1 i_2 \ldots i_n$ and $w = w_1 w_2 \ldots w_n$. We also select a collision-resistant hash function $H : \{0,1\}^* \to \{0,1\}^n$. The master public key is

$$mpk \leftarrow (g, g_1, g_2, u', u_1, \ldots, u_n, v', v_1, \ldots, v_n)$$

and the master secret[1] is $msk \leftarrow g_2^\gamma$.

Extract(mpk, γ, ID): Pick $r \xleftarrow{\$} \mathbb{Z}_p^*$ and return $d_{\mathsf{ID}} \leftarrow (d_1, d_2) = (g_2^\gamma \cdot F_u(\mathsf{ID})^r, g^r)$.

SetSec(mpk): Return a randomly chosen secret value $x_{\mathsf{ID}} \xleftarrow{\$} \mathbb{Z}_p^*$.

SetPub(x_{ID}, mpk): Return $pk_{\mathsf{ID}} \leftarrow (X, Y) = (g^{x_{\mathsf{ID}}}, g_1^{x_{\mathsf{ID}}})$.

SetPriv($x_{\mathsf{ID}}, d_{\mathsf{ID}}, mpk$): Parse d_{ID} into (d_1, d_2), choose $r' \xleftarrow{\$} \mathbb{Z}_p^*$ and set the private key to

$$sk_{\mathsf{ID}} \leftarrow (s_1, s_2) = (d_1^{x_{\mathsf{ID}}} \cdot F_u(\mathsf{ID})^{r'}, d_2^{x_{\mathsf{ID}}} \cdot g^{r'}) = (g_2^{\gamma x_{\mathsf{ID}}} \cdot F_u(\mathsf{ID})^t, g^t)$$

with $t = r x_{\mathsf{ID}} + r'$.

Encrypt($m, pk_{\mathsf{ID}}, \mathsf{ID}, mpk$): To encrypt $m \in \mathbb{G}_T$, parse pk_{ID} as (X, Y), then check that it has the right shape (i.e. that $e(X, g_1)/e(g, Y) = 1_{\mathbb{G}_T}$). If so, choose $s \xleftarrow{\$} \mathbb{Z}_p^*$ and compute

$$C = (C_0, C_1, C_2, C_3) \leftarrow \left(m \cdot e(Y, g_2)^s, g^s, F_u(\mathsf{ID})^s, F_v(w)^s \right)$$

where $w \leftarrow H(C_0, C_1, C_2, \mathsf{ID}, pk_{\mathsf{ID}})$.

---

[1] In order to ensure security against Type II attacks according to definition 2, the discrete logarithms of elements $g_2, u', u_1, \ldots, u_n, v', v_1, \ldots, v_n$ w.r.t. the base g are not part of the master secret and should be deleted after key generation by the KGC.

Decrypt$(C, sk_{\mathsf{ID}}, mpk)$: Parse C as (C_0, C_1, C_2, C_3) and the private key sk_{ID} as (s_1, s_2). Check that

$$e(C_1, F_u(\mathsf{ID}) \cdot F_v(w)) = e(g, C_2 \cdot C_3)$$

where $w \leftarrow H(C_0, C_1, C_2, \mathsf{ID}, pk_{\mathsf{ID}})$, and reject C if those conditions do not hold. Otherwise, return

$$m \leftarrow C_0 \cdot \frac{e(C_2, s_2)}{e(C_1, s_1)}$$

To check the completeness, we note that private keys (s_1, s_2) satisfy

$$e(g, s_1) = e(Y, g_2) \cdot e(F_u(\mathsf{ID}), s_2) \qquad \text{and so} \qquad e(C_1, s_1) = e(Y, g_2)^s \cdot e(C_2, s_2).$$

To speed up the decryption algorithm using ideas from [23], we observe that the receiver can randomly choose $\alpha \xleftarrow{\$} \mathbb{Z}_p^*$ and directly return

$$m = C_0 \cdot \frac{e(C_2, s_2 \cdot g^\alpha) \cdot e(C_3, g^\alpha)}{e(C_1, s_1 \cdot F_u(\mathsf{ID})^\alpha \cdot F_v(w)^\alpha)}$$

which is the actual plaintext if C was properly encrypted and a random element of $\mathbb{G}_T$ otherwise. The well-formedness of C is thus implicitly checked and a product of three pairings suffices to decipher the message. This is sufficient to satisfy our security models; however, it should be noted that this system has the disadvantage of outputting a random message when presented with an invalid ciphertext. This may be a problem in some applications. In the same way, the public key validation can be made implicit at encryption: given $pk_{\mathsf{ID}} = (X, Y)$, the sender picks $\beta \xleftarrow{\$} \mathbb{Z}_p^*$ and computes $C_0 = m \cdot e(Y, g_2^s \cdot g^{s\beta})/e(X, g_1^{s\beta})$ which actually encrypts m whenever pk_{ID} has the correct shape and results in an invalid ciphertext otherwise.

We have the following security results for this concrete scheme:

Theorem 2. *Suppose $\mathcal{A}$ is a Strong Type I adversary that runs in time t, makes at most q_d decryption queries, q_{ppk} partial private key queries, and q_{pk} private key queries. Then there exists*

- *an adversary $\mathcal{A}'$ against the 3-DDH problem that has advantage $Adv_{\mathcal{A}'}^{3\text{-}DDH}(k)$ and runs in time $O(t) + O(\epsilon^{-2} \ln \delta^{-1})$ for sufficiently small ϵ and δ, and*
- *an adversary $\mathcal{A}''$ against the collision resistance of the hash function H that runs in time $O(t)$ and has advantage $Adv_{\mathcal{A}''}^{CR}(k)$*

such that the advantage of $\mathcal{A}$ is bounded by

$$Adv_{\mathcal{A}}^{CL\text{-}CCA\text{-}I}(k) < 8(q_{ppk} + q_{pk})q_d(n+1)^2 \cdot (8 \cdot Adv_{\mathcal{A}'}^{3\text{-}DDH}(k) + \delta) + Adv_{\mathcal{A}''}^{CR}(k).$$

The proof of this theorem is given in the full version of the paper [14]; it uses ideas from [9,30]. Namely, the mapping F_v is chosen so as to have $F_v(w) = g_2^{J_v(w)} g^{K_v(w)}$, for certain functions J_v and K_v, in the simulation of the attack environment. Hence, for any valid ciphertext $C = (C_0, C_1, C_2, C_3)$, we have $C_1 = g^s$ and $C_3 = F_v(w)^s$, for some $s \in \mathbb{Z}_p^*$, and the simulator can extract

$$g_2^s = (C_3 / C_1^{K_v(w)})^{1/J_v(w)}$$

whenever $J_v(w) \neq 0 \bmod p$. Hence, the simulator can compute $e(Y, g_2)^s$ regardless of whether the public key $pk = (X, Y)$ was replaced or not.

Theorem 3. *Suppose $\mathcal{A}$ is a Strong Type II adversary that runs in time t and makes at most q_d decryption queries and q_{pk} private key queries. Then there exists*

- *an adversary $\mathcal{A}'$ against the 3-DDH problem that has advantage $Adv_{\mathcal{A}'}^{3\text{-}DDH}(k)$ and runs in time $O(t) + O(\epsilon^{-2} \ln \delta^{-1})$ for sufficiently small ϵ and δ, and*
- *an adversary $\mathcal{A}''$ against the collision resistance of the hash function H that runs in time $O(t)$ and has advantage $Adv_{\mathcal{A}''}^{CR}(k)$*

such that the advantage of $\mathcal{A}$ is bounded by

$$Adv_{\mathcal{A}}^{CL\text{-}CCA\text{-}II}(k) < 8q_{pk}q_d(n+1)^2 \cdot (8 \cdot Adv_{\mathcal{A}'}^{3\text{-}DDH}(k) + \delta) + Adv_{\mathcal{A}''}^{CR}(k).$$

The proof of this theorem is given in the full version of the paper [14] and uses similar ideas to the proof of Theorem 2.

The reductions given in the proofs of Theorems 2 and 3 leave definite room for improvement since chosen-ciphertext security is achieved by applying the Boyen-Mei-Waters techniques [9] to a 2-level HIBE.

One solution to improve the reduction is to use the Canetti-Halevi-Katz [11] or Boneh-Katz [8] techniques that significantly lengthen ciphertexts and/or introduce additional assumptions for the security of the scheme. If we borrow ideas from [34] and generate the checksum value $C_3 = F(w)^s$ using a chameleon hash function [24] in instead of Waters' "hash", an interesting tradeoff can be achieved. In the above variant, a single element of $\mathbb{Z}_p^*$ (acting as random coins used to compute of the chameleon hash function) should be appended to ciphertexts and the degradation factor q_d is avoided in both reductions. Using a chameleon hash function built upon Pedersen's discrete-logarithm-based trapdoor commitment [28], the resulting combination does not imply any additional intractability assumption for the security of the final scheme.

Acknowledgements

The authors would like to thank Douglas Wikström for an initial conversation about whether it would be possible to construct strong certificateless encryption using Naor-Yung style techniques, and Eike Kiltz for several discussions on artificial aborts. The authors would also like to thank the PKC referees and David Galindo for their helpful comments. The second author acknowledges the Belgian National Fund for Scientific Research (F.R.S.-F.N.R.S.) for their support. This work was supported in part by the European Commission under Contract IST-2002-507932 ECRYPT.

References

1. Al-Riyami, S.S., Paterson, K.G.: Certificateless public key cryptography. In: Laih, C.-S. (ed.) ASIACRYPT 2003. LNCS, vol. 2894, pp. 452–473. Springer, Heidelberg (2003)
2. Au, M.H., Chen, J., Liu, J.K., Mu, Y., Wong, D.S., Yang, G.: Malicious KGC attack in certificateless cryptography. In: Proc. ACM Symposium on Information, Computer and Communications Security, ACM Press, New York (2007)
3. Baek, J., Safavi-Naini, R., Susilo, W.: Certificateless public key encryption without pairing. In: Zhou, J., López, J., Deng, R.H., Bao, F. (eds.) ISC 2005. LNCS, vol. 3650, pp. 134–148. Springer, Heidelberg (2005)
4. Bellare, M., Rogaway, P.: Random oracles are practical: A paradigm for designing efficient protocols. In: Proc. of the First ACM Conference on Computer and Communications Security, pp. 62–73 (1993)
5. Bellare, M., Yung, M.: Certifying permutations: Non-interactive zero-knowledge based on any trapdoor permutation. Journal of Cryptology 9(1), 149–166 (1996)
6. Bentahar, K., Farshim, P., Malone-Lee, J., Smart, N.P.: Generic constructions of identity-based and certificateless KEMs (2005), http://eprint.iacr.org/2005/058
7. Boneh, D., Franklin, M.: Identity based encryption from the Weil pairing. SIAM J. of Computing 32(3), 586–615 (2003)
8. Boneh, D., Katz, J.: Improved efficiency for CCA-secure cryptosystems built using identity-based encryption. In: Menezes, A. (ed.) CT-RSA 2005. LNCS, vol. 3376, pp. 87–103. Springer, Heidelberg (2005)
9. Boyen, X., Mei, Q., Waters, B.: Direct chosen ciphertext security from identity-based techniques. In: Proc. of the 12th ACM Conference on Computer and Communications Security, pp. 320–329 (2005)
10. Canetti, R., Halevi, S., Katz, J.: A forward-secure public-key encryption scheme. In: Biham, E. (ed.) EUROCRYPT 2003. LNCS, vol. 2656, pp. 255–271. Springer, Heidelberg (2003)
11. Canetti, R., Halevi, S., Katz, J.: Chosen-ciphertext security from identity-based encryption. In: Cachin, C., Camenisch, J.L. (eds.) EUROCRYPT 2004. LNCS, vol. 3027, pp. 207–222. Springer, Heidelberg (2004)
12. Cheng, Z., Comley, R.: Efficient certificateless public key encryption (2005), http://eprint.iacr.org/2005/012/
13. Dent, A.W.: A survey of certificateless encryption schemes and security models (2006), http://eprint.iacr.org/2006/211
14. Dent, A.W., Libert, B., Paterson, K.G.: Certificateless encryption schemes strongly secure in the standard model (2007), http://eprint.iacr.org/2007/121
15. Dodis, Y., Katz, J.: Chosen-ciphertext security of multiple encryption. In: Kilian, J. (ed.) TCC 2005. LNCS, vol. 3378, pp. 188–209. Springer, Heidelberg (2005)
16. Feige, U., Lapidot, D., Shamir, A.: Multiple noninteractive zero knowledge proofs under general assumptions. SAIM Journal on Computing 29(1), 1–28 (1999)
17. Fujisaki, E., Okamoto, T.: How to enhance the security of public-key encryption at minimal cost. In: Imai, H., Zheng, Y. (eds.) PKC 1999. LNCS, vol. 1560, pp. 53–68. Springer, Heidelberg (1999)
18. Galindo, D., Morillo, P., Ràfols, C.: Breaking Yum and Lee generic constructions of certificate-less and certificate-based encryption schemes. In: Atzeni, A.S., Lioy, A. (eds.) EuroPKI 2006. LNCS, vol. 4043, pp. 81–91. Springer, Heidelberg (2006)

19. Gentry, C.: Certificate-based encryption and the certificate revocation problem. In: Biham, E. (ed.) EUROCRYPT 2003. LNCS, vol. 2656, pp. 272–293. Springer, Heidelberg (2003)

20. Hu, B.C., Wong, D.S., Zhang, Z., Deng, X.: Key replacement attack against a generic construction of certificateless signature. In: Batten, L.M., Safavi-Naini, R. (eds.) ACISP 2006. LNCS, vol. 4058, pp. 235–246. Springer, Heidelberg (2006)

21. Huang, Q., Wong, D.S.: Generic certificateless encryption in the standard model. In: Miyaji, A., Kikuchi, H., Rannenberg, K. (eds.) IWSEC 2007. LNCS, vol. 4752, pp. 278–291. Springer, Heidelberg (2007)

22. Huang, X., Susilo, W., Mu, Y., Zhang, F.: On the security of certificateless signature schemes from Asiacrypt 2003. In: Desmedt, Y.G., Wang, H., Mu, Y., Li, Y. (eds.) CANS 2005. LNCS, vol. 3810, pp. 13–25. Springer, Heidelberg (2005)

23. Kiltz, E., Galindo, D.: Direct chosen-ciphertext secure identity-based key encapsulation without random oracles. In: Batten, L.M., Safavi-Naini, R. (eds.) ACISP 2006. LNCS, vol. 4058, pp. 336–347. Springer, Heidelberg (2006)

24. Krawczyk, H., Rabin, T.: Chameleon signatures. In: the Proceedings of the Network and Distributed Systems Symposium (NDSS 2000), pp. 143–154 (2000)

25. Libert, B., Quisquater, J.-J.: On constructing certificateless cryptosystems from identity based encryption. In: Yung, M., Dodis, Y., Kiayias, A., Malkin, T.G. (eds.) PKC 2006. LNCS, vol. 3958, pp. 474–490. Springer, Heidelberg (2006)

26. Liu, J.K., Au, M.H., Susilo, W.: Self-generated-certificate public key cryptography and certificateless signature/encryption scheme in the standard model. In: Proc. ACM Symposium on Information, Computer and Communications Security, ACM Press, New York (2007)

27. Naor, M., Yung, M.: Public-key cryptosystems provably secure against chosen ciphertext attacks. In: Proc. 22nd Symposium on the Theory of Computing, STOC 1990, pp. 427–437. ACM Press, New York (1990)

28. Pedersen, T.: Non-interactive and information-theoretic secure verifiable secret sharing. In: Feigenbaum, J. (ed.) CRYPTO 1991. LNCS, vol. 576, pp. 129–140. Springer, Heidelberg (1992)

29. Sahai, A.: Non-malleable non-interactive zero knowledge and adaptive chosen-ciphertext security. In: 40th Annual Symposium on Foundations of Computer Science, FOCS 1999, pp. 543–553. IEEE Computer Society Press, Los Alamitos (1999)

30. Waters, B.: Efficient identity-based encryption without random oracles. In: Cramer, R.J.F. (ed.) EUROCRYPT 2005. LNCS, vol. 3494, pp. 114–127. Springer, Heidelberg (2005)

31. Yum, D.H., Lee, P.J.: Generic construction of certificateless encryption. In: Laganà, A., Gavrilova, M.L., Kumar, V., Mun, Y., Tan, C.J.K., Gervasi, O. (eds.) ICCSA 2004. LNCS, vol. 3043, pp. 802–811. Springer, Heidelberg (2004)

32. Yum, D.H., Lee, P.J.: Generic construction of certificateless signature. In: Wang, H., Pieprzyk, J., Varadharajan, V. (eds.) ACISP 2004. LNCS, vol. 3108, pp. 200–211. Springer, Heidelberg (2004)

33. Yum, D.H., Lee, P.J.: Identity-based cryptography in public key management. In: Katsikas, S.K., Gritzalis, S., Lopez, J. (eds.) EuroPKI 2004. LNCS, vol. 3093, pp. 71–84. Springer, Heidelberg (2004)

34. Zhang, R.: Tweaking TBE/IBE to PKE transforms with chameleon hash functions. In: Katz, J., Yung, M. (eds.) ACNS 2007. LNCS, vol. 4521, pp. 323–339. Springer, Heidelberg (2007)

35. Zhang, Z., Wong, D.S., Xu, J., Feng, D.: Certificateless public-key signature: Security model and efficient construction. In: Zhou, J., Yung, M., Bao, F. (eds.) ACNS 2006. LNCS, vol. 3989, pp. 293–308. Springer, Heidelberg (2006)

Unidirectional Chosen-Ciphertext Secure Proxy Re-encryption

Benoît Libert[1] and Damien Vergnaud[2]

[1] UCL Crypto Group
Place du Levant, 3
1348 Louvain-la-Neuve
Belgium
[2] École Normale Supérieure – C.N.R.S. – I.N.R.I.A.
Département d'informatique, 45 rue d'Ulm
75230 Paris CEDEX 05
France

Abstract. In 1998, Blaze, Bleumer, and Strauss proposed a cryptographic primitive called *proxy re-encryption*, in which a proxy transforms – without seeing the corresponding plaintext – a ciphertext computed under Alice's public key into one that can be opened using Bob's secret key. Recently, an appropriate definition of chosen-ciphertext security and a construction fitting this model were put forth by Canetti and Hohenberger. Their system is *bidirectional*: the information released to divert ciphertexts from Alice to Bob can also be used to translate ciphertexts in the opposite direction. In this paper, we present the first construction of *unidirectional* proxy re-encryption scheme with chosen-ciphertext security in the standard model (i.e. without relying on the random oracle idealization), which solves a problem left open at CCS'07. Our construction is efficient and requires a reasonable complexity assumption in bilinear map groups. Like the Canetti-Hohenberger scheme, it ensures security according to a relaxed definition of chosen-ciphertext introduced by Canetti, Krawczyk and Nielsen.

Keywords: proxy re-encryption, unidirectionality, chosen-ciphertext security, standard model.

1 Introduction

The concept of proxy re-encryption (PRE) dates back to the work of Blaze, Bleumer, and Strauss in 1998 [5]. The goal of such systems is to securely enable the re-encryption of ciphertexts from one key to another, without relying on trusted parties. Recently, Canetti and Hohenberger [12] described a construction of proxy re-encryption providing chosen-ciphertext security according to an appropriate definition of the latter notion for PRE systems. Their construction is *bidirectional*: the information to translate ciphertexts from Alice to Bob can also be used to translate from Bob to Alice. This paper answers the question of how to secure unidirectional proxy re-encryption schemes against chosen-ciphertext attacks – at least in the sense of a natural extension of the Canetti-Hohenberger definition to the unidirectional case – while keeping them efficient.

R. Cramer (Ed.): PKC 2008, LNCS 4939, pp. 360–379, 2008.

BACKGROUND. In a PRE scheme, a proxy is given some information which allows turning a ciphertext encrypted under a given public key into one that is encrypted under a different key. A naive way for Alice to have a proxy implementing such a mechanism is to simply store her private key at the proxy: when a ciphertext arrives for Alice, the proxy decrypts it using the stored secret key and re-encrypts the plaintext using Bob's public key. The obvious problem with this strategy is that the proxy learns the plaintext and Alice's secret key.

In 1998, Blaze, Bleumer and Strauss [5] (whose work is sometimes dubbed BBS) proposed the first proxy re-encryption scheme, where the plaintext and secret keys are kept hidden from the proxy. It is based on a simple modification of the ElGamal encryption scheme [17]: let $(\mathbb{G}, \cdot)$ be a group of prime order p and let g be a generator of $\mathbb{G}$; Alice and Bob publish the public keys $X = g^x$ and $Y = g^y$ (respectively) and keeps secret their discrete logarithms x and y. To send a message $m \in \mathbb{G}$ to Alice, a user picks uniformly at random an integer $r \in \mathbb{Z}_p$ and transmits the pair (C_1, C_2) where $C_1 = X^r$ and $C_2 = m \cdot g^r$. The proxy is given the re-encryption key $y/x \mod p$ to divert ciphertexts from Alice to Bob via computing $(C_1^{y/x}, C_2) = (Y^r, m \cdot g^r)$.

This scheme is efficient and semantically secure under the Decision Diffie-Hellman assumption in $\mathbb{G}$. It solves the above mentioned problem since the proxy is unable to learn the plaintext or secret keys x or y. Unfortunately, Blaze *et al.* pointed out an inherent limitation: the proxy key y/x also allows translating ciphertexts from Bob to Alice, which may be undesirable in some situations. They left open the problem to design a proxy re-encryption method without this restriction. Another shortcoming of their scheme is that the proxy and the delegatee can collude to expose the delegator's private key x given y/x and y.

In 2005, Ateniese, Fu, Green and Hohenberger [2,3] showed the first examples of *unidirectional* proxy re-encryption schemes based on bilinear maps. Moreover, they obtained the *master key security* property in that the proxy is unable to collude with delegatees in order to expose the delegator's secret. The constructions [2,3] are also efficient, semantically secure assuming the intractability of decisional variants of the Bilinear Diffie-Hellman problem [7].

These PRE schemes only ensure chosen-plaintext security, which seems definitely insufficient for many practical applications. Very recently, Canetti and Hohenberger [12] gave a definition of security against chosen ciphertext attacks for PRE schemes and described an efficient construction satisfying this definition. In their model, ciphertexts should remain indistinguishable even if the adversary has access to a re-encryption oracle (translating adversarially-chosen ciphertexts) and a decryption oracle (that "undoes" ciphertexts under certain rules). Their security analysis takes place in the standard model (without the random oracle heuristic [4]). Like the BBS scheme [5], their construction is *bidirectional* and they left as an open problem to come up with a chosen-ciphertext secure unidirectional scheme.

RELATED WORK. Many papers in the literature – the first one of which being [26] – consider applications where data encrypted under a public key pk_A should eventually be encrypted under a different key pk_B. In proxy encryption schemes

[22,15], a receiver Alice allows a delegatee Bob to decrypt ciphertexts intended to her with the help of a proxy by providing them with shares of her private key. This requires delegatees to store an additional secret for each new delegation. Dodis and Ivan [15] notably present efficient proxy encryption schemes based on RSA, the Decision Diffie-Hellman problem as well as in an identity-based setting [28,7] under bilinear-map-related assumptions.

Proxy re-encryption schemes are a special kind of proxy encryption schemes where delegatees only need to store their own decryption key. They are generally implemented in a very specific mathematical setting and find practical applications in secure e-mail forwarding or distributed storage systems (e.g. [2,3]).

From a theoretical point of view, the first positive obfuscation result for a complex cryptographic functionality was recently presented by Hohenberger, Rothblum, shelat and Vaikuntanathan [21]: they proved the existence of an efficient program obfuscator for a family of circuits implementing re-encryption.

In [19], Green and Ateniese studied the problem of identity-based PRE and proposed a unidirectional scheme that can reach chosen-ciphertext security. Their security results are presented only in the random oracle model. Besides, the recipient of a re-encrypted ciphertext needs to know who the original receiver was in order to decrypt a re-encryption.

OUR CONTRIBUTION. In spite of the recent advances, the *"holy grail for proxy re-encryption schemes – a unidirectional, key optimal, and CCA2 secure scheme – is not yet realized"* [20]. This paper aims at investigating this open issue.

We generalize Canetti and Hohenberger's work [12] and present the first construction of chosen-ciphertext secure *unidirectional* proxy re-encryption scheme in the standard model. Our system is efficient and requires a reasonable bilinear complexity assumption. It builds on the unidirectional scheme from [2,3] briefly recalled at the beginning of section 3. The technique used by Canetti-Hohenberger to acquire CCA-security does not directly apply to the latter scheme because, in a straightforward adaptation of [12] to [2], the validity of translated ciphertexts cannot be publicly checked. To overcome this difficulty, we need to modify (and actually randomize) the re-encryption algorithm of Ateniese *et al.* so as to render the validity of re-encrypted ciphertexts publicly verifiable.

Whenever Alice delegates some of her rights to another party, there is always the chance that she will either need or want to revoke those rights later on. In [2,3], Ateniese *et al.* designed another unidirectional PRE scheme that allows for temporary delegations: that is, a scheme where re-encryption keys can only be used during a restricted time interval. We construct such a scheme with temporary delegation and chosen-ciphertext security.

The paper is organized as follows: we recall the concept of unidirectional proxy re-encryption and its security model in section 2.1. We review the properties of bilinear maps and the intractability assumption that our scheme relies on in section 2.2. Section 3 describes the new scheme, gives the intuition behind its construction and a security proof. Section 4 finally shows an adaptation with temporary delegation.

2   Preliminaries

2.1   Model and Security Notions

This section first recalls the syntactic definition of unidirectional proxy re-encryption suggested by Ateniese *et al.* [2,3]. We then consider an appropriate definition of chosen-ciphertext security for unidirectional PRE schemes which is directly inferred from the one given by Canetti and Hohenberger [12] in the bidirectional case. Like [12], we consider security in the *replayable* CCA sense [13] where a harmless mauling of the challenge ciphertext is tolerated.

Definition 1. *A (single hop) unidirectional PRE scheme consists of a tuple of algorithms* (Global-setup, Keygen, ReKeygen, Enc_1, Enc_2, ReEnc, Dec_1, Dec_2)*:*

- Global-setup(λ) $\rightarrow$ par*: this algorithm is run by a trusted party that, on input of a security parameter λ, produces a set* par *of common public parameters to be used by all parties in the scheme.*
- Keygen(λ, par) $\rightarrow$ (sk, pk)*: on input of common public parameters* par *and a security parameter λ, all parties use this randomized algorithm to generate a private/public key pair (sk, pk).*
- ReKeygen(par, sk_i, pk_j) $\rightarrow$ R_{ij}*: given public parameters* par*, user i's private key sk_i and user j's public key pk_j, this (possibly randomized) algorithm outputs a key R_{ij} that allows re-encrypting second level ciphertexts intended to i into first level ciphertexts encrypted for j.*
- Enc_1(par, pk, m) $\rightarrow$ C*: on input of public parameters* par*, a receiver's public key pk and a plaintext m, this probabilistic algorithm outputs a first level ciphertext that cannot be re-encrypted for another party.*
- Enc_2(par, pk, m) $\rightarrow$ C*: given public parameters* par*, a receiver's public key pk and a plaintext m, this randomized algorithm outputs a second level ciphertext that can be re-encrypted into a first level ciphertext (intended to a possibly different receiver) using the appropriate re-encryption key.*
- ReEnc(par, R_{ij}, C) $\rightarrow$ C'*: this (possibly randomized) algorithm takes as input public parameters* par*, a re-encryption key R_{ij} and a second level ciphertext C encrypted under user i's public key. The output is a first level ciphertext C' re-encrypted for user j. In a single hop scheme, C' cannot be re-encrypted any further. If the well-formedness of C is publicly verifiable, the algorithm should output 'invalid' whenever C is ill-formed w.r.t. X_i.*
- Dec_1(par, sk, C) $\rightarrow$ m*: on input of a private key sk, a first level ciphertext C and system-wide parameters* par*, this algorithm outputs a message $m \in \{0,1\}^*$ or a distinguished message 'invalid'.*
- Dec_2(par, sk, C) $\rightarrow$ m*: given a private key sk, a second level ciphertext C and common public parameters* par*, this algorithm returns either a plaintext $m \in \{0,1\}^*$ or 'invalid'.*

Moreover, for any common public parameters par*, for any message $m \in \{0,1\}^*$ and any couple of private/public key pair (sk_i, pk_i), (sk_j, pk_j) these algorithms should satisfy the following conditions of correctness:*

$$\mathsf{Dec}_1(\mathsf{par}, sk_i, \mathsf{Enc}_1(\mathsf{par}, pk_i, m)) = m; \quad \mathsf{Dec}_2(\mathsf{par}, sk_i, \mathsf{Enc}_2(\mathsf{par}, pk_i, m)) = m;$$
$$\mathsf{Dec}_1(\mathsf{par}, sk_j, \mathsf{ReEnc}(\mathsf{par}, \mathsf{ReKeygen}(\mathsf{par}, sk_i, pk_j), \mathsf{Enc}_2(\mathsf{par}, pk_i, m))) = m.$$

To lighten notations, we will sometimes omit to explicitly write the set of common public parameters par, taken as input by all but one of the above algorithms.

CHOSEN-CIPHERTEXT SECURITY. The definition of chosen-ciphertext security that we consider is naturally inspired from the bidirectional case [12] which in turn extends ideas from Canetti, Krawczyk and Nielsen [13] to the proxy re-encryption setting. For traditional public key cryptosystems, in this relaxation of Rackoff and Simon's definition [27], an adversary who can simply turn a given ciphertext into another encryption of the same plaintext is *not* deemed successful. In the game-based security definition, the attacker is notably disallowed to ask for a decryption of a re-randomized version of the challenge ciphertext. This relaxed notion was argued in [13] to suffice for most practical applications.

Our definition considers a challenger that produces a number of public keys. As in [12], we do not allow the adversary to adaptively determine which parties will be compromised. On the other hand, we also allow her to adaptively query a re-encryption oracle and decryption oracles. A difference with [12] is that the adversary is directly provided with re-encryption keys that she is entitled to know (instead of leaving her adaptively request them as she likes). We also depart from [12], and rather follow [2,3], in that we let the target public key be determined by the challenger at the beginning of the game. Unlike [2,3], we allow the challenger to reveal re-encryption keys R_{ij} when j is corrupt for honest users i that differ from the target receiver. We insist that such an enhancement only makes sense for *single-hop* schemes like ours (as the adversary would trivially win the game if the scheme were multi-hop).

Definition 2. *A (single-hop) unidirectional PRE scheme is replayable chosen-ciphertext secure (RCCA) at level 2 if the probability*

$$\Pr[(pk^\star, sk^\star) \leftarrow \mathsf{Keygen}(\lambda), \{(pk_x, sk_x) \leftarrow \mathsf{Keygen}(\lambda)\}, \{(pk_h, sk_h) \leftarrow \mathsf{Keygen}(\lambda)\},$$
$$\{R_{x\star} \leftarrow \mathsf{ReKeygen}(sk_x, pk^\star)\},$$
$$\{R_{\star h} \leftarrow \mathsf{ReKeygen}(sk^\star, pk_h)\}, \{R_{h\star} \leftarrow \mathsf{ReKeygen}(sk_h, pk^\star)\},$$
$$\{R_{hx} \leftarrow \mathsf{ReKeygen}(sk_h, pk_x)\}, \{R_{xh} \leftarrow \mathsf{ReKeygen}(sk_x, pk_h)\},$$
$$\{R_{hh'} \leftarrow \mathsf{ReKeygen}(sk_h, pk_{h'})\}, \{R_{xx'} \leftarrow \mathsf{ReKeygen}(sk_x, pk_{x'})\},$$
$$(m_0, m_1, St) \leftarrow \mathcal{A}^{\mathcal{O}_{1\text{-}dec}, \mathcal{O}_{renc}}(pk^\star, \{(pk_x, sk_x)\}, \{pk_h\}, \{R_{x\star}\}, \{R_{h\star}\},$$
$$\{R_{\star h}\}, \{R_{xh}\}, \{R_{hx}\}, \{R_{hh'}\}, \{R_{xx'}\}),$$
$$d^\star \xleftarrow{R} \{0, 1\}, C^\star = \mathsf{Enc}_2(m_{d^\star}, pk^\star), d' \leftarrow \mathcal{A}^{\mathcal{O}_{1\text{-}dec}, \mathcal{O}_{renc}}(C^\star, St):$$
$$d' = d^\star]$$

is negligibly (as a function of the security parameter λ) close to $1/2$ for any PPT adversary $\mathcal{A}$. In our notation, St is a state information maintained by $\mathcal{A}$ while $(pk^\star, sk^\star)$ is the target user's key pair generated by the challenger that also chooses other keys for corrupt and honest parties. For other honest parties, keys are subscripted by h or h' and we subscript corrupt keys by x or x'. The adversary is given access to all re-encryption keys but those that would allow re-encrypting from the target user to a corrupt one. In the game, $\mathcal{A}$ is said to have advantage

ε *if this probability, taken over random choices of $\mathcal{A}$ and all oracles, is at least* $1/2 + \varepsilon$. *Oracles $\mathcal{O}_{1\text{-}dec}, \mathcal{O}_{renc}$ proceed as follows:*

Re-encryption $\mathcal{O}_{renc}$: *on input (pk_i, pk_j, C), where C is a second level ciphertext and pk_i, pk_j were produced by Keygen, this oracle responds with 'invalid' if C is not properly shaped w.r.t. pk_i. It returns a special symbol $\perp$ if pk_j is corrupt and $(pk_i, C) = (pk^\star, C^\star)$. Otherwise, the re-encrypted first level ciphertext $C' = \mathsf{ReEnc}(\mathsf{ReKeygen}(sk_i, pk_j), C)$ is returned to $\mathcal{A}$.*

First level decryption oracle $\mathcal{O}_{1\text{-}dec}$: *given a pair (pk, C), where C is a first level ciphertext and pk was produced by Keygen, this oracle returns 'invalid' if C is ill-formed w.r.t. pk. If the query occurs in the post-challenge phase (a.k.a. "guess" stage as opposed to the "find" stage), it outputs a special symbol $\perp$ if (pk, C) is a Derivative of the challenge pair $(pk^\star, C^\star)$. Otherwise, the plaintext $m = \mathsf{Dec}_1(sk, C)$ is revealed to $\mathcal{A}$. Derivatives of $(pk^\star, C^\star)$ are defined as follows.*

If C is a first level ciphertext and $pk = pk^\star$ or pk is another honest user, (pk, C) is a Derivative of $(pk^\star, C^\star)$ if $\mathsf{Dec}_1(sk, C) \in \{m_0, m_1\}$.

Explicitly providing the adversary with a second level decryption oracle is useless. Indeed, ciphertexts encrypted under public keys from $\{pk_h\}$ can be re-encrypted for corrupt users given the set $\{R_{hx}\}$. Besides, second level encryptions under $pk^\star$ can be translated for other honest users using $\{R_{\star h}\}$. The resulting first level ciphertext can then be queried for decryption at the first level.

Security of first level ciphertexts. The above definition provides adversaries with a second level ciphertext in the challenge phase. An orthogonal definition of security captures their inability to distinguish first level ciphertexts as well. For *single-hop* schemes, the adversary is granted access to *all* re-encryption keys in this definition. Since first level ciphertexts cannot be re-encrypted, there is indeed no reason to keep attackers from obtaining all honest-to-corrupt re-encryption keys. The re-encryption oracle thus becomes useless since all re-encryption keys are available to $\mathcal{A}$. For the same reason, a second level decryption oracle is also unnecessary. Finally, Derivatives of the challenge ciphertext are simply defined as encryptions of either m_0 or m_1 for the same target public key $pk^\star$. A unidirectional PRE scheme is said RCCA-secure at level 1 if it satisfies this notion.

Remark 1. As in [12], we assume a static corruption model. Proving security against adaptive corruptions turns out to be more challenging. In our model and the one of [12], the challenger generates public keys for all parties and allows the adversary to obtain private keys for some of them. This does not capture a scenario where adversaries generate public keys on behalf of corrupt parties (possibly non-uniformly or as a function of honest parties' public keys) themselves. We also leave open the problem of achieving security in such a setting.

Remark 2. A possible enhancement of definition 2 is to allow adversaries to adaptively choose the target user at the challenge phase within the set of honest players. After having selected a set of corrupt parties among n players at the beginning, the adversary receives a set of n public keys, private keys of corrupt users as well as corrupt-to-corrupt, corrupt-to-honest and honest-to-honest re-encryption keys. When she outputs messages (m_0, m_1) and the index $i^\star$ of a honest user in the challenge step, she obtains an encryption of $m_{d^\star}$ under $pk_{i^\star}$ together with all honest-to-corrupt re-encryption keys R_{ij} with $i \neq i^\star$.

In this setting, a second level decryption oracle is also superfluous for schemes (like ours) where second level ciphertexts can be publicly turned into first level encryptions of the same plaintext for the same receiver. The scheme that we describe remains secure in this model at the expense of a probability of failure for the simulator that has to foresee which honest user will be attacked with probability $O(1/n)$.

MASTER SECRET SECURITY. In [2], Ateniese *et al.* define another important security requirement for unidirectional PRE schemes. This notion, termed *master secret security*, demands that no coalition of dishonest delegatees be able to pool their re-encryption keys in order to expose the private key of their common delegator. More formally, the following probability should be negligible as a function of the security parameter λ.

$$\Pr[(pk^\star, sk^\star) \leftarrow \mathsf{Keygen}(\lambda), \ \{(pk_x, sk_x) \leftarrow \mathsf{Keygen}(\lambda)\},$$
$$\{R_{\star x} \leftarrow \mathsf{ReKeygen}(sk^\star, pk_x)\},$$
$$\{R_{x\star} \leftarrow \mathsf{ReKeygen}(sk_x, pk^\star)\},$$
$$\gamma \leftarrow A(pk^\star, \{(pk_x, sk_x)\}, \{R_{\star x}\}, \{R_{x\star}\})$$
$$: \gamma = sk^\star]$$

At first glance, this notion might seem too weak in that it does not consider colluding delegatees who would rather undertake to produce a new re-encryption key $R_{\star x'}$ that was not originally given and allows re-encrypting from the target user to another malicious party x'. As stressed in [2] however, *all* known unidirectional PRE schemes fail to satisfy such a stronger notion of security. It indeed remains an open problem to construct a scheme withstanding this kind of *transfer of delegation* attack.

The notion of RCCA security at the first level is easily seen to imply the master secret security and we will only discuss the former.

2.2   Bilinear Maps and Complexity Assumptions

Groups $(\mathbb{G}, \mathbb{G}_T)$ of prime order p are called *bilinear map groups* if there is a mapping $e : \mathbb{G} \times \mathbb{G} \to \mathbb{G}_T$ with the following properties:

1. bilinearity: $e(g^a, h^b) = e(g, h)^{ab}$ for any $(g, h) \in \mathbb{G} \times \mathbb{G}$ and $a, b \in \mathbb{Z}$;
2. efficient computability for any input pair;
3. non-degeneracy: $e(g, h) \neq 1_{\mathbb{G}_T}$ whenever $g, h \neq 1_{\mathbb{G}}$.

We shall assume the intractability of a variant of the Decision Bilinear Diffie-Hellman problem.

Definition 3. *The* 3-**Quotient Decision Bilinear Diffie-Hellman** *assumption (3-QDBDH) posits the hardness of distinguishing* $e(g, g)^{b/a}$ *from random given* $(g, g^a, g^{(a^2)}, g^{(a^3)}, g^b)$. *A distinguisher* $\mathcal{B}$ (t, ε)-*breaks the assumption if it runs in time t and*

$$\left| Pr[\mathcal{B}(g, g^a, g^{(a^2)}, g^{(a^3)}, g^b, e(g, g)^{b/a}) = 1 | a, b \xleftarrow{R} \mathbb{Z}_p^*] \right.$$
$$\left. - Pr[\mathcal{B}(g, g^a, g^{(a^2)}, g^{(a^3)}, g^b, e(g, g)^z) = 1 | a, b, z \xleftarrow{R} \mathbb{Z}_p^*] \right| \geq \varepsilon.$$

The 3-QDBDH problem is obviously not easier than the (q-DBDHI) problem [6] for $q \geq 3$, which is to recognize $e(g, g)^{1/a}$ given $(g, g^a, \ldots, g^{(a^q)}) \in \mathbb{G}^{q+1}$. Dodis and Yampolskiy showed that this problem was indeed hard in generic groups [16]. Their result thus implies the hardness of 3-QDBDH in generic groups.

Moreover, its intractability for any polynomial time algorithm can be classified among *mild* decisional assumptions (according to [11]) as its strength does not depend on the number of queries allowed to adversaries whatsoever.

2.3   One-Time Signatures

As an underlying tool for applying the Canetti-Halevi-Katz methodology [14], we need one-time signatures. Such a primitive consists of a triple of algorithms $\mathsf{Sig} = (\mathcal{G}, \mathcal{S}, \mathcal{V})$ such that, on input of a security parameter λ, $\mathcal{G}$ generates a one-time key pair (ssk, svk) while, for any message M, $\mathcal{V}(\sigma, svk, M)$ outputs 1 whenever $\sigma = \mathcal{S}(ssk, M)$ and 0 otherwise.

As in [14], we need strongly unforgeable one-time signatures, which means that no PPT adversary can create a new signature for a previously signed message (according to [1]).

Definition 4. $\mathsf{Sig} = (\mathcal{G}, \mathcal{S}, \mathcal{V})$ *is a strong one-time signature if the probability*

$$Adv^{\mathsf{OTS}} = \Pr\big[\ (ssk, svk) \leftarrow \mathcal{G}(\lambda); (M, St) \leftarrow \mathcal{F}(svk);$$
$$\sigma \leftarrow \mathcal{S}(ssk, M); (M', \sigma') \leftarrow \mathcal{F}(M, \sigma, svk, St):$$
$$\mathcal{V}(\sigma', svk, M') = 1 \wedge (M', \sigma') \neq (M, \sigma) \ \big],$$

where St denotes the state information maintained by $\mathcal{F}$ *between stages, is negligible for any PPT forger* $\mathcal{F}$.

3   The Scheme

Our construction is inspired from the first unidirectional scheme suggested in [2,3] where second level ciphertexts $(C_1, C_2) = (X^r, m \cdot e(g, g)^r)$, that are encrypted under the public key $X = g^x$, can be re-encrypted into first level ciphertexts $(e(C_1, R_{xy}), C_2) = (e(g, g)^{ry}, m \cdot e(g, g)^r)$ using the re-encryption key $R_{xy} = g^{y/x}$. Using his private key y s.t. $Y = g^y$, the receiver can then obtain the message.

The Canetti-Hohenberger method for achieving CCA-security borrows from [14,10,23] in that it appends to the ciphertext a checksum value consisting of an element of $\mathbb{G}$ raised to the random encryption exponent r. In the security proof, the simulator uses the publicly verifiable validity of ciphertexts in groups equipped with bilinear maps. Unfortunately, the same technique does not directly apply to secure the unidirectional PRE scheme of [2] against chosen-ciphertext attacks. The difficulty is that, after re-encryption, level 1 ciphertexts have one component in the target group $\mathbb{G}_T$ and pairings cannot be used any longer to check the equality of two discrete logarithms in groups $\mathbb{G}$ and $\mathbb{G}_T$. Therefore, the simulator cannot tell apart well-shaped level 1 ciphertexts from invalid ones.

The above technical issue is addressed by having the proxy replace C_1 with a pair $(C_1', C_1'') = (R_{xy}^{1/t}, C_1^t) = (g^{y/(tx)}, X^{rt})$, for a randomly chosen "blinding exponent" $t \xleftarrow{R} \mathbb{Z}_p^*$ that hides the re-encryption key in C_1', in such a way that all ciphertext components but C_2 remain in $\mathbb{G}$. This still allows the second receiver holding y s.t. $Y = g^y$ to compute $m = C_2/e(C_1', C_1'')^{1/y}$. To retain the publicly verifiable well-formedness of re-encrypted ciphertexts however, the proxy needs to include X^t in the ciphertext so as to prove the consistency of the encryption exponent r w.r.t. the checksum value.

Of course, since the re-encryption algorithm is probabilistic, many first level ciphertexts may correspond to the same second level one. For this reason, we need to tolerate a harmless form of malleability (akin to those accepted as reasonable in [1,13,29]) of ciphertexts at level 1.

3.1   Description

Our system is reminiscent of the public key cryptosystem obtained by applying the Canetti-Halevi-Katz transform [14] to the second selective-ID secure identity-based encryption scheme described in [6][1].

Like the Canetti-Hohenberger construction [12], the present scheme uses a strongly unforgeable one-time signature to tie several ciphertext components altogether and offer a safeguard against chosen-ciphertext attacks in the fashion of Canetti, Halevi and Katz [14]. For simplicity, the description below assumes that verification keys of the one-time signature are encoded as elements from $\mathbb{Z}_p^*$. In practice, such verification keys are typically much longer than $|p|$ and a collision-resistant hash function should be applied to map them onto $\mathbb{Z}_p^*$.

Global-setup(λ): given a security parameter λ, choose bilinear map groups $(\mathbb{G}, \mathbb{G}_T)$ of prime order $p > 2^\lambda$, generators $g, u, v \xleftarrow{R} \mathbb{G}$ and a strongly unforgeable one-time signature scheme $\mathsf{Sig} = (\mathcal{G}, \mathcal{S}, \mathcal{V})$. The global parameters are

$$\mathsf{par} := \{\mathbb{G}, \mathbb{G}_T, g, u, v, \mathsf{Sig}\}.$$

Keygen(λ): user i sets his public key as $X_i = g^{x_i}$ for a random $x_i \xleftarrow{R} \mathbb{Z}_p^*$.

---

[1] It was actually shown in [24] that, although the security of the underlying IBE scheme relies on a rather strong assumption, a weaker assumption such as the one considered here was sufficient to prove the security of the resulting public key encryption scheme.

ReKeygen(x_i, X_j): given user i's private key x_i and user j's public key X_j, generate the unidirectional re-encryption key $R_{ij} = X_j^{1/x_i} = g^{x_j/x_i}$.

Enc$_1(m, X_i, \mathsf{par})$: to encrypt a message $m \in \mathbb{G}_T$ under the public key X_i at the first level, the sender proceeds as follows.

1. Select a one-time signature key pair $(ssk, svk) \xleftarrow{R} \mathcal{G}(\lambda)$ and set $C_1 = svk$.
2. Pick $r, t \xleftarrow{R} \mathbb{Z}_p^*$ and compute

$$C_2' = X_i^t \quad C_2'' = g^{1/t} \quad C_2''' = X_i^{rt} \quad C_3 = e(g,g)^r \cdot m \quad C_4 = (u^{svk} \cdot v)^r$$

3. Generate a one-time signature $\sigma = \mathcal{S}(ssk, (C_3, C_4))$ on (C_3, C_4).

The ciphertext is $C_i = (C_1, C_2', C_2'', C_2''', C_3, C_4, \sigma)$.

Enc$_2(m, X_i, \mathsf{par})$: to encrypt a message $m \in \mathbb{G}_T$ under the public key X_i at level 2, the sender conducts the following steps.

1. Select a one-time signature key pair $(ssk, svk) \xleftarrow{R} \mathcal{G}(\lambda)$ and set $C_1 = svk$.
2. Choose $r \xleftarrow{R} \mathbb{Z}_p^*$ and compute

$$C_2 = X_i^r \quad C_3 = e(g,g)^r \cdot m \quad C_4 = (u^{svk} \cdot v)^r$$

3. Generate a one-time signature $\sigma = \mathcal{S}(ssk, (C_3, C_4))$ on the pair (C_3, C_4).

The ciphertext is $C_i = (C_1, C_2, C_3, C_4, \sigma)$.

ReEnc(R_{ij}, C_i): on input of the re-encryption key $R_{ij} = g^{x_j/x_i}$ and a ciphertext $C_i = (C_1, C_2, C_3, C_4, \sigma)$, check the validity of the latter by testing the following conditions

$$e(C_2, u^{C_1} \cdot v) = e(X_i, C_4) \tag{1}$$
$$\mathcal{V}(C_1, \sigma, (C_3, C_4)) = 1. \tag{2}$$

If well-formed, C_i is re-encrypted by choosing $t \xleftarrow{R} \mathbb{Z}_p^*$ and computing

$$C_2' = X_i^t \quad C_2'' = R_{ij}^{1/t} = g^{(x_j/x_i)t^{-1}} \quad C_2''' = C_2^t = X_i^{rt}$$

The re-encrypted ciphertext is

$$C_j = (C_1, C_2', C_2'', C_2''', C_3, C_4, \sigma).$$

If ill-formed, C_i is declared 'invalid'.

Dec$_1(C_j, sk_j)$: the validity of a level 1 ciphertext C_j is checked by testing if

$$e(C_2', C_2'') = e(X_j, g) \tag{3}$$
$$e(C_2''', u^{C_1} \cdot v) = e(C_2', C_4) \tag{4}$$
$$\mathcal{V}(C_1, \sigma, (C_3, C_4)) = 1 \tag{5}$$

If relations (3)-(5) hold, the plaintext $m = C_3/e(C_2'', C_2''')^{1/x_j}$ is returned. Otherwise, the algorithm outputs 'invalid'.

Dec$_2$ (C_i, sk_i): if the level 2 ciphertext $C_i = (C_1, C_2, C_3, C_4, \sigma)$ satisfies relations (1)-(2), receiver i can obtain $m = C_3/e(C_2, g)^{1/x_i}$. The algorithm outputs 'invalid' otherwise.

Outputs of the re-encryption algorithm are perfectly indistinguishable from level 1 ciphertexts produced by the sender. Indeed, if $\tilde{t} = tx_i/x_j$, we can write

$$C_2' = X_i^t = X_j^{\tilde{t}} \qquad C_2'' = g^{(x_j/x_i)t^{-1}} = g^{\tilde{t}^{-1}} \qquad C_3''' = X_i^{rt} = X_j^{r\tilde{t}}.$$

As in the original scheme described in [2], second level ciphertexts can be publicly turned into first level ciphertexts encrypted for the same receiver if the identity element of $\mathbb{G}$ is used as a re-encryption key.

In the first level decryption algorithm, relations (3)-(5) guarantee that re-encrypted ciphertexts have the correct shape. Indeed, since $C_4 = (u^{C_1} \cdot v)^r$ for some unknown exponent $r \in \mathbb{Z}_p$, equality (4) implies that $C_2''' = C_2'^r$. From (3), it comes that $e(C_2'', C_2''') = e(X_j, g)^r$.

We finally note that first level ciphertexts can be publicly re-randomized by changing (C_2', C_2'', C_3'') into $(C_2'^s, C_2''^{1/s}, C_3'''^s)$ for a random $s \in \mathbb{Z}_p^*$. However, the pairing value $e(C_2'', C_2''')$ remains constant and, re-randomizations of a given first level ciphertext are publicly detectable.

3.2   Security

For convenience, we will prove security under an equivalent formulation of the 3-QDBDH assumption.

Lemma 1. *The 3-QDBDH problem is equivalent to decide whether T equals $e(g, g)^{b/a^2}$ or a random value given $(g, g^{1/a}, g^a, g^{(a^2)}, g^b)$ as input.*

Proof. Given $(g, g^{1/a}, g^a, g^{(a^2)}, g^b)$, we can build a 3-QDBDH instance by setting $(y = g^{1/a}, y^A = g, y^{(A^2)} = g^a, y^{(A^3)} = g^{(a^2)}, y^B = g^b)$, which implicitly defines $A = a$ and $B = ab$. Then, we have $e(y, y)^{B/A} = e(g^{1/a}, g^{1/a})^{(ab)/a} = e(g, g)^{b/a^2}$. The converse implication is easily established and demonstrates the equivalence between both problems.   □

Theorem 1. *Assuming the strong unforgeability of the one-time signature, the scheme is RCCA-secure at level 2 under the 3-QDBDH assumption.*

Proof. Let $(A_{-1} = g^{1/a}, A_1 = g^a, A_2 = g^{(a^2)}, B = g^b, T)$ be a modified 3-QDBDH instance. We construct an algorithm $\mathcal{B}$ deciding whether $T = e(g, g)^{b/a^2}$ out of a successful RCCA adversary $\mathcal{A}$.

Before describing $\mathcal{B}$, we first define an event F_{OTS} and bound its probability to occur. Let $C^* = (svk^*, C_2^*, C_3^*, C_4^*, \sigma^*)$ denote the challenge ciphertext given to $\mathcal{A}$ in the game. Let F_{OTS} be the event that $\mathcal{A}$ issues a decryption query for a first level ciphertext $C = (svk^*, C_2', C_2'', C_2''', C_3, C_4, \sigma)$ or a re-encryption query $C = (svk^*, C_2, C_3, C_4, \sigma)$ where $(C_3, C_4, \sigma) \neq (C_3^*, C_4^*, \sigma^*)$ but $\mathcal{V}(\sigma, svk, (C_3, C_4)) = 1$. In the "find" stage, $\mathcal{A}$ has simply no information on

$svk^\star$. Hence, the probability of a pre-challenge occurrence of F_{OTS} does not exceed $q_O \cdot \delta$ if q_O is the overall number of oracle queries and δ denotes the maximal probability (which by assumption does not exceed $1/p$) that any one-time verification key svk is output by $\mathcal{G}$. In the "guess" stage, F_{OTS} clearly gives rise to an algorithm breaking the strong unforgeability of the one-time signature. Therefore, the probability $\Pr[F_{\mathsf{OTS}}] \leq q_O/p + Adv^{\mathsf{OTS}}$, where the second term accounts for the probability of definition 4, must be negligible by assumption.

We now proceed with the description of $\mathcal{B}$ that simply halts and outputs a random bit if F_{OTS} occurs. In a preparation phase, $\mathcal{B}$ generates a one-time signature key pair $(ssk^\star, svk^\star) \leftarrow \mathcal{G}(\lambda)$ and provides $\mathcal{A}$ with public parameters including $u = A_1^{\alpha_1}$ and $v = A_1^{-\alpha_1 svk^\star} \cdot A_2^{\alpha_2}$ for random $\alpha_1, \alpha_2 \xleftarrow{R} \mathbb{Z}_p^*$. Observe that u and v define a "hash function" $F(svk) = u^{svk} \cdot v = A_1^{\alpha_1(svk-svk^\star)} \cdot A_2^{\alpha_2}$. In the following, we call HU the set of honest parties, including user $i^\star$ that is assigned the target public key $pk^\star$, and CU the set of corrupt parties. Throughout the game, $\mathcal{A}$'s environment is simulated as follows.

- *Key generation*: public keys of honest users $i \in HU \backslash \{i^\star\}$ are defined as $X_i = A_1^{x_i} = g^{ax_i}$ for a randomly chosen $x_i \xleftarrow{R} \mathbb{Z}_p^*$. The target user's public key is set as $X_{i^\star} = A_2^{x_{i^\star}} = g^{(x_{i^\star}a^2)}$ with $x_{i^\star} \xleftarrow{R} \mathbb{Z}_p^*$. The key pair of a corrupt user $i \in CU$ is set as $(X_i = g^{x_i}, x_i)$, for a random $x_i \xleftarrow{R} \mathbb{Z}_p^*$, so that (X_i, x_i) can be given to $\mathcal{A}$. To generate re-encryption keys R_{ij} from player i to player j, $\mathcal{B}$ has to distinguish several situations:
  - If $i \in CU$, $\mathcal{B}$ knows $sk_i = x_i$. Given X_j, it simply outputs X_j^{1/x_i}.
  - If $i \in HU \backslash \{i^\star\}$ and $j = i^\star$, $\mathcal{B}$ returns $R_{ii^\star} = A_1^{x_{i^\star}/x_i} = g^{x_{i^\star}a^2/(ax_i)}$ which is a valid re-encryption key.
  - If $i = i^\star$ and $j \in HU \backslash \{i^\star\}$, $\mathcal{B}$ responds with $R_{i^\star j} = A_{-1}^{x_i/x_{i^\star}} = g^{(ax_i/(x_{i^\star}a^2))}$ that has also the correct distribution.
  - If $i, j \in HU \backslash \{i^\star\}$, $\mathcal{B}$ returns $R_{ij} = g^{x_j/x_i} = g^{(ax_j)/(ax_i)}$.
  - If $i \in HU \backslash \{i^\star\}$ and $j \in CU$, $\mathcal{B}$ outputs $R_{ij} = A_{-1}^{x_j/x_i} = g^{x_j/(ax_i)}$ which is also computable.

- *Re-encryption* queries: when facing a re-encryption query from user i to user j for a second level ciphertext $C_i = (C_1, C_2, C_3, C_4, \sigma)$, $\mathcal{B}$ returns 'invalid' if relations (1)-(2) are not satisfied.
  - If $i \neq i^\star$ or if $i = i^\star$ and $j \in HU \backslash \{i^\star\}$, $\mathcal{B}$ simply re-encrypts using the re-encryption key R_{ij} which is available in either case.
  - If $i = i^\star$ and $j \in CU$,
    · If $C_1 = svk^\star$, $\mathcal{B}$ is faced with an occurrence of F_{OTS} and halts. Indeed, re-encryptions of the challenge ciphertext towards corrupt users are disallowed in the "guess" stage. Therefore, $(C_3, C_4, \sigma) \neq (C_3^\star, C_4^\star, \sigma^\star)$ since we would have $C_2 \neq C_2^\star$ and $i \neq i^\star$ if $(C_3, C_4, \sigma) = (C_3^\star, C_4^\star, \sigma^\star)$.
    · We are thus left with the case $C_1 \neq svk^\star$, $i = i^\star$ and $j \in CU$. Given

$C_2^{1/x_{i\star}} = A_2^r$, from $C_4 = F(svk)^r = (A_1^{\alpha_1(svk-svk^\star)} \cdot A_2^{\alpha_2})^r$, $\mathcal{B}$ can compute

$$A_1^r = (g^a)^r = \left(\frac{C_4}{C_2^{\alpha_2/x_{i\star}}} \right)^{\frac{1}{\alpha_1(svk-svk^\star)}} . \qquad (6)$$

Knowing g^{ar} and user j's private key x_j, $\mathcal{B}$ picks $t \xleftarrow{R} \mathbb{Z}_p^*$ to compute

$$C_2' = A_1^t = g^{at} \qquad C_2'' = A_{-1}^{x_j/t} = (g^{1/a})^{x_j/t} \qquad C_2''' = (A_1^r)^t = (g^{ar})^t$$

and return $C_j = (C_1, C_2', C_2'', C_2''', C_3, C_4, \sigma)$ which has the proper distribution. Indeed, if we set $\tilde{t} = at/x_j$, we have $C_2' = X_j^{\tilde{t}}$, $C_2'' = g^{1/\tilde{t}}$ and $C_2''' = X_j^{r\tilde{t}}$.

- *First level decryption* queries: when the decryption of a first level ciphertext $C_j = (C_1, C_2', C_2'', C_2''', C_3, C_4, \sigma)$ is queried under a public key X_j, $\mathcal{B}$ returns 'invalid' if relations (3)-(5) do not hold. We assume that $j \in HU$ since $\mathcal{B}$ can decrypt using the known private key otherwise. Let us first assume that $C_1 = C_1^\star = svk^\star$. If $(C_3, C_4, \sigma) \neq (C_3^\star, C_4^\star, \sigma^\star)$, $\mathcal{B}$ is presented with an occurrence of F_{OTS} and halts. If $(C_3, C_4, \sigma) = (C_3^\star, C_4^\star, \sigma^\star)$, $\mathcal{B}$ outputs $\perp$ which deems C_j as a Derivative of the challenge pair $(C^\star, X_{i\star})$. Indeed, it must be the case that $e(C_2'', C_2''') = e(g, X_j)^r$ for the same underlying exponent r as in the challenge phase. We now assume $C_1 \neq svk^\star$.

  - If $j \in HU \backslash \{i^\star\}$, $X_j = g^{ax_j}$ for a known $x_j \in \mathbb{Z}_p^*$. The validity of the ciphertext ensures that $e(C_2'', C_2''') = e(X_j, g)^r = e(g, g)^{arx_j}$ and $C_4 = F(svk)^r = g^{\alpha_1 ar(svk-svk^\star)} \cdot g^{a^2 r\alpha_2}$ for some $r \in \mathbb{Z}_p$. Therefore,

  $$e(C_4, A_{-1}) = e(C_4, g^{1/a}) = e(g, g)^{\alpha_1 r(svk-svk^\star)} \cdot e(g, g)^{ar\alpha_2} \qquad (7)$$

  and

  $$e(g, g)^r = \left(\frac{e(C_4, A_{-1})}{e(C_2'', C_2''')^{\alpha_2/x_j}} \right)^{\frac{1}{\alpha_1(svk-svk^\star)}} \qquad (8)$$

  reveals the plaintext m since $svk \neq svk^\star$.

  - If $j = i^\star$, we have $X_j = g^{(x_{i\star} a^2)}$ for a known exponent $x_{i\star} \in \mathbb{Z}_p^*$. Since $e(C_2'', C_2''') = e(X_{i\star}, g)^r = e(g, g)^{a^2 rx_{i\star}}$ and

  $$e(C_4, g) = e(g, g)^{\alpha_1 ar(svk-svk^\star)} \cdot e(g, g)^{a^2 r\alpha_2},$$

  $\mathcal{B}$ can first obtain

  $$\gamma = e(g, g)^{ar} = \left(\frac{e(C_4, g)}{e(C_2'', C_2''')^{\alpha_2/x_{i\star}}} \right)^{\frac{1}{\alpha_1(svk-svk^\star)}} .$$

  Together with relation (7), γ in turn uncovers

  $$e(g, g)^r = \left(\frac{e(C_4, A_{-1})}{\gamma^{\alpha_2/x_{i\star}}} \right)^{\frac{1}{\alpha_1(svk-svk^\star)}}$$

  and the plaintext $m = C_3/e(g, g)^r$.

In the "guess" stage, $\mathcal{B}$ must check that m differs from messages m_0, m_1 involved in the challenge query. If $m \in \{m_0, m_1\}$, $\mathcal{B}$ returns $\perp$ according to the replayable CCA-security rules.

- *Challenge*: when she decides that the first phase is over, $\mathcal{A}$ chooses messages (m_0, m_1). At this stage, $\mathcal{B}$ flips a coin $d^\star \overset{R}{\leftarrow} \{0,1\}$ and sets the challenge ciphertext as

$$C_1^\star = svk^\star \quad C_2^\star = B^{x_{i^\star}} \quad C_3^\star = m_{d^\star} \cdot T \quad C_4^\star = B^{\alpha_2}$$

and $\sigma = \mathcal{S}(ssk^\star, (C_3, C_4))$.

Since $X_{i^\star} = A_2^{x_{i^\star}} = g^{x_{i^\star} a^2}$ and $B = g^b$, $C^\star$ is a valid encryption of $m_{d^\star}$ with the random exponent $r = b/a^2$ if $T = e(g,g)^{b/a^2}$. In contrast, if T is random in $\mathbb{G}_T$, $C^\star$ perfectly hides $m_{d^\star}$ and $\mathcal{A}$ cannot guess $d^\star$ with better probability than $1/2$. When $\mathcal{A}$ eventually outputs her result $d' \in \{0,1\}$, $\mathcal{B}$ decides that $T = e(g,g)^{b/a^2}$ if $d' = d^\star$ and that T is random otherwise. $\qquad\square$

Theorem 2. *Assuming the strong unforgeability of the one-time signature, the scheme is RCCA-secure at level 1 under the 3-QDBDH assumption.*

Proof. The proof is very similar to the one of theorem 1. Given a 3-QDBDH instance $(A_{-1} = g^{1/a}, A_1 = g^a, A_2 = g^{(a^2)}, B = g^b, T)$, we construct an algorithm $\mathcal{B}$ that decides if $T = e(g,g)^{b/a^2}$.

Before describing $\mathcal{B}$, we consider the same event F_{OTS} as in the proof of theorem 1 except that it can only arise during a decryption query (since there is no re-encryption oracle). Assuming the strong unforgeability of the one-time signature, such an event occurs with negligible probability as detailed in the proof of theorem 1. We can now describe our simulator $\mathcal{B}$ that simply halts and outputs a random bit if F_{OTS} ever occurs. Let also $C^\star = (C_1^\star, C_2'^\star, C_2''^\star, C_2'''^\star, C_3^\star, C_4^\star, \sigma^\star)$ denote the challenge ciphertext at the first level.

Algorithm $\mathcal{B}$ generates a one-time signature key pair $(ssk^\star, svk^\star) \leftarrow \mathcal{G}(\lambda)$ and the same public parameters as in theorem 1. Namely, it sets $u = A_1^{\alpha_1}$ and $v = A_1^{-\alpha_1 svk^\star} \cdot A_2^{\alpha_2}$ with $\alpha_1, \alpha_2 \overset{R}{\leftarrow} \mathbb{Z}_p^*$ so that $F(svk) = u^{svk} \cdot v = A_1^{\alpha_1(svk - svk^\star)} \cdot A_2^{\alpha_2}$. As in the proof of theorem 1, $i^\star$ identifies the target receiver. The attack environment is simulated as follows.

- *Key generation*: for corrupt users $i \in CU$ and almost all honest ones $i \in HU \backslash \{i^\star\}$, $\mathcal{B}$ sets $X_i = g^{x_i}$ for a random $x_i \overset{R}{\leftarrow} \mathbb{Z}_p^*$. The target user's public key is defined as $X_{i^\star} = A_1$. For corrupt users $i \in CU$, X_i and x_i are both revealed. All re-encryption keys are computable and given to $\mathcal{A}$. Namely, $R_{ij} = g^{x_j/x_i}$ if $i,j \neq i^\star$; $R_{i^\star j} = A_{-1}^{x_j}$ and $R_{ji^\star} = A_1^{1/x_j}$ for $j \neq i^\star$.

- *First level decryption* queries: when the decryption of a ciphertext $C_j = (C_1, C_2', C_2'', C_2''', C_3, C_4, \sigma)$ is queried for a public key X_j, $\mathcal{B}$ returns 'invalid' if relations (3)-(5) do not hold. We assume that $j = i^\star$ since $\mathcal{B}$ can decrypt using the known private key x_j otherwise. We have $C_2' = A_1^t$,

$C_2'' = g^{1/t}$, $C_2''' = A_1^{rt}$ for unknown exponents $r, t \in \mathbb{Z}_p^*$. Since $e(C_2'', C_2''') = e(g,g)^{ar}$ and

$$e(C_4, A_{-1}) = e(g,g)^{\alpha_1 r(svk - svk^*)} \cdot e(g,g)^{ar\alpha_2},$$

$\mathcal{B}$ can obtain
$$e(g,g)^r = \left(\frac{e(C_4, A_{-1})}{e(C_2'', C_2''')^{\alpha_2}} \right)^{\frac{1}{\alpha_1(svk - svk^*)}}$$

which reveals the plaintext $m = C_3/e(g,g)^r$ as long as $svk \neq svk^*$. In the event that $C_1 = svk^*$ in a post-challenge query,

- If $e(C_2'', C_2''') = e(C_2''^*, C_2'''^*)$, $\mathcal{B}$ returns $\perp$, meaning that C_j is simply a re-randomization (and thus a Derivative) of the challenge ciphertext.
- Otherwise, we necessarily have $(C_3^*, C_4^*, \sigma^*) \neq (C_3, C_4, \sigma)$, which is an occurrence of F_{OTS} and implies $\mathcal{B}$'s termination.

In the "guess" stage, $\mathcal{B}$ must ensure that m differs from messages m_0, m_1 of the challenge phase before answering the query.

- *Challenge*: when the first phase is over, $\mathcal{A}$ outputs messages (m_0, m_1) and $\mathcal{B}$ flips a bit $d^* \xleftarrow{R} \{0,1\}$. Then, it chooses $\mu \xleftarrow{R} \mathbb{Z}_p^*$ and sets

$$C_2'^* = A_2^\mu \quad C_2''^* = A_{-1}^{1/\mu} \quad C_2'''^* = B^\mu$$
$$C_1^* = svk^* \quad C_3^* = m_{d^*} \cdot T \quad C_4^* = B^{\alpha_2}$$

and $\sigma = \mathcal{S}(ssk^*, (C_3, C_4))$.

Since $X_{i^*} = A_1$ and $B = g^b$, C^* is a valid encryption of m_{d^*} with the random exponents $r = b/a^2$ and $t = a\mu$ whenever $T = e(g,g)^{b/a^2}$. When T is random, C^* perfectly hides m_{d^*} and $\mathcal{A}$ cannot guess d^* with better probability than $1/2$. Eventually, $\mathcal{B}$ bets that $T = e(g,g)^{b/a^2}$ if $\mathcal{A}$ correctly guesses d^* and that T is random otherwise. $\qquad \square$

3.3   Efficiency

The first level decryption algorithm can be optimized using ideas from [23,25]. Namely, verification tests (3)-(4) can be simultaneously achieved with high confidence by the receiver who can choose a random $\alpha \xleftarrow{R} \mathbb{Z}_p^*$ and test whether

$$\frac{e(C_2', C_2'' \cdot C_4^\alpha)}{e(C_2''', u^{svk} \cdot v)^\alpha} = e(g,g)^{x_j}.$$

Hence, computing a quotient of two pairings (which is faster than evaluating two independent pairings [18]) and two extra exponentiations suffice to check the validity of the ciphertext.

It could also be desirable to shorten ciphertexts that are significantly lengthened by one-time signatures and their public keys. To this end, ideas from Boneh and Katz [9] can be used as well as those of Boyen, Mei and Waters [10]. In the latter case, ciphertexts can be made fairly compact as components C_1 and σ

become unnecessary if the checksum value C_4 is computed using the Waters "hashing" technique [30] applied to a collision-resistant hash of C_3. This improvement in the ciphertext size unfortunately comes at the expense of a long public key (made of about 160 elements of $\mathbb{G}$ as in [30]) and a loose reduction.

4 A Scheme with Temporary Delegation

This section describes a variant of our scheme supporting temporary delegation. Like the temporary unidirectional PRE suggested in [2,3], it only allows the proxy to re-encrypt messages from A to B during a limited time period. If the scheme must be set up for T periods, we assume that a trusted server publishes randomly chosen elements $(h_1, \ldots, h_T) \in \mathbb{G}^T$ as global parameters. Alternatively, the server could publish a new value h_i that erases h_{i-1} at period i so as to keep short public parameters.

Global-setup(λ, T): is as in section 3 with the difference that additional random group elements $h_1, \ldots, h_T$ (where T is the number of time intervals that the scheme must be prepared for) are chosen. Global parameters are

$$\mathsf{par} := \{\mathbb{G}, \mathbb{G}_T, g, u, v, h_1, \ldots, h_T, \mathsf{Sig}\}.$$

Keygen(λ): user i's public key is set as $X_i = g^{x_i}$ for a random $x_i \xleftarrow{R} \mathbb{Z}_p^*$.

ReKeygen$(x_i, D_{(\ell,j)})$: when user j is willing to accept delegations during period $\ell \in \{1, \ldots, T\}$, he publishes a delegation acceptance value $D_{(\ell,j)} = h_\ell^{x_j}$. Given his private key x_i, user i then generates the temporary re-encryption key is $R_{ij\ell} = D_{(\ell,j)}^{1/x_i} = h_\ell^{x_j/x_i}$.

Enc$_1(m, X_i, \ell, \mathsf{par})$: to encrypt $m \in \mathbb{G}_T$ under the public key X_i at the first level during period $\ell \in \{1, \ldots, T\}$, the sender conducts the following steps.

1. Choose a one-time signature key pair $(ssk, svk) \xleftarrow{R} \mathcal{G}(\lambda)$; set $C_1 = svk$.
2. Pick $r, t \xleftarrow{R} \mathbb{Z}_p^*$ and compute

$$C_2' = X_i^t \quad C_2'' = h_\ell^{1/t} \quad C_2''' = X_i^{rt} \quad C_3 = e(g, h_\ell)^r \cdot m \qquad C_4 = (u^{svk} \cdot v)^r$$

3. Generate a one-time signature $\sigma = \mathcal{S}(ssk, (\ell, C_3, C_4))$ on (ℓ, C_3, C_4).

The ciphertext is $C_i = (\ell, C_1, C_2', C_2'', C_2''', C_3, C_4, \sigma)$.

Enc$_2(m, X_i, \ell, \mathsf{par})$: to encrypt $m \in \mathbb{G}_T$ under the public key X_i at level 2 during period ℓ, the sender does the following.

1. Pick a one-time signature key pair $(ssk, svk) \xleftarrow{R} \mathcal{G}(\lambda)$ and set $C_1 = svk$.
2. Choose $r \xleftarrow{R} \mathbb{Z}_p^*$ and compute

$$C_2 = X_i^r \qquad C_3 = e(g, h_\ell)^r \cdot m \qquad C_4 = (u^{svk} \cdot v)^r$$

3. Generate a one-time signature $\sigma = \mathcal{S}(ssk, (\ell, C_3, C_4))$ on (ℓ, C_3, C_4).

The ciphertext is $C_i = (\ell, C_1, C_2, C_3, C_4, \sigma)$.

ReEnc$(R_{ij\ell}, \ell, C_i)$: on input of the re-encryption key $R_{ij\ell} = h_\ell^{x_j/x_i}$ and a ciphertext $C_i = (C_1, C_2, C_3, C_4, \sigma)$, the validity of the latter can be checked exactly as in section 3 (i.e. conditions (1)-(2) must be satisfied). If ill-formed, C_i is declared 'invalid'. Otherwise, it can be re-encrypted by choosing $t \xleftarrow{R} \mathbb{Z}_p^*$ and computing

$$C_2' = X_i^t \qquad C_2'' = R_{ij\ell}^{1/t} = h_\ell^{(x_j/x_i)t^{-1}} \qquad C_2''' = C_2^t = X_i^{rt}$$

The re-encrypted ciphertext is $C_j = \big(\ell, C_1, C_2', C_2'', C_2''', C_3, C_4, \sigma\big)$.

Dec$_1$ (C_j, sk_j): a first level ciphertext C_j is deemed valid if it satisfies similar conditions to (3)-(5) in the scheme of section 3. Namely, we must have

$$e(C_2', C_2'') = e(X_j, h_\ell) \tag{9}$$
$$e(C_2''', u^{C_1} \cdot v) = e(C_2', C_4) \tag{10}$$
$$\mathcal{V}(svk, \sigma, (\ell, C_3, C_4)) = 1 \tag{11}$$

If C_j is valid, the plaintext $m = C_3/e(C_2'', C_2''')^{1/x_j}$ is returned. Otherwise, the message 'invalid' is returned.

Dec$_2$ (C_i, sk_i): receiver i outputs 'invalid' if the second level ciphertext $C_i = (\ell, C_1, C_2, C_3, C_4, \sigma)$ is ill-formed. Otherwise, it outputs $m = C_3/e(C_2, h_\ell)^{1/x_i}$.

For such a scheme with temporary delegation, replayable chosen-ciphertext security can be defined by naturally extending definition 2. At the beginning of each time period, the attacker obtains all honest-to-honest, corrupt-to-corrupt and corrupt-to-honest re-encryption keys. At the end of a time interval, she also receives all honest-to-corrupt re-encryption keys if she did not choose to be challenged during that period. When she decides to enter the challenge phase at some period ℓ^*, she obtains a challenge ciphertext as well as honest-to-corrupt keys $R_{ij\ell^*}$ for $i \neq i^*$.

Throughout all periods, she can access a first level decryption oracle and a re-encryption oracle that uses the current re-encryption keys. As she obtains re-encryption keys in chronological order, it is reasonable to expect that queries are made in chronological order as well. Here, a second level decryption oracle is again useless since second level ciphertexts can be publicly "sent" to the first level while keeping the plaintext and the receiver unchanged.

With this security definition, we can prove the security of this scheme under a slightly stronger (but still reasonable) assumption than in section 3. This assumption, that we call 4-QDBDH, states that it dwells hard to recognize $e(g, g)^{b/a}$ given $(g^a, g^{(a^2)}, g^{(a^3)}, g^{(a^4)}, g^b)$. Again, this assumption is not stronger than the q-DBDHI assumption [6] for $q \geq 4$.

Theorem 3. *Assuming the strong unforgeability of the one-time signature, the scheme is RCCA-secure at both levels under the 4-QDBDH assumption.*

Proof. Detailed in the full version of the paper. □

5   Conclusions and Open Problems

We presented the first unidirectional proxy re-encryption scheme with chosen-ciphertext security in the standard model (i.e. without using the random oracle heuristic). Our construction is efficient and demands a reasonable intractability assumption in bilinear groups. In addition, we applied the same ideas to construct a chosen-ciphertext secure PRE scheme with temporary delegation.

Many open problems still remain. For instance, Canetti and Hohenberger suggested [12] to investigate the construction of a multi-hop unidirectional PRE system. They also mentioned the problem of securely obfuscating CCA-secure re-encryption or other key translation schemes. It would also be interesting to efficiently implement such primitives outside bilinear groups (the recent technique from [8] may be useful regarding this issue). Finally, as mentioned in the end of section 2.1, the design a scheme withstanding transfer of delegation attacks is another challenging task.

Acknowledgements

We are grateful to Jorge Villar for many useful comments and suggestions. We also thank anonymous PKC referees for their comments and Susan Hohenberger for helpful discussions on security models. The first author was supported by the Belgian National Fund for Scientific Research (F.R.S.-F.N.R.S.).

References

1. An, J.-H., Dodis, Y., Rabin, T.: On the security of joint signature and encryption. In: Knudsen, L.R. (ed.) EUROCRYPT 2002. LNCS, vol. 2332, pp. 83–107. Springer, Heidelberg (2002)
2. Ateniese, G., Fu, K., Green, M., Hohenberger, S.: Improved Proxy Re-Encryption Schemes with Applications to Secure Distributed Storage. In: NDSS (2005)
3. Ateniese, G., Fu, K., Green, M., Hohenberger, S.: Improved proxy re-encryption schemes with applications to secure distributed storage. ACM TISSEC 9(1), 1–30 (2006)
4. Bellare, M., Rogaway, P.: Random oracles are practical: A paradigm for designing efficient protocols. In: ACM CCS 1993, pp. 62–73. ACM Press, New York (1993)
5. Blaze, M., Bleumer, G., Strauss, M.: Divertible Protocols and Atomic Proxy Cryptography. In: Nyberg, K. (ed.) EUROCRYPT 1998. LNCS, vol. 1403, pp. 127–144. Springer, Heidelberg (1998)
6. Boneh, D., Boyen, X.: Efficient selective-ID secure identity based encryption without random oracles. In: Cachin, C., Camenisch, J.L. (eds.) EUROCRYPT 2004. LNCS, vol. 3027, pp. 223–238. Springer, Heidelberg (2004)
7. Boneh, D., Franklin, M.: Identity-based encryption from the Weil pairing. In: Kilian, J. (ed.) CRYPTO 2001. LNCS, vol. 2139, pp. 213–229. Springer, Heidelberg (2001)
8. Boneh, D., Gentry, C., Hamburg, M.: Space-Efficient Identity Based Encryption Without Pairings. In: FOCS 2007 (to appear, 2007)

9. Boneh, D., Katz, J.: Improved Efficiency for CCA-Secure Cryptosystems Built Using Identity-Based Encryption. In: Menezes, A. (ed.) CT-RSA 2005. LNCS, vol. 3376, pp. 87–103. Springer, Heidelberg (2005)

10. Boyen, X., Mei, Q., Waters, B.: Direct Chosen Ciphertext Security from Identity-Based Techniques. In: ACM CCS 2005, pp. 320–329. ACM Press, New York (2005)

11. Boyen, X., Waters, B.: Anonymous Hierarchical Identity-Based Encryption (Without Random Oracles). In: Dwork, C. (ed.) CRYPTO 2006. LNCS, vol. 4117, pp. 290–307. Springer, Heidelberg (2006)

12. Canetti, R., Hohenberger, S.: Chosen-Ciphertext Secure Proxy Re-Encryption. In: ACM CCS 2007, pp. 185–194. ACM Press, New York (2007)

13. Canetti, R., Krawczyk, H., Nielsen, J.B.: Relaxing Chosen-Ciphertext Security. In: Boneh, D. (ed.) CRYPTO 2003. LNCS, vol. 2729, pp. 565–582. Springer, Heidelberg (2003)

14. Canetti, R., Halevi, S., Katz, J.: Chosen-Ciphertext Security from Identity-Based Encryption. In: Cachin, C., Camenisch, J.L. (eds.) EUROCRYPT 2004. LNCS, vol. 3027, pp. 207–222. Springer, Heidelberg (2004)

15. Dodis, Y., Ivan, A.-A.: Proxy Cryptography Revisited. In: NDSS 2003 (2003)

16. Dodis, Y., Yampolskiy, A.: A Verifiable Random Function with Short Proofs and Keys. In: Vaudenay, S. (ed.) PKC 2005. LNCS, vol. 3386, pp. 416–431. Springer, Heidelberg (2005)

17. ElGamal, T.: A public key cryptosystem and a signature scheme based on discrete logarithms. In: Blakely, G.R., Chaum, D. (eds.) CRYPTO 1984. LNCS, vol. 196, pp. 10–18. Springer, Heidelberg (1985)

18. Granger, R., Smart, N.P.: On Computing Products of Pairings. Cryptology ePrint Archive, Report 2006/172 (2006)

19. Green, M., Ateniese, G.: Identity-Based Proxy Re-encryption. In: Katz, J., Yung, M. (eds.) ACNS 2007. LNCS, vol. 4521, pp. 288–306. Springer, Heidelberg (2007)

20. Hohenberger, S.: Advances in Signatures, Encryption, and E-Cash from Bilinear Groups. Ph.D. Thesis, MIT (May 2006)

21. Hohenberger, S., Rothblum, G.N., Shelat, A., Vaikuntanathan, V.: Securely Obfuscating Re-encryption. In: Vadhan, S.P. (ed.) TCC 2007. LNCS, vol. 4392, pp. 233–252. Springer, Heidelberg (2007)

22. Jakobsson, M.: On Quorum Controlled Asymmetric Proxy Re-encryption. In: Imai, H., Zheng, Y. (eds.) PKC 1999. LNCS, vol. 1560, pp. 112–121. Springer, Heidelberg (1999)

23. Kiltz, E.: Chosen-Ciphertext Security from Tag-Based Encryption. In: Halevi, S., Rabin, T. (eds.) TCC 2006. LNCS, vol. 3876, pp. 581–600. Springer, Heidelberg (2006)

24. Kiltz, E.: On the Limitations of the Spread of an IBE-to-PKE Transformation. In: Yung, M., Dodis, Y., Kiayias, A., Malkin, T.G. (eds.) PKC 2006. LNCS, vol. 3958, pp. 274–289. Springer, Heidelberg (2006)

25. Kiltz, E., Galindo, D.: Direct Chosen-Ciphertext Secure Identity-Based Key Encapsulation without Random Oracles. In: Batten, L.M., Safavi-Naini, R. (eds.) ACISP 2006. LNCS, vol. 4058, pp. 336–347. Springer, Heidelberg (2006)

26. Mambo, M., Okamoto, E.: Proxy Cryptosystems: Delegation of the Power to Decrypt Ciphertexts. IEICE Trans. Fund. Elect. Communications and CS, E80-A/1, 54–63 (1997)

27. Rackoff, C., Simon, D.: Non-interactive zero-knowledge proof of knowledge and chosen ciphertext attack. In: Feigenbaum, J. (ed.) CRYPTO 1991. LNCS, vol. 576, pp. 433–444. Springer, Heidelberg (1992)

28. Shamir, A.: Identity based cryptosystems and signature schemes. In: Blakely, G.R., Chaum, D. (eds.) CRYPTO 1984. LNCS, vol. 196, pp. 47–53. Springer, Heidelberg (1985)
29. Shoup, V.: A proposal for the ISO standard for public-key encryption (version 2.1). manuscript (2001), `http://shoup.net/`
30. Waters, B.: Efficient Identity-Based Encryption Without Random Oracles. In: Cramer, R.J.F. (ed.) EUROCRYPT 2005. LNCS, vol. 3494, pp. 114–127. Springer, Heidelberg (2005)

Public Key Broadcast Encryption with Low Number of Keys and Constant Decryption Time[*]

Yi-Ru Liu and Wen-Guey Tzeng

Department of Computer Science
National Chiao Tung University
Hsinchu, Taiwan 30050
wgtzeng@cs.nctu.edu.tw

Abstract. In this paper we propose three public key BE schemes that have efficient complexity measures. The first scheme, called the BE-PI scheme, has $O(r)$ header size, $O(1)$ public keys and $O(\log N)$ private keys per user, where r is the number of revoked users. This is the first public key BE scheme that has both public and private keys under $O(\log N)$ while the header size is $O(r)$. These complexity measures match those of efficient secret key BE schemes.

Our second scheme, called the PK-SD-PI scheme, has $O(r)$ header size, $O(1)$ public key and $O(\log^2 N)$ private keys per user. They are the same as those of the SD scheme. Nevertheless, the decryption time is remarkably $O(1)$. This is the first public key BE scheme that has $O(1)$ decryption time while other complexity measures are kept low. The third scheme, called, the PK-LSD-PI scheme, is constructed in the same way, but based on the LSD method. It has $O(r/\epsilon)$ ciphertext size and $O(\log^{1+\epsilon} N)$ private keys per user, where $0 < \epsilon < 1$. The decryption time is also $O(1)$.

Our basic schemes are one-way secure against *full collusion of revoked users* in the random oracle model under the BDH assumption. We can modify our schemes to have indistinguishably security against adaptive chosen ciphertext attacks.

Keywords: Broadcast encryption, polynomial interpolation, collusion.

1 Introduction

Assume that there is a set $\mathcal{U}$ of N users. We would like to broadcast a message to a subset S of them such that only the (authorized) users in S can obtain the message, while the (revoked) users not in S cannot get information about the message. Broadcast encryption is a bandwidth-saving method to achieve this goal via cryptographic key-controlled access. In broadcast encryption, a dealer sets up the system and assigns each user a set of private keys such that the

---

[*] Research supported in part by NSC projects 96-2628-E-009-011-MY3, 96-3114-P-001-002-Y (iCAST), and 96-2219-E-009-013 (TWISC).

R. Cramer (Ed.): PKC 2008, LNCS 4939, pp. 380–396, 2008.

broadcasted messages can be decrypted by authorized users only. Broadcast encryption has many applications, such as pay-TV systems, encrypted file sharing systems, digital right management, content protection of recordable data, etc.

A broadcasted message M is sent in the form $\langle Hdr(S, m), E_m(M)\rangle$, where m is a session key for encrypting M via a symmetric encryption method E. An authorized user in S can use his private keys to decrypt the session key m from $Hdr(S, m)$. Since the size of $E_m(M)$ is pretty much the same for all broadcast encryption schemes, we are concerned about the header size. The performance measures of a broadcast encryption scheme are the header size, the number of private keys held by each user, the size of public parameters of the system (public keys), the time for encrypting a message, and the time for decrypting the header by an authorized user. A broadcast encryption scheme should be able to resist the collusion attack from revoked users. A scheme is *fully collusion-resistant* if even all revoked users collude, they get no information about the broadcasted message.

Broadcast encryption schemes can be stateless or stateful. For a stateful broadcast encryption scheme, the private keys of a user can be updated from time to time, while the private keys of a user in a stateless broadcast encryption scheme remain the same through the lifetime of the system. Broadcast encryption schemes can also be public key or secret key. For a public key BE scheme, any one (broadcaster) can broadcast a message to an arbitrary group of authorized users by using the public parameters of the system, while for a secret key broadcast encryption scheme, only the special dealer, who knows the system secrets, can broadcast a message.

In this paper we refer "stateless public key broadcast encryption" as "public key BE".

1.1   Our Contribution

We propose three public key BE schemes that have efficient complexity measures. The first scheme, called the BE-PI scheme (broadcast encryption with polynomial interpolation), has $O(r)$ header size, $O(1)$ public keys, and $O(\log N)$ private keys per user[1], where r is the number of revoked users. This is the first public key BE scheme that has both public and private keys under $O(\log N)$ while the header size is $O(r)$. These complexity measures match those of efficient secret key BE schemes [11,20,21]. The idea is to run $\log N$ copies of the basic scheme in [17,19,22] in parallel for lifting the restriction on a priori fixed number of revoked users. Nevertheless, if we implement the $\log N$ copies straightforwardly, we would get a scheme of $O(N)$ public keys. We are able to use the properties of bilinear maps as well as special private key assignment to eliminate the need of $O(N)$ public keys and make it a constant number.

Our second scheme, called the PK-SD-PI scheme (public key SD broadcast encryption with polynomial interpolation), is constructed by combining the polynomial interpolation technique and the subset cover method in the SD scheme [16].

---

[1] log is based on 2 if the base is not specified.

Table 1. Comparison of some fully collusion-resistant public key BE schemes

	header size	public-key size	private-key size	decryption cost[♮]
PK-SD-HIBE[†]	$O(r)$	$O(1)$	$O(\log^2 N)$	$O(\log N)$
BGW-I [4]	$O(1)$	$O(N)^{♭}$	$O(1)$	$O(N-r)$
BGW-II [4]	$O(\sqrt{N})$	$O(\sqrt{N})^{♭}$	$O(1)$	$O(\sqrt{N})$
BW[5]	$O(\sqrt{N})$	$O(\sqrt{N})^{♭}$	$O(\sqrt{N})$	$O(\sqrt{N})$
LHL[§] [15]	$O(rD)$	$O(2C)^{♭}$	$O(D)$	$O(C)$
P-NP, P-TT, P-YF[‡]	$O(r)$	$O(N)$	$O(\log N)$	$O(r)$
Our work: BE-PI	$O(r)$	$O(1)$	$O(\log N)$	$O(r)$
Our work: PK-SD-PI	$O(r)$	$O(1)$	$O(\log^2 N)$	$O(1)$
Our work: PK-LSD-PI	$O(r/\epsilon)$	$O(1)$	$O(\log^{1+\epsilon} N)$	$O(1)$

N - the number of users.

r - the number of revoked users.

[†] - the transformed SD scheme [6] instantiated with constant-size HIBE [2].

[‡] - the parallel extension of [17,19,22].

[♭] - the public keys are needed for decrypting the header by a user.

[§] - $N = C^D$.

[♮] - group operation/modular exponentiation and excluding the time for scanning the header.

The PK-SD-PI scheme has $O(r)$ header size, $O(1)$ public key and $O(\log^2 N)$ private keys per user. They are the same as those of the SD scheme. Nevertheless, the decryption time is remarkably $O(1)$. This is the first public key broadcast encryption scheme that has $O(1)$ decryption time while other complexity measures are kept low. The third scheme, called the PK-LSD-PI scheme, is constructed in the same way, but based on the LSD method. It has $O(r/\epsilon)$ ciphertext size and $O(\log^{1+\epsilon} N)$ private keys per user, where $0 < \epsilon < 1$. The decryption time is also $O(1)$.

Our basic schemes are one-way secure against *full collusion of revoked users* in the random oracle model under the BDH assumption. We modify our schemes to have indistinguishably security against adaptive chosen ciphertext attacks. The comparison with some other public key BE schemes with full collusion resistance is shown in Table 1.

1.2   Related Work

Fiat and Naor [8] formally proposed the concept of static secret key broadcast encryption. Many researchers followed to propose various broadcast encryption schemes, e.g., see [11,12,16,17,20].

Kurosawa and Desmedt [13] proposed a pubic-key BE scheme that is based on polynomial interpolation and traces at most k traitors. The similar schemes of Noar and Pinkas [17], Tzeng and Tzeng [19], and Yoshida and Fujiwara [22] allow revocation of up to k users. Kurosawa and Yoshida [14] generalized the polynomial interpolation (in fact, the Reed-Solomon code) to any linear code for constructing public key BE schemes. The schemes in [7,13,14,17,19,22] all have $O(k)$ public keys, $O(1)$ private keys, and $O(r)$ header size, $r \leq k$. However, k is a-priori fixed during the system setting and the public key size depends on it. These schemes can withstand the collusion attack of up to k revoked users only. They are not fully collusion-resistant.

Yoo, et al. [21] observed that the restriction of a pre-fixed k can be lifted by running $\log N$ copies of the basic scheme with different degrees (from 2^0 to N) of polynomials. They proposed a scheme of $O(\log N)$ private keys and $O(r)$ header size such that r is not restricted. However, their scheme is secret key and the system has $O(N)$ secret values. In the public key setting, the public key size is $O(N)$.

Recently Boneh, et al. [4] proposed a public key BE scheme that has $O(1)$ header size, $O(1)$ private keys, and $O(N)$ public keys. By trading off the header size and public keys, they gave another scheme with $O(\sqrt{N})$ header size, $O(1)$ private keys and $O(\sqrt{N})$ public keys. Lee, et al. [15] proposed a better trade-off by using receiver identifiers in the scheme. It achieves $O(1)$ public key, $O(\log N)$ private keys, but, $O(r \log N)$ header size. Boneh and Waters [5] proposed a scheme that has the traitor tracing capability. This type of schemes [4,5,15] has the disadvantage that the public keys are needed by a user in decrypting the header. Thus, the de-facto private key of a user is the combination of the public key and his private key.

It is possible to transform a secret key BE scheme into a public key one. For example, Dodis and Fazio [6] transformed the SD and LSD schemes [12,16] into public key SD and LSD schemes, shorted as PK-SD and PK-LSD. The transformation employs the technique of hierarchical identity-based encryption to substitute for the hash function. Instantiated with the newest constant-size hierarchical identity-based encryption [2], the PK-SD scheme has $O(r)$ header size, $O(1)$ public keys and $O(\log^2 N)$ private keys. The PK-LSD scheme has $O(r/\epsilon)$ header size, $O(1)$ public keys and $O(\log^{1+\epsilon} N)$ private keys, where $0 < \epsilon < 1$ is a constant. The decryption costs of the PK-SD and PK-LSD schemes are both $O(\log N)$, which is the time for key derivation incurred by the original relation of private keys. If we apply the HIBE technique to the secret key BE schemes of $O(\log N)$ or $O(1)$ private keys [1,11,20], we would get their public key versions with $O(N)$ private keys and $O(N)$ decryption time.

2   Preliminaries

Bilinear map. We use the properties of bilinear maps. Let G and G_1 be two (multiplicative) cyclic groups of prime order q and $\hat{e}$ be a bilinear map from $G \times G$ to G_1. Then, $\hat{e}$ has the following properties.

1. For all $u, v \in G$ and $x, y \in Z_q$, $\hat{e}(u^x, v^y) = \hat{e}(u, v)^{xy}$.
2. Let g be a generator of G, $\hat{e}(g, g) = g_1 \neq 1$ is a generator of G_1.

BDH hardness assumption. The BDH problem is to compute $\hat{e}(g,g)^{abc}$ from given (g, g^a, g^b, g^c). We say that BDH is (t, ϵ)-hard if for any probabilistic algorithm A with time bound t, there is some k_0 such that for any $k \geq k_0$,

$$\Pr[A(g, g^a, g^b, g^c) = \hat{e}(g,g)^{abc} : g \xleftarrow{u} G; a, b, c \xleftarrow{u} Z_q] \leq \epsilon.$$

Broadcast encryption. A public key BE scheme Π consists of three probabilistic polynomial-time algorithms:

- Setup(1^z, ID, $\mathcal{U}$). Wlog, let $\mathcal{U} = \{U_1, U_2, \ldots, U_N\}$. It takes as input the security parameter z, a system identity ID and a set $\mathcal{U}$ of users and outputs a public key PK and N private key sets $SK_1, SK_2, \ldots, SK_N$, one for each user in $\mathcal{U}$.
- Enc(PK, S, M). It takes as input the public key PK, a set $S \subseteq \mathcal{U}$ of authorized users and a message M and outputs a pair $\langle Hdr(S,m), C \rangle$ of the ciphertext header and body, where m is a randomly generated session key and C is the ciphertext of M encrypted by m via some standard symmetric encryption scheme, e.g., AES.
- Dec($SK_k, Hdr(S,m), C$). It takes as input the private key SK_k of user U_k, the header $Hdr(S,m)$ and the body C. If $U_k \in S$, it computes the session key m and then uses m to decrypt C for the message M. If $U_k \notin S$, it cannot decrypt the ciphertext.

The system is correct if all users in S can get the broadcasted message M.

Security. We describe the indistinguishability security against adaptive chosen ciphertext attacks (IND-CCA security) for broadcast encryption as follows [4]. Here, we focus on the security of the session key, which in turn guarantees the security of the ciphertext body C. Let Enc^* and Dec^* be like Enc and Dec except that the message M and the ciphertext body C are omitted. The security is defined by an adversary $\mathcal{A}$ and a challenger $\mathcal{C}$ via the following game.

Init. The adversary $\mathcal{A}$ chooses a system identity ID and a target set $S^* \subseteq \mathcal{U}$ of users to attack.

Setup. The challenger $\mathcal{C}$ runs Setup(1^z, ID, $\mathcal{U}$) to generate a public key PK and private key sets $SK_1, SK_2, \ldots, SK_N$. The challenger $\mathcal{C}$ gives SK_i to $\mathcal{A}$, where $U_i \notin S^*$.

Query phase 1. The adversary $\mathcal{A}$ issues decryption queries Q_i, $1 \leq i \leq n$, of form $(U_k, S, Hdr(S,m))$, $S \subseteq S^*$, $U_k \in S$, and the challenger $\mathcal{C}$ responds with $Dec^*(SK_k, Hdr(S,m))$, which is the session key encrypted in $Hdr(S,m)$.

Challenge. The challenger $\mathcal{C}$ runs $Enc^*(PK, S^*)$ and outputs $y = Hdr(S^*, m)$, where m is randomly chosen. Then, $\mathcal{C}$ chooses a random bit b and a random session key m^* and sets $m_b = m$ and $m_{1-b} = m^*$. $\mathcal{C}$ gives $(m_0, m_1, Hdr(S^*, m))$ to $\mathcal{A}$.

Query phase 2. The adversary $\mathcal{A}$ issues more decryption queries Q_i, $n+1 \leq i \leq q_D$, of form (U_k, S, y'), $S \subseteq S^*$, $U_k \in S$, $y' \neq y$, and the challenger $\mathcal{C}$ responds with $Dec^*(SK_k, y')$.

Guess. $\mathcal{A}$ outputs a guess b' for b.

In the above the adversary A is static since it chooses the target set S^* of users before the system setup. Let $\mathrm{Adv}_{A,\Pi}^{ind\text{-}cca}(z)$ be the advantage that $\mathcal{A}$ wins the above game, that is,

$$\mathrm{Adv}_{A,\Pi}^{ind\text{-}cca}(z) = 2 \cdot \Pr[\mathcal{A}^{\mathcal{O}}(PK, SK_{\mathcal{U}\setminus S^*}, m_0, m_1, Hdr(S^*, m)) = b :$$
$$S^* \subseteq \mathcal{U}, (PK, SK_{\mathcal{U}}) \leftarrow Setup(1^z, \mathrm{ID}, \mathcal{U}),$$
$$Hdr(S^*, m) \leftarrow Enc^*(PK, S^*), b \xleftarrow{u} \{0,1\}] - 1,$$

where $SK_{\mathcal{U}} = \{SK_i : 1 \leq i \leq N\}$ and $SK_{\mathcal{U}\setminus S^*} = \{SK_i : U_i \notin S^*\}$.

Definition 1. *A public key BE scheme Π=(Setup, Enc, Dec) is (t, ϵ, q_D)-IND-CCA secure if for all t-time bounded adversary $\mathcal{A}$ that makes at most q_D decryption queries, we have $\mathrm{Adv}_{A,\Pi}^{ind\text{-}cca}(z) < \epsilon$.*

In this paper we first give schemes with one-way security against chosen plaintext attacks (OW-CPA security) and then transform them to have IND-CCA security via the Fujisaki-Okamoto transformation [9]. The OW-CPA security is defined as follows.

> **Init.** The adversary $\mathcal{A}$ chooses a system identity ID and a target set $S^* \subseteq \mathcal{U}$ of users to attack.
>
> **Setup.** The challenger $\mathcal{C}$ runs $Setup(1^z, \mathrm{ID}, \mathcal{U})$ to generate a public key PK and private key sets $SK_1, SK_2, \ldots, SK_N$. The challenger $\mathcal{C}$ gives SK_i to $\mathcal{A}$, where $U_i \notin S^*$.
>
> **Challenge.** The challenger $\mathcal{C}$ runs $Enc^*(PK, S^*)$ and outputs $Hdr(S^*, m)$, where m is randomly chosen.
>
> **Guess.** $\mathcal{A}$ outputs a guess m' for m.

Since $\mathcal{A}$ can always encrypt a chosen plaintext by himself, the oracle of encrypting a chosen plaintext does not matter in the definition. Let $\mathrm{Adv}_{A,\Pi}^{ow\text{-}cpa}(z)$ be the advantage that $\mathcal{A}$ wins the above game, that is,

$$\mathrm{Adv}_{A,\Pi}^{ow\text{-}cpa}(z) = \Pr[\mathcal{A}(PK, SK_{\mathcal{U}\setminus S^*}, Hdr(S^*, m)) = m : S^* \subseteq \mathcal{U},$$
$$(PK, SK_{\mathcal{U}}) \leftarrow Setup(1^z, \mathrm{ID}, \mathcal{U}), Hdr(S^*, m) \leftarrow Enc^*(PK, S^*)].$$

Definition 2. *A public key BE scheme Π=(Setup, Enc, Dec) is (t, ϵ)-OW-CPA secure if for all t-time bounded adversary $\mathcal{A}$, we have $\mathrm{Adv}_{A,\Pi}^{ow\text{-}cpa}(z) < \epsilon$.*

3   The BE-PI Scheme

Let G and G_1 be the bilinear groups with the pairing function $\hat{e}$, where q is a large prime. Let $H_1, H_2 : \{0,1\}^* \to G_1$ be two hash functions and E be a symmetric encryption with key space G_1.

The idea of our construction is as follows. For a polynomial $f(x)$ of degree t, we assign each user U_i a share $f(i)$. The secret is $f(0)$. We can compute the secret $f(0)$ from any $t+1$ shares. If we want to revoke t users, we broadcast their shares. Any non-revoked user can compute the secret $f(0)$ from his own share and the broadcasted ones, totally $t+1$ shares. On the other hand, any collusion of revoked users cannot compute the secret $f(0)$ since they have t shares only, including the broadcasted ones. If less than t users are revoked, we broadcast the shares of some dummy users such that t shares are broadcasted totally. In order to achieve $O(r)$ ciphertexts, we use $\log N$ polynomials, each for a range of the number of revoked users.

1. **Setup**$(1^z, \text{ID}, \mathcal{U})$: z is the security parameter, ID is the identity name of the system, and $\mathcal{U} = \{U_1, U_2, \ldots, U_N\}$ is the set of users in the system. Wlog, let N be a power of 2. Then, the system dealer does the following:
   - Choose a generator g of group G, and let $\lg = \log_g$ and $g_1 = \hat{e}(g,g)$.
   - Compute $h_i = H_1(\text{ID}\|i)$ for $1 \le i \le \log N$.
   - Compute $g^{a_j^{(i)}} = H_2(\text{ID}\|i\|j)$ for $0 \le i \le \log N$ and $0 \le j \le 2^i$.
   Remark. The underlying polynomials are, $0 \le i \le \log N$,

$$f_i(x) = \sum_{j=0}^{2^i} a_j^{(i)} x^j \pmod{q}.$$

   The system dealer does not know the coefficients $a_j^{(i)} = \lg H_2(\text{ID}\|i\|j)$. But, this does not matter.
   - Randomly choose a secret $\rho \in Z_q$ and compute g^ρ.
   - Publish the public key $PK = (\text{ID}, H_1, H_2, E, G, G_1, \hat{e}, g, g^\rho)$.
   - Assign a set $SK_k = \{s_{k,0}, s_{k,1}, \ldots, s_{k,\log N}\}$ of private keys to user U_k, $1 \le k \le N$, where

$$s_{k,i} = (g^{r_{k,i}}, g^{r_{k,i} f_i(k)}, g^{r_{k,i} f_i(0)} h_i^\rho)$$

   and $r_{k,i}$ is randomly chosen from Z_q, $1 \le i \le \log N$.
2. **Enc**(PK, S, M): $S \subseteq \mathcal{U}$, $R = \mathcal{U} \backslash S = \{U_{i_1}, U_{i_2}, \ldots, U_{i_l}\}$ is the set of revoked users, where $l \ge 1$. M is the sent message. The broadcaster does the following:
   - Let $\alpha = \lceil \log l \rceil$ and $L = 2^\alpha$.
   - Compute $h_\alpha = H_1(\text{ID}\|\alpha)$.
   - Randomly select distinct $i_{l+1}, i_{l+2}, \ldots, i_L > N$. These $U_{i_t}, l+1 \le t \le L$, are dummy users.
   - Randomly select a session key $m \in G_1$.
   - Randomly select $r \in Z_q$ and compute, $1 \le t \le L$,

$$g^{r f_\alpha(i_t)} = (\prod_{j=0}^{L} H_2(\text{ID}\|\alpha\|j)^{i_t^j})^r.$$

   - The ciphertext header $Hdr(S, m)$ is

$$(\alpha, m\hat{e}(g^\rho, h_\alpha)^r, g^r, (i_1, g^{r f_\alpha(i_1)}), (i_2, g^{r f_\alpha(i_2)}), \ldots, (i_L, g^{r f_\alpha(i_L)})).$$

   - The ciphertext body is $C = E_m(M)$.

3. **Dec**$(SK_k, Hdr(S,m), C)$: $U_k \in S$. The user U_k does the following.
   - Compute $b_0 = \hat{e}(g^r, g^{rk,\alpha f_\alpha(k)}) = g_1^{rr_{k,\alpha} f_\alpha(k)}$.
   - Compute $b_j = \hat{e}(g^{r_{k,\alpha}}, g^{r f_\alpha(i_j)}) = g_1^{rr_{k,\alpha} f_\alpha(i_j)}$, $1 \le j \le L$.
   - Use the Lagrange interpolation method to compute

$$g_1^{rr_{k,\alpha} f_\alpha(0)} = \prod_{j=0}^{L} b_j^{\lambda_j}, \tag{1}$$

   where $\lambda_j = \frac{(-i_0)(-i_1)\cdots(-i_{j-1})(-i_{j+1})\cdots(-i_L)}{(i_j-i_0)(i_j-i_1)\cdots(i_j-i_{j-1})(i_j-i_{j+1})\cdots(i_j-i_L)}$ (mod q), $i_0 = k$.
   - Compute the session key

$$\frac{m\hat{e}(g^\rho, h_\alpha)^r \cdot g_1^{rr_{k,\alpha} f_\alpha(0)}}{\hat{e}(g^r, g^{rk,\alpha f_\alpha(0)} h_\alpha^\rho)} = \frac{m\hat{e}(g^\rho, h_\alpha)^r \cdot g_1^{rr_{k,\alpha} f_\alpha(0)}}{\hat{e}(g^r, h_\alpha^\rho) \cdot g_1^{rr_{k,\alpha} f_\alpha(0)}} = m. \tag{2}$$

   - Use m to decrypt the ciphertext body C to obtain the message M.

Correctness. We can easily see that the scheme is correct by Equation (2).

3.1 Performance Analysis

For each system, the public key is $(\text{ID}, H_1, H_2, E, G, G_1, \hat{e}, g, g^\rho)$, which is of size $O(1)$. Since all systems can use the same $(H, E, G, G_1, \hat{e}, g)$, the public key specific to a system is simply (ID, g^ρ). Each system dealer has a secret ρ for assigning private keys to its users. Each user U_k holds private keys $SK_k = \{s_{k,0}, s_{k,1}, \ldots, s_{k,\log N}\}$, each corresponding to a share of polynomial f_i in the masked form, $0 \le i \le \log N$. The number of private keys is $O(\log N)$. When r users are revoked, we choose the polynomial f_α of degree 2^α for encrypting the session key, where $2^{\alpha-1} < r \le 2^\alpha$. Thus, the header size is $O(2^\alpha) = O(r)$. It is actually no more than $2r$.

To prepare a header, the broadcaster needs to compute one pairing function, $2^\alpha + 2$ hash functions, and $2^\alpha + 2$ modular exponentiations, which is $O(r)$ modular exponentiations.

For a user in S to decrypt a header, with a little re-arrangement of Equation (1) as

$$\prod_{j=0}^{L} b_j^{\lambda_j} = b_0^{\lambda_0} \cdot \hat{e}\left(g^{r_{k,\alpha}}, \prod_{j=1}^{L} (g^{r f_\alpha(i_j)})^{\lambda_j}\right),$$

the user needs to perform 3 pairing functions and 2^α modular exponentiations, which is $O(r)$ modular exponentiations. The evaluation of λ_j's can be done in $O(L) = O(2r)$ if the header consists of

$$\tilde{\lambda}_j = \frac{(-i_1)\cdots(-i_{j-1})(-i_{j+1})\cdots(-i_L)}{(i_j - i_1)\cdots(i_j - i_{j-1})(i_j - i_{j+1})\cdots(i_j - i_L)} \mod q, 1 \le j \le L.$$

The user can easily compute λ_j's from $\tilde{\lambda}_j$'s. Inclusion of $\tilde{\lambda}_j$'s in the header does not affect the order of the header size.

3.2 Security Analysis

We show that it has OW-CPA security in the random oracle model under the BDH assumption.

Theorem 1. *Assume that the BDH problem is (t_1, ϵ_1)-hard. Our BE-PI scheme is $(t_1 - t', \epsilon_1)$-OW-CPA secure in the random oracle model, where t' is some polynomially bounded time.*

Proof. We reduce the BDH problem to the problem of computing the session key from the header by the revoked users. Since the polynomials $f_i(x) = \sum_{j=0}^{L} a_j^{(i)} x^j$ and secret shares of users for the polynomials are independent for different i's, we simply discuss security for a particular α. Wlog, let $R = \{U_1, U_2, \ldots, U_L\}$ be the set of revoked users and the target set of attack be $S^* = \mathcal{U} \backslash R$. Note that S^* was chosen by the adversary in the **Init** stage. Let the input of the BDH problem be (g, g^a, g^b, g^c), where the pairing function is implicitly known. We set the system parameters as follows:

1. Randomly select $\tau, \kappa, \mu_1, \mu_2, \ldots, \mu_L, w_1, w_2, \ldots, w_L \in Z_q$.
2. Set the public key of the system:
   (a) Let the input g be the generator g in the system.
   (b) Set $g^\rho = g^a$.
   (c) The public key is $(\text{ID}, H_1, H_2, E, G, G_1, \hat{e}, g, g^a)$.
   (d) The following is implicitly computed.
      - Set $f_\alpha(i) = w_i, 1 \le i \le L$.
      - Let $g^{a_0^{(\alpha)}} = g^{f_\alpha(0)} = g^a \cdot g^\tau = g^{a+\tau}$.
      - Compute $g^{a_i^{(\alpha)}}$, $1 \le i \le L$, from $g^{a_0^{(\alpha)}}$ and $g^{f_\alpha(j)} = g^{w_j}, 1 \le j \le L$, by the Lagrange interpolation method over exponents.
      - Set $h_\alpha = g^b \cdot g^\kappa = g^{b+\kappa}$.
      - For $j \ne \alpha$, choose a random polynomial $f_j(x)$ and set $h_j = g^{z_j}$, where z_j is randomly chosen from Z_q.
3. Set the secret keys $(g^{r_{i,j}}, g^{r_{i,j} f_j(i)}, g^{r_{i,j} f_j(0)} h_j^\rho)$, $0 \le j \le \log N$, of the revoked user $U_i, 1 \le i \le L$, as follows:
   (a) For $j = \alpha$, let $g^{r_{i,\alpha}} = g^{-b+\mu_i}$, $g^{r_{i,\alpha} f_\alpha(i)} = (g^{r_{i,\alpha}})^{w_i}$, and $g^{r_{i,\alpha} f_\alpha(0)} h_\alpha^\rho = g^{(-b+\mu_i)(a+\tau)} (g^{b+\kappa})^a = g^{a(\mu_i + \kappa) - b\tau + \mu_i \tau}$.
   (b) For $j \ne \alpha$, randomly choose $r_{i,j} \in Z_q$ and compute $g^{r_{i,j}}$, $g^{r_{i,j} f_j(i)}$ and $g^{r_{i,j} f_j(0)} h_j^\rho = g^{r_{i,j} f_j(0)} (g^a)^{z_j}$.
4. Set the header $(\alpha, m\hat{e}(g^\rho, h_\alpha)^r, g^r, (1, g^{r f_\alpha(1)}), (2, g^{r f_\alpha(2)}), \ldots, (L, g^{r f_\alpha(L)}))$ as follows:
   (a) Let $g^r = g^c$.
   (b) Compute $g^{r f_\alpha(i)} = (g^c)^{w_i}, 1 \le i \le L$.
   (c) Randomly select $y \in G_1$ and set $m\hat{e}(g^\rho, h_\alpha)^r = y$. We do not know what m is. But, this does not matter.

Assume that the revoked users together can compute the session key m. During computation, the users can query H_1 and H_2 hash oracles. If the query is of the form $H_2(\text{ID}\|i\|j)$ or $H_1(\text{ID}\|i)$, we set them to be $g^{a_j^{(i)}}$ and h_i, respectively.

If the query has ever been asked, we return the stored hash value for the query. For other non-queried inputs, we return random values in G.

We should check whether the distributions of the parameters in our reduction and those in the system are equal. We only check those related to α since the others are correctly distributed. Since $\tau, w_1, w_2, \ldots, w_L$ are randomly chosen, $g^{a_i^{(\alpha)}}, 0 \leq i \leq L$ are uniformly distributed over G^{L+1}. Due to the random oracle model, their corresponding system parameters are also uniformly distributed over G^{L+1}. Since $\kappa, \mu_1, \mu_2, \ldots, \mu_L$ are randomly chosen, the distribution of h_α and $g^{r_{i,\alpha}}, 1 \leq i \leq L$, are uniform over G^{L+1}, which is again the same as that of the corresponding system parameters. The distributions of g^r in the header and g^ρ in the public key are both uniform over G since they are set from the given input g^c and g^a, respectively. Since the session key m is chosen randomly from G_1, $m\hat{e}(g^\rho, h_\alpha)^r$ is distributed uniformly over G_1. We set it to a random value $y \in G_1$. Even though we don't know about m, it does not affect the reduction. Other parameters are dependent on what have been discussed. We can check that they are all computed correctly. So, the reduction preserves the right distribution.

If the revoked users compute m from the header with probability ϵ, we can solve the BDH problem with the same probability $\epsilon_1 = \epsilon$ by computing the following:

$$
\begin{aligned}
y \cdot m^{-1} \cdot \hat{e}(g^a, g^c)^{-\kappa} &= \hat{e}(g^\rho, h_\alpha)^r \cdot \hat{e}(g, g)^{-ac\kappa} \\
&= \hat{e}(g^a, g^{b+\kappa})^c \cdot \hat{e}(g, g)^{-ac\kappa} \\
&= \hat{e}(g, g)^{abc}.
\end{aligned}
\tag{3}
$$

Let t' be the time for this reduction and the solution computation in Equation (3). We can see that t' is polynomially bounded. Thus, if the collusion attack of the revoked users takes $t_1 - t'$ time, we can solve the BDH problem within time t_1.

4 The BE-PI Scheme with IND-CCA Security

In Theorem 1, we show that the session key in the header is one-way secure against any collusion of revoked users. There are some standard techniques of transforming OW-CPA security to IND-CCA security. Here we present such a scheme Π' based on the technique in [9].

The IND-CCA security of the Fujisaki-Okamoto transformation depends only on the OW-CPA security of the public key encryption scheme, the FG security of a symmetric encryption scheme $\mathcal{E}$, and the γ-uniformity of the public key encryption scheme. The FG-security is the counterpart of the IND-security for symmetric encryption. A public key encryption scheme is γ-uniform if for every key pair (pk, sk), every message x, and $y \in \{0,1\}^*$, $\Pr[E_{pk}(x) = y] \leq \gamma$. Before applying the transformation, we check the following things:

1. The transformation applies to public key encryption, while ours is public key broadcast encryption. Nevertheless, if the authorized set S is fixed, our public

key broadcast encryption scheme is a public key encryption scheme with public key $pk = (PK, S)$. In the definition of IND-CCA security (Definition 1), the adversary $\mathcal{A}$ selects a target set S^* of users to attack in the **Init** stage and S^* is fixed through the rest of the attack. Thus, we can discuss the attack of $\mathcal{A}$ with a fixed target set S^*. Note that $\mathcal{A}$ is a static adversary.

2. Let S be a fixed authorized set of users. For every m and every $y \in \{0,1\}^*$, $\Pr[Hdr(S, m) = y]$ is either 0 or $1/q \simeq 1/2^z$, where z is the security parameter (the public key size). Thus, our broadcast encryption scheme is 2^{-z}-uniform if the authorized set is fixed.

Let $\mathcal{E} : K \times G_1 \to G_1$ be a symmetric encryption scheme with FG-security, where K is the key space of $\mathcal{E}$. Let $H_3 : G_1 \times G_1 \to Z_q$ and $H_4 : G_1 \to K$ be two hash functions. The modification of Π for Π' is as follows.

- In the **Setup** algorithm, add $\mathcal{E}, H_3, H_4$ to PK.
- In the **Enc** algorithm,

$$Hdr(S, m) = (g^r, \sigma \hat{e}(g^\rho, h_\alpha)^r, \mathcal{E}_{H_4(\sigma)}(m),$$
$$(i_1, g^{r f_\alpha(i_1)}), (i_2, g^{r f_\alpha(i_2)}), \ldots, (i_L, g^{r f_\alpha(i_L)})),$$

where σ is randomly chosen from G_1 and $r = H_3(\sigma, m)$.

- In the **Dec** algorithm, we first compute $\bar{\sigma}$ as described in the BE-PI scheme. Then, we compute the session key $\bar{m}$ from $\mathcal{E}_{H_4(\sigma)}(m)$ by using $\bar{\sigma}$. We check whether $\sigma \hat{e}(g^\rho, h_\alpha)^r = \bar{\sigma} \hat{e}(g^\rho, h_\alpha)^{H_3(\bar{\sigma}, \bar{m})}$ and $g^{r f_\alpha(i_j)} = g^{f_\alpha(i_j) H_3(\bar{\sigma}, \bar{m})}$, $1 \le j \le L$. If they are all equal, $\bar{m}$ is outputted. Otherwise, $\perp$ is outputted.

Let q_{H_3}, q_{H_4} and q_D be the numbers of queries to H_3, H_4 and the decryption oracles, respectively. Our scheme Π' is IND-CCA-secure.

Theorem 2. *Assume that the BDH problem is (t_1, ϵ_1)-hard and the symmetric encryption $\mathcal{E}$ is (t_2, ϵ_2) FG-secure. The scheme Π' is $(t, \epsilon, q_{H_3}, q_{H_4}, q_D)$-IND-CCA secure in the random oracle model, where t' is some polynomially bounded time,*

$$t = \min\{t_1 - t', t_2\} - O(2z(q_{H_3} + q_{H_4})) \text{ and}$$
$$\epsilon = (1 + 2(q_{H_3} + q_{H_4})\epsilon_1 + \epsilon_2)(1 - 2\epsilon_1 - 2\epsilon_2 - 2^{-z+1})^{-q_D} - 1.$$

This theorem is proved by showing that if Π' is not IND-CCA-secure, then either Π is not OW-CPA-secure or $\mathcal{E}$ is not FG-secure directly. The OW-CPA security of Π is based on the BDH assumption. We note that the application of the transformation to other types of schemes could be delicate. Galindo [10] pointed out such a case. Nevertheless, the problem occurs in the proof and is fixable without changing the transformation or the assumption. The detailed proof will be given in the full version of the paper.

5   A Public Key SD Scheme

In the paradigm of subset cover for broadcast encryption [16], the system chooses a collection $\mathcal{C}$ of subsets of users such that each set S of users can be covered by the subsets in $\mathcal{C}$, that is, $S = \cup_{i=1}^{w} S_w$, where $S_i \in \mathcal{C}$ are disjoint, $1 \le i \le w$. Each subset S_i in $\mathcal{C}$ is associated with a private key k_i. A user is assigned a set of keys such that he can derive the private keys of the subsets to which he belongs. The subset keys k_i cannot be independent. Otherwise, each user may hold too many keys. It is preferable that the subset keys have some relations, for example, one can be derived from another. Thus, each user U_k is given a set SK_k of keys so that he can derive the private key of a subset to which he belongs. A subset-cover based broadcast encryption scheme plays the art of choosing a collection $\mathcal{C}$ of subsets, assigning subset and user keys, and finding subset covers.

5.1   The PK-SD-PI Scheme

We now present our PK-SD-PI scheme, which is constructed by using the polynomial interpolation technique on the collection of subsets in [16]. The system setup is similar to that of the BE-PI scheme. Consider a complete binary tree T of $\log N + 1$ levels. The nodes in T are numbered differently. Each user in $\mathcal{U}$ is associated with a different leaf node in T. We refer to a complete subtree rooted at node i as "subtree T_i". For each subtree T_i of η levels (level 1 to level η from top to bottom), we define the degree-1 polynomials

$$f_j^{(i)}(x) = a_{j,1}^{(i)} x + a_{j,0}^{(i)} \pmod{q},$$

where $a_{j,0}^{(i)} = \lg H_2(\mathrm{ID}\|i\|j\|0)$ and $a_{j,1}^{(i)} = \lg H_2(\mathrm{ID}\|i\|j\|1)$, $2 \le j \le \eta$. For a user U_k in the subtree T_i of η levels, he is given the private keys

$$s_{k,i,j} = (g^{r_{k,i,j}}, g^{r_{k,i,j} f_j^{(i)}(i_j)}, g^{r_{k,i,j} f_j^{(i)}(0)} h^\rho)$$

for $2 \le j \le \eta$, where nodes $i_1, i_2, \ldots, i_\eta$ are the nodes in the path from node i to the leaf node for U_k (including both ends). We can read $s_{k,i,j}$ as the private key of U_k for the jth level of subtree T_i. In Figure 1, the private keys (in the unmasked form) of U_1 and U_3 for subtree T_i with $\eta = 4$ are given. Here, we use h^ρ in all private keys in order to save space in the header.

Recall that in the SD scheme, the collection $\mathcal{C}$ of subsets is

$$\{S_{i,t} : \text{node } i \text{ is a parent of node } t, i \ne t\},$$

where $S_{i,t}$ denotes the set of users in subtree T_i, but not in subtree T_t. By our design, if the header contains a masked share for $f_j^{(i)}(t)$, where node t is in the j-th level of subtree T_i, only user U_k in $S_{i,t}$ can decrypt the header by using his private key $s_{k,i,j}$, that is, the masked form of $f_j^{(i)}(s)$, for some $s \ne t$. In Figure 1, the share $f_3^{(i)}(t)$ is broadcasted so that only the users in $S_{i,t}$ can decrypt the header.

For a set R of revoked users, let $S_{i_1,t_1}, S_{i_2,t_2}, \ldots, S_{i_z,t_z}$ be a subset cover for $\mathcal{U} \backslash R$, the header is

$$(m\hat{e}(g^\rho, h)^r, g^r, (i_1, t_1, g^{r f_{j_1}^{(i_1)}(t_1)}), \ldots, (i_z, t_z, g^{r f_{j_z}^{(i_z)}(t_z)})),$$

where node t_k is in the j_k-th level of subtree T_{i_k}, $1 \le k \le z$.

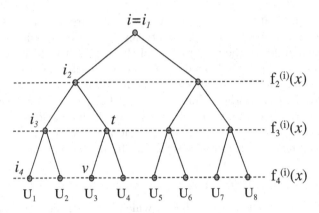

- U_1 holds masked shares of $f_2^{(i)}(i_2)$, $f_3^{(i)}(i_3)$, $f_4^{(i)}(i_4)$
- U_3 holds masked shares of $f_2^{(i)}(i_2)$, $f_3^{(i)}(t)$, $f_4^{(i)}(v)$
- For subset $S_{i,t}$, a masked share of $f_3^{(i)}(t)$ is broadcasted so that U_3 and U_4 cannot decrypt, but others can.

Fig. 1. Level polynomials, private keys and broadcasted shares for subtree T_i

For decryption, a non-revoked user finds $i_k, t_k, g^{r f_{j_k}^{(i_k)}(t_k)}$ (corresponding to S_{i_k,t_k} where he is in) from the header and applies the Lagrange interpolation to compute the session key m.

Performance. The public key is $O(1)$, which is the same as that of the BE-PI scheme. Each user belongs to at most $\log N + 1$ subtrees and each subtree has at most $\log N + 1$ levels. For the subtree of η levels, the user in the subtree holds $\eta - 1$ private keys. Thus, the total number of shares (private keys) held by each user is $\sum_{i=1}^{\log N} i = O(\log^2 N)$. According to [16], the number z of subsets in a subset cover is at most $2|R| - 1$, which is $O(r)$.

When the header streams in, a non-revoked user U_k looks for his containing subset S_{i_j,t_j} to which he belongs. With a proper numbering of the nodes in T, this can be done very fast, for example, in $O(\log \log N)$ time. Without considering the time of scanning the header to find out his containing subset, each user needs to perform 2 modular exponentiations and 3 pairing functions. Thus, the decryption cost is $O(1)$.

Security. We first show that the scheme is one-way secure.

Theorem 3. *Assume that the BDH problem is (t_1, ϵ_1)-hard. Our PK-SD-PI scheme is $(t_1 - t', \epsilon_1)$-OW-CPA secure in the random oracle model, where t' is some polynomially bounded time.*

Proof. The one-way security proof for the PK-SD-PI scheme is similar to that for the BE-PI scheme. In the PK-SD-PI scheme, all polynomials $f_j^{(i)}(x)$ are of degree one. Let (g, g^a, g^b, g^c) be the input to the BDH problem. Let $S_{i_1,t_1}, S_{i_2,t_2}, \ldots, S_{i_z,t_z}$ be a subset cover for $S^* = \mathcal{U} \backslash R$. Due to the random oracle assumption for H_1

and H_2, all polynomials are independent. Thus, we can simply consider a particular $S_{\alpha,t}$ in the subset cover for $S^* = \mathcal{U} \backslash R$, where t is at level β of subtree T_α. The corresponding polynomial is $f(x) = f_\beta^{(\alpha)}(x) = a_1 x + a_0 \pmod{q}$. Wlog, let $\{U_1, U_2, \ldots, U_l\}$ be the set of revoked users that have the secret share about $f(t)$. The reduction to the BDH problem is as follows. Recall that the public key of the PK-SD-PI method is $(\text{ID}, H_1, H_2, E, G, G_1, \hat{e}, g, g^\rho)$.

1. Let g be the generator in the system and $g^\rho = g^a$.
2. Set $f(t) = w$ and compute $g^{f(t)} = g^w$, where w is randomly chosen from Z_q.
3. Let $g^{a_0} = g^{f(0)} = g^a \cdot g^\tau$, where τ is randomly chosen from Z_q.
4. Compute g^{a_1} from $g^{f(t)}$ and g^{a_0} via the Lagrange interpolation.
5. The (random) hash values $H_2(\text{ID}\|\alpha\|\beta\|0)$ and $H_2(\text{ID}\|\alpha\|\beta\|1)$ are set as g^{a_0} and g^{a_1} respectively.
6. Set $h = g^b \cdot g^\kappa$, where κ is randomly chosen from Z_q.
7. The $f(x)$-related secret share of $U_i, 1 \leq i \leq l$, is computed as $(g^{r_i}, g^{r_i f(t)}, g^{r_i f(0)} h^\rho)$, where $g^{r_i} = g^{-b} \cdot g^{\mu_i}$ and μ_i is randomly chosen from Z_q. Note that $g^{r_i f(0)} h^\rho = g^{a(\mu_i + \kappa) - b\tau + \mu_i \tau}$ can be computed from the setting in the previous steps.
8. The non-$f(x)$-related secret shares of $U_i, 1 \leq i \leq l$, can be set as follows. Let f' be a polynomial related to subtree α' and level β', where t' is in the β'-th level and $U_i \in S_{\alpha',t'}$. The secret share $(g^{r'_i}, g^{r'_i f'(t')}, g^{r'_i f'(0)} h^\rho)$ of U_i is computed from $(g^{r_i}, g^{r_i f(t)}, g^{r_i f(0)} h^\rho)$. Let $f'(t') = w'$, $f'(0) = f(0) + a'$ and $r'_i = r_i + r'$, where w', a', and r' are randomly chosen from Z_q. Thus, $g^{r'_i} = g^{r_i} \cdot g^{r'}$, $g^{r'_i f'(t')} = (g^{r'_i})^{w'}$ and $g^{r'_i f'(0)} h^\rho = (g^{r_i f(0)} h^\rho) \cdot g^{r' f(0)} \cdot g^{r_i a'} \cdot g^{r' a'}$. Note that the hash values $H_2(\text{ID}\|\alpha'\|\beta'\|0)$ and $H_2(\text{ID}\|\alpha'\|\beta'\|1)$ can be answered accordingly.
9. Set the challenge as

$$(y, g^c, (i_1, t_1, g^{cf_{j_1}^{(i_1)}(t_1)}), (i_2, t_2, g^{cf_{j_2}^{(i_2)}(t_2)}), \ldots, (i_z, t_z, g^{cf_{j_z}^{(i_z)}(t_z)})),$$

where y is randomly chosen from G and thought as $m\hat{e}(g^\rho, h)^c$. Note that $g^{cf_{j_k}^{(i_k)}(t_k)}, 1 \leq k \leq z$, can be computed since $f_{j_k}^{(i_k)}(t_k)$ is a number randomly chosen from Z_q, as described in Step 2.

If the revoked users $U_1, U_2, \ldots, U_l$ can together compute the session key m from the challenge with probability ϵ_1, we can compute

$$y \cdot m^{-1} \cdot \hat{e}(g^a, g^c)^{-\kappa} = \hat{e}(g^\rho, h)^c \cdot \hat{e}(g, g)^{-ac\kappa}$$
$$= \hat{e}(g^a, g^{b+\kappa})^c \cdot \hat{e}(g, g)^{-ac\kappa} = \hat{e}(g, g)^{abc} \qquad (4)$$

with the same probability ϵ_1. This contradicts the BDH assumption.

Let t' be the time for the reduction and solution computation in Equation (4), where t' is polynomially bounded. Thus, if the collusion attack takes $t_1 - t'$, we can solve the BDH problem in time t_1.

Similarly, we can modify our PK-SD-PI scheme to have IND-CCA security like Section 4

5.2   The PK-LSD-PI Scheme

The LSD method is an improvement of the SD method by using a sub-collection $\mathcal{C}'$ of $\mathcal{C}$ in the SD method. The basic observation is that $S_{i,t}$ can be decomposed to $S_{i,k} \cup S_{k,t}$. The LSD method delicately selects $\mathcal{C}'$ such that each $S_{i,t} \in \mathcal{C}$ is either in $\mathcal{C}'$ or equal to $S_{i,k} \cup S_{k,t}$, where $S_{i,k}$ and $S_{k,t}$ are in $\mathcal{C}'$. The subset cover found for $\mathcal{U} \backslash R$ in the SD method is used except that each $S_{i,t}$ in the cover, but not in $\mathcal{C}'$, is replaced by two subsets $S_{i,k}$ and $S_{k,t}$ in $\mathcal{C}'$. Thus, each user belongs to a less number of $S_{i,t}$'s in $\mathcal{C}'$ such that it holds a less number of private keys.

We consider the basic case of the LSD method, in which each user holds $(\log n)^{3/2}$ private keys. There are $\sqrt{\log n}$ "special" levels in T. The root is at a special level and every level of depth $k \cdot \sqrt{\log n}$, $1 \leq k \leq \sqrt{\log n}$, is special. A layer is the set of the levels between two adjacent special levels. Each layer has $\sqrt{\log n}$ levels. The collection $\mathcal{C}'$ of the LSD method is

$$\{S_{i,t} : \text{nodes } i \text{ and } t \text{ are in the same layer, or node } i \text{ is at a special level}\}.$$

There are two types of $S_{i,t}$'s in $\mathcal{C}'$. The first type is that node i is in a special level and the second type is that nodes i and t are in the same layer. Every non-revoked set $\mathcal{U} \backslash R$ can be covered by at most $4|R| - 2$ disjoint subsets in $\mathcal{C}'$.

Our PK-LSD-PI scheme is as follows. Since $\mathcal{C}'$ is just a sub-collection of $\mathcal{C}$ in the SD method, our PK-LSD-PI scheme is almost the same as the PK-SD-PI scheme except that some polynomials for type-2 $S_{i,t} \in \mathcal{C}'$ are unnecessary. Consider a user U_k (or its corresponding leaf node). For his ancestor node i at a special layer (type-1 $S_{i,t}$'s), U_k is given the private keys (corresponding to subtree T_i) by the same way as the PK-SD-PI method. There are $\sqrt{\log n}$ such i's and each T_i has at most $\log n$ levels. In this case, U_k holds $(\log n)^{3/2}$ private keys. For his ancestor node i and nodes t in the same layer (type-2 $S_{i,t}$'s), choose degree-1 polynomials for the levels between i and its (underneath) adjacent special level only. There are at most $\sqrt{\log n}$ such polynomials and U_k is assigned corresponding $\sqrt{\log n}$ private keys as the PK-SD-PI scheme does. In this case, U_k holds at most $\log n \cdot \sqrt{\log n}$ private keys since U_k has $\log n$ ancestors. Overall, each user U_k holds at most $2(\log n)^{3/2}$ private keys.

Security. We show that the scheme described in this subsection is one-way secure.

Theorem 4. *Assume that the BDH problem is (t_1, ϵ_1)-hard. Our PK-LSD-PI scheme is $(t_1 - t', \epsilon_1)$-OW-CPA secure in the random oracle model, where t' is some polynomially bounded time.*

Proof. The collection of $S_{i,t}$'s for covering $\mathcal{U} \backslash R$ in the LSD method is a sub-collection of that in the SD method. The way of assigning private keys to users is the same as that of the PK-SD-PI scheme except that we omit the polynomials that are never used due to the way of choosing a subset cover in the LSD method. In the random oracle model, we can simply consider a particular $S_{\alpha,t}$ in the subset cover for $\mathcal{U} \backslash R$. Since all conditions are the same, the rest of proof is the same as that in Theorem 3.

With the same extension in [12], we can have a PK-LSD-PI scheme that has $O(1)$ public keys and $O(\log^{1+\epsilon})$ private keys, for any constant $0 < \epsilon < 1$. The header size is $O(r/\epsilon)$, which is $O(r)$ for a constant ϵ. The decryption cost excluding the time of scanning the header is again $O(1)$.

6   Conclusion

We have presented very efficient public key BE schemes. They have low public and private keys. Two of them even have a constant decryption time. Our results show that the efficiency of public key BE schemes is comparable to that of private-key BE schemes.

We are interested in reducing the ciphertext size while keeping other complexities low in the future.

Acknowledgement

We thank Eike Kiltz and Michel Abdalla for valuable comments on the manuscript.

References

1. Attrapadung, N., Imai, H.: Graph-decomposition-based frameworks for subset-cover broadcast encryption and efficient instantiations. In: Roy, B. (ed.) ASIACRYPT 2005. LNCS, vol. 3788, pp. 100–120. Springer, Heidelberg (2005)
2. Boneh, D., Boyen, X., Goh, E.-J.: Hierarchical identity based encryption with constant size ciphertext. In: Cramer, R.J.F. (ed.) EUROCRYPT 2005. LNCS, vol. 3494, pp. 440–456. Springer, Heidelberg (2005)
3. Boneh, D., Franklin, M.: An efficient public key traitor tracing scheme. In: Wiener, M.J. (ed.) CRYPTO 1999. LNCS, vol. 1666, pp. 338–353. Springer, Heidelberg (1999)
4. Boneh, D., Gentry, C., Waters, B.: Collusion resistant broadcast encryption with short ciphertexts and private keys. In: Shoup, V. (ed.) CRYPTO 2005. LNCS, vol. 3621, pp. 258–275. Springer, Heidelberg (2005)
5. Boneh, D., Waters, B.: A fully collusion resistant broadcast, trace, and revoke system. In: Proceedings of the ACM Conference on Computer and Communications Security - CCS 2006, pp. 211–220. ACM Press, New York (2006)
6. Dodis, Y., Fazio, N.: Public key broadcast encryption for stateless receivers. In: Feigenbaum, J. (ed.) DRM 2002. LNCS, vol. 2696, pp. 61–80. Springer, Heidelberg (2003)
7. Dodis, Y., Fazio, N.: Public key broadcast encryption secure against adaptive chosen ciphertext attack. In: Desmedt, Y.G. (ed.) PKC 2003. LNCS, vol. 2567, pp. 100–115. Springer, Heidelberg (2002)
8. Fiat, A., Naor, M.: Broadcast encryption. In: Stinson, D.R. (ed.) CRYPTO 1993. LNCS, vol. 773, pp. 480–491. Springer, Heidelberg (1994)
9. Fujisaki, E., Okamoto, T.: Secure integration of asymmetric and symmetric encryption schemes. In: Wiener, M.J. (ed.) CRYPTO 1999. LNCS, vol. 1666, pp. 537–554. Springer, Heidelberg (1999)

10. Galindo, D.: Boneh-Franklin identity based encryption revisited. In: Caires, L., Italiano, G.F., Monteiro, L., Palamidessi, C., Yung, M. (eds.) ICALP 2005. LNCS, vol. 3580, pp. 791–802. Springer, Heidelberg (2005)
11. Goodrich, M.T., Sun, J.Z., Tamassia, R.: Efficient Tree-Based Revocation in Groups of Low-State Devices. In: Franklin, M. (ed.) CRYPTO 2004. LNCS, vol. 3152, pp. 511–527. Springer, Heidelberg (2004)
12. Halevy, D., Shamir, A.: The LSD broadcast encryption scheme. In: Yung, M. (ed.) CRYPTO 2002. LNCS, vol. 2442, pp. 47–60. Springer, Heidelberg (2002)
13. Kurosawa, K., Desmedt, Y.: Optimum traitor tracing and asymmetric schemes. In: Nyberg, K. (ed.) EUROCRYPT 1998. LNCS, vol. 1403, pp. 145–157. Springer, Heidelberg (1998)
14. Kurosawa, K., Yoshida, T.: Linear code implies public-key traitor tracing. In: Naccache, D., Paillier, P. (eds.) PKC 2002. LNCS, vol. 2274, pp. 172–187. Springer, Heidelberg (2002)
15. Lee, J.W., Hwang, Y.H., Lee, P.J.: Efficient public key broadcast encryption using identifier of receivers. In: Chen, K., Deng, R., Lai, X., Zhou, J. (eds.) ISPEC 2006. LNCS, vol. 3903, pp. 153–164. Springer, Heidelberg (2006)
16. Naor, D., Naor, M., Lotspiech, J.: Revocation and tracing schemes for stateless receivers. In: Kilian, J. (ed.) CRYPTO 2001. LNCS, vol. 2139, pp. 41–62. Springer, Heidelberg (2001)
17. Naor, M., Pinkas, B.: Efficient trace and revoke schemes. In: Frankel, Y. (ed.) FC 2000. LNCS, vol. 1962, pp. 1–20. Springer, Heidelberg (2001)
18. Shamir, A.: How to share a secret. Communications of the ACM 22(11), 612–613 (1979)
19. Tzeng, W.-G., Tzeng, Z.-J.: A public-key traitor tracing scheme with revocation using dynamic shares. In: Kim, K.-c. (ed.) PKC 2001. LNCS, vol. 1992, pp. 207–224. Springer, Heidelberg (2001)
20. Wang, P., Ning, P., Reeves, D.S.: Storage-efficient stateless group key revocation. In: Zhang, K., Zheng, Y. (eds.) ISC 2004. LNCS, vol. 3225, pp. 25–38. Springer, Heidelberg (2004)
21. Yoo, E.S., Jho, N.-S., Cheon, J.J., Kim, M.-H.: Efficient broadcast encryption using multiple interpolation methods. In: Park, C.-s., Chee, S. (eds.) ICISC 2004. LNCS, vol. 3506, pp. 87–103. Springer, Heidelberg (2005)
22. Yoshida, M., Fujiwara, T.: An efficient traitor tracing scheme for broadcast encryption. In: Proceedings of 2000 IEEE International Symposium on Information Theory, p. 463. IEEE Press, Los Alamitos (2000)

Author Index

Lecture Notes in Computer Science

Sublibrary 4: Security and Cryptology

For information about Vols. 1– 2742
please contact your bookseller or Springer

Vol. 4341: P.Q. Nguyên (Ed.), Progress in Cryptology - VIETCRYPT 2006. XI, 385 pages. 2006.

Vol. 4332: A. Bagchi, V. Atluri (Eds.), Information Systems Security. XV, 382 pages. 2006.

Vol. 4329: R. Barua, T. Lange (Eds.), Progress in Cryptology - INDOCRYPT 2006. X, 454 pages. 2006.

Vol. 4318: H. Lipmaa, M.M. Yung, D. Lin (Eds.), Information Security and Cryptology. XI, 305 pages. 2006.

Vol. 4307: P. Ning, S. Qing, N. Li (Eds.), Information and Communications Security. XIV, 558 pages. 2006.

Vol. 4301: D. Pointcheval, Y. Mu, K. Chen (Eds.), Cryptology and Network Security. XIII, 381 pages. 2006.

Vol. 4300: Y.Q. Shi (Ed.), Transactions on Data Hiding and Multimedia Security I. IX, 139 pages. 2006.

Vol. 4298: J.K. Lee, O. Yi, M.M. Yung (Eds.), Information Security Applications. XIV, 406 pages. 2007.

Vol. 4296: M.S. Rhee, B. Lee (Eds.), Information Security and Cryptology – ICISC 2006. XIII, 358 pages. 2006.

Vol. 4284: X. Lai, K. Chen (Eds.), Advances in Cryptology – ASIACRYPT 2006. XIV, 468 pages. 2006.

Vol. 4283: Y.Q. Shi, B. Jeon (Eds.), Digital Watermarking. XII, 474 pages. 2006.

Vol. 4266: H. Yoshiura, K. Sakurai, K. Rannenberg, Y. Murayama, S.-i. Kawamura (Eds.), Advances in Information and Computer Security. XIII, 438 pages. 2006.

Vol. 4258: G. Danezis, P. Golle (Eds.), Privacy Enhancing Technologies. VIII, 431 pages. 2006.

Vol. 4249: L. Goubin, M. Matsui (Eds.), Cryptographic Hardware and Embedded Systems - CHES 2006. XII, 462 pages. 2006.

Vol. 4237: H. Leitold, E.P. Markatos (Eds.), Communications and Multimedia Security. XII, 253 pages. 2006.

Vol. 4236: L. Breveglieri, I. Koren, D. Naccache, J.-P. Seifert (Eds.), Fault Diagnosis and Tolerance in Cryptography. XIII, 253 pages. 2006.

Vol. 4219: D. Zamboni, C. Krügel (Eds.), Recent Advances in Intrusion Detection. XII, 331 pages. 2006.

Vol. 4189: D. Gollmann, J. Meier, A. Sabelfeld (Eds.), Computer Security – ESORICS 2006. XI, 548 pages. 2006.

Vol. 4176: S.K. Katsikas, J. López, M. Backes, S. Gritzalis, B. Preneel (Eds.), Information Security. XIV, 548 pages. 2006.

Vol. 4117: C. Dwork (Ed.), Advances in Cryptology - CRYPTO 2006. XIII, 621 pages. 2006.

Vol. 4116: R. De Prisco, M.M. Yung (Eds.), Security and Cryptography for Networks. XI, 366 pages. 2006.

Vol. 4107: G. Di Crescenzo, A. Rubin (Eds.), Financial Cryptography and Data Security. XI, 327 pages. 2006.

Vol. 4083: S. Fischer-Hübner, S. Furnell, C. Lambrinoudakis (Eds.), Trust and Privacy in Digital Business. XIII, 243 pages. 2006.

Vol. 4064: R. Büschkes, P. Laskov (Eds.), Detection of Intrusions and Malware & Vulnerability Assessment. X, 195 pages. 2006.

Vol. 4058: L.M. Batten, R. Safavi-Naini (Eds.), Information Security and Privacy. XII, 446 pages. 2006.

Vol. 4047: M.J.B. Robshaw (Ed.), Fast Software Encryption. XI, 434 pages. 2006.

Vol. 4043: A.S. Atzeni, A. Lioy (Eds.), Public Key Infrastructure. XI, 261 pages. 2006.

Vol. 4004: S. Vaudenay (Ed.), Advances in Cryptology - EUROCRYPT 2006. XIV, 613 pages. 2006.

Vol. 3995: G. Müller (Ed.), Emerging Trends in Information and Communication Security. XX, 524 pages. 2006.

Vol. 3989: J. Zhou, M.M. Yung, F. Bao (Eds.), Applied Cryptography and Network Security. XIV, 488 pages. 2006.

Vol. 3969: Ø. Ytrehus (Ed.), Coding and Cryptography. XI, 443 pages. 2006.

Vol. 3958: M.M. Yung, Y. Dodis, A. Kiayias, T.G. Malkin (Eds.), Public Key Cryptography - PKC 2006. XIV, 543 pages. 2006.

Vol. 3957: B. Christianson, B. Crispo, J.A. Malcolm, M. Roe (Eds.), Security Protocols. IX, 325 pages. 2006.

Vol. 3956: G. Barthe, B. Grégoire, M. Huisman, J.-L. Lanet (Eds.), Construction and Analysis of Safe, Secure, and Interoperable Smart Devices. IX, 175 pages. 2006.

Vol. 3935: D.H. Won, S. Kim (Eds.), Information Security and Cryptology - ICISC 2005. XIV, 458 pages. 2006.

Vol. 3934: J.A. Clark, R.F. Paige, F.A.C. Polack, P.J. Brooke (Eds.), Security in Pervasive Computing. X, 243 pages. 2006.

Vol. 3928: J. Domingo-Ferrer, J. Posegga, D. Schreckling (Eds.), Smart Card Research and Advanced Applications. XI, 359 pages. 2006.

Vol. 3919: R. Safavi-Naini, M.M. Yung (Eds.), Digital Rights Management. XI, 357 pages. 2006.

Vol. 3903: K. Chen, R. Deng, X. Lai, J. Zhou (Eds.), Information Security Practice and Experience. XIV, 392 pages. 2006.

Vol. 3897: B. Preneel, S. Tavares (Eds.), Selected Areas in Cryptography. XI, 371 pages. 2006.

Vol. 3876: S. Halevi, T. Rabin (Eds.), Theory of Cryptography. XI, 617 pages. 2006.

Vol. 3866: T. Dimitrakos, F. Martinelli, P.Y.A. Ryan, S. Schneider (Eds.), Formal Aspects in Security and Trust. X, 259 pages. 2006.

Vol. 3860: D. Pointcheval (Ed.), Topics in Cryptology – CT-RSA 2006. XI, 365 pages. 2006.

Vol. 3858: A. Valdes, D. Zamboni (Eds.), Recent Advances in Intrusion Detection. X, 351 pages. 2006.

Vol. 3856: G. Danezis, D. Martin (Eds.), Privacy Enhancing Technologies. VIII, 273 pages. 2006.

Vol. 3786: J.-S. Song, T. Kwon, M.M. Yung (Eds.), Information Security Applications. XI, 378 pages. 2006.

Vol. 3108: H. Wang, J. Pieprzyk, V. Varadharajan (Eds.), Information Security and Privacy. XII, 494 pages. 2004.

Vol. 2951: M. Naor (Ed.), Theory of Cryptography. XI, 523 pages. 2004.

Printed in the United States
By Bookmasters